ROUTLEDGE HANDBOOK OF CONTEMPORARY AFRICAN WOMEN

The *Routledge Handbook of Contemporary African Women* highlights the achievements and progress being made by African women across a wide range of sectors in society. Without glossing over the very real challenges which women in Africa continue to face, this landmark handbook demonstrates how women across the continent are deploying their agency to achieve notable progress in areas as diverse as:

- Pandemics
- Climate Change
- Science and Technology
- Entrepreneurship
- Higher Education
- Youth and Older People

Challenging prevailing narratives and stereotypes about African women, this handbook provides a more positive perspective on African women's progressive actions for sustainable development. It will be an essential read for readers across the fields of gender, environment, political science, history, development studies, religious studies, and African studies.

Anna Chitando (PhD) is an Associate Professor in the Department of Languages and Literature, Faculty of Arts, Culture and Heritage Studies at the Zimbabwe Open University. She holds a Doctor of Literature and Philosophy in English from the University of South Africa. Her research interests include African literature, children's literature, peacebuilding, and gender studies.

Eunice Kamaara, a Professor of Ethics with over 30 years' experience in transformative research for holistic health development, holds a Master of Science in International Health Research Ethics and a doctorate in African Christian Ethics. She co-directs the African Character Initiation Programme (ACIP), a community participatory organization which mentors adolescents to lead with character values for holistic health and wellbeing. ACIP is recognized by the World Health Organization among the Top 30 Africa Health Innovations, http://innov.afro.who.int/innovators/professor-eunice-kamaara-25. She also co-directs the Chaplaincy Training Centre at Mo University/Moi Teaching and Referral Hospital which mainstreams spirituality in teaching, research, and care in hospital settings.

Ezra Chitando serves as Professor of History and Phenomenology of Religion at the University of Zimbabwe. He is also an extraordinary Professor at the Desmond Tutu Centre for Social Action, University of the Western Cape, South Africa.

ROUTLEDGE INTERNATIONAL HANDBOOKS

THE ROUTLEDGE HANDBOOK OF ACCOUNTING FOR THE SUSTAINABLE DEVELOPMENT GOALS
Edited By Andrea Venturelli and Chiara Mio

THE ROUTLEDGE HANDBOOK OF THE UNCERTAIN SELF, 2ND EDITION
Edited by Patrick J. Caroll, Kimberly Rios and Kathryn C. Oleson

ROUTLEDGE HANDBOOK ON TRANSNATIONAL COMMERCIAL LAW
Edited by Bruno Zeller and Camilla Baasch Andersen

THE ROUTLEDGE HANDBOOK OF IDENTITY AND CONSUMPTION
Edited by Ayalla A. Ruvio and Russell Belk

THE ROUTLEDGE INTERNATIONAL HANDBOOK OF PSYCHOANALYSIS AND JEWISH STUDIES
Edited by Stephen Frosh and Devorah Baum

THE ROUTLEDGE HANDBOOK OF ARTIFICIAL INTELLIGENCE AND INTERNATIONAL RELATIONS
Edited by Diego Brasioli, Laura Guercio, Giovanna Landini and Andrea de Giorgio

THE ROUTLEDGE INTERNATIONAL HANDBOOK OF DISABILITY, CRIME, AND JUSTICE
Edited by Stephen J. Macdonald and Donna Peacock

ROUTLEDGE HANDBOOK OF CONTEMPORARY AFRICAN WOMEN
Edited by Anna Chitando, Eunice Kamaara and Ezra Chitando

ROUTLEDGE HANDBOOK OF CONTEMPORARY AFRICAN WOMEN

Edited by
Anna Chitando, Eunice Kamaara and Ezra Chitando

LONDON AND NEW YORK

First published 2025
by Routledge
4 Park Square, Milton Park, Abingdon, Oxon OX14 4RN

and by Routledge
605 Third Avenue, New York, NY 10158

Routledge is an imprint of the Taylor & Francis Group, an informa business

© 2025 selection and editorial matter, Anna Chitando, Eunice Kamaara and Ezra Chitando; individual chapters, the contributors

The right of Anna Chitando, Eunice Kamaara and Ezra Chitando to be identified as the authors of the editorial material, and of the authors for their individual chapters, has been asserted in accordance with sections 77 and 78 of the Copyright, Designs and Patents Act 1988.

All rights reserved. No part of this book may be reprinted or reproduced or utilised in any form or by any electronic, mechanical, or other means, now known or hereafter invented, including photocopying and recording, or in any information storage or retrieval system, without permission in writing from the publishers.

Trademark notice: Product or corporate names may be trademarks or registered trademarks, and are used only for identification and explanation without intent to infringe.

British Library Cataloguing-in-Publication Data
A catalogue record for this book is available from the British Library

ISBN: 978-1-032-53818-1 (hbk)
ISBN: 978-1-032-53821-1 (pbk)
ISBN: 978-1-003-41382-0 (ebk)

DOI: 10.4324/9781003413820

Typeset in Times New Roman
by SPi Technologies India Pvt Ltd (Straive)

To the countless contemporary African women, whose remarkable strength, tenacity, and resilience have shattered barriers, empowered communities, and transformed societies. May this handbook continue to be read as an acknowledgement, celebration, and amplification of your accomplishments and inspire many.

CONTENTS

List of Boxes   xiv
List of Illustrations   xv
List of Contributors   xvi
Acknowledgements   xxiii

SECTION 1
Introduction   1

    Introduction   3
    Anna Chitando, Eunice Kamaara and Ezra Chitando

1 Contemporary African Women: An Appreciation   15
    Anna Chitando, Eunice Kamaara and Ezra Chitando

SECTION 2
Empowering Images of African Women in Literary Works   27

2 "Like flowers blooming from an ice bucket": Contemporary Anglophone Cameroonian Women Writers   29
    Naomi Nkealah

3 Sex, Resistance and Agency: (Queer) Young Women in Selected North African Novels and Films   45
    Gibson Ncube

4 Glimpses of African Women's Autonomy as Represented in
Selected African Literature 58
Clemence Rubaya

5 Interrogating the contradictory portrayal of women in African Drama:
Uche Nwaozuzu's *Ajari* and *Ebibi* in Perspective 70
Godstime Eze, Favour Ayozie and Somtochukwu Metu

SECTION 3
African Women Navigating Multiple Pandemics and Climate Change **85**

6 Women, Spirituality/Religion, and Pandemics in Africa 87
Eunice Kamaara

7 Feminine Wisdom as a Resource for Facing Pandemics in Africa 109
Anthony Okeregbe and Muyiwa Falaiye

8 Catholic Religious Women and COVID-19: Tracing the Role of
Sr Astridah Banda – A Dominican Religious Sister – in Curbing the
Pandemic in Zambia 122
Nelly Mwale and Tomaida Milingo

9 Christian Women in Africa and the COVID-19 Pandemic in the
Democratic Republic of Congo and Nigeria 134
Jessie Ini Fubara-Manuel, Yossa Way and Emma Wild-Wood

10 Women's Leadership in the Face of COVID-19: The Case of
Agnes Mahomva in Zimbabwe 145
Mutsawashe Chitando

11 Ellen Johnson Sirleaf's Rhetorical Leadership: The Fight to
Rebuild Liberia, Empower Women and Conquer Ebola 155
Julia A. Spiker

12 Young African Women's Responses to the Impact of Climate Change 169
Ngozi Nwogwugwu and Elizabeth Oluwafunmiso Ngozi

13 Catholic Women Navigating the Challenges of Climate Change in Rural
Manicaland Province, Zimbabwe: An Appreciative Inquiry Approach 184
Milcah Mudewairi and Caroline Dimingu

SECTION 4
Defying the Odds: African Women in Science, Technology, Engineering and Mathematics — **197**

14 Overcoming Difficulties as a Woman Scientist in Africa — 199
Jennifer Thomson

15 The Trajectory of Rwandan Women in Science and Technology: From the Colonial Period to the Digital Era (1894–2023) — 209
Liberata Gahongayire and Innocent Iyakaremye

16 Depatriarchalising the Media Coverage of Science in Uganda: Recovering Women's Voices — 225
Ivan Nathanael Lukanda, Gerald Walulya, Nakiwala Aisha Sembatya and Amon Ashaba Mwiine

17 African Women and Leadership in Science Academies — 243
Jacqueline Kado

18 Eastern Market Women Activism in Colonial Nigeria: A Historical Perspective — 250
Grace Atim

19 Globalization and African Women: Challenges and Opportunities — 260
Josephine Mukabera

20 Pathways to Power: Religiosity, Economic Opportunities, and IlParakuyo Maasai Women — 283
Lucy W. Massoi and Parit O. Saruni

SECTION 5
African Women in Entrepreneurship, Academia and Politics — **301**

21 Thriving in New Lands: Migrant Women Doing Business in South Africa — 303
Vivian Ojong and John Mhandu

22 Church Women and Entrepreneurship: A Case Study of the Evangelical Lutheran Church in Zimbabwe, Western Diocese — 316
Mbongeni Proud Dube

23 The Role of Young Women in Promoting Economic
   Development in Africa   332
   Cherifa Klaa

24 Women in Higher Education Management in Africa: Trends, Policies,
   and Practices   345
   Elizabeth A. Owino and Donald Lwala

25 An Unbalanced Equation: Exploring Gender Disparity among Academics
   in Southeast Universities, Nigeria   362
   Abel T. Ugwu and Ngozika Anthonia Obi-Ani

26 Women's Political Participation and the Place of Patriarchy in Political
   Institutions in Osun State, Nigeria   375
   Abidemi Abiola Isola

27 Young Professional Women's Performative Agency in Challenging Media
   (Mis) Representations of Women in Politics: The Case of Zimbabwe   390
   Kuziwakwashe Zigomo

SECTION 6
African Women Thriving and Struggling In Historical Times, Older Age, Diplomacy and Religion **409**

28 Empowering Images of Older Women in African Literature   411
   Pepetual Mforbe Chiangong

29 Women's Experiences of Growing Older in a Rural Economy in Ghana   424
   Abdul-Aziz Seidu, Joshua Okyere and Bright Opoku Ahinkorah

30 The Role of Elderly Women in Botswana: A Perspective from African
   Theological Feminist Gerontology   437
   Tshenolo Jennifer Madigele

31 Young African Women's Leadership in Religious Studies and Theology:
   A Review with Special Reference to the School of Religion, Philosophy,
   and Classics, University of KwaZulu-Natal, South Africa   453
   Lindiwe Princess Maseko

32 *Aluta Continua!* African Women Theologians' Contributions to Inclusive
   Theological Education: Towards the African Union's Agenda 2063   474
   Moses Iliya Ogidis

33 Calling the Church to Account: A Theological Response to the Silent Pandemic of Sexual and Gender-Based Violence against Women in Nigeria's Mainline Evangelical Churches   486
Henry Marcus Garba and Moses Iliya Ogidis

34 African Women in Diplomacy and the Quest for Gender Justice   500
Primrose Z.J. Bimha

Index   *514*

BOXES

6.1	The Case of Ms U	90
6.2	The Case of Ms V	92
6.3	The Case of Ms W	94
6.4	The Case of Ms X	95
6.5	The Case of Ms Y	96
6.6	The Case of Ms Z	99

ILLUSTRATIONS

Figures

23.1	Gender gap index in Sub-Saharan Africa as of 2023, by country	336
24.1	PRISMA Diagram	353
24.2	Factors that cause women's under-representation in HEM	355
27.1	2018 Gender Distribution of National Assembly Results by Province	397
27.2	2023 Gender Distribution of National Assembly Results by Province	398

Tables

21.1	Participants' profile	305
23.1	Leading African countries in the MasterCard Index of Women Entrepreneurs (MIWE) in 2021	339
24.1	Inclusion and exclusion criteria	351
24.2	A list of some female Vice-Chancellors in Africa (past and present)	360
24.3	List of the first managers (Vice Chancellors) of HEIs in Africa	361
26.1	Women Titled Chiefs and their Complementary Roles in the Precolonial Era in Nigeria	383
27.1	Numbers of Female Political Candidates Who Contested for Local Council by Province (2018 and 2023)	396
27.2	Numbers of Female Political Candidates Who Contested for National Assembly by Province (2018 and 2023)	397

CONTRIBUTORS

Bright Opoku Ahinkorah is a Research Officer at the University of New South Wales Sydney. His research interests include sexual and reproductive health, maternal and child health, implementation science, and communicable and non-communicable diseases.

Grace Atim is a Chief Research Fellow, Gender and Social Safeguards Specialist in the Department of Internal Conflict Prevention & Resolution, at Institute for Peace and Conflict Resolution Abuja. She holds a Doctorate in Gender Security Studies University of Jos. Her research interests include gender studies, peacebuilding, security, child protection, and strategic communication.

Favour Ayozie is in the Department of Theatre and Film Studies, University of Nigeria. She holds a Bachelor of Arts Degree in Theatre and Film Studies. Her research interests include cultural studies, theatre, and gender studies.

Primrose Z.J. Bimha is a Postdoctoral Research fellow in the Department of Sociology and Social Anthropology at Stellenbosch University. She holds a PhD in Political Studies from the University of Cape Town (UCT). Her research interests include women in politics and international relations, gender and the politics of development, and gender inclusion policy research.

Pepetual Mforbe Chiangong worked as an Assistant Professor of African Literatures and Cultures at the Department of African Studies, Humboldt University, from 2012 to 2023. She holds a PhD in African theatre and drama from the University of Bayreuth. She is currently completing her Habilitation project at the Humboldt University on "Old Age in African Drama and Theatre: Perspectives, Practices, and Expectations."

Mutsawashe Chitando is pursuing her PhD studies in Public Health – Health Economics at the University of Cape Town, Health Economics Division. Her research interests include public health, women's leadership, and human capital development.

Contributors

Caroline Dimingu is a Lecturer in the Department of Theology and Religion at Zimbabwe Ezekiel Guti University. She holds a Master of Science degree in Gender and Policy Studies (Great Zimbabwe University) and a Master of Arts in Religious Studies (University of Zimbabwe). She is a member of various professional organizations such as the European Research Network on Global Pentecostalism (Glopent). She is the current Vice Secretary of Forum for African Women Educationalists Zimbabwe (Fawezi). Her research interests include contemporary issues in systematic theology, transformative feminist liberation theology, religion, intersectional gender and women's rights. She received an award of the researcher of the year from Zimbabwe Ezekiel Guti University in 2017. She has published several book chapters and research articles in high-impact journals.

Mbongeni Proud Dube is an ordained minister of religion and a theologian within the Evangelical Lutheran Church in Zimbabwe (ELCZ). He holds two Diplomas, one in Theology from the United Theological College and another in Religious Studies from the University of Zimbabwe. His research interests encompass the realms of religion and gender, religion and politics, and the role of the Church in the public sphere.

Godstime Eze is a Lecturer in the Department of Theatre and Film Studies, and a Research Fellow at the Institute of African Studies, University of Nigeria. She holds a Master of Arts Degree in Theatre and Cultural Administration. Her research interests include African and Caribbean Drama, Igbo Anthroponyms, and Women and Performance Studies.

Muyiwa Falaiye is a Professor of African Philosophy & African Studies and Director, Institute of African and Diaspora Studies, University of Lagos. He holds a doctorate in Philosophy from the University of Lagos, Nigeria. He is an expert in Sage Philosophy, with research interests in African Socio-Political Philosophy, Afro-American Philosophy and diaspora studies.

Jessie Ini Fubara-Manuel is an Adjunct Lecturer at Essien Ukpabio Presbyterian Theological College, Itu, Nigeria. She holds a PhD in World Christianity from the University of Edinburgh, UK. Her research interests include faith, gender, HIV and disability studies.

Liberata Gahongayire is a Lecturer in the Centre for Conflict Management (CCM), College of Arts and Social Sciences (CASS) at the University of Rwanda (UR). She holds a Doctorate in History, Arts History and Archaeology from Université Libre de Bruxelles. Her research interests include history, genocide prevention, conflict transformation, women in history and gender subjects.

Henry Marcus Garba is a Clergyman with the Evangelical Church Winning All (ECWA) in Nigeria. He is a graduate of Igbaja ECWA Theological Seminary. He also holds a master's degree in Church History from Africa International University (AIU), Nairobi, Kenya, and is currently a PhD Candidate in World Christianity at AIU.

Abidemi Abiola Isola (PhD) is an Associate Professor in the Department of Political Science and Public Administration, Babcock University, Nigeria. Her teaching, research interests and area of specialization include public administration, sociology, women and gender studies. She has several publications to her credit, some of which have appeared in respected international journals such as the *Journal of Interdisciplinary Feminist Thought and Information, International Journal of Women's Studies, and Development in Africa (JGIDA)* and others.

Innocent Iyakaremye is an Associate Professor of Gender Studies in the Centre for Gender Studies, College of Arts and Social Sciences at the University of Rwanda. He holds a Doctorate in Gender and Religion from the University of KwaZulu-Natal. His research interests include gender and religion, adolescents' parenthood, gender-based violence, violence against children, and forced migration.

Jacqueline Kado is the Executive Director of the Network of African Science Academies (NASAC). She holds a Doctorate in Human Development from Atlantic International University. Her professional interests include science diplomacy, sustainable development, and gender inclusivity.

Cherifa Klaa is a Professor of Higher Education in the Department of International Studies, Faculty of Political Science and International Relations, University of Algiers 3 (Algeria). She holds a PhD in Political Science from the same university. Her research interests include development in Africa, women's empowerment, security and regional studies, and migration issues in Africa.

Ivan Nathanael Lukanda is a Senior Lecturer in the Department of Journalism and Communication at Makerere University. He has a PhD in journalism obtained from Stellenbosch University, South Africa. His research areas include science and technology communication, gender and the media, climate change, food as communication, and journalists' safety on and offline.

Donald Lwala is a graduate student at Mount Kenya University, where he is currently pursuing a Master's degree in Early Childhood Studies. He is driven by a profound passion for research and is dedicated to exploring the realms of educational research, social justice, and inclusive education. His academic journey is deeply rooted in a commitment to advancing early childhood education, with a particular focus on creating inclusive and equitable learning environments. He aspires to contribute meaningfully to the field, combining academic rigour with a genuine desire to make a positive impact on the lives of young learners.

Tshenolo Jennifer Madigele is a Theology Senior Lecturer in the Department of Theology and Religious Studies at the University of Botswana. Her teaching areas include systematic theology and pastoral care and counselling. Her research interests include human sexuality, gerontology, gender and community building, health and spirituality, and Botho Pastoral Care and Counselling.

Lindiwe Princess Maseko is a second-year doctoral candidate in the Gender and Religion Program at the University of Kwa-Zulu Natal in South Africa. Her research work focuses on gender and religion, African women theology, sexual and reproductive, health and rights, and indigenous knowledge system(s), gender and pandemics, women and peacebuilding, and women and leadership. She has eight professional certificates in theology, gender justice and leadership, ecumenism, and peacebuilding. She is currently involved in a research project to publish a peer-reviewed African Theology student book on pandemics, and Transformative Masculinities and Femininities in Africa.

Lucy W. Massoi is a Senior Lecturer in the School of Public Administration and Management at Mzumbe University, Tanzania. She holds a PhD in Political Science from Ghent University. Her research centres around political ecology, with a particular focus on pastoralism, resource conflicts and gender studies.

Somtochukwu J. Metu is a Lecturer in the Department of English and Literary Studies, University of Nigeria. She is a 2019 CODESRIA Doctoral Fellow. Her research interests are in Poetry, Queer Studies, Gender and Feminist Studies. Her poems are published in *The Muse: A Journal of Critical and Creative Writing*.

John Mhandu is a Senior Lecturer at the University of Mpumalanga, Sociology Department. He holds a Doctorate in Sociology from the University of KwaZulu Natal. He is a self-motivated and results-driven intellectual with a background in social theory and research methodology (both qualitative and quantitative). His research interests include migration, migrant labour, informality, informal economy, and social change.

Tomaida Milingo is a Lecturer in the Department of Religious Studies at the University of Zambia. She holds a Doctorate in Religious Studies from the University of Zambia. Her research interests include religion and society and religion and gender.

Milcah Mudewairi is a PhD student at Great Zimbabwe University and a Senior Lecturer in the Department of Religion and Theology at Zimbabwe Ezekiel Guti University. She is also a Research Associate in the Department of Religion and Theology at the University of Pretoria in South Africa and a short-term Researcher at the University of Religions and Denominations in Iran. She is a specialist in Religion and the Conservation of the environment. To date, she has eight publications in the Area of Eco-theology.

Josephine Mukabera is a Lecturer and Director of the Centre for Gender Studies, College of Arts and Social Sciences, University of Rwanda. She holds a doctorate of Philosophy in Interdisciplinary Gender Studies from Seoul National University. Her research interests include Women in Politics, Gender and Intersectionality, Development and Gender Studies.

Nelly Mwale is a Senior Lecturer in the Department of Religious Studies at the University of Zambia. She holds a Doctorate in Religious Studies from the University of Zambia. Her research interests include religion in the public sphere, Christian higher education, religion and gender, and African Indigenous Knowledge Systems.

Amon Ashaba Mwiine is a Lecturer in the School of Women and Gender Studies, Makerere University. He holds a PhD (Sociology) from Stellenbosch University, South Africa. At Makerere University, he teaches on courses that include; Men Studies: Masculinities and Development; Gender and Sexuality and Feminist Theory. His research interests are in Critical studies of men and Masculinity; ethnographic and narrative forms of qualitative research; gender and politics.

Contributors

Gibson Ncube lectures in the Department of Modern Foreign Languages at Stellenbosch University. His broad research interests are in comparative literature, gender/queer studies and cultural studies. He has published widely in these areas.

Elizabeth Oluwafunmiso Ngozi is a Senior Lecturer in the Department of Nutrition and Dietetics, Ben Carson School of Basic Medical Sciences, Babcock University, Ilishan-Remo, Nigeria. She holds a Doctor of Philosophy degree in Nutrition and Dietetics from the Federal University of Agriculture, Abeokuta, Nigeria. Her primary areas of research interest are Community Nutrition and Public Health.

Naomi Nkealah is a Senior Lecturer of English in the Division of Languages, Literacies and Literatures in the School of Education at the University of the Witwatersrand, Johannesburg. She teaches courses in Shakespearean drama, modern South African drama and African feminist literature. Her research specializes in African feminisms and critical pedagogies for English education. She is co-editor of the book *Gendered Violence and Human Rights in Black World Literature and Film* (Routledge, 2021), co-edited with distinguished professor, Obioma Nnaemeka.

Ngozi Nwogwugwu is a Professor of Political Science in the Department of Political Science and Public Administration at Babcock University, Ilishan-Remo, Nigeria. His primary areas of research interests include Comparative Politics, Governance, Gender Studies, and Public Administration. Professor Nwogwugwu has published over 80 journal articles and peer-reviewed chapters in books in international and national outlets. He is currently the Editor, *Journal of International Politics and Development* (JIPAD).

Ngozika Anthonia Obi-Ani is a PhD holder and a Senior Lecturer in the Department of History and International Studies at the University of Nigeria, Nsukka. She is an interdisciplinary historian whose research lies at the intersection of gender, memory, and conflict, providing valuable insights into the complexities of African history.

Moses Iliya Ogidis is a lecturer at ECWA Theological Seminary Karu Abuja Nigeria. He holds a Doctor of Philosophy in Theology from St Paul's University in Kenya. His research interests include the New Testament, gender and disability studies.

Vivian Ojong is a Full Professor in the Discipline of Anthropology, at the College of Humanities University of KwaZulu-Natal (UKZN), Durban, South Africa. She is currently the Dean and Head of the School of Social Science and the Interim Dean of Research for the College of Humanities at the University of KwaZulu-Natal, Durban. Professor Ojong's research areas are identity politics, migration and internationalization, globalization and diaspora studies, gender, feminism, research methodology and methods, entrepreneurship as well as culture and religion.

Anthony Okeregbe is an Associate Professor in the Department of Philosophy and, an associate of the Institute of African and Diaspora Studies, University of Lagos, Nigeria. He holds a doctorate of Philosophy from the University of Lagos. His research interests include Phenomenology/Existentialism, Contemporary African Philosophy, and transdisciplinary studies of African lifeworlds.

Contributors

Joshua Okyere is a Research Fellow at Challenging Heights, a non-governmental organization dedicated to empowering women, eliminating human trafficking, modern slavery, and all forms of violence. His research interests include women's health, non-communicable disease prevention and management, and palliative care.

Elizabeth A. Owino has been a Lecturer in the Department of Educational Psychology, Moi University for over 15 years. Currently, she is serving as the Director of Quality Assurance at the University of Kigali, Rwanda. She is also an enrolled student at Namibia College of Open and Long Distance Learning (NAMCOL) for postgraduate studies in Open School Operations and Management (PDOSOM). She holds a Doctorate in Educational Psychology. Her research interests include gender studies, human development, and e-learning.

Clemence Rubaya is a Lecturer in the Department of Educational Foundations and Curriculum Development, School of Heritage and Education at Great Zimbabwe University. He is a PhD holder with the University of KwaZulu Natal (UKZN), RSA. His research interests lie in literature and gender studies, with particular bias towards the area of women empowerment. He is also passionate about language-related issues and education in general.

Parit O. Saruni is a Senior Lecturer in the Department of Social Studies at the Mwalimu Nyerere Memorial Academy. He has a Doctorate in Rural Development from Sokoine University of Agriculture. His research interests are on pastoralism, natural resource issues and rural development.

Abdul-Aziz Seidu is an Associate Lecturer at the College of Public Health, Medical and Veterinary Sciences, James Cook University, Australia. He is also the Research and Development Coordinator for the Centre for Gender and Advocacy at Takoradi Technical University, Ghana. His research interests include sexual and reproductive health and rights, disability and health, maternal and child health, gender-based violence, women's empowerment, and social determinants of health.

Nakiwala Aisha Sembatya is a Senior Lecturer and Head of the Department of Journalism and Communication at Makerere University. Her research focuses on social and behaviour change in health contexts as well as communication, women and gender.

Julia A. Spiker, PhD, is a Professor in the School of Communication at The University of Akron. She holds a doctorate from the University of Oklahoma. Her research focuses on political communication, especially the rhetoric of women leaders and the political empowerment of women and girls. Her book entitled, *Empowering Women: Global Voices of Rhetorical Influence* (2019), presents an overarching, global picture of women's empowerment through the lens of elite women political leaders' speeches. She has over 25 journal and book chapter publications and more than 55 conference presentations.

Jennifer Thomson is an Emeritus Professor in the Department of Molecular and Cell Biology at the University of Cape Town, South Africa. She is President of the Organization for Women in Science for the Developing World. Her research is in the development of drought-tolerant maize using genetic modification.

Contributors

Abel T. Ugwu graduated with a Bachelor of Arts degree in 2021 from the Department of History and International Studies at the University of Nigeria Nsukka. He is currently a graduate student in History at the University of Southern Mississippi. His research interests are in Colonial Africa as well as post-colonial migration and gender studies. He is currently working on a thesis exploring the role of colonial policing in southeastern Nigeria.

Gerald Walulya is a Senior Lecturer in the Department of Journalism and Communication, Makerere University. He holds a PhD in Political Communication from the University of Oslo, Norway. His research interests include political communication, freedom of expression, and journalists' safety.

Yossa Way is Academic Secretary General and Professor at the Anglican University of Congo (UAC) and Rector of the Anglican University in Central Africa (UNAAC).

Emma Wild-Wood is a Professor of African Religions and World Christianity at the University of Edinburgh. She co-directs the Centre for the Study of World Christianity and is an editor of the journal, *Studies in World Christianity*.

Kuziwakwashe Zigomo is a Lecturer in the Department of Politics and International Relations at the University of Kent. She holds a Doctorate in Politics from Royal Holloway, University of London. Her research interests include southern African politics (particularly Zimbabwe, South Africa and the overarching SADC region), gender, development, migration, citizenship and belonging, peacebuilding and security studies.

ACKNOWLEDGEMENTS

At the time that this handbook was conceptualized and completed, Eunice Kamaara and Ezra Chitando were African collaborating partners in the Humboldt Research Hub, "Fighting Pandemics with Religion? How Female Religious Actors in Africa Contribute to ensuring Healthy Lives" at the University of Zimbabwe. They would like to register their profound gratitude to the Alexander Humboldt Foundation for the support.

SECTION 1

Introduction

INTRODUCTION

Anna Chitando, Eunice Kamaara and Ezra Chitando

The *Routledge Handbook of Contemporary Women in Africa* draws attention to the profound progress made by African women in sectors that are often neglected in scholarly analyses. It highlights the achievements of African women, placing emphasis on African women's agency. Methodologically, it adopts an Appreciative Inquiry approach by prioritising the positives in African women's lived experiences. The most striking dimension of Appreciative Inquiry is its emphasis on the assets that people have, employing a positive and empowering perspective (see, for example, Demeshane and Nel 2018). Consequently, the handbook shows how African women have deployed their agency to post notable results in such areas as responding to pandemics and climate change, as well as focusing on older and younger women in Africa. Further, it sustains the conversation on the theoretical model that can best advance African women's interests, while showing the progress made by African women in entrepreneurship, Science, Technology, Engineering, Mathematics, and higher education. Its theoretical and ideological take-off point is that despite facing substantial odds, the story of African women cannot be reduced to one of moaning and paralysis. If anything, the handbook utilises the notion of agency to illustrate how African women are contributing to the continent's resilience and occasional flourishing. Acknowledging the progress that Africa has made due to women's transformative leadership, voice, and power (see, for example, Brown 2021), the handbook provides fresh material on hitherto overlooked themes. Contributors reflect on how African women are defying the narratives of never-ending poverty, disease, corruption, and death (Bunce et al. 2016) and show how African women are making progress in the emerging areas of engagement.

Chapters in this handbook are in unison as they show how African women from various spheres, social locations, skill set, and personalities have been achieving notable progress in diverse areas. Overall, the distinctive contribution of the volume is that it seeks to highlight the impact of African women's agency in specific areas, without glossing over the very real and concrete challenges they continue to face from global, national, and local forces.

Chapters in This Volume

Section 1: Introduction

This section presents the chapters in the volume. African women and girls have often been presented as the most disadvantaged people in the world. Global media images tend to beam negative images of African women and girls, associating them with disease, suffering, and death. While it remains true that Africa as a continent continues to wrestle against multiple exclusions, mostly associated with colonialism and ongoing exploitation by the global North (now with China joining in), the story of African women is a story of courage, tenacity, resilience, achievement, and flourishing in the midst of formidable challenges.

The opening chapter seeks to communicate this alternative image of African women. While acknowledging the notable struggles that African women are waging, Chapter 1 concentrates on outlining the different areas where African women are registering notable successes. The chapter summarises the various fields of engagement where African women are exposing "the danger of a single story" (Adichie, 2009) and explicating the sections that constitute this volume. It provides overviews of these sections and prepares the reader to approach the volume with a more positive, refreshing, and empowering approach to the lived experiences of African women from diverse walks of life.

Section 2: Empowering Images of African Women in Literary Works

Progressive representations of African women in literary works are crucial in promoting diverse narratives, challenging stereotypes, and amplifying their voices. Literary works have the power to shape public perceptions and influence societal norms, making it essential to portray African women in a positive and empowering light. The chapters in this section celebrate African women's strength and agency as they challenge the dominant narratives and provide alternative perspectives when they write their own stories.

In Chapter 2, Naomi Nkealah reflects on how African women's voices have become more audible and powerful in the 21st century than ever before as their feminist texts speak to audiences across the world. Nkealah notes that these powerful expressions are the voices of Anglophone Cameroonian women writers whose literary productions in the past three decades have made significant contributions to discourses on gendered violence, women and migration, women's economic empowerment, women's sexuality, polygamy, women and pandemics, and women's indigenous cultures. While the writings of these women are largely invisible in mainstream African literature scholarship, the strength of their voices sears through the silence once one encounters their texts. Nkealah argues that put together, these women create a symphony of voices singing an inspirational song of African women's ability to flourish even under systems determined to break them down – patriarchy, colonialism, and capitalism. The chapter traces the flowering moments in the development of Anglophone Cameroonian women's literature and maps out the emerging areas of engagement in contemporary women's writing, exploring contesting conceptualisations of feminist discourses. In line with the vision of this handbook, Nkealah demonstrates how Anglophone Cameroonian women writers of various backgrounds and social standing have written literature that paints a variegated image of African women's agency.

Chapter 3 examines a selection of North African literary texts and films. Gibson Ncube analyses three novels and two films. The three novels are *L'Enfant de Sable* (1985) by Tahar

Introduction

Ben Jelloun, *Le Garçon Manqué* (2000) and *Mes Mauvaises Pensées* (2005), both by Nina Bouraoui. The two selected films are Nadia El Fani's Bedwin Hacker (2003), as well as Raja Amari's *Al Dowaha* (2009). The chapter focuses on how these selected cultural productions, in their divergent iterations, depict what it means to be a young woman in Arab Muslim societies of North Africa. Arab Muslim societies of North Africa place great value on virginity and as such, young women are expected to behave and perform embodiment in specific ways that ensure that they do not tarnish the name of their families when they get married. The selected texts depict young women protagonists who defy heteropatriarchal dictates. These protagonists show that young women can be sensuous and sexual beings who do not reduce the sum of their being to simply an intact hymen. By focusing on queerness, these cultural productions give agency to the young women and highlight that they can be independent of men and masculinity. The selected novels and films demonstrate that female sexuality in young women can exist beyond the grip and control of phallocracy. The queer young womanhood that emerges from the selected novels and films presents a new way of performing and embodying young womanhood in a region of the African continent where religious dogma and cultural practices continue to oppress women.

In Chapter 4, Clemence Rubaya observes that the power of women to make important decisions in many areas of life has historically been undermined. No society can be exempted from the guilt of being repressive of its women and undervaluing them. Men have been accused of devising strategies and tactics to oppress women. This gross injustice and violation of women's human rights has produced so much misery – not just for the women themselves but for society in its entirety. Despite history being beleaguered with evidence of underestimation of the power of women, there are many indications, both in real life and as represented in literary works, of emerging women who confront diverse challenges, refuse silencing and show great creativity to qualitatively improve the lives of others. This chapter adopts content analysis of selected literary works by African women writers to show the portrayal of women's agency as imperative to ensuring survival of families. It argues that in Africa (as elsewhere), women's value should never be downplayed since the well-being of deprived families in Africa depends fundamentally on the survival strategies implemented by women.

Chapter 5 interrogates the contradictory portrayal of women in African drama using Uche Nwaozuzu's *Ajari* and *Ebibi*. The authors of this chapter, Godstime Eze, Favour Ayozie, and Somtochukwu Metu, examine and analyse various representations of women in African drama, pointing out the contradictory portrayals of women characters in the two drama texts of Uche Nwaozuzu, *Ajari* and *Ebibi*. The study juxtaposes the playwright's representation of women as resilient or fragile to the perceived situation in African societies, owing to the fact that drama is a mirror that reflects the society. The chapter weighs the aforementioned stereotypical representations of womanhood in *Ajari* and *Ebibi*. It also pays attention to the individual and collective roles portrayed, as either regarded or disregarded, strong and opinionated or marginalised and weak in the two drama texts. The focus is on feminism and its ideologies as they concern African women in traditional African society. The chapter analyses different representations of women characters and their contradictory portrayals in the abovementioned drama texts, citing related examples from other literary works. It concludes that most male playwrights in Nigeria, including the ones discussed in the chapter, trod the same direction of deconstructive, stereotypical, and contradictory portrayal of women characters in their works.

Section 3: African Women Navigating Multiple Pandemics and Climate Change

Chapters in this section demonstrate how African women have shown great resilience and adaptability in navigating multiple pandemics and climate change, which have both significant and intersecting impact on their lives and communities. Despite the immense challenges they face, African women are resilient agents of change. They have been actively involved in community-led initiatives to address the impact of pandemics and climate change. African women are organising and advocating for gender-responsive policies, access to healthcare, economic empowerment, and sustainable environmental practices. Their knowledge, leadership, and contributions are critical in building resilient communities and shaping sustainable development in Africa.

In Chapter 6, Eunice Kamaara argues that the dominant story on gender and pandemics in Africa is that there is a disproportionate impact, with pandemics exacerbating existing gender inequalities; women suffer the brunt of pandemics in all aspects. This has been the story with Ebola, HIV and lately, the coronavirus disease (COVID-19). However, women have translated their challenges and vulnerability into remarkable resourcefulness, resilience, and strength to cope better as they (are) mobilise(d) to respond to pandemics. Chapter 6 demonstrates how women deployed religion/spirituality during COVID-19 to cope and promote the health of their families and communities. In addition, the chapter seeks to understand how women as religious/spiritual actors might be equipped in preparedness for future pandemics.

Chapter 7 analyses the multiple dimensions of female agency in tackling two major pandemics in Africa, namely the Ebola epidemic and the COVID-19 pandemic. The authors, Anthony Okeregbe and Muyiwa Falaiye, examine how African women, within performative male interventions and undeserving structures, carried out practical actions that helped in positively transforming lives during pandemics and setting the agenda for positive engagements in their communities.

Nelly Mwale and Tomaida Milingo use the narrative of Sr. Astridah Banda to explore the role of Catholic religious women in curbing the COVID-19 pandemic in Zambia. Chapter 8 argues that through her utilisation of radio, and leadership skills, as inspired by the Dominican charisma to evangelise, Sr Astridah's mediatised COVID-19 responses. The authors contend that this provides lessons for a gendered role in curbing the pandemic, centred on exploiting existing opportunities for the good of humanity.

In Chapter 9, Jessie Ini Fubara-Manuel, Yossa Way, and Emma Wild-Wood discuss the findings of a study they carried out in Nigeria and the Democratic Republic of Congo, focusing on the challenge of conflict and insecurity during the COVID-19 pandemic. The study revealed that in both countries Christian women relied on parachurch and humanitarian organisations for support during the pandemic. Professional women in particular were critical of the way church leadership responded to the pandemic. The authors maintain that this reaction may suggest a trend at the intersection of gender/education responses that requires more attention.

Chapter 10 describes how the emergence of the COVID-19 pandemic raised serious concerns worldwide, particularly on how it threatened to reverse the gains made towards the realisation of the Sustainable Development Goals. However, embedded in the challenges presented by COVID-19 were unique opportunities for women and girls to assume leadership in responding to the pandemic. In this chapter, Mutsawashe Chitando explores the role of women during the COVID-19 pandemic. She highlights women's effective leadership in the

Introduction

face of COVID-19, with a focus on the leadership of Agnes Mahomva who was the Chief Coordinator of the COVID-19 Task Force in responding to the pandemic in Zimbabwe.

In Chapter 11, Julia A. Spiker explores Ellen Johnson Sirleaf's leadership. As the first woman to be democratically elected to lead an African nation, Ellen Johnson Sirleaf served two terms as president of Liberia (2006–2018). Spiker presents Sirleaf as a global leader who fights for democratic rule and women's empowerment. Her determination and leadership successfully fought through the challenges of rebuilding Liberia after a 14-year civil war and overcoming an Ebola epidemic. Sirleaf's political rhetorical leadership offers an opportunity to understand better the intersection of transformative rhetorical leadership and women's agency in a health crisis. Sirleaf's determination and political leadership demonstrate how an African woman successfully expresses power rhetorically.

In Chapter 12, the two authors, Ngozi Nwogwugwu and Elizabeth Oluwafunmiso Ngozi, contend that while the majority of the activities that contribute to climate change are conducted in the West, Africa is the region that is being most affected by its effects. The authors further argue that the participation of women and girls in any meaningful response to the climate change impacts (CCI) is essential. The study concludes that young African women have a variety of options for coping with and mitigating CCI, including using renewable energy sources, managing water resources effectively, practising environmentally friendly agriculture methods, and joining advocacy groups for environmental conservation.

Chapter 13 is an appreciative inquiry into the protest of Catholic women against riverbank cultivation by tobacco farmers in Manicaland Province, Zimbabwe. Milcah Mudewairi and Caroline Dimingu maintain that gendered climate change continues to have a negative effect on women in the rural areas of Manicaland Province in Zimbabwe. The chapter traces and justifies the need to appreciate the roles of women in climate change mitigation despite the gender-related impediments they face in responding to climate change. Utilising the theological appreciative inquiry method, the chapter celebrates the triumphs of the leading role by the Catholic women in Makoni West District in the campaign for climate change resilience against tobacco farmers. The chapter is anchored on the notion that despite the setbacks of gender in climate change mitigation, women are diverting from "weeping" to becoming active participants, hence the need to appreciate such efforts.

Section 4: Defying the Odds: African Women in Science, Technology, Engineering, and Mathematics

Defying the odds, African women in science, technology, engineering, and mathematics (STEM) are making remarkable contributions and breaking barriers in these fields across the continent. Chapters in this section review how African women are contributing to advancement in various scientific disciplines. They are involved in STEM as they challenge stereotypes and make significant strides. Their work is essential for addressing local challenges and driving sustainable development in Africa.

Chapter 14 hinges on Jennifer Thomson's story of overcoming difficulties and obstacles as a woman scientist in Africa. It emphasises the importance of following one's dreams and aspirations against all odds. The chapter is also about sticking to what one is good at and asking for help when necessary. Furthermore, the story is about taking on every opportunity that arises no matter how challenging. The chapter traces Jennifer's achievements from the time she graduated with a PhD from Rhodes University in South Africa up to the time she worked with a number of International Organisations.

In Chapter 15, Liberata Gahongayire and Innocent Iyakaremye reflect on the progress that has been made by women in Rwanda in the fields of Science, Innovation, and Technology (SIT), after having been excluded for a long time. They assert that in recent years, there has been much focus on increasing the representation of women in schools and professions in these fields. This effort is especially pronounced as governmental institutions, non-governmental organisations, and the private sector have made significant investments in supporting and empowering women. Thus, programmes were developed to encourage young women to pursue careers in Information and Communication Technology (ICT) and other fields related to STEM. The chapter also examines the contribution of various initiatives to promote women's access, use, and ownership of SIT, while underlining women's significant involvement in all these ingenuities.

Chapter 16 is an exploration of how female voices are marginalised in media coverage of Science in Uganda, both as authors and sources. The authors of this chapter, Ivan Nathanael Lukanda, Gerald Walulya, Nakiwala Aisha Sembatya, and Amon Ashaba Mwiine, offer insight into the appreciative inquiry for women's voices about Science and Technology in Uganda's media. Based on interviews with women scientists, gender scholars, and women in the media, the chapter focuses on how media can construct women in more meaningful and fulfilling ways by highlighting women's growth at personal and professional levels in the areas of Science and Technology. The chapter suggests ways of bridging theory, evidence, and practice in training and initiating women into Science and Technology leadership. Through this, they can garner more prominence alongside the men who often occupy such positions as a way of depatriarchalizing media coverage in Uganda.

Chapter 17 is an interrogation of why very few women serve in leadership positions in academia, through the lens of the Network of African Science Academies (NASAC). The NASAC is a consortium of Science academies in Africa and is no exception to this phenomenon. Leadership is predominantly male. In this chapter, Jacqueline Kado interrogates why African women scientists do not take up leadership roles in these Science organisations. She reflects on what hurdles deter female leadership or discourage actions that promote gender equity in leadership within academies. The chapter articulates the factors that make the realisation of Sustainable Development Goal 5 (Achieve gender equality and empower all women and girls) almost impossible in Science organisations in Africa, and attempts to explore possible remedial actions.

In Chapter 18, Grace Atim provides historical perspectives on the activism of Eastern market women in colonial Nigeria from 1900 to 1960. She highlights the significant contributions and challenges faced by these women in their pursuit of social, political, and economic rights during this period. The chapter explores the diverse forms of activism undertaken by Eastern market women, including their involvement in nationalist movements, political organisations, and women's associations. It examines the strategies employed by these women to mobilise communities, raise awareness, and advocate for their rights. In addition, it sheds light on the impact of their activism against colonial policies, which brought about political reforms in the region and broader struggle for independence and social justice in Nigeria.

Chapter 19 argues that despite the potential benefits of globalisation, such as increased economic growth and cultural exchange, there is evidence that the process has resulted in uneven and gendered outcomes for women in Africa. Through a systematic review of thirty-eight papers, written on globalisation and African women, Josephine Mukabera answers the question of how globalisation has affected the socio-economic empowerment of African women, and the strategies employed by women to face challenges associated with globalisation processes. She avows that although the legacy of colonialism perpetuated gender inequalities, the postcolonial era is characterised by a strong women's agency and resilience of African women, which challenged biased gender structures by their active participation in economy, politics, and cultural development.

In Chapter 20, the authors, Lucy W. Massoi and Parit L. Saruni, present a comprehensive analysis of the transformations taking place within the Kilosa Ilparakuyo Maasai community in Tanzania, with a particular focus on the progress made by Maasai women. The Maasai people, who traditionally lived in a society characterised by male supremacy and the habit of having multiple spouses, are presently undergoing a significant cultural transformation driven by the complex interaction of increasing religious devotion and economic prospects. The chapter highlights how these changes have promoted the advancement of Maasai women.

Section 5: African Women in Entrepreneurship, Academia, and Politics

Chapters in this section are a demonstration of how African women's participation and success in entrepreneurship, academia, and politics are driving forces behind social and economic progress across the continent. In entrepreneurship, African women have been increasingly breaking barriers, establishing and leading successful businesses. In academia, African women are making significant contributions as researchers, scholars, and educators. Their research and expertise contribute to the development of solutions for local and global challenges, fostering innovation and progress. The achievements of African women in entrepreneurship, academia, and politics are paving the way for a more equitable and prosperous future. However, it is important to acknowledge that significant challenges and barriers still exist. Efforts must continue to be made to address gender disparities, provide equal opportunities, and support the advancement of African women in these fields. By empowering African women in entrepreneurship, academia, and politics, their full potential can be unlocked to contribute to the overall development and transformation of the continent.

In Chapter 21, Vivian Ojong and John Mhandu argue that African migration scholarship appears to reduce women's agency and willpower by linking women's migration processes to those of men, thereby reducing women's agency and determination resulting in their positionalities remaining on the peripheries of literature. There is also the tendency of treating women as a homogeneous group. The fact that their experiences are not the same as those of local (South African women in this case) who occupy the same informal entrepreneurial space is recognised. In the "New Lands" they find themselves, they can utilise the opportunity structures in the South African economy and a cultural disposition for business in their countries of origin to thrive in an environment which is not designed to enable their success. Through the concepts of "bounded solidarity and enforceable trust," they are creating specific niche entrepreneurial spaces that serve as a form of "protected market." The authors conclude the chapter by highlighting the different coping and adaptation mechanisms the women utilise to deal with challenges created by acculturation in the host nation-state.

Mbongeni Proud Dube, in Chapter 22, stresses that contemporary studies on entrepreneurship have shown that female entrepreneurs in Africa encounter various barricades such as traditional socio-cultural influences. Most African societies have made it easier for men to thrive in business than women. Despite this, women in religious spaces have made significant progress in entrepreneurship compared to previous years and they deserve to be credited. Thus, the study is an appreciation of the achievements by female entrepreneurs in the Evangelical Lutheran Church in Zimbabwe (ELCZ), Western Diocese. The author recognises the significant progress made by churchwomen in the business sector. Dube also acknowledges the lived experiences of Church business-women in the ELCZ Western Diocese.

Chapter 23 examines how, in recent years, many African countries have been working to promote the status of women in the society and involve them in development processes. Nevertheless, the policies pursuing this aspired goal have been different from one country to another, given the specificities of each country, and the extent of male domination in the different settings. In this chapter, Cherifa Clan assesses the role of African women in economic development, particularly in the sector of small and medium enterprises. The chapter highlights the constraints facing African women in starting, operating, and expanding projects. The results of this study indicate that there is a great awareness of the challenges facing women in Africa, besides the improvements that have been attained recently in the economic development journey.

In Chapter 24, Elizabeth A. Owino and Donald Lwala affirm that increasing the representation of women in higher education management (HEM) is key to realising gender equality. The chapter aimed to determine the changes experienced in the HEM landscape in Kenya, Rwanda, South Africa, and Tanzania in the last two decades. The results from the study conducted by the two authors indicated that barriers such as socio-cultural factors, institutional factors, and individual factors impede the advancement of women to HEM. The authors advance the argument that the underrepresentation of women in HEM has far-reaching consequences in realising gender equality. The study recommends that effective national and institutional policies be implemented across the continent and globally and, where possible, ineffective policies be reviewed.

Abel T. Ugwu and Ngozika Anthonia Obi-Ani investigate the shifting educational destinies of women in Igboland, concentrating on the dynamics of gender relationships among scholars in chosen universities in Southeastern Nigeria since 1970. Following the conclusion of the Nigeria-Biafra conflict (1967–1970), there has been a relative rise in the count of female academics in higher educational institutions within Igboland. However, this increase has yet to produce the sought-after parity in gender relations essential for substantial societal transformation. Therefore, Chapter 25 is an inquiry into the nature of gender interactions among educators in universities of Southeastern Nigeria. The authors employ the theoretical framework of relative deprivation to analyse the historical backdrop of female academics, simultaneously evaluating the institutional and societal elements obstructing their progress. Beyond acting as a manual for emerging female academics, this chapter also reveals the evolving educational trajectories of women.

Abidemi Abiola Isola, in Chapter 26, brings in another topical theme of women's participation in politics. Isola states that diversity in social, political, and cultural situations in each country of the world has led to variation in women's political participation. In spite of this, the author argues that there is one common feature of women's political experiences across the world. This is with regard to politics, a field that seems to be reserved for men. Consequently, in many parts of the world, most particularly in developing countries, the level of women's political participation is low when compared to their male counterparts. The chapter concludes that there is a need for urgency to protect women from patriarchal subordination starting from the family where patriarchy originated. There is also the need for courage to put an end to male discrimination, and promote equal respect for both male and female in all aspects of life. This would curtail marginalisation, and underrepresentation of women in decision-making, thereby enhancing women's participation in politics among the Yorubas, with Osun State in focus.

In Chapter 27, Kuziwakwashe Zigomo affirms that women's under-representation in politics is a global challenge and the Southern African region has been no exception in this regard. She argues that unbalanced media reporting has contributed to this low representation by reinforcing negative stereotypical images of women in politics. In this chapter, Zigomo explores how young professional women in Zimbabwean politics are challenging these trite renderings in terms of how they epitomise themselves on and offline during electoral periods. The chapter draws on Butler's theory of performative agency and postcolonial feminist theory to highlight their performances of femininity in the public sphere of politics. It also shows how these women have employed their agency to subvert and indeed challenge patriarchal discourses, which serve to exclude them from the political sphere. Whilst young professional women's agency is considerable in this regard, this chapter argues that virtual political spaces on social media in particular have both widened the space for their political participation and engagement whilst still being hostile spaces for women. Ultimately, this chapter challenges society to move beyond conventional stereotypical media representations of women in politics to consider the new and dynamic ways in which young professional women are engaging with politics on and offline to subvert patriarchal discourses that seek to exclude them.

Section 6: African Women Thriving in Older Age, Diplomacy, and Religion

In older age, African women often embody a wealth of knowledge and experience, serving as pillars of their communities and families. In diplomacy, African women have made significant contributions as leaders, negotiators, and peacemakers. They have played crucial roles in conflict resolution, peacebuilding, and promoting social justice. Religion holds a central place in the lives of many African women, providing them with spiritual guidance, strength, and a sense of community. African women have been leaders in various religious traditions. They bring their unique perspectives and insights to religious practices, addressing societal challenges, promoting gender equality, and advocating for the rights and well-being of women and marginalised communities. The chapters in this section explore the thriving of African women in older age, diplomacy, and religion, viewing the involvement of African women in these different aspects of life as testament to their resilience, leadership, and contributions to their communities and societies. Recognising and celebrating their achievements in these areas is crucial for building a more inclusive and equitable society that values the diverse talents and experiences of African women.

In Chapter 28, Pepetual Mforbe Chiangong avers that older women have been known to overturn the course of events and history in some African societies, yet this subject has barely been explored from an African literary perspective. This chapter thus takes a critical angle to explore the political, social, and cultural movements by elderly women in African and African Diaspora literature, underscoring how they have unsettled existing normative ideologies and actions. The author reflects on Jennifer Makumbi's (2020) notion of *mwenkanonkano* "balancing" feminism and follows up from there to locate older women's agency and resistance but also rebellious acts at the grassroots and cosmopolitan spaces in their role, status, and character. Chiangong considers old age and gender as relevant categories necessary to explore older women's empowering role in the society, and what motivates their move towards empowerment. The chapter closely examines elderly women's actions as an attempt to locate their move towards empowerment, but more importantly, underscores that their feminist agenda emerges from their different cultural contexts. Therefore, ritual, the body, words, and action will determine the direction of the debates as old age is employed to position women in select African and African Diaspora literature.

Chapter 29 analyses women's experiences of growing older in a rural economy in Ghana. The authors, Abdul-Aziz Seidu, Joshua Okyere, and Bright Opoku, assert that for years, African women have struggled to gain social recognition and autonomy. This challenge with autonomy has truncated the socio-economic status and exacerbated adverse health outcomes among African women. Using an intersectionality lens as a theoretical framework, the authors explore the experiences of Ghanaian women in relation to ageing in a rural economy. The chapter discusses the social, economic, and health challenges that women experience as they grow older. Furthermore, the authors discuss how gender and rurality intersect to influence Ghanaian women's experiences with ageing. The chapter also identifies existing opportunities that can be leveraged at the individual, household, community, and national levels to improve the quality of life of women as they navigate through their later years. The chapter concludes by calling for greater attention to the experiences of older women in rural economies. It argues that policies and programmes must be designed with a gender-sensitive and intersectionality lens.

In Chapter 30, Tshenolo Jennifer Madigele explores the significant and often overlooked role of elderly women in Botswana through the angle of African Theological Feminism. The chapter delves into the intersectionality of age, gender, and spirituality, shedding light on their multifaceted contributions to the community, family structure, and cultural preservation. Through an in-depth examination of their roles as caregivers, knowledge keepers, and community pillars, the chapter explores the unique challenges elderly women face and emphasises the need for a comprehensive understanding of their significance. Drawing upon African theological perspectives that prioritise the experiences of women, the chapter enriches the discourse surrounding the empowerment, agency, and resilience of elderly women within the broader framework of feminist theology.

Chapter 31 reviews African women's leadership in Religious Studies and Theology, with special reference to the School of Religion, Philosophy and Classics, University of KwaZulu-Natal, South Africa. In this chapter, the author, Lindiwe Princess Maseko, insists that the discipline of religion and theology has often been dominated and influenced by men in African contexts, both institutional or the church. She argues that until the birth of the Circle of Concerned African Women Theologians in 1989, different scholars had reflected upon and interpreted religion and theology in Africa from a patriarchal point of view. Nonetheless, in the midst of this breakthrough, there is still the need for an ongoing recognition of diverse emerging young women and their visible participation in academic religion and theology. This chapter, therefore, reviews the academic contribution of young female students in the Department of Gender and Religion at the University of KwaZulu Natal, in South Africa. The chapter adopts the African Women's Theology framework to appreciate Gender and Religion young female students' scholarly and experiential work as a source of theology that celebrates the visible participation of young women in religious and theological academic institutions. Thus, it argues that the impact of this contemporary scholarship on young women doing religion and theology in shaping the terrain of religion in institutions, communities, and the church has to be acknowledged as a life-affirmation toolkit to young African women.

Henry Marcus Garba, in Chapter 32, calls the church to account and challenges it to respond to the silent pandemic of sexual and gender-based violence (GBV) on women in Nigeria's mainline evangelical churches. Garba argues that the church is believed to be a custodian of truth and to fight for justice and liberation of the oppressed through its theological engagements. However, mainline evangelical churches in Nigeria appear to be silent on the issues that women and young girls are going through regarding sexual and GBV and its effects on the lives of the survivors. The chapter utilises narratives and storytelling within African women theologians' framework in calling the church to account for the nature of theological education being taught, especially in evangelical seminaries and churches. This helps bring to the realisation how sexual and GBV against women is eating the fabric of the church, in which preachers and teachers tend to pay less attention to the silent pandemic or preach and teach the theology of perseverance that appears to be one-sided. Consistent with the central theme of this handbook, the chapter highlights how many Nigerian women are also fighting the pandemic and surviving within the oppressive patriarchal system and interpretation of the Bible that seeks to rob them of their dignity.

In Chapter 33, Moses Iliya Ogidis highlights how men have dominated theological education and scholarship in Africa for centuries, thus creating a large vacuum for women's participation. He gives an example from church history, where African church fathers were discussed and nothing was said about church mothers' contribution to the formation of the church or theology. He maintains that most of the theology that emanates from Africa tends to be "ontological epistemology." However, the emergence of the African women theologians challenges the status quo of male dominance in theological education. The chapter uses descriptive method within the framework of African women theologians in accessing the contributions of African women in theological education. It focuses on the great contributions of some African women theologians for theological education to be inclusive of women who are also experiencing the call of God for their lives, either as ordained ministers or as lecturers in seminaries and universities. The chapter considers the contributions of two women: Mercy Amba Oduyoye and Esther Moraa Mombo. Their contributions to theological education cannot be undermined because their theology is more "functional" through the experiences and realities of women, especially in Africa. The author contends that to achieve the African Union's Agenda 2063, there is a need for an inclusive theological education and the use of African women theologians' methodologies.

Primrose Z.J. Bimha, in Chapter 34, asserts that women remain underrepresented in diplomacy and their inclusion thus far has not resulted in a shift from the heavy preference for male diplomats and masculine diplomatic traits. This chapter adds to existing knowledge on how African women in diplomacy navigate masculinised norms and gendered division of labour. Bimha presents a feminist analysis of the experiences of African women in diplomacy based on perspectives shared by women who occupy roles in diplomacy at various levels (as personal assistants, political desk officers, Foreign Service officers, and ambassadors). She notes that simply including women in diplomatic roles does not rid the sector of elitist patriarchal values and practices that perpetuate gender bias in appointments, heteropatriarchal dynamics, and GBV. Bimha maintains that to ensure transformative inclusion, governments should ensure gender parity at all levels, universal access to education (and more specifically gender education from as early as childhood), promote sociocultural transformation through legal reforms and community education processes, and put in place relevant GBV prevention and survivor support frameworks.

References

Adichie, C. N. 2009. "The Danger of a Single Story | Chimamanda Ngozi Adichie." *YouTube*, TED, 7 October, www.youtube.com/watch?v=D9Ihs241zeg, accessed on 5 April 2024.

Brown, C. 2021. Women, Voice and Power: How transformative feminist leadership is challenging inequalities and the root causes of extreme vulnerability. Full Report. Oxford: Oxfam GB for Oxfam Global. Available at https://oxfamilibrary.openrepository.com/bitstream/handle/10546/621202/dp-women-voice-power-061021-en.pdf;jsessionid=3AD4B6745EEBC03318A09728067E9C8C?sequence=22, accessed on 28 March 2024.

Bunce, M., C. Paterson and S. Franks. 2016. *Africa's Media Image in the 21st Century: From the 'Heart of Darkness' to 'Africa Rising'*. London: Routledge.

Demeshane, J. and H. Nel. 2018. "Applying the Process of Appreciative Inquiry in Community Development". *Southern African Journal of Social Work and Social Development* 30 (3):17 pages. https://doi.org/10.25159/2415-5829/3599

1
CONTEMPORARY AFRICAN WOMEN
An Appreciation

Anna Chitando, Eunice Kamaara and Ezra Chitando

Introduction

Still, they stand. Still, they move and forge ahead. Still, they refuse to stand still. African women, occupying diverse locations and facing multiple exclusions and oppressions (see, e.g., Meer and Alex Müller 2017; Budoo-Scholtz and Johnson 2023; Mohammed 2023; Okpokwasili and Dukor 2023; Leath et al. 2023), provide a classic (counter)example of the danger of a single story that Chimamanda Ngozi Adichie (2009) so ably signalled and articulated with eloquence and panache. The story of African women (past and contemporary) is not one. Even if it were, it would not be one of disease, pain, and suffering. Indeed, it would be one of agency, leadership, and ongoing engagement with all the pressing issues of the day. Often cast as perpetual victims in need of saviours from elsewhere (see, e.g., Khan et al. 2023; Pallister-Wilkins 2021), African women are positively shaping a continent and lives beyond the continent. True, they sometimes hurt (see, e.g., Parsitau et al. 2021). They do face formidable odds in the form of a resilient and devious patriarchal system, insensitive political actors, exclusive economic formations, oppressive religious authorities, and other challenges (see, e.g., Ogundipe-Lesley 1994). Yet, they are critical players within the African continent's peacebuilding architecture (see, e.g., Chitando 2021).

African women writers (see further below) have been particularly active in communicating the agency of African women, as articulated in the following citation: "Women depicted in the literary works of African women writers do not accept passively the conditions or situations which have been imposed on them, be they cultural or political" (Begum 2006: 114). Defying colonial images, many black African women are proudly embracing their Indigenous identity and celebrating their natural hair (see, e.g., Knight and Long 2019). In their fields in rural Africa, market places in urban areas, mining and sports fields, boardrooms and in cockpits, African women are contributing towards the transformation of lives. As the volume *African Women and Intellectual Leadership* (Amutabi et al. 2024) illustrates with special reference to women from western Kenya, African women are making significant achievements in various pursuits. However, as a few chapters in this current volume highlight, the struggle for African women's full liberation is far from being won. Greater investments are required if Africa's women and girls are to achieve their total emancipation. Although there are numerous factors that prevent women in various parts of the world, including in the Global South, from achieving their full potential (see, e.g., Emordi et al. 2021), women continue to defy the heavy odds stacked against them.

Contemporary African women continue to exercise their agency by negotiating multiple stumbling blocks and contributing to human flourishing in the continent. Most of their stories remain untold, with most narratives concentrating on the struggles and pains of African women or the achievements of men. This volume seeks to contribute to the recovery and prioritisation of her stories of agency, empowerment, accomplishment, and principled standing for life by African women in their diversity. It is inspired by African women's effective leadership in families, communities, nations, the continent, and globally. African women are negotiating shame (Brown 2007) and taking up leadership in various sectors. The volume acknowledges the validity of the citation below:

> African women have played integral roles in advancements that have shaped the course of history on the African Continent. They have provided sound leadership as freedom fighters, philosophers, business moguls, human rights defenders, and other change-making roles. In addition, they have been envisioning, motivating, building, and inspiring others to accomplish significant achievements continentally and globally.
>
> (Ngom et al. 2022: 5)

Consequently, this volume is built on the contention that in the face of formidable odds, African women have refused to be written off. As they contend with multiple death-dealing forces that include their continent's multiple exclusions and inequalities, rampant racism and persistent patriarchal oppression, they remain unbowed (Maathai 2006). Even as pandemics such as HIV threaten their very lives, they continue to weave stories of hope. In particular, young women living with or affected by HIV have demonstrated remarkable levels of resilience (see, e.g., Muzenda 2020). Despite battling COVID-19 (see, e.g., Adeola 2021; Manyonganise 2023), sexual and gender-based violence (Muluneh et al. 2020), struggling for formal leadership positions (see, e.g., Poltera 2019) and other forms of oppression, African women and girls remain standing. Like their forebear Africa Queens and women leaders from centuries gone by (Achebe 2020), contemporary African women are demonstrating resilience and creativity. As Wane (2008: 186) declares, "…African women are the guardians of traditional knowledge and leaders in resistance struggles." Contemporary African women are channelling the energy generated by their foremothers (Chitando et al. 2023; Dube et al. 2024) to express themselves in challenging contexts.

Choosing life where death abounds, contemporary African women are making valuable contributions at individual, family, community, national, continental, and global levels. Particularly since the turn of the century, African women have taken up significant leadership positions at global and continental levels. These include Phumzile Mlambo-Ngucka (UN Women), Winnie Byanyima (UN Women), Ngozi Okonjo-Iweala (UN WTO) and others. Nkosazana Dlamini-Zuma has served as the Chairperson of the African Union Commission, while at the time of writing, Samia Suluhu Hassan was the President of Tanzania. African women leaders are joining their peers from other parts of the world (see, e.g., Sueda et al. 2020).

Rejecting stories of perpetual submissiveness (Eze et al. 2016), contemporary African women are leading from the front. The available evidence confirms that African women are effective entrepreneurs. They are active in the creative sectors, sports, nongovernmental organisations (FBOs) and the public sector. African women are defying the odds to be influential in science, technology, and mathematics (STEM). Only the most biased of reviewers can miss African women's leadership in the higher and tertiary education sector. As the chapters in this volume confirm, African women are actively involved in personal, community, national, continental, and global transformation. We anticipate that the volume is making a contribution towards meeting the call in the sub-title of a recent publication: "Beyond Lack, Peripherality, and Failure" (de Heredia and Wai 2018). We are in fundamental agreement with Twasiima Patricia Bigirwa when she asserts that African feminist activism must take on board the rights and interests of all women, while recognising the importance of intersectionality. Thus:

> There are also many strong radical women who have walked this struggle before us, whose practices and experiences can help us as we continue to shape the alternative. Contemporary feminism has to emerge from the consciousness of the past and the thirst for innovation. It has to bring about knowledge production as well as new radical action.
>
> (Bigirwa 2018: 3)

Summarising the Areas of African Women's Engagement Covered in This Volume

From the onset, it is strategic for us to declare that our focus on "contemporary" African women is not meant to suggest a radical rapture with African women from earlier times. If anything, we are acutely aware of the inspiration that contemporary African women draw from women in times gone by (see, e.g., Gabriel 1995; Dube et al. 2024). Consequently, the concentration on African women must not be read as suggesting that African women's past be written off. While we concede that recovering the voices of African women from the past is difficult (Ndlovu-Gatsheni 2005), we retain the argument that African women have always played key roles in African societies. Our focus on the achievements and struggles of contemporary African women must be understood as an effort to understand the present, as well as to contribute towards future generations' appreciation of the present (which will be their past). We are hopeful that as more stories of African women's leadership are told (African Union Commission-Women, Gender and Youth Directorate (AUC-WGYD) 2022), more African women from diverse life settings will be inspired to take up their rightful places and flourish. We are particularly impressed by the few men who have contributed to this volume. They are confirming that the outreach to men is succeeding, as they have demonstrated appreciable levels of gender sensitivity and commitment to African women's full liberation.

Although we have divided the chapters into different sections, it is important to uphold an open and flexible approach regarding these sections. Thus, there are many overlaps across the different sections in this volume. For example, while we have a section focusing on African women and pandemics, we have another section that pays attention to older African women. In reality, older African women are playing a major role in responding to pandemics. In this regard, reflections on older women and their contribution to the care economy could have been included in either section. This pattern is replicated in other sections, underscoring the pragmatic rather than dogmatic approach that we have adopted in this volume.

We are acutely aware of the significant differences that characterise Africa, making generalisations difficult. However, we are inspired by the ideology of a united, peaceful, and prosperous Africa, where women and girls actively contribute to development (African Union Commission 2015: 8). We also challenged the contributors to this volume to invest in ethical story telling in relation to Africa (see, e.g., Pointer 2021). This was not designed to suppress the challenges that African women continue to struggle against, but to highlight the extent to which African women are making progress in a difficult context. The inequality that Africa experiences in the global (dis)order compounds the situation, although African women have demonstrated remarkable resilience and creativity. We are also acutely aware of the diversity that characterises the category "African women" that we are using in this volume. As Cohn (2013) has outlined so effectively, there are numerous factors that shape women. These include age, economic class, race, ethnicity, caste, religion, sexuality, physical ability, culture, geographic location, state citizenship, and national identity. We admit that all these variables imply that there is no generic or stereotypical "African woman."

However, it would be misleading to conclude that the struggle is over and that African women are enjoying their rights and dignity in full. As some of the chapters in this volume confirm, African women continue to face many challenges. The chapters that portray the struggles that African women face in various sectors (see, e.g., chapters on African women and higher education) serve as a poignant reminder that although there have been many breakthroughs, the struggle for African women's full liberation continues unabated.

Images of African Women in Artistic Works and the Media

African women creative writers are making a critical contribution to African women's advancement. Writing from diverse African contexts, they are contesting oppressive socio-cultural and religious norms that prevent women from expressing themselves fully (see, e.g., Tulasi 2022). This is a task that older African women writers have bequeathed to the younger African women. Alongside women journalists, they are contributing towards presenting more positive and dynamic images of African women. They are doing this against the backdrop of consistently negative coverage that Africa endures. The following citation brings this out quite clearly:

> Thus, foreign/western media's portrayals of Africa have…perpetually associated the continent with such hurtful phenomena as famine, hardship, recessions, backwardness, (extreme) primitivism, inter-religious and inter-ethnic wars, genocides, deadly pandemics, totalitarian regimes and corruption among other stereotypes which conform to the racist colonial era depictions of the continent. Such skewed and negative media representations of the African continent have partly been responsible for the persistence among foreign audiences of questionable myths. Some of these questionable beliefs relegate Africa exclusively to a land of disasters, catastrophes, and internecine wars.
> (Edong 2021: 601)

These negative images of African women are being challenged in various publications coming out of Africa. There is a growing awareness of the need to achieve balance and communicate more positive images of African women, including in commercial video films (Owusu and Kwansah-Aidoo 2021). One-dimensional presentations of African women sustain the notion of perpetual victims, thereby denying or minimising the agency of African women. Contributors to this volume have taken up a similarly positive stance and are contributing towards decolonising images of Africa (see, e.g., Mano and Milton 2021).

African Women in the Context of Multiple Pandemics and Climate Change

Pandemics are not gender neutral. They are gendered, with women often enduring the negative effects more than men. For example, women academics were more affected by COVID-19 than men (see, e.g., King and Frederickson 2021). Women in the informal sector were also more adversely affected by the pandemic (see, e.g., Chingono 2021). Similarly, HIV has affected more women than men in Africa (see, e.g., Kiguri and Barungi 2007; Tlou 2007; Jewkes 2009). However, it is also true that class considerations show that men from lower social classes are more vulnerable to pandemics than women from higher social classes. Overall, however, women tend to have more negative experiences of pandemics than men. On the other hand, women's leadership is crucial for effective responses to pandemics, as demonstrated during the COVID-19 pandemic (see, e.g., Garikipati and Kambhampati 2020; UN Women 2021; Ozdenerol et al. 2023). Thus:

> Women played critical roles as governors and mayors; as cabinet ministers, especially ministers of health; as members of parliament; and as COVID-19 task force members and experts. Importantly, women in these roles have not received the same publicity or attention as women presidents and prime ministers, and so their work often goes undocumented or unrecognised. Yet women leaders demonstrated that strong pandemic leadership combined competence with compassion and decisive actions that strengthened state capacity while attending to the needs of vulnerable groups.
>
> (UN Women 2021: 4)

Like their counterparts in other parts of the world, African women's leadership was visible during the COVID-19 pandemic. They led from the front; in the informal sector when mostly African male political leaders uncritically embraced the harsh lockdown measures (see, e.g., Zhanda et al. 2022); providing household food (see, e.g., Matanga and Mukurazhizha 2023); in faith communities (see, e.g., Olufemi and Labeodan 2021); in savings clubs (see, e.g., Adegbite et al. 2022); and in other sectors. This leadership by African women is often either not acknowledged or receives minimal attention to the deep-seated patriarchy that continues to focus attention on male leaders. To emphasise the achievements of African women leaders during COVID-19 is not to overlook the extent to which girls and women were exposed to higher levels of sexual and gender-based violence, loss of income and increased mental health challenges during the pandemic. Our contention, however, is that African women, like their counterparts in other parts of the world, but particularly in the Global South, did not succumb to resignation. Instead, they demonstrated their resilience, capabilities, and leadership to respond to COVID-19. We identify with the following observation:

> Southern women have more or less cracked the tallest and most violent glass ceilings in global masculine politics. The pandemic has proven to the sceptical observer that women can lead successfully. Hopefully, this pandemic will open new gates to a more equitable gender, especially in terms of political empowerment and involvement in the Global South. In the end, based upon the best practice and comparisons that have been done in this research, challenging the underrepresentation of women in COVID-19 decision-making leadership in the Global South is plausible.
>
> (Hanifa 2020: 90)

The same leadership that African women have demonstrated in relation to pandemics has been witnessed in the response to climate change. There is a growing realisation that gender equality is critical for greener and bluer futures (IUCN 2024). Although African women remain vulnerable to climate change (Statistics Department, AfDB 2011), particularly with the increasing drought and food insecurity, they have not accepted their fate and done nothing about it. If anything, they have demonstrated remarkable levels of creativity and resilience. Where most narratives present adolescent girls and young women in Africa as mostly vulnerable, there is a need to acknowledge their proactive approach towards addressing the challenges associated with climate change (see, e.g., Tanner et al. 2022). Due to their productivity in the agricultural sector, African women are making significant contributions to the overall response to climate change by promoting food security and food sovereignty in Africa (Chitando 2024).

This volume includes essays on African women's responses to pandemics and climate change because we are convinced that these areas provide some of the most strategic platforms for demonstrating African girls and women's leadership capabilities. Although there are many factors that increase African women's vulnerability during pandemics, embracing feminist/womanist approaches, including within religious institutions, shows a lot of promise (see, e.g., Mawerenga 2023). The following citation summarises the emergence and confirmation of African women's leadership in the face of multiple pandemics:

> Because women have borne the brunt of both the HIV/AIDS and COVID-19 pandemics, this has resulted in stronger women's mobilisation for purposes of implementing actions to address their unique challenges. This is a positive impact of the pandemics and one of the silver linings that has resulted from the negative impacts that the pandemics have had on women. Thus, in the close to 40 years that Kenya has had to deal with HIV/AIDS, there has emerged a strong movement comprising women who are self-advocates; women's organisations that deal specifically with gender and health rights; and women's groups that offer support at different levels to women who have been infected and affected by the virus. This women's movement has worked closely with other civil society organisations that deal with the right to health more generally to further strengthen women's right to health.
>
> (Kameri-Mbote and Meroka-Mutua 2023: 27)

African Women in Science, Technology, Engineering, and Mathematics

Globally, the perception that the arena of STEM constitutes the domain of men, while the Arts and Humanities are for women remain dominant. In most instances, socially prescribed gender expectations have resulted in the belief that the "hard sciences" require masculine stamina, while the social sciences are better suited for women (see, e.g., Nosek et al. 2022). This stereotype persists to the extent that in many settings, even when women dare to "storm the heavens" and take up jobs within STEM sectors, they get paid less than their male counterparts. Admittedly, African women continue to struggle to take up their rightful places in the STEM spaces. However, change is clearly underway.

Defying the odds, African women are making giant strides in STEM. They have made ground breaking discoveries in the continent and beyond, contributing to knowledge globally. Examples such as Francisca Okeke, a professor of Physics at the University of Nigeria, Nsukka, confirm the remarkable steps that African women have taken. In particular, young African women are bridging the gender gap in STEM. Strategies, such as motivating the girl child to be interested in STEM subjects, utilising role models (see, e.g., Babalola et al. 2023), the development of learning resources that portray the girl child in STEM, further capacitating teachers and changing classroom dynamics (Founou et al. 2023), are contributing towards this shift.

As the world continues to invest in science and technology, it is heartening to observe that African women are making steady progress in this direction. This progress can also be attributed to the role of institutions of higher education that are devoted to women (Garwe and Chikwiri 2021), the increase in the number of organisations supporting African women in STEM (such as the African Institute for Mathematical Sciences (AIMS) and African Women in Science and Engineering (AWSE)), as well as investments by non-governmental organisations (NGOs) in the sector. There is a growing realisation that promoting African women's participation in the digital and tech economy makes good business sense. Thus:

Women's full participation in the digital and tech economy will result in more diverse product creation, higher financial returns, and access to new markets and sectors. For investors, women-led firms experience a 34% higher return on investment than those led solely by men. This is particularly true in innovative fields like technology…Women-led tech start-ups can help reach the women and girls that have historically been left without access to digital markets. This is especially important for business as African women have increasing spending and consumer power.

(Porfido and Marks 2020: 5)

African Women in Entrepreneurship and Management

Without glorifying the precolonial era, it can be stated with confidence that African women were actively involved in entrepreneurship and management. Whereas the dominant view suggests that women were under patriarchal oppression and confined to the home, evidence shows that women were adventurous in business and were active in leadership. Women "… were active in traditional leadership, governance, production, and reproduction in precolonial societies, way before the advent of colonists" (Moadi and Mtombeni 2021: 1130). Although colonialism had a negative impact, women in contemporary Africa have emerged as competent entrepreneurs. By mobilising human, social, spiritual, and financial capital (Ojong et al. 2021: 238), they are contributing to the advancement of the continent. Where many associate Africa with doom and gloom, the continent has one of the highest rates of women entrepreneurs in the world (Nwakanma 2021: 1584).

Although there is room for improvement (Nkomo and Ngambi 2009), African women are also doing well in management. Through increased access to education, they are studying management and leadership and are putting the knowledge they have acquired to good use. They have taken up management positions in both the private and public sectors (Abate and Woldie 2022). According to Amina and Ibrahim (2019), some of the variables that have facilitated women's leadership include visualising new options, mentorship, advanced leadership training, communication skills, financial resources, support, and entrepreneurship. In higher and tertiary education, for example, African women are making significant strides in management. However, as with the other sectors, more can still be achieved (Adewale and Potokri 2023).

African Women in Historical Times, Older Age, Diplomacy, and Religion

As noted earlier, contemporary African women are building on the successes of African women from previous generations who have demonstrated high levels of resilience, resistance to oppression and leadership. Across different African contexts, generations of African women have defied socio-cultural and religious norms that are designed to privilege men and to exclude them. A number of chapters in this volume do evoke the memory of distinguished individuals and groups of African women who serve to inspire contemporary African women.

The fact that Africa has a young population has tended to lead to a general neglect of women in older age. To say this is not to instigate some competition for trauma between older and younger African women, but to recognise that there is a need for greater balance, including from policy makers and academics. This is because African women in older age retain their rights (Thabethe and Usen 2012) and are a strategic resource for their families, communities, their nations, the continent, and globally. Although older women, often classified as women aged 60 and above, face many challenges in different parts of the world (see, e.g., Shankardass 2021), it is helpful to approach them from the perspective of their capabilities (Kuhumba 2022) and appreciate them as resources (Kimuna and Makiwane 2007). While older African women face poverty, poor health, loneliness, discrimination, and other challenges, this is "a single story." The other story is that of older African women leading in providing care to families and communities through their deployment of Ubuntu (Chisale 2018). They are peacebuilders and diplomats, although this is often overlooked in scholarship and policy.

The field of diplomacy has been dominated by men for a long time. However, globally, women have demanded, and taken up, a seat at the table (Sloan 2020) and there is a growing appreciation of the gender turn in diplomacy (see, e.g., Aggestam and Towns 2019). Although African women have been doing very well in diplomacy (see, e.g., Dlamini-Mntambo et al. 2020), there is only very limited scholarly work on their achievements. We contend that this is largely due to the stereotypical presentation of African women as perpetual victims. For example, at the time that this volume was being finalised, Naledi Pandor, the South African Minister of International Relations and Cooperation, was featured prominently in the global media while driving her country's call for peace in Gaza. This is consistent with African women's roles as effective peacebuilders (Chitando 2021). However, deep-seated patriarchal norms and insensitive work practices must be overcome for African women to excel in diplomacy.

Religion continues to be an important factor in the lives of African women. Although they tend to be excluded from formal leadership positions, they participate actively in religious affairs. As more women, including young women, acquire theological education, they are successfully challenging oppressive patriarchal ideologies and taking up leadership roles. Indeed, many older African women and African women in diplomacy regard religion as a powerful resource that they fall back on and utilise in their endeavours (Ngunjiri 2010). Whereas there is still more work to be done to ensure that religion contributes more fully to African women's advancement, it is important to acknowledge that there is notable possible in this direction. Through leadership development programmes (see, e.g., Wakahiu and Salvattera 2012), women are having their capacities further strengthened.

Conclusion

Africa continues to face multiple challenges. These include a global system skewed in favour of the Global North, the negative effects of climate change, pandemics, and wars. African women tend to be at the receiving end of these challenges. However, African women are demonstrating high levels of resilience and agency. They are emerging as key actors in different sectors, defying images of passivity and perpetual victims. While they must still confront and overcome oppression in diverse forms, they are demonstrating effective leadership in the midst of major stumbling blocks. Alongside acknowledging the ongoing struggles of African women, this volume particularly appreciates and presents their creativity, effective leadership, salutary achievements, and successes.

References

Abate, G. B. and A. T. Woldie. 2022. "Breaking barriers to women's advancement in the public sector in Sub-Saharan Africa." *Canadian Bureau for International Education*. Available at https://cbie.ca/wp-content/uploads/2022/04/ALT-Research-Report-Begashaw-EN-FINAL.pdf, accessed 4 April 2024.

Achebe, N. 2020. *Female Monarchs and Merchant Queens in Africa*. Athens, OH: Ohio University Press.

Adegbite, O. et al. 2022. "Women's groups and COVID-19: An evidence review on savings groups in Africa," *Gates Open Research*, 6, 47, Apr 12. doi: 10.12688/gatesopenres.13550.1

Adeola, O. Ed. 2021. *Gendered Perspectives on Covid-19 Recovery in Africa Towards Sustainable Development*. Cham: Palgrave Macmillan.

Adewale, S. and O. C. Potokri. 2023. "Integrating African women academics in leadership: A systematic review," *Journal of Higher Education Policy and Leadership Studies* 4(3), 53–73.

Adichie, C. N. 2009. "The danger of a single story | chimamanda Ngozi Adichie." YouTube, TED, Oct. 7, www.youtube.com/watch?v=D9Ihs241zeg, accessed 5 April 2024.

African Union Commission. 2015. Agenda 2063: The Africa We Want. Popular Version. Addis Ababa: African Union Commission. Available at https://au.int/sites/default/files/documents/36204-doc-agenda2063_popular_version_en.pdf, accessed 5 April 2024.

African Union Commission-Women, Gender and Youth Directorate (AUC-WGYD). 2022. *Women of Impact: Inspiring Stories of African Women Leaders*. Addis Ababa: African Union Commission-Women, Gender and Youth Directorate (AUC-WGYD). Available at https://au.int/sites/default/files/documents/43035-doc-Women_of_Impact-_Inspiring_Stories_of_African_Women_Leaders.pdf, accessed 5 April 2024.

Aggestam, K. and A. Towns. 2019. "The gender turn in diplomacy: A new research agenda," *International Feminist Journal of Politics* 21(1), 9–28.

Amina, B. J. Z. and S. G. Ibrahim. 2019. "Role of African women leaders in inspiring women participation in leadership: An analysis," *African Journal of Social Sciences and Humanities Research* 2(3), 12–27.

Amutabi, M. N. et al. 2024. *African Women and Intellectual Leadership: Life Stories From Western Kenya*. London: Routledge.

Babalola, O.O. et al. 2023. "Power of shared success: How can sharing success and roles of others motivate African women in STEM?" *International Journal of Education Vocational Guidance*. doi: 10.1007/s10775-023-09583-1

Begum, S. H. 2006. "Against all odds: African womanhood in postcolonial African women writing," *Marang* 16, 103–119.

Bigirwa, T. P. 2018. "The social inclusion of women and challenges for a contemporary African feminist activism," *Feminist Dialogue*, 6. Available at https://library.fes.de/pdf-files/bueros/mosambik/14622.pdf, accessed 25 April 2024.

Breton, N. N. 2023. "Reflecting on our good intentions: A critical discourse analysis of women's health and empowerment discourses in sexual and gender-based violence policies relevant to southern Africa," *Global Public Health* 18(1), 2120048. doi: 10.1080/17441692.2022.2120048

Brown, C. 2021. Women, voice and power: How transformative feminist leadership is challenging inequalities and the root causes of extreme vulnerability. Full Report. Oxford: Oxfam GB for Oxfam Global. Available at https://oxfamilibrary.openrepository.com/bitstream/handle/10546/621202/dp-women-voice-power-061021-en.pdf;jsessionid=3AD4B6745EEBC03318A09728067E9C8C?sequence=22, accessed 28 March 2024

Brown, C. B. 2007. *I Thought It Was Just Me: Women Reclaiming Power and Courage in a Culture of Shame*. New York: Gotham Books.

Budoo-Scholtz, A. and A. Johnson. 2023. *COVID-19 and Women's Intersectionalities in Africa*. Pretoria: Pretoria University Law Press.

Chingono, M. 2021. "The impact of the COVID-19 pandemic on women in the informal sector in Southern Africa: A case study of Lesotho," *Journal of Gender and Power* 16(2), 15–37.

Chisale, S.S. 2018. "Ubuntu as care: Deconstructing the gendered Ubuntu," *Verbum et Ecclesia* 39(1), a1790. doi: 10.4102/ve.v39i1.1790

Chitando, A. 2021. Ed., *Women and Peacebuilding in Africa*. London: Routledge.

Chitando, E. 2024. "African women, religion, climate change and food security in the context of pandemics," in L. Maseno et al, eds., *Religion, Climate Change, and Food Security in Africa*. Cham: Palgrave Macmillan, 219–235.

Chitando, E. et al. 2023. Eds., *Chihera in Zimbabwe: A Radical African Feminist Principle*. Cham: Palgrave.

Cohn, C. 2013. "Women and wars: A conceptual framework," in C. Cohn, ed., *Women and Wars: Contested Histories, Uncertain Futures*. Cambridge: Polity Press, 1–35.

De Heredia, M. I. and Z. Wai. (2018). Eds., *Recentering Africa in International Relations: Beyond Lack, Peripherality, and Failure*. Cham: Palgrave Macmillan.

Demeshane, J. and H. Nel. 2018. "Applying the process of appreciative inquiry in community development," *Southern African Journal of Social Work and Social Development* 30(3), 17 pages. doi: 10.25159/2415-5829/3599

Dlamini-Mntambo et al. 2020. *African Women in Diplomacy: Selected Perspectives from Kenya, Rwanda, South Africa and Zimbabwe*. Available at http://www.southafrica-canada.ca/wp-content/uploads/2020/05/Women-in-Diplomacy-in-Africa-website.pdf, accessed 5 April 2024.

Dube, Musa W. et al. 2024. Eds., *African Women Legends and the Spirituality of Resistance*. London: Routledge.

Edong, F. P. C. 2021. "Images as Afro-positivist narratives and counter hegemonic strategy: A study of #TheAfricaTheMediaNeverShowsYou," *International Journal of Modern Anthropology* 2(16), 601–628.

Emordi, A. T. O. et al. 2021. "Women, marginalisation and politics in Africa and Asia," *Integrity Journal of Arts and Humanities* 2(2), 27–35.

Founou, L. L. et al. 2023. "African women in science and development, bridging the gender gap," *World Development Perspectives* 31(3), 1–4.

Gabriel, A. D. 1995. "African women in history: A universalist approach," *Dialogue and Universalism* 4, 83–95.

Garikipati, G. and U. Kambhampati. 2020. Leading the Fight Against the Pandemic: Does Gender 'Really' Matter? Discussion Paper No. 2020-13, Department of Economics, University of Reading. Available at https://www.reading.ac.uk/web/files/economics/emdp202013.pdf, accessed 22 March 2024.

Garwe, E. C. and E. Chikwiri. 2021. "De-gendering STEM: Best practices from a case study of a women's university in Africa," *Global Scientific Journals* 9(1), 576–593.

Hanifa, L. 2020. "Challenging underrepresentation of women leadership in global south during COVID-19," *Global South Review* 2(1), 78–96.

IUCN. 2024. "Gender equality for greener and bluer futures: Why women's leadership matters for realising environmental goals." Available at https://www.iucn.org/sites/default/files/2024-03/2024-gender-equality-for-greener-and-bluer-futures.pdf, accessed 18 April 2024.

Jewkes, R. 2009. "HIV and women," in P. Rohleder et al, eds., *HIV/AIDS in South Africa 25 Years On Psychosocial Perspectives*. New York: Springer Science+Business Media, 27–40.

Kameri-Mbote, P. and A. Meroka-Mutua. 2023. "From one pandemic to another through women's eyes: An analysis of the impacts of Kenya's responses to HIV/AIDS and Covid-19," *Pathways to African Feminism and Development: Journal of the African Women Studies Centre* 8(1), 16–36.

Khan, T., K. Dickson and M. Sonderjee. 2023. Eds., *White Saviorism in International Development Theories, Practices and Lived Experiences*. Wakefield, Québec: Daraja Press.

Kiguri, S. N. and V. Barungi. 2007. Eds., *I Dare to Say: Five Testimonies of Women Living Positively with HIV/AIDS*. Kampala: Femrite Publications Limited.

Kimuna, S. R. and M. Makiwane. 2007. "Older people as resources in South Africa: Mpumalanga households," *Journal of Aging and Social Policy* 19(1), 97–114.

King, M. M. and M. E. Frederickson. 2021. "The pandemic penalty: The gendered effects of COVID-19 on scientific productivity," *Socius: Sociological Research for a Dynamic World* 7, 1–24.

Knight, S. M. F. and W. Long. 2019. "Narratives of Black women on hair in the workplace," *PINS: Psychology in Society* 58, 27–49.

Kuhumba, K. S. 2022. "Towards women's empowerment in Africa: Insights from the capability approach," in E. Chitando et al., eds., *Women and Religion in Zimbabwe: Strides and Struggles*. London: Lexington Books, 237–254.

Leath, J. S. et al. 2023. "Black feminism, womanism, and intersectionality discourse: A theo-ethical roundtable," *Journal of Moral Theology* 12(Special Issue 1), 157–175.

Maathai, W. 2006. *Unbowed: A Memoir*. New York: Alfred A. Knopf.

Mano, W. and V. C. Milton. 2021. Ed., *Routledge Handbook of African Media and Communication Studies*. London: Routledge.

Manyonganise, M. 2023. "COVID-19, gender and health: Recentring women in African indigenous health discourses in Zimbabwe for environmental conservation," *HTS Teologiese Studies/Theological Studies* 79(3), a7941. doi: 10.4102/hts.v79i3.7941

Matanga, S.Y. and M.R. Mukurazhizha. 2023. "The impact of the COVID-19 restrictions on women's responsibility for domestic food provision: The Case of Marondera Urban in Zimbabwe," *HTS Teologiese Studies/Theological Studies* 79(3), a8053. doi: 10.4102/hts.v79i3.8053

Mawerenga, J. H. 2023. "The trilogy of the coronavirus disease, religion, and the health of African women," *Pathways to African Feminism and Development: Journal of the African Women Studies Centre* 8(1), 57–73.

Meer, T. and A. Müller. 2017. "Considering intersectionality in Africa," *Agenda* 31(1), 3–4.

Moadi, A. L. and B. Mtombeni. 2021. "Women in pre-colonial Africa: Southern Africa," in O. Yacob-Haliso and T. Falola, eds., *The Palgrave Handbook of African Women's Studies*. Cham: Palgrave Macmillan, 1113–1132.

Mohammed, W. F. 2023. "Intersectionality in African digital organizing: A Ghanaian perspective," *Communication, Culture and Critique* 16(2), 107–109. doi: 10.1093/ccc/tcad007

Muluneh, M. D. et al. 2020. "Gender based violence against women in Sub-Saharan Africa: A systematic review and meta-analysis of cross-sectional studies," *International Journal of Environmental Research and Public Health* 17(3), 903. doi: 10.3390/ijerph17030903

Muzenda, T. 2020. "The stories of young resilient women." Available at https://www.aids2020.org/the-stories-of-young-resilient-women/, accessed 15 March 2024.

Ndlovu-Gatsheni, S. J. 2005. "Can women's voices be recovered from the past? Grappling with the absence of women voices in pre-colonial history of Zimbabwe," *Wagadu* 2, 1–19.

Nkomo, S. M. and H. Ngambi. 2009. "African women in leadership: Current knowledge and a framework for future studies," *International Journal of African Renaissance Studies – Multi-, Inter- and Transdisciplinarity* 4(1), 49–68.

Ngom, M. et al. 2022. "Foreword," in African Union commission-women, gender and youth Directorate (AUC-WGYD), ed., *Women of Impact: Inspiring Stories of African Women Leaders*. Addis Ababa: African Union Commission-Women, Gender and Youth Directorate (AUC-WGYD), 5–6. Available at https://au.int/sites/default/files/documents/43035-doc-Women_of_Impact-_Inspiring_Stories_of_African_Women_Leaders.pdf, accessed 15 March 2024.

Ngunjiri, F. W. 2010. *Women's Spiritual Leadership in Africa: Tempered Radicals and Critical Servant Leaders*. Albany: State University of New York Press.

Nosek, B. A., M. R. Banaji and A. G. Greenwald. 2022. "Math = Male, Me = Female, therefore math ≠ me," *Journal of Personality and Social Psychology* 83(1), 44–59.

Nwakanma, A. P. 2021. "Women, entrepreneurship, and economic development in Africa," in O. Yacob-Haliso and T. Falola, eds., *The Palgrave Handbook of African Women's Studies*. Cham: Palgrave Macmillan, 1583–1599.

Ogundipe-Leslie, M. 1994. "African women, culture and another development," in Ogundipe-Leslie M. *Recreating Ourselves: African Women and Critical Transformations*. Trenton: Africa World Press, 21–42.

Ojong, N. et al. 2021. "Female entrepreneurship in Africa: A review, trends, and future research directions," *Journal of Business Research* 132, 233–248.

Okpokwasili, O. A. and M. Dukor. 2023. "The intersectionality of culture in gender relation in Nigeria," *Nigerian Journal of African Studies* 5(2), 52–59.

Olufemi, O. A. and H. A. Labeodan. 2021 "'Locked-Down but not 'Locked Out': Experiences of Nigerian Women during the COVID-19 Pandemic," in H. A. Labeodan et al., eds., *COVID-19: African Women and the Will to Survive*. Bamberg: University of Bamberg Press, 15–38.

Owusu, J. O. and K. Kwansah-Aidoo. 2021. "Gender and/in film reading: A comparative analysis of male and female readings of ties that bind," *Participations: Journal of Audience & Reception Studies* 18(2), 124–158.

Ozdenerol, E. 2023. "Female leadership during COVID-19: The effectiveness of diverse approaches towards mitigation management during a pandemic," *International Journal of Environmental Research and Public Health* 20(21), 7023. doi: 10.3390/ijerph20217023

Pallister-Wilkins, P. 2021. "Saving the souls of white folk: Humanitarianism as white supremacy," *Security Dialogue* 52(1_suppl), 98–106. doi: 10.1177/09670106211024419

Parsitau, D. et al. 2021. "'Mama I can't breathe!': Black/African women of faith groaning for social justice and gender equality," *Mission Studies* 38, 448–469.

Pointer, R. 2021. *How to Write About Africa in 8 Steps: An Ethical Storytelling Handbook*. Johannesburg: Africa No Filter

Poltera, J. 2019. "Exploring examples of women's leadership in African contexts," *Agenda* 33(1), 3–8. doi: 10.1080/10130950.2019.1602977

Porfido, D. and Z. Marks. 2020. "Policy brief: Women and the digital economy in Africa," Available at https://africa.harvard.edu/files/african-studies/files/women_entrepreneurship_in_africa_policy_brief_-_digital_economy_final.pdf, accessed 4 April 2024.

Shankardass, M. K. 2021. Ed., *Older Women and Well-Being a Global Perspective*. Singapore: Springer Nature Singapore.

Sloan, S. 2020. *A Seat at the Table: Women, Diplomacy, and Lessons for the World*. Washington, DC: New Degree Press.

Statistics Department, AfDB. 2011. "The link between climate change, gender and development in Africa," *The African Statistical Journal* 12, 119–140.

Sueda, K. et al. 2020. "Women in global leadership: Asian and African perspectives," *The Aoyama Journal of International Politics, Economics and Communication* 104, 39–59.

Tanner, T., L. Mazingi and D. F. Muyambwa. 2022. "Youth, gender and climate resilience: Voices of adolescent and young women in Southern Africa," *Sustainability* 14, 8797. doi: 10.3390/su14148797

Thabethe, N. and L. C. Usen. 2012. "Women's rights are older women's rights too: Narratives of grandmothers in home-based care," *Agenda: Empowering Women for Gender Equity* 4(94), 114–121.

Tlou, S. 2007. "Gender and HIV/AIDS," in M. Essex et al, eds., *AIDS in Africa*. 2nd ed. New York: Springer Science + Business Media, 654–663.

Tulasi, L. 2022. "African women writing and gender identities: A review," *The Review of Contemporary Scientific and Academic Studies* 2(1), 1–4.

UN Women. 2021. Effective, decisive, and inclusive: Women's leadership in COVID-19 response and recovery. Working Paper. New York: Leadership and Governance Section, UN Women. Available at https://www.unwomen.org/sites/default/files/Headquarters/Attachments/Sections/Library/Publications/2021/Effective-decisive-and-inclusive-Womens-leadership-in-COVID-19-response-and-recovery-en.pdf, accessed 22 March 2024.

Wakahiu, J. and M. Salvattera. 2012. "Sustainable leadership: Lessons and implications of a leadership development program for women religious in Africa," *The Journal of Pan African Studies* 12(2), 150–167.

Wane, N. N. 2008. "Mapping the field of Indigenous knowledges in anti-colonial discourse: A transformative journey in education," *Race Ethnicity and Education* 11(2), 183–197. doi: 10.1080/13613320600807667

Zhanda, K. et al. 2022. "Women in the informal sector amid COVID-19: Implications for household peace and economic stability in urban Zimbabwe," *Cities & Health*. doi: 10.1080/23748834.2021.2019967

SECTION 2

Empowering Images of African Women in Literary Works

2
"LIKE FLOWERS BLOOMING FROM AN ICE BUCKET"

Contemporary Anglophone Cameroonian Women Writers

Naomi Nkealah

Introduction

African feminists have long argued that literary texts are not just cultural productions to which we apply theory, but also enriching art forms from which we draw theoretical ideas. Adopting this feminist approach to texts, I attempt in this chapter a conceptualisation of contemporary Anglophone Cameroonian women writers by looking at what their literary productions suggest about what they stand for, as well as analysing how they surmount their challenges to create literature that contributes to enhancing African feminist knowledge.

Boswell (2020:4) has argued that African women's literature must be read not just as creative pieces but also as sites of theory making. Her argument echoes the voices of Lewis (2001:7), Nnaemeka (2003:366), Gqola (2011:7) and Nkealah (2017a:123) who have iterated in different ways the importance of reading African women's literary and cultural texts as expressions of theoretical intervention in feminist thinking. From this conceptual point of view, I see Anglophone Cameroonian women's literature as a site of theory making, specifically in relation to defining the identity of contemporary Anglophone Cameroonian women writers and framing their contributions to African feminist theorisation. Contemporary Anglophone Cameroonian women writers are a formidable force in the African literary landscape because they have flourished despite adverse circumstances. Speaking about South African women's writing, Lewis and Baderoon (2021:1–2) note the significance of acknowledging black women's writing that has "flourished in different regions and cultural forms": such acknowledgement not only corrects omissions in literary historiographies but also brings to critical limelight "key connections and dialogues among perspectives and voices that continue to be sidelined in publishing, scholarship and public debates in South Africa". Applying this insight, I note that it is crucially important for me as an Anglophone Cameroonian feminist to acknowledge the flourishing of Anglophone Cameroonian women writers as they are producing works of art amidst a plethora of socio-economic challenges that can easily stifle literary creativity. The poetry of Joyce Ash offers me an appropriate metaphor for conceptualising this state of flourish. The following poem in Ash's poetry collection *Beautiful Fire* is poignant in imagery:

Imperfection

There's something beautiful about imperfection;
It never claims to be that which it is not,
Like flowers blooming from an ice bucket
Instead of a flower vase,
Like crumpled sheets bearing witness
To a sweet sinful "yes".
Like knowing we are still God's children,
Naked. Imperfect…

(Ash 2018:45)

Although this poem is about the paradoxical beauty of human imperfection, it offers an image that in my view palpably embodies the identity of Anglophone Cameroonian women writers. These writers are "like flowers blooming from an ice bucket / Instead of a flower vase" (Ash 2018:45). This image conveys the thought that Anglophone Cameroonian women writers have braved harsh conditions to produce works of art that speak to the everyday lived realities of women in a country crippled by corruption, violence, economic stagnation and social problems, as well as in various diasporic spaces plagued with racism, sexism and xenophobia. The stories they write may be imperfect, but embedded in that imperfection is the beauty of their characters' defiance of disempowering narratives to be able to tell their own empowering stories. Similarly, their own life experiences may be imperfect, but along with that imperfection is the beauty of their resilience to forge ahead creatively. A flower, after all, will always be a flower, whether in an ice bucket or a flower vase.

Contemporary Anglophone Cameroonian women writers at home and abroad, like flowers from an ice bucket, are adding their voices to the advancement of transnational African feminism by writing literature "that highlights African women's multilayered exploration of subalternity and their nuanced visions of gendered subaltern agency" (Henaku 2021:76). In this chapter, I draw on the many meanings offered by this image to conceptualise contemporary Anglophone Cameroonian women writers as a subgenre of African women writers, looking at their literary works for clues to the form and substance of their feminism. Before I do that, I provide some context to my arguments by looking at the historical evolution of Anglophone Cameroonian women writers and their literature.

Locating the Flowers: The Historical Context of Anglophone Cameroonian Women Writers

In the introduction to her book *Feminism and modernity in Anglophone African women's writing*, Pucherová (2022:5–6) states that African women's voices have become more audible and powerful in the 21st century than ever before as their feminist texts speak to audiences across the world. Agreeing with this statement, I identify the voices of Anglophone Cameroonian women writers as particularly resounding in the past two or so decades. From the year 2000 to 2023, these women have registered literary productions that make significant contributions to feminist knowledge production on gendered violence, women and migration, women's economic empowerment, women's sexuality, polygamy, motherhood, women and HIV and AIDS, women and COVID-19, human rights, divorce, single parenthood, widowhood, and mental illness. However, their published texts are largely invisible in mainstream African literature scholarship.

This invisibility is part of what Nsah (2017:97) calls the triple marginality afflicting Anglophone Cameroonian literature. According to Nsah, Anglophone Cameroonian literature suffers from triple marginality in the sense that at the international level, it is given less critical attention compared to other literatures from Africa and the world; at the national level it is undermined compared to Francophone Cameroonian literature which is dominant owing to the linguistic dominance of French; and at the intra-group level, it is riddled with ethnic and gender differentiation such that writers from certain Anglophone ethnic groups are more prominent than others, while men are more prominent than women. Thus, I argue that the marginality of Anglophone Cameroonian women's literature starts from the intra-group level because of gender bias and spirals all the way through the national level to the international level where the literature becomes eclipsed. Gender bias is evident in the dearth of scholarly attention given to women's works by Anglophone male critics. For example, Emmanuel Fru Doh's book *Anglophone-Cameroon literature: An introduction* (Doh 2015) does not include a single prose, poetry or dramatic text by a woman. Thankfully, the strength of women's voices in their writing pervades the silence of their invisibility to arrest feminist readers who encounter their texts. These texts exist in various genres, from novels to poems, from plays to short stories, from memoirs to folktales, from children's fiction to science fiction. Versatile in their artistic prowess, these women write across genres and are by no means confined to a single writing style.

Anglophone Cameroonian women writers are spread across the world, writing from different geo-political locations, including Cameroon, and centring the Anglophone Cameroonian woman's experience. Contemporary established writers include Makuchi (Juliana Makuchi Nfah-Abbenyi's pen name), Joyce Ash (also writing as Joyce Ashuntangtang), Anne Tanyi-Tang, Margaret Afuh, Eunice Ngongkum, and Ngoh Agnes Nzuh. I classify these ones as established writers, not based on the volume of works they have published, but on the length of time they have been known in the Anglophone Cameroonian literary scene. These writers have been producing literature over decades, even if sporadically. As early as 1977, Makuchi published three short stories in the literary journal *The Mould* edited by the late Bole Butake (Lyonga & Butake 1982:50). These stories were "The Applicant" in *The Mould 1*, "The Visiting Card" in *The Mould 2*, and "Fonki's Plight" in *The Mould 4* (Lyonga & Butake 1982:76). Standing adjacent to these pioneer women writers is a group of writers whose literary presence has been felt only in the last ten or so years. These writers include Imbolo Mbue, Florence Ndiyah, Grace Fien Ngong, Pochi Tamba, Pepertua K. Nkamanyang Lola, Mary Fosi Mbantenkhu, Nnane Ntube, Mary Ngwebong Ngu, Beatrice Fri Bimo, Joffi Ewusi, Dione Precious Betika, and Geraldine Sinyuy. As a published poet, I locate myself among this talented group of emerging writers. Some of these writers however resist confinement to the term "emerging", so I use the term here with caution.

While my classification of established and emerging writers recognises the long-term service of the pioneer women writers to the development of Anglophone Cameroonian women's literature, it nonetheless becomes limited, considering that being a prolific writer is part of what makes a writer established. Some of the newer writers have become established owing to their high productivity in publishing texts across several genres, and are more well known in contemporary Cameroon than their pioneer sisters. Examples here are Perpetua K. Nkamanyang Lola who is author of the novel *Rustles on Naked Trees* (2015), the poetry anthology *Healing Stings* (2016) and the play *The Lock on My Lips* (2023), and Joffi Ewusi who has published the poetry anthology *Inklings from My Ink* (2018) and the novels *Going Home* (2019a) and *Christmas Carols in June* (2019b). Thus, Anglophone Cameroonian women writers challenge notions of what it means to be an established writer. Similarly, this group of writers complicate the meaning of the expression "contemporary writers". While the expression is often used loosely to mean current writers or writers existing now, it is not so easy to pin down contemporarity: is a writer contemporary because they are still alive or because they are actually publishing texts, or because they are both alive and still publishing? McFadden (2021:286) gives contemporarity a fresh meaning in arguing that it is not "the opposite of the modern or the Western" but rather "it is about finding the innovative feminist energies and sensibilities that will enable each of us to live the new politics of this moment in African time". Adopting this view, I use the term contemporary writers to refer to Anglophone Cameroonian women writers whose published texts enable readers to understand the politics of gender in the present time as it plays out for women in Cameroon and abroad.

A succinct paradox in the history of Anglophone Cameroonian women writers is that, while writing in English, these writers have often had to rely on Francophone publishing houses for the publication of their works. It must be remembered that owing to colonisation by the British and French, Cameroon has two official languages, English and French. English, though, is spoken by a minority population – people of Anglophone descent largely located in the North West and South West regions of the country. The linguistic challenges associated with women's publishing are rooted in this colonial history. In 1980, Benedicta Muffuh, one of the early Anglophone women writers, published *The Rebel: A Play in Two Acts* (Muffuh 1980). *The Rebel* was however published by Société de Presse d'edition du Cameroun (SOPECAM) which, according to Joyce Ashuntantang (2009:60), was a state-owned publishing house whose editors did not take time to read or edit submitted manuscripts but simply typeset and printed them. The SOPECAM case illustrates one of the major challenges that early women writers faced: besides having mainly state-owned publishing outlets whose unstated censorship role ensured that texts published did not stir political activism of any sort, women writers also had to deal with publishing texts for which there were no quality assurance processes in place.

Over the years, many Anglophone women writers, like their male counterparts, have had their works published by either Éditions CLÉ in Yaounde or Éditions Véritas in Douala, both of which are located in French-speaking cities. The problem of poor copyediting of texts, or possibly no editing at all, points to the reality that lack of proficiency in the English language is a major setback in publishing with these outlets. Yet, women have had to depend on these publishers for their writing to see the light of day, or resort to self-publishing. In an interview with Nfah-Abbenyi, playwright Bole Butake states that in the colonial days

> there were no publishers in Cameroon. Even after independence, the few publishers who started publishing like Buma Kor abandoned it along the way, so in effect, most of the people who published after independence were mostly self-published.... it's only these days that I can say, the literature is blooming.
>
> (Nfah-Abbenyi & Butake 2016:14)

These are some of the complexities that make a study of Anglophone Cameroonian women writers a compelling scholarly project. Even more compelling is the observation that these writers create a symphony of voices singing an inspirational song of African women's ability to flourish even under systems determined to break them down, foremost among which are patriarchy, colonialism and imperialism.

African women's flourishing in the area of literary publishing is a significant indicator of their agency, resilience and entrepreneurship in the face of colonial, patriarchal and imperialist oppressions over the centuries. Owing to colonial gender bias which privileged men's education over women's, women entered into the field of writing later than their male counterparts (Nkealah 2009:109). Moreover, the missionary education that girls received aimed at training them to be good domestic workers at home (Mougoué 2019:44), thus limiting their potential to venture into public activities such as writing and publishing. In the early post-independence era, gendered state politics and the patriarchal undervaluing of women's voices continued to suppress women's literary production (Pucherová 2022:86). While colonialism is no longer a problem for contemporary women writers who can access higher education and are breaking out of gendered roles to assert their identities in public and private spaces, its legacy is pervasive. The legacy of colonialism in Cameroon was notable in the absence of Anglophone publishing houses that could publish literary works in English, as French remained the dominant language of the country (Ashuntantang 2015:246; Nfah-Abbenyi & Butake 2016:14). Moreover, socio-economic conditions in Cameroon have deteriorated since the 1990s, further jeopardising the development of publishing in Anglophone Cameroon. Despite this gloomy state of affairs, it can be noted that Anglophone Cameroonian women have been publishing steadily from the 1960s. Jedida Asheri, the first Anglophone woman to publish a novel, *The Promise* (1969), did so in Nigeria (Ashuntantang 2009:91), showing women's initiative in transcending publishing challenges. With the emergence of Anglophone publishing houses in Bamenda (Langaa Publishing), Yaounde (Nyaa Publishers) and overseas (Spears Media, USA) over the last two decades, there has especially been a burgeoning of women's literary works since 2000.

Flowers Blooming from an Ice Bucket: Contemporary Anglophone Cameroonian Women Writers

It is expected that flowers rooted in ice rather than soil should look different, smell different and serve a different purpose. Anglophone Cameroonian women writers produce literature that distinguishes itself from male-authored literature through the construction of female characters contending with various forms of patriarchal oppression, such as domestic violence, spousal betrayal and sexual exploitation, and yet finding ways to overcome these challenges, assert their subjectivities, and transform their lives for the better. Speaking about Anglophone Cameroonian literature of the mid-1980s to the 1990s, Ashuntantang (2016:121) states that "while the Anglophone male writer during this phase was concerned with the plight of Anglophones in Cameroon, the women writers dealt with their double marginalization as Anglophones and as women". Contemporary Anglophone Cameroonian women writers are not only writing about the double marginalisation of women but they are also transforming the very ways in which women have been written into texts by the patriarchal hegemonic breed of writers. I argue that these writers practice a feminism of fortitude, which is evinced by both their lived experiences and the female characters they depict in their literary texts. My study of their thematic concerns, ideological positionings and writing styles point to an understanding of Anglophone Cameroonian women writers as relentless in their quest for gender justice in a society that has trampled on women's humanity for a very long time. Nevertheless, I equally note the limitations in some of the solutions proffered in their writing and the shortcomings in some texts in terms of their literariness.

Women Writing under Punitive Socio-economic Conditions

Flowers growing in an ice bucket challenge the orthodox notion that flowers must always be rooted in soil. Soil is a natural resource that makes plants grow. Unlike soil, ice in a bucket is man-made. This analogy suggests that Anglophone Cameroonian women writers have not experienced the luxury of a naturally conducive environment for literary writing and publishing. With the high cost of publishing, the limitation of publicity and dissemination channels, the shortage of government subsidies for artistic, literary and cultural productions, the benign censorship of radical literary voices, and a patriarchal education system that continues to privilege male-authored literature in school and university curricula (Ambanasom 2013:7), women writers have been producing their creative works in largely unnatural socio-economic conditions. These women pursue writing as a means of self-empowerment within a society riddled with economic stagnation, poor transport systems, poor education systems, violence against women and girl children, and ineffective legal systems that render women vulnerable to patriarchal manipulation and domination (Nkealah 2015:61). Many pursue self-publishing as the only alternative in an environment where cultural production is the least urgent project for government subsidisation. The crippling economic situation that makes even self-publishing difficult is a man-made problem; it is the result of corruption, greed and tyrannical political leadership in Cameroon. Operating within this ice bucket environment that stagnates, forestalls and immobilises creative growth, it is impressive that Anglophone Cameroonian women still have the capacity to write and publish. These women are the metaphoric flowers blooming out of an ice bucket. The literature they write captures the harsh conditions under which they pursue their creativity and simultaneously their agency in conquering hurdles.

Margaret Afuh's novel *Flowers in the desert* (2009) uses the metaphor of a desert – an arid, unproductive land – to convey the unfulfilling lives that Anglophone Cameroonians have to endure even though they live in a country blessed with natural resources that could be exploited to create jobs for young people. These resources are "fruits, food stuff, natural resources on land, under the earth, in the sea, in the air, all over the world; beautiful flowers, fauna, flora, beautiful solar system, animals and you name it" (Afuh 2009:84–85). Rudolph, the male protagonist of the novel, calls these resources flowers, and describes Cameroon as "a desert full of flowers" (Afuh 2009:85). His meaning is that the political elite, out of greed, have turned a fertile country full of potential into a desert land devoid of economic development. It is within this kind of stagnating socio-economic space that Anglophone women like Afuh are producing literary texts. The irony in the novel is a pointer to punitive conditions of living under which women write and publish literary texts. However, Afuh's novel title *Flowers in the desert* can equally be interpreted as embodying possibilities of women's triumph over their harsh conditions; that flowers can blossom in a desert suggests that even deserts have oases that offer possibilities of growth and regeneration.

In the preface to her collection of poems titled *I will fly*, Florence Ndiyah (2012) equally describes the horrible socio-economic conditions that many ordinary Cameroonians and especially Anglophone Cameroonians have to endure on a daily basis. Their experiences are what inform the poems she includes in this collection. About the anthology, she states the following:

> It opens with a first set of poems on difficulties faced by Cameroonian citizens. The characters fall in two groups. First, ordinary Cameroonians who simply cannot make ends meet, who daily entertain hardship. Unemployment, underemployment and

related consequences darken their general demeanour. The second group are English-speaking Cameroonians. As the minority population, they constantly bear the weight of marginalisation.

(Ndiyah 2012: vii)

As Ndiyah points out here, her poems capture the lives of citizens suffocated by the crippling economic air of Cameroon that offers little promise of a better tomorrow. The Anglophone minority suffers even more as opportunities for these citizens are further shrunk merely on the basis of their Anglophoneness. Ndiyah (2012:vii) notes in her preface how these conditions push people out of Cameroon to seek better lives in Europe and North America. For women, the situation is even more dire as those who cannot emigrate tend to resort to marriage as a route to escape poverty (Ndiyah 2012:viii), thus reducing themselves to cheap labour for patriarchal men. Ndiyah's poem "Anglo!" included in this collection conveys the misfortune of being an English-speaking Cameroonian in a French-speaking dominated Cameroon. She states that "colonial tongues/stunt our growth" because English is constructed by the Francophone majority as "the wrong language, like one which came in through the back door" (Ndiyah 2012:9). The metaphor of coming in through the back door poignantly conveys the thought that Anglophones are not recognised as legitimate citizens fully entitled to the wealth of Cameroon, that they will always come second in the hierarchy of things, and that they can only work their way to the top of the civil service through stealthy and self-sacrificial means. This situation of being handicapped by an Anglophone identity paradoxically encourages creativity among Anglophone Cameroonian women as they write to give expression to these experiences of substandard living, to vent their frustrations with the political and patriarchal systems within which they operate, and to sound possibilities of hope for the suffering masses.

The effects of the punitive socio-economic conditions on the youth emerge strongly in the writing of Eunice Ngongkum whose short story collection *Manna of a life time and other stories* (2007) presents stories in which young people are completely disillusioned by the prevailing hardships in Cameroon. In the story "Race of hope", the readers meet a widow, Cecilia Kendong, who is desperately looking to loan money so that her daughter, Jeminda, can obtain a visa to study in England on a scholarship. In her quest for the much-needed finances, Cecilia reflects on how the country had collapsed economically as "many of the commercial banks became bankrupt", how corruption had become normalised as "state funds became private funds with impunity" (Ngongkum 2007:75). Salary cuts for civil servants further disempowered parents to provide education for their children, as Cecilia notes that "the buying power of the citizens had been reduced but children had to be sent to school" (Ngongkum 2007:76). For the young people, the consequences of economic stagnation were especially demoralising as "many of the young degree holders [were] roaming the streets" doing nothing; these young people "who were the hope of their families were now the principal architects of desolation" (Ngongkum 2007:78). In addition, "intelligent students get disillusioned and the less intelligent work their way through fraud" (Ngongkum 2007:78). Thus, Cecilia is determined to obtain a loan from the Advocate Sisters' Social Group through her friend Bihmbong who is their member.

The story "Petite amie" in the same collection is about a young Anglophone girl who leaves her home in Tiko to pursue higher education in Yaounde and in the process falls in love with a Francophone man who betrays her in the end by going to marry someone else. The story speaks of the unique challenges Anglophones encounter at the University of Yaounde just because they cannot speak French. Rose, the protagonist, states that "the hurdles had been overwhelming especially for them who were Anglophone" (Ngongkum 2007:87). The story paints a horrid picture of life for Anglophone students in the prestigious University of Yaounde I. Significantly, Ngongkum had attended the same university and ended up working there as a lecturer. The stories she writes about the place are therefore not observations made from a distant place or reports garnered through news media; they are stories borne out of personal experiences with Anglophobia in Yaounde. Writers like Makuchi, Tanyi-Tang, Afuh and Ashuntantang all went through the University of Yaounde I, bringing into the space their Anglophoneness which remained a source of apathy. Like these compatriot writers, Ngongkum wrote her fiction under the duress of acute awareness of her place as an outsider in Francophone Cameroon. That these women could thrive under these conditions attests to the boundlessness of their resilience.

Beside the debilitating national conditions which compel women to write under constraints, the family unit as a patriarchal structure further enforces icy – painful – conditions for women's writing. The case of Pepertua K. Nkamanyang Lola is instructive in showing how Anglophone Cameroonian women are pursuing writing amidst the limitations imposed on them by their gender, Anglophone identity, and social status as wives and mothers. In the preface to her play, *The lock on my lips*, Nkamanyang Lola (2023) narrates an incident that took place on 8 March 2009 which got her to write the play. It was the hostility from her husband about her preparedness to go out and celebrate International Women's Day in Cameroon like all other women. Rather than complimenting her in her beautiful celebratory *kaba* (a long free-flowing dress commonly worn by Cameroonian women), her husband lashed out in anger about the wastefulness of Women's Day, asking "what is even the essence of this Women's Day?…what can women do?" and ordered her to stay at home and tend to their young children (Nkamanyang Lola 2023:xv). Not wanting to risk losing her food allowance, Nkamanyang Lola did her husband's bidding to stay at home, but rebelliously used the time to write a play that challenges men's misconceptions about feminism, women's rights and gender equality. She applied Ezeigbo's snail-sense feminism here by going around the problem of patriarchal domination rather than confronting it (Ezeigbo 2012). By writing and publishing *The lock on my lips*, Nkamanyang Lola gives a direct answer to her husband's question "what can women do?": she shows him that women can write, and through their writing, they not only sensitise ignorant patriarchal men about gender justice but also more importantly assert their right to creative autonomy. While Nkamanyang Lola's experience illustrates the harrowing family circumstances under which Anglophone Cameroonian women writers produce feminist literature, it also elucidates these women's determination to arrest the male shortsightedness, bias and gender insensitivity that pervades Anglophone Cameroonian societies.

Women's Writing as Imperfect Perfections

With the punitive socio-economic conditions under which women in Cameroon are writing, it is no surprise that the quality of some of the texts they publish tends to be substandard, even though the texts themselves address relevant gender issues in Cameroon today. Ash's poem quoted at the beginning of this chapter suggests that flowers blooming in an ice bucket instead of a vase present an imperfect picture: the flowers are not where they naturally belong. Yet, these flowers thrive in spite of the iciness surrounding them. Similarly, the literature that Anglophone women publish in Cameroon is often not where it should be in terms of quality as the writing is beset by imperfections. These imperfections are evident in the numerous language errors that litter the pages of texts. However, as Ash's poem suggests, imperfection can be beautiful in its unpretentiousness. Anglophone Cameroonian women writers similarly embody beauty in their honest appraisals of their societies, shielding no sector of society – least of all women – from the strokes of criticism that writing is capable of wielding. They are writers not on a quest for perfection but for that which is beautiful in writing. Several texts illustrate this notion of women's writing as imperfect perfections.

The novel *Nostalgia* by Grace Fien Ngong (2014) is replete with uncountable grammatical, spelling, vocabulary and punctuation errors that make reading it more of a chore than a delight. Its other problem is a structural weakness, with a plotline that is episodic and fragmentary. The writing style indicates poor mastery of the technique of polyvocality. However, at its core, it is an inspirational story of a young woman, Jessica, who develops the willpower to leave her promiscuous husband, Brandon, for fear of contracting HIV through him. Jessica acknowledges that "living with him was as if I was gradually taking in slow poison with my eyes open" (Ngong 2014:143). Thus, she resolves to end her marriage rather than die whilst trying to keep it. Divorce saves her as eventually both Brandon and his mistress die of AIDS.

The plays of Tanyi-Tang also illustrate the imperfect perfections in women's writing. Tanyi-Tang's play collection *Ewa and other plays* (2000) makes use of many clichéd expressions such as "our dad gave up the ghost" (2000:9), "the joy of motherhood" (2000:41), "it is only a woman who knows the father of her child" (2000:55), "where there is a will, there is a way" (2000:71), "someone seriously sick will soon give up the ghost" (2000:74), and men are "such necessary evil" (2000:95). The clichés suggest a limited linguistic repertoire. In addition, Tanyi-Tang's plays tend to have very utopian endings as evident in "My bundle of joy" included in *Ewa and other plays* in which Kechen, the main character, ends up giving birth to twins after many years in a childless marriage. Similarly, in the play "Visiting America" included in the collection *Two Plays: Visiting America and Marienuelle* (2006), the protagonist, Coco, bears triplets – two boys and a girl – which cements her relationship with her Nigerian lover, Yomi. In *Eneta vs Elimo* (2007), utopianism is seen when Eneta and Enoh reconcile in the end after several years of separation. Despite these weaknesses, Tanyi-Tang's plays present female characters who embody successful self-empowerment. These characters project "a sense of personhood attained through self-emancipatory initiatives" (Nkealah 2014:125). They emerge as role models because "they are successful career women who work hard to acquire positions of authority and respect within their societies" (Nkealah 2014:125). With the depressing socio-economic situation in Cameroon under which women write, Tanyi-Tang's plays are significant because they offer possibilities of women's economic and social empowerment, "which are truly inspirational at a time when the state cannot create adequate job opportunities for young people" (Nkealah 2017b:10549). The plays then, with their shortcomings, are the very epitome of flowers blooming out of an ice bucket.

Besides poor editing, there is also the problem of poor crafting of stories where some narratives tend to read like social commentary pamphlets, journalistic reports or self-help books rather than literary texts. Good examples here are Afuh's *Flowers in the desert* mentioned earlier and Pochi Tamba's *Best friends* (Tamba 2009). In both novels, the authors indulge in moralisation rather than presenting the complexity of women's experiences, as a result of which they have to make tough decisions. These two novels also read like religious testimonies rather than literary texts. The ideological landscape in them is flat as all roads lead to the Christian God. These novels also tend to reinforce gender stereotyping. This is especially true of Afuh's novel in which women like Brenda and Clara are portrayed as incapable of finding happiness outside of marriage and religion, while wives like Wendy meticulously maintain house for their husbands in spite of prevailing poverty. There is hardly any agency displayed by these women as they cannot find self-fulfilment without recourse to patriarchy-defined gender roles of wives and mothers. Even with all these faults, these novels embody perfection as stories of hope. Hope is sorely needed in the social climate of Cameroon where women's lives are a daily struggle against the stigmatisation of people living with HIV as well as of single, divorced, childless and widowed women. The overt and unstated social conspiracies against women who find themselves experiencing any of these predicaments weigh women down, and a novel that offers possibilities for respite, even if it is only through one medium – the church, is very likely to energise women sufferers. The depiction of HIV/AIDS in male-authored texts such as *The deadly honey* by Eugene Kongnyuy (2003) has been particularly gender-biased, devoid of what Eze (2016) calls feminist empathy – the ability of men to feel women's pain in their writing and reading of women. By contrast, women writers like Tamba in *Best Friends*, Afuh in *Flowers in the Desert* and Ngong in *Nostalgia* have re-written women's experiences of HIV infection with empathy, imbuing their narratives with what I call feminist humaneness and define as "women's capacity to care, nurture and heal others in times of crisis" (Nkealah 2022:4). Women's writing therefore attempts to perfect the distorted image of women dealing with HIV infection pandered in male-authored Anglophone literature by projecting survivors as living testimonies of hope.

Writing as Reflections and Recreations of Women's Fortitude

An ice bucket seems incapable of producing anything, least of all flowers. That a plant can take root in an ice bucket and produce flowers speaks to the sheer willpower of the plant to live. In line with this metaphor, contemporary Anglophone Cameroonian women's literature, as well as the lived experiences of the writers themselves, point to fortitude as a central concept in Anglophone Cameroonian feminism. More than just perseverance or the ability to endure hardship, the women writers epitomise the courage to live through pain, personal and collective, and to turn that pain into projects for self and collective recovery. I define feminist fortitude here as the ability of women to defy dominant narratives of pain and create new ones, doing so on their own terms. Florence Ndiyah is a writer who has displayed magnanimous strength in her everyday life and writing career. I first encountered her work as an external examiner of her PhD thesis in Creative Writing which she completed at the University of Pretoria in 2021. From her acknowledgements, I learned that she had lost her husband during the course of the PhD, a man who had been very supportive of her writing career. That she completed the PhD despite this traumatic experience was inspiring to me personally. And so was born the beginning of a beautiful friendship. Significantly, Ndiyah does not have a background in English literary studies. Her undergraduate degree was in microbiology; it was only later that she moved away from the sciences and began to pursue a career in writing (Nkealah & Ndiyah 2021).

Ndiyah writes her fiction with a linguistic flair that makes reading her works a complete delight. The novel she wrote for her PhD is titled *The things we don't talk about* (Ndiyah 2020) and it presents the stories of two women, Valery and Kehmia, who manage to forge a friendship under very difficult circumstances. It is a story of war, love, emotional struggle and women's fortitude in the face of individual and collective crises. The sophistication of the novel lies not only in the complex characterisation of its protagonists but also in its inclusion of dialogue in Cameroonian indigenous languages such as Itaŋikom and Mungaka. The novel challenges the idealisation of monogamy and criminalisation of polygyny, while positing the view that contemporary educated women's choice to enter into polygynous marriage should be understood in the context of their quest for self-fashioning in an era in which getting married is a competition. Kehmia chooses to enter a polygynous marriage but refuses to have children; marriage takes away the stigma of singleness while polygynous marriage gives her the freedom to pursue her career unburdened by the demands of motherhood since her co-wife had already produced children for her husband. Reminiscent of Lola Shoneyin's novel *The secret lives of Baba Segi's wives* (2010), Ndiyah's *The things we don't talk about* foregrounds African women's ability to "overcome several obstacles by combining the ego identity principles of stability, flexibility and independence, as well as ego strength" (Ndiyah 2021:72). Ndiyah's fictional characters, who may be considered extensions of women she is familiar with and simultaneously creations existing solely in her imagination, exemplify women's fortitude in the face of stringent political, social and economic conditions in Cameroon.

Feminist fortitude conjectures women's capacity to resist patriarchal ideologies on women's sexuality by rewriting women's sexuality with unapologetic honesty. This is in line with transnational African feminism which no longer sees sexual politics as only the concern of Western feminists. Pucherová (2022:10) highlights the place of women's sexuality in transnational African feminism when she states: "sexuality, once considered a Western feminist concern by African women, is brought centre-stage and recognized as the location of women's freedom and victimization". Evidence of this claim is found in Anglophone Cameroonian women's poetry. In Ash's poem quoted in the introduction above, the reference to "crumpled sheets bearing witness / To a sweet sinful 'yes'" alludes to the raw honesty of her poems about women and their sexual experiences. *Beautiful Fire* has a whole section titled "Nuggets of passion" in which Ash explores women's desire for orgasmic experience with their partners as in the poem "Into the beautiful fire", their indulgence and enjoyment of cybersex as in the poem "A digital moment", and their erotic desire for past lovers as in "The pulse of love".

My own poetry collection *And they call themselves feminists* (Nkealah 2017c) echoes sentiments about women's sexuality very similar to Ash's. In the poem "Making love in springtime", the speaker enjoys orgasmic pleasure with her partner but rejects his request for her to bear a child for him. The poem "In the chatroom", like Ash's poem "A digital moment", presents the pleasures of cybersex in the very language used within that erotic space. In "A heart's desire", the speaker confesses her insatiable desire for her married lover. Lastly, "There's a woman in my man's life" hints at a lesbian relationship developing between a wife and her husband's second wife, a subversive act of sexuality that comes as a slap on the face of patriarchal heterosexuality. These poems, in their bluntness about what women desire and who they desire it with, remove the patriarchal veil on women that keeps their sexuality shrouded in shamefulness. In writing uninhibitedly about sexual desire and experience, Anglophone women writers construct women as agents of their sexual autonomy who fully express their humanity, "knowing we are still God's children, / Naked. Imperfect" (Ash 2018:45).

Women's courage to rewrite patriarchal histories is also visible evidence of their feminist fortitude. Maidem Kayem, the Kumba-born author of the historical novel *Balumakazi* (2018), believes that Africans must write their own stories to glorify their own heroes and not learn about them through the skewed visions of western historians (Kayem 2019). Like her foremothers Jedida Asheri whose novel *Promise* (1969) presents an autobiographical account of her childhood under the attack of colonial and patriarchal systems of oppression (see Ashuntantang 2016:114) and Azanwi Nchami whose *Footprints of Destiny* (1985) focalises anti-colonial nationalism in African fiction (see Ambanasom 2009:66), Kayem writes African history from a woman-centred African perspective. *Balumakazi* reconceives 500 years of African history, from slavery to colonialism to imperialism, and its characters bring to life forgotten African heroes who staged successful resistance against the slave trade (Kayem 2019). As Kayem (2019) points out, the female character Farra in the novel, who joins the movement to fight colonialism, represents women who fought in armed struggles to gain independence for African countries. In the case of Cameroon specifically, Farra represents Anglophone women like Gwendoline Burnley, Anna Foncha and Josepha Mua who "sought to foster Anglophone nationalism and to improve women's lives even as they navigated the political landscape in which [President] Ahidjo increasingly subjugated Anglophone personhood" (Mougoué 2019:27). The important role women played in resisting colonialism and neo-colonialism is central to *Balumakazi*, and according to Kayem (2019) that role is not emphasised enough in history textbooks emanating from the so-called global north. Thus, Anglophone Cameroonian women's re-writing of history using their feminist biros is most significant.

Women's role in writing history from a feminist perspective that advocates for gender justice is equally resounding in the short stories of Makuchi. Makuchi's feminist fortitude is seen in how she tells the story of the Anglophone crisis in Cameroon from the perspective of the women and girls who suffer unjustly for a war they did not start. In the short story "Land of my dreams" which she published using her full name this time (Juliana Makuchi Nfah-Abbenyi), the reader encounters a beautifully crafted polyvocal narrative that presents the story of an Anglophone family in war-torn Bamenda. According to Murray (2021:112), the changeable, unpredictable narrative voices in stories of war "give credence to forms of trauma so variable and multi-directional as to elude simple solutions". The interlocking relationship between gender and trauma which Murray speaks about in relation to the short fiction of Ugandan writer Beatrice Lamwaka is also evident in Nfah-Abbenyi's story through the separate accounts of the Anglophone crisis presented by the two narrative voices. Angela and her mother, Mami Angela, are victims of the civil war in Cameroon between the Francophone government and the Anglophone insurgents fighting for secession (the Ambazonia).

When the story opens, 10-year-old Angela has wet her bed, something that had not happened in a long time and only started happening when an Ambazonia leader comes to their house demanding 500,000CFA from her father as his compulsory contribution to the Anglophone cause. By the time the story ends, Mami Angela, who thought she had entered menopause as her womb had "stitched its mouth shut" after her brother had disappeared, suddenly finds herself drenched in "a crimson tide" when she realises that Angela has sneaked out of the house to go to school on a day that the Ambazonia leaders had declared lockdown in Bamenda (Nfah-Abbenyi 2021:105). The persistent image of fluid and leaking bodies in this story comes to signify women's vulnerability in the face of oppressive forces over which they have no control. However, in telling a story of gender and war, and precisely how war displaces women, changes them into bitter individuals and destroys their sense of protectiveness over their children, Nfah-Abbenyi enacts a feminism of fortitude, displaying the courage to speak up against a crisis and not remain aloof as a distant observer. She, in this story, vividly captures what Nnaemeka (2021:184) would describe as "the human dimension and cost of the war".

Women Writing in and of Icy Foreign Lands

The expression "like flowers blooming in an ice bucket instead of a vase" in Ash's poem also embodies Anglophone Cameroonian women who are writing their stories of living woman-ness from icy foreign lands. This iciness is both in terms of the cold climates they have to endure in wintery seasons while trying to produce fictional works and the anti-immigrant, racist, and xenophobic attitudes they often encounter while living in their immigrant homes. Instead of blooming as flowers in a vase which would symbolise their birthplace Cameroon, they are blooming in ice buckets by creating success stories in unhomely homes. The ice bucket may be cooler than the hot soil in the vase but the ice cannot be said to be completely comfortable. This has been my personal experience living in South Africa for the past 20 years. Writers such as Tanyi-Tang, Nfah-Abbenyi, Ashuntantang, Kayem, Ngu, Nkamanyang Lola and myself have experienced life in foreign lands and although some of us have made homes in these places, we continue to deal with unhomeliness. The challenges Anglophone Cameroonian women writers experience as immigrants in the United States of America is well articulated by New York based writer Imbolo Mbue in an interview about her novel *Behold the dreamers* (2016a). In this interview, Mbue (2016b) speaks about the anti-immigrant rhetoric in the US that sees immigrants as numbers rather than the human beings they are. She notes that her novel is about the challenges that immigrants like herself experience in New York and the US at large, and even though the novel has made her a successful writer, that success does not take away the challenges she has been through or the reality that she still goes through, because she will always be a black woman, a working class and an immigrant in the US (Mbue 2016b). She also highlights the issue of shame as immigrants tend to feel ashamed for not achieving the American dream despite working very hard to get it (Mbue 2016b). She conveys women's experience of this sense of shame vividly in *Behold the dreamers* through the main female character, Neni, who does not want to return to Cameroon despite her husband's inability to secure legal documents for them to stay on in the US.

In one of her ruminations towards the end of the novel, Neni convinces herself that her unwillingness to return to Cameroon is not because she loves New York too much but because she wants her children to stay in the US and better their lives through the many opportunities they would enjoy as citizens, something she and Jende could not have, and because "no one journeyed far away from home to return without a fortune amassed or dream achieved" (Mbue 2016a:316). This experience of dreams unattained is what Mbue (2016b) says breeds shame among immigrants in the US. One notes here "shame's power to engender a strongly felt (both in the emotional and physical meaning) sense of inferiority, and consequently a need to avoid or even actively flee society" (Bishop 2021:14). For women in particular, this shame comes on top of other kinds of gender-based shame inflicted on them in Cameroonian societies, as Neni states: "she needed to fight so she and her children would never become objects of ridicule the way she'd been when she'd gotten pregnant and dropped out of school" (Mbue 2016a:316). Neni's fear of shame is therefore triggered by previous experiences of shaming as a teenage mother in Cameroon. The multiple forms of shame that African immigrant women have to contend with is a feminist concern here as it points to the double pressure that they are under, as women and as mothers, to make a success of immigrant life. Thus, the metaphor of flowers blooming in an ice bucket suggests that *unlearning* shame is an important feminist project for Anglophone Cameroonian women in the diaspora.

Seeds Popping: Prospects for Anglophone Cameroonian Women's Literature

There exists huge prospects for Anglophone Cameroonian women's literature as new writers are emerging every day and old ones are reinventing themselves. In the context of Ash's metaphor, the blooming flowers are popping seeds into the air, creating opportunities for new flowers to germinate and for creative cross-pollination to take place. Between 2015 and 2023, many women have published their works in Cameroon and abroad. Poetry collections published during this period include those by Nkamanyang Lola (2016), Taku (2016), Ewusi (2018), Ntube (2020), Bime (2021), and Ngu (2021). The last eight years have seen the publication of several novels and short story collections. These include texts by Nkamanyang Lola (2015), Ndiyah (2018, 2019), and Ewusi (2019a, 2019b). Collections of folktales are also on the increase. A newly published collection is *Music in the wood & other folktales* by Sinyuy (2023) which revitalises the folktale tradition already established in collections by Nzuh (1999), Makuchi (2008) and Afuh (2011). The genre of children's fiction also continues to grow with texts by Betika (2021) and Mbantenkhu (2022) making entry into the world of published literature. In the field of drama, new plays continue to visit stages across cities and it is likely that these will eventually make their way into the bookshops as printed texts. Equally worthy of mention in this concluding section are several edited anthologies that have brought together women's writing on pressing concerns in Cameroon, such as the poetry anthologies by Ashuntantang and Tande (2020) and Atanga and Mboumien (2022). Literary awards designed specifically for Anglophone writing, such as the EduART Literary Awards for Cameroon Literature in English founded by Ashuntantang, are encouraging increased literary outputs from women (Barringer 2012:620). With publishers like Langaa Research & Publishing Common Initiative Group, Spears Media Press and Nyaa Publishers churning out works by Anglophone women, the future promises to be even brighter for them. It is envisaged that rather than reverting to blooming in a vase, these flowers will continue to produce colourful petals out of the ice bucket.

Acknowledgements

This work is based on research supported wholly by the National Research Foundation of South Africa (Grant Number 136135). I am equally grateful to Florence Ndiyah, Eyong Tiku, Pepertua Nkamanyang Lola and the wonderful members of the Cameroon Anglophone Writers Association who drew my attention to their published works.

References

Afuh, M., 2009, *Flowers in the desert*, Bamenda, Patron Publishing House.
Afuh, M., 2011, *Fireside stories*, Bamenda, Patron Publishing House.
Ambanasom, S., 2009, *The Cameroonian novel of English expression: An introduction*. Bamenda, Langaa.
Ambanasom, S., 2013, *Perspectives on written Cameroon literature in English*, Bamenda, Langaa.
Ash, J., 2018, *Beautiful fire*, Denver, CO, Spears Media Press.
Asheri, J., 1969, *Promise*, Lagos, African University Press.
Ashuntantang, J., 2009, *Landscaping postcoloniality: The dissemination of Cameroon Anglophone literature*, Bamenda, Langaa.
Ashuntantang, J., 2015, 'The publishing and digital dissemination of creative writing in Cameroon', in C. Davis & D. Johnson (eds.), *The book in Africa: Critical debates*, pp. 245–266, Basingstoke, Hampshire, Palgrave Macmillan.
Ashuntantang, J., 2016, 'Anglophone Cameroon literature 1959–90: A brief overview', *Tydskrif vir Letterkunde* 53(1), 109–127.

Ashuntantang, J. & Tande, D. (eds.), 2020, *Bearing witness: Poems from a land in turmoil*, Denver, CO, Spears Media Press.
Atanga, L. & Mboumien, S. (eds.), 2022, *When the sun turns red: Women's tears from a land of despair*, Denver, CO, Spears Media Press.
Barringer, T.A., 2012, 'West Africa', *The Journal of Commonwealth Literature* 47(4), 619–623.
Betika, D.P., 2021, *Love wins*, Yaounde, Nyaa Publishers.
Bime, B.F., 2021, *Shades of sorrow, tears and laughter*, Denver, CO, Spears Media Press.
Bishop, L.B., 2021, *Scripting shame in African literature*, Liverpool, Liverpool University Press.
Boswell, B., 2020, *And wrote my story anyway: Black South African women's novels as feminism*, Johannesburg, Wits University Press.
Doh, E.F., 2015, *Anglophone-Cameroon literature: An introduction*, London, Lexington Books.
Ewusi, J., 2018, *Inklings from my ink*, Yaounde, Nyaa Publishers.
Ewusi, J., 2019a, *Going home*, Yaounde, Nyaa Publishers.
Ewusi, J., 2019b, *Christmas carols in June*, Yaounde, Nyaa Publishers.
Eze, C., 2016, *Ethics and human rights in Anglophone African women's literature: Feminist empathy*, Cham, Palgrave Macmillan.
Ezeigbo, A., 2012, *Snail-sense feminism: Building on an indigenous model*, Lagos, University of Lagos Press.
Gqola, P.D., 2011. 'Whirling worlds? Women's poetry, feminist imagination and contemporary South African publics', *Scrutiny2* 16(2), 5–11.
Henaku, N., 2021, 'Transnational African women as voices of conscience: Aidoo's *Our sister killjoy*, Adichie's *Americanah*, and Atta's *A bit of difference*', in R.A. Sackeyfio (ed.), *Transnational perspectives in the twenty-first century*, pp. 73–87, London, Lexington Books.
Kayem, M., 2018, *Balumakazi: Native*, Milton Keynes, Xlibris.
Kayem, M., 2019, 'Interview with Maidem Kayem on *Balumakazi: Native*,' viewed on 8 September 2023 from https://kayemwrites.com/media/
Kongnyuy, E., 2003, *The deadly honey*, Yaounde, AMA-CENC.
Lewis, D., 2001, 'African feminisms', *Agenda* 16(50), 4–10.
Lewis, D., & Baderoon, G., 2021, 'Introduction: Being black and feminist', in D. Lewis & G. Baderoon (eds.), *Surfacing: On being black and feminist in South Africa*, pp. 1–14, Johannesburg, Wits University Press.
Lyonga, N., & Butake, B., 1982, *Cameroon literature in English: An appraisal*, pp. 38–40. Yaounde: *ABBIA*.
Makuchi., 2008, *The sacred door and other stories: Cameroon folktales of the Beba*, Ohio, Ohio University Press.
Mbantenkhu, M.F., 2022, *Sibi's adventures in Alahtene*, Denver, CO, Spears Media Press.
Mbue, I., 2016a, *Behold the dreamers*, London, 4th Estate.
Mbue, I., 2016b. 'Imbolo Mbue interview: Everybody has a story', viewed 10 September 2023 from https://www.youtube.com/watch?v=7vDDq4t2h5A
McFadden, P., 2021, 'Living a radical African feminist life: A journey to sufficiency through contemporarity', in D. Lewis & G. Baderoon (eds.), *Surfacing: On being black and feminist in South Africa*, pp. 284–301, Johannesbur, Wits University Press.
Mougoué, J.T., 2019, *Gender, separatist politics, and embodied nationalism in Cameroon*, Ann Arbor, University of Michigan Press.
Muffuh, B., 1980, *The rebel: A play in two acts*. Yaounde, SOPECAM.
Murray, S.A., 2021, 'Gender, disruption and reconciliation in the Ugandan short fiction of Beatrice Lamwaka', in N. Nkealah & O. Nnaemeka (eds.), *Gendered violence and human rights in black world literature and film*, pp. 109–126, New York, Routledge.
Nchami, A., 1985, *Footprints of destiny*, Alfresco, n.p.
Ndiyah, F., 2012, *I will fly: A collection of poems*, Bamenda, Langaa.
Ndiyah, F., 2018, *When tomorrow comes*, Douala, Edition Veritas.
Ndiyah, F., 2019, *To reach a place of peace*, Douala, Edition Veritas.
Ndiyah, F., 2020, 'The things we don't talk about', PhD thesis, Unit for Creative Writing, University of Pretoria.
Ndiyah, F., 2021, 'The emotional well-being of African wives: Perceiving the Generalised Resistance Resources (GRRs) in stress management by co-wives in Lola Shoneyin's novel *The secret lives of Baba Segi's wives*', *Journal of Literary Studies* 37(3), 66–82.

Nfah-Abbenyi, J.M., 2021, 'Land of my dreams', *Feminist Africa* 2(2), 95–107.
Nfah-Abbenyi, J.M. & Butake, B., 2016, 'Anglophone Cameroon literature: A conversation with Bole Butake', *Tydskrif Vir Letterkunde* 53(1), 12–29.
Ngong, G.F., 2014, *Nostalgia*, Bamenda, Royal Publishers.
Ngongkum, E., 2007, *Manna of a life time and other stories*, Yaoundé, Éditions CLÉ.
Ngu, M.N., 2021, *Escape from prison*, Denver, CO, Spears Media Press.
Nkamanyang Lola, P.K., 2015, *Rustles on naked trees*, Paris, L'Harmattan.
Nkamanyang Lola, P.K., 2016, *Healing stings*, Denver, CO, Spears Media Press.
Nkamanyang Lola, P.K., 2023, *The lock on my lips*, Denver, CO, Spears Media Press.
Nkealah, N., 2009, 'Women, power and literature: Negotiating gender in Anglophone Cameroon drama', in Kolk, M. (ed.), *Performing gender in Arabic/African theater: Between cultures, between gender*, pp. 107–125, Amsterdam, Intercultural Theatre 4.
Nkealah, N., 2014, 'Women's contribution to the development of Anglophone Cameroonian drama: The plays of Anne Tanyi-Tang', *Research in African Literatures* 45(2), 122–134.
Nkealah, N., 2015, 'Anne Tanyi-Tang and Bole Butake: Two Anglophone Cameroonian playwrights with contrasting visions of women', *Imbizo: International Journal of African Literary and Comparative Studies* 6(2), 57–73.
Nkealah, N., 2017a, 'Cameline agency: A new agenda for social transformation in South African women's writing 2012–2014', *Current Writing: Text and Reception in Southern Africa* 29(2), 121–130.
Nkealah, N., 2017b, 'The dynamics of women's empowerment and disempowerment in Cameroon: A study of Anne Tanyi-Tang's play, *Ewa*', *Gender & Behaviour* 15(4), 10542–10551.
Nkealah, N., 2017c, *And they call themselves feminists: A poetry collection*. East London, The Poets Printery.
Nkealah, N., 2022, 'Being human in a time of catastrophe: African feminism, feminist humaneness, and the poetry of Joyce Ash', *Journal of Literary Studies* 38(1), 1–17.
Nkealah, N. & Ndiyah, F., 2021, 'Naomi Nkealah in conversation with Florence Ndiyah', Zoom interview, 20 November.
Nnaemeka, O., 2003, 'Nego-feminism: Theorizing, practicing and pruning Africa's way', *Signs: Journal of Women in Culture and Society* 29(2), 357–385.
Nnaemeka, O., 2021, 'Gendered spaces and war: Fighting and narrating the Nigeria-Biafra war', in N. Nkealah & O. Nnaemeka (eds.), *Gendered violence and human rights in black world literature and film*, pp. 175–193, New York, Routledge.
Nsah, K.T., 2017, 'Triple marginality in Cameroon Anglophone literature', in V.N. Gomia & G.S. Ndi (eds.), *Re-writing pasts, imagining futures: Critical explorations of contemporary African fiction and theater*, pp. 96–110, Denver, CO, Spears Media Press.
Ntube, N., 2020, *Litany of a foreign wife*, Denver, CO, Spears Media Press.
Nzuh, N.A., 1999, *Tales from the grassland and the forest*, Yaoundé, Éditions CLÉ.
Pucherová, D., 2022, *Feminism and modernity in Anglophone African women's writing*, New York, Routledge.
Sinyuy, G., 2023, *Music in the wood & other folktales*, Yaoundé, Nyaa Publishers.
Shoneyin, L., 2010, *The secret lives of Baba Segi's wives*, London, Serpent's Tail.
Tamba, P., 2009, *Best friends*, Limbe, Cosmos Educational Press.
Taku, O.K., 2016, *Tears of the innocent: Poems*, Buea, Shiloh Printers.
Tanyi-Tang, A., 2000, *Ewa and other plays*, Yaounde, Éditions CLÉ.
Tanyi-Tang, A., 2006, *Visiting America and Marinuelle*. Yaounde, Éditions Sherpa.
Tanyi-Tang, A., 2007, *Eneta vs Elimo*. Yaounde: Éditi.

3
SEX, RESISTANCE, AND AGENCY

(Queer) Young Women in Selected North African Novels and Films

Gibson Ncube

Introduction

This chapter focuses on a selection of works of fiction, novels, and films, from North Africa, and examines their depiction of (queer) young women. Women have featured sparsely in the production of cultural products such as novels and films in North Africa. In her analysis of the marginalisation of women in francophone North Africa, Mildred Mortimer explains two factors that have led to such a situation:

> Two factors contributed to the dominance of male francophone African writers. Throughout Africa, the colonial educational system made greater efforts to educate boys than girls on the assumption that schools should prepare an educated male elite to serve the colonial administration. In addition, traditional African societies viewed European education, particularly higher education, as superfluous training for girls, who would become dutiful wives and attentive mothers.
>
> (1990:133)

During colonisation, and indeed after, young women were typically excluded from formal education. Socialisation emphasised that young women were prepared for their roles as mothers, wives, and administrators of households. The considerable contributions made by women writers and filmmakers in North Africa, as argued by scholars like Fatima Sadiqi (2016), have mostly gone unnoticed and unacknowledged. The contributions of women writers and filmmakers have often been dwarfed by the exploits of their male counterparts. This adds a different layer and presents another manifestation of the marginalisation of women. Of course, women writers and filmmakers have not and should not confine their contributions to topics only affecting women. Their writings and films have been crucial in articulating and making sense of the daily difficulties of common people throughout history in this region of Africa. By exploring various social and political issues through their writing and films, women writers and filmmakers have provided a unique perspective that has often been overlooked. Their ability to shed light on the struggles and experiences of ordinary individuals has played a significant role in shaping our understanding of North African society.

It is essential to recognise and appreciate the diverse range of topics that women's writing encompasses, as it offers valuable insights into the human condition as a whole. For example, in her book *Nomadic Voices of Exile: Feminine Identity in Francophone Literature of the Maghreb* (1999), Valérie Orlando examines how postcolonial literature has reshaped perceptions of Maghrebian feminine identity. Examining authors residing in the Maghreb or seeking asylum in France due to political persecution, Orlando analyses how they transcend gender-based dialogues, providing nuanced perspectives on the evolving sociocultural and political landscapes of Tunisia, Algeria, and Morocco. In another book, *Of Suffocated Hearts and Tortured Souls: Seeking Subjecthood Through Madness in Francophone Women's Writing of Africa and the Caribbean* (2003), Orlando examines the literary representation of madness and shows how Francophone women writers navigate ever-shifting social realities, influencing feminine identity amid political pressures, traditional norms, historical events, and economic challenges. Orlando contends that the literary trope of madness serves as an extended metaphor for the complex female social condition and the daily alienation experienced by women in the postcolonial era. Naomi Nkealah in the article "Reconciling Arabo-Islamic culture and feminist consciousness in North African women's writing: Silence and voice in the short stories of Alifa Rifaat and Assia Djebar" (2008) explores the theme of silence and voice in the short stories of North African women writers Alifa Rifaat and Assia Djebar. Nkealah demonstrates how Rifaat's characters embrace silence for self-preservation, while those of Djebar's use techniques from writing to open protest to reject gender-based segregation.

While these preceding studies provide valuable insights into the reshaping of North African feminine identities, there appears to be a notable gap in the absence of an exploration of how literary works engage with the question of intersectionality. These preceding studies primarily focus on gender dynamics and oppression but do not extensively examine the intersections of gender with other social factors such as race, class, sexuality, gender, or ethnicity. Moreover, it is also important to focus on the question of agency of women. While existing scholarship touches upon the challenges faced by women and the strategies that they employ to resist oppression, a more nuanced exploration of moments of empowerment, resilience, and agency could offer a more complete and rounder understanding of the complexities of women's lives. In this chapter, I am therefore interested in thinking through the questions of intersectionality and the agency of women characters. I also attempt to show how an examination of literary and filmic texts could potentially offer productive avenues of understanding the lives of women in North Africa.

In this chapter, I will focus on three novels: *L'Enfant de Sable* (1985) by Tahar Ben Jelloun and *Le Garçon Manqué* (2000) and *Mes Mauvaises Pensées* (2005), both by Nina Bouraoui, as well as two films: Nadia El Fani's *Bedwin Hacker* (2003) and Raja Amari's *Al Dowaha* (2009). Although I include a novel by a male writer, Tahar Ben Jelloun, I find that it offers interesting perspectives on how young women negotiate their identities in Morocco. The selected literary and film texts cover three North African countries: Algeria, Morocco, and Tunisia. *L'Enfant de Sable* (The Sand Child) is a novel set in Morocco and tells the story of Zahra, the eighth-born girl child in her family. Because of her father's desire for a male heir, she is raised as a boy named Ahmed. The setting is patriarchal and traditional Moroccan society where boy children are valued more than girl children. It considers the psychological and emotional struggles that Ahmed/Zahra faces throughout his/her life, as well as the complexities of relationships within his/her family. As Ahmed/Zahra matures, (s)he grapples with his/her identity and the desire to live authentically as a woman.

Writing semi-autobiographical books with a focus on women's sexuality, identity, and belonging, Nina Bouraoui is an author of Algerian descent. In her book *Le Garçon Manqué* (The Tomboy), the young protagonist deals with issues of not quite fitting in with the stereotypical ideals of femininity as she matures. The protagonist, a young woman who violates gender norms and acts more like a boy, raises tension and concerns about her identity, as suggested by the book's title. Themes of identity and self-discovery are further explored in *Mes Mauvaises Pensées* (My Bad Thoughts). In this book, Bouraoui explores the mind of the main character, who struggles with inner conflict and a sense of alienation. She considers her own desires and thoughts, which are frequently regarded as unconventional or taboo by social conventions. The protagonist of the book embarks on a voyage of self-discovery as she faces diverse anxieties and insecurities. She attempts to balance her inner world with external social expectations. Both of these books employ intimate and introspective narrative techniques, giving readers an inside look into the protagonist's personal quest for self-awareness and her thoughts on gender, sexuality, and identity in the context of her Franco-Algerian background.

Although its focus is on the effects of technology on traditional societies, *Bedwin Hacker* by Nadia El Fani provides a nuanced take on women's roles and lives in Arab-Muslim communities of Tunisia. The film depicts Kalt, a strong-willed woman who has relationships with a man and a woman. Kalt's character defies the traditional definition of how a woman should behave, dress, and perform her femininity. Kalt's character embodies the intersection of tradition and modernity, reflecting evolving roles and choices available to women within Arab-Muslim communities as they navigate changing cultural landscapes. While *Bedwin Hacker* primarily focuses on cultural clashes, it prompts viewers to consider the agency, as well as complexities and diversity of women's experiences in these societies.

Raja Amari's film, *Al Dowaha* (Buried Secrets), revolves around the lives of three women. They are headed by a widowed matriarch whose express goal is to uphold the expectations that patriarchy has for women, particularly in terms of what they are allowed and not allowed to do with their bodies and sexualities. Aïcha, her older sister Radhia, and their matriarchal mother are the three main characters of the movie. The daughters stand for an effort to challenge conventional ideas about what women ought to be and what they ought to do. The film explores themes of female empowerment, societal constraints, and the clash between tradition and modernity in a rural Tunisian setting. The film offers a poignant and provocative-provoking look at the struggles and aspirations of its central characters.

As highlighted in the above synopses of the selected novels and films, the central themes are the questions of being young women in Arab-Muslim countries which are deeply entrenched in patriarchy, as well as religious and cultural practices. This chapter, therefore, focuses on the various ways in which these selected cultural creations in North Africa's Arab-Muslim civilisations represent what it means to be a young woman. Because virginity is highly valued in Arab-Muslim countries in North Africa, young women are required to act and perform duties in particular ways to protect the reputation of their family when they get married. The chosen novels feature young women as the main characters who resist heteropatriarchal expectations. These women demonstrate how young girls may be sensual, sexual beings who do not lower themselves to nothing more than an intact hymen. These cultural productions empower young women by emphasising their queerness and showing that they can be independent of men. The chosen books and movies show that young women's sexuality can exist outside of the grasp and control of phallocracy, which is contrary to heteropatriarchy, which places emphasis on the penis and its satisfaction.

As is the case in many other parts of the continent, in North Africa, women are still subject to cultural and religious traditions that oppress them, the queer young womanhood that emerges from the chosen novels and films offers a creative manner of performing and embodying young womanhood. This new method of portraying and embodying young womanhood challenges the conventional gender norms and expectations set by society. Young women are given the freedom to explore their own desires, identities, and sexualities while escaping the restrictions of heteronormativity. These books and movies empower young women by displaying a variety of storylines and experiences, encouraging them to embrace their own special routes to self-discovery and satisfaction.

Understanding the Place of (Queer) Young Women in North Africa

The enduring representations of women in North Africa have often reproduced orientalist gazes of women in this region as passive and subordinate. As argued by Jasmin Zine, "we have seen how the images of Muslim women have been represented in the Western male imaginary as sensual, harem girls as well as debased, voiceless and universally oppressed victims, forming a complex nexus of desire and disavowal" (2016: 35). Such a representation of women in cultural productions has been influenced by and enmeshed in a variety of cultural, historical, and religious variables. It is, therefore, important to consider that women's experiences are diverse when addressing the place of women in North Africa. There is not a single story of women's experience in this region of the continent. It is particularly important, as I point out in a previous study, "to be wary of the often-restrictive orientalist narratives that frame gender relations in a monolithic binary that pits abusive, violent, and oppressive men against docile, passive, and taciturn women" (Ncube, 2021: 1923).

There are, indeed, opposing views on how Islam and cultural practices have affected the lives and lived experiences of women in North Africa. On the one hand are scholars who find Islam as offering women freedom. Anouar Majid, for example, contends that:

> While the widely held assumption that women have been historically persecuted by all patriarchal cultures is, to a large extent, incontestably true, the discourses of Western feminism, largely shaped by gender relations in Christian capitalist cultures and by the exhausted paradigms of Western social thought, have hindered a more subtle appreciation of women's issues under Islam.
>
> (1998: 322)

Such a situation has indeed bypassed and short-cut the nuance that is needed in understanding the impact of Islam on women's lives in North Africa, as is certainly the case in other Arab-Muslim regions of the world. On the other hand, such a need to think of the possible progressive treatment of women in Arab-Muslim societies is pitted against the Western gaze which frames these women as being nothing more than oppressed and abused beings. This binary overlooks the diverse experiences and agency of women in Arab-Muslim societies, who actively navigate and negotiate their roles within the context of their religion and culture. This perspective has especially been intensified within prevailing Islamophobic discourses which have multiplied in the aftermath of the 11 September 2011 terrorist attacks. Iman

Hashim appositely argues in this regard that: "there are many problems with the representation of veiling in Western, and early feminist, literature, which has helped to perpetuate an image of Muslim women as victims and denied the diversity of meaning and practice associated with this tradition" (2010: 10). This misrepresentation of veiling has led to the marginalisation and stereotyping of Muslim women, further perpetuating Islamophobia. It is, thus, crucial to recognise the complexity and agency of Muslim women in their choices to wear the veil, as it is not solely a symbol of oppression but also a reflection of their religious and cultural identity.

Despite such circumstances, it should be accepted that Islam, like all the other Abrahamic religions, remains patriarchal in its epistemological grounding. What this means is that although there are possibilities for women to exercise their agency, Islam remains a religion fashioned by "a patriarchalised view of God as Father/male, and a theory of father-right, extending to the husband's claim to rule over his wife and children" (Barlas, 2002: 12). Such a dynamic has been central in perpetual sociocultural conditions in which "women […] are usually represented as inferior, submissive and dependent, living in a male-dominated patriarchal society" (Naciri, 2003: 20).

Moreover, cultural practices have also operated in such a way that they place immense focus on young women's sexualities. Traditional societal expectations place a heavy burden on young women to uphold their family's honour and reputation by preserving their virginity until marriage (Skalli, 2016). The notions of "shame" and "family honour" are deeply entrenched in Arab-Muslim societies, as is certainly the case in other patriarchal communities. This inadvertently leads to surveillance and policing of young women's sexualities. As Caitlin Killian explains that surveillance of "virginity remains strong, even for those women with the most 'tolerant' parents. Virginity constitutes the honour of the family. It's the honour of the family that's riding on it, so if a girl loses her virginity, the family has lost its honour" (2006: 48–49). Families often closely monitor and control young women's activities, including their interactions with men, to ensure they conform to societal norms. This surveillance and control are manifested in various ways, such as restricting young women's access to social events or imposing curfews. These measures aim to uphold the perceived importance of virginity and maintain the family's reputation within the community. This importance placed on young women's virginity has, in recent years, seen the emergence and proliferation of surgical procedures such as "hymen repair" or "hymen reconstitution." These are procedures done on women who have lost their virginity and who wish to ensure that their families are not shamed when they got married. Sawitri Saharso (2022) explains that these surgical procedures achieve two diametrically opposed goals. On the one hand, these practices seemed "to accommodate a patriarchal norm of female virginity that denies women sexual autonomy" (2022: 198). On the other hand, "the surgery actually makes the underlying value of chastity meaningless and is thus subverting the tradition" (2022: 198). In this argument, these surgical procedures perpetuate a patriarchal expectation of female virginity, which restricts women's sexual agency and autonomy. However, paradoxically, by undergoing such surgeries, women are challenging and undermining the very notion of chastity as a valuable virtue within traditional norms. This suggests a complex and contradictory relationship between these practices and the values they claim to uphold.

In this chapter, I focus on what I call "queer young women." I take queer not simply to refer to young women whose sexual and gender identities challenge heteronormative framings of gender and sexuality. I use the term to make sense of the out-of-placedness of young women whose gender and sexual identities are deemed to not fit within what is considered normal or socially desirable behaviour. Ju Hui Judy Han expounds that "to be out of place [...] is an affliction of inconvenience, discomfort, pain, and far worse" (2022: 127). The idea of being out of place suggests that there is literally no room for those young women who fail or refuse to fit within the existing framework of what is viewed as normal identity performance.

In the following sections of the chapter, I will examine how the selected novels and films grapple with how young women grapple with the diverse issues highlighted above such as gender identity, sexuality, as well as agency. The selected novels and films, I will show, provide a nuanced exploration of the challenges faced by young women in navigating their gender identities and sexualities in societies where their agency is often undermined. These fictional narratives shed important light on the complex ways in which societal expectations and norms intersect with personal experiences. Delving into the characters' journeys offers deeper understandings of the multifacetedness of these issues and how they shape the lives of young women in North Africa.

What Does It Mean to be a Young Woman?

In this section, I will read the two novels by Nina Bouraoui in conversation with that of Tahar Ben Jelloun. These three novels deal with different questions of what constitutes a young woman within the cultural spaces of Algeria (for Bouraoui) and Morocco for Ben Jelloun. These novels especially show that there isn't a single way of being a young woman or of experiencing young womanhood. Instead, they call attention to the fact that there are many ways of being a young woman.

Tahar Ben Jelloun's novel *L'Enfant de Sable* grapples with the question of what being a woman, or man, means. The protagonist is a girl child who is raised as a boy because her father needed a male heir. In this specific society, girl children could not inherit any of their father's wealth. Called Ahmed, the child is socialised to become a man. All rituals that are done for boy children are done for Ahmed, including the circumcision ceremony where the father cuts off part of his thumb so that blood can be seen. Ahmed assumes this imposed masculinity and finds that it provides opportunities which would not ordinarily be available for girl children: "I don't just accept my condition and endure it, I actually like it. It is interesting. It opens doors for me, and I like that, even if it then locks me in a glass cage" (Ben Jelloun, 1985: 34). However, with the passage of time, Ahmed's body changes and it begins to betray traits of femininity: breasts and menstruation. This compels Ahmed to move towards embracing her feminine identity and the name Zahra. Ahmed has been socialised to consider himself a man to look down upon everything that is feminine. Ahmed sees himself superior and different from other women in his family, his mother and his sisters. However, despite this socialisation, he is unable to escape his female or feminine essence.

What I find particularly interesting about this novel is the fact that attempts to suppress femininity do not seem to work. Ahmed's father attempts to create a boy child who would inherit his wealth. Despite his efforts, femininity refuses to be suppressed. Ahmed embraces his femininity by acknowledging that the socialisation that he has received has not made a man of him. Even as I write this, the difficulty in choosing pronouns, between him and her or between he and she, highlights the protagonists' struggle in defining their gender. What *L'Enfant de Sable* manages to do is reflect on the fluidity as well as the fragility of the social construction that is gender. Through Ahmed's journey, the novel challenges the rigid societal norms that dictate how one should express one's gender. It explores the notion that gender is not a fixed identity, but rather a complex and ever-evolving spectrum. By embracing his femininity, Ahmed defies the constraints imposed by society and asserts his right to self-expression. *L'Enfant de Sable* ultimately invites readers to question and challenge their own preconceived notions about gender, encouraging a more inclusive and accepting understanding of identity.

If *L'Enfant du Sable* highlights the fragility of gender construction, then Nina Bouraoui's novels are more overt in challenging these imposed gender identities. Bouraoui's literary works offer an invaluable opportunity for reimagination and revaluation of what it means to be a woman within the specific context of Tunisia. This reimagination stands in stark contrast to the prevailing narrative that subjects women's bodies and sexualities to patriarchal control and imposes an orientalised perspective on the Arab-Muslim womanhood. Bouraoui's novels both present and interrogate the manifold manifestations of marginalisation to which women's bodies are subjected.

In the novels *Mes Mauvaises Pensées* and *Garçon Manqué*, Nina, the central character in her narratives, demonstrates a sharp awareness of her liminal identity, a realisation that has accompanied her from a young age due to her status as a mixed-race individual, rendering her neither entirely Algerian nor French. This liminality is further amplified by her gender identity which refuses to be neatly put into the heteropatriarchal binary of either masculine or feminine. Her unconventional desires, which she terms *mauvaises pensées* (bad thoughts), highlight how her socialisation makes her think of her identity is deemed incorrect. Consequently, she grapples incessantly with the need to reconcile and validate her existence, physicality, gender, sensuality, and sexuality. This constant struggle to find validation and acceptance leads her to question societal norms and challenge the traditional notions of gender and sexuality. She seeks to break free from the constraints imposed by society and embrace her true self, even if it means navigating through a world that often rejects or misunderstands her. In the novel *Mes Mauvaises Pensées*, Nina, the protagonist-narrator, explains that she continuously has to negotiate the identity contradictions which characterise her being in a haunting way: "*Il y a deux flux en moi, que je ne pourrai jamais diviser, je crois n'être d'aucun camp. Je suis seule avec mon corps*" (*Mes Mauvaises Pensées*, 2004: 52) (There are two streams in me which I will never be able to divide, I think I am not of any side. I am alone with my body). This same idea is echoed in *Garçon Manqué* where Nina states: "*Tous les matins, je vérifie mon identité. J'ai quatre problèmes. Française? Algérienne? Fille? Garçon?*" (*Garçon Manqué*, 2000: 163) (Every morning, I check my identity. I have four problems. French? Algerian? Girl? Boy?). In negotiating this fluidity and fluctuation, Nina refuses for her identity to be boxed into either masculine or feminine as well as between French and Algerian. She embraces the complexity of her identity and challenges societal norms by rejecting the binary categorisation of gender. Instead, she navigates the space between these categories, embracing her own unique and fluid sense of self. This refusal to conform to traditional expectations allows Nina to explore and express her true identity in authentic ways.

Another salient observation to highlight pertains to the challenging of heteropatriarchal ways of thinking which seek to rigidly define the gender and sexual identity of Bouraoui's protagonist. It also underscores how the protagonist-narrator resists the conventional perspectives that attempt to categorise her in a fixed manner. This is acutely articulated through the following passage from *Garçon Manqué*, where the protagonist recounts an incident where an old woman mistakes her for a boy: "*Brio contre la femme qui dit: Quelle jolie petite fille. Tu t'appelles comment? Ahmed. Sa surprise. Mon défi. Sa gêne. Ma Victoire*" (*Garçon Manqué*, 2000: 51) (I am Brio to the woman who says: What a pretty little girl. What's your name?

Ahmed. Her surprise. My challenge. Her embarrassment. My victory). This passage illustrates Bouraoui's defiance against societal expectations and gender norms. By identifying as Ahmed, a traditionally masculine name, she challenges this woman's assumption that she should be seen as a *jolie petite fille* (pretty little girl). Nina's victory lies in her ability to assert her own identity and reject the fixed categorisation imposed on her.

Through this steadfast refusal to conform to pre-established gender norms, Nina Bouraoui conveys the idea that gender identities are fluid and inherently resistant to rigid categorisation. They are, in fact, in a constant state of evolution, negotiation, and construction. Nina herself embraces a fluid and liminal identity that defies easy classification as exclusively male or female. This is particularly evident in her relationship with her father, who raises her in a manner that transcends traditional gender expectations: "*Il m'élève comme un garçon. Sa fierté. La fierté. La grâce d'une fille. L'agilité d'un garçon*" (*Garçon Manqué*, 2000: 24) (He raises me like a boy. His pride. Pride. The grace of a girl. The agility of a boy). In her father's eyes, Nina embodies both feminine grace and masculine physicality and agility simultaneously. Unlike Ahmed's father in *L'Enfant de Sable* who is adamant on raising his girl child as a boy, Nina's father is more interested in letting his child live out her difference. He recognises and values the unique qualities that Nina possesses, appreciating her ability to embody both femininity and masculinity. By allowing her to embrace her individuality, he fosters a sense of self-acceptance and freedom for Nina to explore her own identity. This contrast with Ahmed's father highlights the importance of parental support and acceptance in allowing children to fully express themselves.

This section has shown young women in novels who question the idea of what a "normal" woman is and what a "normal" woman should do. The novels analysed in this section present young women who are comfortable in occupying a liminal space in terms of their gender and sexual identities. These young women challenge societal expectations and norms by embracing their individuality and refusing to conform to traditional gender roles. They navigate their own paths, exploring different aspects of their identities and forging their own definitions of what it means to be a woman. Through their stories, these novels highlight the importance of self-discovery and the empowerment that comes from embracing one's true self.

Refusal and Challenging of Imposed Purity

The literary and film texts which I examine in this chapter show that young women are socialised to think of marriage as the principal objective of their lives. As argued by Jenny Birchall (2018), early marriages, which are often arranged, lead young women to drop out of school. Dropping out of school limits the possibilities of imagining a professional life, one that is not tied to domestic work in the home. As pointed out in one of the previous sections, there is excessive pressure for young women to safeguard their virginity and purity as these are held highly when young women get married. In this section, I will examine the film *Al Dowaha* by Nadia El Fani to show how young women refuse to accept the purity that is imposed on and demanded of them.

Al Dowaha focuses on the lives of a mother and her two young daughters. They occupy a room in a deserted house. The mother is traditional and strict in the way she brings up her two daughters, Radhia and Aïcha. The two young women do not have any interaction with the outside world except on the few days that they go to the market with their mother. The arrival of the owners of the house, a young couple, upsets the protected lives of these three women. This couple, particularly the young wife, exerts a distinctive influence on Radhia and Aïcha, affording them exposure to a different manifestation of femininity hitherto beyond their immediate reach. When Selma, the young wife, inadvertently discovers the presence of these three women, she is forcibly abducted and kept within the confines of the single room that is occupied by the three women. Selma imparts a disruptive element into the clandestine and private existences hitherto cultivated by Aïcha, her sister, and their mother. The two young are especially compelled to rethink what it means for young women to maintain purity and chastity. Selma's presence especially compels them to confront their bodies and their eroticism.

This film is replete with silence and there is very minimal dialogue. This silence accentuates the proximity and intimate space that the three women share. For Radhi and Aïcha, the constant proximity of their own bodies forces them to think of themselves as young women who have sexual feelings. In one scene, Radhi is captured giving her younger sister a bath. There is a sensuality to the way in which Radhi touches her sister's naked body. In another scene after, we find Aïcha alone in the bathroom. She is shaving her legs. The camera zooms in on the Aïcha legs as the razor blade glides over her skin. I explain elsewhere that this focus on the skin is important in that it allows a rethinking of the young woman's relationship with her body:

> Closely related to how the film depicts the negotiation of sexual identity is how the skin is presented not just as a sensuous surface but, more importantly, as a site that articulates the protagonist's attempt to break free from the restrictions placed on what women can do with their bodies. In Aïcha's case, the skin becomes a transgressive site through which she asserts her agency by showing that she actively forges her own pleasure.
>
> (Ncube, 2022: 36)

I want to push this idea further and contend that the representation of the skin is especially important in allowing young women to rethink what the imposed purity and chastity mean to them. The way in which Radhia and Aïcha touch each other and relate to each other pushes the limits of what is socially permissible and certainly highlights what is considered taboo. The way in which they relate to each other is quasi-incestuous. However, what I find productive in this relationship is the fact that the two young women challenge what is expected of them. By exploring their physical connection and defying societal norms, Radhia and Aïcha break free from the confines of traditional expectations of young women who are supposed to live chaste lives in which sex and eroticism do not exist. Their quasi-incestuous bond serves as a powerful tool for redefining their own identities and reclaiming control over their bodies. This defiance not only challenges the imposed and perceived purity and chastity of young women but also opens a space for critical reflection and personal growth, ultimately empowering them to question and reshape societal constructs. They defy societal norms and expectations by embracing their own desires and exploring their own definitions of purity and chastity. Their intimate connection challenges the oppressive boundaries imposed on them, ultimately empowering them to redefine their identities on their own terms, and even if this involves engaging, what may be considered incorrect and taboo ways of being.

Singleness and the Challenging Heteropatriarchy

In the face of young women being expected to be married and fulfil what is almost considered their sacrosanct role of being wives and mothers, choosing to remain single and unmarried becomes an act of defiance and of challenging heteropatriarchy. Judith Bennett explains that in patriarchal societies, there is a "constant pressure on single women to make marriage and family their main career" (2006: 21). The pressure articulated by Bennett stems largely from the deeply ingrained belief that a woman's worth is tied to her ability to fulfil traditional gender roles. Therefore, women who choose to remain single challenge this societal expectation and assert their autonomy and independence. Moreover, remaining single and unmarried allows women to prioritise their own goals of self-actualisation, rather than conforming to societal norms that limit their choices and potential.

Tunisian filmmaker Nadia El Fani grapples with some of these complex questions of Arab-Muslim women who choose to remain single in the face of pressure to conform to societal demands to get married and assume their roles as wives and mothers. In this section, I will focus on her film *Bedwin Hacker* which tells the story of a young woman named Kalt, who is a hacker and orchestrates multiple cyberattacks against Tunisia and Western countries, especially France. Although as I argue in a previous study, "Kalt's sexuality is framed as a subplot that runs parallel to the main storyline" (Ncube, 2022: 31), the focus on this protagonist is important in thinking of what it means for young women to remain single and to be in control of their sexual lives. This is especially relevant considering how women's bodies have become the site of thinking through the implications of the Islamisation of North African countries like Tunisia. Abdessamad Dialmy explains in this regard that:

> An example of this intricacy is the body of the Muslim woman, which becomes a tool for resistance to the globalisation of dress and the individual, liberal sexual values it symbolises. The feminine body becomes entrusted with Arab culture and identity more than ever before, so that the movement of Islamisation of Arab society begins initially with the Islamisation of the woman's body through the call for the veil.
>
> (2005: 16–17)

In the face of such a situation, Kalt refuses to do several things which challenge societal norms of what young women should be, should do, and should aspire to be and do. First, she refuses to wear a veil which covers not just her face but her body. Instead, she is filmed dressed in military camouflage and also clothing which reveals her skin. Robert Lang in an analysis of this film explains that:

> From the very first shot we see of Kalt, with her short-cropped hair and decisive gait, and wearing a military combat cap, she not only confounds the stereotype of conservative Arab femininity so often depicted in terms of veiled modesty, but she also offers a contrast to the images of 'liberated', sometimes sexually provocative women that can be seen on advertising billboards throughout Tunisia.
>
> (2014: 200)

In her portrayal of Kalt, El Fani challenges the stereotype of Arab women as veiled sensual beings who are perpetually submissive and subjugated victims. Kalt, unlike the majority of the other women in the film, is never seen wearing a veil. Instead, she wears items of clothing that expose the contours of her body and skin, claiming her agency. This agency allows her to question what is judged acceptable and hence the correct means of deploying and clothing the female body. In the representation of Kalt, there is especially a double challenge of the sexualising gazes of men in Tunisia as well as the Western orientalising gazes in which "the covered Arab woman appears to be a victim, unable to express herself in word and deed" (Buller,

2007: 16). Western imaginings exclusively tie the veil to the representations of Arab-Muslim women from North Africa, and indeed from other parts of the Arab world. Through her words and deeds, especially what she does with her body, Kalt forces the viewer to rethink the idea of Arab-Muslim women as being merely veiled and oppressed beings.

In addition to what she does with her body and its dressing, Kalt chooses to remain single and unmarried. This decision is further amplified by the fact that she chooses to have a sexual relationship with a woman. A lesbian relationship poses a set of important yet unsettling questions: What does it mean when women experience sexual pleasure in the absence of a penis? What does such an experience of pleasure say about women's sexuality in these societies where women's sexuality is hardly ever spoken about? What does women's sexual pleasure do to the supremacy of the penis as the phallic representation of patriarchy and the diverse forms of real and symbolic powers invested in the penis and masculinity? In several scenes in the film, Kalt is captured engaging in lovemaking with her white French partner, Julia. Although the scenes are often cut short, they do represent an attempt to show women experiencing sexual pleasure in the absence of men. By depicting women experiencing sexual pleasure in the absence of men, these scenes challenge the traditional narrative that positions men as the sole providers of sexual satisfaction. This portrayal disrupts the patriarchal notion that women's sexuality is solely for the pleasure and validation of men. It opens a space for discussions and exploration of women's sexual agency and pleasure, ultimately questioning the supremacy of the penis as a symbol of power in society. As I elaborate elsewhere, "depicting women pleasing each other sexually transgresses heteropatriarchal ideals, which place men and masculinity at the centre of all forms of sexual activity and sexual pleasure" (Ncube, 2022: 34).

Singleness, as depicted in *Bedwin Hacker*, has the potential to challenge patriarchy in Arab-Muslim societies of North Africa through various means. To begin with, women who choose to remain single and especially choose to be in lesbian relationships challenge the heteropatriarchal consideration of women as nothing more than sacred uteruses whose role is to produce children. Once women, like Kalt, refuse to assume this (re)productive role, their lives and bodies are deemed unproductive and therefore easily disposable. This, of course, is the kind of reasoning that is used to justify violence against queer young women. It is precisely because "outside of the family and the familial framework, one becomes a free-floating pleasure machine released from the clutch of paternalistic authority and the capitalistic logic of the private property of the body" (Sikora, 2008: 386). In such a representation of single young women, the film shows that they can experience being and embodiment in diverse and multifaceted ways. This representation challenges societal norms and expectations, highlighting the agency and autonomy of queer young women. By depicting them as free from patriarchal control and capitalist exploitation, the film promotes a more inclusive understanding of identity and sexuality and encourages viewers to question the justification of violence against marginalised communities based on outdated notions of family and societal structures.

Conclusion

In this chapter, I have explored a selection of novels and films from North Africa, shedding light on the depiction of queer young women within complex cultural, religious, and societal contexts. I have discussed the profound impact of historical, religious, and cultural factors on the lives of young women in this region. Historically, North Africa's colonial education system (as was the case in many other regions of the continent) favoured boys over girls, perpetuating gender disparities and limiting opportunities for women's education and emancipation. This, coupled with traditional societal expectations that prepared young women for roles as wives and mothers, has created an environment that marginalises women, especially in their roles in producing diverse cultural products such as literature and film.

Through an analysis of three novels and two films, I demonstrated how different young women negotiate their identities in Algeria, Morocco, and Tunisia. These stories challenge conventional gender norms and provide a platform for young women to explore their desires, identities, and sexualities outside the constraints of heteronormativity and phallocracy. By highlighting the "queerness" or out-of-placedness and independence of young women in North Africa, these cultural productions empower them to break free from the shackles of societal expectations. Young women like Kalt in the film *Bedwin Hacker* and Aïcha in *Al Dowaha* take ownership of their bodies, sexualities, and eroticism. They use their agency to experience sexual pleasure which does not hinge on heteropatriarchal imaginings of sex. These characters embark on unique journeys of self-discovery, challenging the traditional roles and expectations placed upon them. Through these narratives, these works of fiction and film offer a powerful and transformative representation of young womanhood in North Africa.

The exploration of these selected novels and films has underscored the importance of acknowledging and celebrating the diverse voices and experiences of young women in North Africa. It reminds us of the capacity of literature and film to challenge and reshape societal norms, offering new perspectives and possibilities for young women in the region and beyond. By amplifying the voices of young women in North Africa, these novels and films also serve as powerful tools for the empowerment and self-expression of young women.

References

Barlas, A. (2002). *Believing Women in Islam: Unreading Patriarchal Interpretations of the Qur'an*. Austin: University of Texas Press.
Ben Jelloun, Tahar. (1985). *L'Enfant de Sable*. Paris: Seuil.
Bennett, J. M. (2006). *History Matters: Patriarchy and the Challenge of Feminism*. Philadelphia: University of Pennsylvania Press.
Birchall, J. (2018). "Early Marriage, Pregnancy and Girl Child School Dropout." *Journal of Education*, 5(2), 17–31.
Bouraoui, N. (2000). *Garçon Manqué*. Paris: Éditions Stock.
Bouraoui, N. (2004). *Mes Mauvaises Pensées*. Paris: Éditions Stock.
Buller, R. E. (2007). "Un/veiled: Feminist Art from the Arab/Muslim Diaspora." *Al-Raida*, 24(116–117), 16–20.
Dialmy, A. (2005). "Sexuality in Contemporary Arab Society." *Social Analysis*, 49(2), 16–33.
Han, J. H. J. (2022). "Out of Place in Time: Queer Discontents and Sigisangjo." *The Journal of Asian Studies*, 81(1), 119–129.
Killian, C. (2006). Stanford: Stanford University Press.
Lang, R. (2014). *Tunisian Cinema: Allegories of Resistance*. New York: Columbia University Press.
Majid, A. (1998). "The Politics of Feminism in Islam." *Signs: Journal of Women in Culture and Society*, 23(2), 321–361.
Mortimer, M. (1990). *Journeys through the French African Novel*. London: James Currey.
Naciri, R. (2003). "The Women's Movement in the Maghreb: With An Emphasis on Tunisia, Morocco and Algeria." Al-Raida, 20, 20–28.
Ncube, G. (2021). "Women in North African Literature" In O. Yacob-Haliso & T. Falola (Eds.). *The Palgrave Handbook of African Women's Studies* (pp. 1919–1935). Cham: Palgrave-Macmillan.
Ncube, Gibson. (2022). *Queer Bodies in African Films*. Makhanda: NISC.

Nkealah, N. (2008). "Reconciling Arabo-Islamic culture and feminist consciousness in North African women's writing: Silence and voice in the short stories of Alifa Rifaat and Assia Djebar." *Tydskrif vir letterkunde*, 45(1), 19–41.

Orlando, V. (1999). *Nomadic Voices of Exile: Feminine Identity in Francophone Literature of the Maghreb*. Ohio: Ohio University Press.

Orlando, V. (2003). *Of Suffocated Hearts and Tortured Souls: Seeking Subjecthood through Madness in Francophone Women's Writing of Africa and the Caribbean*. Lanham, MD: Lexington Books.

Sadiqi, F. (2016). "Gendering political agency in the Maghreb." *Journal of Middle East Women's Studies*, 12(1), 88–92.

Saharso, S. (2022). "Hymen 'Repair': Views from Feminists, Medical Professionals and the Women Involved in the Middle East, North Africa and Europe." *Ethnicities*, 22(2), 196–214.

Sikora, T. (2008). "Queer/Waste." In T. Rachwal (Ed.). *Rubbish, Waste and Litter: Culture and Its Refuse/als* (pp. 376–388). Warszawa: Wydawn. Szkoły Wyższej Psychologii Społecznej.

Skalli, L. H. (2016). "Young Women and Social Media against Sexual harassment in North Africa." In A. Khalil (Ed). *Gender, Women and the Arab Spring* (pp. 114–128). London: Routledge.

Zine, J. (2016). "Between Orientalism and Fundamentalism: Muslim Women and Feminist Engagement." In K. Hunt & K. Rygiel (Eds.). *(En)Gendering the War on Terror: War Stories and Camouflaged Politics* (pp. 27–50). New York: Routledge.

Filmography

Amari, R. dir. (2009). *Al Dowaha [Buried Secrets]*. Paris: Les films d'ici.
El Fani, N. dir. (2003). *Bedwin Hacker*. Tunis: Z'Yeux Noirs Movies.

4
GLIMPSES OF AFRICAN WOMEN'S AUTONOMY AS REPRESENTED IN SELECTED AFRICAN LITERATURE

Clemence Rubaya

Introduction

In an ideal society, possessing power, freedom and being at liberty to make one's own decisions in all areas of life without being held in check by anyone is a basic human right that must be promoted to "reduce unmet needs" (Sougou et al. 2020:1). However, due to patriarchy and other structural and coercive systems of privilege that have intersected with it, in "most of the South East Asian and Sub-Saharan countries, women have inferior position[s] and less power for making household decisions as well as seeking healthcare for their own and children" (sic) (Dangal and Bhandari 2014:1, citing Hogan et al. 2010). Denying women the power to make important decisions while expecting men to wield and monopolise all decision making power has often compromised the quality of decisions made. In the context of Africa, a continent facing and battling many catastrophes and crises, including drought, war, poverty, disease and many others that have dented the quality of life and livelihoods, denying some members of society the agency, autonomy and power to act, is a catalyst for worsening the quality of life for everyone.

Despite society's disregard and pretended obliviousness to women's powerful contribution to addressing the ills faced by society, history remains littered with recorded evidence that shows women at the forefront of so many struggles, not as spectators but as leaders. Ama Ata Aidoo has observed how, "After the Second World War, many women stayed in the forefront of the agitation for independence. Some, like General Muthoni (of the Mau Mau Rebellion) became guerrilla leaders whom the enemy feared even more than their male insurgents" (1998:41). Similarly, "the story of South Africa's fight against the institutionalized horrors of [apartheid] conquest would be different if women had not been prepared to get actively involved" (Aidoo 1998:41). What this proves is how noteworthy women's powerful responses and interventions towards addressing challenges faced by different societies have been. "A number of women [have] acted [and continue to act] with powerful sense of their priorities and agendas to create new roles for women, citizens and leaders, and negating stereotypes of being passive, submissive or muted" (Narismulu 2012:68). It is, therefore, unfortunate that the patriarchal heritage, handed down from generation to generation, endorses women's dependence on men "as a key element of the cultural constitution of female identity" (Mumtaz and

Salway 2009:1350). Such disregard for women's human rights is not just a violation of their God-given rights, but a gross injustice that has produced so much misery, not just for the women themselves but for society at large. Worryingly, it is women and children who are usually the most seriously affected victims of this societal mindset that wants to undervalue women.

It is against the above background that this chapter seeks to challenge patriarchy's false claims about the nature of womanhood. The chapter draws from literature written by women feminists which it views as a space of contrasts as it disputes patriarchal thinking about women. The purposively selected focal texts for this discussion are Tsitsi Dangarembga's *Nervous Conditions* and Lauretta Ngcobo's *And They Didn't Die*.

Discoursing Women's Autonomy in the Context of Patriarchy

Autonomy relates to the freedom and capacity of an individual to make independent and personal decisions without any fear of inhibitions from anyone. This freedom is God granted right that must be protected. According to Mumtaz and Salway (2009:1349), autonomy relates to "a set of multiple but inter linked domains including, but not limited to, decision-making authority, economic, social, emotional and physical autonomy." This definition suggests that there are many different spaces through which autonomy can be expressed. In this chapter, focus is on two areas of autonomy as it is difficult to discuss and do justice to them all in this short chapter. It is important to note that if one has autonomy, then one has the freedom to act as one sees fit. This underscores definitions that situate autonomy as the "enacted ability to influence decisions, control economic resources, and move freely" (Dangal and Bhandari 2014:1). In simple terms, to possess autonomy is to have control over one's own life and power of choice. Going by this definition, autonomy becomes a catalyst for self-determination without the fear of being held back by anyone. Without autonomy, it means one is subject to control by another. The danger of being controlled by others is that one begins to worry about meeting other people's expectations at the expense of one's own. One major advantage of encouraging autonomy in society is that every individual is likely to feel accountable and want to perform at one's best. Where autonomy abounds, there is mutual respect, greater happiness around and more engagement. Resultantly, there will be greater productivity from which the whole community or family will benefit.

However, in patriarchal dictum, autonomy has been viewed as a prerogative of men. As a consequence of patriarchy, many men often claim to have the authority to determine what is ideal for women without seeking their input (Offen 1998). Patriarchy is a *male-centred* and *male-identified* socially constructed system where men predominantly enjoy *unearned* advantages over women as is observable in how "positions of authority – political, economic, legal, religious, educational, military, domestic – are generally reserved for men" (Johnson 2014:6). Within the patriarchal system, "core cultural ideas about what is considered good, desirable, preferable, or normal are culturally associated with how we think about men, manhood and masculinity" (Johnson 2014:7). Some of these core values include "qualities such as control, strength, competitiveness, toughness, coolness under pressure, logic, forcefulness, decisiveness, rationality, autonomy, self-sufficiency…" (Johnson 2014:7). Over the years, patriarchy's unfairness has been noted in its attempts to socialise men and women to "behave, think, and aspire differently because they have been taught to think of masculinity and femininity in ways which condition difference" (Sultana, 2011:10). This has made some men want "to see themselves as separate, autonomous, and disconnected from others" [i.e. women and children] (Johnson 2014:14). Patriarchy's "association of manhood with control" (Johnson 2014:213) and womanhood with lack of it has, over time, diminished the true value of womanhood. Thus, historically, many women have endured oppression as men have exercised "control over women's labor and women's bodies – their sexuality and reproductive potential – especially in families" (Johnson 2014:118). Due to patriarchal engineering, historically, as a result of patriarchal structuring of society, many women "have not been allowed the chance or space to articulate their thoughts, fears and hopes on the subjects of labour, reproduction, child-bearing and sexuality" (Obbo, 1986:1). Furthermore, the wife was denied spatial freedom as her space was limited since she was tied to the home. The irony of patriarchal logic is that it undervalues a woman's labour at the home front but has a different perspective of men's labour. It claims that "work defines manhood" and treats the work that men do not just "as energy spent but as labor that supports life, constructive labor" (Gilmore 1990:110). Such disproportionate views of men and women affirm how much the patriarchal system distrusts women with responsibility, reducing women to "little more than passive performers of insignificant tasks whose main function is to free men to do the real work of providing for families" (Johnson 2014:134). It is as if womanhood exists in contrast to manhood. Serious questions borne out of that patriarchal "logic" include the following: if the husband fails in his breadwinning duties, doesn't that leave the family exposed to the harshness of life? Can't a family survive without the man of the house? What chances at life do families headed by women as single parents have? If the woman is "homebound" and lacks the freedom and autonomy to venture out of the home space to work, how will the family survive if the husband dies or the husband who is the provider of the family's daily bread divorces his wife? Answers to all these questions reveal that there is definitely something wrong with patriarchal thinking that restricts women from economic activity and autonomy, denying them space to contribute towards bringing food on the table and improving their families' livelihoods. Unfortunately, today, just like it was in nonindustrial societies, social response to women who aspire to be autonomous continues to be hostile or, at best, just ambivalent.

To imagine that it is man's intervention that has associated God-given hominoid qualities such as rationality, ability to organise, power to make decisions and courage with men highlights the amount of cruelty and injustice that follow the lives of women. Homogenisation of attributes that are purely human by tying them to natural anatomical differences between men and women should be contested. Women do not lack the capacity to act rationally or organise. And as highlighted by Lee (2017:1) highlights this: "[a]gency, activism and organisation have been [and continue to be] central and constant themes in women's and gender history. Both separately and in combination, they constitute a valuable analytical framework for the study of women's lives, culture and experience." The two novels selected to discuss these issues resonate well with these objectives as both writers have produced insightful gender-sensitive literature that portrays women's autonomy.

For this chapter, literature has been specifically chosen to mediate the issues under discussion given the close link that exists between it and the real world. According to Duhan (2015:192), literature

> reflects the society, its good values and its ills. In its corrective function, literature mirrors the ills of the society with a view to making the society realize its mistakes and make amends. It also projects the virtues or good values in the society for people to emulate. Literature, as an imitation of human action, often presents a picture of what people think, say and do in the society.

These views are emphasised by Tsaaior (2011:98) who stresses that writers are members of society. Tsaaior argues that in writing,

> writers inscribe their distinct individualities and existential experiences within the fabrics of their writings as veritable members of their societies. In strict fidelity to the protocols of their trade, writers live above society, outside of it; a kind of self-imposed exile, while at the same time remaining part of it, as a function of the compulsion to objectively focus on society in its motions in the historical continuum... interpreting its moods and temperaments, defining its present, and divining its future of (im)possibilities.
>
> (2011:98)

These views underpin the perspective that though literature may be fiction, it still draws from real lived life and captures people's historical or time milieu of which the writer is part of. "What writers of literature do is to transport the real-life events in their society into fiction and to present it to the society as a mirror with which people can look at themselves and make amends where necessary" (Duhan 2015:192).

For feminist women writers, literature is an arena of struggle to champion women's interests and campaign for justice and social transformation. Narismulu (2012:71) views (literary) art as "a powerful source of innovation, advancing justice and transformation." This reflects what Ngugi wa Thiong'o (2012:1) has said about literary writers:

> like prophets and seers, writers are driven by a force, an irresistible desire to give to the inner impulses, the material form of sound, color and word. This desire cannot be held back by laws, tradition or religious restrictions. The song that must be sung will be sung; and if banned, they will hum it; and if humming is banned, they will dance it; and if dancing is banned, they will sing it silently to themselves or to the ears of those near, waiting for the appropriate moment to explode.

In other words, literature creatively deals with real-life issues that society grapples with in ways that provoke social transformation and promote justice.

However, because this chapter is about women's autonomy and agency, literature by men will not be examined. This is because literature by men, arguably, speaks from the outside on issues that affect women. Flora Nwapa, two decades ago, decried the reduced role that women characters consistently seemed to receive in literature by men. This made her ask: "How do African literary texts [by men] project women?" (1998:91). She criticised the fact that very few men writers "tried to project an objective image of women, an image that actually reflects the reality of women's role[s] in society" (1998:91). Her analysis of the situation obtaining led her "to conclude that there is a difference between the African male writer and his female counterpart" (1998:92). This provoked my interest in this chapter, to examine how selected women writers espouse a "revisionist" slant in their portrayals of women's autonomy, and my findings are given below.

Feminist women writers' portrayal of women and reproductive autonomy

Women's maternal or reproductive autonomy constitutes a thematic presence that looms large in feminist literature by women. Reproductive autonomy relates to women having the freedom to make decisions regarding their marriage, whether to have sex or not, how many children to have and when, among others. Such power is fundamental to women's welfare "because childbearing takes place in women's bodies" (Purdy 2006:287). Unfortunately, for women, "such autonomy is a low priority for most societies" (Purdy 2006:287). Nwapa (1998:95) has also observed that, for most women, "there are not too many alternatives to being married and having children." In other words, women, without exception, are expected to get married and have children, especially the boy child (Uwakweh 1998). Regrettably, patriarchy has no allowed them" the chance or space to articulate their thoughts, fears and hopes on the subjects of labour, reproduction, child-bearing and sexuality" (Obbo 1986:1). Despite women bearing the brunt and marks of child-bearing, as well as assuming the responsibility of carrying babies in their wombs and greater roles in child-rearing, ironically, men continue to possess unjust power, as husbands and partners, to speak on behalf of women regarding issues of maternity. Silencing women's voices in areas of their own reproductive capacities is a serious violation of women's rights that many feminist scholars and writers have contested.

Tsitsi Dangarembga, in her novel *Nervous Conditions*, has successfully tackled the issue of women fighting for maternal autonomy through her portrayal of the character of Lucia. Through Lucia, she succeeds in demonstrating that women can choose against marriage if they so wish and not feel bad about it. Lucia is the direct opposite of women characters in the same novel such as Mai Tambu and, to some extent, Maiguru, who have consistently been denied voice to speak up on many issues affecting their lives. For instance, in a private talk with her daughter, Mai Tambu acknowledges how difficult life is for women:

> This business of womanhood is a heavy burden. How could it not be? Aren't we the ones who bear children? When it is like that you can't just decide today I want to do this, tomorrow I want to do that, the next day I want to be educated! When there are sacrifices to be made, you are the one to make them. And these things are not easy (p. 16).

This private mother-and-daughter conversation reveals how constraining a woman's life is. Mai Tambu underlines that women, who are "the ones who bear children," are denied freedom of voice to make decisions. However, through the life of Lucia, Dangarembga depicts an independent woman with voice to speak and the autonomy to make personal decisions.

In spite of the patriarchal dictation that women should marry (Uwakweh 1998), Lucia actually decides against marriage. Though she came from a very poor family and "had been brought up in abject poverty, she had not, like my mother, been married … at fifteen. Her spirit, unfettered in this respect, had experimented with living and drawn its own conclusions" (p. 127). That Lucia did not allow the poverty of her family to restrain her voice is a loud statement about her strength. To highlight her autonomous behaviour, the narrator describes her as "a much bolder woman" and "strong" (p. 127). This description defies patriarchy which associates *boldness* and *strength* with manhood and not womanhood (Johnson 2014).

Lucia's boldness is demonstrated in that she challenged her patriarchal society by choosing to fall pregnant out of wedlock, something that her society did not take kindly to. Yet, Lucia seemed unconcerned. Takesure was responsible for the pregnancy but, though "Lucia was carrying his baby… Lucia who had grown shrewd in her years of dealing with men, denied that the foetus was Takesure's" (p. 126). She accredited Jeremiah to be responsible even if the latter "had sensibly not allowed himself to enjoy Lucia's voluptuousness until after she had fallen pregnant" (p. 126). This was a very deliberate move by Lucia to escape getting married to Takesure. Her estimation of Takesure was that he was not responsible enough to be a husband and let alone a father. She says of Takesure to the family council while holding him by his ears: "Tell me Babamukuru, would you say this is a man? Can *it* be a man that talks this nonsense? A man should talk sense, isn't it? So what can *this* be? And she tweaked *its* ears to find out what *it* would say" (p. 144; original emphasis).

She speaks ill about Takesure who was ready to take her for a wife and actually dehumanises him through use of the pronoun 'it' to describe him. She had budged into the Sigauke family council that had convened to discuss the issue of her pregnancy, uninvited. Having the audacity to budge into the meeting uninvited reveals her unpreparedness to hand over to the family patriarchy the power to decide her fate in her absence. It is a statement to women that: at times, they should not be soft and pliant if men are to take them seriously. Men will want to continue their domination but women should learn to take a stand against being sidelined. Lucia, is an interesting character because she was going to determine her own future.

Interestingly, Lucia was not against motherhood but wifehood. Like Jezile in Ngcobo's *And They Didn't Die* who "did not see motherhood as a bind, a fulfilment of other people's expectations" (p. 6), Lucia was ready to raise the child all by herself but not be tied in matrimony to an irresponsible man, just to satisfy patriarchal expectations. Raising her child alone meant she would enjoy unhindered access (by the husband) to the child and the power to decide what was good for her baby. Lucia's actions communicate to many women the possibilities of taking charge of their own and children's lives. Many single parents (perhaps due to divorce or death of spouse) can draw strength from the actions of Lucia to embolden their resolve to survive on their own and not feel helpless if abandoned by their husbands.

Lucia was proud of her own capabilities as a woman. She would rather live independently than with a husband. Hence, she says: "As for Takesure, I don't know what he thinks he can give me. Whatever he can do for me, I can do better for myself" (p. 145). Even if Takesure was responsible for the pregnancy, Lucia was not going to marry him just to appease society's ego that a woman was incomplete without a husband. She was not afraid to confront head-on all the shame and censure that society associated with raising a child as a single mother. What Lucia craved for was the freedom that she would get out of this arrangement, which she knew marriage would not afford her. She was able to recognise the colossal opportunities that this freedom presented her. For example, she would not have to consult anybody before making personal decisions as seen in how she looked for employment at the mission, enrolled for Grade One classes where she excelled and could freely move between home and the mission school where she worked, without seeking permission from anyone. Choosing to live outside marriage and its restrictions gave her spatial autonomy. Like Oduche in Achebe's fiction, *Arrow of God*, Lucia who had enrolled for Grade One classes "recognized the self-actualizing potential of the new education and its enormous possibilities for enhanced social freedom" (Ogwude 2011:111). For instance, during Lucia's conversation with Babamukuru, she spoke to him in a very candid and blunt manner that other women (and men) were not capable of, given Babamukuru's social stature. She attributed her ability to speak her mind to her remaining unmarried:

Well, Babamukuru, maybe when you marry a woman, she is obliged to obey you. But some of us aren't married, so we don't know how to do it. That is why I have been able to tell you frankly what is in my heart. It is better that way.

(p. 171)

Thus, Dangarembga, through literary representation, succeeds in creating space for women to exercise freedom and challenge socially constructed rules and practices instituted by patriarchy.

Another way through which Dangarembga discusses women's reproductive autonomy is depicted in the way that she portrays Lucia as someone who has power over her own body. Although she had flatly rejected Takesure's hand in marriage, that did not stop Lucia from engaging in a sexual relationship with him, only when it was convenient to her. She was in control of the relationship and not the other way around. For instance, at one point, she chose to sleep with the girls and not join Takesure (who desperately wanted her to come) in the bedroom. However, a few weeks down the line, when she felt the time was right, she moved on her own accord and joined him. All this shows how the kind of relationship Lucia had created with Takesure gave her space, autonomy and freedom to be in control of her body. No one had some kind of "proprietary" ownership over her body. She was in charge, and that is autonomy. After securing employment at the mission, Lucia took her reproductive autonomy to another level. Her newly found economic autonomy saw her discontinuing her relationship with Takesure altogether. When she returned from the mission, "Takesure was very pleased [to see her back]… but Lucia *did not even see him*" (p. 185, original emphasis). She chose to sleep with Mai Tambu in the kitchen, "which annoyed Takesure, who had invited Lucia to the *hozi*" (p. 186). Clearly, power over one's own body is something that women should struggle for.

Reproductive autonomy is a subject that should not be taken for granted as it is critical for women to possess it as an important right. "People with reproductive autonomy can control whether and when to become pregnant" (Bixby Centre 2014). Without reproductive autonomy, a woman may be objectified by some men who reduce women to automated childbearing machines and "toys" for their sexual pleasure. This sad situation is what Ngcobo depicts in her portrayal of Zenzile who keeps having babies against her will. Zenzile was married "to that good for nothing Mthebe" (p. 5) who was extravagant in Durban yet neglected his family's financial needs back home. This left Zenbzile being responsible for the provision of the day-to-day needs of the family. This is a call for society to recognise how much women require economic autonomy "because they are generally expected to take primary responsibility for child rearing" (Purdy 2006:288). Women's autonomy, in this respect, would be very valuable for the children's welfare since there is evidence of many irresponsible fathers just like Mthebe in Ngcbo's novel.

Zenzile lacked maternal autonomy. It was Mthebe, her husband, who controlled her reproductive behaviour: "Each time Mthebe came home from leave he found a new baby, and he left another growing, ready to find on his next visit" (p. 5). Giving birth yearly left Zenzile "haggard and despondent" and made her "a captive in her house, with children who whimpered and hung around her skirts" (p. 5). She confided to Jezile that she no longer wanted another child. Yet, because she lacked reproductive autonomy, her yearly ordeal persisted. She was perennially ill, confirming what scholars on reproductive health have stated. "Contemporary scholarship and policy responses in diverse developing-country settings emphasize women's limited autonomy as a key barrier to improvements in their reproductive health" (Mumtaz and Salway 2009:1349). Later in the story, Zenzile's death was wrought by pregnancy complications, as if Ngcobo was making a statement of the detrimental impact of women's lack of maternal autonomy on their lives. Comparing the two women, Zenzile and Lucia, it is clear that lack of reproductive autonomy is a site of oppression for women that must be overcome in line with the aims of the fifth Millenium Development Goal: to reduce maternal mortality, which has been "extremely high in low income countries of sub-Saharan Africa" (Dangal and Bhandari 2014:1).

Women and Educational Autonomy

For women to break free from positions of marginality and dependence on men, education has been posited by feminist scholars as a critical variable that will lead to their realization of economic independence and other freedoms (Uwakweh 1998; Mama 2001). Autonomous livelihoods are achievable if women "receive modern education and participate, along with the men, in productive activity outside the home" (Bernstein, 1978:19). Unfortunately, in order to keep women down, patriarchy continues to refuse women and girls education, which remains, particularly in some African families, a male preserve. Patriarchy urges women to view marriage as a pinnacle of their attainment and something that fulfils their lives.

However, in Dangarembga's *Nervous Conditions*, Tambudzai, an eight year old girl at the beginning of the narrative, refuses marriage, choosing education instead. Her father, a staunch representative of the patriarchal system, tries hard to dissuade Tambu from pursuing education while encouraging her to think about getting married as a better alternative. While talking to Mr Matimba who was Tambu's teacher, Jeremiah was resolute that Tambu should opt out of school and his patriarchal reasoning made him ask: "Have you ever heard of a woman who remains in her father's house? She will meet a young man and I will have lost everything" (p. 30). To Tambu, he said, "Is that [education] anything to worry about? Ha-a-a, it's nothing.... Can you cook books and feed them to your husband? Stay at home with your mother. Learn to cook and clean. Grow vegetables" (p. 15).

However, Tambu "loved going to school and ... was good at it" (p. 15). She would not let her father stop her as she dared to be different from her mother who was uneducated and had, as a consequence, been reduced to a slave who toiled daily to feed the family while Jeremiah, her husband, was not only "a lazy hand" who "doesn't want to work" but a devotee to the formulation of cunning strategies that helped him avoid all forms of domestic work (p. 145). The life that her uneducated mother led, where she was tied to the domestic space, was not appealing to Tambu. Young as she was, she despised becoming another patriarchal victim, "Maiguru's educational achievement, lifestyle, and [relative] freedom from the drudgery of domesticity inspired her [want] to escape from the threat of her own mother's condition and poverty" (Uwakweh 1998:18, 19). She was determined to rescue herself from patriarchal victimhood and not be like her own mother who was located in a repulsive and invidious position where, even if she saw the injustice suffered by women, lacked the power to act and challenge the injustice openly. Tambu saw her mother as "an obstacle in the path of my departure" (p. 58). This was because Mai Tambu, like the "dutiful" wife that she was, had already taken upon herself the duties of a "good" wife and mother as she lectured and prepared Tambu "to learn to carry your burdens with strength" (p. 16) and "accept your lot" as a woman within patriarchy (p. 20). In Tambu's words, "my mother began to prepare me for disappointment long before I would have been forced to face up to it. To prepare me she began to discourage me" to aspire for "unwomanly" vocations (p. 20). Dangarembga's message is clear: some women, not out of choice but due to patriarchal tutelage, may participate alongside men in opposing the struggle for women's autonomy. In the novel, no matter how much "people were prejudiced against educated women" (p. 181), Tambu remained adamant that education would rescue her and help her attain autonomy.

Denying women educational autonomy is a pervasive theme in literature by feminist women writers. It is also discussed in Buchi Emecheta's *The Bride Price* (1978) through the mistreatment faced by Aku-nna. In Emecheta's story, Auntie Matilda highlights the predicament that awaits Aku-nna due to the patriarchal attitudes of her society when she remarks, "The pity of it all is that they will marry her off very quickly in order to get enough money to pay Nna-nndo's school fees" (p. 38). Just like the education of Nhamo, a boy child, is preferred in *Nervous Conditions*, the same obtains in *The Bride Price* where the education of Akunna's brother, Nna-nndo, is considered a priority concern by the African patriarchal normativity.

In *Nervous Conditions*, Tambu's response to her situation where patriarchy blocked her education was quite remarkable. Having connected her education to her future liberation and viewing it as a fundamental attainment that would avail enormous opportunities to her, she looked far ahead and daydreamed of the future that education would offer her. As she envisions her future self, Tambu says:

This new me would not be enervated by smoky kitchens that left eyes smarting and chests permanently bronchitic. This new me would not be frustrated by wood fires that either flamed so furiously that the sadza burned, or so indifferently that it became mbodza. Nor would there be trips to Nyamarira… where we drew our water…. I could not pretend to be sorry to be leaving the water-drums whose weight compressed your neck into your spine, were heavy on the head even after you had grown used to them and were in need of refilling (p. 59).

Tambu's desire to break free from domesticity affirms Mama's (2001) view where she urges women not to "relish the idea of being kept at home" but rather to fight to gain admission into the greater society where they truly belong. As Tambu later points out, education offered her an "opportunity for mental and eventually, through it, material emancipation" (p. 87). She did not just envision herself as the sole beneficiary of the economic freedom that her education offered her. She dreamt of her father and brother being emancipated alongside her. She was frustrated by the picture of her own father living in the shadow of rich men like Babamukuru. Thus, she dreamt of improving her father's condition and so she states: "I wanted my father and Nhamo [her brother] to stand up straight like Babamukuru, but they always looked as though they were cringing" (p. 49, 50). This shows how society as a whole stands to benefit from women achieving autonomy.

The fact that Tambu has to fight for educational autonomy shows that society will never hand over autonomy to women on a silver platter without them having to fight for it. For Tambudzai, her struggle included having to work for her own school fees as her parents could not afford to send her to school. Her father abused the money for fees sent by Babamukuru. Given the little money for school fees that she managed to raise, Tambu's mother, in true patriarchal fashion, prioritized sending Nhamo, the boy child, to school. Much as we may blame Mai Tambu for preferring the education of the boy child to that of the girl child, we cannot lose sight of what the decisiveness of a mother can do. Tambu narrates how her mother kept Nhamo in school:

my mother was determined in that year. She began to boil eggs, which she carried to the bus terminus and sold to passengers…. She also took vegetables – rape, onions and tomatoes – extending her garden so that there was more to sell…. In this way she scraped together enough money to keep my brother in school.

(p. 15)

Without Mai Tambu's interventions, Nhamo would not have been able to continue with school. She defended her son's interests where her husband had failed, thus confirming Aina's assertion in her study of African women at the grassroots, where she has concluded that "the survival of poor families from the devastating socio-economic situation on the continent depends largely on the strategies adopted by women" (1998:71). This argument demonstrates what women's agency can achieve. If women were to be allowed more freedom to make important decisions in the home and society, and were provided with the resources for capital projects, clearly, much more good would be achieved.

There is a fascinating disparity in the way that Dangarembga portrays the actions of the two children affected by the news that there was no money for fees. Nhamo's response is summed up in two words: "He cried" (p. 15). Crying reflects lack of creativity and resourcefulness on his part. Apparently, no amount of tears would change the situation for him. In sharp contrast, once it dawned on Tambu that there were no fees, she set about planning ways to address the challenge rather than feel sorry for herself. She did not beg or plead with anyone, determined to find fees somehow. If her parents would not send her to school, she would send herself to school. Her resolve was "to be like Maiguru, who was not poor and had not been crushed by the weight of womanhood" but "looked well-kempt and fresh, clean all the time" (p. 16). Tambudzai thought through her course of action "for several days" (p. 16) and then one day she "*announced*" to her parents: "I shall go to school again" (p. 16) and "I will earn the fees" (p. 17). Her father's immediate response to his daughter's announcement was "by laughing and laughing in an unpleasantly adult way" (p. 17). Jeremiah's laughter was meant to demoralize his daughter and dissuade her from pursuing her dream, confirming Aidoo's argument that "Much of the putting down of women" comes mostly from men (1998:47). Yet, Tambu remained resolute. The use of the word "announced" underlines her decisiveness: her capacity to make important decisions. She did not intend to rely on anyone to find the fees for her. There she was, a young girl ready to chart the course of her own life rather than have others charting it for her. The two statements she uttered to her parents – "I shall go to school again" and "I will earn the fees" – though not concomitant with her age, are significant markers of her search for agency and self-determination. She has the strength of character to seek to address her situation rather than accept defeat. Defying her age, she asked for a small plot where she planted maize for sale. This was going to be her escape route. Explaining her age-defying antics and resilience, Tambu says:

> That year I grew older, stronger and sturdier than any eight year old can usefully grow. More often than not I woke up before dawn, the first lifting of the darkness occurring while I was sweeping the yard. Before it was fully light I would be on my way to the river and then returning along the footpath through the trees and past other homesteads, where the women were just waking, my water-drum balanced on my head-pad of leaves and green twigs.... By the time the sun rose I was in my field, in the first days hoeing and clearing; then digging holes thirty inches apart, with a single swing of the hoe, as we had been taught in our garden periods at school (pp. 19–20).

This reflects her industry. It was a fight for her future economic autonomy and nothing could stop her. However, when Tambu's green mealies had ripened and were ready for sale, Nhamo, started stealing maize from her plot and freely distributed the maize to other children at school. This incensed Tambudzai who engaged him in a brutal fistfight. She could not passively watch as Nhamo, a young representative of the patriarchal system, acted in ways that would have derailed her ambition to go back to school. Once she learnt what Nhamo was doing, in raging anger, she

> took off from the pada game like a dog after a buck. I remember at one moment playing pada, the next Nhamo and I rolling about in the dirt of the football pitch… I went straight for my brother and brought him down in a single charge… I sat on top of him, banged his head into the ground, screamed and spat and cursed…. I charged again, intending this time to kill (pp. 22–23).

Fighting her brother who felt had unearned entitlements to decide for his sister underscores the idea highlighted earlier that women need not expect freedom to be freely offered to them but that they have to fight for it since many men are not prepared to give up the privileges they have enjoyed historically (Johnson 2014). Later, with the help of Mr Matimba, she went to Umtali to sell her maize. Mr Matimba taught her how to sell her wares. The help that Mr Matimba offered is a testament to men that they too can play a role to help women around them attain independence. Feminist writers agree that men should not see themselves as outsiders but as participants with roles to play in women's fight for their liberation. Bell Hooks has emphasised the need for inter-gender solidarity in the fight against patriarchal abuses and stated more than three decades ago that "time has come for women active in feminist movement to develop new strategies for including men in the struggle against sexism" (1984:72). In Umtali, Tambu was able to earn (through the benevolence of Doris, a white woman) enough fees to keep her in school for a few years. Her mental resourcefulness, boldness and possession of courage to overcome the limitations imposed by the poverty of her family and the patriarchal system are quite inspiring. She refused silencing and exclusion even by the poverty of her family, an affirmation of her search for autonomy. In a critique of Yvonne Vera's *Under the Tongue*, Kizito Muchemwa has equated women's muted voices in the face of exclusion "with absence, death, negation and repression; and [their] speech with presence, life, affirmation and freedom" (Muchemwa 2002:9). Women have to choose voice and presence in order to win the battle, not just for themselves but for the benefit of society at large.

Conclusion

It is clear from this Chapter's discussion that patriarchy is a horrid evil that needs purging to allow women space to redefine themselves outside its precincts that continue to deny them autonomy over their own lives. The chapter has shown that, no matter how much society may attempt to underestimate the power of women, it is undeniable that women continue to make powerful decisions and exercise autonomy in ways that benefit society as a whole. This is a view underscored by Kimmel (2005:107) who has pointed out how the life of every member of society "will be better if women have more freedom and better jobs and work." All humanity will experience a more fulfilling existence as long as women's autonomy and agency are not restrained.

References

Aidoo, A. A. (1998) The African Woman Today. In O. Nnaemeka (ed.) *Sisterhood, Feminisms and Power: From Africa to the Diaspora*. Trenton, NJ: Africa World Press. 39–50.

Aina, O. (1998) African Women at the Grassroots. In O. Nnaemeka (ed.) *Sisterhood, Feminisms and Power: From Africa to the Diaspora*. Trenton, NJ: Africa World Press. 65–88.

Bernstein, H. (1978) *For Their Triumphs and for Their Fears: Women in Apartheid South Africa*. London: International Defence and Aid Fund.

Bixby Centre for Global Reproductive Health (2014) Measuring women's reproductive autonomy, March 17, 2014. San Francisco: University of California. [Internet Access: http://bixbycentre.ucsf.edu]

Buchi, E. (1978) *The Bride Price*. Glasgow: Fontana.

Dangal, G. and Bhandari, T. R. (2014) Women's Autonomy: New Paradigms in Maternal Health Care Utilization. *Global Journal of Medicine and Public Health*, 3(5). Internet Access: www.gjmedph.org.

Dangarembga, T. (1988) *Nervous Conditions*. Harare: Zimbabwe Publishing House.

Duhan, R. (2015) The Relationship between Literature and Society. *Language in India*, 15(4), 192–202.

Gilmore, D. (1990) *Manhood in the Making: Cultural Concepts of Masculinity*. New Haven: Yale University Press.

Johnson, A. (2014) *The Gender Knot: Unravelling our Patriarchal Legacy*. New York: Temple University.

Kimmel, M.S. (2005) Why Men Should Support Gender Equity. In S. Freedberg, E. Haghighat and B. Ngo-Ngijol-Banoum (eds.) *Women's Studies Review, special Edition: The Role of Women in World Peace and the Role of Men and Boys in Gender Equity*. New York: Women's Studies Program, Lehman College. 102–114.

Lee, C. (2017) Women's Agency, Activism and Organisation. 831–834. Internet Access: https://doi.org/10.1080/09612025.2017.1346880

Muchemwa, K. Z. (2002) Language, Voice and Presence in *Under the tongue* and *Without a name*. In R. Muponde and M. Maodzwa-Taruvinga (eds.) *Sign and Taboo: Perspectives on the Poetic fiction of Vera*. Oxford: James Currey. 3–14.

Mumtaz, Z. and Salway, S. (2009) Understanding Gendered Influences on Women's Reproductive Health in Pakistan: Moving beyond the Autonomy Paradigm. *Social Science & Medicine* 68, 1349–1356.

Narismulu, P. (2012) For my Torturer': An African Woman's Transformative Art of Truth, Justice and Peace-making during Colonialism. *Journal of International Women's Studies*, 13(4), 67–81.

Ngcobo, L. (1999) *And They Didn't Die*. New York: The Feminist Press.

Ngugiwa, Thiong'o (2012) Speaking My Language: gugi wa Ta Thiong'o's Address at the 2012 Sunday Times Literary Awards by Sophy on June 25th, 2012 *The Media Online*.

Nwapa, F. (1998) Women and Creative Writing in Africa. In O. Nnaemeka (ed.) *Sisterhood, Feminism and Power: From Africa to the Diaspora*. Trenton, NJ: Africa World Press. 89–99.

Obbo, C. (1986) *African Women: Their Struggle for Economic Independence*. London: Zed Press.

Offen, Karen. 1998. Defining Feminism: A Comparative Historical Approach. *Signs: Journal of Women in Culture and Society*, 14(1), 119–157.

Ogwude, S. O. (2011) History and Ideology in Chimamanda Adichie's fiction. *Tydskrif vir Letterkunde: Nigerian Literature, Triumphs and Travails: A Journal for African Literature*, 48(1), 110–123.

Purdy, L. (2006) Women's Reproductive Autonomy: Medicalisation and Beyond. *Journal of Medical Ethics*, 32(5), 287–291.

Sougou, N. M., Bassoum, O., Faye, A. and Leye, M. M. M. (2020) Women's Autonomy in Health Decision-making and Its Effect on Access to Family Planning Services in Senegal in 2017: A Propensity Score Analysis. *BMC Public Health*, 20, 1–9. Available: https://doi.org/10.1186/s12889-020-09003-x

Sultana, Abeda. 2011. Patriarchy and Women's Subordination: A Theoretical Analysis. *The Arts Faculty Journal*, July 2010–June 2011, 1–18.

Tsaaior, J.T. (2011) Exile, Exilic Consciousness and the Poetic Imagination in Tanure Ojaide's Poetry. *Tydskrif vir Letterkunde: Nigerian Literature, Triumphs and Travails: A Journal for African Literature*, 48(1), 98–109.

Uwakweh, P. (1998) Carving a Niche: Visions of Gendered Childhood in Buchi Emecheta's *The Bride Price* and Tsitsi Dangarembga's *Nervous Conditions*. In E. D. Jones and M. Jones (eds.) *Childhood in African Literature*. Oxford: James Currey, (21), 9–21.

5
INTERROGATING THE CONTRADICTORY PORTRAYAL OF WOMEN IN AFRICAN DRAMA
Uche Nwaozuzu's *Ajari* and *Ebibi* in Perspective

Godstime Eze, Favour Ayozie and Somtochukwu Metu

Introduction

Women in a typical African society are expected to be well behaved, be good wives, and not to speak when the men elders are talking, while their male counterparts have a humongous amount of freedom (Yeseibo 2013). Our prehistoric nomadic fore-parents lived in a less equal society. With the advent of agriculture and the idea of property, men wanted to keep track of their progenies. Women were kept as baby-making machines. Their contribution was confined to the premises of a household for centuries (163). Their roles varied depending on class and context. In a work by Florence Ebila on the construction of gender and nationalism, in Wangari Maathai's autobiography "*Unbowed*", she opines that "in a typical African traditional setting, the definition of a 'proper' woman is influenced by socio-cultural and patriarchal ideologies that construct the ideal African woman as the docile one who does not question male authority" (2015). Women have been relegated to the background, and their lives have revolved around upholding family values as virtuous women, having "wife material", and being answerable to the men in their lives. Most women appear comfortable with their lives being dictated by men perhaps to align with the societal construct of how a woman should live or to have a peaceful environment either as an understanding wife or girlfriend. This is a clear case of the slave falling in love with her chains. According to Fwangyil (2012):

> Women are subjected to male oppression and suppressed at various stages of life. Unfortunately, female oppression is deeply ingrained in the culture of the society which ensures the continuation of patriarchal control. This situation makes it almost impossible for women to seek ways of liberating themselves because doing so would be tantamount to challenging the age long tradition and custom of the people.
>
> (15)

The above claim is a result of a generational pattern of upbringing that is gender based in an African society and other parts of the world. In the same vein, Chimamanda Adichie expresses her dissatisfaction with the treatment of women and girls lamenting that much disservice has been done to girls at the very point of upbringing. They are raised to always make reference to the fragile egos and validations of men. In her words (2009), "we teach girls to shrink themselves, to make themselves smaller. We say to girls: you can have ambitions, but not too much. You should aim to be successful but not too successful; otherwise, you will threaten the man".

These facts stated above have caused several problems among women, some of which include negligence to political participation, religious deprivation, and societal depression. These serve as hindrances to women achieving development and determining their positions in the society. However, a good number of women are now rising above the embargos placed on women by the society, tradition, and the men in their lives. Numerous advocacies for women and lots of feminist movements and ideologies have been developed over the years. Efforts for the active involvement of women in decision-making have increased over the last decades as can be seen in the proposition of several women right laws. As Jennifer Breen (1990) states:

> The reality is that women are still far from attaining 30 per cent of women parliamentarian in most post conflict contexts, which is the first step to resolve women's problems. In Africa, there are only two key successful examples of women's participation in governance: Liberia with a female president and Rwanda with 50 per cent of female parliamentarians. Nonetheless, the legal recognition of women's rights has led to a greater awareness, advocacy and mobilization.
>
> (60)

With the progression of female activism and movement, there is a need for women to begin to see themselves as agents of greater achievements. With these developments, one can see the contrasting image of women from one generation to the other. These developments have attracted the attention and focus of many playwrights in Africa and Nigeria as well.

Deconstructive Representation of Women in African Drama

The representation of women in most Nigerian dramas is often defined by how men see them, or how the society expects them to behave because patriarchal societies lionise men and denigrate women (Azunwo and Ejiro, 2015). As such, women suffer both self and social marginalization and this is a result of the training and upbringing of women, which has greatly been influenced by the patriarchal construct that the will of women is submerged in the needs and expectations of the society. Nelly Furman (cited in Makama, 2013) notes that, "In a world defined by man, the trouble with woman is that she is at once an object of desire and an object of exchange, valued on the one hand as a person in her own right and on the other hand considered simply as a relational sign between the controllers of the society" (61). This goes to show that the distinctive feminine qualities of a woman are not seen as a necessary balance to the male but rather as a complementary accessory.

Over the years, women have been treated unfairly in Africa, and sometimes have had to deal with various forms of degradation and abuse from men because right from when they are born, they are taught by tradition and the society that they are just tools for men. It is not arguable to say that a woman's oppression begins from the cradle. Jean Damascene (2019) admits that:

> Boys and girls grew up knowing what is required of them in the society. Boys grew up knowing that they had to be strong and wise in order to take care of and provide for their wives. Similarly, the girls grew up knowing that they had to be hardworking and submissive in order to appeal to a man as a wife.
>
> (60)

From our observation of most literary works by men, the female gender is usually depersonalized and socially constructed as secondary and subservient to the generic male gender. Women are often represented in these literary works as tamed sexual beings that are weak vessels, obligated to produce children, cook food for the household, and tend to the needs of the man. Nnolim Charles (2009) captures the way some playwrights like Achebe paint the image of women in a degraded manner. Women are portrayed as weak, helpless, brutalized, and victimized or they are prostitutes or seductive mistresses destined to cater for the man's needs. Nnolim further notes that:

> Right from the Edenic era to modern times, women have been depicted as angels with feet of clay, as purveyors of unhappiness both for themselves and for their male counterparts. The image of women in African literature is a gloomy one compounded by the helpful hand of tradition and patriarchy.
>
> (165)

The above assertion implies that the actions and inactions of women bring unhappiness to both themselves and the men and so should not be left to their own devices, but rather follow the guidance of the men and tradition, that even though women are admirable they are still vulnerable. A raft of male writers such as Chinua Achebe, Wole Soyinka, Ahmed Yerima, Ola Rotimi, Esiaba Irobi, Emeka Nwabueze, and Sam Ukala, to mention a few, represent women poorly in their works as docile virtuous people, tempests, wretches of the earth, properties to be acquired by men, avaricious fellows who were predetermined by fate, and in Ogunyemi's words "to carry foo foo and soup to men dealing with important matters". This is a result of the exaction of traditional values in them which saw women as inferior to the man, and in light of this, it is also reflected in the ways they write their dramatic texts as they give negative attributes to the female characters.

Chinua Achebe, in *Things Fall Apart*, captures life in a prehistoric African village where the women are portrayed as weak and marginalized while the male gender exercises humongous influence over them. Achebe builds the plot of the story in such a way that it colours the journey of a man alone; keeping women's suffering normal, as if that is how they should be treated. For instance, Okonkwo and Nwakibie are said to have barns of yam and wives. Okonkwo is portrayed as a typical wealthy man who is a great wrestler and an industrious man who exacts absolute control over his wives and rules his household with an iron fist. This is in direct contrast with the women as they are portrayed as docile, weak, and emotional creatures that are dependent and in need of a man's protection and provision. The wives of Okonkwo could be used as a representation of how women were viewed in the book. Their only role was to give birth to children, cook, and serve food. The position of women in Umuofia is very low. In fact, Okonkwo nearly killed one of his wives when she went to her friend's house and forgot to come back on time to prepare his meal, irrespective of the fact that it was the week of peace. Graburn, Nelson (2008) states that a man finds it "okay" to beat and abuse women because they are inferior to the superior men who can do everything.

The only woman who seems to have authority and command the respect of the men is Chielo, the Priestess of Agbala, the oracle of the hills and caves. She is a simple trader who sells in the market with the other women but when she is possessed by the power of her gods, she speaks with no fear or intimidation. Her voice is described as a sharp knife cutting through the night and even men like Okonkwo heed her warnings and instructions. The representation and image portrayal of women above show the flawed allegation of femininity as a mere figment of the men's imagination and undeserving of a woman's reputation as women can be more than flippant gossip who are weak and absolutely dependent on the protection and guidance of the men.

Examples also can be seen in the character of the nameless young helpless bride in Wole Soyinka's *Death and the King's Horseman*. In *Kongi's Harvest*, we see that Segi is described by Soyinka as "a right cannibal of female species" who sucks the vigour and vitality of men leaving them like "sugar pulp squeezed dry". In *The Trials of Brother Jero*, Soyinka portrays Amope in a negative light, as a troublesome and quarrelsome woman who drives her husband crazy all the time. To date, men still see women as available sex commodities. In Emeka Nwabueze's *Parliament of Vultures*, the only female character is not only a whore but also a dunderhead who is ill-tempered and uneducated.

Constructive Representation of Women in African Drama

Women dramatists like Zulu Sofola, Flora Nwapa, Buchi Emecheta, Ama Ata Aidoo, Julie Okoh, Tess Onwueme, Irene Salami, and Chimamanda Adichie, to mention a few, used their works to protest against patriarchal stereotyping. They have, in every given opportunity, advocated for women's empowerment and also used their writings to voice out these concerns by writing women into significance. Therefore, women dramatists' writings seek to put to light the real place of women in the chronicles of mankind to redefine and reconstruct the former image created by men. Gerda Lerner (1987) opines that it is the responsibility of women to affect the importance of femininity in historical processes when she explains thus:

> Women have been left out of history not because of the evil conspiracy of men in general or male historians in particular, but because we have considered history only in male centred terms. What would history be like if it were seen through the eyes of women and ordered by the values they define?
>
> (52)

Rolf Solberg (1983) recommends that "one of the ways of correcting one's faulty image of the African woman would be through the African woman seen from the 'inside', in other words, rendered by women" (249). This includes women giving a wide assessment to the female writing as it has its own unparalleled unique characteristics. Irene Salami is optimistic that:

> As female writers resort to writing themselves by rewriting these negative portrayals, they will creatively begin to express their discontent and correct the misinterpretation of women. Through their writings, they will erase images of women as victims in the society.
>
> (47)

However, there have been many scenarios where women have been declined access to opportunities for trainings, practice, and a chance to advancement and development in public spaces especially in Nigerian politics. Nevertheless, amidst these challenges, most women have taken extraordinary steps to distinctively make themselves unique, and different from other women with the significant effect of the mark they have left imprinted in the sand of time. According to Godstime Eze and Dilichukwu Agu (2023), "feminist thinkers have argued and are still arguing that western feminism derived much of its inspiration from Africa." Some societies in Africa have had women who ruled kingdoms and led victorious wars. Examples of such documented women include: Ahebi Ugbabe, a Warrant Chief and king of Enugu Ezike (the only female king in the history of Igboland), as accounted by Nwando Achebe (2011). Others are Queen Amina of Zazzau in the 16th century, Nzinga of Angola in the 17th century, Nehanda of Zimbabwe in the 19th century, Queen Kambasa of Bonny, who one time led her army on an expedition to the town of Opuoko where the town was razed to the ground, and Emotan of Benin, who equally unseated the Oba who had usurped her brother from the throne. There are also iconic mythic heroines like Inikpi of Igala and Moremi of Ife (Eze, 2019).

In recent times, there are renowned women playwrights who have rivalled the likes of Chinua Achebe and Wole Soyinka. In an interview with Ezenwa Ohaeto, Flora Nwapa admitted that when she wrote her first novel *Efuru* in 1966, she unconsciously put into writing her personal life experiences. The novel was quite different from what used to be written at that time, and that was because it was written by a woman, and it had a female protagonist. The male critics even asked why she should write about a woman. In Stella Oyedepo's *The Rebellion of the Bumpy-Chested*, a picture is painted of aggressive women who are willing to use guns to fight because of the rights they have been denied. It is a rebellion by women in solidarity against male domination. Irene Salami's *More than Dancing* exhibits strong women who engage in politics that is "supposedly for the men" and overcome their male rivals. Nona, who exudes a high level of political discernment, overwhelms her male counterparts and emerges victorious after they had underestimated her. All these women have succeeded in defining the ideology and wistful desires of the Nigerian woman; they have showcased women as the injured party in the society that gives them little space to develop. Xaviere Gauthier (2010) emphasizes why women should not keep silent but speak up. She states that:

> Women are in fact caught in a very red contradiction throughout the course of history, they have been mute and it is doubtless by virtue of this mutism that men have been able to speak and write. As long as women remain silent, they will be outside the historical process.
>
> (162)

As Rowland C. Amaefula (2019) rightly pointed out, "the beginning of women's accomplishment of heroism through protest is traceable to the renowned amazons of the classical Greek society" (6). Colonialization stifled the voices of women and entrenched a gender-oriented control mechanism that preserves despite decolonization; however, the events of colonialism inform the reconstruction of gender roles in protest drama in postcolonial Nigeria. The colonial masters at their arrival engineered the imposition of gender definition as they mostly ignored the women in their decisions and only involved the men. They turned a blind eye to the women and consulted the men even in matters that required the consultation of both genders. Florence Stratton, as cited in Ellsworth (1991), identifies that:

> Colonialism was a patriarchal order, sexist as well as racist in its ideology and practices. What these studies (of feminism under colonialism) indicate is that women's position relative to men deteriorated under colonialism. Under colonialism, then African women were subjected to the racism of colonialism and to indigenous and foreign structures of male dominance.
>
> (7)

Gloria Chuku (2009) points out women's emancipation from the political angle when she states that:

> The colonial officers regrettably failed to perceive the political contribution of women, believing that politics is a man's exclusive domain. Consequently, warrant chief's symbols of the destructive elements of indirect rule were created and women particularly suffered under the arbitrary jurisdiction.
>
> (4)

The statement above shows how women were not included in government matters in the community. The events of colonialism gave rise to the "protest" drama genre in postcolonial Nigeria. Some of these protest plays, although written by male playwrights, were dominated by feminist messages. Examples include Emeka Nwabueze's *The Dragon's Funeral* and John Pepper Clark's *The Wives Revolt*. *The Dragon's Funeral* fictionalized the Aba women's riot and the tax policy imposed on them in 1929. These women formed a women's league and commenced a riot to nullify the taxation policy imposed on them. Their protest yields its fruit when the colonial masters and the collaborators fail to extinguish or subdue the revolt. *The Wives Revolt* intercepts the oppression against women. When Okoro, the leader of the men's dictatorship in the Erhuwaren community, gives a proclamation on the sharing pattern of the money given to the community by the oil companies, the women made a protest. This was because this "money sharing pattern" had policies and ways to emasculate the women's income. We see the portrayal of feminine strength in how the women revolted against the decision. Women's identity has been denigrated by traditional practices and societal stereotypes. Breen further responded to these issues as thus:

> Only when women have remade their own view of themselves and internalized a new scale of values will they be free of that masculine super ego which through socio-cultural training, they have more or less imposed on themselves.
>
> (4)

Therefore, women's empowerment becomes necessary as it entails not only transmogrification and concrete change, but also dissemble cultural and traditional values that derogate, vilify, and abase women. As acclaimed by Matthew Umuokoro, as cited in Nwanya and Ojemudia (2014) on the issue of feminism in a patriarchal society:

> ...for the African woman, female empowerment is seen neither as a negation or denial of the fundamental attributes of womanhood, nor the abdication of obvious natural and cultural responsibilities. The goals and objective of women empowerment are meant to be conscientiously pursued within the broad context of womanly dignity and social responsibility.

At the midpoint of Alice Walker's womanist theory is the concern for women and their role in their immediate surroundings and more global environment. Walker explains a womanist as a "black feminist or feminist of color" who loves other women nonsexually; appreciates and prefers women's culture, women's emotional flexibility, and women's strength; and is committed to "survival and wholeness of entire people, male and female" (Walker 1983). In Nwaozuzu's *Ebibi*, priorities are given to collective emancipation over individual choices and desires, but in *Ajari*, the reverse is the case. Adopting qualitative and comparative analytical approaches as its methodology, the need to compare the representations of women in both drama texts becomes imperative. At this juncture, the study moves to introduce the women characters, and their roles and development that clearly define the tenets of African women and their struggles before delving properly into the business of examining the playwright's contradictory representations of women.

Characterization of Selected Women Characters in *Ebibi* and *Ajari*

Okiki: She is the protagonist and the heroine of the play. She is a 20-year-old university undergraduate who was married off to the priest of Ebibi in accordance with the customs and traditions of her people. She is also the former fiancée and love interest of Obiudo, the king's son, who is an accountant. Her family fought tooth and nail with the help of Obiudo as they refused to give her out to be married to the priest of Ebibi. Threatened to be ostracized with his family from the village, her father Ogbuefi Idume tricks her into coming back to the village where she is forced to marry the priest of Ebibi, while Obiudo is told to give up his feelings for her and find another girl. One year later, as Ebibi makes preparations to take another virgin bride, Obiudo prepares to fly Okiki out of the country in order to save her from this hideous tradition. The success of this plan is disturbed when Ebibi chooses Obiudo's only sister as his next bride. Okiki in order to stop this tradition kills the priest of Ebibi and kills herself.

Lolo Obiaku: She is the wife of Igwe Echeodo and the mother of Prince Obiudo and Princess Obianuju. She is a typical example of a submissive wife who would do anything to please her husband and the community. Even though she tries to see reasons with the women right representatives on the abolition of Ebibi, her loyalty to her husband makes her think of his reaction first and that of the villagers too.

Obianuju: She is Igwe Echeodo and Lolo Obiaku's daughter, who had recently completed her studies in London and is back to serve her father's land as a qualified lawyer, a solicitor of the supreme court of the country. On the day of her arrival in the village, Ebibi chooses her as his next bride. Her parents fight to make sure she is not given to Ebibi. Eventually, when Obianuju arrives at the village, she tries to put a stop to the tradition by inviting soldiers to her aid. When the elders and villagers hear the soldiers have been invited, everybody takes to their heels.

Ajarinwanyi: She is the antagonist of the play. She is the wife of Abaliebuka the brave, mother of Otunwa and stepmother to Odinchezo. She is a nefarious conniving schemer, who is not afraid of any man, not even the mischievous medicine man Ogirisi. Other characters in the play like Ugebedi Ezealamba's wife and an elder Chimereze are not ignorant of her devices as they both suspect she may have a hand in with what was going on in the village. Ajari's sole ambition is to make her husband the next Onowu of the village, and she would go to any length to make sure she installs him even at the cost of her life. Ajari visits a powerful deity Izugbe Dike and vows to be the deity's slave if the deity helps her in making her husband Onowu. The deity promises to help her but warns her about letting her ambition ruin her. She invites Igunkwu, a native doctor in the village to her house, to prepare a charm for her husband, kills him, and uses his head to concoct the preparation of the charm. She manipulates and hypnotizes her kinsman Mkpisi and the prince Akwakata into doing her bidding. She also tries to sell her stepdaughter Odinchezo into the hands of head hunters. In the end, she achieves her goal of installing her husband as Onowu before she confesses her wrongdoings, falls down on the floor, and dies.

Odinchezo: She is the daughter of Abaliebuka the great and stepdaughter to Ajari. She looks out for the good of the family, a promoter of peace, as portrayed in the text. When Ajari confronts and abuses Ogirisi, the medicine man, Odinchezo goes to plead with him and ask for forgiveness on behalf of her stepmother. Ogirisi gives her a charm that would protect her father which, unknown to her, will kill him. Ajari decides to sell her off to head hunters because she does not join her in her evil scheming. The head hunters took pity on her and tied her to a tree for wild beasts to devour but the prince found her and helped her escape. Another woman in the play who played a very important role, though in the background, is Ugegbedi.

Ugegbedi: She is Ezealamba Ejiofor's wife, the Lolo, and the mother of Prince Akwakata. She notices the changes in Akwakata when he comes back from Abaliebuka's house and she suspects that Ajari must have something to do with it. She eventually visits Ogirisi in his shrine to get a charm that would cure her son of the supposed aliment and, in turn, promises to make Ogirisi the next Onowu.

Analysis of the Portrayal of Women in *Ebibi* and *Ajari*

Nelson Graburn (2008) postulates that "tradition was the name given to those cultural features which in situation of change, were to be handed on, thought about, preserved and not lost". In other words, traditions are symbols, stories, and memories that can give both identity and status. In *Ebibi*, the playwright, Uche Nwaozuzu, uses this story to confront a long-held tradition imposed on the people of Umuidem. This tradition, according to Igwe Echeodo, is a legend which has even restricted Christianity and western civilization. He goes ahead to add that:

IGWE: A deity that was brought to these parts in the dim distant past by the smallest village in this town, out of fear that the other bigger villages were going to subjugate them. Legend has it that when this people brought Ebibi, a great plague befell Umuidem. We went to Ibiniukpabi, and it was revealed that the only way to forestall further calamity was to give Ebibi a virgin girl…So my friend, that was how it started. We gave Ebibi a virgin and surprisingly, the plague abated. Ever since then, four villages that make up Umuidem have been giving Ebibi one virgin girl every year (24).

This was the origin and history of how the Ebibi tradition came into the village. The playwright develops female characters that are left at the mercy of tradition in a patriarchal society. Florence Ebila (2015) states that "in a typical African traditional setting, the definition of a proper woman is influenced by socio cultural and patriarchal ideologies that construct the ideal African woman as the docile one who does not question male authority". As opposed to the above assertion, in *Ebibi*, the playwright presented other women representing women in a wider spectrum, Onie, Hope, and Iruka, representatives of the women's rights advocate in the local chapter who have visited Igwe Echeodo in his palace regarding the Ebibi tradition and its abolishment. Although their visit could not yield instant fruit as the Igwe insists that he cannot abolish a long-standing tradition of his forefathers on his own, it was a bold step in the right direction of emancipation.

Okiki is a young girl aged 20 whose dreams and aspirations are cut short by a long-held custom and traditions of her community. Her academic dreams and social life are put on hold immediately after Ebibi chooses her as a bride. She is not given the privilege to choose who to get married to as tradition has already handpicked a ready husband for her. When she puts up resistance against this tradition by following Obiudo to the city, her family, unknown to her, is threatened to be ostracized. With her father's conviction, she returns to the village where she is bundled and married off to the priest of Ebibi. She remembers and narrates the ordeal as thus:

Okiki: Just like last year when I was chosen. How time flies…do you remember how my father fought for my freedom? How he pleaded with your father to spare me?
Obiudo: Yes, I remember.
Okiki: Do you remember how he threatened my father with ostracism if he invited the police to look into the affair?
Obiudo: I remember Okiki. Even after I went and reported to the police myself, the divisional police officer told me that it was a local matter to be settled in the traditional way.
Okiki: Settle they did. They gave me to the priest of Ebibi to be his virgin bride… (10–11).

It is evident from the above how institutions foster some negative traditions against women under the guise that it is a traditional affair and should be settled traditionally, or turn a blind eye to some harmful traditional and social practices against women in the name of tradition.

Eventually, Okiki decides to take her destiny into her hands to achieve the freedom she so desires, even if it means paying with her life. She kills the chief priest and equally stabs herself. By killing the priest, she emancipates not only herself but the other women from the traditional bondage.

Just like Okiki, Lolo Obiaku is another woman character whose hands are traditionally tied. She is torn between remaining a faithful and loyal wife to her husband and the village at large and doing something about changing the tradition. But the narrative changes when her daughter Obianuju is chosen to be a bride to Ebibi. She is filled with anxiety as she finds ways to stop her daughter from being married off to Ebibi. But when her husband resolves to let tradition take its course, she is devastated and still remains hands-tied as she cannot go against her husband's wishes. But we see her blossom in joy towards the end of the play as her daughter, Obianuju, shows up to put a stop to the tradition. Obianuju is another character that oozes a high level of confidence and exhibits attitudes of a fearless and courageous woman. She decides without informing anyone to put a stop to the barbaric tradition by calling on the help of a Brigade commander who is a family friend. She disperses the crowd of villagers by telling them she has invited soldiers to the community. In the characters of Okike and Obianuju, we see fearlessness and determination to rewrite histories and place women in the right perspectives as legal members of the society who partake in decision-making, especially in matters that concern them and not being regarded as things without identity. Like the nameless young bride in Soyinka's *Death and the King's Horseman*, not much is known about the other six wives of Ebibi. In fact, we do not even know their names. The only time they appear in the play, they match in a procession as part of the chief priest's acolytes to pluck the scared feathers that would be presented to the family of the chosen bride.

In *Ajari*, the playwright builds a woman who is powerful, determined, and strong in the character of Ajarinwanyi, who is the antagonist in the play, the wife of Abaliebuka the brave hunter. She is determined to install her husband as the next Onowu of the Alamba kingdom, no matter what it takes. Her determination takes her to Izugbe Dike, the strongest *dibia* in the community to find a means of achieving her aim of making her husband the Onowu.

Ajari: I have come to you wise one. I have made my vow and ready to hold onto it.
Izugbe: Very well. Remember, human life is very sacred. If you take any, you are bound to give yours in return.
Ajari: Yes Izugbe Dike.
Izugbe: I can see that you are very determined, that is why I counsel you to invoke a medium made of herbs, roots and animal not human and I shall always be there for you.
Ajari: I promise to do all these things wise one, just help me make my husband the Onowu of this land and I shall be a slave to you (6).

Ajari is so powerful and fearless that she had to use the *dibia* that prepared the charm for her and gave the instruction that the most potent way to activate the charm is to sacrifice a human being and sprinkle the blood on the medicine pot which he (the *dibia*) already handed over to her. She kills the *dibia* to use his head and make her charm the most potent.

Otunwa: *(Frightened)* Oh mother you have killed him, he is dead, you know he is a medicine man... You know he is a medicine man.
Ajari: And that is why he has to die, so that we can use his head for the medicine pot. The head of a great medicine man would be the most potent. So he told me... (16).

She is also a nefarious schemer who craftily weaves her net to ensnare as many as would fall for her tricks. She manipulates her kinsman Mkpisi into looking into the pot, hence turning him into her minion. Her ambitions become so big that they made her greedy. She not only wanted to make her husband the Onowu, but she also had other dubious plans, including marrying her daughter off to the Prince of Alamba so that she could become the Queen Mother.

Otunwa, just like her mother Ajarinwanyi, is a conniving schemer. As Igbo adage says, *Agwọ aghaghị imụta ihe toro ogologo* (A snake will always give birth to something that is long). She conceals every evil that her mother commits. A daughter of a lion is also a lion, Otunwa helps her mother kill Igunkwu, another medicine man, and hide his body. She is also aware that her mother plans to kidnap and sell her step-sister Odinchezo to head hunters. Even though she feels a little bit sorry at first, after her mother rebuffs her, she does not stop the evil from taking place.

Ajari is not intimidated by anyone and knows how to hold her own. She talks to the men as she pleases and is not afraid of any intimidation whatsoever. She puts Odikpo straight when he tries to threaten her husband, Abaliebuka.

Odikpo: You can't be serious. I will deal with that hunter of rats and rabbits… that wretched village charlatan. Look let me tell you, you and your husband are treading on dangerous ground.

Ajari: You cannot do anything Odikpo. I have done more than exchange words with effeminate men like you. My hands have done mightier things on greater men than you and can still do more because I am Izugbe. Now state your business to this house and leave (50).

There is also another woman character, Ugegbedi, who just like Ajarinwanyi seeks to protect what is hers. Ugegbedi notices the change in her son after he pays a visit to the household of Abaliebuka. Like a concerned mother, she takes precautionary measures to protect her son from the evil claws of Ajarinwanyi against her husband's wishes to do nothing for the time being. She consults Ogirisi, a medicine man, to unravel the mystery behind her son's sudden bewitchment.

Ogirisi: Consider it done Lolo! I am Ogirisi Ngidingi, the man who meditates between men and spirit. I will bring your son back. I will defeat Ajarinwanyi. I have your word for it?

Ugegbedi: You have my word, Ogirsi. I am the queen; I will be with my lord Ezealamba when the stool will be brought out and it will be yours to receive (58).

Odinchezo is the only woman character in the text that both man and gods speak kindly of. From the beginning of the play, Izugbe, the deity, warns Ajarinwanyi to love her stepdaughter and do her no harm as her melodious voice can withstand even the medicine pot. She is a child of goodwill and cannot condone any evil of any kind:

Izugbe: Let me repeat again, love your step daughter Odinchezo. She is a prodigy. In her voice, in the songs she sings are locked potent powers that abhor evil but love goodness. Her voice can with stand any evil ordeal or intentions.

Ajari: And even the power of the medicine pot?

Izugbe: Yes, even the power of the medicine pot. Desist from harming her, she is a child of goodwill... (8).

Ogirisi considers her a sensible child who is in no way like her stepmother. Even Ugebedi agrees she has a dainty voice that has rattled the core of her heart. She is the only person who, because of her goodwill and the purity of her heart, is able to withstand Ajari and her evil devices. Even when she is kidnapped, the spirit of good fortune smiles at her and she is rescued by Prince Akwakata.

Comparative Analysis of the Contradictory Representations of Women in *Ebibi* and *Ajari*

In Uche Nwaozuzu's *Ebibi* and *Ajari*, we see a clear portrayal of women in both negative and positive light. We see the women in the light of what the society expects of them, what their husbands expect of them, and what they expect for themselves. The playwright uses both plays to show how women in a patriarchal society can decide to either ruin or make themselves. Both plays are set in an African environment, the Igbo land to be precise. Perhaps unconsciously, the playwright portrays strong bread kind of women characters who take up tasks without the influence or persuasion of anyone.

Phenomenal women like Okike, Ajarinwanyi, Oni, Hope, Obianuju, Ugegbedi, and Obiaku in the drama texts figure out what they want to achieve and go for it. They set to demystify what Lerner (1987) refers to as the unnatural and nonbiological dominance over women, but the product of historical development which she argues can also be ended by the historical process. This is what the abovementioned women have achieved in one way or the other in both plays. In *Ebibi*, the playwright uses the character of Okiki to give an insight on how tradition can make women hapless and helpless but, at a greater level, projects women who achieved their desires of rewriting the history even when their lives were the prize for the emancipation of the generation of women yet to come. Okiki's dreams and aspirations are cut short the moment Ebibi chooses her to be his bride, but embarking on that journey gives her the platform to carry out a task that every member of the community felt was an impossible mission. Not only does the tradition render her helpless, but the patriarchal or social construct wearing the lens of patriarchy, whose head is the Igwe, joins to arm-twist her father into giving his daughter away.

Becoming the wife of Ebibi and his favourite avails Okike the opportunity of getting sufficient information about the laws and traditions of the land. Armed with this information, she seeks freedom. She decides to make a change and, if necessary, pay the ultimate price with her life. She decides to not be like the other wives in Ebibi's harem. The playwright uses the characters of Dr Onie, Hope, and Iruka to speak out on how the lives of these women have been affected negatively by tradition.

However, their pleas fall on deaf ears as the Igwe blatantly ignores them, until the onus falls on him to give his own daughter away and let tradition prevail. He even tries to thwart tradition to protect his daughter's interest, all to no avail. He brings someone else who would impersonate his daughter and this plan equally backfires and everything goes haywire. This is until Okiki pays the ultimate price of killing the chief priest and herself. By killing the priest, she attains the freedom of the other women both for the past and the future and by killing herself she breaks out of the traditional bondage and gets the freedom she so desires even if it means sojourning to the other realm.

In *Ajari*, the narrative is different as the playwright builds the character of Ajari as a phenomenal force to reckon with. He uses her to show that women could be powerful, wicked and manipulative achievers if they set their minds to what they want. Ajari, in contrast to Okiki, knows what she wants from the beginning of the play. She seeks to install her husband as the Onowu of the kingdom of Alamba and she would stop at nothing until she achieves her aim. She takes the bull by the horns and moves heaven and earth to achieve her aim.

Ajari: (*Seemingly possessed*) No! I can't, I cannot die (*she gets up*). Whoever you may be, I must leave to see my husband's glory. I will leave to be the mother of the queen and the mother in-law of the king. I am your servant Izugbe Dike, you cannot kill your own. (56).

All the women in *Ajari* are proactive and sometimes do not need the men to dictate most of their decisions. Ajari tells her husband of all the necessary preparations she has made towards his successful instalment but Abali warns her to beware not to be faster than the gods, or try to twist the hands of nature. Yet she goes behind his back to do what she pleases:

Ajari: Oh, gods of our forefathers. Oh Izugbe, god of the harvest... Oh most ungrateful husband. Look at my ambition melting like the harmattan oil and my heart pierced with sorrow. The Odu stool must come to this house and Abaliebuka my husband will be the new Onowu... (29).

The playwright uses the names of the characters as metaphorical innuendos to convey special image meaning. Ajarinwanyi means a proactive woman, a woman who acts as though she were a man, and the character of Ajari embodies all of this. Just like Otunwa connotes, she is the only child of her mother. The name Odinchezo in English means "will it be forgotten?" and we cannot forget in a hurry how both god and man seem to be in awe of the good-willed girl. "Ebibi" in Igbo language means to pass a proclamation or a declaration. For instance, when a person's present life is bad, he or she would pass an "Ebibi" (a strong claim of affirmation) employing the next life to be better than the previous one. Put in another definition, Ebibi could also mean to destroy or annihilate.

Conclusion

The contradictory representations of women in African drama are quite broad as they relate to women of all ages. Women, as seen in this work, have been portrayed both in negative and positive lights by some Nigerian playwrights. Uche Nwaozuzu used his two plays *Ebibi* and *Ajari* to expound appropriately the different perspectives and perceptions on the representation and portrayal of women in African drama. In *Ebibi*, light is thrown on the objectification and inhumane treatment of women in Umuidem village. Okiki, the protagonist, however, emancipates herself when she confronts an old tradition imposed on the people by their ancestors. She decides to become her generational agent of change by taking the decision to killing the old chief priest and courageously killing herself too, in order to end the outrageous long age-held tradition. This action of hers makes the Igwe's daughter acknowledge her as "brave" and a true hero. It also shows self-evidently that women can step up against male dominance in the society and that since tradition was made by men, it could also be changed by men. This, however, is in complete contrast with *"Ajari"* where we see a woman (Ajari) already taking the front seat at the helm of affairs. She contends with her male counterparts and makes sure they bend to her will. The character of the woman Ajari is portrayed in a negative light as she is the antagonist of the play. The playwright creatively shows us the contrasting image of women using the characters of Okiki and Ajari.

References

Achebe, C. (1958) *Things Fall Apart*: USA: Penguin Classics.
Achebe, N. (2011) *The Female King of Colonial Nigeria*: Indiana University Press.
Adichie, C. N. (2009) *Danger of a single story* http://www.ted.com/talks/chimamanda-adiche-the-danger-of-a-single-story accessed 7th October, 2021.
Amaefula, R. C. (2019) "Gender Performance, Fluid Identities and Protest in Tess Onwueme's *Then She Said It*". *Journal of Language and Cultural Education* 7(1), 118–138.
Azunwo, E. E. and Ejiro, K. O. (2015) "Female Dramatists, Distinction and The Nigerian Society: An Examination of Zulu Sofola ad Tess Onwueme's Select Plays". *Journal of African studies* 4(1), 102–105.
Breen, Jennifer. (1990) *In Her Own Write: Twentieth Century Women's Fiction*. London: Macmillan.
Chitauro-Mawema, M. (2006) Gender sensitivity in shona language use: a lexicography and corpus-based study of words in context. Zimbabwe: ALLEX project.
Chuku, G. (2009) "Igbo Women and Political Participation in Nigeria, 1800s–2005". *The International Journal of African Historical Studies*, 42(1), 81–103.
Chukwuma, Helen. (1994) *Feminism in African Literature: Essay on criticism*. Ibadan: Heinemann Educational Books Nigeria (HEBN).
Clark, J. P. (1991) *Wives Revolt*, Ibadan: University Press Plc.
Damascene, Jean. (2019) *The Impact of Women oppression on the societal destruction*. A case study of Ijem U. Blessing and Agbo I. Isaiah. "Language and Gender Representation in Chinua Achebe's *Things Fall Apart*."
Ebila, Florence. (2015) "A proper woman in the African tradition: The construction of gender and Nationalism in Wangari Maathai's autobiography Unbowed". *Tydskrif Vir Letterkunde*. 52(1), 109–121.
Ellsworth, Kirstin Lynne (1991) "Buchi Emecheta: A Novelist's Image of Nigerian Women". *Undergraduate Honors Thesis Collection* https://digitalcommons.butler.edu/ugtheses/
Fwangyil, Gloria Ada (2012) "Cradle to Grave: An Analysis of Female oppression in Nawal El Saadawi's at point zero". *An International Journal of Language, Literature and Gender Studies* 1(1), 76–79.
Eze, Godstime and Agu, Dilichukwu (2023) "Women Are Not Marginalized in Igboland: A Critical Interpretation of Uche Nwaozuzu's *Ajari*." *Indiana Journal of Humanities and Social Sciences*, 4(1), 5–11.
Eze, Godstime (2019) "Women in Conflict Management: A Review of the Female Characters in Nwabueze's *The Dragon's Funeral* and Irobi's *Nwokedi*". *Ikenga: International Journal of Institute of African Studies* 20(1), 296–311.
Graburn, Nelson. (2008) "What Is Tradition"? *An article in museum Anthropology*, 2008.
Gauthier, Xaviere (2010) *Women of Consequences: Heroines who Shaped the World*. New York: Rizzoli International Publications, 256.
Hornby, A. S. (2015) *Oxford Advanced Learner's Dictionary of Current English*. 7th Edition. London: Oxford University Press.
Lerner, Gerda. (1987) *The Creation of Patriarchy*. London: Oxford University Press, 368
Longley, R. (2006) "Womanist: Definition and Examples". http://www.thoughtco.com/womanist-feminism-definition Accessed 11 September, 2022.
Makama, Godiya Allanana. (2013) "Patriarchy and Gender Inequality in Nigeria: The way Forward". *European Scientific Journal* 9(17). 57–69.
McNabb, D. E. (2009) *Research Method for Political Science: Qualitative and Quantitative Methods*. New Delhi: PHL Learning Private Limited.
Methuselah, S. (2010) "Women's Playwright and Female Imaging in Nigerian Literary Drama: An Overview". *Journal of The Nigerian English studies Association* 13(2), 102–105.

Nnolim, Charles. (2009) *Issues in African Literature*. Yenagoa: Treasure Resource Communication Limited.
Nwabueze, Emeka. (2013) *Research Methods: An Integrated Approach*. 2nd Edition. Enugu: ABIC.
Nwabueze, Emeka (2011) *A Parliament of Vultures*. Enugu: ABIC Books and Equipment Ltd.
Nwabueze, Emeka (2005) *The Dragon's Funeral*. Enugu: ABIC Books and Equipment Ltd.
Nwanya, Agatha Njideka and Ojemudia, C. Chris. (2014) "Gender and Creativity: The Contribution of Nigerian Female Writers". *Global Journal of Art Humanities and Social Sciences* 2(1), 65–67.
Nwaozuzu, Chinemere Uche (2021) *Ajari*. Enugu: CNC Publication.
Nwaozuzu, Chinemere Uche (2020) *Ebibi*. Enugu: CNC Publications.
Oyedepo, Stella. (2002) *Rebellion of the Bumpy-Chested*. Accra, Ghana: Delstar Publishers.
Saadawi (2012) "Woman at Point Zero". *An International Journal of Language, Literature and Gender Studies* 1(1), 98–99.
Salami, Irene Isoken (2003) *More Than Dancing*. Ibadan Saniez Publications.
Solberg, Rolf (1983) "The woman of Black Africa, Buchi Emecheta: The Woman's Voice in the New Nigerian Novel". *English Studies* 64(3), 247–262, DOI: 10.1080/00138388308598254
Walker, Alice. (1983) Womanist Theory. https://www.vanderbilt.edu/olli/classmaterials/Alice_Walkers_Womanist_Trope.pdf Accessed 11 November, 2023.
Wole, Soyinka (1975) *Death and the King's Horseman*. London: Methuen.
Wole, Soyinka (1967) *Kongi's Harvest*. London: Oxford University Press.
Wole, Soyinka (1973) *The Jero plays*. London: Methuen Press.
Yeseibo, John Ebimobowei. (2013) "Portrayal of Women in Male Authored Plays in Nigeria". *Journal of Philosophy, Culture and Religion* 1, 157–165.

SECTION 3

African Women Navigating Multiple Pandemics and Climate Change

6
WOMEN, SPIRITUALITY/ RELIGION, AND PANDEMICS IN AFRICA

Eunice Kamaara

Introduction

In 2012, Phillips, Craig, and Dean recorded the song, *Tell Your Heart to Beat Again*. Later in 2014, American singer, Dean (Danny Gokey), recorded it in his studio album, *Hope in Front of Me*. In 2016, Gokey released it as a single and it rose to second position on the Billboard Christian Songs chart. Gokey's song was inspired by the death of his wife, Sophia Martinez. Sophia died while having a heart surgery in 2009. Reeling from the loss of his wife, fear engulfed him and he could not let go of his wife. Suffering from depression and insomnia due to his doubts about God's love, Gokey experienced profound sorrow and pain. Unaware of her imminent death, Sophia had pleaded with Gokey and made him promise her that he would try out American Idol because she was convinced that he was excellent at singing. Gokey had obliged and registered for American Idol, only for Sophia to die a month before the event. Therefore, in spite of his deep sorrow, he tried it out only to fulfil his promise to his late wife. He made it to the top 50. The rest is history.

Come 2016 and Gokey was inspired to release the song by another real-life story. The story involves a sick woman, Ms Johnson, an Ohio-based Pastor and a heart surgeon. As with the initial purpose of the song, the song would inspire hope in the midst of deep pain, sorrow, and hurt to support individuals to overcome their challenges, let go of their past, and embrace new beginnings. This has parallels to the story of women in Africa in the context of COVID-19. In the midst of profound pain and sorrow occasioned by a pandemic that was sweeping through the continent with no cure, a disease which dictated conditions that were impossible to keep (Nderitu and Kamaara, 2020), rather than sink into hopelessness, women turned to religion/spirituality for resilience, resourcefulness (innovation), and strength. Religion/spirituality, presented as prayer and positive self-talk, was often expressed through music. Often this was combined with sharing and trying out different complementary home therapies.

Spirituality is, in this context, defined as the invisible component of human reality that relates to belonging (not what belongs to humans but what humans belong to) and interconnectedness (Rosmarin et al., 2021), and therefore relationships in the context of seeking meaning in life events. It is borne out of the recognition that humans are limited and generally lack control over life. Spirituality relates to efforts to respond to ultimate questions of human existence related to identity, purpose, and destiny of human persons. Spirituality emerges most strongly in moments of crisis when humans recognize their limitations and lack of control. This perspective of spirituality concurs with that expressed by Mwenda Ntarangwi. He notes that spirituality refers to

> … that realm of our consciousness as humans that says there is something greater than us in the world which defines or orders life. I argue that when confronted with unknown phenomena people turn to this knowledge, this spirituality, however diverse it is, in order to make sense of that unknown.
>
> (Ntarangwi, 2021: 15–16)

Many scenarios create crises that render humans powerless. Among these are pandemics or communicable diseases. The worst of pandemics cross borders, leaving trails of mortalities and morbidities to become epidemics. Pandemics have existed since time immemorial and as long as there were national borders, there were epidemics. The earliest recorded epidemic (suspected to be typhoid fever) occurred in 430 BCE during the Peloponnesian War and swept across Greece, Libya, Ethiopia, and Egypt killing two-thirds of the population in these countries. The latest is the COVID-19 pandemic, which has been recorded in nearly all countries of the world. In between the two have been many pandemics, the worst of which is believed to be the first and the second bubonic plagues that killed 26% and over 33% of the world's population, respectively. Historical experience suggests that pandemics are gendered in terms of causes, methods of spread, and impact, and therefore any analysis of the phenomenon should be done with a gender lens for effective preparedness and response (Simba & Ngocobo, 2020).

Initial gender analysis of COVID-19 indicated that more men than women were being infected and more men than women succumbed to the disease (Global Health, 2020). However, in-depth analysis suggested that while this remained true, women were suffering much more from the impacts of the pandemic than men (Maula, 2021; UNFPA, 2021; Wenham et al., 2020). For example, gender-based violence, including sexual violence against females, increased exponentially and women were carrying the burden of care for COVID-19 victims. Women had to intensively care for their fathers, husbands, and sons alongside their female relatives with occasional fatalities. Cumulatively, COVID-19 affected women more than it affected men. At its height, African women suffered the brunt of the pandemic, as they watched devastating news of people in Europe and America dying of COVID-19 in highly equipped intensive care units; COVID-19 presented an enormous crisis. If those with bulging economic muscle, technological biomedical infrastructure, and expertise were dying as portrayed in both print and electronic media, what chances did women in resource-poor settings have, who could not afford masks and whose only choice was between staying home to die of hunger and going out to work and get infected with COVID-19? Religion/spirituality came in handy. Unlike what had been predicted, Africa registered relatively few cases of COVID-19 deaths in spite of the general infeasibility of "international best practices" (Nderitu & Kamaara, 2020).

In this chapter, I present preliminary findings on the experiences of women who were infected with COVID-19 and/or their significant others who were infected and/or died of COVID-19 in relation to their response to and coping with the situation. How did they build their resilience and what resourcefulness/innovations supported their response to provide them with strength? From these findings, I draw inferences on how women as religious/

spiritual actors may be equipped to prepare for future pandemics. Before presenting the findings, I present the methods used in the study in the following section.

Methods

From a constructionist philosophical approach, I used a lived experience approach to explore how diverse women experienced and responded to their own COVID-19 infection as well as infection and/or death from COVID-19 of their significant others (children or husbands). Six women were purposively selected based on their socio-demographic characteristics and on their adverse experiences with COVID-19. They were interviewed in depth using an unstructured interview schedule and consequently engaged through focus group discussions (FGDs) lasting close to two hours. All interviews were recorded with written informed consent from each of the participants. Except for one interview where the participants could not speak in English, all interviews were conducted in English. For the exception, data were collected in Kikuyu, one of the indigenous languages in Kenya. All data were transcribed (and the one in Kikuyu translated into English) before analysis. Electronic thematic data management and analysis with the support of NVivo software was done. This was complemented with manual analysis to capture contextual and members' meanings. Data were coded using NVivo codes.

Findings from one-on-one in-depth interviews are reported in the form of cases using verbatim reports after which the key findings are discussed alongside those from data collected through FGD. From this, I draw out lessons on building individual and group solidarity, resourcefulness, and resilience in preparation for future epidemics.

Following the in-depth oral interviews, two FGDs were conducted. Each group had six women with age ranges 23–75. The sample population was accessed through snowballing guided by gender and intersectionality (Shield, 2008) and also critical diverse literacy theory (Steyn, 2015). This involved identifying one woman whose husband had died of COVID-19 and requesting her to lead to another woman whose husband was reported as having died or survived after COVID-19 infection. Those who fit into the social-demographic characteristics were recruited to participate in the FGDs. Purposive selection ensured the inclusion of Christians, Muslims, African indigenous, and at least one nonaffiliated to any religion into each of the groups.

A FGD guide informed by the findings of the in-depth oral interviews was used to run the FGDs. Data collected using FGDs were transcribed, translated, coded, and categorized thematically using NVivo as well as analytic codes. Findings from the two FGDs are reported in prose with occasional voices from the groups. Thereafter, the different findings are merged and discussed as we draw lessons for preparedness for future pandemics.

Findings in Cases

This section will present six cases, capturing their social and demographic information, their experiences of COVID-19 infection (their infection and/or death of their husbands and/or children), and their responses to prevent or manage infection, as well as their coping strategies.

In total, 18 women of different socio-demographic characteristics were interviewed: age (24–88); rural and urban; rich and poor; of different religious and educational backgrounds (Christian, Muslim, African indigenous religion, and nonaffiliated). Out of the six women whose cases are presented below, five reported at the time of the interview that they were initially married but one was widowed well before COVID-19 while the other three were widowed by COVID-19. One was single. Three of the six women experienced at least three of the symptoms that were associated with COVID-19 to different levels of severity and suspected that they were infected with COVID-19. However, only two of them were diagnosed through testing and admitted to hospital settings. For all six women, their husbands or/and sons tested positive for COVID-19 suffering various symptoms to different levels of severity, and some were admitted in isolation in hospital settings.

Box 6.1   The Case of Ms U

Miss U is a 65-year-old female from central Kenya. She is a housewife and a small-scale farmer. She lives with her seven children (one son and six daughters) and with five grandchildren. Four of the children work in Nairobi, commuting daily from her house. Her husband was a long-distance driver and was often home for two or three days, often in the middle of the week when there was not a lot of demand for travel. But even on those three days, he was home for short periods, mostly a few hours in the night—arriving late in the evening and leaving early the following day.

Ms U is a strong practicing Roman Catholic Christian. She describes herself as a prayerful person who believes in God's provision and protection in all situations. Her conversation with me confirms this as it is punctuated by a reference to God as the source of all good things. Below is an extract from our conversation that is most relevant to this chapter.

When COVID *broke out in Kenya in 2020, my family was enjoying life as usual. We first heard about* COVID-19 *on TV in early 2020. There were reports that a disease that was spread from bats and rats was killing people very quickly in China and was spreading quickly to other countries. …We didn't think much about this news. We dismissed this as a Chinese problem and joked that this was because Chinese eat anything, including rodents like rats. None of the Kenyan people eat rodents.*

… then the government reported that a young woman coming from the US had arrived in the country with the disease and the government was looking for her to isolate her. But she had already mixed with people. The government found the woman and isolated her, but in a few weeks, there were more and more cases reported… When the cases were too much, the government closed travel and people were ordered to stay at home. For us in the village, this was not for us. We assumed that this was a disease of town.

… another man who is a son of my friend and works in Mombasa came home. In two days, he died. We were told by my friend that this man came home feeling unwell. He was coughing and shivering. They thought it was a cold but before they could even think of taking him to hospital, he was unable to breathe and by the time they took him to hospital it was too late. He died. …

The government sent policemen to the home with some doctors and they picked everybody in the home for testing. But none of the people had COVID. *Then came the burial. There were policemen all over and people wearing plastic overalls were in charge. They ordered that everyone stay away from the body as they collected it from the car they had come with and took it straight to the grave. The body was all covered up in a big black plastic chapter bag. They threw the body of the man into the grave and quickly put the soil to bury him.* (Ughh! She sighs). *The family was not allowed anywhere near. My friend, the mother of the man, could not be consoled. She screamed and tossed herself to the ground while her husband and other relatives watched helplessly. (Ughh! sighs). The whole village came out to watch this event but from a distance because the police and the men in plastic overalls looked very scary…. there were rumors that the family was also infected and would pass on* COVID *to other people if people went near. From where we stood, I prayed hard for this woman that God would console her. I believed that God would help her.*

… when we in the village realized that COVID *was real. And it was dangerous. It would kill. We were all very scared. And we were shocked that the men had thrown the body into the grave so badly. That man was not buried. He was thrown away, which is very bad. And as soon as he was buried, everybody left and the family was left to mourn lone. It was so sad.*

… we went home, my husband and I discussed the issue with my husband who was now home throughout the day because the government had locked the country. My husband said he did not believe in COVID *and that the man must have had another disease. He said European travelers may be putting stuff in people's hands and in the air to get some kind of poisoning.*

… I requested my husband to take me to visit my friend and console her now that people were keeping away…. we went late in the evening to avoid people seeing us to see my friend whose son had died. When we went there we prayed with her and I sang a song that she loves very much, telling her not to be discouraged and that God knows everything. Otherwise, we just sat there…. just to show them we were standing with them. Then we prayed and left.

… few months later, now in early 2021, my husband who had resumed his transport business came home one late Wednesday. He said he was feeling tired and did not want to eat. He went straight to bed. He was coughing a little so I made some concoction (hot lemon water mixed with honey, garlic, and ginger). We use this to fight the common cold. And it works. …. He took a big cup of this and then we slept. As usual, he woke up very early. He used not to take breakfast so after taking a bath, he took his car keys and went out. I assumed he had gone…. was just beginning to feel sleepy when one of my children knocked at my door and said her dad was not well. She said he was trying to open the car door but he wasn't succeeding. By the time I went out to see, he was sitting down on the ground by the car. I panicked. I ran out to a neighbor who is a driver and called him to come and help…… He came and we drove my husband to the hospital. As we drove, I prayed to God to help my husband reach the hospital for help.

… my husband was saying he doesn't want to go to the hospital, and that he is ok. But we drove. When we got to the hospital, he told me he doesn't want the nurses to take blood from him. He was behaving like a small child … looking very restless. I comforted him and encouraged him that all will be well. But I noticed that the nurses were kind of avoiding us. Then it occurred to me that my husband was probably having COVID. *I was not afraid of* COVID. *I did not think I could be infected. And anyway, I couldn't just watch him or avoid him. He is my husband. I kept holding him close to my chest as we waited for the doctor to come. … I was thinking I can't desert him—it is even better we die together than I desert him.*

…. The doctor came wearing those plastic overalls that we had seen at the funeral of my friend's son. The nurses also came now wearing the same plastic clothes. They seemed so scary.

The doctor put my husband on an oxygen mask and then he and the nurses left ….. My husband now seemed comfortable and was lying peacefully on the bed. Then one of the nurses came and said my husband needed to be admitted. They led us into a ward and when my husband was now admitted,

I prayed for him, I told him he would be okay then I requested to run back home to see that the children were ok and come back immediately after.

… before I got home, I received a call from hospital… my husband had died. How? I asked God. I couldn't believe it. I didn't even continue home, I turned and returned to the hospital. … It was a difficult journey back. I actually can't remember how I found my way back. …. Back in hospital, they did not want me to see my husband…. They said he had died and they suspected it was COVID *so they were not going to allow people to see him. I told them I am not 'people'. He is my husband. …, I had been with him and insisted that I wanted to see him…. Finally, they allowed me to see the body. When I confirmed it I was him Mhhhh! and he was dead, I felt like my legs could not hold me. I told God, please God give me the courage to face this situation. That is how my husband died. In spite of rumors that he had died of* COVID, *even now (I don't think it was* COVID, *and rumors that my children and I were all sick, we prayed to God to keep us safe and to give us courage.*

People started talking behind my back to say that my children and I and all the people who interacted with my husband, including the man who helped us take him to the hospital, were all infected and were going to die, I had no option but to turn to God. …. I turned to God because God was the only place I could turn to and God is able to deal with any situation so I know he could deal with my situation. I pleaded with …. God not to bring shame to my faith and to my family…. I prayed for the protection of my children, my neighbors, and the man who helped us take my husband to the hospital, and all the people who had met or touched my husband so that they may not get sick because of their good works of helping us. There was no other trick…. I would kneel before God and pray but even when I was not kneeling, I would sing songs of praise and worship and feel very empowered, feel very strong, I would actually feel a flash of power run through my body from head to toe and I always believed that I would make it and that I was ready to face the situation. And it worked. None of us got sick. I had some bad flu and I took medicine but it never was COVID.

….I prayed to God to help me cope with the death of my husband. And God did. We buried my husband and all went well. I felt deep sorrow but I was sure God would help me cope. I kept singing praises to God to keep my children encouraged. And God is merciful. He did. None of us got sick. At some point, I felt I had a cold and feared that I was getting COVID. *…….I prayed even harder to God asking him, "if you take me who will take care of these children?" But I never showed my children that I was sick. I even went to the garden to dig while I was sick. I took many cups of the concoction every day until I felt well. God is merciful and gracious. That's my experience.*

Box 6.2 The Case of Ms V

Ms V is a 24-year-old widow. At the time, she was a volunteer teaching music at a private boarding school. She had been married for two years at the time COVID-19 struck. She was living with her husband. They had no children. She described herself as "not religious" until after her COVID-19 experience. Probed to explain what she means by "nonreligious," she said she was baptized when she was a baby but in her adult life, she had not been to church. She narrated to me her experience of COVID-19 as follows:

At first, we did not believe there was COVID-19. It seemed to be a disease in Europe, Asia, and America. It is only when schools were ordered closed and children went home that we began to take COVID seriously. ...My husband owned a pub and when bars were ordered closed, they would close people inside to show the police that they were closed but drinking continued inside the bar. When the police learnt about this, people started drinking in the lodging rooms. Then we started hearing of people we know that had been admitted in the hospital with the disease and some of them died. But we didn't know anybody that we knew who had died.

... a friend of ours called to tell me that he had taken my husband to hospital because he was not feeling well. It was about 9 pm. He added that I did not need to worry, that my husband might be late coming home but he would come home anyway. He assured me that my husband would come home later. So I stayed in bed listening to music. Although I was used to my husband coming home late, I felt that something was not right. ...... I kept calling our friend to ask how my husband was doing and he kept saying he is being observed and he will bring him home after the doctors were done. As it got later and later, I requested our friend to come and take me to the hospital to be with my husband as he was being treated. But he insisted that I wait for him at home. I kept trying to call my husband but his phone was off. When I called our friend .... later, our friend's phone was also off. I was now getting very anxious. But it was already too late for me to go to the hospital on my own. It was already 3 am. I kept calling but the phones were off...I decided to wait for morning then I went to the hospital. At some point, I realized that I didn't even know to which hospital he had been taken, but I assured myself that I would go to all the hospitals nearby.......

The trouble is that I could not sleep. I did not feel like sleeping. My mind kept wandering all over. I imagined that my husband had died in a road accident. That is what I could imagine because he left home very fine. No. I am not a religious person, I don't go to church, but on this day I prayed and asked God to forgive me for the times I had ignored him and lived like he did not exist. I prayed that in the morning I find my husband alive and well. At 4.30 am, I called my friend who lives about a kilometer from where we live. I explained to her what our friend had told me. My friend is good. She came. She came to our house immediately. She walked through the night on her own to my place. She sat with me and together we tried to call our friend who had told me about my husband being sick. His phone remained off. So was my husband's phone. .... We kept calling my husband's friends whose phone numbers we had. But none of them knew anything about my husband's sickness. My friend sat with me. She comforted me and assured me that all would be well. She asked me to pray with her for my husband. We prayed over and over again....... When it was getting a little bright, my friend called a Little Cab and we left for the nearest hospital. .....We checked with reception if a patient by the name of my husband had come in the night. There hadn't been. We were just driving out of the parking to the next hospital when our friend switched on his phone. As many messages as the number of times I had tried to call him came into my phone. "You tried calling me..." Then before I could call, he called.

.....He requested that we meet at another hospital. My friend who was with me told the driver to stop the car so that we would pray and thank God that we don't have to look everywhere. That our friend had called to direct us. She attributed this to God's doing which seemed strange to me. But I was desperate so I didn't question anything. She also prayed that we find my husband well.

... We drove to the hospital and found our friend who took us to where my husband was—in the ICU—unconscious. Our friend explained that we were not allowed to enter the ICU so we looked

through the glass. I could see one doctor and a nurse walking up and about from one cubicle to the next. They were wearing clothes that covered all their bodies and had big glass googles. I have never seen anything like this. It seemed like a dream. …. The next thing is that I felt dizzy and tried to sit to avoid falling down. The next time I woke up I was in ICU. My body was all numb and my hands were tied to the bed in white bandages around my wrists. My mouth was very very dry. I could feel something inside my mouth that was making it difficult for me to make any saliva. My throat was in pain. I could hear something ticking loudly behind my head. I tried to keep my eyes open but it was difficult. I wondered where I was. … in brief, my husband and I were in hospital in ICU for two weeks. He died. Nobody told me until I came out of ICU a week later. It was bad…. Bad bad bad! Anyway, I prayed to God to help me. My friends prayed with me. They came and stayed with me in the hospital. My husband was buried when I was still in hospital. I had come out of the ICU but was still in the general ward with oxygen. … I owe it to my female friends. They came and ensured I followed the funeral on Facebook streaming. Every time I broke down, they comforted me. They were not afraid of being infected with COVID *but we always had our masks on. …. Hey. That was tough. If it was not for God and my women friends, I was going to hit a depression. I don't know where I would be today.*

Box 6.3   The Case of Ms W

Ms W is a Muslim woman aged 50. She lives in Mombasa Kenya. Her husband used to live with her and was a headmaster. She and her husband have two children who were both in college when corona got to Kenya. She is a housewife. She used to make table clothes for a living but now sells (in) a shop. Below is her experience of the coronavirus as she narrated it:

Corona *was terrible…. I have no idea who between me and my husband infected the other or even how we were infected in the first place. We just got sick almost at the same time. I was the first to tell my husband that I was feeling tired for nothing and my head was very painful… He said that he too was feeling tired. He attributed his state to staying idle all day when he was used to a strict work schedule…. The following morning, I woke up feeling normal and did not remember that I slept feeling unwell. I started doing my household chores. Then I realized that my husband was still in bed, which is unusual… When I went to check on him, I found he had vomited by the bed side and was sweating a lot. I threw the bedsheet off his body and tried to fan him as I shook him and asked him how he was feeling and if he was well. He tried to speak but words were not coming out. He gestured that he needed a glass of water. I quickly brought him water, which he quickly drank. Then he seemed to feel better. He could not talk. … he was feeling very bad and needed to get to the hospital immediately. I called the school driver and we drove my husband to the hospital. Up to this point, I had not even thought about Corona. … but when we reached the hospital, I saw doctors and nurses dressed in plastic gear and it occurred to me that my husband maybe was suffering from Corona. My husband was admitted and the doctors put an oxygen mask on his nose. Then the doctors said they need to test both my husband and me. It was only at that point that I realized that both my husband and I may have been suffering from Corona. I turned to Allah, the merciful, and prayed for healing for my husband to get well and for me not to be sick. Since I woke up feeling well, I thought I would not be sick. By this time, my husband had improved and was feeling well. He would even remove the mask for some minutes to talk and laugh. Both of us were tested and unfortunately, both of us had Corona. I did not panic. I knew we would be well and I told myself that I was going to be well. Both my husband and I were isolated. We called our children who were away in Nairobi (both were in college at the time) and explained that we had fallen a little sick but they need not worry because we would be well. My husband talked to them and we felt relaxed…. I knew it was only for a few days and we would be discharged. We kept taking our medication.*

A few of our friends would call us and tell us to be strong and to get well soon. We would talk on phone and assure them that we were on the road to recovery. Meanwhile, a second Corona test showed that my Corona had cleared but my husband remained positive. …It was on the tenth day early in the morning when the doctors came for the usual round. He attended to me and said I was all fine and would be discharged. Then he went to my husband's bed and they spoke. I heard the doctor tell my husband that he was doing well. My husband said he was feeling much better and had slept for much of the night without oxygen. I had the doctor tell my husband not to remove the mask unless the nurses say so. "Then the doctor made to go then took a step back and turned the knob to increase the oxygen flow." Then he left. As he left, I felt a strong urge to turn the knob and reduce the oxygen flow. Up to now, I don't know why I felt like that. But I did not. In less than five minutes, my husband complained that he was having very sharp pains in his chest. He held onto his chest with both hands and tightly closed his eyes. I dashed out to call the nurse. … When I returned with the nurse, the nurse pulled the curtains around my husband's bed and pushed me to the next room. I was shaking and praying that merciful Allah has mercy on us. I was afraid and I felt like I was not breathing. Then I saw a doctor get behind the curtains with the nurse and could see him touching my husband. Then the doctor came to the room where the nurse had left me and said "I am sorry. We have lost him". What! I could not believe it. Just like that? How? Did the doctor kill my husband with too much oxygen? Why did I not turn it down after he left? …. I started crying. I regretted not having turned backwards the knob when the doctor left. I had killed my husband. I could not be consoled. The nurse came and gave me some hot water to drink. She comforted me and explained that my husband may have seemed fine but his lungs were badly affected and they doubted that he would get well. She said even if he got well, he would have been disabled. I didn't understand why the nurse was telling me all this. I guess she was trying to comfort me. …

Anyway, eventually I came to terms and told myself "Allah is in charge. We leave it to Allah." I am at peace knowing that Allah knows every one of us and has a destiny for each of us.

Box 6.4 The Case of Ms X

Ms X is an 88-year-old widow living in a rural village in the Rift Valley area of Kenya. She describes herself as an African traditional religion believer. Despite her age, she looks strong and lives alone. She told me that a young lady comes to help her during the day but she goes away in the evening. The only day the lady didn't come is on Sunday. I interviewed this widow on a Sunday so she was not with her. She is all alone at night. In spite of her age, she wakes up early (at about 4.30 am). She boils water for milking her one cow and prepares breakfast for herself and the young lady. Then the young lady who helps her during the day comes in at about 5 am. She milks the cow, takes breakfast, then goes to take milk to the dairy cooperative factory at about 6 am. The old woman usually goes back to bed and wakes up at about 8 am when the young lady returns from the dairy factory. She lives in the same homestead (but different houses) with her last-born son. His house is about 100 meters away from hers. Her son is married and they have three children. The oldest girl was in her third year of high school in 2020, while the other two were in primary school. All of them were at home during that year.

She shared her experience of COVID-19 as partly reproduced: early last year, I learnt that this woman died in her sleep. The lady who worked for her came early as usual to milk the cows only to find that the woman was still asleep. She called but she did not respond. She nagged the widow by her bed and she did not respond. She went away and came back at about 7 am. The house was still locked from inside. They had to break the house only to find the woman had died in her sleep. Her son died from kidney disease only a week after her death. Below is the experience of the old lady as she narrated it to me. We spoke in Kikuyu, so I had to translate the transcript into English. I interpreted the conversation verbatim.

… I knew my son had contracted the strange disease because he kept going to the hospital for dialysis. He had a kidney disease. Besides, his wife is not a careful woman and she would not do what I was advising her to do to ensure that he was warm when they went to the hospital. I also advised her to give him boiled chicken soup all the time, but she rarely did. Occasionally, I would make the soup in my house and put various herbs but she would not come for it. So when his wife called me to say he had difficulties breathing, I knew it was COVID. *I rushed out to where my son was. They had put him in a car to take him to the hospital. I looked at him once and said: "Ngai Njega (good God). Please come and help us. Come now". I looked up to the skies, spit on my chest, and requested God of the Agikuyu to hear my plea. I prayed that they would go safely to the hospital and that they would find a wise doctor who would treat my son well. …Then I left them to go to the hospital. I went back to my house and pleaded with God to intervene. I was talking to myself all through telling me that all would be well because the God of our forefathers had revealed to me that my son would not die ahead of me. The year before I had lost a daughter and a son and it was very very painful. … this time God heard me and saved my son. They found a good doctor who insisted that my son should not be tested for* COVID *because he already had a kidney disease. He said the test would be positive even if he did not have* COVID. *So he treated him and sent him back home and asked the wife to give him a lot of white porridge, boiled chicken, and a lot of cabbage. When they came home, I made it my work to cook the things for my son and I would put various herbs in the boiling chicken and the cabbage. … He got well. I believe without God's help, he would have died.*

Box 6.5 The Case of Ms Y

Ms Y is a 45-year-old woman. She is a teacher in a national school in a town in rural western Kenya. She and her family live in a house in the school compound. The house belongs to the school. She lived with her husband in a rural town in western Kenya. Her husband works as a purchasing officer in a government office in the town. She is a Christian who worships with the Seventh-day Adventist Church. Her husband is a Christian too but he hardly practices—he doesn't go to church and he doesn't pray with the family. He used to drink a lot of alcohol but he has since stopped drinking. They have three teenage children, two boys and a girl. All of the children were in boarding schools when COVID-19 spread to Kenya and government agencies introduced measures to manage its spread. She narrated to me the following:

When we heard about COVID *from a friend, we thought she was joking. It didn't seem possible that with all the scientific and technological advancements, there would be a disease that can terrorize people like that without control. And even when we heard that it was spreading fast to other countries, we did not think much about it. …We believed that people, especially in Europe and America, have a lot of knowledge and would soon beat the disease. … the government declared all schools closed and we sent all children home. My children also came home. It began to appear true. News, especially from abroad, for example, from Italy and America, were especially very frightening. We, that is my children and I, began to feel very scared and personally I stopped watching the news…. I told God to give me faith that all would be well. And I knew God would protect us. But my husband was either not frightened or he was not showing. He continued with life as usual. He would even go out and drink a lot even though bars were supposed to be closed. He seemed not to be bothered. I silently prayed to God to keep him safe because I kept having this feeling that he would bring the disease home because he was out drinking and he was not wearing a mask. …Then another teacher who lived in the school compound with us got sick when she travelled to her rural home and she died. I was even more frightened. …The more frightened I got, the more I pleaded with God to save us. I would gather the children in the evening and early in the morning to pray. My husband would mock us and say this is not a matter of God but of science to intervene. This did not stop us from praying.*

… one day, my husband woke up much earlier than usual. It was about 4.30 am because when checked my phone later it was 5 pm. He went to the bathroom. Then I heard him call once from the bathroom and when I went to see what it was I found him leaning on the wall inside the toilet. He said he was feeling like falling and he had chest pains. I put my hand under his arms and helped him back to bed. As he lay on bed groaning in pain, which seemed to be increasing, I went to the bathroom, locked myself in and prayed to God to ensure that this was not COVID. *Yet, at the back of my mind, I was sure that my husband had* COVID *since he always went out without a mask, drank a lot, and mixed with many people…called our friend to come and help take him to the hospital. I could not stay long in the bathroom because my husband was groaning even more and I feared that the children would hear and come over. My instinct was to ensure that they don't come near him lest they get infected.*

… After the prayer, I wanted to take a shower but then I heard God tell me to wear my mask and take my husband to hospital immediately before I take a shower. I thought to myself that God did not want him to be home and make the children worry. I called my boda boda man (motorcycle public transport) and I made my husband sit on the saddle, I sat behind him to hold him between the driver and myself because he was not stable and threatened to fall. After a few kilometers, we realized that we would not make it to the hospital on the motorcycle because I could no longer hold my husband steadily…. The boda boda man was very kind—oh God bless him! He told us to sit at the side of the road and wait while he went to look for a vehicle. As we sat there I spoke to my husband to keep him

awake. I feared he would die if I didn't keep him engaged. … came back with a vehicle and we rushed to hospital. My husband was immediately attended because some of the nurses knew him through his work office. He was admitted and immediately given oxygen. I stayed by his side and spoke to him encouraging words. I told him that he would be fine. I told him that God loves him. I told him that since he was now in hospital, everything would be fine.

At lunchtime, I went home. I needed to go and see that the children were fine. I got home and we prayed some more after I told them that their daddy was very sick and had been admitted. They said they wanted to go and see him, but I told them we need to wait for him to be strong. I told them that the doctor had said he needs to rest for two or three days without anybody exciting him but that he would be well in three days. I hid from the children and went back to the hospital alone to see him. I found that he had gotten worse and had been transferred to isolation in the ICU. I was shocked. Then they told me that they had done a COVID test. If his test turned positive, they would have to test me as well. Meanwhile, they asked me to stay away and only see him from afar. I prayed hard to God that my husband would not test positive for COVID. The following two days were tough as I prayed with the children for their dad to get well. I kept paying and promising God that my husband and I would serve him forever if God saved us. Then the COVID results were out. My husband tested positive. I then had to be tested. Even as I was testing, I told myself that I would not be positive. Meanwhile, I developed some sharp dryness in my mouth, a slight headache, and some occasional minor pains in my chest. I feared I had contracted COVID. … still, I prayed to God to spare me and my children.

My results came out and I was positive. I was immediately admitted and put in isolation. I started coughing and experienced shivers. Initially, I felt like God had betrayed me. Why did God not hear my prayer? But I told myself that God has a reason for everything and that I should persevere and pray to get well. … my children came to see me; they were denied entry so they could only see me from far. I assured them that I was fine and all would be well. …The next time the children came, they were with my sister. I felt so happy to see my sister with my children because I knew she would take good care of them. She passed me a note in which she said she was praying for me and my husband and that we would get well. She referred me to many Bible verses that promised healing. She assured me that many people get well from COVID and I and my husband would be one of those lucky ones. I was under medication and in isolation for two weeks. …, my husband improved and was transferred from the ICU to the HDU and eventually to the isolation ward where I was. By this time, I was almost feeling fine. Many of the symptoms had disappeared. However, I could not smell things or taste food. My husband was weak and not eating well but in due course, he improved day by day. When I was next tested for COVID, I tested negative and so I was discharged. I comforted my husband that I had to leave him behind and encouraged him to look up to God who had helped him this far. He agreed with me that God had saved him and he promised me that if he gets well he will never drink again, and will worship God…. my husband was discharged on a Friday.

The following day was the Sabbath and he woke up early to go to church. Since then, he goes to church without failure and thanks God for saving his life. He also thanks me for praying for him over the years because that is why he believes God saved both of us. For me, I have a testimony that God is a great healer and he works in mysterious ways. …This was his way of making my husband turn to him and worship him. I am grateful that it happened though I still wish we didn't have to go *through that.... It was very difficult, especially when my children came to see me and I would see them from afar crying. I would not cry when they were there because I didn't want them to lose hope, but as soon as they left, I would cry a lot.... I am very grateful to my sister who took care of my children while we were in hospital, and kept coming every day to see me. She brought me avocados, oranges, and hot water with ginger, which she said was good for* COVID. *She too would pray with my children for me every day. I believe this is how I didn't get too sick and recovered quickly. Prayer changes things.*

Box 6.6   The Case of Ms Z

Ms Z is a 29-year-old woman from Eastern Kenya who is living with physical disabilities. She lived in Machakos with her son, then 15 years old. She got the child when she was a teenager in her second year of secondary school, upon which she dropped out of school. Later on, she did her end of secondary school examination as a private candidate and proceeded to do a secretarial course at a business school. She works as a messenger for a private law firm. She shared her story as follows:

I remember boss sent us away because COVID started. He said he did not have money to pay us. He said he could not pay us and we were not working. I could not afford rent, so I went to stay with my mother in the village. My son also. It was very boring living in the village. It was difficult also. I was happy in town. There is electricity in the house. There is water in the house. And the toilet was good, especially with disability. In the village, you get water from the river and the toilet is outside with an open hole (referring to a long drop latrine). My son did not like it also. I told him that we would soon go back to our house .... To tell you the truth, I was very worried. I knew my work was gone. But I didn't want to make my son sad. I wondered how I would live here. But what to do? Nothing. So I told my son we were ok. We would go back to town. I didn't want to worry him. Anyway, we tried. I was ok. We lived ok.

Sometimes towards the end, ... about November 2020, my brothers came home also. He was working in Kisumu. He said there was no job and he was sent away. He looked very tired. ...I thought it was travelling. He did not eat. The next day he was tired also. And coughing. Sleepy also. He went back to bed. But coughing also. I looked at him. He had running nose and complained of headaches also. I suspected COVID. When I told my mother, she said no. It cannot be. Still, she said we pray. We prayed that it was not COVID .... She went away and came back with many bottles of Vicks Vaporub (menthol). She boiled water. She put boiled water in a bucket. She added a drop of Vicks. She covered me with a blanket over the bucket of hot water and said it would help us not to get COVID from my brother. She told me "breathe in and breathe out" many times. I sweated a lot. And I felt very good. She called my brother also. Did the same also. My brother almost refused. Mother insisted. She said, "God help those who help themselves." ... We pray to God to save us. We try what we know. My mother told us "We were told in a chama (women's group) that this is good medicine to prevent and to stop COVID." My brother agreed. He covered himself and sweated. He sweated very much also. When he came out of the blanket, he asked mother "how did you know I have COVID? I was tested and the results came today. I have COVID, I was to go to isolation. I hid and ran away to come home..." We were shocked. My mother and I. Mother exclaimed "Wooooi my God, my son." .... Then mother hugged my brother. I was shocked. I tried to pull her. But she hugged tightly. I stepped away fearing to catch COVID. Mother prayed and prayed. She prayed and told God to cure her son. She held my brother on the shoulders. She looked him straight and told him "Do not be afraid, son. Do not worry. You will be ok. I will take care of you. And God is faithful. God will heal you. You hear me?" My brother started to cry. My mother boiled more water. She put more Vicks. She asked my brother to put his head under a blanket. He sweated a lot also. My brother said he now felt good. He said his chest was heavy but he feels good. My mother said it was God answering her prayers. My mother boiled other water. She put on Vicks and also covered herself. All through she was praying, "God help us." ... When my son came home. He was to the shops or somewhere. My mother treated him with boiled water and Vicks also. She said it was to prevent COVID.

She ordered us to eat. She had cooked rice with beans. Even my brother ate. He said he was ok now. We ate. Then mother made strong tea with a lot of lemon covers (rind). She told us to drink without sugar. She prayed. She thanked God. She said God had healed her son. God had sent her son home so she could pray. She had prayed. He had begun healing. We all go to sleep. I hear my mother praying from her bed.

...Mother woke us up the next morning. Very early. She prayed and prayed and prayed. She thanked God for healing her son, my brother. She thanked God for giving us medicine. Mother had water boiling. She made us all use it with Vicks. We all did. My brother said he slept well. My mother had made fruits. She said we eat fruits. We eat. Then she gave us black tea with lemon covers and arrowroots. Boiled eggs also. She made sure we eat much. We did this. Imagine mother kept doing this like four times every day for the week. Then later once, in the evening every day. My brother got well. My son and I did not get sick. Mother did not get sick also. Mother said God has favored us. My brother said he was sure he came home to die. He was very happy. He said his mother had saved his life. Mother said, "No. It is God. And my women in chama who told me what to do."

Findings from Focus Group Discussions

In this section, I present the data that was collected using two FGDs in response to women's experiences of COVID-19 infection (their infection and/or death of their husbands and/or children), and their responses to prevent or manage infection, as well as their coping strategies.

In total, 18 women of different socio-demographic characteristics participated in FGDs. Their socio-demographic characteristics were as follows: age (20–75); rural and urban; rich and poor; of different religious and educational backgrounds (Christian, Muslim, African indigenous religion, and nonaffiliated). Out of the 12 involved in 2 FGDs, eight had been married but had been widowed, four by COVID-19 and four by other causes, and four were single. One was cohabiting with her "boyfriend" as she described him, and three were living with their families of upbringing during COVID-19.

In both FGDs, prayer emerged as the most common practice that women used to prevent or manage COVID-19. A 75-year-old woman (in Group 1, which comprised older women—50 and above) who described herself as an adherent of traditional African religion though with some elements of Christianity had this to say:

… you see, many of these diseases come from white people. I don't know why they do this. Now this one defied them and they were suffering more than we were suffering. I think our ancestors protected us. Many of us prayed individually but also as a group…I remember this day when we went to a sacred place and we fasted and prayed the whole day. At that time, COVID *had come into the country but it was not common in our place in the village. But our religious leader told us to go out and resist any efforts of the evil one to destroy us. … and when they said they had tested my husband and had found that he had it, we went out again with a group of women in our religious groups and we prayed and fasted all day. I left the prayer session feeling that my husband would be ok. I told myself it was okay and everything would be okay. The next day I went to hospital hoping to see my husband but they refused me to go in. right at the gate. That was very kind…*

Another woman in the group interjected demonstrating a lot of anger:

Exactly. The doctors and nurses were very cruel. They said the government did not allow. They refused me to see my husband's body. But God is good. I finally accepted my fate. I said 'let him rest. We will meet again'.

In FGD 2, made up of younger women (below 50), a similar discussion was undertaken. The youngest in the group, a 20-year-old woman, spoke of how women experienced and responded to COVID-19. She said:

You know what, many women, many more than men survived COVID *because of prayer. When my parents and one of my brothers were sick, our mother prayed all the time, pleading with God to save him. And my mother has a lot of faith. It is not surprising that she was cured and my brother was also cured. Although my brother is yet to be himself. He still gets sick just like that. My father was always a non-believer, so he did not believe it when my mother prayed and said they would be well. So he died. …*

Another participant, aged 46, who had been silent for much of the time, suddenly said:

No no. Don't say that about your father. Your father was a good man. I am sure he went to heaven. Even if he didn't believe, God would have saved him if he wanted to. In my view, it was his time to go so he went.

Yet another interjected:

…It is only by God's grace that we survived. You know, when my husband died and they tested me, they said I did not have COVID. *How? But I stayed with my husband all through, sleeping in the same bed, eating from the same cups and plates …and my children too but we did not get* COVID. *How is that? Something was not adding up. I kept telling myself that this thing is not true. God is greater than any forces and God will win the*

battle. So I kept praying and praying. With these prayers, COVID *could not attack me or my children. We covered ourselves with the blood of the lamb.*

Many of the other women in both groups kept referring to how they prayed to prevent or manage COVID and its negative consequences.

Worth of special mention is that women did not pray and wait for miracles to happen. They punctuated prayer with action, as will be presented in the next theme. Besides, the women resisted some of the responses that the government adopted that were culturally not sensitive such as not treating human bodies with respect. For example, Maseno (2024) documents the case of a woman and her daughter-in-law who dramatically sat on the grave of their dead son/husband in defiance of a call to exhume his body after he was hurriedly buried by the state in the night (Maseno, 2024).

Another theme that emerged from the FGDs, as from the one-on-one oral interviews, is self-talk. This is closely related to prayer. The voices cited above also illustrate this aspect where individual persons comforted themselves and encouraged themselves to remain positive even in difficult situations.

A 33-year-old Muslim woman said that after her husband was taken ill and hospitalized, she and her four children got to some point when they had no food. Her husband had been the sole breadwinner. One day she woke up and there was nothing to cook for the children who were at the time aged 2, 4, 5, and 8. She shared:

I turned to Allah and asked: Why did you give me these children only to kill them with hunger? Where do I go now with all the stigma? People were pointing at us saying we were infected. So they stopped coming to our house when my husband was admitted (in hospital). I could not dare go out. But can you imagine, Allah is full of mercy. Another woman came to visit us and when she found we had nothing to eat she went back and brought us a lot of food—cooked and raw- we had enough for almost a week. And she kept coming and giving us food. Especially food which she said was good like fruits (oranges and avocados) and millet porridge until my husband got well and returned home. Then I kept telling myself: "Allah Akba". And it is not just me. Many women were helping young mothers like me. They came with food and powdered milk for babies. They prayed with us. They told us what to drink.

A 26-year-old added:

But this was only in some areas. In others, people kept away. The stigma was so so bad. I remember when the government came in the night to bury another woman who had died of COVID, *people became even more afraid of one another. Even Muslims who are always very good to one another, this time they kept away. Stigma is a bad thing.*

Another participant said:

But it can be understood. When someone is covered all over and then they are thrown into a grave just like that, a like a log, you feel afraid. It is like during the days of AIDS. People were afraid.

A third response, common across the different methods of data collection, was the sharing of resources but also of home remedies, including foods to prevent or manage COVID-19 infection.

> *Participants in both groups persistently referred to how women shared 'formulas' like taking dawa (concoction made of lemon, ginger, garlic, sweetened with honey), steaming as soon as one felt any slight dryness of the throat, and not lying in bed when one felt sick.*

A participant in Group 1 emphasized:

> *Something that helped women cope was working. You know, when you fell sick, like homa (common cold), you don't go to bed and cover yourself with a blanket and start thinking of how you are sick. You will die. This message spread a lot among women. So when my sister started feeling like she had a cold, she would wake up, go for a walk, come back, clean) the house and generally keep working. Then at night because she was tired she would just sleep pah! Like a log. And her cold went. Within that week, a friend who she had closely associated with tested positive and in a few days she was dead. The difference is that her friend went to hospital and was admitted and put on oxygen which means she could not move. She was just there idle thinking of how she is sick. And it is not just with COVID. Any disease worsens with idleness. ...*

These sentiments compare with the experience of Ms U, the 65-year-old participant, in the in-depth interview who said that she would go to the garden even when she was feeling unwell.

In summary, findings from the two FGDs suggest that women relied a lot on spiritual resources such as prayer and self-talk, and they also relied on sharing information and resources on home remedies that they could use to prevent or manage COVID-19.

Results and Discussions

The results suggest that all the women applied various spiritual/religious resources (prayer, self-talk, and pastoral care) and shared experiences and resources with other women on what complementary therapy was working well and what was not working well to provide holistic care to themselves and their significant others to prevent and manage COVID-19 infection and its consequences. They are all convinced that it is these spiritual resources on their own or combined with biomedical treatment that enabled them to make meaning of what was happening to them and/or their significant others, to successfully respond to COVID-19 and to cope effectively with their own ill health but also with the ill health and/or death of their loved ones. These findings are discussed in the following section.

We discuss prayer, self-talk, and sharing independently as resources for spiritual (self) care, even though most of the time their expressions of these interact in a complex way. In the discussion section that follows, each of these resources is discussed in relation to the extant literature in terms of their (re)constructions and expressions and how they changed or did not change in the course of the progress of infection and/or consequent death of significant others. In all situations, all participants expressed a process of (re)negotiation in thoughts, beliefs, and practices.

Prayer

A spiritual resource that was commonly applied across all participants (regardless of religious affiliation) as they (re)negotiated and (re)interpreted what was happening as they sought to find or express value, meaning, and hope is prayer. Hamman (2023) defines prayer simply as communication between humans and the supernatural and identifies four types of prayer: petition (request), confession, intercession, and mystical union (ecstasy). However, these are not mutually exclusive. One session of prayer may cover all the different types to serve all the different purposes.

According to Roberts et al. (2007),

"Prayer is an ancient and widely used intervention for alleviating illness and promoting good health. Whilst the outcomes of trials of prayer cannot be interpreted as 'proof/disproof' of God's response to those praying, there may be an effect of prayer not dependent on divine intervention. This may be quantifiable; which makes this investigation of a widely used health care intervention both possible and important."

(Abstract)

Roberts *et al* are accurate. Prayer may be quantified and investigated and it is critically important. A number of studies quantifying prayer have been done (see, e.g., Koenig and Büssing, 2010; Mathai & Bourne, 2004; Matthews et al., 2000; Poloma & Pendleton, 1990; Zarzycka et al., 2022). While the science of studies measuring the relationship between religion and health has been queried as not being robust (Ragle, 2006; Vincent, 2015), lack of robustness is not unique to studies on prayer. Studies on otherwise obviously quantifiable realities have been questioned. The challenge is to seek to study prayer better rather than dismiss it as unquantifiable.

Commonly cited among women involved in this study, though to different levels, was the use of music as a medium of all these types of prayers, as a way of preventing COVID-19 infection as well as of managing infections. Many said they were significantly exposed to infection because they did not have an option but to closely take care of their loved ones when they fell sick—even when they themselves were infected. Aware of their vulnerability, many women petitioned God to protect them from infection.

Self-Talk

Self-talk refers to communication with oneself or internal dialogues (Latinjak et al., 2023; Puchlska-Wasyi and Zarzycka, 2021), that is, a situation where an individual has a conversation with the self in their thoughts. Psychologists distinguish between different kinds of self-talk and suggest that self-talk is normal and part of human nature (Latinjak et al., 2023; Puchlska-Wasyi and Zarzycka, 2021; Tod et al., 2011). Various studies have been done on the subject across different disciplines. Every person will often be involved in self-talk. It is only when it becomes pronounced to become explicit because of reduced inhibition that self-talk becomes a source of concern. Self-talk is often pronounced when one is faced with crises, for example, when one is anxious because they have a difficult decision to make and the consequences of their decision are enormous. These thoughts may be positive or negative, for example, affirming to the self that a certain outcome is possible or not possible. In Kenya, the popular reference to self-talk is "calling oneself to a meeting" to address a critical issue. In this chapter, we consider self-talk as spirituality because it is about the relationship with the self.

Through their experiences of COVID-19, all six women indicated that they constantly engaged in self-talk, especially with regard to how to prevent COVID-19, particularly for those who were directly caring for their infected husbands and/or children. In their view, this was effective in helping them cope.

Spiritual Care-Sharing Knowledge and Resources

Two key resources were applied by all participants to different levels, although some of the participants did not express them until they were probed. These came out very strongly in the FGDs, but also with some of the participants.

There was a lot of sharing of knowledge, perspectives, and resources with feelings of togetherness, even as COVID-19 policies promoted isolation and social distancing and even though there were reports of stigma. The majority of the participants were of the view that sharing and togetherness were positively associated with healing and well-being. This compares with the observations of Kimani Njogu in a special issue of Jahazi on Culture, Arts, and performance in the context of COVID-19 resilience:

> Nonetheless, there were numerous instances of local community solidarities and empathy, sharing of basic needs, and caring for each other. COVID-19 has not just been a medical calamity; it has been a wake-up call for us all to look at our political path, our economic choices and our social practices. At the core of this wake-up call is the urgent need to invest... (Njogu, 2021: 4)

All 24 women who participated in this study reported that sharing of knowledge on various homemade remedies, including the use of herbs and specific foods and fruits, steaming, and use of inhalants, was common and effective. This compares with other studies that have been done on home remedies and COVID-19 (Adebiyi et al., 2022; Azam et al., 2020; Makua, 2022; Malapela et al., 2022; Marevesa et al., 2021; Mshana et al., 2021; Negi and Bala, 2020).

Women reported sharing their experiences with other women (those with experience of COVID-19 infections and those with not) and explicitly said that this sharing was effective in helping them prevent and manage infection, as well as cope with their situations. While some of them said they feared stigmatization and were therefore careful with who they shared, generally they trusted that their friends would provide more support than stigma and so they freely shared with friends and relatives. Upon sharing, almost all of them felt that the people they shared with listened to them with love and compassion, which was demonstrated in that they shared their resources like food and money, shared their knowledge and beliefs like on what concoctions to take or give to those in danger of infection or those already infected, and prayed with and for them throughout their COVID-19 experience. All 24 of them reported that the spiritual care that they received from their fellow women was significantly important to their recovery and coping with COVID-19 for the women, as well as for their significant others.

The most valuable gifts that humans share are not things. Instead, these are sharing of their time and energies, sharing of themselves. In the experiences shared above, we see a lot of women sharing their time just to sit and listen to those who were sick or had sick relatives, and we see a lot of sharing of people's energies. We read of neighbors taking sick ones to hospital; we hear of mothers and wives cooking for their sons; and we hear of relatives and friends visiting in hospital or at home in spite of the measures that were put in place by the government. This confirms what we all know: prevention of spread and management of epidemics, including COVID-19, is more of a spiritual health issue, an issue of relationships with God, with self, and with others. Biomedical responses on their own will not help, especially in contexts where the so-called international best practices are not practical.

Yet, in spite of (or perhaps because of) major advancements and innovations in health, human health remains largely a spiritual matter that is largely addressed with technical biomedical resources.

Communicable diseases are even more about relationships in terms of prevention, care, and outcomes. On social medicine in the context of COVID-19, Trout and Kleinman (2020) note:

> Covid-19 is an inherently social disease, with exposure, illness, care and outcomes stratified along familiar, social, economic and racial lines. However, interventions from public health and clinical medicine have focused primarily on the scale-up of technical, biomedical solutions that fail to address the social contexts driving its distribution and burden.

While social medicine is increasingly receiving some attention, spiritual care is often dismissed as superstition and not empirical. Yet, as observed in the findings from both in-depth interviews and FGDs, individual men and women connected with religious/spiritual communities during the COVID-19 crisis. This concurs with what Borkataky-Varma *et al.* (2024) have suggested that in times of personal and collective crises, such as pandemics, individuals tend to connect with their religious/spiritual communities.

Lessons Learned

Given the design of the study, particularly that the study relies on self-reporting, and given the small sample that is context specific, it may be difficult to draw lessons from the cases with much confidence. However, the study provides lessons that can lay a foundation for more widespread and more systematic studies on women, religion/spirituality, and pandemics. These lessons include:

1 There is a link between religion/spirituality on the one hand and healing and coping with COVID-19/pandemics on the other.
2 Religious women played fundamental roles in preventing and managing COVID-19 and we can learn from them how to share spiritual resources, including prayer, self-talk, and popular and contextually available and effective remedies to communicable epidemics.
3 Spirituality as healthy relationships: sharing and togetherness (relationships) even in contexts of communicable pandemics may have more positive health outcomes than biomedical interventions.
4 Drawing from the findings and the lessons learned, we stipulate that there is a need for robust studies in religion/spirituality and pandemics with a special focus on the role of women as the primary caregivers in the first tier of health systems, the home. Clearly,

African women's resilience, care and compassion, pragmatic problem-solving, and spirituality are resources that would be useful in preparing for the next epidemic.

5 Strengthening religion/spirituality, especially sharing of information and resources, may be effective in creating resilience, innovativeness, and strength to respond to outbreaks of and cope effectively with pandemics.

References

Adebiyi, B. O., G. T. Dong, B. Omukunyi, and N. V. Roman. (2022). "How South African families protected themselves during the COVID-19 pandemic. A qualitative study," *Sustainability* 14, 1236. DOI: 10.3390/su14031236

Azam, M. N. K., R. A. Mahamud, A. Hasan, R. Jahan, and M. Rahmatullah. (2020). "Some home remedies used for treatment of COVID-19 in Bangladesh," *Journal of Medical Plants Studies*. 8(4), 27–32.

Borkataky-Varma, Sravana, Christian A. Eberhart, and Marianne Bjelland Kartzow (Eds). (2024). *Religious Responses to Pandemics and Crises Isolation, Survival, and #Covidchaos*. London, New York: Routledge.

Global Health. (2020). *COVID-19 Sex-disaggregated Data Tracker: Sex, Gender and COVID19 USA* (2020). Available online at: https://globalhealth5050.org/covid19/sex-disaggregated-data-tracker/ (30 July, 2020).

Hamman, Adalbert G.. (2023). "Prayer," *Encyclopedia Britannica*, 25 July. https://www.britannica.com/topic/prayer. Accessed 16 September 2023.

Koenig, Harold G., and Arndt Büssing. (2010). "The Duke University Religion Index (DUREL): A five-item measure for use in epidemiological studies," *Religions* 1: 78–85.

Latinjak, Alexander T., Alain Morin, Thomas M. Brinthaupt, James Hardy, Antonis Hatzigeorgiadis, Philip C. Kendall, Christopher Neck, Emily J. Oliver, Małgorzata M. Puchalska-Wasyl, Alla V. Tovares, and Adam Winsler. (2023). "Self-Talk: An interdisciplinary review and transdisciplinary model," *Review of General Psychology* 0, 1–32. DOI: 10.1177/10892680231170263

Makua, T. (2022). "The use of mušukutšwane with kwena and matlapaneng to manage covid-19," *ASMS*. 6(7), 223–226. DOI: 10.31080/ASMS.2022.06.1335

Malapela, R. G., G. Thupayagale-Tshweneagae, and W. M. Baratedi. (2022). "Use of home remedies for the treatment and prevention of coronavirus disease: An integrative review," *Health Science Report* 6(1), e900. DOI: 10.1002/hsr2.900.

Marevesa, T., E. Mavengano, and P. N. Nkamta. (2021). "Home remedies as medical development in the context of the COVID-19 pandemic in Zimbabwe: A cultural memory paradigm," *Gender Behaviour* 19(1), 17379–17391.

Maseno, Loreen. (2024). "Sitting on a Grave: Female Agency and Resistance During the COVID-19 Pandemic. Sravana Borkataky-Varma et al. in Chiga Village, Kenya," in *Religious Responses to Pandemics and Crises Isolation, Survival, and #Covidchaos*, edited by Borkataky-Varma, Sravana, Eberhart, Christian A. and Bjelland Kartzow, Marianne. London, New York: Routledge.

Maula, Johanna. (2021). *The Impact of COVID-19 on women and men*. Nairobi: UN Women and UNFPA, East and Southern Africa Regional Offices.

Mshana, G., Z. Mchome, D. Aloyce, E. Peter, S. Kapiga, and H. Stöckl. (2021). "Contested or complementary healing paradigms? Women's narratives of COVID-19 remedies in Mwanza, Tanzania," *Journal of Ethnobiology and Ethnomedicine*, 17(1), 30. DOI: 10.1186/s13002-021-00457-w

Mathai, J. and A. Bourne. (2004). "Pilot study investigating the effect of intercessory prayer in the treatment of child psychiatric disorders," *Australasian Psychiatry*, 12(4), 386–389. DOI: 10.1111/j.1440-1665.2004.02132.x

Matthews, D. A., S. M. Marlowe, and F. S. Macnutt. (2000). Effects of intercessory prayer on patients with rheumatoid arthritis, *Southern Medical Journal*, 93(12), 1177.

Nderitu, David and Eunice Kamaara. (2020). "Gambling with COVID-19 makes more sense: Ethical and practical challenges in COVID-19 responses in communalistic Resource-Limited Africa," *Bioethical Inquiry*.DOI: 10.1007/s11673-020-10002-1

Negi, S., and L. Bala. (2020). "Natural home remedies may act as potential immunomodulators to protect against SARS-CoV-2 infection," *Journal of Experimental Biology and Agricultural Science* 8(1):S176–S189. DOI: 10.18006/2020.8

Njogu, Kimani. (2021). Publishers Note in *Jahazi*: Special Issue on Culture, Arts, *Performance*. 9(1), 4–6.

Ntarangwi, Mwenda. (2021). "Reflections on COVID-19 and spirituality in Kenya," *Jahazi*: Special Issue on Culture, Arts, Performance 9(1), 15–21.

Poloma, Margaret, and Brian Pendleton. (1990). "The effects of prayer and prayer experiences on Measures of general well-being," *Journal of Psychology and Theology* 19, 71–83. DOI: 10.1177/009164719101900107.

Puchlska-Wasyi, M. M., and B. Zarzycka (2021). "Why do we have internal dialogues? Development and validation of the functions of dialogues–revised questionnaire (FUND-R)," *Journal of Constructivist Psychology*. DOI: 10.1080/10720537

Ragle, Brian. (2006). "Prayerful science: more on the relationship between prayer and healing," *Skeptic* [Altadena, CA], 12(4), 11. https://go.gale.com/ps/i.do?id=GALE%7CA155735524&sid=googleScholar&v=2.1&it=r&linkaccess=abs&issn=10639330&p=AONE&sw=w&userGroupName=biola_alumni&aty=ip. Accessed 24 Feb. 2024.

Roberts L, I. Ahmed, and S. Hall. (2007). "Intercessory prayer for the alleviation of ill health," *Cochrane Database of Systematic Reviews*, 1. Art. No.: CD000368. DOI: 10.1002/14651858

Rosmarin, David H. Kenneth I Pargament, and Harold Koenig. (2021). "Spirituality and mental health: challenges and opportunities," *The Lancet Psychiatry* 8(2), 92–92.

Shield, A. (2008). "Gender: An intersectionality perspective," *Sex Roles* 59, 301–311. DOI: 10.1007/s11199-008-9501-8

Simba, H., and S. Ngocobo (2020). "Are pandemics gender neutral? Women's health and COVID-19," *Frontiers in Global Women's Health*, 1, 570666. DOI: 10.3389/fgwh.2020.570666

Steyn, Melissa. (2015). "Critical diversity literacy: Essentials for the twenty-first century," in *Routledge International Handbook of Diversity Studies*, edited by Steven Vertovec. London: Routledge, 379–389.

Tod, David, James Hardy, and Emily J. Oliver. (2011). "Effects of self-talk: A systematic review," *Journal of Sport and Exercise Psychology*. 33(5):666–687. DOI: 10.1123/jsep.33.5.666

Trout, L. J. and A. Kleinman (2020). "Covid-19 requires a social medicine response," *Frontier in Sociology* 5, 579991. DOI: 10.3389/fsoc.2020.579991

UNFPA. (2021). *Impact of COVID19 on Gender Equality and Women's Empowerment in East and Southern Africa*. UN Avenue Nairobi, Kenya: UN Women East and Southern Africa Regional Office Gigiri Complex.

Vincent, Savannah. (2015). "Livin' on prayer: An analysis of intercessory prayer studies," *Dialogue & Nexus* 3(1), 8.

Wenham, C., J Smith, and R Morgan. (2020). "COVID-19: The gendered impacts of the outbreak," *Lancet*. 395, 846–848. DOI: 10.1016/S0140-6736(20)30526-2

Zarzycka, B, D. Krok, K. Tomaka, and R. Rybarski. (2022). "Multidimensional prayer inventory: Psychometric properties and clinical applications," *Religions* 13(1), 79. DOI: 10.3390/rel13010079

7
FEMININE WISDOM AS A RESOURCE FOR FACING PANDEMICS IN AFRICA

Anthony Okeregbe and Muyiwa Falaiye

Introduction

Until recently, the question of women and leadership in Africa, which has attracted and engaged public opinion moulders, social activists and academics, was viewed as a settled matter purportedly superintended by the patriarchal hegemony of traditional and conservative institutions. One influential doctrine of social organisation arising from patriarchal mentality is one that views leadership as a capacity to authoritatively achieve goals through some form of strategy and competitiveness based on special sapiential qualities and personality traits. In traditional African social settings where this position gains traction, it is assumed that such qualities are predominant in men. In a study of the role of female chiefs and rulers in Angola, Ghana, Nigeria, Benin and Uganda, among other African countries, it was found that although women traditionally held significant authority in the governing structures of their political entities, their participation in governance with men is one of the greatest challenges in contemporary African socio-political history. This has been attributed to colonialism (Day, 2021). While women are more likely to be welcome in active participation in the economic and social sectors than in the political governance arena of power, decision-making and leadership are considered as a natural prerogative of men (Amadi-Njoku, 2021).

Behind this thinking is the apologetic rhetoric on gender role categorisation that appeals to benign sexism. Without sufficient qualification, this sympathetic tendency posits that nature has destined man and woman for different roles in society on the basis of their biological classification as male and female. Women, based on this theorising, are homemakers confined to domesticity and have been naturally endowed with facilities amenable to homemaking. The combination of these natural attributes and a gracious biology prepares the woman as a being that personifies compassion, perseverance and patience. By this argument, therefore, it would be injurious to either of the sexes, particularly, and society in general, if one sex takes over the natural role of the other.

However, this thinking develops cracks under serious rational scrutiny as scholars and activists interrogate whatever justification impels patriarchy and its institutions to dominate narratives about human nature and social existence, more especially when it comes to matters of leadership. While it is true that women have played a significant role in the creation and nurturing of life, it is important to note that this view is not universally accepted and can be seen as controversial. It is, therefore, essential to recognise that both men and women have unique qualities and abilities that contribute to society's growth and development. Although gender roles are different, they are not necessarily in competition and should not be. Oftentimes, they are complementary. Thus, it is important to celebrate and respect these differences rather than perpetuate gender stereotypes.

This chapter seeks to examine what has been termed feminine wisdom as a resource in facing pandemics. The aim of this chapter is to examine how African women, within performative male interventions and undeserving structures, carried out practical sapiential actions that helped in positively transforming lives during pandemics and setting the agenda for positive engagements in their communities. It does this by analysing the multiple dimensions of female agency in tackling two major health challenges in Africa, namely, the Ebola epidemic and the COVID-19 pandemic. In adopting a qualitative research approach, this chapter relies on media monitoring and purposive sampling of instances of enactive female agency during both major health challenges. It also deploys hermeneutical and phenomenological analyses to identify and explore sapiential resources that were amenable in tackling the pandemics.

Furthermore, the theoretical framework for this chapter is feminist personalism. Feminist personalism is a philosophical approach that combines feminist theories with personalism (Urban, 2022; Schroeder, 2014), a theory that emphasises the significance, uniqueness and inviolability of the individual and also recognises the importance of individual subjective experiences in shaping reality (Williams and Bengtsson, 2022). It is concerned with the ways in which gender inequality affects women's experiences and seeks to promote gender equality through the recognition of women's unique experiences and perspectives (Schroeder, 2014). While this chapter affirms such resources or resourcefulness as female agency, it problematises the implication of this position by raising questions concerning in what sense they may be termed feminine.

Women and Pandemics

One area in which women's leadership capacity has been very pronounced in recent times is in addressing the menace of pandemics. This is especially true of Africa, where both the Ebola virus disease (EVD) and the coronavirus disease (COVID-19) health challenges have had a significant impact. While the global community exercised some hesitant caution as EVD decimated people in West Africa, where it blew up to become a major concern in 2014, the early predictions of the impact of the COVID-19 pandemic on Africans by some public health scientists painted a gloomy picture. It was speculated that the continent was heading for a harvest of deaths, owing to its huge population, poor healthcare system and its governments' lack of foresight (Byanyima & Kende-Robb, 2021). However, these predictions did not hold true. Africa did not only experience fewer deaths than predicted but also had been much less affected than many other parts of the world.

As widespread infectious and contagious disease conditions that affect a great number of people at the same time, pandemics have been known to exacerbate gender disparities. Pandemics not only undermine women and their health but also entrench prevalent gender prejudices. As observed in three examples of pandemics examined by Simba and Ngcobo (2020), gender norms, obsolete healthcare services and the political system characterised by patriarchy and privileged masculinist power structures not only entrench the gender disparity between the sexes but also increase the vulnerability of women (Ahinkorah et al., 2021; Simba & Ngcobo, 2020).

Although pandemics adversely alter personal routines and an individual's management of time and resources, in light of the imposition of stringent measures such as lockdowns, hygiene routines and physical distancing, their effect in communal spaces tended to be more pronounced. According to reports, in many homes in sub-Saharan Africa, women, especially mothers, were saddled with multiple responsibilities, such as caring for the elderly, the sick and the vulnerable. All this created additional burden in terms of domestic engagement and family responsibility (Ahinkorah et al., 2021), with recorded incidences of domestic violence, sexual assaults and truncated education for girls owing to housework overload (Bwzynska & Contreras, 2020).

Using Burkina Faso and Ghana as case studies, Darkwah et al. (2022) analyse the ripple effects of the containment measures during the COVID-19 pandemic on gender. According to their analysis, the closures of borders, markets, schools and workplaces disproportionately affected women since their immediate income was impacted due to changes in domestic chores and care work. Furthermore, the extended closures of borders damaged trade networks, which directly affected women involved in informal trade, all of which were underreported by a large section of the mainstream media and unrecognised by state institutions.

Female Agency, Feminine Wisdom and Pandemics

In response to the situation of women during the COVID-19 pandemic, many feminist advocacy groups and organisations, sympathetic to women's cause, laboriously highlighted the plight of women and the girl-child with lavish media coverage. A report by the Brookings Institution, a nonprofit organisation concerned with policy research on governance, listed five ways African female agencies faced the pandemic (Byanyima & Kende-Robb, 2021). The commentary revealed that African women propelled the continent's transformation by driving the emergency response and leading at the forefront of the COVID-19 response in Africa, with empathy and compassion. African women were said to have been instrumental in delivering equitable, gender-responsive and inclusive health systems and also educated girls with knowledge and skills to lead the transformation. They also fostered deepened economic integration of the continent through the African Continental Free Trade Area (afCTFA) to transform Africa's informal economy, of which 70 per cent is controlled by women. Furthermore, they were also prominent in innovating across the tech spectrum, from fintech to agtech, and driving the continent's digital transformation.

In the same advocacy mode, Columbia University's Earth Institute highlights important lessons from African feminists' grassroots mobilisation against COVID-19 (Forsyth, 2020). In the report, leaders of grassroots women's organisations across Nigeria, Uganda, the Democratic Republic of the Congo, Lesotho and Sudan mobilised to give visibility to frontline work that women did to care for their communities. In this way, they magnified the critical but unrecognised peace-building work and contributions they made to care for their community in times of crisis. They also mobilised to prioritise women and girls as those disproportionately affected during crises and consequently build solidarity and equity. Lastly, in line with solidarity, they considered taking a feminist approach to leadership, including self-care.

Some Expressions of Female Agency

Besides the widely publicised care-giving actions carried out by women during the Ebola virus epidemic and the COVID-19 pandemic, two examples of female agency from West Africa demand some brief elaboration. First is the intervention of the physician, Dr. Stella Ameyo Adadevoh, at the height of the EVD pandemic, and the other is the recorded engagement of female film-makers, who, in telling the stories of female COVID-19 survivors, displayed certain qualities that expressed sapiential resources for addressing the pandemic. What informs the choice of these two examples of female agency is that both cases illustrate the value of feminine initiative amidst government inaction and underperformance in crisis situations that should demand holistic and integrated social action. Besides, in both the Ebola virus epidemic and the COVID-19 pandemic, many mainstream and official government media presented women and girl children as mere victims, thereby glossing over the heroic aspect of female social action. Thus, there is a need to engage this position for its patriarchal prejudice and chauvinism.

Stella Adadevoh: The Heroine Who Trapped Ebola with Her Life

Dr. Ameyo Stella Adadevoh was a Senior Consultant of First Consultant Clinic in Lagos, Nigeria, who, in a display of uncommon courage and exemplary sense of commitment, prevented a possible Ebola virus epidemic that would have ravaged the whole of the West African region like a cataclysmic holocaust (Kareem, 2023). Notwithstanding the conspiracy theory about the EVD being an artificial creation from some laboratory, the 2014 West African outbreak of the disease was first detected when, in December 2013, a two-year-old boy from Meliandou village in the Gueckedou region of Guinea fell sick and died within a few days of showing some strange symptoms. Gueckedou is a few kilometres from the Sierra-Leonian and Liberian borders. A month later, after his health attendants fell sick and his three-year-old sister, mother and grandmother also fell ill and died, the domino effect caused by this "mysterious illness" spiralled into an outbreak that grew exponentially to remote towns and villages. However, a wave of denial and hesitation initially swept over the minds of Guinea's power bloc, and before one knew it, Ebola had spread like wildfire until it hit the capital Conakry with a devastating blow.

With the Guinean outbreak and its attendant humanitarian crisis, people started trooping to neighbouring Sierra Leone and Liberia, carrying with them the deadly virus. Before long, Sierra Leone and Liberia had begun to record many deaths. With the latest official records putting its confirmed cases at 7,862 and its recorded deaths at 3,384, Liberia had the highest fatality rate of EVD in the West African subregion. However, owing to the absence of political will and indiscipline in maintaining travel bans, some top government functionaries sought ways of either fleeing from the imminent pestilence or searching for a cure. While a few found their way to the United States, some contemplated travelling to Nigeria. Of the latter, one former high-ranking official found his way to Lagos, becoming the vector of the EVD in Nigeria.

As the Nigerian newspaper, *The Guardian*, commented when it made Dr. Stella Adadevoh its Person of the Year 2014 (*The Guardian*, January 1, 2015): had Dr. Adadevoh, Consultant Physician and Endocrinologist, not held down the late visitor and Ebola virus vector, and perhaps if he found his way to Calabar for the sub-regional meeting he was ostensibly to attend or sneaked into the Synagogue Church of All Nations as many sick but influential

African leaders are wont to do, Nigeria, given its population size, might have witnessed many deaths far more absurd, ravaging and pestilential than the bubonic plague. One can only imagine what monumental tragedy it would have been if Nigeria, a nation overwhelmed by terrorism, crime and political tension, hamstrung by a vast population and a decrepit healthcare system characterised by incessant industrial action, was ravaged by a disease without a cure. The paper's comment on her heroism captured the sorry state Nigeria would have been.

> Between (the visitor's) case and the possibility of a pandemic in Nigeria, Ameyo Adadevoh was the rock that stood and prevented death from assuming a national reign. Hers was an uncommon story of diligence, exceptional ability, sacrifice, heroism, self-lessness and an unwavering commitment to the Hippocratic oath. In saving Nigeria from a crisis by that exemplary conduct, she taught all citizens the finest ideals of service to humanity, and she is now in the caravan of the greats. Adadevoh has made history and has changed the course of Nigeria's history.
>
> Her simplicity, inner and outer beauty were legendary and her devotion to her duty as a physician made her the poster girl for the culture of service that Nigeria so desperately needs. Her therapeutic pleasantness in relating to patients was widely attested to by all. Yet, she was so humble and never got carried away by her illustrious background and enviable qualities.
>
> (*The Guardian*, January 1, 2015, p. 6)

Female Filmmakers on COVID-19 Stories

Drawing in on the disproportionately drastic impact which the COVID-19 pandemic had on women, the Ladima Foundation, in partnership with DW Akademie, invited African women to share their stories about the personal, economic and social impact of COVID-19 in Africa. While the project does not directly address the resources of women in fighting COVID-19, it does provide a platform for African women to share their experiences during the pandemic. By sharing their stories, these women are able to raise awareness about the challenges they face and the resources they need to overcome them. The project also highlights the resilience and strength of African women in the face of adversity. An article that captured the essence of the film project states:

> The brave and powerful films that were submitted sadly have reflected the extremely difficult circumstances that many African women are facing. The stories have shown how in too many cases that the pandemic has indeed impacted women harder and in different ways than on their male counterparts.
>
> (Modern Ghana, 2020)

The project aims to showcase the diverse and powerful voices of African women filmmakers and to raise awareness of the challenges and opportunities they face during the pandemic. Some examples of the films that convey this message are: "Love, Zawadi" by Wambui Gathee, which tells the story of how the enforced lockdown puts women and girls at risk of sexual violence and how one girl escapes her abusive uncle with the help of a friend; "Worlds Apart" by Yehoda Hammond, which depicts the contrast between the privileged and the poor in Ghana, and how a wealthy woman decides to help a struggling mother who sells food on the street. Others worthy of mention include Hellen Samina Ochieng's "Moyo," where the story is told of Achieng, a young single mother working as an underpaid nurse in Mbagathi Hospital, Nairobi. She struggles with the grim financial, mental and physical realities of being a single mother and the pressures of being a front-line, essential worker in a country crippled by a pandemic. When Achieng is called into the hospital at midnight to attend to a COVID-19 emergency, she must turn to Mike, her abusive ex-boyfriend, to take care of her daughter Waridi.

Also with a similar plot and theme, Chioma Divine Favour Mathias'
"My Sunshine" is a short story about the struggle of a single mother with a disabled child, trying to fend for herself and her baby at the same time surviving the effect of the pandemic. She did all she could to stay strong and sharp even in the face of tribulations. This story depicts the true strength of an African woman. Faith Ilevbare's short film "Loop: Every End Has a Beginning" highlights the negative effect of domestic violence on children exposed to such violence during the lockdown.

In our opinion, the message of feminine wisdom in this project is that African women are resilient, creative and courageous in the face of adversity. They are not passive victims but active agents of change and hope. They use film as a tool to express their emotions, experiences and aspirations and to inspire others to take action. They also demonstrate solidarity, compassion and support for each other, especially for the most vulnerable and marginalised groups. These films, and the others in the project, are examples of how African women use their creativity, talent and wisdom to cope with the COVID-19 crisis and to make a positive difference in their communities and beyond. They are also a testament to the diversity and richness of African women's stories and perspectives, which deserve more recognition and support in the global film scene.

Having analysed the engagements of female agents during both pandemics, can the resources dispensed by these women be described as feminine wisdom? In what way do these resources reflect wisdom as feminine?

Of Wisdom and Its Being Feminine

In both specialist literature and general writings, wisdom is often portrayed as a cherished virtue traversing moral, religious, psychological and even economic planes. Although the word "wisdom" is commonly used in reference to expert knowledge, personality characteristics (Ardelt, 2004: 305), admonition and warning (Kekes, 1983), it is difficult to explicate in generally accepted terms (Ardelt, 2004: 207; Taranto, 1989: 2). Coupled with this is the fact that wisdom has also been identified in many cultures with spiritual connotations and religious symbolisms associated with femininity. From the Jewish rendition of *hokmah*, the grammatically feminine for wisdom, to the biblical portrayal of wisdom as a "she," down to the Greek Sophia (wisdom) personified in the goddess Athena, and to the *Tao Te Ching*, which personifies wisdom as the "eternal mother," cultural history quickly reminds us of the gendered personification of wisdom as a female; that lady standard-bearer of divine attributes just as Boethius' Lady Philosophy bearing wisdom (Boethius & Goins, 2011). In Ghanaian art, the old woman (ewu, abrewa, mama and pɔnyaale) is famously depicted as wisdom aiding men in decision-making. Thus, wisdom is "personified as a female virtue to endow the elders with the prowess to adjudicate in intractable cases" (Okyerefo, 2019: 14), thereby predicating male decision-making on female acumen.

What does this feminisation of wisdom mean in everyday life? What attributes does it reveal in the one who is said to be wise? What does wisdom mean to the different users of the term? Despite this symbolism, there was nothing from the earliest times, suggesting femininity in the meaning of wisdom. Socrates, who bequeathed onto philosophy the truth-searching mission for the transformation of individuals and society, saw wisdom as epistemic humility. He argued that genuine wisdom is the acknowledgement of one's ignorance and how little one knows about life and existence. Plato developed this epistemic notion of wisdom by submitting that wisdom is the expert knowledge of the individual to master self as well as the transcendent ability of the quintessential statesman to not only contemplate eternal truths but also to pass ethical judgement, balancing the psychic components of individuals, and thereby maintain social equilibrium. Building on this tradition, Aristotle sought to explain how a wise person acts by distinguishing between theoretical wisdom and practical wisdom. While theoretical wisdom is intellectual, a priori and esoteric, practical wisdom, which he identified as *phronesis* on the other hand, is action-guiding. Aristotle stresses the latter not only because of its emphasis on intuition and practical knowledge but also for its dynamic balance of prudence, discernment, insight and realistic judgement (Kekes, 1983: 281; Kekes, 1995: 16; Rooney & McKenna, 2008: 711). Kekes develops this action-guiding conception of wisdom by positing it as a humanistic attitude that guides how we face adversities and evaluate the often conflicting possibilities and limits of life in the context in which we live (Kekes, 2020). Concerning the kind of knowledge applicable to wisdom, Kekes explains:

What a wise man knows, therefore, is how to construct a pattern that, given the human situation, is likely to lead to a good life. This knowledge is not esoteric, for it is within everyone's reach; nor does it require a special skill or talent, for it concerns the recognition of possibilities and limitations that are the same for everyone.

(1984: 280)

Following Kekes' simple but detailed explications, Oruka had to contend that wisdom "is a quality which enables a person to utilize knowledge of his traditions and human nature in general for the purpose of making mature and objective judgement about life and human relations" (Oruka, 1991: 40).

On the Question of Wisdom Being Feminine

If this is the case, it is pertinent to ask: "In what way could wisdom be said to be feminine? Does it even make sense to speak of feminine wisdom?" In recent times, attempts have been made to construct an idea of feminine wisdom. In mainstream academic discourse, it is difficult to grapple with the notion of wisdom being feminine. Can the ability to navigate through the vagaries of existential situations be gendered? How is a woman's sapiential action distinct from a man's? What are the distinguishing features? Because these questions are constructed from a masculinist mindset, it becomes pertinent to ask whether it makes sense to pose the questions in the first place. As certain feminist scholars have noted, the notion of interpretation with its traditional goal of objectivity and disinterestedness has been laced with androcentric biases and patriarchal interests (Joseph, 2013: 24). The canons of interpretation, on the basis of which terms and concepts make sense, are rooted in mainstream epistemology of the traditional patriarchal reasoning. If the interpretation of wisdom as feminine is to make sense in its own right, it can only be from the standpoint of an eco-feminist hermeneutics that regards mainstream theories of interpretation with suspicion and therefore deconstruct them to reveal the dynamics of power and the embodied state of all epistemologies. As Joseph asserts: "Feminists have highlighted that traditional epistemologies neglect women's ways of knowing and being and feminine aspects of understanding, many of which are essential to sound interpretation and theorizing" (2013: 25).

While there are novels, blogs and sapiential literature on feminine wisdom or female wisdom in the form of activistic narratives (Okyerefo, 2019), theorising on feminine wisdom, which has been a controversial subject in wisdom psychology and human development for over two decades (Orwoll and Achenbaum, 1993; Ardelt, 2004; Xiong and Wang, 2021), is just emerging in African public intellectual space as people raise questions about being wise and its relationship with African human development. If particular human experiences are socially conditioned and culturally rooted, it does make sense to say that there are ways human experiences affect females and women in virtue of the fact that they are women.

On What Constitutes Feminine Wisdom

Judging by the engagements of the female actors presented, certain qualities may be identified as resources women brought to bear in tackling both pandemics. These qualities are empathy, intuition, nurturing and resilience. When viewed under the prism of patriarchy, these qualities tend to fit into the patriarchal narrative that women lack the capacity to think rationally like men. However, as stated earlier as per Kekes, the kind of sapiential resource needed for knowledge production or intellectual exercises is different from that required as an action-guiding principle. Theoretical wisdom or the capacity for ratiocination is not an embodiment of wisdom in its entirety; in the same way, there are other dimensions of what it means to be wise. Resources deployed by women who faced pandemics in Africa, including empathy, intuition, nurturing and resilience, are candidates for feminine wisdom.

Empathy

Empathy, which is the ability to understand or share the feelings of someone else, is an act in which foreign experience is grasped. At face value, it is generally assumed that women possess a deep sense of fellow feeling, which allows them to understand and connect with others on a profound level. Based on this assumption, inferences are drawn to conclude that the regime of caregiving, sacrifice and solidarity dispensed by African women during pandemics are indications that empathy is a peculiar feminine quality. In their explication of an integrative model of wisdom comprising three domains of personality, cognition and conation and operative at the intrapersonal, interpersonal and transpersonal levels, Orwoll and Achenbaum (1993) highlight possible differences in the way men and women attain and express wisdom. Concerning the affective dimension of wisdom, which refers to the emotional or feeling aspects of wise behaviour, and the conative dimension which refers to the motivational or volitional aspects of wisdom, they, like other theorists, suggest that women may be more likely to exhibit wise behaviour in both domains than men, as women are often more socialised to be more nurturing and empathetic (Orwoll and Achenbaum, 1993: 276–281; Xiong and Wang, 2021). In a psychological study that examines the role of gender stereotypes in influencing people's perceptions and expressions of empathy, Löffler and Greitemeyer (2023) argue that women are not inherently more empathetic than men, but rather that they are expected to be more empathetic by society and thus conform to this expectation. They also suggest that men may suppress their empathic responses due to the pressure to appear masculine and avoid being seen as weak or feminine. It follows from this study that the trait of empathy exhibited by women and often construed as feminine wisdom is consistent with the general social expectations.

Amplifying this conative aspect of wisdom in a rather practical manner, Avivah Wittenberg-Cox suggested that during the COVID-19 pandemic, feminine wisdom was candidly expressed as a valuable resource (Cutruzzula, 2020). According to her, women leaders have demonstrated four common threads in their leadership during the pandemic: trust, decisiveness, tech and love. She emphasises that good leaders from both genders all used the first three (trust, decisiveness and tech), but the fourth factor—love —is what really sets the women apart (Cutruzzula, 2020). Her argument is that women leaders were observed to be more empathetic and inclusive in their leadership style. They were more likely to include everyone in their plans and made it very explicit that they cared for everybody. They were also more authentic and shared their personal experiences to connect with other people. This empathetic nature enabled African women to offer support, compassion and a listening ear to those around them.

Intuition

Intuition has been described as a powerful aspect of feminine wisdom. It has been so widely publicised by wellness and self-care feminists that the common impression is that it is an exclusively female faculty. This intuitive sense is said to allow women to navigate complex situations, anticipate challenges and find creative solutions. But is the sense of intuition an exclusively female faculty? Right from Thomas Aquinas through Thomas Kuhn to Miranda Fricker, intuition has enjoyed respect as a special faculty, but devoid of the gendered qualification it is currently receiving in pop psychology and new age spirituality. As far back as over a century ago, Christine Franklin made the point that the gendered association of parts of the mind rests on a misleading, ancient psychology that ascribes reason to men and intuition to women (Franklin, 1893: 211). She argues:

> It is not true that men's minds and women's minds have a different way of working; but it is true that upon certain occasions (and by far the greatest number of occasions) we all men, women, ... act from intuition...
>
> (Franklin, 1893: 211)

In the same vein, Miranda Fricker, who draws on the work of Kuhn to convincingly challenge the reason-intuition dualism, argues for a relationship of complementarity between intuitive and the rationalist modes of cognition. In further supporting Kuhn, she submits that intuition, which is appropriated in certain quarters and associated with the female, is described by Thomas Kuhn as a feature that is "at the heart of rational inquiry" (Fricker, 1995: 235).

While we maintain that intuition is both an androgynous quality and not inferior to reason, we nonetheless identify this quality as a resource deployed in tackling the pandemics. Once again, Dr. Adadevoh, just like many initiators of interventions during and post-COVID-19 pandemic, deployed her intuition. Her conviction about her intuitive capacity might have triggered the courage with which she spoke truth to power. By that singular act of defiance against the pleas of officials of the Economic Community of West African States (ECOWAS) and influential persons who wanted the infected visitor out of the hospital, she gave hope to the Nigerian people. This is an exemplary gesture given the prevalent circumstance and political situation, where those who call themselves leaders and opinion moulders have either sided with the oppressive political class or are too weak and compromised to stand up forcefully against inept leadership and speak truth to power.

Nurturing

Another fundamental quality of feminine wisdom displayed by Adadevoh and also by Achieng in Ochieng's "Moyo" is nurturing or nurturance. While the concept retains the connection in the mother-child relationship, its feminist interpretation expands the concept to accommodate such description as to support or strengthen "the unique will of each individual to form open, trusting, creative bonds with others..." (Trebilcot, 1996: 360). Generally, in common African settings, African women are socialised to possess a nurturing instinct that drives them to care for and support others. As Fawole et al. (2016) admit, "African women are culturally revered and almost glamorized for their care-giving roles," and this, in turn, leads to the "feminization of many epidemics due to the social customs." This nurturing nature is evident in the way women tend to prioritise the well-being of their loved ones and communities. In certain quarters, this ascription of nurturing as an expression of feminine wisdom has been viewed as a patriarchal instigation from the standpoint of domesticity.

In the management of the lives of women in Africa, domesticity plays a very important role in maintaining the dominance of patriarchy. For women who want to make their mark publicly, the translocation of domesticity to the public space has been a recurrent phenomenon. In the corporate setup, women are valued for the commercialisation of their bodies as salespersons, marketing officers and such positions that demand economic management of the female body or what might be termed body economics. In the political arena, they are deployed as protocol managers, a euphemism for older women who scout around for comfort girls for politicians. Not even in wars and conflicts does this change. While the Nigerian civil war saw women being used as spies and comfort girls for soldiers (Alabi-Isama, 2013), Boko Haram insurgents saw women as spies, human explosives in the form of suicide bombers and comfort companions. It is even probable, as speculated by the media, that the abducted Chibok girls and Dapchi girls might have been deployed for these purposes. In all of the aforementioned cases where female agency has succeeded in the translocation and reconstruction of domesticity in the public space, they have done so at the instigation and superintendence of male control.

Contrarily, in pandemics, there is a deconstruction of domesticity in the public space in a manner initiated and superintended by women. Women thought through the crisis situation, mobilised themselves, sourced resources for their agencies and managed them. Adadevoh and the many women who faced pandemics as caregivers and comfort providers exemplified the spirit of sacrifice which caregivers muster as they carry out their responsibilities at the expense of their health and even their lives. By this endeavour, these African women tended to have countered the inhibitive, patriarchy-inducing spaces of domesticity which undermine the role of women in the public space by transforming them into women-dominated spaces for care (Tamale, 2014: 57).

Resilience

Still another remarkable quality exhibited by the women is resilience. As defined by Parmar (2021), "Resilience is the ability to quickly recover from stress, whether it is physical, mental, or emotional. It is a reflection of how flexible we are in adapting to problems that involve family and relationships, health, work, or finances" (par. 7). According to Greitens (2016), who identifies resilience as some kind of wisdom, resilience is a virtue that enables people to move through hardship and become better. A profound submission in Greitens' position is the belief that while no one escapes pain, fear and suffering, from pain can come wisdom, from fear can come courage and from suffering can come strength. African women have demonstrated incredible strength and resilience throughout history, overcoming adversity and breaking barriers. In demonstration of this truth, it seems that the thoughts and actions of female filmmakers, who, in a courageously intentional manner, created awareness about the plight of women, are attestations to the virtue of resilience. Resilient thinking was demonstrated in how women viewed and engaged with the world by deconstructing erstwhile patriarchal spaces into initiatives of care advocacy. It was demonstrated by the mobilising power and strength of women's social resources and their ability to cope with external and internal demands, despite disproportionate equality.

Therefore, it seems that resilience can be a form of wisdom. The ability to bounce back from challenges, adapt to change and persevere in the face of obstacles is a testament to the resilience of feminine wisdom. By embracing their resilience, the Ladima filmmakers can inspire others, shatter stereotypes and create a more inclusive and equitable society. By enabling other women to learn from experiences, they can make them develop the ability to cope with adversity and become wiser and more resilient individuals.

Conclusion

From this analysis, it could be inferred that feminine wisdom is a multifaceted and empowering concept that encompasses the qualities and perspectives which women bring to the world. But as points to ponder, what difference does all this make concerning women's agency and leadership in Africa? It does make a difference. While it is true that sapiential attributes apply to both men and women, the fact remains that the initiative of the African women to face pandemics the way they did was entirely and purely an expression of female agency and initiative. Despite the under-reporting of these expressions of female agency by the mainstream media, the documentation of the interventions by non-governmental organisations that promote women's interests represents a positive step in the right direction. This should be encouraged through proper education, but it should be devoid of hyperfeministic tendencies that tend to put the genders in needless competition.

To this end, women's leadership in Africa needs to be forceful and strong and should challenge socialised gender prejudices that affect leadership. The interpretation of wisdom or what it means to be wise should be deconstructed and exorcised of entrenched and privileged masculinist epistemology. So far, this is what this chapter has attempted to achieve by looking into and bringing to light how African women, despite undeserving socio-political and cultural structures, carried out practical sapiential actions that helped in positively transforming lives during pandemics and setting the agenda for positive engagements in their communities. These practical actions were made possible by the initiative and self-generated qualities of empathy, intuition, nurturing and resilience, which have been rightly recognised as attributes of feminine wisdom.

References

Ahinkorah, B. O., Budu, E., Seidu, A.-A., Agbaglo, E., Adu, C., Ameyaw, E. K., et al. 2021. "Barriers toHealthcare Access and Healthcare Seeking for Childhood Illnesses Among Childbearing Women in sub-Saharan Africa: A Multilevel Modelling of Demographic and Health Surveys," *PLoS ONE* 16(2): e0244395, DOI: 10.1371/journal.pone.0244395.

Alabi-Isama, G. 2013. *The Tragedy of Victory: On-the-spot Account of the Nigerian -Biafran War in the Atlantic Theatre*. Ibadan: Spectrum Books.

Amadi-Njoku, R. 2021. "Representation & Gender in Africa: Role of women in leadership," viewed on October 17, 2023 from https://www.africanpressclub.com/stories/representation-gender-in-africa-role-of-women-in-leadership

Ardelt, M. 2004. "Where can Wisdom Be Found? A Reply to the Commentaries by Baltes and Kunzmann, Sternberg, and Achenbaum," *Human Development* 47(5), 304–307.

Boethius, A., Goins, S. 2011. *The Consolation of Philosophy: With an Introduction and Contemporary Criticism*. San Francisco, CA: Ignatius Press.

Burzynska, K., and Contreras, G. 2020. "Gendered effects of school closures during the COVID-19 pandemic," *Lancet* 395(10242): 1968. DOI: 10.1016/S0140-6736(20)31377-5.

Byanyima, W. and Kende-Robb, C. 2021. "5 Ways Women Are Driving Africa's Transformation and Contributing to a Global Reset," *The Brookings Institution*, viewed on October 10, 2023 from https://www.brookings.edu/articles/5-ways-women-are-driving-africas-transformation-and-contributing-to-a-global-reset/

Cutruzzula, K. 2020. "6 Things We Can Learn from How Women Leaders Have Handled the Pandemic," viewed on October 11, 2023 from https://ideas.ted.com/6-things-we-can-learn-from-how-women-leaders-have-handled-the-pandemic/

Darkwah, A. K., Thorsen, D. and Wayack P. M. 2022. "Gender Blind Spots in COVID 19: Containment and Mitigation Measures in Burkina Faso and Ghana," *Feminist Africa*, 3, 71–98.

Day, L. R. 2021. "African Women Traditional Chiefs and Rulers," In: Yacob-Haliso, O., Falola, T. (eds), *The Palgrave Handbook of African Women's Studies*. Palgrave Macmillan, Cham. DOI: 10.1007/978-3-030-28099-4_28

Fawole, O. I., Bamiselu, O. F., Adewuyi, P. A., and Nguku, P. M. 2016. "Gender Dimensions to the Ebola Outbreak in Nigeria," *Annals of African Medicine* 15 (2016): 7–13.

Fiorenza, E. S. 2001. *Wisdom Ways: Introducing Feminist Biblical Interpretation*, Maryknoll, NY: Orbis Books.

Forsyth, M. 2020. "Lessons from African Feminists Mobilizing Against COVID-19", *State of the Planet: News from the Columbia Climate School*, April 3, viewed on October 10, 2023 from https://news.climate.columbia.edu/2020/04/03/african-feminists-mobilizing-covid-19/

Franklin, Christine Ladd. 1893. "Intuition and Reason," *The Monist* 3(2), 211–219.

Fricker, M. 1995. "Why Female Intuition?" *Women: A Cultural Review*, 6(2), 234–248.

Greitens, Eric. 2016. *Resilience: Hard-won wisdom for Living a Better Life*, New York: Harper Collins.

Joseph, Pushpa. 2013. "Eco-Feminism and Faith: Reclaiming a Subverted Global Wisdom," *SANYASA: Journal of Consecreted Life* VIII(2), 21–31.

Kareem, Itunu Azeez. 2023, "Remembering Ameyo Stella Adadevoh: A mother who paid the ultimate price," *The Guardian* (Nigeria). March 19, viewed on November 6, 2023 from https://guardian.ng/life/remembering-ameyo-stella-adadevoh-a-mother-who-paid-the-ultimate-price/

Kekes, John. 1983. "Wisdom," *American Philosophical Quarterly*, 20(3), 277–286, viewed on September 19, 2023 from http://www.jstor.org/stable/20014008.

Kekes, John. 1995. *Moral Wisdom and Good Lives*, Ithaca: Cornell University Press.

Kekes, John. 2020. *Wisdom: A Humanistic Conception*. New York: Oxford University Press.

Löffler, C. S. and Greitemeyer, T. 2023. "Are Women the More Empathetic Gender? The Effects of Gender Role Expectations," *Current Psychology*, 42, 220–231.

Mawere, M., and Mayekiso, A. 2014. "Traditional Leadership, Democracy and Social Equality in Africa: The Role of Traditional Leadership in Emboldening Social Equality in South Africa," *International Journal of Politics and Good Governance*, 5(5.3), 1–22.

Modern, Ghana. 2020. "African Women Have COVID-19 Stories To Tell: Let's Watch Them," viewed on September 10, 2023 from https://www.modernghana.com/news/1014893/african-women-have-COVID-19-stories-to-tell-lets.html

Okyerefo, M. P. K. 2019. "Feminine wisdom as an axis to traditional knowledge in Africa," *Open Air African Innovation Research*, July 11, viewed on September 10, 2023 from https://openair.africa/feminine-wisdom-as-an-axis-to-traditional-knowledge-in-africa/

Oruka, O. H. 1991. *Sage Philosophy: Indigenous Thinkers and Modern Debate on African Philosophy*. Nairobi: African Centre for Technology Studies.

Orwoll, L. and Achenbaum, W. A. 1993. "Gender and the Development of Wisdom," *Human Development*, 36 (5), 274–296.

Parmar, R. 2021. "The Wisdom of Resilience," *Psychiatric Times*. December 23, viewed on November 9, 2023 from https://www.psychiatrictimes.com/view/the-wisdom-of-resilience

Rooney, D. and McKenna, B. 2008. "Wisdom in Public Administration: Looking for a Sociology of Wise Practice," *Public Administration Review* 68(4), 709–721.

Schroeder, S. 2014. "Feminist Personalism," *ethikapolitika.org*, November 11, viewed on December 27, 2023 from https://www.academia.edu/10464530/Feminist_Personalism/

Simba, H., and Ngcobo, S. 2020 "Are Pandemics Gender Neutral? Women's Health and COVID 19," *Frontier in Global Womens Health*. Oct 19; 1:570666. DOI: 10.3389/fgwh.2020.570666

Tamale, S. 2014. "Gender Trauma in Africa: Enhancing Women's Links to Resources," *Journal of African Law* 48(1), 50–61.

Taranto, M. A. 1989. "Facets of Wisdom: A Theoretical Synthesis," *International Journal of Aging and Human Development* 29, 1–21.

Trebilcot, J. 1996. "Conceiving women: Notes on the logic of feminism," In Marilyn Pearsall (ed.), *Women and Values: Readings in Recent Feminist Philosophy*, pp. 358–364. Belmont, CA: Wadsworth.

Urban, P. 2022. "Care Ethics and the Feminist Personalism of Edith Stein," *Philosophies* 7(3):6. DOI: 10.3390/philosophies7030060

Williams, T. D., and Bengtsson, J. O. 2022. "Personalism," *The Stanford Encyclopedia of Philosophy* (Summer 2022 Edition), Edward N. Zalta (ed.), April 27, viewed on December 27, 2023 from https://plato.stanford.edu/archives/sum2022/entries/personalism/

Xiong, M., and Wang, F. 2021. "Gender Effect on Views of Wisdom and Wisdom Levels," *Frontiers in Psychology* 12, 725–736.

8

CATHOLIC RELIGIOUS WOMEN AND COVID-19

Tracing the Role of Sr Astridah Banda – A Dominican Religious Sister – In Curbing the Pandemic in Zambia

Nelly Mwale and Tomaida Milingo

Introduction

As the world continued to grapple with the surge in the number of confirmed cases of COVID-19, religious sisters in Africa moved in to support their government's efforts to combat the pandemic in the areas they served (Ajiambo, 2020). This is because, among other things, the onset of the COVID-19 pandemic raised global panic. At the same time, as the cases of people who had contracted the virus began to rise in Zambia, different spheres of life were negatively affected. For example, businesses such as bars, restaurants, gyms, and casinos had to shut down in order to minimise social interaction, which directly contributed to the spread of the virus. Those in the informal economy, such as market traders, were also negatively impacted as people avoided going to crowded places. This resulted in heightening levels of vulnerability and, more importantly, leading to changes in the livelihoods of individuals at household and community levels. Similarly, public religion was affected as places of worship had to be closed and alternative ways of worship had to be sought.

This chapter prioritises the contributions of women to the well-being of society with specific reference to African women's lived experiences during the pandemic. For example, despite the role of women in curbing the pandemic and in particular the contributions of women religious to the early response to the pandemic, they have not been the focus of much scholarly attention. This chapter, therefore, explores the role of women in addressing contemporary challenges with specific reference to how individual women responded to the COVID-19 pandemic. The chapter focuses on the narrative of Astridah Banda, a Zambian Dominican religious sister, given that the collective portrayal of Catholic religious women's responses to COVID-19 often obscures the role of individual personalities in managing the crisis. For example, while the Church was applauded for contributing to the fight against the pandemic, the individual narratives of the religious sisters behind the church's response remained unnoticed in the wider responses of the church, as shown by Mwale's (2022) analysis of the response of Catholic religious women to the pandemic. More importantly, Mwale

(2022, 2019) points to the need to identify and celebrate the women who made a difference during the pandemic and in public life.

The chapter is also driven by having observed lapses in the emerging literature on religion and the pandemic, which have tended to sideline the contributions of women. For example, some studies focused on the Church in general to neglect the voices of women, as demonstrated by Mwale and Chita (2022) in the responses of the Church mother bodies to the pandemic. In Zambia, all religious groups must affiliate with the umbrella body referred to as the "Mother body," under which individual churches and denominations are gathered under one administrative authority. The key mother bodies include the Council of Churches in Zambia (CCZ), the Evangelical Fellowship of Zambia (EFZ), and the Zambia Conference of Catholic Bishops (ZCCB). Other studies in Zambia that have addressed the gender and pandemic nexus have not been grounded in religion. For example, Malambo, Singogo, Kabisa, and Ngoma (2020) focus on a policy response dimension of the pandemic in Zambia, while Saasa and Spencer (2020) focus on the implications of the pandemic on the family's social, economic, and psychological well-being. Other studies are situated in the educational sphere (Mwale and Chita, 2020; Sintema, 2020).

Although the chapter focuses on a single narrative of Sr Astridah, she represented her work as a representation of Catholic religious women. She noted, "I am convinced that sisters are doing great works, and I feel that if I can represent the sisterhood, then our service to the people of God is recognized" (Interview with Ajiambo, 2020). The intent of the chapter is also to show the unique roles of women as exemplified by Sr Astridah Banda. The chapter, therefore, draws on a qualitative narrative research design in which document analysis was used to construct the representation of Sr Astridah Banda in response to COVID-19 in Zambia. This was supplemented by a member check.

Brief Overview of Related Literature

The review of related literature is situated in gender, religion, and pandemic scholarship. In this regard, studies have focused on the gendered impacts of COVID-19. For example, Pearce (2022) dwells on gendering the impacts of COVID-19 in Zambia and shows that COVID-19 has the potential to increase negative social vices such as intimate partner violence, stigma, and discrimination, as well as unequal access to information, financial and social protection, and access to sexual and reproductive health services. Accordingly, it was recommended that global and national strategic plans for COVID-19 preparedness and response must be backed by strong gender analysis and ensure meaningful participation of affected groups, including women and girls, in decision-making and implementation. Ford et al. (2022) also show that COVID-19 revealed the deep-rooted socio-economic vulnerabilities that exist due to gender inequality and how they are further perpetuated during times of crisis, particularly among women and girls.

Similarly, Manda (2022) explores the impact of the COVID-19 pandemic on rural livelihoods in Zambia from a gendered perspective and demonstrates that the pandemic and the measures to contain it induced livelihood struggles in rural economies. Despite this, livelihood impacts across gender and wellbeing remain under-researched. As such, Manda's study shows that for women, the pandemic-related inflationary pressures further induced challenges of access to inputs, leading to a general scale down of their agricultural activities, retreating to their domestic spheres. Additionally, the intra-household analysis further revealed deeper insights into COVID-19 impacts on household provisioning, labour, and caring burdens. Whereas provisioning responsibilities, labour demands, and care burdens increased generally for households, more impacts were felt by women. For example, the loss of jobs among men (e.g., in mining areas) meant women had to work even harder towards their daily subsistence and care for the members, while the closure of schools increased supervision responsibilities for women, thereby affecting time allocation.

Other gendered studies on the impacts of COVID-19 include Mukuka's (2021) study, which provides a gender-sensitive cultural hermeneutics analysis on COVID-19 and violence against women and children in Zambia. Her study highlights the value of human dignity, womanhood, culture, religion, and the misuse of male power or male dominance in the communities and homes and consequently calls for gender-sensitive responses. Similarly, Munyao and Kithuka (2021) writing from the Kenyan context, argue that gender-based violence (GBV) cases increased during the pandemic, hence the need for continued provision of GBV response services during the pandemic.

The major themes on religion and COVID-19 have focused on both the positive and negative roles of religion in the pandemic. For example, Chiluba and Shula (2020) analysed the COVID-19 epidemiological thought on why politics and religion were compromising the fight in Zambia and showed that deliberate and unnecessary political and religious gatherings inaction carried the risk of dire consequences, some of which had already led to suspected COVID-19 deaths of members of parliament and hospitalisation of a sizeable number of political leaders. Religious leaders were also not immune to this vice, as a number of COVID-19-related deaths passed through churches with body viewings being conducted. The duo concluded that such behaviours led to preventing action against COVID-19 outrunning evidence, or at least helping evidence to catch up, and that a myopic continued action of ignoring COVID-19 guidelines by politicians and religious leaders was a disservice to epidemiology.

Other studies that have analysed the intersection of religion and the pandemic include Mutemwa, et al. (2021) who explore the role of religion, philosophy of life, global health, traditional medicine, and past experiences in the COVID-19 pandemic response in Zambia. Their study demonstrates that contrary to expectations, Zambia protected public health against COVID-19 relatively successfully, at least during the first year of the pandemic. They concluded that this success was attributed to the possible role of religion, philosophy of life, global health approach, traditional medicine, and experiences with previous deadly epidemics that might have contributed to Zambia's public health success.

While the foregoing studies show the intersection of religion, gender, and the pandemic, the role of women in addressing the pandemic remains inadequately studied. This is because the few gendered studies on COVID-19 are devoid of the individual narratives of women. Hence, this chapter seeks to contribute to this emerging scholarship on the ways in which individual actors played a role towards addressing the pandemic from the Zambian context. This is deemed significant for complementing emerging scholarship on the intersection of religion, gender, and the pandemic, as addressed by a few notable scholars. For example, writing from the Zimbabwean context, Manyonganise (2023) links religion, gender, and health through her analysis of the role played by women in the utilisation of African Indigenous Medicine within the context of COVID-19. She demonstrates the ways in which women safeguarded plants and trees whose leaves, roots, and barks were considered effective in dealing with the disease in Zimbabwe. Manyonganise (2022) also explores how religion influenced the experiences of women during the COVID-19 pandemic in Zimbabwe. Similar approaches have been used by scholars in the Circle of Concerned Women Theologians (such as Hadebe, 2021; Hadebe et al., 2021).

Approach to Methods and Theory

The chapter is informed by insights from a qualitative narrative research design, here understood as a specific type of qualitative design in which narrative is understood as a spoken or written text giving an account of an event/action or series of events/actions, chronologically connected (Czarniawska, 2004:17). This is because the focus was on the narrative of a single person in relation to her role in responding to the COVID-19 pandemic in its early phases. Accordingly, biographical narrative research was used, in which the work of Sr Astridah Banda was gathered through document analysis. This was supplemented by Sr Astridah's review of the gathered media stories about her work during the pandemic. The data were analysed through the process of restoring, in which stories were gathered, analysed for key elements of the story (e.g., time, place, plot, and scene), and then rewritten to place them within a chronological sequence (Ollerenshaw and Creswell, 2002).

Theoretically, the chapter employs mediatisation as a framework to aid the understanding of the representations of Sr Astridah Banda's role in responding to the pandemic. Mediatisation is a social and cultural process through which the mass media influences the social changes that occur in any given society (Hjarvard 2017; Faimau and Lesitaokana, 2018; Mwale and Chita, 2016). Similarly, mediatisation is also influenced by changes in society. Accordingly, the presence of new media changed the ways in which women responded to the pandemic in the context of COVID-19. Of the four kinds of processes in which the media can change human communication and interaction identified by Schulz (2004), the chapter engages more with the ways in which the media makes actors in many different sectors adapt their behaviour to accommodate the media's valuations, formats, and routines. This is because the other three processes, namely, extending human communication abilities in both time and space, substituting social activities that previously took place face-to-face, and instigating an amalgamation of activities, are more inclined to other spheres than the context of pandemics. In this regard, the mediatisation theory as a framework has been used to make meaning of how media work as channels for conveying COVID-19-related messages.

The chapter takes the view that the interaction of media could be linked to gender, religion, and pandemic based on the gendered ways in which COVID-19 was mediatised by Catholic religious women. As such, this interaction would not only be influenced by the availability of media but also by the circumstances in the material world, which demand repackaging the content to be conveyed through the media in the context of the pandemic. Accordingly, the chapter pays attention to how the media act as conduits of communication, as the interest was to understand how Catholic religious women, through the narrative of Sr Astridah Banda, used the media to respond to COVID-19 in the early weeks of the pandemic in the country.

Sr Astridah Banda's Responses to COVID-19

To start with, Sr Astridah Banda's biography was not often linked to her narrative in the media. In this regard, she was simply represented as a member of the Dominican Missionary

Sisters of the Sacred Heart of Jesus. The Dominican Missionary Sisters of the Sacred Heart of Jesus came to Zambia in 1924. They minister to people in education, health, pastoral, and social services. Sr Astridah Banda started her journey as a religious sister in 2001. She has a Bachelor's degree in Social Work and Counselling and has been practising as a social worker since 2012. She has vast experience in working with rural and peri-urban communities and her passion is working with vulnerable women and children with a special focus on empowering vulnerable groups to be self-sustaining. Her belief is that life invites everyone every day to make a difference and as a social worker, one has many opportunities to make a positive and noticeable difference in society. She worked for the Zambia Association of Sisterhoods at the Secretariat as project manager for the Strengthening Capacity of Religious Women in Early Childhood Development (SCORE ECD) Project, a project through which Catholic Relief Services (CRS) worked through National Associations of Sister congregations to support Catholic Sisters in Kenya, Malawi, and Zambia to expand the provision of early childhood development services for children aged 0–2. Her work under the SCORE-ECD project encompassed building capacity in community health volunteers and mothers who provide key early childhood development messages to caregivers so that children under the age of 2 attain developmental milestones. The key messages consisted of health, nutrition, and WASH [water, sanitation, and hygiene] as well as parenting and stimulation messages [that encourage someone to grow, develop, or become active] (Ajiambo, 2020). After working at the Zambia Association of sisterhoods as project manager for an Early Childhood project in partnership with Catholic Relief Services (CRS) for 8 years, Sr Astridah Banda was (at the time of writing this chapter) the Regional Projects Coordinator for the Dominican Missionary Sisters of the Sacred Heart of Jesus.

Sr Astridah's representation of the roles she played during COVID-19 is seen through the major themes, which revolve around networking, conveying COVID-19 on radio, pastoral care, donation of protective equipment, and mediatising the work of the nuns/sisters.

Networking

Sr Astridah's role in curbing the pandemic was demonstrated through networking. For example, she collaborated with the humanitarian organisation, *Alight*, to create the COVID-19 awareness programme. This quest for partnership was situated in a context of fear and anxiety, which characterised the early phases of the pandemic. She recalled that she became alarmed following the news of deaths in the United States and Zambia's weak healthcare system. "I think on my part I was alarmed. It was scary. We were seeing reports from the European countries and America of people dying…. I was wondering how we were going to keep ourselves safe, how the community would be safe" (Interview with Ajiambo, 2020).

Her quest to make a difference during the pandemic was also motivated by the prevailing myths and misconceptions about the virus which were spreading in the community, contributing to the fear. As such, Sr Astridah partnered with the non-profit organisation, Sisters Rising Worldwide, to obtain personal protective equipment for her community and to better understand the available information on the coronavirus. This was followed by undergoing training on COVID-19, which was sponsored by Alight and Sisters Rising Worldwide. The training not only resolved her fears about the disease but also inspired her to make a difference in the community.

The moment I finished the training I really felt empowered.... the fear left me immediately and I felt I needed to do something about it. [I thought] how do I tell my neighbour and the next neighbour and those at home and everyone in the community that actually we can prevent this virus from spreading.

(Banda, Interview with ASEC staff, 20 April, 2021)

Her ability to network also shows how women take up leadership roles during a crisis. As affirmed by ASEC (2021), the citizens of Zambia had the tools and ability to combat COVID-19 but needed a community leader who appreciated their circumstances to guide them. In the case of the Catholic religious women, Sr Astridah's role was prominent as she took up the leadership role to guide the needy community in times of need. Her abilities to network demonstrate religion's ability to be a resource during a pandemic. This was demonstrated in the partnerships that were centred on religious institutions, as was the case when the Dominican Sisters in Lusaka worked with Alight and participated in the Sisters Rising Worldwide programme in the fight against coronavirus. The linkage was made possible by the Justice Coalition for Religious (JCOR), and the community took up the initiative of making a difference and contributing to the fight against COVID-19 (Banda, 2020). Networking also went hand in hand with mobilising resources to respond to COVID-19 in different communities and to raise awareness about prevention measures for the pandemic (Banda, 2020). Her leadership role affirms that faith-based organisations had a pivotal role during the COVID-19 pandemic and that faith leaders were seen as having an immense influence on people's health-related social behaviours (Heward-Mills et al., 2018) and in turn played a key role in strengthening community participation during a pandemic (Marston et al., 2020).

Conveying COVID-19 Messages on Radio

Besides partnering with like-minded organisations, Sr Astridah was represented as having played a role in curbing the pandemic through her radio show. Sr Astridah took up a community leadership role by tapping into her prior experience as a radio host to organise and produce the COVID-19 Awareness Programme through which she broadcasted public health messages and pandemic guidelines. Sr. Astridah believed this innovative idea was the most efficient way to reach underserved communities. She approached Yatsani Community Radio in March 2020 and asked to start broadcasts where she could translate health bulletins into Zambia's local languages and provide other critical news on the coronavirus. Her show, which aired several times each week, was produced in a talk show format with various guests who discussed specific health topics and answered questions from callers.

Sr Astridah's use of radio to convey COVID-19 messages was situated in her broader concern for the poor. In this regard, Sr Astridah realised that accessing public health information could be extremely challenging for the poor. Even for those with access to the internet, she observed that it could be difficult to know what information is valid and trustworthy. Most importantly, the health messages tended to be conveyed in English, and this meant that in a context like Zambia, where there are more than 70 languages, many people could not benefit from COVID-19-related information in English. As such, Sr Astridah set out to make a difference and reach people with essential information about COVID-19. Her use of radio was also a way of widening access to COVID-19 information to more people who otherwise may not have access to other media platforms such as the television or the internet. As has been well described by Musgrave (2020: n.p):

> In the radio show, Banda speaks about critical COVID-19 information and updates in multiple languages. In addition to telling listeners to wash their hands, wear masks, and stay home, the show also answers questions that listeners send in. Banda was able to create this multilingual show with the help of panelists, usually other nuns/sisters from the Association of Sisters in Zambia, each of whom speaks a designated local language. Knowledge is power, and access to critical information can often be the difference between life and death. Through the resourceful radio show, Banda and her fellow nuns/sisters ensure Zambians have the necessary means to fight the virus. For impoverished communities without advanced technologies, the radio show offers them access to essential information about the COVID-19 pandemic and how to protect themselves from the disease. The nuns and sisters in Zambia are making a difference in Zambia's fight against COVID-19 by spreading critical information and hope, two of which are crucial to surviving the pandemic.

Opting for the poor and adapting the message of COVID-19 to their needs also points to Catholic social teachings and Dominican ideals in ways that demonstrate how women responded to the pandemic by exploiting religious ideas or teachings. Additionally, the show on the radio not only points to how Catholic media was used as a tool to mediatise COVID-19 but also the role of Catholic religious women in the production of the programme. As concluded by Wijesinghe et al. (2022), the role of religious persons in conveying COVID-19 information was significant as it was a way of building trust through the sharing of timely and trustworthy health information and preventive behaviours via the media.

Pastoral Care

Sr Astridah also offered pastoral care through the media. For example, she recounted that the radio programme was based on COVID-19 messages and counselling and psychosocial support: "We could support our callers with spiritual support as well on issues that were affecting them because of the virus, like lack of money, loss of loved ones, and boredom" (Banda, 2020). As observed by Magezi (2016), pastoral care has been consistently concerned with the caring ministry of religious communities. It also entails the thorough care of people in their existential situations (Lartey, 1997). In the context of the pandemic, there was a need for targeted pastoral care, an aspect which the radio programme sought to accomplish. As argued by Hove (2022), the church has the mandate to provide pastoral presence to proclaim the gospel and provide care and healing to those who are suffering due to the effects of COVID-19. This was significant in that there was an increased demand for pastoral care resulting from people's experiences of anxiety, loneliness, and depression during the pandemic (Mwale, 2023).

Most importantly, Sr Astridah's drawing on online-based platforms not only entailed a shift in the mode of pastoring but also affirmed how media was used as a resource in the context of the pandemic. This was similar to other contexts, as concluded by Pavari (2021), that church leaders raised awareness and shared biblical and encouragement messages and prayers to assist members in overcoming fear during the pandemic, respectively. In the case of Sr Astridah's work, she relied on the common form of media, the radio, as a tool to reach out to those who would otherwise not benefit from social media.

Providing Preventive Equipment

Sr. Astridah also empowered communities through the distribution of protective gear. For example, during the radio programme, Sr Astridah was able to provide callers to the show with face masks in an effort to increase engagement. The distribution of masks was accompanied by explanations of the importance of face masks. Sr. Astridah noted that they were overwhelmed by phone calls during each broadcast:"…we had so many people phoning in. It would be like one after another and we couldn't even manage to receive all the calls during our talk show" (ASEC, 20 April 2021). This role of distributing face masks was similar to the roles that religious leaders are portrayed to have played during the pandemic. For example, from the Zimbabwean context, Dziva (2020) shows that religious leaders distributed protective gear. Similar conclusions have been drawn in Zambia, where Mwale and Chita (2022) show that Church mother bodies responded to the pandemic by making donations to the state and other needy communities. What is remarkable about Sr Astridah's work is the gendered response, which highlights the role of women in the pandemic. As observed by Essa-Hadad et al. (2022), religious leaders serve as a bridge between health authorities and communities and can be mediators who reconcile science, policy, and religious perspectives.

Mediatising the Work of the Nuns

Besides responding to the pandemic by way of spreading the COVID-19 preventive messages, Sr Astridah also reported on what the Catholic religious women were doing. For example, Sr Banda reported on the work of the Dominican Sisters and their partners during the pandemic:

> On Palm Sunday, the sisters participated in the Campaign to encourage people to stay home and it was broadcasted on American National television…The Trainings provided by Alight has given us the confidence to provide correct information to the communities and we are planning on having Radio programs to sensitize the community and provide Key messages shared by Alight. The supplies will help our vulnerable communities to keep to the recommended government guidelines on COVID-19 prevention which most of these communities cannot even afford. Gratitude goes to Alight and Sisters Rising Worldwide for these initiatives and the great work they are doing for humanity.
>
> (Banda, 2020: n.p)

Sr Astridah's contributions during the pandemic were also recognised at the global level. In this regard, Bill Gates named her as one of the seven unsung heroes of the pandemic. This was in view of the radio show which had an impact in Zambia and other parts of Africa, "In September, 2020, Bill Gates named Sr. Astridah as one the unsung heroes of the pandemic, featuring her in his popular Gates Notes newsletter and praising her work on FM 99.1" (ASEC, 20 April 2021).

Emerging Lessons from Sr Astridah Banda's Narrative

The narrative of Sr Astridah's role in curbing the pandemic brings to the fore lessons on how women have been active actors in moments of crisis. To start with, Sr Astridah's role demonstrates her utilisation of religious ideas or teachings, which enabled her to make a difference during a crisis. These teachings were centred on love for one's neighbour and opting for the poor, among others. Most importantly, her narrative signifies the religious mandate of her congregation:

> Our charism is evangelization. We praise, bless, and preach God's goodness everywhere. Reading the signs of times is a Dominican culture, and if preaching is by media, then why not? I have great support from my congregation, as most of the work has been done with sisters within the congregation and in different communities.
> (Ajiambo, 2020)

As observed by Isiko (2020), prayers and divine interventions brought hope to the people. The pandemic, however, brought about practical needs at both individual and community levels, which were to be met if the disease was to be defeated. Apart from the bodily harm of the disease, society had been affected economically and mentally, necessitating a holistic approach to the pandemic. The pandemic presented an opportunity for churches to fill the glaring gaps and practically serve the people in alternative ways, as did Sr Astridah in Zambia.

Sr Astridah's narrative also points to the utilisation of her religious organisation in the form of structures. For example, through the available apostolates, the religious sisters used their facilities and organisational structures to respond to the pandemic, as was the case in their health and education centres, including the use of Catholic media services. The Zambia Association of Sisterhoods (ZAS) as a structure was also a platform through which the interventions were coordinated and implemented. As observed by ASEC (2021), Catholic nuns hold a unique position in their local communities as they live among their neighbours, see who is in need and what is needed, and, perhaps most importantly, they are trusted. It is this rare combination of skills, trust, and working on the ground that places these sisters in a critical role during times of emergency response. This also relates to what other sisters were doing in the region, as thousands of the more than 38,000 Catholic religious women in the African countries of ASEC find themselves on the front lines of crises ranging from the current COVID-19 pandemic and other infectious diseases to medical care for trauma emergencies and responding to the fallouts of war (ASEC, 2021). The leadership training facilities also contributed to empowering Sr Astridah to serve the community in the manner she did:

> A number of sisters from ASEC programs have taken their skills and education to respond to the over 4 million cases of COVID throughout Africa. Sr Astridah Banda… participated in a web design course through SLDI. Through the course, she not only further her IT skills, but also learned the importance of telling a good story and how quality communication can build community and spread information. This training was key when the first cases of COVID-19 were discovered in her area. Most of the COVID-19 prevention messages were distributed in English and Sr. Astridah felt a sense of urgency to act and translate the information into local languages. She started a weekly radio program that disseminated prevention information, reaching over 1.5 million people.
> (ASEC, 3 May 2021)

Her narrative further shows the critical role of religious leadership in the pandemic. As observed by Marshall (2022), millions of people worldwide look more to religious authorities than health officials for guidance on how to behave and what to believe during a crisis. As such, the leadership role played by Sr Astridah cannot be downplayed as she affirmed that people tend to trust sisters when they provide messaging of such a nature. This is affirmed by the impact her engagement had. For example:

> After three months of our live broadcasts, we expanded the radio programs to three more provinces, where sisters got on the radio in their local languages and provided preventive messages to their communities, as well. The children participated in providing live radio programs to engage their fellow young people.
> (Banda interview with Ajiambo, 2020)

As concluded by Isiko (2020), the COVID-19 fight in Uganda demonstrated that religion and its institutions were instrumental in mobilising citizens to abide by government programmes, especially public health programmes. Therefore, whereas medical interventions were critical in the fight against disease, Isiko argues that Uganda's scenario demonstrated that religion and its institutions could be the tranquilliser in the whole medical response to an epidemic. In the Zambian context, this is demonstrated by the trust accorded to religious leaders and to religious women like Sr Astridah in particular.

Conclusion

The chapter trailed the intersection of religious women and the pandemic through the exploration of Sr Astridah Banda's role in curbing COVID-19. Given that Sr Astridah's roles were characterised by hosting a multi-language radio show on a Catholic-based radio station (with approximately over 1.5 million listeners), which addressed different themes related to the pandemic, her narrative shows that women were active players in addressing the pandemic. Through her network of Catholic religious sisters, she mobilised sisters from the community and other congregations to participate in her radio program, which translated information about proper handwashing, social distancing, and wearing masks into local languages, among other issues.

The chapter further showed that based on the impact of her radio show, she was named as one of the seven unsung heroes of the pandemic by Bill Gates. Through her utilisation of radio, leadership skills, and Dominican charism to mediatise COVID-19 responses, the chapter argues that her narrative underscores lessons for a gendered role in curbing the pandemic centred on exploiting existing opportunities for the good of humanity.

Bibliography

African Sisters Education Collaborative(ASEC)., 2021. "Nun's Radio Show Disseminates COVID-19 Info to Zambians in Multiple Languages." *ASEC News*, 20 April.

Ajiambo, D., 2020. "Q & A with Sr. Astridah Banda, 'unsung hero' for educating on COVID-19," pp. 1–11, Global Sisters Report, 17 November, viewed 27 July 2020, from https://www.globalsistersreport.org.

Aluko, O. P., 2020. 'COVID-19 pandemic in Nigeria: The response of the Christian Church', *African Journal of Biology and Medical Research*, 3(2), 111–125.

ASEC, 2020. "Bringing Light to the Darkness: Catholic Sisters on the Front Lines in Africa," *ASEC News*, 3 May, Accessed from http://asec-sldi.org/news 27 June 2023

Banda, A., 2020. "The Zambian Region joins the fight against COVID-19." Justice Coalition for Religious. Accessed form https://jcor2030.org/wp-content/uploads/2020/04/The-Zambian-Region-joins-the-fight-against-COVID-Dominican-Sisters.pdf

Chiluba, B. C., and Shula, H., 2020, "Zambia: Editorial Comment-COVID-19-Epidemiological Thought on Why Politics and Religion Are Compromising the Fight," *Journal of Preventive and Rehabilitative Medicine*, 2(1), 1–4.

Czarniawska, B., 2004. *Narratives in Social Science Research*. London: Sage.

Dziva, C., 2020. "The Potential and Challenges for Traditional Leadership in Combating the COVID-19 Pandemic in Rural Communities of Zimbabwe." *African Journal of Governance and Development*, 9(2), 510–523.

Essa-Hadad, J., Abed Elhadi Shahbari N., Roth, D., and A. Gesser-Edelsburg. 2022. "The impact of Muslim and Christian religious leaders responding to COVID-19 in Israel," *Frontier in Public Health* 10, 1061072

Faimau, G and Lesitaokana, W. O. eds. 2018. *New Media and the Mediatisation of Religion: An African Perspective*. Cambridge: Cambridge Scholars Publishing.

Ford, J. D., Zavaleta-Cortijo, C., Ainembabazi, T., Anza-Ramirez, C., Arotoma-Rojas, I., Bezerra, J., Chicmana-Zapata, V., Galappaththi, E. K., Hangula, M., Kazaana, C., and Lwasa, S., 2022. "Interactions between Climate and COVID-19." *The Lancet Planetary Health*, 6(10), e825–e833.

Hadebe, M., 2021. *Social Insurance Protection in South Africa during COVID-19: A Legal Perspective*. Johannesburg: University of Johannesburg (South Africa).

Hadebe, N., Gennrich, D., Rakoczy, S., and Tom, N., 2021. *A Time Like No Other: COVID-19 in Women's Voices*. Johannesburg: University of Johannesburg (South Africa).

Heward-Mills, N. L., Atuhaire, C., Spoors, C., Pemunta, N. V., Priebe, G., and Cumber, S. N., 2018. "The Role of Faith Leaders in Influencing Health Behaviour: A Qualitative Exploration on the Views of Black African Christians in Leeds, United Kingdom," *Pan African Medical Journal*. https://doi.org/10.11604/pamj.2018.30.199.15656

Hjarvard, S. 2017. "Mediatisation." In Patrick, Rössler, Cnythia A. Hoffner and Liesbert van Zoonen (eds). *The International Encyclopaedia of Media Effects*, Malden, MA: Wiley-Blackwell, 1221–1241.

Hoezee, S., 2020. "The Pandemic and Homiletics 101: A Reflection," *Acta Theologica* 40, 2: 82–95. https://jcor2030.org/wp-content/uploads/2020/04/The-Zambian-Region-joins-the-fight-against-COVID-Dominican-Sisters.pdf) Accessed 27th June 2023

Hove, R., 2022. "The Pastoral Presence in Absence: Challenges and Opportunities of Pastoral Care in the Context of the Global Corona Virus Pandemic." *Pharos Journal of Theology*, 103(1), 1–11.

Isiko, A. P., 2020. "Religious Construction of Disease: An Exploratory Appraisal of Religious Responses to the COVID-19 Pandemic in Uganda," *Journal of African Studies and Development*, 12(3), 77–96.

Lartey, E. Y., 1997. *In Living Colour: An Intercultural Approach to Pastoral Care and Counselling*. London: Cassell.

Magezi, V., 2016, "Reflection on Pastoral Care in Africa: Towards Discerning Emerging Pragmatic Pastoral Ministerial Responses," *In die Skriflig* 50(1), 1–7.

Malambo, M., Singogo, F., Kabisa, M., and Ngoma, H. 2020, "Balancing Health and Economic Livelihoods: Policy Responses to the COVID-19 Pandemic in Zambia," IFPRI COVID-19 Policy Portal. https://www.ifpri.org/project/COVID-19-policy-response-cpr-portal

Manda, S., 2022. Mainstreaming Gender for Enhanced COVID-19 Rural Livelihood Recovery in Zambia,' Policy Brief. IDRC/OXFAM-006

Manyonganise, M., 2022, "'When a pandemic wears the face of a woman': Intersections of religion and gender during the COVID-19 pandemic in Zimbabwe," In F. Sibanda et al, eds., *Religion and the COVID-19 Pandemic in Southern Africa* (pp. 232–243). London: Routledge.

Manyonganise, M., 2023. "COVID-19, Gender and Health: Recentring Women in African Indigenous Health Discourses in Zimbabwe for Environmental Conservation." *HTS Teologiese Studies/ Theological Studies*, 79(3), 1–9.

Marshall, K., 2022. "COVID-19 and Religion: Pandemic Lessons and Legacies." *The Review of Faith & International Affairs*, 20(4), 80–90.

Marston, C., Renedo, A., and Miles, S., 2020. "Community Participation Is Crucial in a Pandemic," *The Lancet*, 395(10238), 1676–1678.

Mukuka, N. N. M., 2021. "COVID-19 and Violence Against Women and Children in Zambia," In C. J. Kaunda, ed., *Religion, Gender, and Wellbeing in Africa*, (pp. 49–62). Lanham: Rowman & Littlefield.

Munyao, M., and Kithuka, E., 2021, *The Role of Religion in Public Life: COVID-19 and Gender-based Violence in Kenya*. Lanham: Rowman & Littlefield.

Musgrave, P., 2020. "How Nuns in Zambia are Fighting COVID-19 with Knowledge." *Boregn Magazine*, 7 July. Accessed from https://www.borgenmagazine.com/nuns-in-zambia/

Mutemwa, D., Zvánovcová, V., Helová, A. and Novotný, D. D., 2021. "The Role of Religion, Philosophy of Life, Global Health, Traditional Medicine, and Past Experiences in the COVID-19 Pandemic Response: Zambia Case Study." *Caritas et Veritas*, pp. 34–49.

Mwale, N. and Chita, J., 2016. "Religion and the Media: The Portrayal of Prophecy in the Zambian #." *Prophecy today: Reflections from a Southern African context*, Special edition of Word and Context Journal, 41–63.

Mwale, N., and Chita, J., 2020. "Higher Education and Programme Delivery in the Context of COVID-19 and Institutional Closures: Student Responses to the Adoption of e-Learning at a Public University in Zambia," In N. Mkhize et al., eds., *Technology-based Teaching and Learning in Higher Education during the Time of COVID-19* (pp. 9–33), Durban: CSSALL

Mwale, N., and Chita, J., 2022. "Standing Together in Faith through the Time of COVID-19: The Responses of Church Umbrella Bodies in Zambia," in F. Sibanda et al, eds., *Religion and the COVID-19 Pandemic in Southern Africa* (pp. 155–171), London: Routledge.

Mwale, N., 2019. "The Nature and Significance of a Muslim Woman's Contest for Mayor of Lusaka, Zambia." *African Journal of Gender and Religion*, 25(2), 63–85.

Mwale, N., 2023. "'Be Spiritual and Employ Technology in your Ministry': An Experience of Sermons Amid COVID-19 by Bishop Harrison Sakala of Tabernacle of David Assembly of God in Zambia." *Studia Historiae Ecclesiasticae*, 49(3), 1–16.

Ollerenshaw, J. A. and Creswell, J. W., 2002. "Narrative Research: A Comparison of Two Restorying Data Analysis Approaches." *Qualitative Inquiry*, 8(3), 329–347.

Pavari, N., 2021. "The Role of Pentecostal Church Leadership to the COVID 19 Pandemic in Zimbabwe. *Global Journal of Management and Business Research*, 21(5), 32–38.

Pearce, A., 2022. *Gendering the Impacts of COVID-19: Equitable Policy Responses for Zambia-Policy Brief*. Lusaka: Policy Monitoring Research Centre.

Saasa, S., and Spencer, J., 2020. "COVID-19 in Zambia: Implications for Family, Social, Economic, and Psychological Well-Being," *Journal of Comparative Family Studies*, 51(3/4), 347–359. https://www.jstor.org/stable/26976656

Schulz, W. 2004. "Reconstructing Mediatisation as an Analytical Concept." *European Journal of Communication*, 19(1), 87–101.

Sintema, E. J., 2020, 'Effect of COVID-19 on the Performance of Grade 12 Students: Implications for STEM Education,' *EURASIA Journal of Mathematics, Science and Technology Education*, 16(7), em1851.

Wijesinghe, M. S. D., Ariyaratne, V. S., and Gunawardana, B. M. I., 2022, "Role of Religious Leaders in COVID-19 Prevention: A Community-Level Prevention Model in Sri Lanka," *Journal of Religion and Health*, 61, 687–702.

9
CHRISTIAN WOMEN IN AFRICA AND THE COVID-19 PANDEMIC IN THE DEMOCRATIC REPUBLIC OF CONGO AND NIGERIA

Jessie Ini Fubara-Manuel, Yossa Way and Emma Wild-Wood

Introduction

Across the globe, women, girls, and other vulnerable members of society were adversely affected by the COVID-19 pandemic in 2020–2022 and the social repercussions of the public health measures introduced to retard the spread of disease. African women were no exception. By mid-2020, humanitarian groups and economic organisations, like UN Women (n.d.), Partners (July 2020), and Social Science Analytics Cell (2023), produced evidence of a significant negative impact on job security, education, safety in the home, and maternal health for women and girls. Whilst international groups, like The Elders (June 2020) and the World Bank (2022), called for improved, accessible social service systems and the addressing of harmful social norms, many women were finding ways of coping on a daily basis with these unprecedented circumstances. This chapter acknowledges the significant role played by African religious institutions in health delivery and in shaping gender norms (Sibanda et al. 2022; Manyonganise 2022), and it specifically examines how Christian women in two African countries, the Democratic Republic of Congo ("Congo" in this chapter) and Nigeria, were able to respond to the pandemic and its social effects. It adds to previous research on faith communities and the pandemic, which concluded that churches possessed high levels of trust and many of them were ready to assist with pandemic measures (Igwe 2021), yet governments and Ministries of Health worked with international humanitarian agencies and rarely engaged well with churches directly (Wild-Wood et al. 2021). Many church leaders said they did not understand the public health messages they were asked to transmit; their ability to offer social and spiritual support to vulnerable people was compromised by the closure of buildings; and digital communication was not readily available to all, and many lost incomes (Kangamina et al. 2022; Baba et al. 2022).

Using a mixture of methods and interviewing a majority of women from Protestant churches,[1] we identified the important role of humanitarian and parachurch organisations in the contemporary empowerment of women faced with disease. There was also a criticism of church leadership that resonated with the self-critique of leaders (Baba et al. 2022). Women continued to meet in church groups during the pandemic, albeit with restrictions, and took succour from the teaching and sense of community they provided. Other Christian women met in groups outside the church setting whilst drawing strength from their Christian faith and their solidarity with one another. Their story is one of familiarity with disease and of resilience to living in a context with multiple threats to life. Our findings suggest that the social effects of public health measures impacted women more than the disease itself. These measures may have successfully reduced COVID-19 infections, but they also exacerbated social challenges. For this reason, the social background is presented first.

Christianity, Health, and Conflict in Congo and Nigeria

Congo and Nigeria will see a significant increase in their population in the next 30 years (UN Dept of Social and Economic Affairs 2022). Nigeria is anglophone and Congo is francophone. In both countries, religious faith is public, and there are many Christian denominations. Churches are often regarded as patriarchal institutions with predominantly male leadership and a tendency to promote traditional values like obedience to a male household head. However, they are very diverse institutions with opportunities for female empowerment. The majority support female-led associations, development activities, and discourses that encourage women to use their gifts, even though for some denominations these gifts are gendered and associated with work in caring professions or in informal employment. In Congo, the population is estimated to be 95.1% Christian (Johnson and Zurlo 2020). The Catholic Church is the largest church. The federation of Protestant churches (*Eglise du Christ au Congo*, ECC) and the Pentecostal churches (*Eglises du Reveil*, EdR) are large alliances of different denominations. There are also independent churches, including the Kimbanguist church, one of the largest African Instituted churches.

In Nigeria, the Catholic Church and the Protestant churches make up the Christian Association of Nigeria, which offers a public, united Christian presence. Among the Protestant churches, there is a distinction between mission-led churches and African Instituted churches, which are often offshoots of the mission-led churches. In both Congo and Nigeria, Christian churches have delivered health care since the Western missionary era (Kangamina et al. 2022), and women have been recruited and trained as nurses and medical assistants, allowing them new forms of economic independence from their families (Meier zu Selhausen 2014: 74–5).

In Congo, faith-based health facilities manage health delivery on behalf of the Ministry of Health (Seay, 2013; Lindstrom 2019: 79). For Nigeria, the state regulates health care services, and the private sector offers a major contribution to health delivery. Some health facilities are managed by churches and faith-based organisations; others are run by individuals and medical organisations. Over the years, the use of traditional or alternative medicine has also increased, especially in rural areas (Asakitikpi 2016: 30–31). The health facilities run by the Catholic church particularly played a strategic role during the pandemic. In Nigeria, some of the large Pentecostal churches, like the Redeemed Christian Church of God, are involved in nationwide medical care (Wild-Wood et al. 2021: 66–67). However, in Congo, the Pentecostal Churches, with some notable exceptions of influential congregations, have little involvement with formal health care and are likely to rely solely on divine healing. Divine healing by prayer alone, or accompanied by exorcism, is also attractive to some members of Protestant and Catholic churches, who develop prayer groups for this purpose, both in Congo and Nigeria.

In both countries, the COVID-19 pandemic arrived in situations of significant political conflict. Nigeria and Congo were 6th and 17th, respectively, on the Global Terrorism Index (2022). In Nigeria, conflict can be stirred up by the religious divide across ethnic groups, with the south being predominantly Christian and the north predominantly Muslim. Since 2009, the insurgencies of Boko Haram and Islamic State in West Africa Province (ISWAP) in the north-eastern part of Nigeria have resulted in over 20,000 fatalities and over 2 million refugees and displaced people (Amwe 2023; Fubara-Manuel and Ngwobia 2021). In the Niger Delta, where Fubara-Manuel's research takes place, conflict continues to surround a quest for resource control. Nigerians wanting to control the oil-rich region's resources resorted to militancy and protested to force multinationals to address the underdevelopment of the area (Fubara-Manuel 2014). Violence by the police, including police brutality against those who did not comply with lockdown restrictions (Gruzd et al. 2020), has also been met with protest and come under international scrutiny (*Human Rights Watch*, 2023). In Congo, conflict and the resultant insecurity are found particularly in the east of the country where our research took place. Conflicts are prompted by access to mineral resources, land, involvement of neighbouring states, and ethnic tensions. Women and girls have been targets of rape during this time. 130 armed groups were reportedly active in 2019, just prior to the arrival of COVID-19 (Wells et al. 2019). In June 2021, the number of internally displaced people in Ituri was 1.7 million, almost half the province's estimated population. Displaced women often rely on prostitution as a readily available source of income. Yet there is also a growing recognition of the importance of strengthening the legal rights of women and of ensuring parity in governance roles in the country (Milemba 2019).

The Democratic Republic of Congo

Background to the Pandemic

From 19th March to 22nd July 2020, the government of Congo prohibited all gatherings of more than 20 people in public places. Schools, universities, and churches were closed until 10 August 2021. When they reopened social distancing, handwashing and the wearing of face coverings were required. In June 2021 and January 2022, there was a significant rise in COVID-19 cases, but, overall, the number of recorded deaths remained low compared with other countries.[2] Some women remembered the challenges of being confined to the home and trying to occupy and teach the children. They considered that they had greater responsibility than men for ensuring the care of children and the home. Although markets remained open, there was a reduction in trade, which affected stall holders (many of them women), and certain goods were not available. When children returned to school, parents were expected to provide children with face coverings and encourage the washing of hands. Again, this task fell disproportionately on women. To give one example, a headmistress we interviewed sewed face coverings so that those pupils whose parents did not provide them would still be able to attend school. She did this in addition to monitoring the daily school regime of handwashing and temperature measuring. Professional status influenced the reactions to COVID-19. Teachers and health agents considered themselves to be working together, helped by humanitarian agencies, to comply with government measures they understood to be in the best interests of the population. They expressed concern that many people resisted the measures because they lacked the resources to comply with them.

Some women in Ituri province said that they were worried about catching COVID-19 and were particularly frightened when the death toll rose in June 2021 and prominent businessmen died.[3] One said that to keep her family safe, she preferred not to attend funerals. This fear of the disease was, however, a less common reaction in the general population.

For many people, the threat of the spread of COVID-19 was the least of their worries. They complied with measures only to avoid being fined. Other illnesses and insecurity seemed more pressing. Congo experienced significant Ebola outbreaks in 2017–2018 and 2019–2020. Bubonic plague is endemic, and there is limited health assistance for widespread illnesses like malaria and cholera. Familiarity with diseases in general reduced the anxiety of COVID-19 for many, particularly when other continents were more immediately impacted. For those living in the insecure eastern provinces of Congo, the threat of armed groups, curfews, and military rule were pressing issues. A group of internally displaced people in a camp in Bunia made their opinions clear to a vaccination team. While many people were wary of being vaccinated, this group refused the vaccine on the grounds that 'The real COVID (i.e., crisis) is at Djugu.' Their priority was a peace settlement in order to be able to go home. Some people thought the public health measures were futile because COVID-19 was a spiritual disease caused by the devil or evil spirits and, thus, required prayer to combat it (Wild-Wood et al. 2023). The women we interviewed were most directly affected by the preventative measures rather than the disease itself. It added another layer of complexity to their lives, sometimes reducing their income. Many regretted the reduction in social activities, like those run by the church.

Women in Church

While churches were shut, women continued to meet in small groups of up to 20 people, seated at a distance. In the Anglican Church, the Mothers Union met every week, and women attended a monthly prayer meeting, *Maombi ya Umoja* (prayer of unity). In the same way, the Federation des Femmes Protestants (FFP), the parachurch organisation that unites women members of the Protestant *Eglise du Christ au Congo*, arranged small groups of different women each week for prayer and support. The FFP operates at local, provincial, and national levels. During the COVID-19 pandemic, provincial FFP officers were in touch with one another across the country. They were already sharing experiences learnt from the recent Ebola epidemics about how to raise awareness of the disease and its prevention. Furthermore, the FFP used prior relations with humanitarian organisations to provide advice and personal protective equipment to vulnerable groups.[4]

The FFP has, in recent years, worked closely with humanitarian organisations that focus on development for women and girls. During the pandemic, some FFP leaders collaborated with organisations to raise awareness of the disease among their members and among those vulnerable to the spread of diseases, like displaced people and the taximen.[5] In Ituri province, the FFP facilitated the delivery of handwashing stations to displaced people living in cramped conditions with limited sanitation. The FFP was also involved in encouraging vaccination take-up in a country which was generally hesitant about having the vaccine. In the north-east of the country, relationships between FFP and humanitarian agencies were already established because of the regional conflicts. In 2016, the FFP of Ituri (FFPI) organised a team of twenty people to visit an area where violence against women was particularly acute. MONESCO (the UN peacekeeping force) supported the venture with finance and protection. Subsequent meetings with women and the armed groups reduced the violence in the region (FFPI et al. 2016). The relationship with MONESCO and humanitarian organisations over several years allowed the leaders of the FFPI to respond quickly and effectively to COVID-19 because they were already working with those organisations that were able to provide messaging and basic protective equipment.

Church leaders were criticised by some members of the FFP and women working in education and health: Some church leaders were accused of negligence or of not taking the spread of disease seriously. Others preached that COVID-19 did not exist, that it was caused by evil spirits, or that prayer alone would cure it. That such views were held is unsurprising in a country where the government fails to protect its people from violence and where medical facilities are often too limited or too expensive to respond to health needs (Lindstrom 2019: 77–79). Yet this rhetoric established a situation in which trust in God was diametrically opposed to trust in medical advice.

Professional women and FFP leaders, however, were concerned about the health of women who were persuaded by arguments that COVID-19 need not be taken seriously or was a spiritual disease. The women we spoke to compared unfavourably those church leaders who preached these views or gave little guidance with the humanitarian organisations, whose intervention they welcomed in providing health messages and basic protective equipment. Furthermore, many humanitarian organisations have a central aim of empowering women because female decision-making and education have long been seen as key to healthy populations (UN Women(a) n.d). They often seek out local women's organisations when requiring representatives from civil society. Adverts for local or national jobs with humanitarian organisations often prioritise female candidates.

For professional Christian women, churches that have traditionally provided education and medical care are perceived to be falling behind humanitarian organisations in a number of ways. Churches in Congo have supported women's education and advancement since their inception, but in specific ways. Female leadership is visible mainly in female-only spaces, in children's work, or in schools and medical facilities. Very few Protestant denominations ordain women. Those who are ordained rarely take high office. The Catholic Church is the largest denomination and also does not ordain women. This limited leadership by women is replicated in other sectors of society, with humanitarian organisations offering a stark contrast in their practical assessment of women's public skills and abilities. During COVID-19 humanitarian, organisations provided a space for professional women to be active in supporting public health messaging as volunteers and in their capacities as teachers and health professionals when many (male) church leaders were unsure how to respond or were dismissive of the disease.

Nigeria

Background

Like Congo, the Nigerian government responded to the pandemic by adopting many of the global measures advised by the WHO to stem the spread of the infection. The first case of infection was recorded by Nigeria on 27 February 2020, just as the Federal Government (2020) announced lockdown in major cities such as Lagos and Abuja. The fact that the nation was in lockdown did not mean that women's gender-based concerns and responsibilities ceased; instead, they multiplied in ways that made women vulnerable to domestic abuse (Olufemi and Labeodan 2021). Whilst it has been acknowledged that women bore the brunt of the consequences of COVID-19 because of care responsibilities and patriarchal systems that impinge on their rights, many women with disabilities suffered more, were more vulnerable to abuse, and were often treated very badly. For some, this increased level of vulnerability was because of the prevailing stigma associated with disabilities. Discrimination because of disability often increases when there is fear or disease. For others, it was simply because their impairments made it difficult for them to protect themselves or to cope by themselves (Ekiikina, 2021). Some women with disabilities explained that they were often treated as though their disability made them more susceptible to infection. Those with other health conditions, especially those who live openly with HIV, spoke of receiving disdainful and hostile stares.

The Federal Government began to give out basic relief items, and those with disabilities were not included. Many churches, collaborated with faith-based NGOs to organise support for the poor without any direct response to those with disabilities. Disabled women pushed for the allocation of portions accordingly, but the distribution process was fraught with corruption (Salaudeen 2020). People who needed basic food and medical supplies were expected to go to designated locations for pickup, a feat that women living with mobility challenges said was difficult without assistance. COVID-19's social distancing measures deprived many disabled women of the assistance they needed to carry out routine duties. Married women living with disabilities reported that increased dependence on their spouses caused friction in the marriage. A single woman blamed COVID-19 for making 'her do things to survive' such as sleeping with her neighbour in exchange for assistance. Those who had to move back home with family because they could not stay without help spoke of feeling 'degraded' and having to deal with paternalistic behaviours as though they were not capable of taking care of themselves. The NGO Support Group that they belonged to was beyond physical reach, and the church had never been of much help. There were a few women living with disabilities who described themselves as 'blessed' because they had help from family and friends.

UN Women(b) (n.d.) acknowledged that women with disabilities also faced challenges adhering to other preventive measures such as handwashing and wearing of face masks/covering of face, for example. Deaf people found that face covering impaired communication because sign language also involves different parts of the face. Those who used their hands to manage their walking aids found public handwashing frustrating. The challenges with these directives make the dread of the disease minimal. For women with disabilities, the fear of the spread of COVID-19 was less worrisome than the heightened level of stigma and discrimination due to their disability, increased vulnerability to domestic abuse because of their inability to protect themselves, lack of assistance and ensuing poverty, and the difficulty with adhering to preventive measures. To cope with these challenges, women with disabilities would find greater succour in support groups with shared experiences and spiritualities than the church, whose attention to disadvantaged groups has been limited.

Women with Disabilities in Church

With the lockdown came the closure of all public places including the churches. Many women with disabilities did not find church closure particularly discomforting, as ableist assumptions and infrastructure had often marginalised their participation in church activities. Some church leaders preached that COVID-19 was a sin, a punishment from God, and those who were infected were facing the wrath of God – a teaching similar to that used to explain disability. Women with disabilities had already experienced the rejection and stigma of such misleading theology when they were expected to be delivered and healed from their disability. A few who sang in a church choir said they missed choir rehearsals during the pandemic and the friendships they had developed with some of the choristers. Many had struggled to find a place of belonging among churches' women's groups, often being told they would be unable to take part sufficiently in the women's activities such as cleaning the church, visiting members, or cooking for church events.

Women with disabilities from different churches found an alternative sense of church belonging to a humanitarian non-governmental organisation (NGO) for women with disabilities: Bold Hearts Initiative for Beautiful Outstanding Ladies with Disabilities (Bold Hearts). Whilst there are many NGOs in Nigeria addressing the concerns of disability, Bold Hearts has a focus on gender and disability, and it is run primarily by women with disabilities themselves. It provides a safe place for members to live positive lives when support from the church or society is inadequate. Members spoke of Bold Hearts as the place of belonging, of friendship, and of mutual support. As all members of Bold Hearts in Port Harcourt are Christians, their support group meetings, prior to the pandemic, took the form of church fellowship meetings.[6] It was these meetings with Bold Hearts that the women missed and for which they longed, as it provided solidarity and sharing of a common faith.

At its May 2020 meeting, the executive members of Bold Hearts decided to start an online discussion forum called BoldTV. The Secretary of Bold Hearts mentioned that members wanted a space in the public domain where women with disabilities could control the narrative of their experiences with COVID-19 and other issues.[7] By producing their own material, they also intended to educate the public about their challenges and perspectives on life. On 13 June 2020, the first weekly episode of BoldTV went live on Facebook (www.youtube.com/@boldtv_boldhearts). When BoldTV celebrated its first anniversary on 12 June 2021, it had broadcast 44 episodes, launched itself on YouTube, and spread beyond Port Harcourt to the national stage. Members testified to a sense of 'camaraderie.' Sign language interpreters were employed for every episode to ensure better inclusion. Unfortunately, in Nigeria, as elsewhere in the world, there were those who were still left out by the rapid adoption of digital measures (Goodall and Meakin, 2021). The digitalised world was not helpful to those in rural areas or those who were unable to afford phones. As lockdown rules were relaxed and public gatherings opened, Bold Hearts obtained sponsorship from the World Council of Churches (WCC), the Ecumenical HIV and AIDS Initiative and Advocacy, to hold a workshop to address gender-based violence. They wanted a physical space for women with disabilities who had been abused during lockdown to share their experiences and find a space for healing. At the end of the workshop held on 30 October 2020, the women made an advocacy promotional video with the slogan, 'Gender-based violence against women and girls with disabilities: Silence is not golden.'[8] Bold Hearts continues to offer an enabling space where religious faith informs and motivates coping strategies.

Ignoring the church's neglect, women with disabilities in Bold Hearts are replicating their expectations of the church by supporting one another and sharing their lives together. They started a platform to educate the public on disability and, in doing so, dispel stigma around disability, speak against domestic abuse, educate its members on economic empowerment, and offer enlightenment on ways of coping in a pandemic. They claim a relationship with a loving God, who is with them through the challenges of disability, and some with disability and disease, and who was with them through COVID-19. It was a shared faith, but it was also one to which they confessed a personal reality.

Christian Women and Humanitarian Organisations

Women in Nigeria and DR Congo displayed resilience and adaptability during the COVID-19 pandemic. Their criticism of churches and their ability to work with – and even to found – humanitarian organisations before and during the pandemic suggests a possible trend in the attitudes of educated Christian women when faced with social challenges. Women were able to navigate and create organisations to bring about change they regarded as necessary.

Our findings support those of humanitarian organisations, like UN Women (n.d.) and The Elders (June 2020) Partners (July 2020), who identified how women were adversely affected by the pandemic. However, the women we interviewed – most of them professional and Protestant – also displayed an ability to protect their families and workplaces against disease whilst adapting to the public health measures, which often had a constraining effect on economic activity and social support. Women living with disabilities found this particularly challenging, but together in an organisation like BOLD Hearts, they could display great tenacity.

Christian faith played a significant role in their resilience: Women used their membership in fellowships and parachurch organisations for prayer and moral support. Some also used these groups to support others in the community. It was striking, however, to hear a significant level of criticism levelled at the churches of which they were part. Their high expectations of church leaders were not met. In Nigeria, before the pandemic, women living with disabilities had formed the NGO Bold Hearts in response to a society and churches that stigmatise disabled women. The pandemic highlighted the level of societal stigma and increased the criticism of the institutional church by members of Bold Hearts, even as they remained members of their churches. Bold Hearts became a place of support and refuge for women living with disabilities. It proved to be a place where they could express their Christian faith without the expectation that they should be healed or delivered from evil spirits. In Congo, women also compared favourably the actions of national and international humanitarian organisations and parachurch organisations with the actions of church leaders during the pandemic. They expected guidance from church leaders but felt that many were unclear and some gave unwise advice. The gendered norms of caregiving, often reinforced by churches, were particularly onerous for women during the pandemic.

Professional women, who are members of mainstream churches that run schools and medical facilities, some of whom are living with disabilities, were critical of church leaders and felt empowered by the humanitarian sector, having already connected with humanitarian organisations before the pandemic. They used these prior connections to offer mutual support and raise awareness of COVID-19 prevention measures among members and vulnerable people.

Conclusion

In studying the response of Christian women to the pandemic, our findings suggest an intersection between gender and education in faith communities' response to the pandemic. Personal faith and membership in parachurch organisations were significant for women during the pandemic in coping with the challenges of health, inequality, and disability. Yet they were critical of institutional church leadership.

Professional, Protestant women sought guidance and support from humanitarian organisations that had been intentional about promoting female education and opportunities or establishing their own. Whilst they did not directly raise the issue of female leadership in churches, some of them felt better able to act in the humanitarian space rather than in churches, which may suggest a problem with limited commitment by many churches to female leadership. Their reactions also support the previous research on COVID-19 and faith communities that found that despite the high social capital of religious communities among the general population, church leaders were overlooked by governmental organisations and thus felt disempowered to offer advice or pastoral support during the pandemic (Baba et al. 2022). Professional women responded to this sense of disempowerment from church leaders by looking to humanitarian agencies for help. It seems from these professional women's perspective, that even before the pandemic, the church leaders were unprepared to act in a health emergency. Yet both professional Christian women and church leaders were disappointed by this situation because of the public and social role of Christianity. There appeared to be an expectation that church leaders ought to be able to respond quickly and appropriately to the pandemic, an expectation which was not replicated in other parts of the globe.

Of course, differentials in educational attainment and the social and economic advantages that accompany it, play a role in how Christianity and disease control are understood among women and men. Not all Christian women in Nigeria and Congo would level this sort of internal critique at their churches, preferring instead to criticise the state-sanctioned public health measures that closed churches or to identify ways in which their denomination rose appropriately to the challenges of the pandemic. Further study is needed to appreciate how these elements intersect to create differences of opinion.

The responses to COVID-19 from the women in this study may suggest a fissure between different sectors of society – government, humanitarian organisations, and churches. This fissure may arise from several factors, including unequal resources to achieve similar health goals, distrust between different sectors, and a lack of gender and disability awareness in churches. Whatever the reasons, during the pandemic, Christian women who were brought up and educated in church institutions considered that the church leadership did not show the guidance they expected when faced with a multi-faceted crisis. They looked to humanitarian organisations and women-only fellowships for social and spiritual support. They adapted models from their relationships with humanitarian organisations rather than their churches to shape the immediate decision-making required for an appropriate public and primary health care approach during the pandemic.

Notes

1 Qualitative interviews, focus groups, and participant observation were carried out in-person and on-line to ascertain Christian women's perceptions of the pandemic and the response of churches during 2023 in accordance with ethical procedures. Details of the interviews are not recorded here to protect anonymity, except where participants wished to be named. We thank the health workers, teachers, small-scale retailers, women living with disability, and leaders of women's organisations for their cooperation. For Congo, the interviews were part of a larger project funded by the University of Edinburgh, 'Maximising public health responses of faith communities in DRC.' For Nigeria, new data complemented research carried out for Fubara-Manuel's doctoral thesis, 'The Role of Christian Faith for Women Living with Disabilities and HIV in South-south Nigeria,' 2022.
2 95,645 confirmed cases and only 1,464 deaths. It is likely that reporting was limited. World Health Organisation. https://COVID19.who.int/region/afro/country/cd (accessed 25/02/23).
3 In Africa, COVID-19 was often seen as a rich person's disease, see, for example, Reuters. COVID-19 kills 32 members of DR Congo's parliament [Internet]. 2021. https://www.reuters.com/business/healthcare-pharmaceuticals/COVID-19-kills-32-members-congos-parliament-2021-05-28.
4 In our interviews, many women spoke of 'NGOs' (non-governmental organisations) in general terms rather than mentioning specific organisations. They were referencing humanitarian organisations that were international or national or local groups that had close associations with international organisations. Some of the organisations were connected to governments.

5 Private reports from FFPI office verified this statement.
6 Port Harcourt in South-south Nigeria is predominantly Christian, so it is no surprise that members of Bold Hearts are all Christians. This is not the case in many of the Northern and Western States, predominantly Muslim in which Bold Hearts has mixed religious affiliations.
7 Personal Interview, Osaki Georgewill, 15 April 2023.
8 Personal Interview, Osaki Georgewill, 15 April 2023.

Bibliography

Amwe, Ruth Vida. 2023. '"Womanhood on the Street": African Women at the Crossroads of Religious Violence and Social Justice,' *Studies in World Christianity* 29 (1), 37–56.

Asakitikpi, Alex E. 2016. 'Healthcare Delivery and the Limits of the National Health Insurance Scheme in Nigeria,' *Africa Development/Afrique et Développement* 41(4), 29–45.

Baba, A., Grant L., Pearson N., Wild-Wood, E., Falisse, J. B., Way, Y., and Kangamina, S. 2022. 'Engaging Faith Communities in Public Health Messaging in Response to COVID-19: Lessons Learnt from the Pandemic in Ituri, Democratic Republic of Congo.' *Frontier in Public Health* 10, 916062. doi: 10.3389/fpubh.2022.916062.

Ekiikina, Peter O. 2021. 'A Co-Produced Response to COVID-19,' in *COVID-19 and Co-Production in Health and Social Care Research, Policy, and Practice*, ed. Oli Williams et al. Bristol: Policy Press, pp. 51–56.

FFPI (Federation des Femmes Protestantes de l'Ituri), Promotion de la Femme Pour la Reconstruction de l'Ituri, Espace D'Echange des Femmes de l'Ituri. 2016. 'Rapport de Formation sur la Mediation et Sensibilitations au Sude-Irumu Chefferie des Walendu-Bindi.'

Fubara-Manuel, Jessie. 2022. 'The Role of Christian Faith for Women Living with Disabilities and HIV in South-south Nigeria,' PhD thesis, University of Edinburgh.

Fubara-Manuel, Jessie and Ngwobia, Justina Mike. 2021. "Women with Disabilities, Peacebuilding and Development in Adamawa State, Nigeria," in *Women and Peacebuilding in Africa*, ed. Anna Chitando. London and New York: Routledge, pp. 124–135.

Fubara-Manuel, Jessie. 2014. *Giver of Life, Hear Our Cries!* Geneva 2, Switzerland: World Council of Churches Publications.

Global Terrorism Index 2022, viewed 5 July 2023. https://reliefweb.int/attachments/a62d4dc4-c69b-49ee-8ef5-50d98205e70d/GTI-2022-web_110522-1.pdf

Goodall, Adam and Meakin, Becki. 2021. 'Locked in or Locked Out,' in *COVID-19 and Co-Production in Health and Social Care Research, Policy, and Practice*, ed. Oli Williams et al., Bristol: Policy Press, pp. 67–76.

Gruzd, Steven, Bosman, Isabel and Zikalala, Nhlakanipho Macmillan, 2020, 'Regions Apart: How South Africa and Nigeria Responded to COVID-19,' Research report, *South African Institute of International Affairs*, www.jstor.org/stable/resrep28259.

Human Rights Watch. 2023. 'Nigeria: A Year On, No Justice for #EndSARS Crackdown.' viewed 8 June 2023. https://www.hrw.org/news/2021/10/19/nigeria-year-no-justice-endsars-crackdown.

Igwe, Oliver. 2021 'Not my Portion: An Appraisal of Religions Responses to the COVID-19 Pandemic in Nigeria,' *International Journal of Arts and Social Science* 13, 106–122.

Johnson, Todd and Zurlo, Gina. 2020. *World Christian Encyclopedia*, viewed 1 March 2022. https://www.academia.edu/download/66253713/Lindsay_Jenn_World_Christianity_Encyclopedia_2020_Italy.pdf.

Kangamina, S., Falisse, J. B., Baba, A. Way, Y., Grant, L., Pearson, N., and Wild-Wood, E. 2022. 'Conflict, Epidemic and Faith Communities: Church-State Relations during the Fight against COVID-19 in North-eastern DR Congo.' *Conflict and Health* 16 (56). https://doi.org/10.1186/s13031-022-00488-4.

Lindstrom, Camilla, 2019, 'Donors and a Predatory State: Struggling with Real Governance.' In Tom De Herdt and Kristof Titeca (eds), *Negotiating Public Services in the Congo*. London, Zed Books, pp. 74–95.

Manyonganise M., 2022, '"When a pandemic wears the face of a woman," Intersections of Religion and Gender during the COVID-19 Pandemic in Zimbabwe.' In F. Sibanda et al, (eds), *Religion and the*

COVID-19 Pandemic in Southern Africa. London, Routledge, pp, 232–243, DOI: 10.4324/ 9781003241096-16

Meier zu Selhausen, Felix, 2014, 'Missionaries and Female Empowerment in Colonial Uganda: New Evidence from Protestant Marriage Registers, 1880-1945,' *Economic History of Developing Regions*, 29 (1), 74–112.

Milemba, Phidias Ahadi Senge. 2019. 'Parite homme-femme en RD Congo: Vers Quel Ordre Sociopolitique?' *Congo-Afrique*, 533, 236–246.

Mukwege, Denis. 2022. 'Rape as a Weapon of War in the Democratic Republic of the Congo: From Holistic Care to Transitional Justice,' *Revue LISA/LISA e-journal*, 20, 53. Accessed 15 February 2023. http://journals.openedition.org/lisa/13875; doi.org/10.4000/lisa.13875

Nigerian Federal Government. 27 February 2020. 'Health Minister: First Case Of COVID-19 Confirmed in Nigeria,' viewed June 18, 2023. www.health.gov.ng/index.php?option=com_k2&view=item&id= 613:health-minister-first-case-of-COVID-19-confirmed-in-nigeria.

Olufemi, Olusola A. and Labeodan, Helen A., 2021, '"Locked-Down" But Not "Locked Out": Experiences of Nigerian Women During the COVID-19 Pandemic,' in Labeodan, H.A. Amenga-Etego, Rosemary, Stiebert, Johanna, Aidoo, Mark S. et al. (eds) *COVID-19: African Women and the Will to Survive*, ed. Bamberg: University of Bamberg Press, pp. 16–38.

Partners, 31 July 2020, 'The Impacts of COVID-19 on Nigerian Women, viewed 11 February 2023. https://www.partnersnigeria.org/the-impacts-of-COVID-19-on-nigerian-women/

Salaudeen, Aisha, 2020, 'Government, Banks and Wealthy Individuals Contribute Billions to Fight Coronavirus in Nigeria,' CNN, March 27. Accessed 7th July 2023. https://www.cnn.com/2020/03/27/ africa/coronavirus-nigeria-fund/index.html.

Seay, L. E. 2013. 'Effective Responses: Protestants, Catholics and the Provision of Health Care in the Post-war Kivus'. *Review in African Political Economy*, 40, (135), pp. 83–97.

Sibanda, Fortune, Muyambo, Tenson, Chitando, Ezra, 2022, 'Introduction Religion and public health in the shadow of COVID-19 pandemic in Southern Africa,' In Fortune Sibanda, Tenson Muyambo, Ezra Chitando (eds), *Religion and the COVID-19 Pandemic in Southern Africa* London, Routledge, pp. 1–24. DOI: 10.4324/9781003241096-1

Social Sciences Analytics Cell. 2023. The Impacts of COVID-19 outbreak response on women and girls in DRC, viewed 11 February 2023. https://www.unicef.org/drcongo/media/5416/file/COD-CASS-impacts-COVID-response-women-girls.pdf

The Elders. 18 June 2020. COVID-19 and the impact on African women: all responses must respect the gendered impacts of the pandemic. viewed 10 February 2023. https://theelders.org/news/COVID-19-and-impact-african-women-all-responses-must-respect-gendered-impacts-pandemic

UN Dept of Social and Economic Affairs. 2022. *World Population Prospects 2022: Summary of Results*. New York, UN, pp. 5–6, viewed 15 February 2023 https://www.un.org.development.desa.pd/sites/ www.un.org.development.desa.pd/files/wpp2022_summary_of_results.pdf.

UN Women a. n.d. 'UN Women. About us,' viewed 6 July 2023, https://www.unwomen.org/en/about-us.

UN Women b. 2023. 'Women with Disabilities in a Pandemic (COVID-19)' Country Support Policy Brief 1, viewed 29 May 2023. https://www.unwomen.org/sites/default/files/Headquarters/Attachments/ Sections/Library/Publications/2020/Policy-brief-Women-with-disabilities-in-a-pandemic-COVID-19-en.pdf.

UN Women c. 2023. 'Women in Informal Economy,' viewed 11 February 2023. https://www.unwomen. org/en/news/in-focus/csw61/women-in-informal-economy

Wells, C. R., Pandey, A., Ndeffo Mbah, M. L., Gaüzère, B. A., Malvy, D., Singer, B. H. et al. 2019. 'The Exacerbation of Ebola Outbreaks by Conflict in the Democratic Republic of the Congo'. *Proceedings of the National Academy of Science USA* 116, 24366–24372.

Wild-Wood, Emma, Way, Yossa, Baba, Amuda, Kangamina, Sadiki, Falisse, Jean-Benoit, Grant, Liz, and Pearson, Nigel, 2023. 'Perceptions of COVID-19 in faith communities in DR Congo', *Journal of Eastern African Studies*, DOI: 10.1080/17531055.2023.2235659

Wild-Wood, Emma, Grant, Liz, Adedibu, Babatunde, Barnard, Alan, Ajore, Aloys, and Way, Yossa. 2021. 'The Public Role of Churches in Early Response to COVID-19 in Africa: Snapshots from Nigeria, Congo, Kenya and South Africa'. *Studies in World Christianity* 27(1) 63–84.

World Bank. 2022. *Assessing the Damage: Early Evidence on Impacts of the COVID-19 Crisis on Girls and Women in Africa*, viewed 10 February 2023, https://openknowledge.worldbank.org/handle/ 10986/37347 License: CC.

10
WOMEN'S LEADERSHIP IN THE FACE OF COVID-19
The Case of Agnes Mahomva in Zimbabwe

Mutsawashe Chitando

Introduction

The COVID-19 pandemic affected various facets of society, including health systems, economies, and social protection structures. It revealed long-standing vulnerabilities, including gender inequality, pay and educational disparities, limited access to healthcare, and employment challenges worldwide (Mutanda, 2022, OECD, 2020, Bwire et al., 2022, Chitungo et al., 2022). Among the, most affected were women, girls, the elderly, and other marginalised groups, particularly those in low-middle-income countries. Unfortunately, the pandemic threatened and in many ways reversed, the gains made in pursuit of the Sustainable Development Goals (SDGs) (Ekwebelem et al., 2021, Odey et al., 2021). According to a study quantifying the impact of the pandemic on the SDGs, the goals of eradicating poverty (SDG 1), achieving zero hunger (SDG 2), good health and well-being (SDG 3), decent work and economic growth (SDG 8), and reduced inequality (SDG 10) were directly impacted the most (Yuan et al., 2023).

Individuals working in informal sectors were acutely affected by the pandemic. Globally, 58% of employed women work in the informal sector and are likely to be in low-paid categories of informal employment (IMF, 2021). In South Asia, over 80% of women in non-agricultural jobs are in informal employment; in sub-Saharan Africa, 74%; and in Latin America and the Caribbean, 54% (UNWOMEN, 2022). In low-middle-income countries, 92% of all employed women are in informal employment compared to 87% of men (OECD, 2019). COVID-19 restrictions rendered those in the informal sector unable to earn a livelihood, plunging many into economic uncertainty. Gender inequality was prevalent during the pandemic, as millions of women in informal work were forced to stop working when the pandemic emerged. Women make up 80% of domestic workers globally, and 72% of them lost their jobs following the pandemic. Forty-one per cent of women-owned businesses in sub-Saharan Africa closed, compared to 34% of those owned by men (IMF, 2021).

Tragically, the pandemic also brought about a surge in cases of sexual and gender-based violence, a grim consequence of women and girls spending extended periods in confined spaces. Researchers have referred to this surge as "shadow pandemic" (Felten 2023), "trapped between two pandemics" (Uzobo and Ayinmoro, 2023), and "a twin pandemic to COVID-19"

(Dlamini, 2021). Furthermore, the closure of schools in response to the pandemic led to substantial learning losses among women and girls, exacerbating existing disparities in educational outcomes. In many instances, women bore the burden of home schooling due to cultural and religious norms that project mothers as the teachers of the children, including formal schooling.

Despite the challenges that COVID-19 presented, it also created unique opportunities for women and girls to respond to the pandemic. Women occupied different positions from the highest positions in decision-making, frontline service delivery, and community champions. They exhibited remarkable resilience and adaptability, challenged traditional gender norms, and showcased their ability to become exceptional leaders. This is in defiance of the social construction of men as leaders and women as followers. Women's leadership, as this chapter will highlight, is critical for the development of countries and the continent. Having more women in leadership will inspire young women and girls to take up leadership positions. Thus:

> Despite the continent's long and rich history of female leaders, particularly pre-colonisation, the political, social, and cultural systems and beliefs do not currently promote leadership qualities or aspirations in young girls. Concerted efforts over the last two decades have expanded access to quality education and health for many, but women's political participation must also be a priority to ensure good governance. Half of the population cannot be side-lined in decision-making for continued and more expansive progress on the continent. If only half of the potential leaders are identified and supported, policy solutions remain only halfway forged.
>
> (Ngwenya 2022: 4)

This chapter explores women's pivotal roles during the COVID-19 pandemic, focusing on Dr. Agnes Mahomva's leadership in Zimbabwe. The chapter is structured to outline the methods used, discuss the findings, and conclude with valuable insights from the pandemic.

Methods

This study was an exploratory qualitative scoping review, aiming to gain insights into the multifaceted aspects of women's leadership during the COVID-19 pandemic. To accomplish this, a scoping review of the literature was performed across various electronic databases, including PubMed, Semantic Scholar, and Google Scholar. Keyword searches and Boolean operators were employed to collate available resources. The inclusion criteria included both published articles and grey literature. Language restriction was applied, and only articles published in English were included. The study period spans from 2019 to 2023, capturing the dynamic landscape of the pandemic. However, to offer a broader context, relevant literature pertaining to previous pandemics is included.

It is key for the reader to note that while this study does not present an exhaustive overview of women's leadership in the context of COVID-19, it serves as a valuable indicator of the several ways in which leadership was exhibited and provides a foundational understanding of this subject matter. The chapter is built on the conviction that it is critical for conversations on women's leadership in Africa to be intensified to ensure that the many gifts and skills that women bring can be utilised. As the continent invests in democracy, good governance, and inclusive development, it must take women's leadership seriously. The chapter has benefited immensely from the following reflections:

> The project of engendering democracy has to be deeper and wider than just adding women to existing political structures and processes and expecting gendered transformations to follow. While not downplaying the importance of these formal structures or indeed the importance of more diverse representation within them, focus and attention also needs to spread to the many other sites and spaces of everyday politics in which the discussions, deliberations, negotiations, bargaining and decision-making which take place have immediate impacts on peoples' daily lives.
>
> (Gaynor 2022: 175)

Women's Leadership during Pandemics in Africa

Over the years, the African continent, like the rest of the world, has experienced different shocks, including fragility and conflict, natural disasters, poverty, and health threats. What has emerged in these challenging times is the remarkable and multifaceted role of women. Women's leadership in Africa is not a new phenomenon, and throughout Africa's history, women have been critical problem solvers, leading militaries, freedom fighters, and transitional leaders (Sirleaf, 2022).

The Ebola Virus outbreak in West Africa in 2014–2016 serves as an example of women's contributions despite several obstacles. In Liberia, the outbreak resulted in women being out of work for extended periods due to their overrepresentation in the sectors hardest hit by the outbreak (WorldBank, 2014). In Sierra Leone, school closures and diminished economic opportunities increased the risk of early pregnancy and girls dropping out of school (Powers and Azzi-huck, 2016, Bandiera et al., 2020). The Ebola outbreak resulted in the loss of lives of healthcare personnel, disruptions in maternal and child healthcare services, and a subsequent surge in maternal and child mortality (Kassa et al., 2022). Additionally, the pandemic magnified existing issues of sexual and gender-based violence, prompting women's groups and associations to advocate for strengthened response mechanisms and engage in community education and mobilisation efforts to curb the spread of the virus.

Similar trends unfolded during the human immunodeficiency virus (HIV)/acquired immunodeficiency virus (AIDS) pandemic in sub-Saharan Africa, where women played pivotal roles in responding to the crisis but also faced barriers. Women have been at the forefront of providing care for people living with and affected by HIV, especially when no treatment is available (UNAIDS, 2017). They have also been at the forefront of HIV treatment and prevention efforts, including community mobilisation. However, structural and cultural factors often impede women's participation and increase their vulnerability to HIV. Examples include limited access to education and healthcare, unequal economic opportunities, discrimination, stigma, and gender-based violence. The caregiving roles assumed by women and girls as wives, mothers, and daughters often come at significant opportunity costs.

The emergence of COVID-19 mirrored these patterns, with women and girls assuming caregiving responsibilities while acting as mobilisers and catalysts for change in their communities. The pandemic illuminated existing gender inequalities while fuelling alarming levels of gender-based violence and economic setbacks. Despite these challenges, numerous documented success stories showcase African women's effective leadership in the fight against

COVID-19. The former President of Liberia, Ellen Johnson Sirleaf, acknowledged several outstanding African women for their exceptional leadership during the pandemic (Sirleaf, 2020). Among these remarkable leaders were Yvonne Aki-Sawyerr, the mayor of Freetown, Sierra Leone, and Dr. Zaneta Agyeman-Rawlings, a Ghanaian Member of Parliament, who played pivotal roles in behaviour change communication. In Ethiopia, Blen Sahilu harnessed social media to disseminate public information messages in multiple languages (Pikramenou and Mahajan, 2021).

Women were also instrumental in strengthening infrastructure in response to the pandemic. Clare Akamanzi, a cabinet member in Rwanda, played a central role in organising isolation centres, sourcing testing kits, and developing post-COVID-19 recovery plans. In Liberia, Cornelia Kruah-Togba recognised the urgency of the situation and orchestrated the installation of handwashing stations at gathering places. The nation also benefited from the efforts of Kula Fofana, who initiated a program to support pregnant women during crises, mobilising essential items needed by expectant mothers. Aïda Alassane N'Diaye-Riddick, the Côte d'Ivoire Country Manager at Teaching at the Right Level, facilitated children's access to education through radio programmes in response to the closure of schools and limited internet access (Sirleaf, 2020).

One such phenomenal leader is Dr. Agnes Mahomva of Zimbabwe, whose work is explored in the following section.

Dr Agnes Mahomva's Leadership in Responding to COVID-19

Dr. Agnes Mahomva was the Chief Coordinator of Zimbabwe's COVID-19 response in the Office of the President and the Cabinet, where she demonstrated effective leadership during the crisis. Her role placed her at the forefront of the government's strategy, where she exhibited exemplary abilities to navigate the challenges that arose following the COVID-19 pandemic. Her position was backed by her extensive work as a specialist public health physician with over 30 years of experience in managing, directing, and leading public health programmes.

When Zimbabwe recorded its initial COVID-19 case in early 2020, the nation was gripped by shock and apprehension. There was an urgent need for a robust and well-coordinated response as the virus spread rapidly (UNICEF, 2023). Fortunately, before the pandemic, the Ministry of Health had undertaken significant efforts to bolster the country's healthcare system in preparation for epidemic responses. Dr. Mahomva's pivotal role as the Permanent Secretary of the Ministry of Health became invaluable in the coming months.

The pandemic's transboundary nature and rapid transmission demanded swift action, and Zimbabwe displayed an efficient response. An international survey by the Partnership for Evidence-Based COVID-19 Response (PERC) in 2020 highlighted the effectiveness of early public health and social measures, including the March 2020 lockdown, in delaying the epidemic's impact (PERC, 2020). This success underscored Zimbabwe's adept crisis management and decision-making.

Central to this achievement was the government's commitment to real-time data. Dr. Mahomva and the national COVID-19 task force recognised that informed decisions hinged on accurate information. Consequently, they established a 24-hour COVID-19 response centre, enabling the collection, processing, analysis, and real-time evaluation of critical data. This commitment not only curbed the spread of the virus but also fostered trust and credibility between the government, stakeholders, and the communities it served (UNICEF, 2023).

As newly reported COVID-19 cases surged, peaking in July 2021 at 2325, the government exhibited agility in its response. Governments were racing to flatten the curve by increasing testing for the virus and developing and deploying a vaccine. The national preparedness and response strategic plan required the government to strengthen its health system to be implemented effectively, and this required resource mobilisation. About 84% of the total response funding was domestic funding spearheaded by the Government of Zimbabwe, and 16% was received from its partners. USD 100 million was set aside for vaccine procurement (UNICEF, 2023). Resources were diverted towards a pandemic response, particularly those from infrastructure development. The Government of Zimbabwe also partnered with domestic partners, such as universities who produced personal protective clothing and hand sanitisers.

Furthermore, Dr. Mahomva's leadership extended to the realm of information dissemination and public awareness. Misinformation and rumours regarding COVID-19 and vaccines are widespread (Larsson et al., 2023). Dr. Mahomva and the task force recognised the paramount importance of effective communication in debunking rumours. They used mainstream media for communication, social media, and traditional channels to communicate health messages. Religious and traditional leaders played a pivotal role in debunking myths regarding the virus in various communities (Chitando and Chitando, 2023). Under her guidance, committees and training workshops were established with healthcare professionals within the church community actively engaging in awareness-raising efforts.

In addition, the pandemic response also necessitated a significant expansion of healthcare infrastructure. Dr. Mahomva's leadership was instrumental in this regard. She worked closely with her colleagues in the inter-ministerial task force to secure the resources necessary for expanding case management and isolation facilities (Reliefweb, 2020). Another critical component was the training of health personnel at quarantine facilities through the Ministry of Health and Child Care (MoHCC). Dr. Mahomva expressed that identifying the quarantine facilities was not good enough on its own; there was a need to manage them efficiently and effectively with the growing numbers of returnees in the centres (WHO, 2020). Returning residents were allowed to return to Zimbabwe from neighbouring countries, despite the borders being closed. The guidelines stipulated that every returning citizen be subjected to symptomatic screening and referred to a nearby hospital if they presented with symptoms. Law enforcement agents were positioned at various ports of entry to provide support and ensure that people complied (UNICEF, 2023). Communities also worked closely with the authorities to report those who entered the country illegally. These efforts were crucial in ensuring that Zimbabwe had the capacity to effectively detect cases and care for patients.

Another remarkable achievement was the expansion of testing for COVID-19 in all ten provinces, from one central testing laboratory to more than 1,000 testing centres (Gudza-Mugabe et al., 2022). This not only increased the testing capacity but also facilitated quicker and more decentralised testing, allowing for faster identification of cases and contact tracing. This expansion was pivotal in controlling the spread of the virus and reducing the burden on centralised testing facilities.

As frontline health workers were working long shifts, it became necessary to keep them motivated because they played a critical role in the COVID-19 response (Jimu et al., 2023). Under Dr. Mahomva's leadership, there was the introduction of a risk allowance, a financial incentive recognising the dedication and sacrifices of healthcare professionals who put their lives on the line to care for COVID-19 patients (Chitungo et al., 2022). The risk allowance served as both a practical form of support and a symbol of appreciation for their tireless efforts.

Dr. Mahomva's leadership extended beyond the immediate healthcare response to the pandemic. She recognised that the pandemic's impact had a ripple effect in various sectors of Zimbabwe. Education, for instance, faced unprecedented challenges, as schools closed to curb the spread of the virus. The closure of educational institutions meant that learners were deprived of their regular learning environments, which posed a significant threat to their academic progress (Maphosa, 2021). In response to this challenge, collaboration was fostered between the Ministry of Health and the Ministry of Education. This collaboration led to the establishment of a rapid response team within the Ministry of Health, prepared to address COVID-19 cases should they arise in schools. The Ministry of Education, on the other hand, initiated measures to enable remote learning, including televised lessons, radio broadcasts, and digital resources (Nhongo and Tshotsho, 2021). Dr. Mahomva's leadership facilitated a seamless exchange of ideas and resources between these critical sectors, ensuring that children continued to have access to education despite challenging circumstances.

Another initiative that emerged during this period was the "learning passport." The learning passport was provided by the Ministry of Primary and Secondary Education to ensure that children could continue their education, irrespective of their physical location or access to conventional classroom settings. By leveraging digital technologies and distance learning approaches, Zimbabwean educators created a system in which students could access learning materials and assessments remotely. This approach not only mitigated the immediate disruptions caused by the pandemic but also laid the foundation for more flexible and inclusive education systems in the future.

Additionally, the pandemic has underscored the importance of learner welfare and well-being. The task force under Dr. Mahomva's leadership recognised that the abrupt closure of schools could have unintended consequences for the psychological and emotional well-being of students. The learner welfare department under the Ministry of Education was tasked with monitoring the well-being of students and providing necessary support, including counselling services, to address any emotional or psychological challenges that students might face during this unprecedented period (Cluster, 2020). Dr. Mahomva's commitment to the holistic development of Zimbabwean youth was evident in these efforts, which aimed not only to maintain academic progress but also to safeguard the mental and emotional health of the nation's future leaders (Mbunge et al., 2020). Closely related was the social welfare program rolled out by the Government of Zimbabwe to support vulnerable households during the pandemic. Cash transfers also included US $20–25 per person in a household monthly and fee payments for children from vulnerable households (UNICEF, 2023). The government's food deficit mitigation program was also scaled up across the country.

Dr. Mahomva's leadership during the COVID-19 pandemic transcended the boundaries of traditional healthcare roles. Her visionary approach and ability to foster collaboration across sectors were instrumental in guiding Zimbabwe through a challenging period. Her commitment to information dissemination and public welfare ensured that the pandemic's impact was mitigated not only in terms of public health but also across various aspects of Zimbabwean society, leaving a legacy of resilience and adaptability in the face of adversity. What truly set her apart was her remarkable balance and composure, unwavering confidence, and exceptional communication skills during a time marked by widespread panic and pandemonium. She exhibited these qualities while navigating through the waves of the pandemic. In doing so, she effectively challenged the stereotype that women leaders might succumb to panic in the face of adversity.

In 2023, she was honoured with the prestigious Star of Zimbabwe in silver, recognising her outstanding leadership in the successful coordination of COVID-19 response efforts across the country (Chidakwa, 2023). Additionally, in the same year, the President of Zimbabwe, Emmerson Mnangagwa, appointed Dr. Mahomva as public health advisor to the President and Cabinet, which was a newly created post (Ndlovu, 2023). Her appointment to this post signifies her expertise and commitment to the country's healthcare sector.

The Landscape of Women in Public Health

Exceptional women leaders, such as Dr. Mahomva, are a source of inspiration for many. In the landscape of women in public health, these inspirational figures contribute to a growing trend of increased female representation in positions of authority. The ability to identify and acknowledge the presence of such women, their effectiveness in leadership positions, and their influence on public health marks a significant milestone. This is proof of the evolving landscape of gender dynamics in this critical field. However, even as we acknowledge these milestones, it becomes increasingly apparent that there is still much work to be done to fully harness the potential of African women to shape the future of public health across the continent.

While we witness a gradual shift towards greater inclusivity and representation, the pace of integrating women into leadership roles within public health remains slow. Women are still underrepresented in this field, spanning from policymaking to ground-breaking research initiatives (Baobeid et al., 2022, Ilesanmi, 2018). This underrepresentation stifles the diversity of perspectives in critical decision-making processes and creates disparities in healthcare delivery and resource allocation. The urgency of this issue cannot be overemphasised. For the world to realise its collective goals, gender equality and the empowerment of women and girls should be at the centre of these goals. For instance, SDG 3, "Ensure healthy lives and promote well-being for all at all ages," hinges upon creating environments where women play pivotal roles in shaping policies around healthcare, services, and research agendas. Moreover, SDG 5, "Achieve gender equality and empower all women and girls," underscores the intrinsic value of women's contributions in all spheres, public health being no exception.

To accelerate progress and bridge the gender gap in public health leadership, it is imperative that governments, development partners, and stakeholders take deliberate and concerted action. Policymakers play a role in ensuring that gender disparities are addressed systematically when designing pandemic prevention and response programs (Gordon et al., 2022). Such programmes must safeguard not only women's lives but also their livelihoods, recognising that the well-being of communities and nations hinges upon the well-being of their women. Increasing women's leadership in public health presents a profound opportunity to enhance the resilience and responsiveness of healthcare systems (Muktar et al., 2022). It is not merely a matter of representation, but one of efficacy and innovation. When women are actively engaged in leadership, health policies and interventions become more attuned to the diverse needs of the population, addressing the multifaceted health challenges that Africa faces.

Realising this potential necessitates comprehensive investments in training programmes and educational opportunities for women and girls across the continent. These investments are instrumental in empowering women to lead themselves. By recognising and rectifying the current imbalances and investing in the development of women leaders, Africa can chart a course towards a more equitable, resilient, and responsive future for public health.

Limitations and Future Directions

It is important to reiterate that this work does not present an exhaustive portrayal of the extensive contributions of African women in response to the challenges posed by the COVID-19 pandemic. The research approach employed here is a scoping review chosen for its ability to provide an exploratory overview of the topic. A systematic literature review (Higgins, 2019), characterised by a more structured and rigorous methodology, could have offered a more comprehensive perspective on this subject, which future researchers can employ.

Furthermore, it is essential to recognise that this study relies solely on secondary sources of data, drawing from existing literature and research. Although these sources provide valuable insights, they may not capture the full spectrum of experiences and actions of women during the pandemic. Incorporating primary data collection methods, such as surveys, interviews, or case studies, could have enriched the research by offering first-hand accounts and a more detailed understanding of women's responses to COVID-19.

In essence, this chapter serves as an introductory exploration of the topic, laying the groundwork for more comprehensive and in-depth research endeavours that may follow the vital roles played by African women in the face of the COVID-19 pandemic. Generating such evidence could ultimately inform and enhance the opportunities awarded to women in Africa and beyond, recognising their pivotal roles in crises.

Conclusion

It is undisputed that women's leadership and contributions must take the central stage in pandemic preparedness and response, health system strengthening, and resilience. The invaluable work undertaken by inspirational women like Agnes Mahomva in Zimbabwe, along with numerous others across the African continent, serves as a testament to the untapped potential and indispensable role of women in responding to multifaceted challenges, such as pandemics.

In a world that has become increasingly interconnected, it is crucial to recognise that pandemics are not confined to borders or geography. When one country is affected, the effects are transboundary. Conversely, the effective response of one country not only safeguards its own population but also extends a helping hand to others. This interdependence underscores the critical importance of documenting and sharing lessons learned during these periods.

While the contextual nuances of each country's responses may vary, the underlying principles of effective crisis management and leadership often remain consistent. The lessons distilled from the experiences of women leaders in Africa are invaluable not only to the continent but also to the entire world. In the face of future challenges, we should heed these lessons and leverage the potential of women leaders in our collective pursuit of resilience and preparedness. Stories such as those of Agnes Mahomva and her contemporaries remind us that women's leadership is not an option but a necessity, a force that can drive transformative change and lead us towards a more equitable, inclusive, and resilient world. We must continue to celebrate, support, and amplify the voices and leadership of women in public health, as they are at the forefront of our shared journey towards health, well-being, and global solidarity.

Bibliography

Bandiera, O., Buehren, N., Goldstein, M., Rasul, I. & Smurra, A. 2020. "Do school closures during an epidemic have persistent effects." in Abdul Latif Jameel ed. *Evidence from Sierra Leone in the time of Ebola*. Cambridge (MA): Poverty Action Lab Research Paper.

Baobeid, A., Faghani-Hamadani, T., Sauer, S., Ii, Y. B., Hedt-Gauthier, B. L., Neufeld, N., Odhiambo, J., Volmink, J., Shuchman, M., Ruggiero, E. D. & Condo, J. U. 2022. "Gender equity in health research publishing in Africa." *BMJ Global Health*, 7, e008821.

Bwire, G., Ario, A. R., Eyu, P., Ocom, F., Wamala, J. F., Kusi, K. A., Ndeketa, L., Jambo, K. C., Wanyenze, R. K. & Talisuna, A. O. 2022. "The COVID-19 pandemic in the African continent". *BMC Medicine*, 20, 1–23.

Chidakwa, B. 2023. "Hall of fame for the outstanding." *The Herald*, August 15 2023.

Chitando, M. & Chitando, E. 2023. "Bridging the 'social distance' between public health and religion: insights from responses to COVID-19 vaccines in Zimbabwe." in T. Muyambo et al, eds., *Religion and COVID-19 Vaccination in Zimbabwe*. London: Routledge.

Chitungo, I., Dzinamarira, T., Tungwarara, N., Chimene, M., Mukwenha, S., Kunonga, E., Musuka, G. & Murewanhema, G. 2022. "COVID-19 response in Zimbabwe: The need for a paradigm shift? *COVID*, 2, 895–906.

Cluster, Z. E. 2020. Zimbabwe COVID-19 preparedness and response strategy. Available at https://planipolis.iiep.unesco.org/sites/default/files/ressources/zimbabwe_education_cluster_covid_strategy_12.05.2020_final.pdf

Dlamini, N. J. 2021. "Gender-based violence, twin pandemic to COVID-19." *Critical Sociology*, 47, 583–590.

Ekwebelem, O. C., Ofielu, E. S., Nnorom-Dike, O. V., Iweha, C., Ekwebelem, N. C., Obi, B. C. & Ugbede-Ojo, S. E. 2021. "Threats of COVID-19 to achieving United Nations sustainable development goals in Africa." *The American Journal of Tropical Medicine and Hygiene*, 104, 457.

Felten, G. 2023. "Recognising the shadow pandemic in the humanitarian sector: Ending violence against women in the aftermath of COVID-19." *International Journal of Humanitarian Action*, 8(9). http://doi.org/10.1186/s4018-023-00142-5

Gaynor, N. 2022. *Engendering Democracy in Africa: Women, Politics and Development in Africa* (in Italics). London: Routledge.

Gordon, R., Cheeseman, N., Rockowitz, S., Stevens, L. M. & Flowe, H. D. 2022. "Government responses to gender-based violence during COVID-19." *Frontiers in Global Women's Health*, 3, 857345.

Gudza-Mugabe, M., Sithole, K., Sisya, L., Zimuto, S., Charimari, L. S., Chimusoro, A., Simbi, R. & Gasasira, A. 2022. "Zimbabwe's emergency response to COVID-19: Enhancing access and accelerating COVID-19 testing as the first line of defense against the COVID-19 pandemic." *Frontiers in Public Health*, 10, 871567.

Higgins, J. P. T. 2019. *Cochrane handbook for systematic reviews of interventions*, Hoboken, NJ: Cochrane.

Ilesanmi, O. O. 2018. "Women's visibility in decision making processes in Africa—Progress, challenges, and way forward." *Frontiers in Sociology*, 3, 38.

IMF. 2021. *Five things to know about the informal economy* [Online]. International Monetary Fund. Available: https://www.imf.org/en/News/Articles/2021/07/28/na-072821-five-things-to-know-about-the-informal-economy [Accessed 11 October 2023].

Jimu, C., Kanyemba, R., Tarisayi, K. S., Shumba, K. & Govender, K. 2023. "An exploration of female healthcare workers' experiences during the COVID-19 pandemic in Bindura, Zimbabwe." *Cogent Social Sciences*, 9, 2218725.

Kassa, Z. Y., Scarf, V. & Fox, D. 2022. "The effect of Ebola virus disease on maternal health service utilisation and perinatal outcomes in West Africa: A systematic review." *Reproduction Health*, 19, 35.

Larsson, L., Dziva Chikwari, C., Simms, V., Tembo, M., Mahomva, A., Mugurungi, O., Hayes, R. J., Mackworth-Young, C. R. S., Bernays, S., Mavodza, C., Taruvinga, T., Bandason, T., Dauya, E., Ferrand, R. A. & Kranzer, K. 2023. "Addressing sociodemographic disparities in COVID-19 vaccine uptake among youth in Zimbabwe." *BMJ Glob Health*, 8(7), e012268. doi: 10.1136/bmjgh-2023-012268

Maphosa, V. 2021. "Teachers' perspectives on remote-based teaching and learning in the COVID-19 era: Rethinking technology availability and suitability in Zimbabwe." *European Journal of Interactive Multimedia and Education*, 2, e02105.

Mbunge, E., Fashoto, S., Akinnuwesi, B., Gurajena, C., Metfula, A. & Mashwama, P. 2020. "COVID-19 pandemic in higher education: critical role of emerging technologies in Zimbabwe." Available at SSRN 3743246.

Muktar, S. A., Desta, B. F., Damte, H. D., Heyi, W. K., Gurmamo, E. M., Abebe, M. G., Mesele, M. G. & Argaw, M. D. 2022. "Exploring the opportunities and challenges of female health leaders in three regional states of Ethiopia: A phenomenological study." *BMC Public Health*, 22, 1471.

Mutanda, D. 2022. "Challenges and opportunities for Zimbabwe's responses to COVID-19." *Cogent Social Sciences*, 8, 2084890.

Ndlovu, B. 2023. President appoints first female AG. *Chronicle*. www.chronicle.co.zw/president-appoints-first-female-ag/

Ngwenya, P. 2022. "Foreword." In African Union 20 Years. Women of Impact: Inspiring Stories of African Women Leaders (italics, "African Union…"). Addis Ababa: African Union Commission-Gender and Youth Directorate (AUC-WGYD), 4–6.

Nhongo, R. & Tshotsho, B. P. 2021. The shortcomings of emergency remote teaching in rural settings of Zimbabwe during COVID-19 school closures: Lessons from China's experience. *Africa's Public Service Delivery & Performance Review*, 9, 9.

Odey, G. O., Alawad, A. G. A., Atieno, O. S., Carew-Bayoh, E. O., Fatuma, E., Ogunkola, I. O. & Lucero-Prisno, D. E. 2021. COVID-19 pandemic: impacts on the achievements of sustainable development goals in Africa. *Pan African Medical Journal*, 38. 10.11604/pamj.2021.38.251.27065

OECD. 2020. *COVID-19 and Africa: Socio-economic implications and policy responses* [Online]. OECD. Available:https://www.oecd.org/coronavirus/policy-responses/COVID-19-and-africa-socio-economic-implications-and-policy-responses-96e1b282/ [Accessed 11 October 2023].

OECD, I. 2019. Protecting informal economy workers and their dependents. *Tackling Vulnerability in the Informal Economy*.

PERC. 2020. *Effective Implementation of Public Health and Social Measures in Zimbabwe: Situational Analysis* [Online]. Partnership for Evidence-Based Response to COVID-19. Available: https://preventepidemics.org/wp-content/uploads/2020/05/Zimbabwe_perc-countrybrief_mobility.pdf [Accessed 11 October 2023].

Pikramenou, N. & Mahajan, S. 2021. "Make every African woman leader count." *Agenda*, 33, 82–96.

Powers, S. & Azzi-Huck, K. 2016. "The impact of Ebola on education in Sierra Leone" [Accessed 11 October 2023].

RELIEFWEB. 2020. *COVID-19 response: Weekly UN in Zimbabwe upfate issue VIII* [Online]. Reliefweb. Available: https://reliefweb.int/report/zimbabwe/COVID-19-response-weekly-un-zimbabwe-update-issue-viii-19-june-2020 [Accessed 11 October 2023].

Sirleaf, E. J. 2020. *Opinion: African women are leading the fight against COVID-19* [Online]. DEVEX. Available: https://www.devex.com/news/opinion-african-women-are-leading-the-fight-against-COVID-19-97980 [Accessed 11 October 2023].

Sirleaf, E. J. 2022. "The art of the pivot: African women as critical problem solvers in the 21st century". *Brookings Foresight Africa*. Available at https://www.brookings.edu/articles/african-women-and-girls-leading-a-continent/#:~:text=Throughout%20Africa%27s%20history%2C%20women%20were,crises%20of%20the%2021st%20century [accessed 22 April 2024].

UNAIDS 2017. When Women Lead Change Happens: Women advancing the end of AIDS. UNAIDS.

UNICEF. 2023. *Fighting the wave - How a nation united to fight the COVID-19 pandemic*. Directed by UNICEF. Zimbabwe.

UNWomen. 2022. *Women in informal economy* [Online]. UN WOMEN: UN WOMEN. Available: https://www.unwomen.org/en/news/in-focus/csw61/women-in-informal-economy [Accessed 11 October 2023].

Uzobo, E. & Ayinmoro, A. D. 2023. "Trapped between two pandemics: Domestic violence cases under COVID-19 pandemic lockdown: A scoping review." *Community Health Equity Research & Policy*, 43, 319–328.

WHO. 2020. *MoHCC enriches Zimbabwe's quarantine staff's capacity to manage individuals in quarantine facilities* [Online]. World Health Organisation. Available: https://www.afro.who.int/news/mohcc-enriches-zimbabwes-quarantine-staffs-capacity-manage-individuals-quarantine-facilities [Accessed 11 October 2023].

Worldbank. 2014. *Nearly half of Liberia's workforce no longer working since Start of Ebola crisis* [Online]. World Bank. Available: https://www.worldbank.org/en/news/press-release/2014/11/19/half-liberia-workforce-no-longer-working-ebola-crisis [Accessed 11 October 2023].

Yuan, H., Wang, X., Gao, L., Wang, T., Liu, B., Fang, D. & Gao, Y. 2023. Progress towards the sustainable development goals has been slowed by indirect effects of the COVID-19 pandemic. *Communications Earth & Environment*, 4, 184.

11
ELLEN JOHNSON SIRLEAF'S RHETORICAL LEADERSHIP
The Fight to Rebuild Liberia, Empower Women, and Conquer Ebola

Julia A. Spiker

Fighter for Transformational Change

"We always say as women, 'We don't believe in power; we believe in influence'—But there comes a time as a woman leader when you have to exercise power. When that time comes, don't be afraid to use it," stated former Liberian President Ellen Johnson Sirleaf (2023: para. 11). Sirleaf was unafraid to exercise power throughout her long political career. She used her political voice to exercise her agency. Sirleaf has been a leader who uses her political agency to fight for transformational change.

A key foundation of Sirleaf's agency is her use of power, specifically empowerment. Carr (2003:18) describes empowerment as a "cyclical process of collective dialogue and social action that is meant to effect positive change." Empowerment involves "change or transformation toward an expansion of choices, self-determination, and enhanced health and wellbeing" (Whiteside et al. 2011:115). Sirleaf drew her source of power from her gender, her experiences as a woman in African politics, and her interpersonal connections with Liberian women. From these power sources, Sirleaf fought to empower others. Sirleaf's rhetorical power is shaped by her political ethos. Her popular nicknames such as "Old Ma" and "Iron Lady" illustrate the fighting spirit within Sirleaf. "Old Ma" represents a traditional authority within the African culture. Sirleaf as "Old Ma" fights for her people as a mother who cares for her children. The "Iron Lady" depicts a strong leader who fights for her people. Throughout her political career, Sirleaf's political agency is woven into her rhetorical leadership style, engaging her citizens and global audiences in compelling ways to achieve shared goals and create a sense of collectivity. Sirleaf sought transformational changes in Liberian society as she fought to empower the Liberian people, especially women.

This and the following paragraph frame the scope and methods of this chapter. Sirleaf's rhetoric offered insight into the rhetorical agency of a woman leading the West African nation of Liberia. Sirleaf's political communication style has been examined from various perspectives such as how she used rhetoric to craft a cosmopolitan nationalism, her political influence on women's rights, and how the media used language to frame her political leadership (Stillion Southard 2017; Kodila-Tedika & Asongu 2017; Anderson et al. 2011). This case study on rhetorical leadership analyzes Sirleaf's rhetoric to better understand the political agency of an African woman political leader. Sirleaf's speeches, interviews, official statements, and media reports between 2006 and 2023 are examined to understand her rhetorical leadership style and messages. Her rhetoric is analyzed using empowerment theory to frame her rhetorical style and key thematic messages in her fight narrative. Sirleaf is a global leader who fights for democratic rule and women's empowerment. Her determination and leadership successfully fought through the challenges of rebuilding Liberia after a 14-year civil war and overcoming an Ebola epidemic. Sirleaf's rhetorical style projects an image of a leader who fights for others. This image is distinguished by a fight narrative. Her rhetorical style of the fight narrative developed during her presidency as she fought for women's empowerment. She fought for other women to enter politics and express their political voices. Her rhetorical style during the Ebola crisis strengthened the fight narrative with powerful war metaphors. Even now, as a global leader, Sirleaf's fight narrative threads throughout her rhetorical leadership style as she tackles new global health crises.

Rhetorical leadership incorporates leadership and rhetoric elements. "Leadership is realized in the process whereby one or more individuals succeed in attempting to frame and define the reality of others" (Smircich & Morgan 1982: 257). Leadership through rhetorical style engages leaders with their citizens as they share the journey of reaching collective goals. Rhetorical style incorporates a deliberate framing of a message for a distinct outcome. Cohen (1998: 35, 38) argues that "style is the verbal clothing of ideas" and that a "clear style is often aided by 'methods of amplification,' that is, word choices and word arrangements that emphasize and enliven ideas." According to Stoner and Perkins (2005: 141), "the pattern of word choice is what makes a 'style' of discourse." Rhetorical devices such as narratives and metaphors are important tools of style. Palczewski, Ice, and Fritch (2012: 44) argue that "Narratives play a significant role in public communication. They form and maintain public memory and teach cultural values." Sirleaf uses a fight narrative to frame her leadership messages. "Metaphors explicitly or implicitly say that two things are the same" (Cohen 1998:39). Mio et al. (2006:288) explain why a political leader uses metaphors, "The ability to clarify and perhaps arouse emotions in followers may be a key reason why leaders use metaphors in political speeches." "Metaphors draw on shared cultural experiences to give meaning to ideas" and influence "our understanding of the world around us" (Atuhura 2022:3). The continued use of war metaphors in recent health crises' rhetoric such as COVID-19 supports how such methodological tools provide a framework to analyze communication style (Atuhura 2022; Seixas 2021). During the 21-month Ebola crisis, Sirleaf exercised her political agency as a woman political leader fighting to save her country from an "unknown enemy" using war metaphors. The war metaphor was a useful rhetorical strategy to manage the Ebola crisis by challenging Liberians to change their behavior, bring the nation together, and enlist the support of other countries in the battle against Ebola. Sirleaf's political rhetorical leadership offers an opportunity to better understand the intersection of transformative rhetorical leadership and women's agency in a health crisis.

Campbell and Huxman (2009: 165) connect style to the rhetor by elaborating on "what is distinctive about the language of a rhetorical act reflects the attitudes and character of the rhetor and hints at feelings about the subject being explored or advocated." Sirleaf's rhetorical style provides insight into her worldview as a political leader who is unafraid to do battle for Liberians. Sirleaf's rhetorical leadership style includes her determination to fight for Liberia, being a warrior for women's empowerment, battling Ebola to save Liberians, and challenging global pandemics.

Sirleaf the Fighter to Rebuild Liberia

Her lengthy career of political experience led Sirleaf to become the first woman elected to head an African country. The 24th president of Liberia, Ellen Johnson Sirleaf served two terms from 2006 to 2018. Liberia, the oldest African Republic, is a West African nation of about four million people founded by freed American and Caribbean slaves in 1847 (Liberia Country Profile 2015). Political turmoil in Liberia erupted in a raging civil war that lasted from 1989 to 2003. BBC News reported,

> Around 250,000 people were killed in Liberia's civil war and many thousands more fled the fighting. The conflict left the country in economic ruin and overrun with weapons. The capital remains without main electricity and running water. Corruption is rife and unemployment and illiteracy are epidemic.
> (Liberia Country Profile 2015: para. 9)

The political turmoil of Liberia's history provided the context for Sirleaf's rhetorical message of fighting for transformational change for her people and Liberia. This context of Liberian wars provided a rhetorical framework which Sirleaf used to connect to her citizens who have endured the struggles for democracy.

Educated in the United States, Sirleaf earned bachelor's degrees in accounting and economics and a master's degree in public administration. By 1979, Sirleaf served as the Minister of Finance under President William Tolbert in Liberia. Sirleaf continued to work in the Liberian government after a military coup, briefly serving as the president of the Liberian Bank for Development and Investment under President Samuel Doe before resigning and fleeing into exile in Kenya (Ellen 2009). She later returned to Liberia to win a seat in the Senate but then refused to take office in protest of Doe's policies. As a member of the political opposition to Doe, Sirleaf was detained, arrested, and sentenced to 10 years in prison. However, international protests led to her release after seven months in jail, and again she fled into exile (Ellen 2009).

Sirleaf returned to Liberia again and became chair of the Governance Reform Commission (GRC). She was "responsible for designing and implementing a thorough reorganization of the country's governing structures, which had been weakened by years of corruption and mismanagement" (Ellen 2009: para. 11). In 2005, the first elections since the civil war ended were held and Sirleaf was elected as the first woman president of Liberia. "For many of her supporters, Sirleaf personified the nation's ability to recover from the long nightmare of civil war" (Ellen 2009: para. 13). In 2011, Sirleaf was re-elected to a second term. Her victory celebrations were short-lived as Liberia still needed much rebuilding. She recognized her unique political position as well as the challenges she faced to rebuild Liberia as she stated,

> Today I stand proud, as the first woman president of my country, Liberia. This has allowed me to lead the processes of change, change needed to address a long-standing environment characterized by awesome challenges: a collapsed economy, huge domestic and external debt arrears, dysfunctional institutions, destroyed infrastructure, poor regional land international relationships, and social capital destroyed by the scourge of war.
> (2011a: para. 10)

By 2011, "perhaps the greatest achievement of her administration has been negotiating the write-off of nearly $5bn (L3.2bn) in crushing foreign debt, enabling Liberia to borrow again. The government's annual budget has risen six fold from $80m to $516m" (Ford, 2011: para. 7). Sirleaf regenerated Liberia's economy as evidenced by the gross domestic product rising to "$2.1 billion in 2016 from $500 million in 2005" (Bariyo 2018: para. 9). Sirleaf voiced pride in Liberia's willingness to transform from a nation devastated by war to one with a bright future as she stated,

> Today I stand equally proud, as the first woman president of our African continent, a continent that has embraced the process of change and transformation. I am proud that Liberia became a beacon of hope in Africa.
>
> (2011a: para. 14)

Sirleaf's narrative of fighting for the Liberian people engaged Liberians to make transformational changes in their country. Sirleaf's rhetoric embraces change with positivity.

Sirleaf the Fighter for Women's Rights

Having risen to power after a devastating 14-year-long civil war, Sirleaf focused heavily on rebuilding the nation's physical infrastructure as well as re-establishing the intangible bond between the government and the people. Her determination to fight for the Liberian people was central to her political ethos, which she built through her personal narrative. Sirleaf offered the story of her grandmother's values as a parallel narrative to establish the foundation for the values which guide her professional mission. Sirleaf stated,

> Both of my grandmothers were farmers and village traders. They could not read or write any language—as more than three-quarters of our people still cannot today—but they worked hard, they loved their country, they loved their families and they believed in education.
>
> (2006b: para. 8)

The values of hard work, patriotism, family, education, and determination to lead form the foundation of Sirleaf's political leadership style. Sirleaf's determination to succeed is a key pillar in her rhetorical leadership style's narrative of a leader who fights for others. Her grandmothers serve as her role models. As Sirleaf stated, "They inspired me then, and their memory motivates me now to serve my people, to sacrifice for the world and honestly serve humanity. I could not, I will not—I cannot—betray their trust" (2006b: para. 8). Another component of Sirleaf's political ethos is developed in the narrative of her identity. The humble roots of her youth grew because of education and international experience to blossom into her current professional success. Sirleaf stated,

> So my feet are in two worlds—the world of poor rural women with no respite from hardship, and the world of accomplished Liberian professionals, for whom the United States is a second and beloved home. I draw strength from both.
>
> (2006b: para. 11)

Sirleaf's political ethos narrative associated her as a leader who can identify with poor rural women as well as educated professionals. Based upon her personal life story, Sirleaf's rhetoric created a powerful lens through which she argued for equal rights and opportunities for women.

Sirleaf used rhetorical messages to rebuild the people's trust in the government after years of civil war. She also chose to target women with specific political messages of empowerment and of challenging women to participate in politics. Sirleaf used her office to fight for women's rights, opportunities, and equality and enacted policies benefiting women. She wanted to improve women's status from second-class citizens to individuals with basic human rights. Furthermore, Sirleaf linked gender equality to economic prosperity as she stated,

> We also know for long-term growth and development to occur, to be sustainable the role and contribution of women must be taken into account. This is because when women are poor, uneducated, and have low participatory roles in the wider areas of governance and leadership, the family size tends to be larger, population growth and the effect on sustainable growth seem to be higher. Poverty reduction and gender equality are thus inextricably linked.
>
> (2008: para. 1, 2)

Sirleaf's rhetoric combined her goals to rebuild her nation while also fighting for gender equality. Her fight narrative used the argument that gender equality is a necessary component of economic and political success.

After her election in 2006, Sirleaf set a high goal for gender equality in her first inaugural address as she stated, "My Administration shall thus endeavor to give Liberian women prominence in all affairs of our country. My Administration shall empower Liberian women in all areas of our national life" (Sirleaf 2006a: para. 74). Sirleaf targeted policy changes to achieve this goal as she stated, "We will support and increase the writ of laws that restore their dignities and deal drastically with crimes that dehumanize them. We will enforce without fear or favor the law against rape recently passed by the National Transitional Legislature" (Sirleaf 2006a: para. 74). By 2012, in her second inaugural address, Sirleaf stated, "My administration remains particularly committed to achieving equality for women and girls in all areas of life: education, business, and in the family itself" (2012: para. 34).

Sirleaf did not speak for women, rather she used her office as a platform to speak to women. She encouraged women to exercise their political agency and realize their empowerment. Sirleaf fought to express her political voice in her career and fought to empower women so they could also express their political voices. A key component of her fight narrative focused on voice as evidenced when Sirleaf stated, "My sisters, my daughters, everywhere, find your voices!" (2011b: para. 28). The focus on voice charged women to activate their personal agency for the betterment of themselves, for all women, and for society. Sirleaf stated,

> Each of us has her own voice, and the differences among us are to be celebrated. But our goals are in harmony. They are the pursuit of peace, the pursuit of justice. They are the defense of rights to which all people are entitled.
>
> (2011b: para. 28, 29)

The political agency of Liberian women is a battle worth fighting to achieve gender equality, which can occur with active political participation by Liberian women expressing their rights via their voices. Sirleaf stated, "Today, an unprecedented number of women hold leadership positions in our country, and we intend to increase that number" (2011a: para. 34).

Liberian women want the same equal rights as men and Sirleaf described these rights in her speeches. She stated,

> Women, my strong constituency, tell me they want the same chances that men have. They want to be literate. They want their work recognized. They want protection against rape. They want clean water that won't sicken and kill their children.
>
> (2006b: para. 17)

Sirleaf illustrates women's needs with concrete examples to help the audience visualize equal rights in everyday life. Her narrative of fight and determination helped her to transform her political accomplishments to the potential of Liberian women's political ambitions as she stated, "Women know not only that they can compete, but also that they can excel. They can be mothers and also professionals. They know that we don't have to be stuck in the backyard" (Hammer & Polier 2006: para. 29).

The poor condition of Liberia's infrastructure greatly affected the rights of women and girls. Sirleaf tied the rebuilding of Liberia's infrastructure to the opportunity to fight for the empowerment of Liberian women, targeting such issues as healthcare, illiteracy, rape, human trafficking, and abuse to raise awareness of the tremendous challenges associated with them. Women have less access to healthcare and infant mortality rates are high. Girls were denied education and also became the targets for gender-based violence. Sirleaf stated,

> Girls were kept home instead of going to school because they have to help their mothers or go to the market place to be able to provide assistance to their mothers as a result they become vulnerable to gender-based violence.
>
> (2008: para. 2)

Sirleaf described how "the madness that wrought untold destruction" (2011b: para. 19) during the Liberian Civil War "found its expression in unprecedented levels of cruelty directed against women" (2011b: para. 19). Sirleaf noted the impact of rape, "The number of our sisters and daughters of all ages brutally defiled over the past two decades staggers the imagination, and the number of lives devastated by such evil defies comprehension" (2011b: para. 20). Sirleaf described the war's brutality on girls as she stated, "Our girls, capable of being anything they could imagine, were made into sex slaves, gang-raped by men with guns, made mothers while they were still children themselves" (2006b: para. 14). The lost potential of girls, individuals who could contribute positively to society, was lost because of abuse. Sirleaf stated,

> In too many parts of the world, crimes against women are still under-reported, and the laws protecting women are under-enforced. In this 21st century, surely there is no place for human trafficking that victimizes almost a million people, mostly girls and women, each year. Surely there is no place for girls and women to be beaten and abused. Surely there is no place for a continuing belief that leadership qualities belong to only one gender".
>
> (2011b: para. 23)

Sirleaf challenged Liberians to empathize with her depictions of what happens when women are treated unequally. Her fight narrative style described the after-effects of war on human lives. She challenged Liberians to join her battle for gender equality, and she implored the audience to reject any level of tolerance for permitting dehumanizing behavior which depreciated the basic human rights of women and girls.

Sirleaf recognized the importance of education for girls so "that we begin to bring that crop of women up right from the beginning" (Sirleaf 2008: para. 2). Under Sirleaf's leadership, Liberia introduced "literacy micro-loan programs," "training programs in leadership, home economics, agri-processing," "the Liberian education trust," and the "market women fund" to educate and to improve working conditions for women and girls (Sirleaf 2008: para. 2). Significant progress was made in achieving United Nations Millennium Development Goals (MDGs) promoting gender equality in Liberia due to Sirleaf's political leadership (Hanna & Alfaro 2012).

Sirleaf's determination to be treated as equal in society paved the way for her achievements as a political leader in Liberia and now globally. Through the Ellen Johnson Sirleaf Foundation, she continues to advocate for women's empowerment and leadership. Sirleaf stated, "Women are not asking for favors. Women are competent, able, knowledgeable, courageous, and have the tenacity to be able to stand up and claim leadership" (2023: para. 7). Aware of the challenges and obstacles that women political leaders face, Sirleaf challenged women to exercise their political power. Sirleaf's personal determination and the use of the fight narrative in her rhetorical style motivate other women to compete in political leadership.

War metaphors such as "fight," "warriors," and "battling" are used by Sirleaf to advance women's empowerment issues with the goal of women's equality. The fight narrative in Sirleaf's rhetorical style has been an integral component of her political leadership. As Sirleaf battled to rebuild Liberia upon principles of gender equality, she faced off against another enemy. The "unknown enemy" of Ebola had invaded Liberia. Sirleaf's rhetorical fight narrative transformed into an all-out war narrative as she battled to save Liberians from this new threat.

Sirleaf the Fighter Against Ebola

Rebuilding Liberia's infrastructure and political systems was a challenge for Sirleaf; however, she also fought to save her country from a health crisis of epidemic proportions from 2014 to 2016. Sirleaf stated, "Liberia was struck by a terrifying virus, an unseen enemy more fearsome than war" (2017: para. 21). Ebola, a viral hemorrhagic fever, first surfaced in 1976 in the Democratic Republic of Congo (DRC). Ebola "is spread through contact with the bodily fluids of Ebola patients showing symptoms," and it has a fatality rate of between 55% and 90% (Liberia Declares 2014: para. 6). Ebola returned with a vengeance in 2013. The Ebola Outbreak in West Africa was traced to patient zero, a two-year-old child who died from it in Guinea in December 2013 but it was not recognized until March 2014. The outbreak reached Liberia on March 31, 2014, when two cases of Ebola were confirmed. By July 30, 2014, Ebola had been declared out of control by Doctors Without Borders (MSF), the international, medical, humanitarian organization; and on August 8, 2014, the World Health Organization (WHO) declared "the Ebola epidemic 'a public health emergency of international concern'" (Ebola: Timeline 2015). The West African Ebola epidemic peaked in August and September 2014.

Liberia was declared free of the deadly Ebola virus on May 9, 2015 by WHO and the epidemic was thought to have ended; however, additional cases of Ebola in July 2015 fueled fears of a resurgence of it in Liberia (Zoroya & Fallah 2015). In a second declaration, the WHO declared Liberia free of Ebola on January 14, 2016 because "all known chains of transmission have been stopped in West Africa" (Latest Ebola 2016: para. 1). The WHO urged continued vigilance as flare-ups of the Ebola virus were expected. Over 28,000 people were infected, and Ebola has taken the lives of over 11,000 people in the countries of Liberia (4809), Sierra Leone (3955), Guinea (2536), Nigeria (8), and Mali (6) (Ebola: Mapping 2016).

Sirleaf's messages and communication style influenced her rhetorical leadership during the Ebola crisis and beyond. She crafted a fight narrative built on war metaphors to stir Liberians to act against Ebola. Sirleaf called the Ebola virus the "unknown enemy" (Gladstone 2015). Her rhetorical goal was to unmask the "unknown enemy," make it known, and defeat it. Once her rhetoric made known the "unknown enemy," Sirleaf worked to convince Liberians that together they could fight and win the battle against Ebola. In addition, ethos, pathos, and logos appeals were used by Sirleaf to strengthen her persuasive messages. Sirleaf framed her rhetorical style with her political ethos, an appeal to her credibility and authority. She fought to convince Liberians and the world community that she had the credibility and authority to lead Liberia through the rebuilding of the country, to conquer Ebola, and to address global pandemics. Sirleaf applied pathos—emotional appeals—to convince the global community to help Liberians who were its victims and to protect their own citizens from the spread of the disease. She applied logos by reasoning with Liberians to work with her and convincing other nations to join the fight to save Liberia from Ebola and other global pandemics. The combination of the fight narrative and the appeals of ethos, pathos, and logos created a powerful, persuasive rhetorical style for a leader.

Powerful war metaphors in Sirleaf's fight narrative described the effect of Ebola on Liberia. Sirleaf described Ebola as an invader attacking Liberia, and her persuasive approach intertwined a public health crisis with the survival of the political state in her war narrative. She stated, "it attacks our way of life, with serious economic and social consequences" (Paye-Layleh 2014a: para. 6). She stated, "As such we are compelled to bring the totality of our national resolve to fight this scourge" (Christensen 2014: para. 3). Sirleaf's reaction to the invasion of the disease mirrored a leader's actions in wartime to protect the country from an "unknown enemy." She stated, "controlling borders and controlling places where we put quarantine is difficult because of the free movements that people are accustomed" (Tapper 2014: para. 43). She declared a 90-day state of emergency in August 2014, which gave her extraconstitutional powers (Leaf 2014). Sirleaf claimed her action was for "the very survival of our state and for the protection of the lives of our people" (Maclean 2014: para. 7). Her official policies reflected a wartime approach. She closed a newspaper critical of her efforts to fight Ebola. She ordered a night-time curfew, sealed off an area of West Point, and used military forces to surround the area preventing people from leaving. She fired government officials who refused to return to Liberia and canceled national elections. In response, many Liberians withdrew money from the banks, stocked up on food, and fled to the countryside (Maclean 2014). Also, Liberians kept the sick at home instead of taking them to treatment centers (Liberia Declares 2014).

Sirleaf's response to the public panic brought about by the Ebola virus used a strong war narrative to frame her communication style. In June 2014, she warned that "anyone caught hiding suspected Ebola patients will be prosecuted" (Johnson 2014: para. 1). Sirleaf stated,

Here, we're talking about a deadly disease—a disease that can kill people. And we're obliged to also protect the lives of people. And so this is just bringing to their attention that there's a law that says they must do that, and if they don't, then there are penalties.
(Quist-Arcton 2014: para. 4)

Sirleaf ascribed the peoples' lack of knowledge for creating panic when she stated, "Our people know nothing. There's no cure. There was denial. It's now turned into fear and panic..." (Tapper 2014: para. 43). Traditional and cultural practices such as the sick going to prayer rooms or witch doctors and families engaging in burial practices in which the bodies were washed in rituals clashed with Ebola healthcare procedures (Quist-Arcton 2014; Ward 2014). In July 2014, a regional response was formed by West African health ministers; however, "public fear and lack of knowledge about Ebola" were obstacles (Quist-Arcton 2014: para. 1). Sirleaf acknowledged that "there was quite a bit of denial. People did not respect the health authorities' advice. They thought this was just a scam. But now they are seeing people die. People are dying in their communities" (Tapper 2014: para. 45). Building upon a war narrative, Sirleaf stirred Liberians to reflect upon their individual duty to protect the country and to trust her leadership when she stated, "Denying that the disease exists is not doing your part, so keep yourselves and your loved ones safe" (Ebola outbreak 2014: para. 3).

Sirleaf's messages to her world allies called for help to support her efforts to protect Liberia from the "unknown enemy." She framed the Ebola "war" in Liberia as a threat to the international community. She argued that she was unable to control the virus due to internal confusion, a lack of medical knowledge among officials and the people, few resources, charges of corruption, and the highly contagious nature of the disease. She based her argument on these factors as she stated,

Liberia has tried. We've used our own resources, but obviously we have limitations in our own resources and we hope the international community will see this as a grave international disease, an international catastrophe and will respond to it in kind.
(Tapper 2014: para. 52)

Sirleaf argued that the threat of Ebola spreading to other parts of the world could be stopped if the international community would respond and give aid. Her rhetorical style framed the call for international aid with a fear appeal. She stated, "The message we sent to everybody is that Ebola is not just a threat to Liberia and West Africa. It's a global threat...Today it's Liberia, but tomorrow it could be any other country, including the U.S." (Doughton 2015: para. 27). In other words, the international organizations should help the Liberian people out of fear for their safety because the disease might spread to their own countries. International organizations should give aid to help Liberians in ways that Liberians were unable to do. For example, she stated, "What we need is to build our capacity in terms of technical assistance, for training, technical assistance for treatment in the form of doctors and nurses" (Tapper 2014: para. 49). She also asked for help with logistics and supplies to help with hygiene. Sirleaf "noted that with limited understanding of the disease, low human capacity and a slow international response, the virus quickly outpaced the country's ability to contain it" (Wesee 2014). She needed to identify and isolate patients to curb the virus, which required construction of treatment centers (Northam 2014). In addition, Sirleaf's rhetoric framed the call for international aid to fight the Ebola epidemic as a duty of the world community. She stated,

> This fight requires a commitment from every nation that has the capacity to help whether that is with emergency funds, medical supplies or clinical expertise…It is the duty of all of us, as global citizens, to send a message that we will not leave millions of West Africans to fend for themselves against an enemy that they do not know, and against whom they have little defence.
>
> (Paye-Layleh 2014b: para. 12)

Liberia's war on Ebola gained traction with the influx of international support merging with the country's internal efforts. Sirleaf's war rhetoric engaged Liberians as partners in the battle against Ebola. Sirleaf stated, "Fear brought unity. Everybody came together to fight this common enemy" (Doughton 2015: para. 23). Sirleaf's rhetorical leadership was strengthened by her acknowledgment of the importance of empowering Liberia's citizenry. She stated, "Now I know that people's ownership, community participation, works better in a case like this. I think that experience will stay with us" (Gladstone 2015: para. 12). To win a war, political leaders need the people to join the fight. She acknowledged the power of working with the Liberian people as equal partners in the fight against Ebola as she said,

> Liberians took on the challenge to save our country. A Coordinating Body was established to include all stakeholders—leaders of the three Branches of Government, the international community, civil society, traditional and religious leaders to reinforce the responsibility to solve the problem rested essentially with ourselves.
>
> (President of Liberia 2015: para. 3)

Sirleaf seized rhetorical moments and modified her communication style throughout her fight to save Liberians during the Ebola crisis (Spiker 2017). Sirleaf's ability to critically assess, shape, and meet the communication needs of Liberians went a long way to establishing a meaningful connection between the leader and her citizens and thereby building a level of trust needed to combat the disease. Sirleaf stressed how important the people's "buy-in" is to a leader who strives for transformational change as she stated,

> It must be demand-driven by citizens empowered through civic education, decentralization of government and democracy practiced at the community level. The only sustainable power must come from the support of one's people.
>
> (2019: para. 15)

Her fight narrative illustrated how she fought for the Liberian people and with the Liberian people against common enemies. Sirleaf stated, "Indeed, my most proud accomplishment is that after decades of violent conflict, the power in Liberia now rests where it should—with the people, who must assure that it is grounded in the rule of law and upheld by institutions" (2019: para. 16). Sirleaf's rhetoric embraced the relationship between a political leader and citizens. Her voice challenged and motivated the Liberian people to work together to fight

Ebola while also drawing worldwide attention to the plight and the fight of the Liberian people.

Sirleaf the Fighter Against Global Pandemics

This research examined Sirleaf's communication style to better understand her rhetorical leadership as an African woman leader. Sirleaf crafted a fight narrative in her messages of determination as she built her rhetorical agency and rose to political leadership. She continued to use a fight narrative in her messages as a political leader who faced and overcame tremendous challenges. An analysis of her rhetoric offered insight into the ways that Sirleaf engaged in a fight narrative to help others, specifically to rebuild Liberia after a civil war, to empower Liberian women, to save Liberians from Ebola, and to protect people throughout the world from health crises.

In 2018, Sirleaf followed the country's constitution, stepping down to become "Liberia's first president ever to peacefully relinquish power" (Bariyo 2017: para. 1). This action was extraordinary as Baker (2020:126) stated, "For all the expectations, and inevitable failures, she (Sirleaf) did achieve something unprecedented in 70 years of leadership by Liberian men: she stepped aside for someone else when her time in power was up." Sirleaf stated, "I will preside over the election of a new Liberian leader. I have served faithfully my two terms. I respect our constitution, and am making way for a new leadership" (2017: para. 37). Sirleaf's actions led to a peaceful 2017 presidential election and are seen as a positive sign that Liberia's democracy is maturing (Macdougall 2018). Looking forward to her retirement, Sirleaf stated that she is "proud that she will be the country's only former president enjoying retirement at liberty" (Bariyo 2017: para. 19).

Since she left office, Sirleaf's experience and leadership during Liberia's Ebola crisis have placed her in a unique position to contribute to international responses to global health crises. She serves as an international leader for the World Health Organization as a Global Ambassador for the Health Workforce and as a co-chair of WHO's Independent Panel for Pandemic Preparedness and Response (IPPR), among other appointments. SARS, Ebola, and COVID-19 have revealed weaknesses in the global response structure. Sirleaf collaborates with world leaders such as Gro Harlem Brundtland, Helen Clark, Jakaya Kikwete, and Ban Ki-Moon to argue for the need to build a "pandemic-proof system" in the form of a "Global Pandemic Threats Council" established through a U.N. resolution (Brundtland et al. 2023). Sirleaf and Dr. Raj Panjabi offered key lessons from their experiences battling Ebola to offer help during the COVID-19 pandemic (Sirleaf & Panjabi 2020). Sirleaf and Panjabi stated,

> When epidemics strike, fear, anxiety and despair can be agonizing. But we are not defined by the conditions we face, no matter how hopeless they seem—we are defined by how we respond to them. Decisive political leadership and global cooperation will determine if we win the war against this invisible enemy.
>
> (2020: para. 8)

The fight narrative continues to dominate Sirleaf's rhetorical style in the years after Ebola as she keeps battling global health crises from her position as a world leader.

The rhetorical warrior, Sirleaf, is a woman political leader whose victory as the first woman President of an African nation transformed Liberian society by reimagining what a leader could be like. She recognized the impact of her election as transformative for other women because she understood the obstacles. She stated,

> As we know, African women, by definition, are political outsiders; they threaten the governing status quo—a status quo that for too long has held onto power at all costs, while their citizens live in want and deprivation, with their untapped potential never fully realized.
>
> (2021: para. 9)

Her rhetorical leadership changed the dynamic of women's roles and rights in Liberian society, but it may take years to fully appreciate her impact. Sirleaf's messages challenged Liberians and other nations to rebuild Liberia after the civil war's destruction. Her statements urged women to fight for their rights, to find their voices, and to participate in politics. Her communication style engaged war metaphors to make known and conquer the "unknown enemy" of Ebola. Her persuasive approach continues to engage countries throughout the world to work together in the fight against global pandemics. Sirleaf, the rhetorical warrior, continues to fight for transformational change and to empower others.

Bibliography

Anderson, J. A., Diabah, G., & Mensa, P. A. 2011. 'Powerful women in powerless language: Media misrepresentation of African women in politics (the case of Liberia)', *Journal of Pragmatics* 43, 2509–2518.

Atuhura, D., 2022. 'The Metaphor of war in political discourse on COVID-19 in Uganda', *Frontiers in Communication* 6, 1–19. doi: 10.3389/fcomm.2021.746007

Baker, A., 2020. 'Ellen Johnson Sirleaf: A first for Africa', *Time*, 16–23 March, p. 126.

Bariyo, N., 2017. 'Liberian Leader Ellen Johnson Sirleaf yields as voters choose her successor: While breaking a violent tradition by relinquishing power, president leaves moribund economy behind', *The Wall Street Journal Online*, 8 October. Retrieved from https://www.wsj.com

Bariyo, N., 2018. 'World News: Liberia's Ex-President wins leadership prize', *The Wall Street Journal Online*, 13 February. Retrieved from https://www.wsj.com

Brundtland, G. H., Clark, H., Kikwete, J., Ki-Moon, B. & Sirleaf, E. J., 2023, 'Opinion: Patchwork reforms won't stop pandemic threats', *devex*, 23 January. Retrieved from https://www.devex.com/news/opinion-patchwork-reforms-won-t-stop-pandemic-threats-104856

Campbell, K. K. & Huxman, S. S., 2009. *The Rhetorical act: Thinking, speaking, and writing critically*, Wadsworth Cengage Learning, Belmont, CA.

Carr, E. S., 2003. 'Rethinking empowerment theory using a feminist lens: The importance of process', *Affilia* 18(1), 8–20.

Christensen, J., 2014. 'Liberia closes its borders to stop Ebola', *CNN*. 22 August. Retrieved from https://CNN.com

Cohen, J. R., 1998. *Communication criticism: Developing your critical powers*, SAGE Publications, Thousand Oaks, CA.

Doughton, S., 2015. 'Liberia's president visits Seattle with thanks, warnings on Ebola', *The Seattle Times*, 4 October. Retrieved from www.seattletimes.com

'Ebola: Mapping the Outbreak', 2016, *BBC*, 14 January. Retrieved from http://www.bbc.com/news/world-africa-28755033

'Ebola outbreak: "out of control…and can get worse"; Nigeria's Asky airline stops flying to Liberia, Sierra Leone; Liberia closes schools', 2014, *International Business Times*, 31 July. Retrieved from http://eds.a.ebscohost.com

'Ebola: Timeline of a Ruthless Killer', 2015, *Agence France-Presse*, 31 January. Retrieved from http://reliefweb.int

'Ellen Johnson Sirleaf', 2009. In *Contemporary Black Biography*. Retrieved from http://www.encyclopedia.com

Ford, T., 2011, 'Ellen Johnson Sirleaf—profile', *The Guardian*, 7 October. Retrieved from http://www.theguardian.com

Gladstone, R., 2015. 'Liberian leader concedes errors in response to Ebola', *The New York Times*, 11 March. Retrieved from http://www.nytimes.com

Hanna, H., & Alfaro, A. L., 2012. 'The Future of development in Liberia: Keeping women on the agenda', *Women's Policy Journal of Harvard*, 9, 77–79. Retrieved from https://www.academica.edu

Hammer, J., & Polier, A., 2006. 'Healing powers', *Time*, 3 April, 147(14), 30–39. Retrieved from https://time.com

Johnson, G., 2014. 'Liberia vows prosecution for hiding Ebola patients', *The Associated Press: AP Top News Package*, 30 June. Retrieved from http://eds.a.ebscohost.com

Kodila-Tedika, O., & Asongu, S. A., 2017. 'Women in power and power of women: The Liberian experience', *International Feminist Journal of Politics*, 19(1), 86–101.

'Latest Ebola outbreak over in Liberia; West Africa is at zero, but new flare-ups are likely to occur', 2016, *World Health Organization*, [Press release], 16 January. Retrieved from http://www.who.int/

Leaf, A., 2014. 'Ebola spotlights Liberians' distrust of their political leaders', *Al Jazeera*, 14 October. Retrieved from http://america.aljazeera.com

'Liberia Country Profile', 2015, *BBC News*, 30 June. Retrieved from http://www.bbc.com

'Liberia declares state of emergency over deadly Ebola virus outbreak', 2014, *Arabia 2000*, 7 August. Retrieved from http://eds.a.ebscohost.com

Macdougall, C., 2018. 'The President of Liberia is ousted in a party brawl', *The New York Times*, 15 January. Retrieved from https://www.nytimes.com/

Maclean, R., 2014. 'Ebola panic sweeps across Liberia as president declares state of emergency', *Time*, 8 August, p. 32. Retrieved from http://eds.a.ebscohost.com

Mio, J. S., Riggio, R. E., Levin, S., & Reese, R., 2006. 'Presidential leadership and charisma: The Effects of metaphor', *The Leadership Quarterly*, 16, 287–294.

Northam, J., 2014. 'Three forlorn presidents bring Ebola wish list to the World Bank', *All Things Considered (NPR)*, 9 October. Retrieved from http://eds.a.ebscohost.com

Palczewski, C. H., Ice, R., & Fritch, J., 2012. *Rhetoric in Civic Life*, Strata Publishing, Inc., State College, PA.

Paye-Layleh, J.. 2014a, 'Liberia president orders new anti-Ebola measures', *The Associated Press: AP Top News Package*, 28 July. Retrieved from http://eds.a.ebscohost.com

Paye-Layleh, J. 2014b, 'Liberia's president calls for more aid as Ebola toll rises', *New Zealand Herald*, 21 October. Retrieved from http://eds.a.ebscohost.com

'President of Liberia praises international community's support to Liberia over tackling Ebola disease', 2015, *Arabia 2000*, 23 February. Retrieved from http://eds.a.ebscohost.com

Quist-Arcton, O., 2014. 'In West Africa, officials target ignorance and fear over Ebola', *All Things Considered (NPR)*, 10 July. Retrieved from http://eds.a.ebscohost.com

Seixas, E. C., 2021. 'War metaphors in political communication on COVID-19', *Frontiers in Sociology*, 5, 1–11. doi: 10.3389/fsoc.2020.583680

Sirleaf, E. J., 2006a. *Inaugural Address of H. E. Ellen Johnson Sirleaf*, 16 January. Retrieved from https://awpc.cattcentre.iastate.edu

Sirleaf, E. J., 2006b. *President Ellen Johnson-Sirleaf's Speech to the U.S. Congress*, delivered at US Joint Session of Congress, 15 March. Retrieved from https://awpc.cattcentre.iastate.edu

Sirleaf, E. J., 2008, *Gender & Infrastructure*, Keynote speech at Gender & Infrastructure Workshop at World Bank sponsored Fourth International Conference on African Development, June. Retrieved from http://www.youtube.com

Sirleaf, E. J., 2011a. 'Text of Ellen Johnson Sirleaf's speech: Harvard commencement remarks', *The Harvard Gazette*, 26 May. Retrieved from https://news.harvard.edu/gazette/story/2011/05/text-of-ellen-Johnson-sirleafs-speech

Sirleaf, E. J., 2011b. *A Voice for freedom!* Nobel Lecture, Oslo, 10 December. Retrieved from https://www.nobelprize.org

Sirleaf, E. J., 2012. 'Inaugural Address "The Values of a Patriot"', *Embassy of the Republic of Liberia in the United States*, 16 January. Retrieved from https://www.liberianembassyus.org/in-the-news/presiden-ellen-johnson-sirleafs-inaugural-address

Sirleaf, E. J., 2017. 'Remarks by Her Excellency Ellen Johnson Sirleaf', *U.S. Institute of Peace*, 25 September. Retrieved from https://www.usip.org/sites/default/files/Remarks-by-Her-Excellency-Ellen-Johnson-Sirleaf-September-25-2027.pdf

Sirleaf, E. J., 2019. 'Centre for global development keynote address', *Centre for Global Development*, 4 November. Retrieved from https://www.cgdev.org/publication/centre-global-development-keynote-address

Sirleaf, E. J., 2021. 'The Inaugural Kofi Annan Geneva Peace Address with Nobel Laureate Ellen Johnson Sirleaf', *The Kofi Annan Foundation*, 4 November. Retrieved from https://www.kofiannanfoundation.org/articles/the-inaugural-kofi-annan-geneva-peace-address-with-nobel-laureate-ellen-johnson-sirleaf/

Sirleaf, E. J., 2023. 'Former President Ellen Johnson Sirleaf makes a clarion call for women's leadership at the Women Deliver 2023 conference', *Women Deliver*, 26 July. Retrieved from https://ejscentre.org/former-president-ellen-johnson-sirleaf-makes-a-clarion-call-for-womens-leadership-at-the-women-deliver-2023-conference/

Sirleaf, E. J., & Panjabi, R., 2020. 'Five key lessons from the fight against Ebola', *Time*, 19 March. Retrieved from https://time.com

Smircich, L., & Morgan, G., 1982. 'Leadership: The Management of meaning', *The Journal of Applied Behavioral Science*, 18(3), 257–273.

Spiker, J. A., 2017. 'Conquering the unknown enemy: Sirleaf's evolving rhetorical leadership during Liberia's Ebola crisis', *African Journal of Rhetoric*, 9, 143–176.

Stillion Southard B. A., 2017. 'Crafting cosmopolitan nationalism: Ellen Johnson Sirleaf's rhetorical leadership', *Quarterly Journal of Speech*, 103(4), 395–414.

Stoner, M. & Perkins, S., 2005. *Making sense of messages: A Critical apprenticeship in rhetorical criticism*, Houghton Mifflin Company, Boston.

Tapper, J., 2014. 'Interview with Liberian Pres. Ellen Johnson Sirleaf', *CNN*, 31 July. Retrieved from http://eds.a.ebscohost.com

Ward, R., 2014. 'Ebola's public health remedy', *Harvard Political Review*, 15 October. Retrieved from http://harvardpolitics.com

Wesee, B. P., 2014. 'Liberia: Ellen speaks on impact of Ebola crisis', *AllAfrica*, 13 October. Retrieved from http://allafrica.com

Whiteside, M., Tsey, & Earles, W., 2011. 'Locating empowerment in the context of indigenous Australia', *Australian Social Work*, 64(1), 113–129.

Zoroya, G. & Fallah, S., 2015. 'Re-emergence of Ebola in Liberia remains a mystery', *USA Today*, 16 July. Retrieved from http://usatoday.com

12
YOUNG AFRICAN WOMEN'S RESPONSES TO THE IMPACT OF CLIMATE CHANGE

Ngozi Nwogwugwu and Elizabeth Oluwafunmiso Ngozi

Introduction

Globally, climate change has over the last two decades become a priority subject in discourses on environmental issues in the international arena. Climate change impacts (CCI) reverberate across several facets of the society, such as health, water resources, and agricultural production and trigger displacements as CCI induced conflicts over resources (International Centre for Research on Women, 2023). Although not a completely new phenomenon, there appears to be an increasing level of warming being experienced across the globe as a result of natural disasters such as volcanic eruptions, earthquakes, tsunamis and human-induced catastrophes through the emission of greenhouse gases, flooding and deforestation (Gashaw et al., 2014).

Despite having the lowest level of global gas emissions, Sub-Saharan Africa (SSA) has been identified as the region of the globe that will be most affected by the effects of climate change (CCI) (Nwogwugwu, 2020a; Intergovernmental Panel on Climate Change (IPCC), 2014; Niang et al., 2014). The majority of SSA nations have shown a lack of political will to see policy and action plans, with limited funding for climate change adaptation and mitigation strategies, despite the fact that the region is the most vulnerable to CCI. Given their many roles, women are more susceptible to CCI than males, according to research on the gender features of CCI (Nelson, 2010; Lambrou & Piana, 2006; Rohr, 2005; Denton, 2002). The suggestion is that gender-sensitive adaptation and mitigation methods for CCI have been proposed in order to ensure that initiatives aimed at women would address their unique requirements (Nwogwugwu, 2020a; Lambrou & Piana, 2006; Rohr, 2005; Denton, 2002). The majority of African nations' responses have, at best, been inconsistent, lacking the necessary deeds to support their declarations.

Some of these African nations prefer reactive action instead of pro-active action. As such, the vast financial outlay required to fund strategies to mitigate CCI has been lacking in many of these countries. CCI are long-term due to environmental and ecosystem degradation as well as short-term due to natural calamities such as drought, floods, landslides, and earthquakes (UN Women, 2022). The implication is that the adoption of ad hoc or emergency measures, which African countries are specialists in, cannot effectively tackle CCI.

According to the International Centre for Research on Women (2023), "women and girls are both more likely to be killed, injured, and displaced by severe climate-related disasters, and are more likely to face detrimental economic, educational, and security consequences as a result of long-term climate change". CCI is reported to worsen existing gender inequities for the female gender, especially in patriarchal societies such as Africa. Women are especially susceptible to CCI because of the intersections of gender, power dynamics, socio-economic systems, and sociocultural norms and expectations (Andrijevic et al., 2020; Hoffman, 2009).

Africa's high vulnerability to CCI has been attributed, in part, to the continent's predominantly non-mechanized subsistence agriculture (World Bank, 2015; Dercon, 2009). Given that women make up the majority of individuals working in the agricultural sector and that CCI is expected to have a negative impact on agricultural production, health, and the ocean and Savannah ecosystems (Nwoke & Ibe, 2015), women are more susceptible to CCI on the continent than men. The inference is that young African women will become the group most affected by CCI because they make up the bulk of individuals working in the agriculture sector, and being in their reproductive years, they are more vulnerable to CCI on their health. A changing climate puts sexual and reproductive health and rights in jeopardy. Given their status as mothers and expectant mothers, it is anticipated that women in their reproductive years will be particularly susceptible to CCI. They must take care of their own, their children's health, the health of their other family members, and the endemic health issues brought on by climate fluctuation.

Evidence suggests that the mortality rate among women, girls, and children during catastrophes, including severe weather events like hurricanes, wildfires, and flooding, is up to 14 times higher than that of men (Zeid, 2015; World Health Organization, 2014; Plan International, 2013), even though some nations, like Nigeria, are not at the forefront of compiling climate-related gender-disaggregated data.

Similar to this, young women, especially those in Africa, may suffer from malnutrition and/or undernutrition as a result of CCI-induced shortages in macro- and micronutrients, particularly in those who are pregnant. Low-weight births, miscarriages, and perinatal mortality may arise from this, as well as effects on pregnancy, nursing, and neonatal outcomes (Asian-Pacific Resource & Research Centre for Women, 2014; Sorensen et al., 2018; Centre for Climate Change and Health, 2016).

Climate change is associated with an increase in the spread of vector-borne diseases because it causes temperature variations that some vector-borne diseases benefit from. Young women of reproductive age who are exposed to vector-borne diseases have an increased risk of spontaneous abortion, early delivery, stillbirth, low birth weight, eclampsia, and cesarean delivery. Some researchers (Nwogwugwu, 2020a, Stevens, 2010) have concentrated on women, while others have examined the gender component of CCI in Africa (Kumar & Quisumbing, 2014; Meinzen-Dick et al., 2014; Villamor et al., 2015; Lambrou & Piana, 2006; Rohr, 2005; Denton, 2002). There is a dearth of material devoted to the CCI's effects on young African women and the particular adaptation and mitigation measures that are appropriate for them. This chapter seeks to close that gap in the literature.

The chapter focuses mostly on CCI on young African women with an emphasis on agricultural production/food security and health (reproductive and maternal health). The specific context that is examined is four countries that are among the most vulnerable to CCI from different sub-regions of the content: the Democratic Republic of Congo, Ethiopia, Madagascar, and Nigeria. However, examples of successful interventions by young women from other African countries will also be presented. These examples can inspire young women in the focus countries and beyond to recognize the agency and capacity of young women to be effective frontline actors in responding to climate change.

The Democratic Republic of Congo

The Democratic Republic of Congo (DRC), which spans 2,345,410 km², is Central Africa's biggest and the continent's second largest nation. It has a small opening to the Atlantic Ocean and nine neighbors: Angola, Burundi, the Central African Republic, the Republic of the Congo, Rwanda, South Sudan, Tanzania, Uganda, and Zambia. The DRC is characterized by extreme political unpredictability, lack of access to food, extreme poverty, and social instability. These issues are projected to get worse due to predicted temperature rises, an increase in the frequency of extreme weather events, and the location of the countries of Uganda, Rwanda, Burundi, and the United Republic of Tanzania in the east; the Central African Republic and Sudan in the south; Angola and Zambia in the west.

Along the country's eastern border, particularly in the Great Lakes region, climate vulnerability is further exacerbated by poor governance and high population density (Doty, 2011). In recent years of strife, the security and governance situation in the region has gotten worse. The DRC is home to an estimated 7.7 million refugees and internally displaced persons, and 524,000 of its citizens reside in refugee camps outside of the nation, according to the UN. Conflicts increase marginalized communities' vulnerability by causing poverty, displacement, immobility, and social network erosion. Additionally, the paucity of water and the scarcity of arable land could be contributing factors to future wars (Office of the Deputy Prime Minister DRC, 2022).

The United Nations Framework Convention on Climate Change, the Paris Agreement, and the Kyoto Protocol were all ratified in 1997, 2005, and 2015, respectively. The Nationally Determined Contribution (NDC), a pledge to reduce emissions by 21 percent between 2021 and 2030, of which 19 percent will be accomplished with external assistance and 2 percent through national efforts (USAID, 2019), ensures that the nation's efforts at adaptation and mitigation of CCI are primarily driven by external factors. The estimated total for the NDC of the DRC is USD 48.68 billion; of this sum, USD 25.60 billion will be used to implement agreed mitigation measures and USD 23.08 billion will be used to prioritize adaptation initiatives (Office of the Deputy Prime Minister DRC, 2022).

About 90% of the people in the DRC depend on agriculture as their primary source of income; however, the sector is predominantly subsistence-based and largely rain-fed. Communities that are impoverished and vulnerable face threats to social development and food security.

Variations in rainfall, shortening of the rainy seasons, rising heat waves as well as increases in average soil temperature "affect crop growth, harvests will be unreliable and the people who rely on rainfed agriculture will be extremely vulnerable" (Office of the Deputy Prime Minister DRC, 2022, pp. 30–31). Women in the DRC are responsible for producing or providing water and food, and young women in the DRC are more dependent on resources connected to the climate than males are. Due to their limited mobility, lack of empowerment and restrictive land laws, as well as the low degree of employment in the formal sector, they also face a double burden of low adaptive ability (Nwogwugwu, 2020b; African Development Bank Group, 2013).

Ethiopia

Due to its vulnerability to the effects of climate change, Ethiopia is particularly concerned about them. As a result of climate change and fluctuation, Ethiopia is one of Africa's most susceptible nations and frequently experiences drought and flooding (NAPA, 2007). Land degradation, reliance on rain-fed agriculture, and weak institutions make the nation more susceptible to natural calamities. Among the countries rated for 2015 by the Global Climate Change Adaptation Index (GAIN), Ethiopia is placed as the 36th most vulnerable and the 40th least ready to adapt to climate change (Mc Sweeney et al., 2008).

According to Burnett (2013, cited in Gashaw et al., 2014), one of the nations with the greatest vulnerability to climate change and variability is Ethiopia. It frequently endures tragedies brought on by the climate, primarily drought and flooding. A drop in agricultural output, lack of water, an increase in the frequency of pests and illnesses, flooding, the development of desertification, the loss of wetlands, the extinction of species, and recurrent droughts and famines are all effects of climate change. Climate change is expected to worsen Ethiopia's environmental degradation, food insecurity, water scarcity, disease epidemics, and poverty (World Bank, 2010). The temperature is rising (maximum, lowest, and mean), but there is no clear pattern because of the significant variability of the rainfall (NMSA, 2007; Bewket & Conway, 2007; McSweeney et al., 2008; Bewket, 2011).

Ethiopia is extremely vulnerable to CCI, similar to other African nations (Gashaw et al., 2014), linked to factors in the social, economic, and environmental. The nation is especially sensitive to climate change due to a number of characteristics, including high levels of poverty, rapid population growth, rain-fed subsistence agriculture, high levels of environmental degradation, ongoing food insecurity, and recurrent natural drought cycles (Aklilu et al., 2009). According to Gashaw et al. (2014), the most vulnerable sectors are agriculture, water resources, and human health.

Impacts on Agricultural Production and Food Security

As previously mentioned, Ethiopia's agriculture, like that of most African countries, is primarily rain-fed and subsistence-based, making it particularly vulnerable to CCI, especially droughts (which are very common in the country), which result from increased temperature levels (Zegeye, 2018). In Ethiopia, rainfall patterns are becoming more irregular due to climate change, which also leads to greater soil erosion from heavy rains, changes in crop sowing and harvesting dates due to delayed and earlier rainfall, adjustments to agricultural systems, and an increase in pest and disease incidence.

Crop output in Ethiopia will be impacted by CCI, which might result in subpar harvests or even crop failures for national staples like wheat and maize, as well as cash crops like coffee. It is probably going to have a negative impact on agricultural yields and, as a result, food security (Muluneh et al., 2016). Due to the frequent droughts in the region, indigenous wheat and barley varieties are dwindling in the Menz Gera Midir District (Kassa, 2013). The lack of pastures (animal feed) and water brought on by climate change has an impact on livestock productivity as well. Pests and illnesses that affect crops and livestock are expanding to regions that were formerly too cold for them to survive (Getu, 2010).

According to data obtained from the World Bank by Trading Economic (2023), women make up 55.9% of the workforce in Ethiopia's agricultural industry. This suggests that women will be more adversely affected by CCI in the agricultural sector than males. The implication is that young women are more susceptible to CCI than other groups in the agriculture sector. Climate change would exacerbate people's susceptibility and livelihood insecurity, which could ultimately force a significant portion of the population to rely on food handouts (Troeger, 2010). Since the bulk of the population works in agriculture, its implications on the national economy are more extensive.

Impacts on Human Health

The health of the population will be significantly impacted by climate change and variability. Pests and diseases will become more prevalent and more severe as a result of climate change. This could result in a rise in the prevalence of tropical diseases that are susceptible to fluctuations in temperature, precipitation, and humidity, such as malaria, cholera, yellow fever, meningitis, and others (Adem & Bewket, 2011). Climate change will affect some disease vectors' ecology, which will change the temporal and spatial patterns of disease transmission. By way of illustration, the temperature rise has caused the mosquito belt to significantly extend to higher elevations, and as a result, malaria is now spreading to highland regions that were formerly malaria-free. Due to their responsibilities as mothers who must care for their children who are prone to these diseases, homemakers, and agricultural workers in the subsistence and natural resource-dependent agricultural sector, young women are especially vulnerable.

Evidence suggests that the greatest altitude limit for malaria transmission was 2,000 meters above sea level, although epidemics of the disease have recently occurred in areas with height limitations between 1,600 and 2,150. As a result of rising food and nutrition insecurity brought on by climate change, Ethiopia and other countries in Africa are more likely to experience famine and malnutrition. The prevalence of respiratory conditions like bronchitis and asthma will rise as a result of climate change. Heat waves will also result in more deaths and injuries from heat-related causes. Due to their dependence on the use of wood to build fires for household cooking, young women are also more susceptible to respiratory illnesses. Climate change is expected to compound Ethiopia's health challenges/problems, especially among young women.

Madagascar

The unique geophysical characteristics of islands, according to Nurse et al. (2014), make CCI more severe and acute. Islands, especially those that have separated from the mainlands for a long time, experience sea level rise, fluctuating precipitation, and negative impacts on vital sectors like agriculture, water supply, fisheries, health, biodiversity, and livelihoods as a result of CCI (Nurse et al., 2014; Veron et al., 2019). Given that 90% of its biodiversity is endemic, Madagascar is a nation unusually rich in natural resources (Rakotondravony et al., 2018). A large portion of Madagascar's forest habitat has been lost, making populations, biodiversity, and ecosystem services more vulnerable to climate change (Lee et al., 2008).

Agricultural Production and Food Insecurity

Over the last decade, Madagascar has experienced tremendous increased food insecurity as a result of CCI, 8.8 million people in Madagascar (or around 33 percent of the population) are food insecure as of September 2022. The number of people in food insecurity is particularly higher over the lean season, but the situation remains critical throughout the year (Fayad, 2023).

Given that Madagascar is an island, fishing serves as the nation's main form of agriculture. The fishing sector will employ 57,684,010 people worldwide in 2022 across inland and marine fisheries, pre- and post-harvest work, and subsistence fishing, according to the Illuminating Hidden Harvests (IHH) Initiative. Similar to the majority of countries in continental Africa, where the majority of those in the agricultural sector practice subsistence farming, the majority of people in Madagascar work in the maritime small-scale fishing sub-sector. Additionally, the IHH calculated that a total of 2,496,835 persons depend on fisheries, at least in part, including 1,533,194 SSF, 743,894 SSF, and 219,747 LSF (Wabnitz & Harper, 2023).

According to the Illuminating Hidden Harvests (IHH) Initiative, women are more likely than men to fish for subsistence, making up 66% and 51% of all inland and marine subsistence fishers, respectively. As the majority of people working in the processing and trade of fish—57% and 51%, respectively—across SSF value chains are women—women also play a significant role in the fishing value chain (Wabnitz & Harper, 2023).

Extreme weather and decreased agricultural productivity could exacerbate food insecurity. Extreme events, for instance, have the ability to disrupt food supply systems and diminish agricultural productivity (Rakotoarison et al., 2018). The danger of hunger and malnutrition could rise by 20% by 2050 if significant adaptation efforts are not made (WHO, 2016); this malnutrition can have long-term effects on development and health (Davis-Reddy & Vincent, 2017).

Human Health

As a result of climate change in Madagascar, the frequency and severity of heavy precipitation events and cyclones have already increased. It is anticipated that if climate change becomes more prominent, these repercussions on health will also become more severe as a result of increases in the intensity, duration, and frequency of such events. The deadliest weather-related risks include cyclones and floods, which cause numerous deaths per year, usually from drowning, and affect more than five million people (Fayad, 2023; WHO, 2018).

Malnutrition, extreme poverty, and a lack of access to high-quality healthcare put a lot of individuals in Madagascar at risk for CCI. For instance, 40% of rural residents are unable to get healthcare because they live more than five kilometers away, and poor weather can make it extremely challenging to provide care in these locations. Because of this, most people do not have access to quality medical treatment (Rakotoarison et al., 2018).

Every year, natural disasters can have a significant negative influence on the healthcare industry, and their effects frequently last for years. Generally speaking, the country lacks the resources necessary to respond to, adequately plan for, and repair the harm caused by catastrophic disasters. Diseases are implicated as the major cause of death in Madagascar, according to Rakotoarison et al. (2018), many of which are climate-sensitive. More CCI-induced devastating disasters could lower the quality of life, especially for individuals who lack suitable housing (Davis-Reddy & Vincent, 2017).

The anticipated temperature increase in many areas of Madagascar is likely to hasten the spread of climatically sensitive vector-borne illnesses like malaria, dengue, chikungunya, and yellow fever (Rakotoarison et al., 2018). WHO (2018) predicts that malaria cases will rise across Madagascar, notably in the Menabe and Nosy Be regions. Due to CCI, acute malnutrition is common, and the prevalence of chronic malnutrition is 40%, placing Madagascar as the tenth most stunted country in the world (Fayad, 2023). In the future, CCI is expected to result in acute respiratory infections, diarrheal diseases, malnutrition, and malaria, with young women being more vulnerable, not only for themselves but also for their children that they have to take care of.

It has been established that the Atsimo-Atsinanana, Androy, Anosy, and Analanjirofo regions are particularly vulnerable to the negative effects of climate change on their health.

As a result of their isolation, low population density, poor access to healthcare, and low-income levels, these are the regions with the lowest capacity for CCI adaptation (Rakotoarison et al., 2018; WHO, 2018).

The most vulnerable populations to the health risks posed by climatic hazards are Melaky, Androy, and Atsimo-Atsinanana, principally because of their high rates of household poverty and reliance on subsistence farming. Agriculture, shoddy housing, a generally unhealthy situation (as shown by the low immunization rate), a high frequency of pre-existing diseases, and high malnutrition rates (WHO, 2018). These negative living conditions make them more vulnerable to CCI than other regions of the country.

Effective adaptation measures would include building resilience and low carbon in the health systems of Madagascar. According to WHO (2018):

The health sector must be built strong to meet changing climate pressures (e.g., higher temperatures, increased precipitation, and stronger storms) and also increasing populations, local environmental degradation, and emerging infectious disease outbreaks. Resilience is particularly important in the context of climate change given the complex, unpredictable, and multifaceted ways in which climate change affects health systems and infrastructure. Vulnerable health systems will simply be unable to cope with threats posed by climate change.

(p. 30)

Nigeria

The rate of temperature rise and its accompanying effects, such as desertification, coastal erosion, loss of biodiversity, and saltwater intrusion, are increasing faster than on average throughout the world, and it is widely acknowledged that this has a disproportionately negative impact on Africa (Adelekan et al., 2022). Nigeria was identified as the seventh-most susceptible nation in the world by Verisk Maplecroft in 2016. Nigeria ranked 161 out of 182 nations in terms of its sensitivity to climate hazards and its capability for adaptation, according to the Notre Dame Global Adaptation Initiative (ND-GAIN) in 2021 (Notre Dame University, 2021).

As early as 2012, the country was already experiencing climate unpredictability and high-intensity rainfall events in the country's central and southern areas, which led to repeated flood disasters with losses and damages estimated at USD 16.9 billion (EUR 16.9 billion) (Verisk Maplecroft, 2016).

Agricultural Production and Food Security

Nigeria is currently dealing with difficulties in the form of complicated direct and indirect effects, including food shortages, forced migration, violence, unfavorable health outcomes, and others, which, taken together, provide obstacles to tackling climate change and fostering economic progress. Particularly, local people who practice rain-fed agriculture have suffered disproportionately as a result of droughts and desertification in northern Nigeria's arid and semi-arid regions. Due to dryness and droughts, nomadic Fulani herders are migrating from the north to the south, which has led to a number of violent incidents with local people who cultivate crops. The southern region of the country has been linked to these nomadic herdsmen for spreading zoonotic diseases that can be made worse by climate change (Elelu et al., 2019).

The combined impact of droughts, saltwater intrusion, and sea level rise has negatively impacted crop production and urban infrastructure in other parts of the country, increasing food costs, construction costs, and other associated issues. Crop yields are particularly sensitive to changes and climate variations because there are many different factors influencing crop yields: agriculture is primarily rain-fed, less than 1% of the nation's farmland is irrigated, and more than 70% of farmers practice subsistence farming, which accounts for nearly 23% of GDP (FAO, 2022). If Nigeria does not successfully adapt to climate change, it could lose between USD 100 billion (EUR 100 billion) and USD 460 billion (EUR 460 billion) by 2050 (Federal Ministry of Environment, 2021).

Human Health

At the time of writing, the incidence of diseases was rising due to floods (river and urban) and other climate change-related disasters in the nation. The majority of these diseases are vector-borne illnesses like malaria, which affected 60 million people in Nigeria and caused 200,000 deaths in 2021—32% of all malaria deaths worldwide (WHO, 2022). Additionally, the risk of water-borne illnesses like cholera is rising.

During the baseline year of 2008, there were an estimated 137,600 diarrheal deaths among children under the age of 15 in Nigeria. According to a high emissions scenario, 9.8% of the over 76,000 diarrheal fatalities anticipated in 2030 are expected to be linked to climate change and occur in children under the age of 15. Although it is anticipated that there will be fewer diarrheal fatalities by 2050—around 43,500—the percentage of mortality related to climate change will increase to about 14.2% (Lloyd, 2015 cited in WHO & UNFCCC, 2015).

Climate change impacts health-related issues such as water-borne illnesses, under-nutrition, airborne illnesses, frequent natural disasters like floods, droughts, and acid rain, pollution of water sources, extreme weather conditions, deteriorating forest ecosystems, decreased agricultural output, and declining water quality and quantity, among others (Mustapha et al., 2022).

According to Adepoju (2017), CCI in Nigeria includes rising temperatures, rising sea levels, and erratic weather. Food shortages are caused by poor harvests and increased freshwater shortages for those working in agriculture, the majority of whom are women engaging in subsistence agriculture. According to Borokinni (2017), CCI has an effect on social and environmental factors that affect health in Nigeria, including access to clean water, food security, and clean air. This is particularly true given that people continue to perform archaic anti-environmental behaviors like bush burning, indiscriminate waste disposal, and construction of buildings on approved waterways and canals, leading to flooding. The young women, especially those in the rural areas, are more vulnerable, given their role in taking care of their families, which makes them contributors to the problem as well as victims.

Nwoke et al. (2009) established a relationship between CCI-induced temperature increases and increased secondary pollutant production, which, in turn, raised the incidence of allergies, cardio-respiratory diseases, and fatalities. Additionally, "this study shows that the adverse effect of rise in ambient temperature strongly influences increase in morbidity rate in Nigeria" (confirm). According to Eke and Onafalujo (2013), "four diseases were highlighted as the principal health concerns aggravated by climate change: cholera, meningitis, malaria, and pneumonia" (confirm). According to Mustapha et al. (2022), environmental disasters like the nation's yearly flooding, rising sea levels, and water scarcity that force some populations to move could lead to mental health issues, particularly for young women who are expected to take care of their families.

Activities by Young Women to Mitigate Climate Change Impacts

In recognition of the high level of vulnerability of women, young women have been very active in working toward adaptation and mitigation of CCI across Africa. The strategies and types of activities adopted vary from country to country as a result of the differences in the nature of impacts that are predominant in various countries. In this section, we survey some strategic efforts of young women across some African countries to adapt and mitigate CCI, despite their not being included in the decision-making processes on climate action at the national levels of their countries. As indicated above, it is anticipated that young women in the most affected countries can draw on these experiences and implement similar initiatives.

Campaign for Female Education (CAMFED), launched in 2013, has successfully reached 8,500 young women from poor, marginalized farming communities across sub-Saharan Africa who had been trained as Agriculture Guides—champions of sustainable agriculture. These young women agriculture guides have improved productivity, sustainability and profitability of their own smallholdings, as well as trained and encouraged others to adopt practical, affordable, and locally relevant climate smart techniques. CAMFED aims to reach 50,000 young women across rural Africa by 2028 (United Nations Climate Change, 2023).

In Ethiopia, following the government's climate resilient green economy strategy, the young women in their various youth groups have participated in tree-planting and other activities such as terracing and natural resource-promotion initiatives (Denovald et al., 2022). These activities target the reduction of emissions from the forest sector and promotion of sustainable tree-based production systems (Atani, 2019). In addition, the young women have also been active in advocacy activities to push for efforts at deforestation through charcoal production. This is a delicate area, and charcoal production serves as an alternative source of energy during drought, and equally a source of deforestation (Denovald, 2022).

In Madagascar, young women in various groups are working to increase community knowledge regarding health (e.g., sanitation, vaccine and hygiene), effective farming practices, and the benefits of environmental conservation. Some of the young women are working as community health agents through the healthcare centers located in different rural communities to promote healthy behaviors (Weiskopf et al., 2021).

In Nigeria, young women acting under the umbrella of Youth Climate Clubs, Rivers State, in the country's Niger Delta region, have engaged in advocacy activities, including successful engagement with leadership and members of the state legislature and relevant government agencies. Those engagements have yielded positive results in the form of the eventual domestication of the Climate Change Act in the state and the establishment of the Climate Change Council. The climate clubs organized community clean-up activities and educational sessions to raise awareness and foster local ownership of climate initiatives, as well as tree-planting drives (Ogbanga, 2023). The youth climate clubs have also engaged in enlightenment campaigns on desirable health practices on how to avoid water-borne diseases and other infections by women and girls when the riverine areas are flooded as a result of CCI.

In Uganda, Girls for Climate Action, a local youth movement, has trained 300 women in climate policy and advocacy out of the target 1,000 young women to be trained as part of their 2030 commitment to Generation Equality's Feminist Action for Climate Justice Action coalition. Those trained are from different regions of the country, such as Kasese in the Southwest, Moroto in the Southeast and Manafwa and Bududa in the East, areas that have experienced devastating landlines, floods and drought as a result of climate change. In addition, in Jinja, activists with the group have rallied for the restoration of the Butamira forest against the encroachment of sugarcane growers and sugar companies. In Kasese, they are undertaking advocacy against copper mining that is affecting water resources downstream of the river Nyamwamba, as well as working toward improving the living conditions of those displaced by the river's heavy flooding (UN Women, 2023).

In Zambia's Chembe District, young women groups have actively engaged in tree planting in areas that have been affected by deforestation and various borehole drilling efforts. Young women who are engaged in agricultural production are involved in the growing of drought-resistant crops such as cassava and sweet potato in Luapula and preserving foods such as vegetables, cassava, and cowpeas. Conservation agriculture was reported as one of the strategies in Mambilima, Chembe District, while planting on higher ground in Luapula is one measure that young women have adopted as an adaptation measure to CCIs (Tanner, Mazingi & Muyambwa, 2022). Among the other strategies being adopted as adaptation practices by young women in Zambia are efforts at diversifying from agriculture toward less climate-sensitive livelihoods. In Chipembi, many young women have learned skills such as tailoring and hairdressing which are not affected by CCI. In Temfe and Kasoma, other young women have moved from planting crops that are usually affected by flooding to chicken rearing as an alternative source of income (Tanner et al., 2022).

In both Chiredzi and Tsholotsho in Zimbabwe, as their response to CCI, young women groups are among farmers who have resorted to growing drought-resistant crops such as sorghum, rapoko and millet, peanuts and ground nuts, maize, watermelons, pumpkins, sunflower, mashamba, cotton, and bhondasi. In Chiredzi, Zimbabwe, following advocacy efforts by young women groups, the government is planning to convert the area around Chilonga into a green belt by planting lucerne grass (Tanner et al., 2022).

Conclusion and Recommendations

It should be underlined that since the national plan of action in 2006, the DRC has made significant progress in putting policies for CCI adaptation and mitigation into effect. Thanks to assistance from development partners and other technical and financial partners, the procedures in the DRC have evolved. The following are some of the adopted strategies that are being implemented at various stages: (a) plan for gender mainstreaming; (b) plans for monitoring and evaluation; (c) plans for capacity-building and assessment; (d) plans for institutional reviews to advance the NAP process; and (e) plans for incorporating adaptation into Provincial Development Plans (PDPs) (Office of the Deputy Prime Minister DRC, 2022). Presently, the young women in DRC are not included in the decision-making processes on adaptation and mitigation of CCI, nor is there any framework for them to make input into the processes.

Ethiopia has shown environmental conservation as well as political action to stop climate change. The United Nations Convention on Biological Diversity (CBD), the United Nations Framework Convention on Climate Change (UNFCCC), and the Paris Agreement are just a few of the significant international environmental treaties and protocols that Ethiopia has joined. Additionally, Ethiopia has developed and implemented numerous governmental projects and programs related to climate change. The country has actively taken part in international climate negotiations. Political declarations and pertinent actions have not yet been matched; therefore, the institutional framework required to implement effective policies for climate change adaptation and mitigation does not yet exist.

Nigeria signed the UNFCCC in 1992, ratified the Kyoto Protocol in 2004, created Vision 2020 (with an environmental component) in 2009, and developed a national adaptation strategy and plan of action on climate change in 2011, but it has not given CCI and other environmental issues the high priority they deserve. The Nigerian government's failure to integrate CCI into the main national discourse presents the greatest obstacle to the development of effective measures for CCI adaptation and mitigation. Nigeria has not prioritized gender-disaggregated data on CCI.

African nations must support women's leadership in climate-related activities such as creating peace and security agendas and preparing for climate adaptation, as well as investing in women-led grassroots organizations working to increase climate resilience.

Relevant government agencies in African countries need to formulate policies that would facilitate adopting renewable energy sources, effective management of water, environment-friendly agricultural practices, and involvement with advocacy groups working on environmental protection.

Young African women should be empowered, educationally, economically, and politically, in order for them to participate in the decision-making processes on adaptation and mitigation of CCI.

Bibliography

Adelekan, I. O., Simpson, N. P., Totin, E., & Trisos, C. H. (2022). "IPCC Sixth Assessment Report (AR6): Climate Change 2022 – Impacts, Adaptation and Vulnerability: Regional Factsheet Africa." Retrieved on 10/07/2023 from https://policycommons.net/artifacts/2264240/ipcc_ar6_wgii_factsheet_africa/3023294/

Adepoju, A. A. (2017). "Climate change and health in Nigeria." *Nigerian Tribune*. Retrieved on 10/07/2023 from https://www.tribuneonline.com/climate-change-health-nigeria

Adem, A., and Bewket, W. (2011). *A Climate Change Country Assessment Report for Ethiopia submitted to Forum for Environment (On behalf of ECSNCC) By Epsilon International R and D*. Addis Ababa, Ethiopia.

Africa Development Bank (AfDB). (2011). "Climate change, gender and development in Africa." *Economic Brief*, *1*(1). Retrieved on 10/08/2023 from https://www.afdb.org/sites/default/files/documents/publications/climate_change_gender_and_development_in_africa.pdf

African Development Bank Group. (2013). "2013–2017 – République Démocratique du Congo – Document de stratégie pays." Abidjan, AfDB Group, Regional Centre Department. Retrieved on 10/07/2023 from www.afdb.org/fileadmin/uploads/afdb/Documents/Project-and-Operations/Democratic Republic of Congo – 2013–2017 – Country Strategy Paper.pdf

Aklilu, K., Rovin, K., and Hardee, K. (2009). Linking Population, Fertility and Family Planning with Adaptation to Climate Change: Views from Ethiopia.

Andrijevic, M., Crespo Cuaresma, J., Lissner, T., et al. (2020). "Overcoming gender inequality for climate resilient development." *Nature Communications* 11. 6261. Retrieved on 10/07/2023 from https://doi.org/10.1038/s41467-020-19856-w

Ammer, C. (2019). "Diversity and forest productivity in a changing climate." *New Phytologist*, *221*(1), 50–66.

Asian-Pacific Resource & Research Centre for Women. (2014). *Scoping Study: Identifying opportunities for action on climate change and sexual and reproductive health and rights in Bangladesh, Indonesia, and the Philippines*. Kuala Lumpur: Asian-Pacific Resource & Research Centre for Women. Retrieved on 10/07/2023 from https://arrow.org.my/wp-content/uploads/2015/04/Climate-Change-andSRHR-Scoping-Study_Working-Paper_2014.pdf

Atani, M. (2019, April 22). "Ethiopia plants over 350 million trees in a day, setting new world record." UN Environment Programme, Retrieved on 29/11/2023 from www.unep.org/news-and-stories/story/ethiopia-plants-over-350-million-trees-day-setting-new-world-record

Borokinni, J. (2017). "Climate change and health impacts." *The Nation Newspaper*. Retrieved on 10/07/2023 from https://nationonline.ng.net/climate-change-health-impacts

Bewket, W. (2011). "Farmers' knowledge of soil erosion and control measures in the Northwestern Highlands of Ethiopia." *African Geographical Review*, *30*, 53–70.

Bewket, W., and Conway, D. (2007). "A note on the temporal and spatial variability of rainfall in the drought-prone Amhara region of Ethiopia." *International Journal of Climatology*, 27, 1467–1477.

Centre for Climate Change and Health. Special Focus: Climate Change and Pregnant Women. 2016. Centre for Climate Change and Health. Retrieved from 15/08/2023 from https://climatehealthconnect.org/wp-content/uploads/2016/09/PregnantWomen.pdf

Davis-Reddy, C., and K. Vincent. 2017. *Climate risk and vulnerability: a handbook for Southern Africa* (2nd ed.). Pretoria, South Africa: CSIR. Retrieved on 10/07/2023 from https://www.csir.co.za/sites/default/files/Documents/SADC%20Handbook_Second%20Edition_full%20report.pdf

Denton, F. (2002). "Climate change vulnerability, impacts, and adaptation: Why does gender matter?" *Gender and Development*, 10, 10–20.

Dercon, S. (2009). "Rural poverty: Old challenges in new contexts." *World Bank Research Observer*, 24(1), 1–28.

Devonald, M., Jones, N., Gebru, A. I., and Yadete, W. (2022). "Rethinking climate change through a gender and adolescent lens in Ethiopia." *Climate and Development*. Retrieved 29/11/2023 from https://doi.org/10.1080/17565529.2022.2032568

Doty, B. G. (2011). "Vulnerability to climate change: An assessment of East and Central Africa." The University of Texas at Austin, Robert Strauss Centre for International Security and Law. Available at www.strausscentre.org/ccaps/publications/student-working-papers.html?download=36

Easterling, W., Hurd, B., and Smith, J. (2004). "Coping with global climate change: the role of adaptation in the United States." Pew Centre on Global Climate Change. Available at https://www.pewtrusts.org/~/media/legacy/uploadedfiles/wwwpewtrustsorg/reports/global_warming/pewclimate0704pdf.pdf, accessed on 22 April 2024.

Eke, P. O., and Onafalujo, A. K. (2013). Effects of climate change on health risks in Nigeria. *Asian Journal of Business and Management Sciences*, 1(1), 204–215.

Elelu, N., Aiyedun, J. O., Mohammed, I. G., Oludairo, O. O., Odetokun, I. A., Mohammed, K. M., Bale, J. O., and Nuru, S. (2019). "Neglected zoonotic diseases in Nigeria: Role of the public health veterinarian," *The Pan African Medical Journal* 18, 32:36. doi: 10.11604/pamj.2019.32.36.15659

FAO. (2022). "Nigeria at a glance." Retrieved on 11/07/2023 from https://www.fao.org/nigeria/fao-in-nigeria/nigeria-at-a-glance/en/

Fayad, D. (2023). "Food Insecurity and climate shocks in Madagascar." *IMF e-Library*. Retrieved on 10/07/2023 from https://www.elibrary.imf.org/view/journals/018/2023/037/article-A001-en.xml

Federal Ministry of Environment. (2021). "National Climate Change Policy for Nigeria. Department of Climate Change." Federal Ministry of Environment. Retrieved on 12/07/2023 from https://climatechange.gov.ng/wp-content/uploads/2021/08/NCCP_NIGERIA_REVISED_2-JUNE-2021.pdf

Gashaw, T., Mebrat, W., Hagos, D., and Nigussie, A. (2014). "Climate Change Adaptation and Mitigation Measures in Ethiopia," *Journal of Biology, Agriculture and Healthcare*, 4(15), 148–152.

Habtezion, Z. (2011a). "Gender and climate change capacity development series – Africa." United Nations Development Programme. Retrieved on 10/08/2023 from https://www.uncclearn.org/sites/default/fifiles/inventory/undp117.pdf

Habtezion, Z. (2011b). "Gender and climate change capacity development series – Africa. United Nations Development Programme." Retrieved on 18/08/2023 from https://www.uncclearn.org/sites/default/fifiles/inventory/undp117.pdf

Health Cluster (n.d.). "Gender-based violence in health emergencies." World Health Organization. Retrieved on 12/07/2023 from https://www.who.int/health-cluster/about/work/other-collaborations/genderbased-violence/en/

Hoffman, S. (2009). "Preparing for disaster: protecting the most vulnerable in emergencies." *University of California at Davis Law Review* 42(5), 1491–1547.

Intergovernmental Panel on Climate Change (IPCC). (2014). *Summary for policy makers. In Climate change 2014: Impacts, adaptation, and vulnerability. Part A: Global and sectoral aspects. Contribution of Working Group II to the fifth assessment report of the Intergovernmental Panel on Climate Change.* Cambridge: Cambridge University Press.

International Centre for Research on Women. (2023). "Women and Girls at the Intersection of Climate Change and Economic Empowerment." Womens Economic Empowerment Community of Practice. Retrieved on 10/07/2023 from https://www.icrw.org/wp-content/uploads/2023/07/Technical-Brief-WEE-and-Climate-Change-3_uid_64be3d56c220e.pdf

Kier, G., Kreft, H., Lee, T. M., Jetz, W., Ibisch, P. L., Nowicki, C., Mutke, J., and Barthlott, W. (2009). A global assessment of endemism and species richness across island and mainland regions. *Proceedings of the National Academy of Sciences* 106 (23), 9322–9327. Retrieved on 10/07/2023 from https://doi.org/10.1073/pnas.0810306106

Kumar, N., and Quisumbing, A. (2014). "Gender and resilience." In S. Fan, R. Pandya-Lorch, & S. Yosef (Eds.), *Resilience for food and nutrition security* (pp. 155–168). Washington, DC: International Food Policy Research Institute.

Lambrou, Y., and Piana, G. (2006). *Gender the missing component of the response to climate change*. Rome: Food and Agricultural Organization.

Lee, H., Radhika, D., Lowry, P. P., Andelman, S., Andrianarisata, M., Andriamaro, L. Cameron, A., Hijmans, R., Kremen, C., Mackinnon, J., Randrianasolo, H. H., Andriambololonera, S., Razafimpahanana, A. Randriamahazo, H., Randrianarisoa, J., Razafinjatovo, P., Raxworthy, C., Schatz, G. E., Tadross, M., and Wilme, L. (2008). "Climate change adaptation for conservation in Madagascar." *Biology Letters* 4(5), 590–594. Retrieved on 10/07/2023 from https://doi.org/10.1098/rsbl.2008.0270

Mc Sweeney, C., New, M., and Lizcano, G. (2008). "UNDP climate change country profile for Ethiopia." Retrieved on 10/07/2023 from http://country-profiles.geog.ox.ac.uk

Meinzen-Dick, R. S., Kovarik, C., and Quisumbing, A. (2014). "Gender and sustainability." *Annual Review of Environment and Resources*, 39, 29–55.

Muluneh, A., Stroosnijder, L., Keesstra, S., and Temesgen, B. (2016). Adapting to climate change for food security in the Rift Valley dry lands of Ethiopia: Supplemental irrigation, plant density and sowing date. *The Journal of Agricultural Science*, 155, 1–22. 10.1017/S0021859616000897

Mustapha, M. L. A., Mohammed, S. A., and Yusuf, J. (2022). "Impact of climate change awareness on Undergraduates socio-emotional wellbeing in Nigeria." *International Journal of Emotional Education*, 14(2), 53–67. Retrieved on 10/07/2023 from https://doi.org/10.56300/GDUE5169

Myers, N., Mittermeier, R. A., Mittermeier, C. G., da Fonseca, G. A. B., and Kent, J. (2000). "Biodiversity hotspots for conservation priorities." *Nature*, 403, 853–858. Retrieved on 10/08/2023 from https://doi.org/10.1038/35002501

National Adaptation Programme of Action (NAPA). (2007). *Climate change national adaptation programme of action (NAPA) of Ethiopia*. Addis Ababa: NAPA.

National Meteorological Services Agency (NMSA) (2007). *Climate change National Adaptation Program of Action (NAPA) of Ethiopia*. Addis Ababa, Ethiopia.

Nelson, V. (2010). Climate and gender: What role for Agricultural Research small holder farmers in Africa? *CIAT Working Document No 222*. India: CIAT.

Niang, I., Ruppel, O. C., Abdrabo, M. A., Essel, A., Lennard, C., Padgham, J., and Urquhart, P. (2014). "Africa." In V. R. Barros, C. B. Field, D. J. Dokken, M. D. Mastrandrea, K. J. Mach, T. E. Bilir, M. Chatterjee, K. L. Ebi, Y. O. Estrada, R. C. Genova, B. Girma, E. S. Kissel, A. N. Levy, S. MacCracken, P. R. Mastrandrea, & L. L. White (Eds.), *Climate change 2014: Impacts, adaptation and vulnerability. Contribution of working group II to the fifth assessment report of the Intergovernmental Panel on Climate Change* (pp. 1199–1265). Cambridge: Cambridge University Press.

Noasilalaonomenjanahary, A. L. and Ramaromisa, V. (2020). "Producer-driven economic models of climate resilience in Madagascar." IIED and the National Platform for women, sustainable development, and food security (PNFDDSA), London, UK. Retrieved on 30/11/2023 from https://wrd.unwomen.org/sites/default/files/2021-11/Gender-focused_economic_models_Madagascar.pdf

Nurse, L. A., McLean, R. F., Agard, J., Briguglio, L. P., Duvat Magnan, V., Pelesikoti, N., Tompkins, E., and Webb, A. (2014). "Small islands." In V. R. Barros, C. B. Field, D. J. Dokken, M. D. Mastrandrea, K. J. Mach, T. E. Bilir, M. Chatterjee, K. L. Ebi, Y. O. Estrada, R. C. Genova, B. Girma, E. S. Kissel, A. N. Levy, S. MacCracken, P. R. Mastrandrea, & L. L. White, (eds.), *Climate change 2014: impacts, adaptation, and vulnerability; part B: regional aspects: Contribution of Working Group II to the Fifth Assessment Report of the Intergovernmental Panel on Climate Change*. (pp. 1613–1654). Cambridge, UK: Cambridge University Press, https://doi.org/10.1017/CBO9781107415386

Nwogwugwu, N. (2020a). "Women, climate change and sustainable development." In Yacob-Haliso, & T. Falola (eds.), *The Palgrave Handbook of African Women's Studies*, Switzerland: Palgrave Macmillan. https://doi.org/10.1007/978-3-319-77030-7133-1

Nwogwugwu N. (2020b). "Women's empowerment and women's health in Africa." In Yacob-Haliso, O. & T. Falola (eds.), *The Palgrave Handbook of African Women's Studies*. Cham, Switzerland: Palgrave Macmillan. Retrieved on 10/07/2023 from https://doi.org/10.1007/978-3-319-77030-7160-1

Nwoke, B. E. B., Nwoke, E. A., and Ukpai, O. M. (2009). "Effect of climate change on human health and some adaptive strategies: A review." *Bayero Journal of pure and Applied sciences*, 2(1), 168–172.

Nwoke, E. A., and Ibe, S. N. O. (2015). Climate change impact on the health of African women and adaptation strategies. *International Journal of Public Health and Epidemiology*, 4(6), 162–171.

Office of Deputy Prime Minister, Ministry of Environment & Sustainable Development. (2022). *National Adaptation Plan To Climate Change (2022–2026) Democratic Republic of Congo*. DRC and UNDP. Retrieved on 10/07/2023 from https://unfccc.int/sites/default/files/resource/DRC-NAP_EN.pdf

Ogbanga, M. (2023). "Youth Participation in climate advocacy: A case study of climate change clubs in Rivers State." *The Professional Social Work Journal* 9(9), 1–11.

Plan International. (2013). The state of the world's girls 2013: Adolescent girls and disasters. Retrieved on 10/07/2023 from https://plan-international.org/publications/state-worlds-girls2013-adolescent-girls-and-disasters.

Rakotoarison, N., Raholijao, N., Razafindramavo, L. M., Rakotomavo, Z. A. P. H., Rakotoarisoa, A., Guillemot, J. S., Randriamialisoa, Z. J., Mafilaza, V., Ramiandrisoa, V. A. M. P., Rajaonarivony, R., Andrianjafinirina, S., Tata, V., Vololoniaina, M. C., Rakotomanana, F., and Raminosoa, V. M. (2018). "Assessment of risk, vulnerability and adaptation to climate change by the health sector in Madagascar," *International Journal of Environmental Research and Public Health* 15(12), 2643. Retrieved on 10/07/2023 from https://doi.org/10.3390/ijerph15122643

Rohr, U. (2005). "Gender and climate change: A forgotten issue." In *Tiempo: Climate change newsletter UEA, SEI and IIE*. Retrieved from 10/07/2023 https://wwwtempocyberclimate.org/newswatch/comment0507//htm

Smit, B., Burton, I., Klein, R. J., and Wandel, J. (2000). "An anatomy of adaptation to climate change and variability," *Climatic Change* 45, 223–251.

Sorensen, C. et al. (2018). "Climate change and women's health: Impacts and policy directions," *PLoS Medicine* 15(7), e1002603. https://doi.org/10.1371/journal.pmed.1002603

Stevens, C. (2010). "Are women the key to sustainable development?" *Sustainable Development Insights*, 003, 1–8.

Tanner, T., Mazingi, L., and Muyambwa, D. F. (2022). "Youth Gender and Climate Resilience: Voiced of Adolescent and Young Women in Southern Africa," *Sustainability* 14(14), 8797. https://doi.org/10.3390/su14148797

Trading Economic. (2023). "Ethiopia – Employees, Agriculture, Female (% of Females employment)," Retrieved on 10/07/2023 from https://tradingeconomics.com/ethiopia/employees-agriculture-female-percent-of-female-employment-wb-data.html#:~:text=Employment%20in%20agriculture%2C%20female%20(%25,compiled%20from%20officially%20recognized%20sources.

UN Women. (2022). "Explainer: How gender inequality and climate change are interconnected." Retrieved on 10/07/2023 from https://www.unwomen.org/en/news-stories/explainer/2022/02/explainer-how-gender-inequality-and-climate-change-are-interconnected

UN Women. (2023). "Young women in Uganda lead nationwide action against climate change." Retrieved on 27/11/2023 from https://africa.unwomen.org/en/stories/news/2023/10/young-women-in-uganda-lead-nationwide-action-against-climate-change.

Uneke, C. J. (2008). "Impact of Placental Plasmodium Falciparum Malaria on Pregnancy and Perinatal Outcome in Sub-Saharan Africa," *Yale Journal of Biology and Medicine* 81(1), 1–7. Retrieved on 10/07/2023 from https://www.ncbi.nlm.nih.gov/pmc/articles/PMC2442721/

United Nations (2019, October). "For Every Dollar Invested in Climate-Resilient Infrastructure Six Dollars Are Saved, Secretary-General Says in Message for Disaster Risk Reduction Day." [Press Release]. Retrieved on 10/07/2023 from https://press.un.org/en/2019/sgsm19807.doc.htm

United Nations Climate Change. (2023). "CAMFED: Young women's grassroots climate action in Africa/Sub-Saharan Africa." Retrieved on 25/11/2023 from https://unfcc.int/climate-action/momentum-for-change/women-for-results/camfed

United Nations Population Fund. (2019). *Unfinished Business: The pursuit of rights and choices for all. State of World Population*. New York: United Nations Population Fund. Retrieved on 13/07/2023 from https://www.unfpa.org/swop-2019.

University of Notre Dame. (2021). Notre Dame Global Adaptation Initiative | Rankings. Notre Dame Global Adaptation Initiative, Retrieved on 10/07/2023 from https://gain.nd.edu/our-work/country-index/rankings/.
USAID. (2019). "The Democratic Republic of Congo Climate Change Fact sheet." Retrieved on 10/07/2023 from https://www.usaid.gov/sites/default/files/2023-03/2022-USAID-DRC-Climate-Change-Country-Profile_0.pdf
Verisk Maplecroft. (2016). "Climate Change Vulnerability Index." Retrieved on 10/07/2023 from https://www.maplecroft.com/risk-indices/climate-change-vulnerability-index/
Veron, S., Mouchet, M., Govaerts, R., Haevermans, T., and Pellens, R. (2019). "Vulnerability to climate change of islands worldwide and its impact on the tree of life." *Scientific Reports* 9, 14471. Retrieved on 10/07/2023 from https://doi.org/10.1038/s41598-019-51107-x
Villamor, G. B., Dah-Gbeto, A., Bell, A., Pradhan, U., and Noordwijk, M. V. (2015). "Gender-specific spatial perspectives and scenario building approaches for understanding gender equity and sustainability in climate smart landscapes." In P. Minang, M. Van Noordwijk, O. Freeman, C. Mbow, J. de Leeuw, & D. Catacutan (Eds.), *Climate-smart landscapes: Multifunctionality in practice* (pp. 211–224). Nairobi: World Agroforestry Centre (ICRAF).
Wabnitz, C. C. C. and Harper, S. J. M. (2023). "Gender and Fisheries, Country Factsheet The republic of Madagascar." Retrieved on 10/08/2023 from https://oceanrisk.earth/wp-content/uploads/2023/05/Madagascar_factsheet_fin-1.pdf
Weiskopf, S. R., Cushing, R. A., Morelli, T., and Myers, B. J. E. (2021). "Climate change risks and adaptation options for Madagascar," *Ecology and Society* 26(4), 36. https://doi.org/10.5751/ES-12816-260436
WHO (2018). World health Statistics 2018: Monitoring health for the SDGs, sustainable development goals. Retrieved from https://iris.who.int/handle/10665/272596
WHO (2022). "Fact sheet about malaria." Retrieved on 13/08/2023 from https://www.who.int/news-room/fact-sheets/detail/malaria.
WHO & UNFCCC (2015). Climate and Health Country Profile – 2015 Nigeria. Retrieved on 10/07/2023 from https://apps.who.int/iris/bitstream/handle/10665/208865/WHO_FWC_PHE_EPE_15.11_eng.pdf
Wiebe, K. D., Sulser, T. B., Mason-D'Croz, D. and Rosegrant, M. W. (2017). "The effects of climate change on agriculture and food security in Africa." In A. De Pinto & J. M. Ulimwengu (eds), *A thriving agricultural sector in a changing climate: Meeting Malabo Declaration goals through climate-smart agriculture* (pp. 5–21). Washington, DC: International Food Policy Research Institute (IFPRI). http://doi.org/10.2499/9780896292949_02
World Bank. (2010). *Economics of adaptation to Climate Change, Ethiopia*. Washington, DC: World Bank Group.
World Bank. (2015). "Rainfed agriculture." Retrieved on 20/07/2023 from http://water.worldbank.org/topics/agricultural-water-management/rainfed-agriculture.
World Bank. (2018). *Madagascar Climate Change and health Diagnostic: Risks and Opportunities for Climate-Smart Health and Nutrition Investment*. Washington, DC: World Bank.
World Health Organization (2014). *Gender, Climate Change and Health*. Geneva: World Health Organization. Retrieved on 10/07/2023 from https://www.who.int/globalchange/GenderClimateChangeHealthfinal.pdf?ua=1.
World Health Organization (WHO). (2016). *Climate and health country profile-2015 Madagascar*. Geneva, Switzerland: World Health Organization. Retrieved on 10/07/2023 from https://apps.who.int/iris/handle/10665/246140
Woyessa, Y. E., Pretorius, E., Hensley, M., van Rensburg, L. D., and van Heerden, P. S. (2006). Upscaling of rainwater harvesting for crop production in the communal lands of the Modder River basin in South Africa: Comparing upstream and downstream scenarios. *Water S.A.*, 32(2), 223–228.
Zegeye, H. (2018). "Climate change in Ethiopia: Impacts, mitigation and adaptation," *International Journal of Research in Environmental Studies*, 5, 18–35.
Zeid, S. (2015). "Women's, children's, and adolescents' health in humanitarian and other crises," *British Medical Journal*, 351, 56–60. Retrieved on 10/07/2023 from www.jstor.org/stable/26521866

13
CATHOLIC WOMEN NAVIGATING THE CHALLENGES OF CLIMATE CHANGE IN RURAL MANICALAND PROVINCE, ZIMBABWE

An Appreciative Inquiry Approach

Milcah Mudewairi and Caroline Dimingu

Introduction

The story of an African woman being that of a perpetually weeping person not only reinforces the patriarchal grip, but boldly demotivates and demoralises African women from responding to the climate change crisis. There is a need for a shift of mindset when it comes to coming up with lasting solutions to gender-related climate change in Zimbabwe. What is needed is the practical knowledge capable of resolving the gender obstacles in dealing with climate change crisis. The involvement and celebrating the effective interventions of women as advocates of climate change is strategic and entails coming up with relevant knowledge in addressing climate change from a gender perspective. However, there is limited scholarly work in this regard. There are few and indirect studies with detailed information on the extent to which research on climate change can influence development. For instance, the work by Chazovachii et al. (2010) on rural women growing small grains to adapt to climate change in the rural areas can be complemented by this chapter. On his part, Chagutah (2010) researched the state of preparedness for climate change resilience in Zimbabwe.

Whilst the work by Chaguta is appreciated, it is silent on the need to consider gender issues, which are currently seen as barriers to mitigating climate change. Gukurume's (2013) article on sustainable agriculture in rural areas of Zimbabwe as a means of coping with climate change is helpful. However, Gukurume overlooked the need for gender balance. Bunce et al. (2010) focused on the problems of development projects in mitigating climate change resilience. All the above literature is preoccupied with the problems of climate change and the possible solutions. Unfortunately, many challenges still persist. This is mostly due to the fact that women's contributions have been overlooked. Thus, additional research is needed in order to capture the investment by women in the climate change response (Kipuri and Ridgewell 2008).

Instead of relying on the problem-focused inquiry, this chapter adds value to the quest for acknowledging the positive developments by women through teamwork in addressing gendered ecological problems. The women who happen to be the participants for the study resort to teamwork in dealing with stream bank cultivation problems caused by tobacco farmers who were putting more emphasis on economic benefits at the expense of environmental conservation. Due to the fact that women in the study area were burdened more burdened by problems of water shortages that, in turn, pave the way for deforestation, they agreed that enough was enough as they arose as a team to denounce ecological degradation. It was not an easy task, but teamwork reinforced the action and it was a success; hence, the need to celebrate such notable deeds to be used as a reference guide for motivation and change.

This chapter targets to bring about change by drawing attention to the need to acknowledge what women are doing and capable of doing as a signal for gender inclusive climate change resilience. The key questions being responded to in this chapter are: "What are the problems of gender being encountered by rural women in mitigating climate change in Zimbabwe? How are the women breaking gender barriers in climate change resilience?" This chapter critiques the image of African women as resorting to desperate cries of hopelessness. It underscores the need and importance of acknowledging women's efforts towards mitigating climate change in Zimbabwe. It focuses on the activities of Catholic women in Manicaland province who protested against streambank cultivation and deforestation in their community. Most of the people responsible were the men growing tobacco alongside the Mucheke River. What follows after the introduction is the geographical description of the study area, then the context of the research. The appreciative inquiry as the methodology underpinning the study leads to the explanation of the gendered climate change and finally the discussion of the findings.

As outlined above, the chapter is composed of six main sections. After the introduction, there is the brief background of the study area and then the justification of the research. The presentation of the appreciative inquiry from the definition, background and application comes after the significance of the study. After the methodology, is the lengthy presentation on gender-induced climate change and then the discussion of findings just before the recommendations and conclusion of the chapter. The chapter consistently refers to women's greater vulnerability to the effects of climate change and their positive contributions in responding to the crisis. This strategy has been deployed in order to remind readers of the critical nature of the issues under discussion.

The Physical Geography of the Study Area

The study was carried out over a period of two months (June and July 2022) in Zimbabwe, Manicaland Province, in the jurisdiction of Chief Tandi in Mubvurungwa communal area. The people in the study area are subsistence farmers whose mainstay is the growing of crops like maize, beans and sweet potatoes. However, due to the shifting of seasons and unreliable rainfall as a result of climate change, the rainfed agriculture has been greatly affected. People now rely on the Mucheke River to get water for domestic use and watering of garden crops. The river has also become the major source of drinking water for domestic and wild animals. It is this river that is being defended by women from "abuse" by tobacco farmers who are causing siltation. Having noticed that the river is the only remaining natural feature supporting the women's livelihood, the women decided to team up against tobacco farmers to challenge them to respect the natural resources in response to climate change crisis. Such collective action against climate change indicates that women are capable of reaching greater heights and are better stewards of the environment if given the opportunity. The action by women to conserve the natural resources like water sources justifies the need to appreciate the positive action by women towards halting climate change in spite of the gendered climate change problems they are facing in their context.

The Context of the Research

The background to the need to celebrate the progress of African women in response to climate change is associated with the global call to mitigate the negative effects of climate change worldwide. Human activities are the prime drivers of global climate change. This has been echoed by the United Nations Secretary General, who described the climate change emergency as "a code red for humanity, in need of speedy syndicate response" (UNEP 2021). In this case, the Secretary General is appealing for all hands to be on deck, if we are to win the global war against climate change. The grave effects and impact of climate change are fast approaching at a terrible speed if no effort is put in to mitigate the impending crisis (World Meteorological Organisation, WMO, 2019). Climate change is rated as the major obstacle to meeting the objectives of the United Nations 2030 Sustainable Development Goals and also the 2063 African Union Agenda. A joint report by WMO and the African Union Commission indicates that if nothing practical is imposed to deal with the crisis of climate change, Africa will not be able to withstand the climate pressures come 2030. All this is complicated by the fact that Africa is already weakened by an increase in the instability of weather through ecological disasters and disruption of the economic system. As a result, an estimated 118 million Africans will be extremely poor due to increased heatwaves, unpredictable drought and costly floods by 2030 (WMO 2019). If no practical resolutions are implemented to tackle climate change in Africa, it is estimated that by 2050, climate impacts could cost African nations close to USD 50 billion annually (WMO 2019). In order to avoid or limit the costly and deadly impact of climate change on the economy of Africa, there is a need to lessen the impact of, or adapt to, climate change in Africa.

At this juncture, it is of paramount importance to note that the effects of climate change are not uniform across the globe. Patterson (2022) argues that although climate change threatens everyone, it is not uniform for everyone. It has been noted with concern that, by virtue of poverty, Africa is affected more by climate change in the form of the degradation of the natural environment. There is evidence that women are more prone to natural disasters resulting from climate change, and Zimbabwe is a case in point. Masika (2002) noted that women are more vulnerable to climate change than men, as they are reported to be the majority among the poorest and most disadvantaged groups in society. Indeed, Zimbabwe has not been spared by the crisis of climate change, which is further compounded by gender inequalities.

In Zimbabwe, gender disparities have become an obstacle when it comes to the total involvement of women in responding to the environmental crisis in the form of deforestation, pollution and the general degradation of Earth. In developing countries such as Zimbabwe, women are seen to be more involved in climate change-induced tasks like food producers, fetching water, home managers as well as homework teachers for the new curriculum-related continuous learning assessment. Phiri et al. (2014) echo that disadvantaging women in climate change resilience activities mitigates women's disadvantages when it comes to climate change activism. Climate change is a challenge for women since it increases the inequality between men and women in society. Given the impact of climate change disasters on the part of women, Dankelman (2002) sees the necessity of quantifying the damage of gender when it comes to dealing with climate change problems. However, the challenge of the full realisation of women in alleviating climate change problems is still difficult to reach due to the fact that the knowledge and capabilities of women in the Zimbabwe dimension are not fully recognised. Above all, the socio-political, economic and religious challenges are still a stumbling block to accommodating women in development programmes. The UNDP (2009) highlights that the vulnerability of women to the effects of climate change is mainly because of their over-dependence on natural resources, their responsibility for water and food procurement and their increased risk exposure during times of disasters and severe weather crises. Masika (2002) and Maphosa (2004) concur that rural women are beginning to engage in climate-resilient programmes like growing small grains, water harvesting and keeping drought-tolerant animals like goats. All the moves of women stem from the fact that they rely more on rain-fed agriculture and are the most burdened by climate change. Similar studies in Zimbabwe by Phiri, Ndlove and Chiname (2014) focus on the need to prioritise women in the development programmes as they are the most affected and burdened by climate change.

Contextualising the Response of St Therese Mission Catholic Women to Climate Change in Rural Zimbabwe

As noted above, women are more vulnerable to the effects of climate change. However, this does not justify the portrayal of women, including Zimbabwean women, as passive actors and beggars when it comes to responding to the environmental crisis and the impact of climate change. Women can be key players when it comes to addressing these challenges, assuming leadership positions and contributing to sustainable development in Zimbabwe. Despite the gender imbalances, women are emerging as strategic actors in generating sustainable and effective solutions to mitigate climate challenges in Zimbabwe.

With climate change, everyone is at risk. This has seen the religious sector in Africa emerging to contribute to the overall response to climate change (Chitando et al. 2022). Churches are now seen joining the secular world in coming up with practical solutions to climate change. The Catholic Church remains guided by the papal encyclicals when it comes to spiritual response to climate change. Pope Francis (2015) is the turning point on the need for Catholics to be active citizens responding to the hazards of the environment. For the Pope, it is everyone's duty to take good care of creation. The theological background and argument is that the Earth is the home for everyone, thus Christians should take good care of their home. Failure to conserve the environment is equal to sin. It is within this context that Catholics are seen preaching as well as practising environmental conservation. On many occasions, the green papal encyclical document is read before the congregation.

As part of their praxis, the Catholic women at St Therese fought strategically, not with swords, but through scripture, in order to convince the tobacco farmers on the dangers of riverbank cultivation. For the Catholic women, subduing the earth is equal to effective land conservation (Genesis 1v27–28). Thus, river bank cultivation and deforestation are not part of the plan of God for humanity. In the following section, the chapter outlines the key tenets of appreciative inquiry.

Appreciative Inquiry

Problem-focused approaches in dealing with climate change crisis are so far bringing insignificant results in relation to finding lasting solutions to address gendered climate change problems in Zimbabwe. It is high time that Zimbabweans and the African continent at large are forced to shift mindsets by rethinking approaches that focus on problems to adopting a positive and strength-based approach to motivate collective commitment and actions for change (Hung et al. 2018:1). This chapter is influenced by the call to rethink and reassess responses to climate change. It is action research utilising the theological appreciative inquiry research design. The chapter is qualitative in nature as it seeks to appreciate the role of women in climate change mitigation, making use of key informant interviews and focus group discussions as data gathering techniques.

Appreciative inquiry focuses on the positives in the process of exploring and discovering possibilities with the aim of transforming societies or groups with a shared vision (Cooperrider & Whitney 2001). Focusing on the principles of discussion and partnership, appreciative inquiry is of value in building up solutions to climate change in Zimbabwe. What is unique in appreciative inquiry is its focus on the positive approach, thereby unlocking collective intelligence and team-building capacity (Hung et al. 2017). In communities facing climate change and its impact, appreciative inquiry is of value as it challenges the dominant hierarchical power relations, thus empowering women to become change agents and to explore innovative practice (Trajkovski et al. 2015). As opposed to dealing with negatives, appreciative inquiry supports learning and reflection in a positive way (Curtis et al. 2017).

Despite its promising stance in resolving gendered climate problems, appreciative inquiry has been criticised for focusing on the positive experiences whilst failing to address the negative problems (Reason & Bradbury 2008). It is important to point out that using a positive approach does not mean ignoring problems (Bushe 2011). In fact, a positive approach creates room for improvement. A total focus on the failure to tackle the gendered climate crisis will just compound the problem, leaving no room for success. This chapter is a showcase that despite the gender problems that women face in trying to contribute to climate change resilience, they are not surrendering. They continue to strive against heavy odds. This creates enthusiasm and hope for women to make improvements in the ways they are utilising to protect the environment as they aim to ensure climate change mitigation. Above all, acknowledging the strategic interventions of women to respond to climate change can generate positive conversations, all for bettering the approaches to climate change crisis. Bushe (2011:12) maintains that generative conversation refers to the inquiry that challenges the status quo so that new thinking generates compelling images, thereby leading to change. This is because people like the new options in front of them and want to use them. In this case, the march of women against environmental degradation provides valuable insights that women can positively contribute in responding to the crisis brought about by climate change.

Sampling Procedures and Data Collection

Twenty-eight respondents were purposively selected to participate in the focus group discussions. Key informant interviews were carried out with the founding members of the garden project for the women and other key figures, such as the young women who were equipped with entrepreneurial skills. The affected tobacco farmers as well as the grandmothers who are burdened by taking care of the children whose parents migrated to Mozambique and South Africa due to climate change disasters also participate in the research. The village head was interviewed separately as he refused to be part of the focus groups. All in all, six focus groups were conducted in order to appreciate the contribution of the "single women" in the response to climate change.

The data for the research were gathered utilising the key informant interviews as well as the focus group discussions. The desktop research was also helpful to get scholarly opinions regarding the research problem. Twenty-eight respondents who participated in the study were selected using the purposive sampling. The priest in charge of the Church parish, and the headman of the Mubvurungwa area, were among the key participants. In order to balance the study, the tobacco farmers were also interviewed. To manage the respondents, six focus group discussions were held. Data were presented and analysed using the thematic approach. For objectivity and reliability, during the data collection and presentation period, the ethical considerations for research were upheld.

Discussion of Findings

The following are the research-based findings obtained utilising the key informant interviews as well as the focus group discussions. The presentation is based on the related themes.

Climate Change and Gender in Manicaland, Zimbabwe

Study participants confirmed that there is an imbalance when it comes to how Africans experience the effects of climate change. There is evidence that women tend to suffer more as a result of climate change in Africa (UN Women 2022). Researches that have been conducted in relation to food and nutrition, security matters, the agricultural sector, health issues, as well as water and energy, in addition to climate-linked disasters like migration and conflicts, are all in agreement that women experience more challenges than their male counterparts (Awiti 2022:1). In other words, gender differences are complicating the situation and making women more prone to climate change. For instance, in the agricultural sector, most farmers are now opting for diversity farming due to unreliable rainfed agriculture. However, it should be noted that this is burdening women farmers, as they need to calculate and balance time between work in the fields and household chores such as the preparation of food, fetching water and firewood, as well as child rearing. This is seen as a burden mainly on women because most men are now spending time working in industries and factories, whilst women are confined to the field and home. The burdening of women with both household duties and crop production is associated with social norms and traditional gender roles. This is particularly the case with reference to especially caregiving that undermines women's capacity to reallocate time to work on family plots, diversify crop or livestock production or take up off-farm work (FAO 2015). This is a sad reality currently witnessed in Manicaland, but it is also worth checking on how far women are breaking the chains of gender in practising climate change resilience. This chapter is tracing the achievements of women in dealing with climate change problems. Given that women are impacted more by climate change in the food and security section, the WHO (2002) acknowledges that climate change adaptation action should follow a gender-responsive approach.

The Painful Realities of Climate Change and Its Impact on Gender in Manicaland

Data from the field shows that like other African countries, Zimbabwe is experiencing gender-related climate problems due to the patriarchal nature of the society. The depletion of the natural environment has become the order of the day in Zimbabwe, showing escalating rates in deforestation, water shortages, pollution issues and the vanishing or rare animal and plant species. Compounding matters is the issue of erratic rain, localised droughts and floods. All these factors are threatening food security (Tanyanyiwa & Mufunda 2019:1). In the rural and urban areas of Manicaland Province, firewood has become the major source of energy, whilst the production of farm bricks and charcoal has become the businesses of the moment. The environment is suffering terribly due to wanton cutting down of trees and the ravaging of the environment without limit.

Some groups in society, including the poor, women, elderly, female-headed families and children, are more vulnerable to climate change (Chigwada 2005). The migration of men locally and abroad due to harvest failure as a result of climate change is mainly affecting the women, who are being left with the burden of taking care of the children as well as providing for them and the elderly. The adverse impact of climate change is sometimes forcing women to spend the whole day queuing for water and gathering firewood. The high cost of living and continuous power cuts are also affecting the urban women, whilst the men are generally having better lives. All these markers of gender imbalance, thereby make women vulnerable to climate change. It is only in limited instances that women are fully represented in discussing climate change issues (Ndlovu & Mjimba 2021). Despite all the challenges, it is important to draw attention to the notable achievements of women in responding to climate change. The following section presents the study findings

Gendered Climate Change Crisis in Mubvurungwa Communal Area

The information previously presented on the study area states that Mubvurungwa communal area has not been spared by climate change crisis. In response to the problems of climate change, the women in the study area are actively involved in the campaigns against the depletion of the natural environment. The women who are taking centre stage in the conservation of the environment are affected by forced migration of many men from their families and communities. With the high rate of migration of men to the neighbouring countries of Mozambique and South Africa, many households now depend on the mothers. The men occasionally come back, and at most once annually, during the festive season at the end of the year. However, other men have not come back for a number of years and are not making any effort to send food, clothes and school fees to the family.

"Single": Women and Climate Change Resilience

The idea of women adapting to climate is one of the major findings of the study. This is happening against the backdrop of the painful reality of men migrating due to the harsh effects of climate change. The good news at this stage is that women are learning to be self-sufficient as they are now turning problems into opportunities.

Focus group Number Four participants were clear in narrating that they calculated that Mucheke River had the potential to the desperate women to survive by providing water for their gardens that are about 100 metres away from the river. Since they were single women who were greatly affected by the challenges, they decided to survive and thrive through gardening. They discussed and agreed to grow and sell fresh garden produce like cabbage, beans, peas, carrots and tomatoes to a nearby boarding school that also has a mission hospital. None of the individual farmers in the area was able to meet the demands of the boarding school and the hospital as far as the produce from the gardens was concerned. They realised that they had a ready and vibrant market.

An idea of raising funds to buy thick diamond Marsh wire and metal poles to fence the garden area was initiated by the single Catholic women of St Therese Parish who are part of the women affected by climate change-induced migration. The funds for the fencing project were raised through the sale of homemade buns with the help of the parish priests of St Therese Mission Catholic Church. The profit money was kept secure through the *gaba*[1] strategy until it was enough for the project. Now that the garden area was free from domestic animals that were a problem, especially during the winter and spring seasons when they would be roaming freely, they agreed to grow uniform crops at a particular time so that they could produce enough to supply St Therese Mission Girls High School, as well as the Mission hospital that is also located within the vicinity of the boarding school. By engaging in collective farming, the women were now able to meet the vegetable demands of the boarding school, and this boosted their income. Rather than using their energy to track their husbands in Mozambique who were not providing food on the table, the women now diverted their energy to the garden project that was now viable. Of importance to note is also that the women were aware of the land conservation farming methods to ensure that the environment is not degraded and, at the same time, preserved for the next generations. For instance, the distance from the river to the garden filed was maintained at more than 100 metres. Crop rotation and the use of natural fertilisers form the basis of the land tilling ground rules.

Members of focus group Number Six were keen to share that the rate of single women whose husbands are alive has increased greatly. Such a category of women is suffering a lot as they are forced to take on the double role of being a father and mother of the family. The problems of these "single but married mothers" are being doubled by climate change crisis that is affecting agriculture. It is these women being deserted by their husbands who come up with the idea of doing gardening on a cooperative level, making use of the Mucheke River, the perennial river that flows through the area. The idea of gardening is a result of climate change problems that affect women more than men. Men in this study area easily adapt to climate change by migrating to greener pastures, whilst it was not an easy decision for women who were to remain with the burden of fending for the children alone. The women's ability to engage in joint projects in the face of the impact of climate change confirms the fact that women are beginning to adapt rather than crying out for help from outsiders.

Conservation versus Development: Environmental Justice in Broiler Farming

Focus group five explained how the rearing of broiler chickens became the turning point for the garden project of women. As the income of the project expanded, they started keeping broiler chickens since they now had a ready market. The broilers only need six weeks to reach maturity stage, hence the possibility of quick turnover. The idea of broiler project was initiated by the young women who were sent to attend entrepreneurship workshops and seminars organised by the headmistress of the boarding school, where they supply the garden produce. The first two batches of the broilers did not do well since they were affected by cold winters, as there is no electricity in the village to use the infrared lights to keep the chicks warm. However, the idea of using warm water bottles in the chicken brooders worked very well. The profit from the broiler project was being realised instantly.

However, the fact of intensive broiler farming negatively impacting the environment could not be underestimated at this point. Vaarst et al. (2015), EPRS (2019) and Dróżdż et al. (2020) provide evidence that commercial poultry farming contributes to the depletion of the ozone layer due to the ammonia (NH_3), nitrous oxide (N_2O) and methane (CH_4) emissions. The researchers were keen to know how the women are doing environmental justice in this development project since conservation and development can clash. The focus group was in agreement that with the knowledge of entrepreneurial skills, the waste products like manure and any other litter were being managed in order to reduce the pollution of the environment and contamination of water bodies, as well as risking human and animal health. The poultry manure is used as organic fertiliser for the garden and the fields. After learning more about the hazards of intensive poultry farming to the environment, the women promised to increase their environmental conservation strategies in order to limit the production of gases like ammonia that damage the ozone layer. Indeed, the discussion was sensitive to the politics associated with conservation and development that usually result in development taking precedence over conservation.

Viewing the developments from an indigenous perspective, the rural women opt to keep broiler chickens and not the indigenous breeds that are disease-resistant, locally grown and more nutritious because the indigenous chickens were to be supplied occasionally to the market. At St Therese Mission and other surrounding hospitals and clinics, they serve "road runner" meat occasionally when compared to broiler meat. The kitchen chef at the hospital argues that indigenous chickens are nutritious, but the hospital and high school faced the challenge that they were not getting the quantities they needed. The women were even advised to consider rearing indigenous breeds of chickens, as they were in demand at the time the study was conducted. An analysis of the need to consider intensive farming of indigenous chickens was associated with the growth time, space for free range and birds being predators of the garden and field crops. However, the idea was welcomed as a potential project that could even attract long distance buyers who are into traditional food business.

Catholic "Single Women" on the Frontline of Halting Tobacco Riverbank Cultivation

Another important theme that dominated the focus group discussions as well as the key informant interviews was related to tobacco farming in the area under study. Key informant interview #3 and the other three focus group discussions were in agreement that tobacco growing had become a double-edged sword in the study area, with negative impacts on women. The narration of the sad ordeal by the leaders of the garden project about tobacco farming pushed women to rethink gendered climate change as the women agreed to stand firm against climate change, despite the harassment associated with the patriarchal nature of the society. The tobacco farmers hijacked the garden project as they were now growing tobacco along the river bank, causing siltation and soil erosion, as well as deforestation. This was a significant drawback on the part of women, as their survival strategies were threatened. Using their patriarchal muscle, the men ignored the dangers of streambank cultivation, as they also protested that it was a matter of life and death. It was the youngest age group of the women that finally gathered courage and condemned the tobacco growers for digging a pit to fill another pit.

Two of the grandmothers who were part of the study participants outlined that things turned upside down in 2021 when a group of middle-aged men and school leaver boys started to flock to the river bank, establishing a tobacco seedling nursery and also growing tobacco. The older women added that this affected the garden project as well as water for domestic use. To make things worse, the tobacco growers started to use engines to draw water from the river. Moreover, the surrounding forests were affected by deforestation as the men cut down trees for firewood to dry tobacco. Since firewood is the source of fuel in the rural areas, deforestation affected the women a lot as they were forced to travel long distances to fetch firewood. Efforts to discuss the problems of streambank cultivation and deforestation were futile, as the men were concerned with making money without the conservation of the environment in mind. Upon realising that their lives were at risk because of tobacco farmers, the young Catholic single women who are part of the project decided to bring the parish priests to intervene at their plight using the word of God.

The two parish priests of St Therese Mission Roman Catholic Church accompanied the women to the headmen, who then called for a meeting with all the concerned parties. The meeting was difficult to chair since tobacco growers were of the view that it was a matter of survival, whilst the single women were firm on the need to be climate change resilient by avoiding the depletion of the natural resources. As stated earlier, women were conscious of climate-smart methods like crop rotation, use of organic fertilisers and maintaining the required distance of more than 100 metres from the river. The Catholic priests responded with the 2015 encyclical letter from the Pope entitled **Laudato Si**,[2] which refers to environmental stewardship as mandatory for all Christians. The priests took turns in explaining that the Earth is everyone's home, and by ignoring climate change, human beings are threatening their own lives by destroying their own homes. The headman was surprised and empowered to learn that caring for the environment also has biblical roots. The headman added that, as much as they were facing economic hardships and political instability, the ravaging of the environment could not be the solution because even the indigenous religions take heed of environmental conservation as the land belongs to the ancestors. He went on to explain that the environmental catastrophes like drought, incurable diseases and unpredicted rain patterns were all a result of the anger of the ancestors, who were not happy with the way human beings are ravaging the natural resources. The headman pointed out that there was a need for joint action in taking good care of the natural resources. He even condemned the indiscriminate cutting down of big trees like *muhacha, musasa and mukute*, among others, that should never be cut (*marambakutemwa*) at all costs, as the trees are believed to be the abode of the ancestors.

Tobacco Farmers Resisting Climate Change Resilience

Key informant interviewee Number Four submitted that tobacco farmers in the study area promised to refrain from streambank cultivation and deforestation, but in a very short space the tobacco farmers were preparing the same area for tobacco nursery seedbeds. It was a bitter pill to swallow for the women doing the garden project, as it was a pointer to competition for water and firewood. Probing the respondents during the focus group discussions as to why the tobacco farmers did not take heed of climate change resilience through the conservation of the natural environment revealed that the whole issue was politicised. Once political interests coincide with conservation issues, everything became complicated. Further investigations brought to the surface that political leaders and other officials were allowing the tobacco farmers to practice illegal farming just for political mileage. The political figures were prioritising votes, thereby undermining climate change adaptation through the conservation of natural resources such as water and trees. On condition of anonymity, one respondent pointed out that the issue of bribery between the traditional leaders and the illegal farmers is one of the concrete reasons for the tobacco farmers continuing with river bank cultivation, thereby disadvantaging the women practising gardening through making use of the Mucheke River water.

After a series of meetings on the way forward, the women were frustrated and decided to take bold action by campaigning against the illegal tobacco farmers who were against climate change adaptation. It is important to note that the protest against tobacco farmers was an important step towards climate change resilience through breaking the chains of gender inequalities. A close analysis of the findings associated with tobacco farmers shows that there is a need to address gender disparities in the development programmes that, in turn, impact the environment negatively.

The Women's March: Demonstrating Climate Change Resilience

Two of the key informant interviewees and the rest of the focus groups confirmed that the tobacco growers did not quit riverbank cultivation. The women were frustrated, and they took bold action as they marched to the tobacco seedling section with the intention of destroying the seedlings. This was a protest of its own kind, and the incident happened one month away from the rainy season. The tobacco seedlings were ready for transplanting, and the tobacco farmers were in the final stages of land preparation. The marchers uprooted all the tobacco seedlings without saying a word. It was a coordinated action, with elderly women leading the women. These elderly women were taking care of the children whose parents had gone to Mozambique for good. These elderly women had resorted to the selling of garden produce as a means of survival with their grandchildren. The young women who were empowered with entrepreneurship skills destroyed the engine lines that draw water from the river to the tobacco fields.

On this day, people witnessed the power of women as far as the climate change crisis is concerned. Men learnt that the violence of silence is the worst type of violence. The headman had remarked that the women were not weak and that they would one day revolt if the men pushed them too far. The community people realised that the river and the surrounding forests had become their source of livelihood, not only for the project women, but for all people in the area. The women had managed to transform the lives of people in a very short space of time after the men had left for greener pastures without leaving a survival schedule for their families.

The event marked the end of streambank cultivation and reduced the rate of deforestation in Mubvurungwa rural remote area. It is a very important event, but unfortunately the news did not reach far enough to empower the other women across the province. Surprisingly, some groups of men started to join the women project. The founding members of the project reiterated that the project was flourishing and all the surrounding schools, hospitals, churches and towns were relying on the Mucheke River Garden project. All the nearby fields had been converted into a garden area as they were now growing green mealies for sale utilising the water from the river. The idea of coordinated gardening was the best option since they were only growing scheduled crops that meet the demands of the customers. The march of women protesting against streambank cultivation has become a major lesson for climate change adaptation in the Mubvurungwa area.

It is strategic to note that through arbitration by the headman and the Catholic parish priests, tobacco farmers finally saw the light regarding the need to engage in development programmes that do not harm the environment. The young Catholic women were demonstrating that a good environment is the key to survival on Earth. It should also be highlighted that the men who were into tobacco growing joined the garden project, and others resorted to the keeping of goats with the help of the Member of Parliament of the area. This appreciative inquiry into the contribution of women in mitigating the effects of climate change confirms that women in Zimbabwe are flourishing in the face of major challenges. It is all because of the syndicate effort by women to limit riverbank cultivation that the depletion of the natural resources has decreased in the study area.

Conclusion

This chapter appreciates the role being played by women in climate change resilience in Mubvurungwa communal area in Manicaland Province of Zimbabwe. Although there are gender challenges faced by women in the study area, the women are seen contributing a lot to mitigating the effects of climate change. The Mubvurungwa women managed to drive away tobacco farmers who were illegally cultivating tobacco along the Mucheke River. It was not an easy task, but the women managed to convince men, not with swords but through displaying facts about climate change, hence the need to adapt. Through climate change adaptation, Mubvurungwa women are conserving Mucheke River water, which sustains the garden project that was started by the single but married women whose husbands migrated to neighbouring Mozambique fleeing pressures of climate change. These women have defied patriarchy, demonstrated high levels of resilience and are demonstrating effective leadership in responding to climate change.

Notes

1 Putting money in a sealed container, until one reaches the amount they want.
2 Laudato Si means praise be to you. It is an encyclical letter by Pope Francis that was published in 2015, warning humanity of the dangers of the impending climate change crisis. The Pope alludes that, it is everyone's responsibility to conserve the environment.

Bibliography

Awiti, A.O. (2022). "Climate change and gender in Africa: A review of impact and gender-responsive solutions." *Front. Clim.* 4: 895950. doi: 10.3389/fclim.2022.895950

Bunce, M., Brown, K., and Rosendo, S. (2010). "Policy misfits, climate change and cross-scale vulnerability in coastal Africa: How development projects undermine resilience," *Environ. Sci. Policy* 13: 485–497.

Bushe, G. (2011). "Appreciative inquiry: Theory and critique." In D. Boje, B. Burnes, & J. Hassard (Eds.), *Routledge companion to organizational change*, Oxford, UK: Routledge. Pp 87–103.

Chagutah (2010). *Climate Change Vulnerability and Adaptation Preparedness in Southern Africa Zimbabwe Country Report*. Berlin: Heinrich Boll Stiftung.

Chazovachii, B., Chigwenyu, A., and Mushuku, A. (2010). "Adaptation of climate resilient rural livelihoods through growing of small grains in Munyaradzi communal area, Gutu District," *Afr. J. Agric. Res.* 7: 1335–1345.

Chigwada, J. (2005). "Case study 6: Zimbabwe climate proofing Infrastructure and diversifying livelihoods in Zimbabwe." invulnerability, adaptation and climate disasters, *IDS Bulletin* 36(4), 103–116.

Chitando, E. et al. (2022). Eds. *African Perspectives on Religion and Climate Change*. London: Routledge.

Cooperrider, D. L., and Whitney, D. (2001). A positive revolution in change: Appreciative inquiry. *Public Administration and Public Policy*, 1–36. Retrieved from http://www.tapin.in/Documents/2/AppreciativeInquiry-PositiveRevolutioninChange.pdf [20/08/2023]

Curtis, K., Gallagher, A., Ramage, C., Montgomery, J., Martin, C., Leng, J., and Holah, J. (2017). "Using appreciative inquiry to develop, implement and evaluate a multiorganisation 'Cultivating Compassion' programme for health professionals and support staff," *J. Res. Nursing* 22: 150–165.

Dankelman, I. (2002). "Climate change: Learning from gender analysis and women's experience of organizing for sustainable development," *Gender Dev.* 10(2), 21–29.

Dróżdż, D., Wystalska, K., Malińska, K., Grosser, A., Grobelak, A., and Kacprzak, M. (2020). "Management of poultry manure in Poland – current state and future perspectives," *J. Environ. Manag.* 264: 110327.

EPRS. (2019). "The EU Poultry Meat and Egg Sector: Main Features, Challenges and Prospects: In-depth Analysis," *European Parliamentary Research Service*, Brussels, Belgium.

FAO. (2015). *Regional Overview of Food Insecurity: African Food Insecurity Prospects Brighter Than Ever*. Accra: FAO.

Gukurume, S. (2013). "Climate change, variability and sustainable agriculture in Zimbabwe's rural communities," *Russ. J. Agric. Soc. Econ. Sci.* 14: 89–100.

Hung, L. et al. (2018). "Appreciative inquiry: Bridging research and practice in a hospital setting," *J. Qual. Methods* 17, 1–10.

Hung, L., Phinney, A., Chaudhury, H., Rodney, P., Tabamo, J., and Bohl, D. (2017). "'Little things matter!' Exploring the perspectives of patients with dementia about the hospital environment," *Int. J. Older People Nursing* 12 (3): e12153. doi: 10.1111/opn.12153

Kipuri, N., and Ridgewell, A. (2008). *A double blind: The exclusion of pastoralists' women in the East and Horn of Africa.* London: Minority Rights Group International.

Pope Francis. (2015). *Laudato Si: On care for our common home.* New Jersey: Paulist Press.

Maphosa, F. (2004). The impact of remittances from Zimbabweans working in South Africa on rural livelihoods in the Southern Districts of Zimbabwe. CODESRIA, Dakar International Crops Research Institute for the Semi-Arid-Tropics (ICRISAT.

Masika, R. (ed.) (2002). *Gender, development and climate change.* Oxford: Oxfam.

Ndlovu, T., and Mjimba, V. (2021). "Drought risk-reduction and gender dynamics in communal cattle farming in Southern Zimbabwe," *Int. J. Disaster Risk Reduct.* 58: 1–23.

Patterson, J. J. (2022). *Culture and identity in climate policy.* Available online at https://doi.org/10.1002/wcc.765 [Accessed 14 Nov 2023]

Phiri, K., Ndlove, S., and Chiname T. B. (2014). "Climate Change Impacts on Rural Based Women: Emerging Evidence on Coping and Adaptation Strategies in Tsholotsho, Zimbabwe. p. 22552. http://www.mcser.org/journal/index.php/mjss/article/view/4819/4673

Reason, P., & Bradbury, H. (2008). *The sage handbook of action research: Participative inquiry and practice* (2nd ed.). London: Sage.

Tanyanyiwa, V. I., and Mufunda, E. (2019). "Gendered impacts of climate change: The Zimbabwe perspective," *Climate Action: Encyclopedia of the UN Sustainable Development Goals.* Cham: Springer. https://doi.org/10.1007/978-3-319-71063-1_33-11-13

Trajkovski, S., Schmied, V., Vickers, M., & Jackson, D. (2015). "Using appreciative inquiry to bring neonatal nurses and parents together to enhance family-centred care: A collaborative workshop," *J. Child Health Care* 19: 239–253.

UNDP (2009). "Gender and climate change: Impact and adaptation." *IRADe.* Available online: http://www.csd-i.org/. [Accessed 14 November 2014)

UNDP Zimbabwe, (2022). *Women speak on the disproportionate impact of a changing climate.* Available on https://www.undp.org/zimbabwe/stories/women-speak-disproportionate-impact-changing-climate. [Accessed 21/08/23].

UNEP, (2021). *State of the climate: UNEP climate action note.* Available at org/facts about climate change emergency. [Accessed 11 August 23].

Vaarst, M., Steenfeldt, S., and Horsted, K. (2015). "Sustainable development perspectives of poultry production," *World's Poul. Sci. J.* 71: 609–620.

WHO. (2002). Gender and health in disease. Avenue Appia Geneva, Switzerland: WHO Department of Gender and Women's Health 20. Available online at: https://www.who.int/gender/other_health/genderdisasters.pdf [accessed August 2023]

World Meteorological Organisation (WMO) (2019). *Statement on the state of the global climate in 2019: Collection(s) and series WMO No1248.* Available at https://library.wmo.int/index.php?lvl=notice-display&id=21700

SECTION 4

Defying the Odds

African Women in Science, Technology, Engineering and Mathematics

14
OVERCOMING DIFFICULTIES AS A WOMAN SCIENTIST IN AFRICA

Jennifer Thomson

Introduction

My life as a student was anything but straightforward! In fact, this became somewhat of a problem for funding agencies later on in my career, as I didn't follow a single theme but became involved in what might have seemed to be a somewhat chaotic change of research areas. However, as I hope you will see, to me it was totally logical and certainly not random. Let me explain in the next section.

My "Random" Studies

When I finished school in 1964, I had two major loves: English and biology. Little did I know that by choosing the latter I would end up doing a great deal of the former. In fact, my choice of a BSc was driven largely by the fact that most of my school friends were choosing to do a BA. So I began with a general first-year BSc at the University of Cape Town but soon realised that my love was Zoology, so I majored in that and General Physiology. Shortly thereafter, I had the opportunity to do a degree at Cambridge University, but I found the Zoology Department there totally boring, and to my horror, they expected me to spend my summer vacation working! As I wanted to travel, this was definitely not an option, so I cycled out to the Genetics Department, which, in those days, was a little bit out of Cambridge. I told the head that I had done about a week of genetics in my third year at UCT and could I switch to that subject? He was extremely obliging, and so I left Cambridge in 1970 with an MA (all master's degrees were MA!) in Genetics.

One thing I had learnt during my genetics training was that the organisms we worked on (such as drosophila fruit flies) grew too slowly, so I needed to do my PhD on organisms that grew fast. The only universities in South Africa in those days that offered microbiology at the PhD level were Pretoria and Rhodes. Not being very fluent in Afrikaans, my choice was obvious, so I joined the Botany Department, in which David Woods had just started a microbiology major, having just returned from having obtained a PhD in that subject from Oxford. And so I became his first PhD student. After three years of studying the genetics of bacteria involved in leather decay (there was a leather research institute in Grahamstown) and six months of lecturing when Dave went on sabbatical research, I got married and moved to Boston, USA.

The reason for that move was that I had been extremely fortunate to be awarded a post-doctoral fellowship there in the Department of Medical Microbiology. My initial reaction when I arrived was one of absolute terror, as everyone seemed to know so much and I seemed to know so little. One of the reasons was that in South Africa we spent our entire PhD years working on a single project, while in America they do a longer PhD, which includes coursework. Slowly, by dint of constant reading and questioning, I began to feel more at home, but one of the outcomes was that I told my husband that, as I wanted to become a career scientist, I would not be able to have children. I do not regret this decision, but one of my reasons for standing for election as President of the Organisation for Women in Science (OWSD) in 2016 was that I don't want other women scientists to have to make the same decision. But more of that later!

Getting into Genetically Modified Organisms (GMOs)

At Harvard, I was working on the genetics of the central metabolism of the bacterial "workhorse" called *Escherichia coli* (*E. coli* for short), and after a year of using classical genetics tools, I was getting nowhere. This was in 1974, and a new technology called genetic engineering (or genetic modification) had just started. I went to my supervisor and told him that if I could get hold of the particular gene I was working on, I could solve the problem. He said if I did that, I would be on my own as the science was so new, and, in addition, one of the leaders of the group opposing GMOs, "Science for the People," worked in the lab right above ours! Accordingly, I contacted the scientist who had cloned all the *E. coli* genes, and in due course, he sent me the one I needed. It took me a year to get the answer, but indeed it worked, and I will never forget the thrill of seeing the peak of my protein appearing on the scintillation counter at the dead of night!

I duly wrote up the work for publication and submitted the manuscript to my supervisor. He returned it some days later with many corrections and suggestions, but, to my horror, he had crossed out his name as co-author. "Oh, no!" I thought to myself. "He either thinks the work is useless or he doesn't want to be associated with research using GMOs." "No," he replied. "This is all your own work so my name shouldn't appear on the paper!" So, I am the single author of a chapter from work carried out at Harvard University. It would be great if other supervisors could work on similar principles.

After my 2 years at Harvard, I returned to South Africa to take up a lectureship in 1977 in the Department of Genetics at the University of the Witwatersrand (Wits) in Johannesburg. My husband, who had been studying for a PhD in architecture at Boston University, received a Fullbright Fellowship to carry out his fieldwork in Botswana, after which he got a job in Johannesburg. I immediately applied to the scientific funding agency, which, at the time, was the Council for Scientific and Industrial Research (CSIR). This was the first application for research on GMOs, and they realised that they needed it to be regulated, as was being done in the USA and other countries. They accordingly established SAGENE, the South African Genetic Engineering Committee, with Prof David Woods, my friend and PhD supervisor, as the Chair. They even invited Herb Boyer, the co-founder of the company Genentech in California, which was commercialising cloned insulin, which he had developed with his colleague Stanley Cohen, to visit South Africa. I had the honour of co-hosting him in

Johannesburg, when he was horrified that the CSIR was spending more on the regulations via SAGENE than on giving me and other scientists research grants!

SAGENE actually played an important role in fostering research in GMOs, as universities were forced to comply with the regulations and hence provide research facilities for their scientists. It also ran courses, both for researchers and regulators, on how to work with GMOs, in many of which I participated.

European Molecular Biology Organisation (EMBO) Course in Basel

Shortly after I joined Wits, I received an unexpected invitation to join a course on genetic engineering held by EMBO in Basel. Unexpected, as it was during the South African apartheid regime, and we were not usually invited to such events. I was therefore extremely grateful for what turned out to be a life-changing experience. It was in the early days of GMO research, and we were extremely fortunate to be taught Southern gels by Ed Southern himself, the use of plasmids and virus vectors by the developers Ken and Maureen Murray themselves and so it went on. One evening, while walking to supper, the man who was teaching us about plant genetic engineering, Marc van Montagu from Ghent University in Belgium, asked me what I wanted to work on in the future. When I replied "plants" he said, "Well you'll have to come and work in my lab." And that is precisely what I did for a number of years, spending all my free time learning plant genetic engineering from one of the masters! I cannot describe how helpful and welcoming Marc was, letting me stay with him and his wife, Nora, in their home in Amsterdam, driving me to and from the lab and generally making me feel most welcome. Later on, when the CSIR was becoming seriously interested in plant genetic engineering, they invited Marc to visit South Africa on a number of occasions to help them get the field started.

Marc introduced me to Jeff Schell, another giant in the field, who also became a friend. When the CSIR asked me to invite Jeff to South Africa, he replied that he would as long as he could visit me in Cape Town. Sadly, Jeff died before he could be included in the 2013 World Food Prize that was presented to Marc, Mary-Dell Chilton and Robert Fraley. Much later, when I began to work on GM maize, Marc introduced me to Mary-Dell, who worked in the famous Research Triangle Park in North Carolina, and she and her research group were instrumental in getting my lab geared up to work in this field.

The CSIR and the Laboratory for Molecular and Cell Biology (LMCB)

In 1982/1983, I took a sabbatical year's leave at the Massachusetts Institute of Technology (MIT). I had met Charlie Cooney from their Chemical Engineering Department when he visited Wits, and he invited me to bring my technology to introduce it to his graduate students. This was a really great experience and made me realise that I should possibly consider working in the USA. Word must have got back to the CSIR that I was job hunting, and one day I was asked to meet with their Vice President, Dr Arndt, who was visiting in Washington, DC. He offered me the opportunity to start a new division at the CSIR, called the Laboratory for Molecular and Cell Biology (LMCB). I jumped at this, not only because I would be the first woman to head a CSIR division but also for the opportunities it would give me to run my own lab. However, I stipulated that I would run it from Wits rather than move to the CSIR campus in Pretoria, and, very fortunately, Wits gave me a suite of labs and offices on the top floor of the very building where I had worked in the Genetics Department.

During the course of my four-year LMCB stint, we brought in the CSIR's veterinary research group that was operating at the Onderstepoort Veterinary Research Institute. They remained physically there but we worked as a unit; their interests mainly on ruminant nutrition and the bacteria involved in fibre digestion. During that time, our research gained the interest of the African Explosives and Chemical Industry (AECI), which was starting to diversify into the use of cellulose (plant fibre consisting of glucose molecules) as a source of fuel. They funded us most generously, which became very useful in 1987 when, for personal reasons, I had to leave the LMCB. They generously hired most of my research group and built a lab specifically for their needs. I, in the meantime, became the Head of the Department of Microbiology at the University of Cape Town (UCT).

The Department of Microbiology at UCT

As far as I was concerned, this was the best job for me in South Africa, which I obtained in competition with three men, becoming the first woman head of a department in the Science Faculty. It was quite a daunting task, but I received superb support from my predecessor, who happened to be the very David Woods under whom I had received my PhD. I also received excellent support from the Vice-Chancellor, Stuart Saunders, who put me in touch with the Claude Leon Foundation, who supported my research for many years.

In 1989, SAGENE (mentioned above), which had largely become dormant, suddenly resurfaced to advise the South African Department of Agriculture when it received its first application for a GM crop field trial. This was for insect-resistant cotton and it was authorised in terms of the Pest Control Act. SAGENE had been given the mandate to advise, somewhat informally, on biosafety issues. However, it was legally reconstituted in 1992 and again in January 1994. The latter agreement came into effect just a few months before the first democratic election in South Africa.

SAGENE's new terms of reference included furnishing advice to any Minister, statutory or government body on any form of legislation or controls pertaining to the importation and/or release into the environment of GMOs. As the new South African government, which was ushered in on 27 April 1994, had no particular knowledge or expertise in these areas, regulatory matters were left very much in the hands of SAGENE.

SAGENE continued to act as the regulator until the GMO Act came into effect on 1 December 1999. By the time of the GMO Act, a considerable number of field trial permits had been granted, and a number of GM crops had already been commercialised. I had become the Chair and found that my work for SAGENE was extremely time-consuming but also very rewarding. It was not only the driving force behind a rapid rate of GMO approvals, but it also had the task of drafting the GMO Act.

The World Economic Forum and the United Nations

One day in about 1998, quite out of the blue, I received an invitation to speak at the African event of the annual World Economic Forum (WEF), which is held every January in Davos, Switzerland. From time to time, they hold regional meetings, and this one was in Durban. I remember giving (them) my talk to friends I was staying with nearby and receiving extremely helpful feedback for improvement. It must have worked because the following year I received an invitation to speak at the 2000 Davos WEF, all expenses paid, including a business class airfare.

My main task, as I was involved in a number of meetings, was to participate in a panel discussion on GM crops with a packed audience. During question time, Gordon Conway, then President of the Rockefeller Foundation, was asked what their next focus of funding would be. "Drought tolerant crops for Africa" was his reply. Afterwards, I tapped him on the shoulder and said, "Excuse me, Gordon….." and that was the start of about 15 years of incredible funding, during which Gordon (later Sir Gordon) and I became great friends. On one occasion, I even spent a few wonderful days with him and his wife, Anne, at their beautiful country home in Sussex.

I was invited back the next year, and the highlight of this one was a discussion with world leaders on a Sunday, which is supposed to be a "free day!" On the way over, I had been bumped up to first class, and there I met our then South African Minister of Trade and Industry, Alec Eriwn. He and our then Minister of Economic Development, Trevor Manuel, sat next to me at the discussion and, under their breath, would tell me where each person who asked a question came from. This was because, although I was introduced to them, they were not introduced to me! After a while, however, I became so used to addressing heads of state that Alec and Trevor left me to myself. What an experience!

One of the outcomes of my Davos experiences was that I met the then President of the USA National Academy of Sciences, Bruce Alberts. He, in turn, asked Kofi Annan, then Secretary General of the United Nations, to invite me to speak to the UN General Assembly. This I duly did in 2002, as described in the following section.

Writing Books

Sometime around 2002, I received a request from the UCT Press to write a book on GMOs, specifically from an African perspective. I asked my friend, Prof George Ellis from the Department of Mathematics, who has written widely on a wide range of subjects, for his advice. What he told me I have used for every one of the six books I have written: do a draft outline of the book with chapters identified (these can easily be changed later), create a folder for each chapter (in my case, these were physical folders) and file relevant articles and notes in each one. I also realised that I needed to devote myself entirely to writing this book, and I was extremely fortunate that friends lent me their holiday home at Plettenberg Bay, a beautiful beach resort up the east coast from Cape Town.

I wrote almost every day for four weeks, sending chapters regularly to a scientific editor friend in the USA, Mike Shelby. This was before the days of emails and cell phones, so I would fax them to him and receive these back with copious corrections and questions such as "Would Kaolin (my niece) understand this?" Finally, I sent the book off to UCT Press, only to receive a reply that they no longer existed as they had been taken over by a commercial publishing company, which company told me that they had no interest in publishing my book! Horrified, I immediately contacted George and Mike, who both wrote very strongly worded letters to the publisher saying that if they didn't publish my book, they would be fools! Fortunately, these worked, and both wrote forewords to *Genes for Africa*, which was published under the UCT Press logo in 2002 (Thomson 2002).

My good friend, Gordon Conway, President of the Rockefeller Foundation, wrote a review of the book for the journal *Nature*, in which he stated that it was a gem of a book but that it needed more on the environmental impacts of GM crops. Accordingly, I applied for (and received) a fellowship to write such a book at Rockefeller's Villa Serbelloni in Bellagio, Italy, in July 2005. What a marvellous experience that was, and what a privilege to spend a month with other writers, composers and designers in those glorious surroundings on Lake Como! The product, *GM Crops: The Impact and the Potential*, was copublished by the CSIRO Press in Australia and Cornell University Press (under the title of *Seeds for the Future* 2006 CSIRO Publishing) with a foreword by Gordon, in (Thomson 2006).

My third book, *Food for Africa: The Life and Work of a Scientist in GM Crops*, was published in 2013 by UCT Press, now back in business. The foreword for this was written by Dr Mamphela Ramphele, then Vice-Chancellor of UCT. The first paragraph of the introduction will give you a feel for what the book is about.

> I am having lunch with Kofi Annan in his private dining room on the top floor of the United Nations. In a short while I will try to convince UN ambassadors that GM crops can help to feed hungry Africans. Kofi Annan is jovial, all smiles: 'Nothing happens till I get there'. I sweat slightly as I wait to give what could be the most important lecture I have ever given. Zambia has just said no to food aid because it might contain GM maize. Farmers might plant it, instead of eating it, even though their families are starving. But if they plant it, Zambia might lose its GM-free status for its food exports to Europe. African leaders are thus caught on the horns of a dilemma. Will I be able to convince them to embrace this technology when Europeans and others are telling them it could poison their people or, worse still, make them sterile?
>
> (Thomson 2013: p. 1)

Based on these European/African complications, some years later, I decided to write a book entitled *GM Crops: The West versus the Rest*. Again, the CSIRO Press in Australia agreed to publish it, but under the somewhat less confrontational title of *GM Crops and the Global Divide* (Thomson 2021a) CSIRO Publishing, Australia. This was published in 2021 and led to an online interview with the Chinese GM crop regulators. Whether it had any impact, I don't know, but China commercialised GM crops in 2022.

In the meantime, in 2021, I self-published (at the request of members of the staff of my department at UCT) a book entitled *Travels with my Lab Notebook*, which was a lot of fun. I also wrote book 6 on a completely different, non-scientific, subject. At the moment, at the request of family and friends, I am writing a book called *Life After Retirement*!

Working with the South African Government's Department of Science, Technology and Innovation

In the early 2000s, the South African Department of Science and Technology (DST; now Department of Science, Technology and Innovation) appointed me to their National Advisory Council on Innovation (NACI) to represent biotechnology. After a few years, NACI decided that biotechnology was taking off at such a rate in the country that they needed a special committee to deal with this. As a result, in 2006, the National Biotechnology Advisory Committee (NBAC) was launched as a subcommittee of NACI. I was appointed as Chair, a position I shared with Prof Michael Pepper, then the Director of the NetCare Institute of Cellular and Molecular Medicine at the University of Pretoria.

Over time, NBAC realised that biotechnology needed to be recognised as a contributor to the national economy. As a result, a few of us, joined by leading economists, produced an

Audit on the South African Bioeconomy Sector. This was published in 2022, and time will tell how it will be used to improve the role of this sector in our economy.

DST had, in the past, a programme called the Public Understanding of Biotechnology (PUB). In 2014, they asked me to compile a book on South African biotechnologists. I said, "Boring, unless we can write stories about them." Accordingly, I hired a very talented writer and photographer, Clinton Wittstock (2014), and together we compiled a terrific (says she modestly!) book entitled *Blazing a Biotechnology Trail: Celebrating Biotechnology Excellence in South Africa*. We had a terrific launch in Pretoria at which many of the featured scientists were present, and a great time was had by all.

African Agricultural Technology Foundation (AATF)

Sometime in 2003, I was asked to put my name forward as a potential board member of a newly formed organisation called the AATF based in Nairobi. In due course, I received notification that not only was I a member of this board but I was its Vice-Chair. I have to confess that I could not remember what AATF stood for (the only acronym I could find on the internet stood for the African Association of Teachers of French!) and when, to my horror, I was told that the Chair had resigned and I was, therefore, the Chair. I went cap in hand to one of the organisers to find out what this was all about. I, therefore, went to my first board meeting with considerable trepidation. Well, I needed not have worried, as I soon found that I was now a member of one of the most remarkable organisations. It has ever been my good fortune to be associated with. It aims to transform the livelihoods of sub-Saharan Africans through innovative agricultural technologies, but it is the people of the AATF who are so astoundingly devoted to this aim that made my many years with them such a joy and a privilege.

What we aimed to do, especially in those early years, was to bring technological innovations in agriculture from multinational organisations for use in Africa royalty-free. I had a marvellously supportive board, and Nairobi was like a second home to me. This became even more so when the Executive Director had to resign and I was asked to step off the board (my second term was about to expire) in order to take on the role of ED until a permanent one could be appointed. Thus, I would commute every two weeks between Cape Town and Nairobi for about four months. Not only did I get to know the staff and their dedication even more, but I got to know Kenya a bit better. This included a camel safari near Mount Kenya, a weekend on the tiny island of Lamu, visits to the various game reserves, including Masai Mara, time spent around the coastal town of Mombasa and much more.

The International Consortium of Applied Economic Research (ICABR)

In 2008, I was asked to speak at a meeting of the ICABR, which meets every year in the glorious town of Ravello above the Amalfi Coast in Italy. In the early days, we met in an old monastery looking out over the sea. It was an incredibly beautiful setting for a conference, even if in the venue there was only one toilet, and relief had to be obtained by hiking up a steep set of steps to a nearby hotel. In later years, the meeting moved to the imposing conference centre, but it never lost its charm.

Most of the people attending the meeting were economists and political scientists, from whom I learnt so much that I decided there and then to continue attending these meetings. As I was one of the few scientists who attended regularly, I was soon elected to the board. At one of our meetings, I commented that although we paid lip service to the importance of agricultural biotechnology for developing countries, we did little to influence this, and shouldn't we have a meeting in one of these countries? I should have kept my thoughts to myself, as I was immediately asked to run an ICABR conference in Africa!

This I agreed to do as long as I could run it in Nairobi with the help of the AATF, who was a tower of strength, even committing a staff member full-time to the 2014 conference. It was held in the beautiful Safari Park Hotel and was an astounding success, with the Bill and Melinda Gates Foundation paying for African scholars to attend.

The Alliance for Science

In 2014, I was asked to attend an agricultural biotechnology meeting at Cornell University in the USA. It turned out to be the start of a marvellous organisation called the Alliance for Science (AfS) under the leadership of a truly gifted science communicator, Sarah Evenega. At the time of writing, it was based in the Boyce Thompson Institute for Plant Research and was a global communications and training initiative that combats misinformation about agricultural biotechnology, climate change and other science-related issues.

The flagship programme of the AfS, especially in its early years, was the Science Global Leadership Fellows Programme, a 12-week intensive training course for men and women working in science communication. My role was to spend about a week with these students at the start of their course, teaching them the basics of GMOs so that they could understand the science involved. I thoroughly enjoyed this involvement as I met fascinating young people from many developing countries and was able to learn from them about the problems they faced. We tried to bring a group of 3–5 people from any given country and sent them home with a specific task that they could undertake as a group. From this base, they would then use their training to improve communication regarding GM crops and other related scientific topics.

The CGIAR (Consortium of International Agricultural Research Centres)

In 2016, I was approached by the CGIAR to become part of their Independent Science and Partnership Council (ISPC; now the ISDC – Independent Science for Development Council). This is a panel of scientific experts whose aim is to strengthen the quality, relevance and impact of CGIAR science. Its main purpose was to provide independent advice and expertise to the funders of the CGIAR. My first meeting at the UN Food and Agricultural Organisation (FAO) in Rome was rather a challenge as many of the members were economists who seemed to speak a different language. Fortunately, I was fairly soon given a specific task – to organise their biennial Science Forum in 2018 (SF 18). This we organised in Stellenbosch, a picturesque university town in the Winelands some 50 km from Cape Town.

My term of office ended soon after the conference but my involvement continued, indirectly, when the chair, Holger Meinke, invited me to visit his home Australian province of Tasmania to help them with the review of their GMO policy. I spent a 5-day whistle-stop tour of the various stakeholders in 2019, but I am not sure how much good it did as the government decided to continue their ban on GMOs for another 10 years, although subject to annual reviews.

The L'Oreal/UNESCO Prize

In December 2003, I received a phone call from Paris from a woman who worked for L'Oreal, telling me that I had won the 2004 L'Oreal/UNESCO prize for Africa and the Arab States. What an overwhelming experience this was to be! Apart from the USD 100,000 prize, I spent five glorious days in Paris staying at the Hilton Hotel. The announcement of the five winners was embargoed until the night of the announcement, but while we were gathered in a room under the lights of the Eiffel Tower, someone ran in and said, "the news is out" and, embarrassingly, the news was about me. What had happened was that L'Oreal had engaged a TV film crew to interview me in my lab just before I left for Paris. Although they had been told of the embargo, they obviously had other ideas, and there it was in glorious technicolour on French TV! Fortunately, the organisers decided that the publicity was, in fact, good for the programme, so I was spared any further embarrassment.

Another positive outcome of the TV interview was that shortly after I returned home, I received a letter from the Sorbonne University in Paris asking me whether I would accept an honorary doctorate. What a question! And so, in due course, I returned to Paris to accept this degree.

The Canadian International Development Research Centre and the International Food Security Research Fund

In 2009, I was contacted by the Canadian International Development Research Centre (IDRC) asking me to serve on the selection panel for projects under their new Canadian International Food Security Research Fund (CIFSRF). The projects were aimed at relieving hunger in developing countries, and the main requirement was that they had to be joint projects with a Canadian partner. Serving on the panel was an extremely rewarding experience, as the projects had to show their absolute dependence on all the partners involved. In addition, projects could fail if they did not show the active participation of women in the execution of the project and as recipients of the products or processes being developed.

I served on that panel for about six years and thoroughly enjoyed the experience, including meeting amazing fellow panel members and delighting in the beauty of Ottawa and the rivers that flow through it.

OWSD

In 1996, soon after South Africa's first democratic election, a non-governmental scientific advisory group was formed. A friend and I decided that this needed women's voices, so we started an organisation at UCT called South African Women in Science and Engineering (SAWISE), which had a representative in this group. I was chair of SAWISE for many years, with its main function being to help women scientists at UCT get ahead in their careers.

Many years later, a colleague who ran the SA Academy of Science and knew about my SAWISE work suggested I put my name forward for the position of President of the Organisation for Women in Science for the Developing World (OWSD). I had been involved in the South African National Chapter of OWSD but had never thought of taking any other role. However, she was persuasive, and in 2016, at the General Assembly in Kuwait, I was duly elected President. And what a new life this has given me!

OWSD is an international organisation founded in 1987 and based at the offices of the World Academy of Sciences (TWAS) in Trieste, Italy. It is a programme unit of UNESCO. It is the first international forum to unite eminent women scientists from the developing and developed worlds with the objective of strengthening their role in the development process and promoting their representation in scientific and technological leadership. It provides research training, career development and networking opportunities for women scientists throughout the developing world at different stages in their careers.

Sadly, in March 2023 we heard that the long-standing donors of our PhD programme, SIDA (the Swedish International Development Agency), had cut their funding by about 50%. This has caused us to do a major reshuffle and hope to have a MSc programme in place by the end of this year. Fortunately, the Canadian IDRC (mentioned above) continues to fund our Early Career Fellowships and the Elsevier Foundation our joint awards program. For further information about OWSD, see our website, www.owsd.net.

I have had a marvellous time meeting and working with amazing women (and men!), many of whom work under incredibly difficult and challenging circumstances. I am filled with admiration for all that they continue to do.

Conclusion

Now, at the age of 75 at the time of writing, I still continue to give invited lectures on my research and on GM crops in general. My work for OWSD also continues as my second (and final) term of office as President will end in 2027. Since COVID-19, my travelling has been considerably curtailed, but I am finding that the internet with Zoom and Teams works amazingly well. Thus, my life in retirement is busy, rewarding and extremely interesting.

Bibliography

Thomson, J. 2002. *Genes for Africa: Genetically Modified Crops in the Developing World.* Cape Town: UCT Press.
Thomson, J. 2006. *Seeds for the Future: The Impact of Genetically Modified Crops on the Environment.* Collingwood: CSIRO Publishing.
Thomson, J. 2013. *Food for Africa: The life and work of a scientist in GM crops.* Cape Town: UCT Press.
Thomson, J. 2021a. *GM Crops and the Global Divide.* Collingwood: CSIRO Publishing.
Thomson, J. 2021b. *Travels with my Lab Notebook.* Self-published.
Wittstock, C. 2014. *Blazing a Biotechnology Trail: celebrating biotechnology excellence in South Africa.* Pretoria: Public Understanding of Biotechnology. Available at https://www.pub.ac.za/wp-content/uploads/2015/06/web-NRF%20coffee%20table%20bookwith%20bleed.pdf Retrieved on 25 May 2024.

15

THE TRAJECTORY OF RWANDAN WOMEN IN SCIENCE AND TECHNOLOGY

From the Colonial Period to the Digital Era (1894–2023)

Liberata Gahongayire and Innocent Iyakaremye

Introduction

This chapter highlights the trajectory of Rwandan women in science, innovation, and technology (SIT) from the colonial period to the digital era (1894–2023). Rwanda is situated in the heart of Africa between latitudes 1°04′ and 2°51′ south and longitudes 28°45′ and 31°15′ east, on a land area of 26,338 km², including waters (Republic of Rwanda, 2021). According to the 5th population and housing census of 2022, Rwanda's population was 13,246,394, with 6,817,068 females representing 51.5% of the population, which is slightly higher than 6,429,326 males, representing 48.5% of the population (NISR, 2023). In August 2022, at the time of the census, 8.2 million were adults aged 15 years and above, of whom approximately 79% (6.5 million) could read and write with understanding in any language, and 2,954,770 (22.3%) have never been to school. The overall net attendance rate (NAR) was 89.3% in primary education and 22.3% in secondary education and is consistently higher among females than among males (NISR, 2023).

According to the Education Statistical Yearbook 2021/2022, in Rwanda, the proportion of learners in the education system has always been slightly higher among females than among males from 2017 to 2022 (always about 51%). In science, technology, engineering, and mathematics (STEM) in upper secondary, females' representation is always almost 50% (47.6%, 45.6%, 44.7%, 46.2%, and 47.7%, respectively). But looking at the female population in schools, those in STEM were always more than 50% in all these academic years (MINEDUC, 2023, p. 22).

In higher education, women in STEM studies vary between 31.1% and 36.4%. Considering the female population, their representation in STEM subjects has consistently increased since the academic year 2016/2017, with 29.1%, 29.1%, 32.1%, 38.4%, and 44.8% respectively (MINEDUC, 2023, p. 40).

According to the 2022 census, 14% of the population aged ten years old and above use the Internet, and 64% of them use it from their homes. Sixty-two point nine per cent (62.9%) of residents aged 21 years and above own a mobile phone, and this ownership is slightly higher among the males (86.2% of males aged 21 years and above versus 79% of females of the same age) (NISR, 2023)

Rwanda is currently recognized as a global leader in women's political participation. For the period 2013–2018, 64% of seats in the parliament were occupied by women, and for the period (2018–2023), women's seats were 61% (GMO, 2019). In 2022, this country ranked first in Africa and sixth globally in closing the gender gap.[8] At this point, a slight downfall was observed in 2023 with the coverage of 79.4% and 12th position (World Economic Forum, 2023).

These figures show a high position of the country in terms of covering the gender gap in general and women in SIT in particular, as compared with other countries worldwide and on the African continent (World Economic Forum, 2023). However, this did not happen without the efforts and strategies of various institutions, bodies, and individuals, including women's initiatives as active agents, especially after the 1994 genocide against the Tutsi. It was during colonial times (1894–1962) that formal education started in Rwanda, with German presence first, then with Belgian control, although without noticeable success (Erny, 1974, p. 707). However, from the colonial period until this particular point in time (1994), women's formal education had never been recognized as a priority, and no special attention was drawn to women's studies in science, innovation, and technology.

During the colonial period, girls' education programmes trained them for a variety of professions, such as nursing, teaching, and social work. Girls were also introduced to good household management and housekeeping. In the post-colonial era, the colonial system still influenced girls' education in Rwanda. In the 1960s, children who were completing primary school but could not access secondary education even if they had good results had a programme implemented for them. This was post-primary in this vein, in 1962, a household management programme *(Enseignement complementaire familial)* was introduced. It became a three-year programme in 1969. The focus was on training future housewives for marriage with the new elite. In 1970, an almost similar programme for boys was created as a trial in the form of rural agricultural, technical, and crafting teaching centres (Erny, 1974, p. 716).

However, after the 1994 genocide against the Tutsi, the Rwandan government significantly invested in gender equality promotion in securing a conducive legal, structural, and institutional framework in line with global, continental, and regional orientation, which has allowed other international, national, and local stakeholders to contribute. Women themselves were motivated and contributed with their last energy. Already just after the genocide was stopped, Pro Femmes/Twese Hamwe, a Rwandan organization promoting women's rights, peace, and development, encouraged women's participation in the Gacaca jurisdiction. They advocated a gender sensitive integration in Gacaca law development and implementation and held awareness sessions for 100,000 women leaders, local government representatives, and detainees. Women have played various roles, such as witnesses, judges, advocates, and bridges to local communities, and have even adopted children (Gahongayire, 2016, p. 307).

Women have also contributed to the writing of the 2003 Constitution, which secured them 30% of positions in addition to having the right to compete for the remaining 70% (Republic of Rwanda, 2023). The government's encouragement and guarantee of freedom took women higher and higher in all aspects, including the areas of SIT.

Therefore, the present chapter reconstitutes this trajectory of Rwandan women in SIT from the colonial period to the digital era (1894–2023) in order to appreciate their agency and suggest ways to consolidate it. It responds to three questions: What is the historical background of women's education in SIT in Rwanda? What are the opportunities that have created a conducive environment for women's education and involvement in SIT? And what was women's agency in this journey?

Methods

Marcel Hertfelt's 1968 inaugural lecture emphasizes that history is a disciplined method of interpreting past traces, including human, zoological, botanical, and geological aspects. He highlights Africa's history from the Neolithic era, describing it as the cradle of humankind, characterized by agricultural advancements and animal domestication (*Rwanda Carrefour d'Afrique*, 1969, pp. 5–11). Likewise, this chapter used historical data and methodology to examine secondary data on Rwandan women's education in SIT, both at secondary and higher education levels since the colonial period, as well as the initiated support for this perspective, women's agency on this journey, and challenges faced along the way until the year 2023.

The main highlights are the historical background of women in SIT since the colonial period, opportunities that have contributed to the change of stereotypes, and the agency of women for the improvement of women's access, use, and excellence in SIT. Data collection exploration relied on a wide variety of secondary sources, including published and unpublished materials. To frame the context and insights into the historical period of Rwandan women in SIT, we conducted data search in government archives that have been preserved over time, such as government records, diaries, letters, newspapers, and photographs available in the Rwandan National Library and Royal Museum for Central Africa (RMCA) located at Tervuren in Belgium and in the library of the Dominican Congregation in Kigali City, Rwanda. In the spirit of Marc Bloch (Bloch, 1952) and Antoine Prost (Voldman, 1996), we employ a historical method of data analysis to reveal the real story of women's advancement in science education. We identify, comprehend, and evaluate the efforts of women engaged in educating girls and women in SIT so they can master the modern world through writings and publications from the colonial and post-colonial eras to the present time.

Findings

The findings of this research are structured according to the three questions mentioned above. Thus, they revolve around the historical background of women's education in SIT in Rwanda. The initiatives that have supported women in SIT since the colonial and post-colonial eras up to 2023 and the women's agency as active agents involved in this journey.

The Historical Background of Women's Education in SIT in Rwanda

The historical background of women's education in SIT explores the matter, looking first at the historical context of formal education in Rwanda, especially since the colonial period. Then, the focus is put on women's and men's education in SIT from the colonization era to the 1994 genocide against the Tutsi, and lastly, during the post-genocide period up to 2023.

The Historical Context of Formal Education in Rwanda

Drawing on Denise Bentrovato's (2016) analysis of the politics of education in Rwanda, ethnicity was a central factor that determined access to means of schooling in colonized Rwanda. The establishment of education during the colonial period was slow, especially given the fact that it was imported from outside. However, until 1962, the time of independence of this country, primary education was expanded, although it was not strong. The double shift started in 1959, where one teacher would be in charge of two classes, one in the morning and the other in the afternoon, and in 1962, primary education was compulsory for all children (Erny, 1974, pp. 707, 711, 712).

Bentrovato's analysis informs us that secondary education was initiated in 1929 with the Astrida School complex (Groupe Scolaire d'Astrida), a prestigious secondary school in Ruanda-Urundi (current Rwanda and Burundi) created by the Brothers of Charity, one of the Catholic Church congregations. It educated students who would form an élite to serve as chiefs and medical, agricultural, and veterinary assistants in the Belgian mandate over Ruanda-Urundi. It enrolled students, often the children of chiefs and other dignitaries, from both modern-day Rwanda and Burundi (Bentrovato, 2016, pp. 56–58). However, apart from the importance of the politics of education analysis, this author's work remains insensitive to the gender and women aspect.

At the time, it was not essential for the mother-to-be to know how to read and write or how to calculate in order to be a good mother (Thiry, 1999). In her article, Anne Cornet shows that the missionary sisters worked alongside the Rwandan nuns to teach the women childcare methods and practices. The White Sisters also travelled to the villages to treat Rwandans who were unable to go to the dispensary because of their illness (Cornet, 2014, p. 41).

Therefore, at the beginning of colonial times, education was managed by the Catholic Church, and priority was given to boys in both primary and secondary education. Secondary schools for boys were opened before 1930, including the School of Monitors of Save, Minor Seminary of Kabgayi, and College of Astrida (Groupe Scolaire Officiel). It was not until 1939 that the first post-primary school was opened for girls. All this was due to the patriarchal ideology of colonialists together with the Catholic Church, with which mixing girls and boys in schools was prohibited, and this has limited girls from attending, although it was addressed with time. Thus, in 1952, middle teacher training for lay women teachers colleges like Byimana (Centre) and Rwaza (North West) was opened, and nursing sections were established in Kabgayi (Centre) and Rwamagana (East of the country). Protestant education, which was more tolerant of mixed pupils, was not managed well due to a lack of support from the colonial administration (Pro Femmes Twese Hamwe, 2000, p. 12).

Girls in secondary school were not prepared for higher education, as this required one to complete the first seven years of secondary school education (humanities). This limited access to education for girls was not addressed until 1975, the International Women's Year, when a few women campaigned for greater access (Pro Femmes Twese Hamwe, 2000). From the 1980s onwards, the Rwandan education system, based on ethnic quotas, moved away from a logic of control and allowed the emergence of "initiatives" by parents and others concerned with education and culture to create private secondary schools. This change marked a break from the previous educational philosophy of regional and ethnic quotas. It led to a strengthening of state regulation mechanisms, in parallel with the rise in power of parents' associations and the state's commitment to openness (Rugengande, 2007). Given the fields in which girls are trained, openings and preamble in the STEM field are limited.

Currently, in Rwanda, the preambles preparing the students for their future careers is decided upon after three years of secondary education (lower secondary level). After sitting for the national exam, pupils now select their specialization, which lasts three years before sitting for another national exam, leading to having a secondary school certificate, which is the basis of eligibility to be admitted to particular disciplines in higher education. For this reason, for each period considered, the two following sections shed light on women's education in SIT in secondary education and then in tertiary (higher) education.

Women in SIT Education between Colonization and the 1994 Genocide against the Tutsi

Secondary Education

Since colonization up to the 1994 genocide against the Tutsi, women's education in SIT in secondary schools was overlooked and sometimes contested. The report made by Haguruka in 2001 noted that during the colonial period, educational institutions were created and managed by the Catholic Church but did not accommodate girls adequately (Haguruka, 2001). It qualifies this neglect as a noticeable sign of the reinforcement of gender-based inequality in Rwandan education.

The initial schools created all over the country included schools and seminaries such as Kabgayi, Karubanda, Nyundo, Saint André, Byumba, Save, Collège Officiel de Kigali, Christ-Roi, Groupe Scolaire de Butare, and Musanze. Other schools were opened over the years to promote the role of girls and women in the homes. These schools were given different French names like *Ecole Ménagère, Foyers Sociaux, Ecoles Familiales*, and *Ecole Sociale*, whose meaning revolves around house or family care and household management, thus displaying their ultimate goals. For example, since their arrival in 1909, the Missionary Sisters of Notre Dame d'Afrique, known as the Soeurs Blanches (White Sisters), were involved in the creation of girls' schools, starting with Save and looking after the health of the local population, depending on where the Catholic missions were set up. From the year 1913 up to 1953, they created seven schools in the centre (Save, Kabgayi, Astrida-Butare, Nyanza), the north (Nyundo, Rwaza), and the east (Zaza) of the country (Bashige, 1989, pp. 138–139). For years, the management of these schools passed from the White Sisters to the Rwandan nuns, who were called natives and are now the *Benebikira sisters* and the auxiliary sisters, with the exception of the lay sisters of the girls' scientific school in Nyundo in the north.

Meanwhile, other schools were added to the existing seven schools focusing on social, nursing, housekeeping, and education schools initiated and managed by the White Sisters. These new ones were created by the Bernardine Sisters (Lycée Notre Dame de Cîteaux -1960), the Auxiliary Sisters (Karubanda Social School), the Sisters of St. Francis of Assisi, or Penitent Sisters (Institut Sancta Familia Nyamasheke-1952). With this momentum, girls' schools were built little by little and were created and managed by the sisters from various Catholic congregations established in the national territory. Thus, girls' opportunities for studies evolved slowly and offered almost similar social and care programmes, neglecting the subjects related to science and technology. Until 2008, when the girls' education policy was established, women in SIT were not understood as a priority (MINEDUC, 2008).

Tertiary Education

Tertiary education started in Rwanda in 1963 with the *Université Nationale du Rwanda* (UNR), and the initial students were predominantly males. The University opened its doors to around fifty students in three faculties: *Ecole Normale* (Teacher Training), Social Sciences and Economics, and Medicine (*Rwanda Carrefour d'Afrique*, 1968, p. 2). According to the Rwanda Carrefour d'Afrique in February 1969, the Faculty of Agronomy opened its doors in 1969. UNR planned to offer a bachelor's degree in economics and management. Still, it was not until 1972 that this project came to fruition, with eight candidates, including one girl (*Rwanda Carrefour d'Afrique*, 1972).

In his speech on July 7, 1972, at the closing of the academic year, Mr. Sylvestre Nsanzimana, the then Rector of UNR, highlighted that despite Rwanda's national constitution and school legislation promoting equality in education, the 1972 academic year at the NUR saw a distinct situation: out of 471 students, 46 (9.8%) were female, comprising 19 in the nursing school (not medicine, which was men's portion) and 27 in other faculties, highlighting the unique challenges faced by women in education at that point of time (*Rwanda Carrefour d'Afrique*, 1972, p. 4). The rector did not provide details about the girls in other departments, nor did he mention the issue of science and technology; instead, he focused on promoting equality for access to education under the Rwandan constitution.

It should be pointed out here that apart from a few exceptions for those who had the opportunity to study abroad, the UNR and *Institut Pedagogique National* (IPN) in the 1970s and 1980s were the only places for public tertiary education, in addition to the Catholic Seminary of Nyakibanda (Bureau National de Recensement, 1984:106). The analysis of the annual reports of the UNR from 1982/1983 to 1985/1986 shows a slight increase in the number of girls who graduated from this institution: 63 females versus 464 males (12.0%) in STEM (Medicine, Human Biology, Public health, Nutrition, Pharmacy, Chemistry, Mathematics, Physics, Biology, Civil engineering, Agronomics, and Textile). There were no females in Mathematics, Physics, Biology, and Civil engineering. For non-STEM programmes, there were 121 females against 688 males (15%). In total, the graduates for all four years of bachelor (Baccalaureat) and bachelor with honours (*Licence*) degrees were 1336, of whom 184 (13.8%) were females (UNR, 1986).

During the period prior to the 1994 genocide against the Tutsi, women were less represented than men, who occupied 86% of university posts in both STEM and non-STEM fields. This low representation can be explained by the small number of girls in secondary schools awarding eligible university and science degrees. The high number of graduates were in the faculties of sciences of education and medicine.

Women in SIT Education during the Post-genocide Era: Increase in Strategies and Numbers

Secondary Education

The current government of Unity, led by His Excellency Paul Kagame, is known as a champion in promoting gender equality globally. This was observed right from the introduction of its vision, especially in the 2003 Constitution as revised in 2015 and 2023, where women are granted at least 30% of positions in all decision-making services in addition to their rights to compete for the remaining 70% (Republic of Rwanda, 2023 Art.10:d). This constitutional and political standpoint will influence other legal and strategic development and planning. Thus, both the Rwandan Economic Development and Poverty Reduction Strategies (2008–2012 and 2013–2018), The National Strategy for Transformation 2017–2024 (NST1), and policies and strategies for implementation take gender and women empowerment as a cross-cutting subject that has been mainstreamed in all aspects of development initiatives. It was in this context that the equal integration of women and girls into all programmes and levels of education, including in SIT, was now taken seriously. However, women's adherence to this ultimate initiative has also played a crucial role.

As a result of this vision, the Education Statistics Yearbook 2021/2022 shows that since the year 2017/2018 to 2021/2022, females constitute nearly 50% of the students in SIT education programmes at the secondary school level. They were 47.6%, 45.6%, 44.2%, 46.2%, and 47.7% respectively. Women's percentages in STEM were higher in government-subsidized institutions, where they were more than males, with 54.4%, 54.0%, 54.7%, 54.0%, and 54.9%, respectively. They were less represented in private schools where gender equality is less scrutinized, with 34.2%, 33.8%, 30.6%, 25.7%, and 33.5%, respectively (MINEDUC, 2023, p. 40).

Compared with the population of women in other fields of education, the proportions of women (like men) in SIT are always higher. For the whole country, women in SIT programmes were 51.4%, 51.6%, 50.7%, 48.4%, and 57.4% from 2017/2018 to 2021/2022, respectively. The proportion of women in SIT programme was higher in public institutions, with 55.8%, 55%, 54.2%, 48.1%, and 60.5%, respectively. Still, private institutions are the ones less populated by women in SIT, with 42%, 42.9%, 38.1%, 39.9%, and 51.5%, respectively (MINEDUC, 2023, p. 40).

Nevertheless, in spite of these high numbers, the attitude is yet to be totally positive for the possibility of women's integration into SIT. In this regard, a study conducted by Wuyts et al. (2022) among secondary school students in Kayonza District revealed that males show more interest in the pursuit of STEM programmes in school, while the subjects related to life and health attract more women than men (Wuyts, Meeusen and Draulans, 2022). In addition, both male and female students assert that males are superior in mathematics and ICT. Such thoughts and views that are still noticeable among secondary school students seem to be a reflection of what they live in their community and may constitute an obstacle to women's exploration and extension of their potential in SIT disciplines.

Tertiary Education

The Rwandan tertiary education system has experienced significant growth since 1994, from hundreds of students in four private universities to 31,170 students in 13 private higher learning institutions in 2010. In the same year (2010), the public higher education network had expanded significantly as well, with 17 institutions serving 31,564 students, thus reflecting the country's evolution through a century of reforms (Kamuzinzi, 2012, pp. 4–5). Concerning women's education examined together with men's education in STEM, the MINEDUC report of 2023 (MINEDUC, 2023, p. 40) shows that for five academic years: 2016/2017, 2017/2018, 2018/2019, 2020/2021, and 2021/2022, women were 33.8% and men 66.2% in the country. Women were 30% in public institutions and 40% in private institutions. Comparing women in STEM with women in other fields of studies for the same period, they were higher in the academic year 2021/2022, with 44.8%. Previously, they were 29.1%, 29.1%, 32.1%, and 38.4%, respectively. They were higher in public institutions, with 50.1%, 47.2%, 52.9%, 62.6%, and

68.3%, respectively. For private tertiary education, women's representation in STEM was always lower, with 19.4%, 20.7%, 22.9%, 27.2%, and 25.6%, respectively (MINEDUC, 2023, p. 42).

As regards public tertiary institutions, the University of Rwanda (UR) was established in 2013 by the government through law No 71/2013 of 10/09/2013. It resulted from a merger of seven public tertiary institutions: the National University of Rwanda (NUR), Kigali Institute of Science and Technology (KIST), Kigali Institute of Education (KIE), Institute of Agriculture and Animal Husbandry (ISAE), Kigali Health Institute (KHI), School of Finance and Banking (SFB), and Umutara Polytechnic (UP). Now, they formed one higher learning entity with six colleges: the College of Arts and Social Sciences (CASS); the College of Agriculture, Animal Sciences, and Veterinary Medicine (CAVM); the College of Business and Economics (CBE); the College of Education (CE); the College of Medicine and Health Sciences (CMHS); and the College of Science and Technology (CST) (University of Rwanda, 2018, pp. 5–7).

The 2018 UR report provides a retrospective statistical analysis of the University of Rwanda's graduates, student enrolment, staff, publications, and infrastructure development over the past five years. The report aims to address discrepancies in the University's statistical data bank due to missing or duplicate information. The University of Rwanda graduated 32,938 people, with 54% in non-STEM, 46% in STEM areas, and 36% female and 64% male over five years, from 2013 to 2017. Non-STEM female attendance was 19%, and 16% was in STEM. The percentage of men doing non-STEM was 34%, while 30% were in STEM (University of Rwanda, 2018, pp. 1–11).

The statistical analysis of the area of studies from 2013 up to 2022 at the UR revealed that the enrolment of students in STEM programmes was 57% against 43% in non-STEM subjects (University of Rwanda, 2022, p. 8). Only 35% of these students were women, with a proportion of 19% (versus 38% for men) in STEM and 16% (against 27% for men) in non-STEM disciplines (University of Rwanda, 2022, p. 8). As for graduates for this period, women were 36% (against 64% of men) in STEM and 37% (against 63% of men) in non-STEM, which makes 37% of women and 63% of men graduates in total (University of Rwanda, 2022, p. 36).

Regarding the fields most frequented by women, this report shows that for the year 2021/2022, the proportion of women's enrolment compared to men's enrolment was higher in the College of Business and Economics (CBE) (48.5%) followed by College of Agriculture and Veterinary Medicine (CAVM) (43.4%) and College of Education (CE) (40.1%). Women's propositions were less in the College of Science and Technology (CST) (31.6%) (University of Rwanda, 2022:7). Looking at the level of colleges, women's proportions were higher in CE (29.3%) and CBE (20.0%), followed by CST (15.9%), CAVM (14.4%), and CMHS (13.4%). The CASS was the least represented in the number of women, with 6.9% (University of Rwanda, 2022, p. 7).

At the University of Rwanda graduation on November 17, 2023, females were 3,258 out of 8,321 (39%), all colleges together. In CST, they were 429/1,323 (32%) and 512/1361 (38%) in CMHS. Out of the 38 PhD graduates, 13 (34.2%) were women. In CST, there was only one female out of ten in total (10%), and in CMHS, there were two out of five (40.0%) (Rwanda, 2023).

It is visible here that the proportion of women in tertiary education, as compared with men, is still low. However, compared with the situation before the 1994 genocide against the

Tutsi, there are significant improvements. For example, in secondary education, the low representation of women in science-related subjects is influenced by historical cultural stereotypes toward female capacities in sciences.

As will be highlighted later, the government of Rwanda and the University of Rwanda, in particular, have developed policies to promote education in science and technology. However, many women are still hesitant to select these subjects, thinking that they are beyond their capacities. The journal article published on female students' participation in Higher Education showed that women in the non-pure science-related disciplines are the most privileged (Rubagiza, Umutoni, and Iyakaremye, 2022, p. 137). Students are encouraged to select science-related subjects, and sometimes candidates are admitted to these subjects even when they did not mention them as their preference. In this case, women are more likely to withdraw from this admission in order to find another field of study or to go to private universities, which are more flexible with respect to the candidate's choice.

In addition, 80% of the scholarship loans received from the government are dedicated to STEM (Science) fields of study. Thus, females' under-representation in these subjects leads to the scarcity of female role models in professions related to science and technology. Therefore, from 9.8% representation of women in all public higher learning institutions in Rwanda in 1972 to the average of 12% representation in STEM for the Period 1982/1983–1985/1986, and the average of 35% in STEM for the period 2013–2022 at the University of Rwanda, there is a visible increase of women representation in science that need to be celebrated. All these efforts have resulted in a number of women's figures in the area of STEM careers and professions. However, there is still a need to know what has caused this success that had been missing in previous periods. The following section seeks to highlight the opportunities that have enabled women to participate actively in SIT in Rwanda.

Opportunities That Have Paved the Way for Women's Participation in SIT in Rwanda

As alluded to above, these achievements did not come out of the blue; strategies were developed in order to ensure that women's integration and involvement in SIT are promoted. These strategies start with the 2003 Constitution as revised in 2015 and 2023. Article 10:d of the Constitution stipulates that *"The State of Rwanda commits itself to upholding and ensuring respect for the following fundamental principles: … (d) building a state governed by the rule of law, a pluralistic democratic Government, equality of all Rwandans and between women and men which is affirmed by women occupying at least 30% of positions in decision-making organs…"*. This commitment opened the door to gender equality in all aspects of development to the point that gender equality and women empowerment have been cross-cutting themes in all development programmes ever since.

This principle was respected in all the national development documents, including Economic Development and Poverty Reduction Strategies (EDPRS I: 2008–2012; EDPRS II: 2013–2018) and National Strategy for Transformation (Government of Rwanda, 2017), as well as the Vision 2050 (Minicofin, 2015). These national documents were also aligned with the Continental Agenda 2063 (African Union, 2015) and the global development agendas such as the Millenium Development Goals (MDG) (UN Documentation, 2000) Sustainable Development Goals (SDGs) (The United Nations, 2017), and the UNESCO Convention against Discrimination in Education (UNESCO, 1990), which prohibits actions that jeopardize girls' access to all areas, levels, and acceptable conditions of schooling. The World

Declaration on Education for All (UNESCO, 1990), article 3 prioritizes girls' access to quality education and sufficient conditions, as well as specific groups such as adolescents and disabled persons. In these documents, women and girls and gender are included either as a standalone subject, a cross-cutting theme, or both. Likewise, technology is the pillar that supports every single initiative of the expected outcome of these national, continental, and global instruments.

Women's education in SIT is stipulated also in education sector policies and plans. These include the *Girls' Education Policy* of 2008 (MINEDUC, 2008). This policy seeks to promote and diversify technical and vocational education and training (TVET) and remove all gender stereotypes in the choice of vocation. Thus, the government created technical schools in each province in order to allow offering and diversifying programmes for both boys' and girls' opportunities to participate. In this perspective, the government promised incentives to girls who enter the occupations traditionally known as for boys and to boys who choose to enter those occupations traditionally known as female. In addition, the policy offers to put in place measures to promote the participation of girls in science and technology and other learning opportunities. In secondary and tertiary education, special measures were taken for girls' participation in science and technology-related fields. The government provides two years of free tuition fees for girls in science and technology. Also, it identifies and empowers women role models in teaching science and technology (MINEDUC, 2008, pp. 21–22).

In 2016, Rwanda developed the policy of ICT in education, with four objectives: creating a content and relevant ICT professional base to meet industry needs, increasing ICT penetration and usage at all educational levels, developing education leadership and teachers' capacity and capabilities in and through ICT, as well as enhancing teaching, learning, and research through ICT integration in high learning institutions (MINEDUC, 2016, pp. 5–6).

The National Council for Science and Technology (NCST) was also created by law no 40/2017 of 16/08/2017. It aims to enable Rwanda to become a country based on SIT as a tool for promoting social welfare, sustainable socio-economic development of the country, and competitiveness in the market. The central role involves advising the government on science, technology, research, and innovation policies, setting national priorities, identifying new sectors for innovation, analyzing resource efficiency, regulating innovation and research, managing the National Research and Innovation Fund, promoting outreach activities, preparing annual reports, and collaborating with other institutions of excellence. They also analyze national resources and infrastructures for sustainable use.

In 2020, the *Science, Technology, and Innovation Policy* was developed. One of its objectives is to increase research and development and innovation financing. One of the ways of meeting this objective is diversifying the initiatives in order to promote women in SIT (MINEDUC, 2020, p. 18).

At the lower levels of education, Rwanda has introduced a new "New Competence-Based Curriculum" for pre-primary to upper secondary education in 2019, focusing on STEM and ICT-led education. The Ministry of Education has partnered with technology-enabled companies like Microsoft, O'Genius Panada, Zora Robotics, Class VR, and Keza to incorporate STEM and ICT-enabled education, promoting transferable skills like critical thinking, problem-solving, and creativity (AUDA-NEPAD, 2021). The National Gender Policy revised in 2021 has provided for the promotion of girls' and women's education in science and technology as well. Objective 3 of this policy reads, *"Improve the implementation of gender equality and equity principles in education, health, and social protection"*. The actions associated with this objective include bridging the gender divide gap in ICT, STEM, and TVET education programmes at all levels of education (3.1.1.). In addition, the policy suggests that families should be engaged in promoting such an education (MIGEPROF, 2021, p. 39).

In harmony with this national orientation, the University of Rwanda has developed a Gender Policy (University of Rwanda, 2016) and a strategic plan for 2017–2024 (Government of Rwanda, 2017) where the matters of inclusion in all aspects are catered for. This fact led to the development of projects with high-level gender sensitivity. For example, the Mastercard Foundation project provides scholarships to postgraduate students, and two of its clauses specify that 70% of all the scholarships are accorded to females and that 80% of all the scholarships are given to students in science-related programmes (University of Rwanda, 2022).

Therefore, it is clear here that these development instruments and policies have created an environment where any initiatives towards promoting women and girls in science and technology are encouraged and supported. The following section sheds light on women's contribution to what the country is celebrating in terms of women's education in SIT.

Women's Agency

Women's agency is understood here as women's contribution as active agents in their journey to becoming literate and experts in SIT. Although there were conducive opportunities, as explored above, women were also contributors to the steps they made. Their contributions do not constitute isolated initiatives. They are somewhat connected to each other and are boosted and protected by the political will and conducive environment already created by the international and national community. It implies acknowledging the influence of the Beijing Declaration and Platform of Action (United Nations, 1995) and CEDAW (UN Women, 1979) in making women aware of their rights and daring to reclaim them. It is hard to promise to exhaust all the networks available to women in Rwanda in order to develop the skills in SIT. The following paragraphs mention some of them in order to argue that the terrain is well-prepared for women in STEM perspective.

One of the networks through which women act to mobilize their potential for the agency is the Forum for African Women Educationalists (FAWE). It is a pan-African women's organization, which supports girls and women's education for development. FAWE motivates girls to join the fields of Science, Engineering, and Technology. Together with its partners, FAWE Rwanda has initiated girls' schools and centres of excellence as part of the sensitization of women in these fields. FAWE also provides scholarships of many kinds to women doing science and technology as their field of education (FAWE-Rwanda Chapter, 2021).

Women in Tech Africa (WITA) is another network that supports women in technology in Africa and impacts their communities positively. Women in Tech Africa believe that women can do whatever men can do anywhere, including performing in technology in Africa. Therefore, they seek to enhance African women's capacities to achieve their professional dreams, develop and connect with women leaders and role models, and develop Africa through technology (Womenintechafrica, n.d.). This network was launched in Rwanda in March 2019 by Minister Paula Ingabire, Minister of ICT and Innovation, who requested all women to access and use technology because it is very beneficial.

Moreover, the initiative "Girls in ICT", tries to increase the number of girls and women in ICT-related fields. It is a group of young and adult women who are already in professional life, as well as those who are still in school, who work together to help girls understand, like, and do STEM. It was initiated in Rwanda in 2011 and is celebrated annually together with International Girls in ICT (GMO, 2017, p. 21). The celebration of girls in ICT day brings high school girls together to showcase ICT companies and solutions, promoting STEM career paths. The MsGeek competition inspires female university/TVET students to think critically and design solutions for Rwandan issues. "Girls in ICT" also conducts awareness campaigns in partnership with the Ministry of ICT and Youth, educating girls about STEM career paths and sharing experiences. The Girls in ICT mentorship programme aims to provide high school, university, and newly working young women in Rwanda with the knowledge, skills, and experience of Rwanda's women in STEM. The programme visits schools, organizes events, and conducts one-on-one mentorship for diverse students and women, including business leaders, software engineers, engineers, and policymakers. The programme aims to build partnerships and create a critical mass of Rwandan women in STEM (Girls in ICT Rwanda, 2018).

"Resonate initiative" is another initiative co-founded in 2013 by Ayla Schlosser and Solange Impanoyimana, putting in place the "Rise And STEM" programme to support women and girls to participate and advance in STEM through capacity-building and leadership training (Resonate, n.d.). In Rwanda, the Rise and STEM programme targets rural or disadvantaged girls studying at secondary or tertiary levels, as well as recent graduates in the fields of STEM. They support their training or organize workshops with them on soft skills, lifestyle, self-management, professional life, and other various ways of capacity building and interaction with professional mentors.

The "WeCode", another woman's initiative, is a high-class software development and coding training to support women in the innovation and ICT field. It aims to address the gender digital divide in the ICT sector by providing quality training to women, addressing gender bias from employers, and promoting women's representation. In Rwanda, it involves Moringa, GIZ, and the Rwandan government and has helped many women gain access to the tech sector (Mugabo, 2020).

Furthermore, the "She Can Code" initiative is another women's programme that trains young women aged 18–25 to code and build web design and applications in Rwanda. The programme, funded by UN Women Rwanda and the Multi-Partner Trust Fund/SIDA, has graduated the seventh cohort of 52 students by December 9, 2022. The programme was founded in 2018, focusing on mobile or web application development, leadership, entrepreneurship, and career coaching. The students create projects to solve community problems and are prepared to serve ICT companies and use their skills to solve community problems (UN WOMEN -Africa, 2023).

The Rwandan Association for Women in Science and Engineering (RAWISE) is another women's network that also promotes the participation of women in science, technology, engineering, and decision-making processes. RAWISE suggests that women are still freshly skilled people who can make changes for development. They organize workshops in order to initiate girls STEM-related skills and professions for their future and development (RAWISE, 2023).

These institutions and bodies are numerous, and they work day and night in order to support women in STEM. It is worth observing here that all of them work in synergy, some at the international level and others at national and local levels. It is also observed that none is enough in itself, which means that cooperation and partnership are always necessary. Moreover, individual beneficiaries are not inactive. Otherwise, even these institutions' efforts would yield nothing. In this vein, at the graduation ceremony organized by the University of Rwanda on November 17, 2023, one of the female PhD graduates in the College of Medicine and Health Science, responding to the interview of Rwanda Television, was very excited about having completed her studies. She testified that this was not the end of learning and that it was really feasible rather than what people used to think. She also promised to encourage and support other women who are still hesitating so that they can value and positively use their potential as well (LIVE: University of Rwanda Graduation ceremony, 2023 | Musanze, November 17 2023, 2023). These accounts, as well as this testimony, confirm the view that women are able and can do whatever men can do, although they always need to cooperate with other institutions and bodies.

Discussion

According to Pamela Abbot and Marklin Rocogoza's report, women are not "the second sex". Rwanda is the first country in the world to have more than 50% women in its parliament. The law requires that at least 30% of the positions in decision-making bodies at the national, regional, and local levels be held by women (Abbot and Rucogoza, 2011).

Ever since the colonial period, data has unceasingly illustrated that girls have been sensitized girls to pursue non-STEM related subjects like hospitality, education, and others that did not allow them to venture into scientific fields, going as far as creating a marginalization cycle that made them stall in their development by not equipping them enough for an opportunity to go into these fields and manage to perform as their counterpart males. Academic authorities, such as the heads of schools and religious community-led schools, mainly drove this situation. Regardless of that situation, in 1967, a science school in Nyundo was launched that was specifically for girls, and it saw exponential growth in solving that inequality.

In the post-1994 era of rebuilding the nation, there were reforms that were supposed to eradicate all forms of discrimination and bring equality in education among all students, whether boys or girls, and that started the promotion of equality and its ideology development of women empowerment and its emphasis along the way among Rwandans. It is with that line of thought that Rwanda has put forward a culture of generating solutions for societal challenges from within and from all the people of the country equally. It is in consistency with this idea that the government has put together means to engage everyone in that solution generation, like enabling young girls to access that education easily in many scholarship opportunities to equip them with all the necessary skills to actively take a significant part in the development seeking for inner generated solutions that are inclusive.

Therefore, although women's capacity in SIT was not valued in the former Rwanda, today, most people have come to appreciate the importance of women's participation and leadership in SIT. Through the present discussion, it is understood that such an achievement cannot be attributed to one single entity, institution or individual. It is the result of work in synergy with various partners at international, national, and local levels. However, the government is always expected to support and create a conducive environment to mainstream the matter within policy and law development, as well as planning. In other words, such success does not come on its own. It is fought for, and women are part of it. In addition, even though there was a visible improvement, parity is still yet to be achieved in Rwanda, at least in tertiary education. This means that although there is still a long way to go, there is hope that it will be achieved.

Conclusion

Throughout this chapter, the journey of researching and closely analyzing the deeds of women in SIT from the past was variously described and drawn in the trajectory of Rwandan women in SIT during the last 129 years, from colonial times up to 2023. The chapter highlights challenging moments where women's capacity in SIT was ignored, neglected, and wasted. However, we are now in another era when their potential is being sustained, cared for, and given value. Thus, there were various actions and initiatives to support women in SIT, including mentorship, training, and networking opportunities, as well as efforts to challenge gender stereotypes and biases in these fields. Currently in Rwanda, young and adult women have room to develop their potential and skills in SIT. But gender parity is yet to be achieved, so there is still a long way to go. The achievement will be secured if partners work in synergy and with passion. And much as this chapter has provided rich information, there is no pretence that it has exhausted the issue of women's education in SIT in Rwanda. For example, an empirical study providing first-hand information on each aspect would bring more clarity on some aspects, such as the impact of the increasing numbers of women in SIT in Rwanda. However, as this chapter has highlighted, there has been, and there is, reassuring progress in women's active and meaningful participation in SIT in Rwanda.

Bibliography

Abbot, P. and Rucogoza, M. (2011). *Legal and Policy Framework for Gender Equality and the Empowerment of Women in Rwanda*. Kigali. Available at: https://docplayer.net/64173458-Legal-and-policy-framework-for-gender-equality-and-the-empowerment-of-women-in-rwanda-pamela-abbott-and-marklin-rucogoza.html (Accessed: December 13, 2023).

African Union. (2015). *Agenda 2063. The Africa we want*. Addis Ababa. Available at: https://au.int/sites/default/files/documents/33126-doc-framework_document_book.pdf.

AUDA-NEPAD. (2021). *Rwanda as a Model: Improving STEM Education Curricula In Africa*. Available at: https://www.nepad.org/blog/rwanda-model-improving-stem-education-curricula-africa#_ftn1 (Accessed: October 6, 2023).

Bashige, B. (1989). *Action éducative des soeurs missionaires de notre -dame d'Afrique dans l'enseignement au rwanda 1938-1973*. Mémoire, faculté des sciences de l'éducation. Université Nationale du Rwanda. Campus universitaire de Ruhengeri.

Bentrovato, D. (2016). *Narrating and Teaching the Nation: The Politics of Education in Pre- and Post-Genocide Rwanda*. Göttingen: V&R Academic.

Bloch, M. (1952). *APOLOGIE POUR L'HISTOIRE OU*. 2 e édition. Paris: Armand Colin.

Cornet, A. (2014). 'Soigner et guérir au pays des mille collines: de l'activité sanitaire à la quête d'autonomie', *Histoire, monde et cultures religieuses*, 30(2), pp. 33–49.

Erny, P. (1974). 'L'enseignement au Rwanda', *L'école et le Tiers Monde*, 15(59–60), pp. 707–722.

FAWE-Rwanda Chapter (2021). *FAWE Rwanda Chapter – Annual report*. Kigali.

Gahongayire, L. (2016). 'Essay on the role of women in transitional justice in post conflict societies', *International Journal of Innovation and Applied Studies*, 16(2), pp. 304–308.

Girls in ICT Rwanda. (2018). *Girls in ICT Rwanda - Rwanda Women in Technology - #TechNeedsGirls*. Available at: https://www.girlsinict.rw/ (Accessed: October 6 2023).

GMO. (2017). *Gender Profile in Information and Communication Technology (ICT)*. Kigali.

GMO. (2019). *The state of gender equality in Rwanda from transition to transformation*. Kigali. Available at: https://gmo.gov.rw/fileadmin/user_upload/Researches%20and%20Assessments/State%20of%20Gender%20Equality%20in%20Rwanda.pdf.

Government of Rwanda. (2017). *National Strategy for Transformation (NST1) 2017–2024*. Kigali.

Haguruka. (2001). *La femme rwandaise et l'accès à la justice*. Kigali.

Kamuzinzi, M. (2012). 'L'évolution du système éducatif rwandais à travers un siècle de réformes', *Revue internationale d'éducation de Sèvres*, (59), pp. 25–31. Available at: https://doi.org/10.4000/ries.2251.

LIVE: University of Rwanda Graduation ceremony,2023 | Musanze, November 17 2023 (2023). Musanze. Available at: https://www.youtube.com/watch?v=Sg5EdQIvJ2Y (Accessed: December 13 2023).

MIGEPROF. (2021). 'Revised National Gender Policy'. Available at: https://www.migeprof.gov.rw/fileadmin/user_upload/Migeprof/Publications/Guidelines/Revised_National_Gender_Policy-2021.pdf.

MINEDUC. (2008). *Girls education policy*. Kigali.

MINEDUC. (2016). *ICT in education policy*. Kigali. Available at: https://planipolis.iiep.unesco.org/sites/default/files/ressources/rwanda_ict_in_education_policy_approved.pdf.

MINEDUC. (2020). *Science, Technology, and Innovation Policy*. Kigali. Available at: https://www.mineduc.gov.rw/index.php?eID=dumpFile&t=f&f=17135&token=c64ea84e90450da788598d96cc37bcd124d001e7.

MINEDUC. (2023). *2021/22 Education Statistical Yearbook School year ended in July 2022*. Kigali.

Minicofin. (2015). *Vision 2050*. Kigali. Available at: https://www.minecofin.gov.rw/fileadmin/user_upload/Minecofin/Publications/REPORTS/National_Development_Planning_and_Research/Vision_2050/English-Vision_2050_Abridged_version_WEB_Final.pdf.

Mugabo, A. (2020). 'The WeCode Programme: Teaching women in Rwanda how to code', *Digital Transformation Centre Rwanda*. Available at: https://digicentre.rw/the-wecode-programme-why-teaching-women-in-rwanda-how-to-code-is-crucial-for-the-tech-sector/ (Accessed: October 6 2023).

NISR. (2023). *Fifth Population and Housing Census - 2022. Main Indicators Report*. National Institute of Statistics of Rwanda. Available at: https://statistics.gov.rw/datasource/fifth-population-and-housing-census-2022 (Accessed: December 13 2023).

Pro Femmes Twese Hamwe. (2000). *Recherche sur «les raisons de la non scolarisation des filles au rwanda»*. Kigali.

RAWISE (2023). *Welcome to Rawise*. Available at: https://www.rawise.org.rw/ (Accessed: December 13 2023).

Republic of Rwanda. (2021). 'Presidential Order N° 058/01 of 23/04/2021 establishing the National Land Use and Development Master Plan'. Official Gazette n° 15 bis of 26/04/2021.

Republic of Rwanda. (2023). 'Constitution of the Republic Of Rwanda'. Official Gazette n° Special of 04/08/2023.

Rubagiza, J., Umutoni, J. and Iyakaremye, I. (2022). 'Gender-Related Factors Influencing Female Students' Participation in Higher Education in Rwanda', *International Journal of African Higher Education*, 9(2), pp. 124–149. Available at: https://doi.org/10.6017/ijahe.v9i2.15377.

Rugengande, J. (2007). *Développement et diversification de l'enseignement privé en Afrique subsaharienne: l'enseignement privé au Rwanda*. Thèse de Doctorat en Sciences de l'éducation. Université Catolique de Louvain. Available at: file:///C:/Users/hp/Downloads/TheseDraft.pdf.

Rwanda Carrefour d'Afrique. (1968). 'L'UNR fête le 5ème anniversaire de sa fondation: National University of Rwanda celebrates the 5th anniversary of its foundation.' December, p. 2.

Rwanda Carrefour d'Afrique. (1969). 'L'université d'un pays, c'est son cerveau', February, p. 7.

Rwanda Carrefour d'Afrique. (1972). 'Allocution de Monsieur Nsanzimana Sylvestre, Recteur de l'Université Nationale du Rwanda', pp. 3–6.

Rwanda, University of Rwanda. (2023). *Graduation Ceremony Attendance Confirmation (on Friday, November 17, 2023) at Musanze*. Available at: https://ur.ac.rw/?Graduation-Ceremony-Attendance-Confirmation-on-Friday-November-17-2023 (Accessed: December 13 2023).

Thiry, M.-L. (1999). 'Communautés et œuvres des sœurs missionnaires de Notre Dame d'Afrique (Sœurs blanches) au Rwanda. 1909–1999'. Bruxelles.

UN Documentation. (2000). *Millennium Development Goals, 2000–2015*. Available at: https://research.un.org/en/docs/dev/2000-2015 (Accessed: December 13 2023).

UN Women. (1979). *Text of the Convention on the Elimination of All Forms of Discrimination against Women*. Available at: https://www.un.org/womenwatch/daw/cedaw/cedaw.htm (Accessed: December 13 2023).

UN WOMEN-Africa. (2023). *UN Women Rwanda stirs hope among young women through the SheCanCODE software and web development training program.*, *UN Women – Africa*. Available at: https://africa.unwomen.org/en/stories/news/2023/02/un-women-rwanda-stirs-hope-among-young-women-through-the-shecancode-software-and-web-development-training-program (Accessed: October 6 2023).

UNESCO. (1990). *World Declaration on Education for All and Framework for Action to Meet Basic Learning Needs*. Jomtien, Thailand. Available at: https://unesdoc.unesco.org/ark:/48223/pf0000127583 (Accessed: December 13 2023).

United Nations. (1995). *Beijing Declaration and Platform for Action*. Beijing.

University of Rwanda. (2016). *UR-Gender policy*. Kigali. Available at: https://ur.ac.rw/documents/UR%20Gender%20Policy.compressed.pdf.

University of Rwanda. (2018). 'Facts and Figures 2013–2018'. Available at: https://ur.ac.rw/documents/Facts%20and%20Figures-Final-2018B.pdf.

University of Rwanda. (2022). *Facts and Figures 2013–2022*. Available at: https://ur.ac.rw/?-Facts-Figures- (Accessed: November 10 2023).

UNR. (1986). *Yearbooks 1982/1983-1985/1986*. Butare.

Voldman, D. (1996). 'Prost Antoine, Douze leçons sur l'histoire', *Vingtième Siècle. Revue d'histoire*, 52(1), pp. 174–175.

Womenintechafrica (n.d.) About Women in Tech Africa. http://www.womenintechafrica.com/. Accessed 20/11/2023

World Economic Forum. (2023). *Global Gender Gap Report 2022: Insight Report*. Geneva. Available at: https://www.weforum.org/publications/global-gender-gap-report-2022/in-full/1-2-global-results/ (Accessed: December 13 2023).

Wuyts, C., Meeusen, C. and Draulans, V. (2022). *Understanding gender imbalances in STEM fields in Rwanda: Methodological report*. Belgium.

Wuyts, C. et al. (2022). *Understanding gender imbalance in STEM fields in Rwanda. A survey of secondary school students in Kayonza District, Rwanda*. CESO.

16
DEPATRIARCHALISING THE MEDIA COVERAGE OF SCIENCE IN UGANDA

Recovering Women's Voices

Ivan Nathanael Lukanda, Gerald Walulya, Nakiwala Aisha Sembatya and Amon Ashaba Mwiine

Introduction

Depatriarchalisation involves initiatives aimed at reducing the socially constructed superiority of the male gender and socially imposed inferiority of the female gender by supporting the progress of women through empowerment, and change in mentalities and structures that anchor patriarchy (Hammad, 2013). Depatriachalisation of media coverage of science would then mean breaking the socio-cultural barriers that systematically and latently marginalise women's voices in media spaces with the aim of recovering such voices. The areas that need depatriachalisation include gender disparity in media roles of on-screen talent, writers, directors, and producers (Ward & Grower, 2020; Smith & Choueiti, 2010); gender disparity in media content, production and representation, and inclusive representation (Dragaš, 2012); gender gaps in training (Wotschack, 2019); and gender power relations in media with a focus on sexual harassment (ACME, 2019; North, 2016; Orgeret et al., 2020), among others.

This chapter is a response to a chapter published by the first author that showed that female voices are marginalised in media coverage of science in Uganda, both as authors and sources (Lukanda, 2020). Such margination is against the legal provisions in Uganda. The 1995 Uganda Constitution provides for equality before the law for men and women, as well as women's rights and affirmative action for women (Republic of Uganda Constitution, 1995). Moreover, the Uganda Gender Policy (2007) gives a mandate to the Ministry of Gender, Labour, and Social Development, along with other line ministries, to mainstream gender in all sectors at national, local, and community levels as a way of fostering equal gender relations and elimination of gender inequality across age groups in the political, economic, and socio-cultural spheres. Through its Gender Mainstreaming Directorate established in 2000, Makerere University has been making deliberate attempts to achieve gender equality, women empowerment, and ensuring zero tolerance to sexual harassment and violence against women and girls (Makerere University, 2023). These provisions, however, are not specific to the inclusion of women scientists in media coverage or supporting women to be actors in media practices with a special emphasis on women in science-related topics.

In the artificial intelligence era where traditional and new media forms have become intertwined with many aspects of our lives, the media are crucial platforms for sharing research and scientific information on topics such as health, climate change, agriculture, and nuclear power (Lukanda, 2020). Media also serve as major means of subduing and advocating action (Lester, 2020; Lukanda et al., 2023). Therefore, excluding a group of people based solely on their gender is unfair. Gender in this case refers to the roles assigned to biological men and women in an attempt to organise collective life in society based on social values and norms (Azmawati, 2019). This study is premised on the assumption that promoting a positive image for women in finding a face for science remains a big challenge in a world of patriarchy (Chimba & Kitzinger, 2010). Patriarchy in this study refers to a system of relationships dominated by socially defined men (Pringle, 2020).

Despite women being more than half of the world's population, they are underrepresented in every aspect of society, including political leadership, religion, entertainment, and science. A UN specialised agency on information, communication, and technology (ICTs) (2021) report notes that in spite of global efforts to increase the number of women in science, girls and women remain in the shadow of men as a result of gender biases that determine the quality of girls' education and consequently career:

> Although women have been behind a number of scientific discoveries throughout history, just 30 per cent of researchers worldwide and 35 per cent of all students enrolled in STEM-related fields of study are women.
>
> (UN Women Europe and Asia, 2020, n.p)

Such inequality is reflected in the media. Although the world average in labour force statistics is 46%, only 27% of health specialists appeared in COVID-19 stories in 2020 (Global Media Monitoring Project (GMMP), 2020:2). Moreover, the same report highlights that only 25% of sources in mainstream news media were women, based on a study that covered 116 countries the same year (GMMP, 2020:1).

The media gets patriarchal by reproducing hegemony enacted through history, religion, moral values, and media ownership using text. Patriarchy extends to online news. Women were only 21% of digital news that included tweeting in multinational media (GMMP, 2020:2). The power of patriarchal culture in news and features discriminates against women and portrays them as gender with a consumerist lifestyle (Murtiningsih et al., 2017).

A Geena Davies Institute on Gender in Media (2014) report highlights that almost 90 per cent of characters seen on screen in science, technology, engineering, and mathematics roles were male in more than ten countries. Yet, it is known that media has an influence in creating and preserving unconscious public biases about science (Van Eperen & Marincola, 2011). Therefore, establishing ways of including both women and men is a good avenue for minimising the biases and inspiring other women to participate in the sector in numbers proportional to demographics since science is everywhere and affects everyone in their daily lives. Indeed, extending opportunities for more citizens to express themselves increases the value of news and enhances trust in media platforms.

This chapter suggests ways of bridging theory, evidence, and practice in training and initiating women into science and technology leadership, where they can garner more prominence alongside the men, who often occupy such positions, as a way of depatriarchalising media coverage in Uganda. The key question is: How can women be constructed in meaningful ways?

Gender Bias and Underrepresentation in Media Coverage of Science

During the past decade, researchers have intensified efforts to understand women's representation and voices in science, even though the focus has largely been on STEM. One area of investigation has been the representation of women scientists in particular, and women in general in the media coverage of science and research. In much of this research on Uganda (see, e.g., Lukanda, 2021; Nassanga, 2019; Semujju, 2015), it is indicated that women have fewer chances and opportunities compared to men to appear in media stories about science issues and research. In addition, researchers argue that public communication and media engagement activities about science are done significantly more by men than by women scientists (Crettaz von Roten, 2011). For this reason, women as news actors continue to experience marginalisation and segregation that reinforces their historical exclusion when it comes to commenting on key topics in areas of science.

Research has shown that media coverage of science is highly patriarchal and is consistent with male gender-normative traits, which impedes the attraction and progression of girls and women in science fields and professions (McKinnon & O'Connell, 2020; Ruder et al., 2018). For example, when women scientists are covered in media stories, emphasis is on their roles outside science, in particular their maternal roles and as wives (Chimba and Kitzinger, 2010). They are also depicted in supporting roles to male scientists (Long et al., 2001) and are mainly quoted as secondary sources or with invited comments that focus primarily on their appearance and personal lives (Niemi & Pitkänen, 2017). Researchers also point out that women are often depicted as less competitive, and therefore less likely to have what it takes to succeed in the hard domain of science (Fiske et al., 2002). In so doing, media coverage reinforces dominant social norms that discriminate against women and depict them as unfit to pursue scientific careers (Women's Leadership Institute Australia, 2019; Ratale et al., 2019). This in turn influences public perception of science as a masculine field through shaping the understanding of those who get exposure to scientific news and media information. For example, the media associate science and scientific work more with men more than with women, for example, boys are depicted as being better at science than girls.

Factors such as women principal investigators, postgraduate, and research staff being preoccupied with providing care for children and elderly at a time when options to provide such care have potentially disappeared, especially during COVID-19 (Minello, 2020; Shah et al., 2021), are important to bear in mind. Yet, such care did not take away their roles as academics who had to do extra work supporting students during online learning. The lockdowns, school closures, and quarantines intensified family and professional responsibilities. Such care often takes away the time that would be used in valuable research that would yield results to attract media visibility for academic mothers.

Positive media representation of women and their public communication of science as being important to society could be a constructive force in improving science communication by positively influencing public understanding and visibility of scientific information, innovations, and scientists. However, even in the western world, where gender equality and equity are seemingly at a higher level, gender biases and underrepresentation of women in media coverage of science persist. In Switzerland, for example, media were found to contact women scientists less often than men scientists, regardless of position, age, and faculty (Crettaz von Roten, 2011). In the United Kingdom, an investigation on the coverage of human genetic research by national newspapers and television found that women as sources were much less prominent. In addition, men were quoted four times as often as women in news chapter articles and given as much time on television news (Williams et al., 2003). Although much of the previous research regarding gender representation in science communication, particularly in media, has focused on prejudices as well as the meagre and narrow representations to which women in science are subjected to, it is essential to consider how women's voices can be brought back in media reporting of science and science communication in general, arguably the missing link in science communication discourse.

Gender Representation in the Ugandan Media: A General Overview

Since the 2000s, numerous studies have reported the continued misrepresentation of women in the Ugandan media. Women, regardless of their age, education, and socio-economic status, are reported to suffer from biased and limited coverage in both print and broadcast media. This, however, is not surprising as it reflects the longstanding socio-cultural and structural biases informed by male domination in a society that is underpinned by an old-age patriarchal social system. Based on this, women as a social group attract little positive attention in the Ugandan media. It is, therefore, of no surprise if women scientists are also not positively visible and represented in the Ugandan media.

It should be noted, however, that women's representation is gradually improving as media actors become increasingly aware of the need and importance of gender equality in society. Nevertheless, the representation of women still lacks diversity in terms of topics women are allowed to speak about and how they speak about them. Popular images of women as mothers, weak, subordinate to men, and less industrious still persist in Uganda's media.

Ugandan Women Scientists: Achievements and Challenges

Although gender inequality persists as a major problem in Uganda's education system, the number of women who are receiving qualifications and taking up work in various scientific fields has been increasing over the last two decades (Odaga, 2020). Indeed, women are now recognised for making strides and achievements in occupations related to science. In Uganda, for example, women's contribution has been recognised in a wide range of scientific fields, including social science, medicine and health, agriculture, engineering, and technology, as well as the environment.

Despite these strides, Ugandan women still have challenges that continue to constrain their full scientific potential and success in scientific fields and disciplines. In general, women in science face challenges that are related to gender biases that make it hard for them to venture into male-dominated areas and fields. There are social and cultural barriers that curtail their access and success in higher education (Zink, 2016). Those who are already working in scientific occupations suffer from underrepresentation in leadership roles, limited access to professional networks and mentorship programmes, inadequate recognition and visibility, as well as institutional barriers such as unfavourable work policies and inflexible work environments (Tizikara et al., 2019). Seen together, these challenges work to curtail Ugandan women's contribution to various scientific fields and at other times disable their efforts to stay in science (Batiibwe, 2022; Nyadoi et al., 2023).

Women Voices in Science Media: Intervening Factors

The general exclusion of women in science also bears on their exclusion from media communication and media coverage of science in particular. Although there is almost limited literature that points to the voices of Ugandan women in science, it is not difficult to discern that women in general find it difficult to communicate their scientific work publicly, including through the media (McKinnon & O'Connell, 2020). McKinnon and O'Connell report that women scientists who usually speak publicly about their work in both mainstream and non-mainstream media channels find themselves in a more vulnerable position and face negative stereotypes of being seen as bossy, bitchy, and emotional, including by fellow women. This view consolidates further the ongoing bias and discrimination against women in science.

The underrepresentation of women's voices in the media coverage of science stems from a complexity of individual, social, and cultural factors, including those that are attributable to women themselves and others who operate at institutional and more structural levels. Some studies suggest that at an individual level, women tend to have a scanty inclination to speak in the media or public arena, first due to the burden of domestic responsibilities and second because of their reservations toward activities outside the home. Rohn (2010) posits that women are less confident than men in regard to commenting about scientific issues. She further posits that the provocative nature of the public debate is a hindrance to many women, yet any good pundit must have the ability to handle the charged media environment.

Beyond individual women, studies which focus on the absence of women pundits in the media also note how this gender bias is a result of the widespread patriarchy, male dominancy, and gender biases in our society (GMMP, 2020). For example, although it is hard to find literature that points to why women do not speak specifically about science, researchers who have asked general questions about why women do not make media appearances have revealed some useful insights. In Burkina Faso, a study by Viviane Schönbächler discovered that the existence of traditional structures and patriarchal values that condition women not to speak or be present in the public domain was an obvious deterrent (DW Akademie, 2023). She contends, for example, that a woman talking on the radio is often seen as going against the traditional role of women in society. As such many women are constrained to speak because they are afraid of the consequences, including worries about their husbands and reactions from society. This implies therefore that patriarchy still plays a key role in media operations as well as news and content production, especially in Africa where the patriarchal system still roams large.

Some studies have noted that at the institutional level, the near-absence of women's voices in science news and information is related to newsroom structures, cultures, and practices. It is argued that while some women might have a difficulty that constrains their social and financial accessibility to the mainstream media, media institutions and journalists in particular make very little effort and do not invest time to reach out to women to be used as sources (African Centre for Media Excellence [ACME], 2012). Media outlets are less likely to see women as experts or authorities on various topics and as stories become important on the news agenda, women become even further relegated to the margins as sources. Besides, there is also little that is done by the journalists to gain women's trust. Supporting this viewpoint, ACME, (2019) suggested that due to time and practical constraints, media outlets are likely to reinforce existing stereotypes that perpetuate gender imbalances, if not create new ones. Women may opt not to appear in science stories because of the persistent negative portrayal and misrepresentation, which reduce their confidence and trust and force them to shy away. Attempts to increase women in media in Uganda as a potential way of improving women's visibility in the news, including science, have not yielded fruits because of sexual harassment that keeps driving women out of the media (ACME, 2019). With such constraints, it remains to be seen what mechanisms and interventions can be deployed to bring women's perspectives to science news and information and to make news about science deliberately inclusive. This chapter is an effort in this direction by suggesting strategies to bring women's voices into the media coverage of science.

Efforts to Amplify Women's Voices

Although there have been efforts to promote gender equality and to attract more women into science through the use of role models (García-Holgado et al., 2020), efforts at better mentorship and education opportunities (Anderson, 2005; Chesler & Chesler, 2002) and initiatives to amplify women's voices and to inspire them to speak publicly about scientific issues are rarely reported in the literature. It is reported that institutionally, a small number of media houses are making efforts to reduce barriers to gender equality in news about issues such as science. Such efforts include keeping databases of women experts to make it easy for journalists to contact them for their comments and training of journalists in the consideration of gender in news reporting (ACME, 2019). In addition, there are developments that could potentially tilt the gender balance in news and public information on issues like science, where women lack the space, opportunity, and efficacy to voice their opinions. One such development is the emergence of digital media platforms and their reported potential to amplify women's voices (Nasaba, 2019). Previous studies on the emergence and proliferation of digital media platforms found that the techno-space holds a promise for women's visibility and amplification of their voices, as well as improving their overall coverage in the media on platforms such as X (formerly Twitter), TikTok, and Instagram (Lee-Johnson & Henderson, 2019; Phillips et al., 2022; Huber & Baena, 2023).

Researchers have in particular observed a growing trend among scientists, including women, to present their work and voice their opinions on a range of professional issues through major social media, including platforms such as YouTube, Instagram, and Twitter (Bosslet et al., 2011; Patel et al., 2017). In their chapter on social media and the advancement of women physicians, Shillcutt and Silver (2018) contend that social media platforms may provide non-traditional but far-reaching avenues for women scientists to disseminate their research. This, in turn, may lead to speaking invitations or other traditional career-enhancing opportunities for women in science. It remains to be seen, however, if these are opportunities that women scientists in Uganda and elsewhere in sub-Saharan Africa, where the effects of patriarchy are still strong, can and are relying on to push women to publicly speak about scientific issues.

The potential of media literacy and education for women is another development to be noted. Media literacy can empower women science content creators, consumers, and the general women population to positively participate in challenging and removing gender biases in the media. Research suggests that women who have the know-how to constructively utilise media, including mainstream media, in public communication and are skilled in media relations can challenge and influence the ways in which media content about women is constructed and portrayed (Suwana, 2017). Women who have media literacy skills are normally able to speak for and about themselves and their work and other important issues (McArthur, 2016). Media literacy programmes focused on teaching women to become content creators can be successful in influencing the positive attitudes and behaviours of women towards becoming sources of media information and engaging in media productions. In Zimbabwe, for example, women were found to have increased their participation on the political scene by becoming content creators on Twitter (Mathe, 2023). Although this research demonstrates how critical media literacy skills can help women to become more actively involved and engaged in media productions, and by implication increase their presence and voice in media coverage of public issues including science, research is needed to understand whether this is a strategy that is readily being used to augment women's voices in science media and media coverage of science. Such research would also be useful if it tackled the type of media literacy interventions that can work best in order to increase women's presence in news and media information about science.

Finally, studies that have addressed strategies for challenging gender biases in the media have also noted the important role of education institutions and media training in fostering critical thinking about gender representation. This recognition has shifted focus from just making newsrooms and media institutions gender-sensitive to efforts that can be initiated at the pedagogical level, especially where journalism students can be sensitised about the underlying issues of gender and their impact today before they embark on careers in journalism (Nakiwala & Namasinga-Selnes, 2020). In their case, Stoddard et al. (2021) have shown that engaging in critical media education practices that focus on representation can prepare students and future journalists to begin to recognise and challenge the injustices perpetrated by both mass and social media. This can allow young people and journalists to analyse the perspectives and representations in the sources they use in media content and to produce content that challenges mis- and under-representation based on such categories as gender and race.

Some scholars encourage women principal investigators to network as a way to understand and advance women's careers in science (Kreeger et al., 2020; Feeney & Bernal, 2010). Networking is assumed to improve PI's ability to engage at various levels through physical and virtual meetings. The scholars caution against using their networks to discriminate against fellow women or confront male colleagues.

Considering the foregoing discussion, it is plausible to say that addressing the misrepresentation of women in the media coverage of science requires a systematic focus on challenging prejudices and increasing opportunities for women to voice their views and opinions on a wide range of scientific topics, including sharing their own works. Limited work exists that explores the strategies through which women's voices can be brought into the media coverage of science and science communication in general. Although much of the research has previously focused on women's representation in general, it is clear that it is easier to increase women's visibility in the media coverage of science if the efforts start targeting women scientists themselves and focus on how to implement such strategies. In this chapter, we focus on the perspectives of women scientists at a major university in Uganda to examine what strategies they perceive as important for invigorating the voices of women in media coverage of science. We report on an exploratory evaluation that addresses two primary research questions:

RQ1   What is the experience of women scientists working at Makerere University in communicating their scientific work through the media, if at all?
RQ2   What remedies can be used to increase the voices and visibility of women in the media coverage of science in Uganda?

In answering these research questions, it is hoped that both women scientists and media workers, particularly science journalists, will make a conscious effort to employ some of the strategies discussed in this chapter to improve media coverage and representation of women in science news and information, which in turn would contribute to the visibility of science (and scientific information) and its role in society.

Theory and Methodology

The chapter is based on David Cooperrider and Suresh Srivastva's (1987) appreciative inquiry theory. It is based on the principles of constructionism, simultaneity, poeticism, anticipation, and positivity. It is, therefore, a positive approach to leadership and organisational change that incorporates the involvement of stakeholders in defining problems, designing approaches to solving the problem, discovering the solution, and determining their destiny. Appreciative inquiry is the idea that the solutions to the challenges of organisations and society already exist in those institutions by moving away from the deficit to the strength-based approach (Armstrong et al., 2020; Hall and Hammond, 1998). In that sense, solving problems requires an emphasis on the forces that give life to an institution. For that reason, we chose to ask mainly women for the solutions to their underrepresentation in the media.

The chapter employed semi-structured interviews with women scientists and gender scholars. The study targeted interviewees who have ever appeared in the media on a matter related to their work. The study also purposively targeted women scientists who are either holding or have previously held leadership positions within the university. It was assumed that such leadership comes with prominence that is a critical element in the selection of news. This was important because we wanted to capture the experiences of their previous encounters with journalists and the media. A total of 15 women and one male respondent were interviewed. These included a medical doctor, an electrical engineer, a plant pathologist, a space physicist, a French and African languages scholar, a Bantu languages scholar, a feminist researcher on women's land rights, two media scholars, one female science reporter, and one male gender studies scholar.

The objective of selecting women researchers from a variety of academic fields of STEM, humanities and social sciences was to capture a wide range of experiences based on expertise in the various areas of science. The woman journalist was chosen because of her experience of more than 20 years covering science. A male participant was included in the study because of his experience in women and gender scholarship. Each interview lasted between 20 and 32 minutes. The interviews were conducted in August and September 2023. Most interviews were conducted physically in the interviewees' respective offices during working hours. Two of the interviewees preferred to respond to the interview through written emails. The 13 interviews were transcribed and thematically analysed along with the two emailed interviews.

Findings

The findings are divided into two categories aligned to the two objectives of the study. In the first category, we present findings about women scientists' experiences with journalists and the media. In the second category, we present individual and institutional support mechanisms that enhance coverage of women scientists in the media.

How Women Scientists Promote Their Research

Participants recognised the importance of the interaction between scientists and the general public. They noted that sharing research information allows the public to access new knowledge. Such involvement also gives researchers the opportunity to get new ideas/problems for further research.

Study participants acknowledged that they use various means to promote their academic work. These means include academic and non-academic platforms. Academic platforms include conferences, seminars, webinars, journal articles, book chapters, and actual books. Some of the academic platforms that participants reported using included radio, television, newspapers, and community engagements. Other non-academic platforms included X (formerly Twitter), Facebook, LinkedIn, and Instagram.

> As an academic, I publish in journals, edited books, but I also write books and dictionaries about my work. I do a lot of community engagement for instance, among the Luluuli –Lunyala (one of the local languages) speakers we have trained cadres of linguists on how to document their own languages in areas which my projects could not cover. Scientist A
>
> During engagement workshops or stakeholders' meetings, I call media personnel to cover them and they publish them in the mainstream media or I share them as video clips on Twitter as twitter feeds. Scientist E
>
> Most of the disseminations are interpersonal, for instance if we are working with farmers, we call them back and we inform them what we found out. Scientist D

Online social groups are also important platforms for sharing research with experts and non-expert audiences. Indeed, a scientist indicated that many of the journals they publish in share research using their official social media handles, tag authors and their institutions, and encourage them to re-share with their other audiences as a way of increasing access and therefore impact of the work.

According to participants, the choice of which platform to use for a given dissemination largely depended on several factors. These factors include the attitude of the researcher, the type of target audience, the relevance of a given research to a given audience, and affordability.

> It depends on the kind of work that you are going to disseminate. There is research we could do that a farmer does not care about, yet there is research we do when the farmer is the actual beneficially. So, if the work directly impacts on the farmers, the best way to disseminate that information would be to go back and talk to them face-to-face, or to use platforms like the National Agriculture Research and Farmers' Groups. In the advanced scientists' research, where farmers have no interests but only academics, we present that in the conferences, and professional bodies. However, we also consider

access and affordability of the platform before we chose it. For instance, you might want to go on Television or radio and announce something, but when you do not have the money, yet it would reach more people.

In this study, we note that the new media platforms have increased opportunities for women scientists to engage with fellow scientists and the public. Specifically, X (Twitter), WhatsApp, Facebook, and LinkedIn were cited as key facilitators for engagement.

Further, we note that scientists have become more creative in sharing their research beyond traditional and social media platforms. Rotary Club meetings, schools, and church groups, such as mothers' and fathers' unions, were reported to be some of the platforms scientists use to disseminate their research. Researchers also identified mosques as places where they talk to Sheikhs and their wives about issues such as immunisation and HIV.

Media Construction and Representation of Women Researchers

On the issue of how women scientists are constructed, we observe that there are mixed sentiments ranging from being ignored and remembered on Women's Day to receiving adequate coverage. Compared to other fields such as politics, sport, or business, science is one of the least covered subjects in Uganda regardless of whether the actors are men or women. Participants noted that in the few instances when science is covered in the media, it tends to focus on male scientists.

> The only period I have seen them [journalists], is during Women's Day Celebrations, and that is done because they want profiles to put in their newspapers and promote their readership. And, I do not think that they go and talk to women scientists if they have not done ground breaking research. Scientist D.

However, some participants thought that gender is not an issue when it comes to covering science. For instance, Scientist C reported that "I have not felt that I have not got coverage because I am a woman". This sentiment was more common with women scientists who were also working in prominent positions outside the academia. Emancipation beyond academia seems to be an important factor in empowering women to engage the media. Such emancipation also comes with experience not only in the subject matter but also the comfort of dealing with journalists and the ability to simplify messages for the public that access scientific knowledge via the media.

Participants attributed the prevailing representation of women researchers in the media to three broad factors, namely, cultural, institutional and individual. From a cultural perspective, women scientists note that the patriarchal nature of the Ugandan society largely discourages women from speaking in public, where the media realm falls. Young girls are raised to act under the shadow of men and this shapes their response to issues when they become career scientists. Considering that few women join the male-dominated field of science, cultural factors that limit their public appearance exacerbate the number of women's voices in the media. "Women falling back and leaving men do things is a bit cultural and culturally ladies are brought up like that. So, men become more vocal than women". Scientist J

Institutionally, some of the media schedules are unfriendly to women. As we noted earlier, science issues are not a priority subject in the media. This means that many of the programmes that focus on science issues tend to take place outside the media's prime time. For example, on radio and television, which are the most used media in Uganda, hours such as too early in the morning or too late in the night are unfavourable to women, yet programmes that take place during working hours have less viewership/listenership. Relatedly domestic responsibilities tend to tie down women scientists from participating in knowledge sharing through the media as Scientist B observed. "Another issue arises from balancing other responsibilities of being a good mother, grandmother, looking after the home among other activities that compete for space in our scientific projection of work, yet they are not counted at all".

Further, the news selection criteria discriminate against women because it emphasises prominence, yet, by virtue of culture women are kept under the shadow of men. Because men occupy prominent positions, journalists find it easier to include men than women's voices in their media reporting. Within Makerere University, which is our case study, women scientists are not yet at par with men in leadership positions. Yet, occupying such positions is a major condition for being covered in the media. For example, out of the 10 colleges that form Makerere University, only three were led by woman Principals at the time of writing this chapter. Indeed, the women we interviewed for this study are either currently or previously held (middle-level) leadership positions, as indicated in the selection criteria of participants in the methodology. When women gain leadership positions, it increases their chances of being reported in the media. Indeed, participants noted that women scientists who were PIs on research projects were more likely to be reported about in the media.

At an individual level, participants observed that some of the women scientists lack the confidence to speak in the media. This can be attributed to a culture that forbids women from speaking in the public. Some participants attributed this lack of confidence to fear of criticism arising out of what they say in the media. Some participants noted that some of their women scientists' colleagues have a negative attitude toward the media. As such they do not respond to opportunities of speaking through the media.

> I think it also depends on the aggressiveness of the scientists. We women tend to be laid back and wait until the media come to interview us. I have seen some scientists, when they get a research, they push it, they look for the radio, pay the journalists. Scientist B

Such an attitude can discourage journalists from contacting women scientists for opportunities to be covered in the media in future. However, some participants noted that the Ugandan media gives priority to agriculture and health science issues.

> People always go wrong when they think of science to be only in the medical field, yet, there is science beyond that. They [journalists] look at what the bigger population expects and target to publish what everybody would be excited of. Scientist J

The female journalist selected for this study noted that in addition to women being preoccupied with motherly roles, many of them are very "emotional and are easily angered". She argued that for many female PIs, a disagreement with a journalist about the presentation of facts can lead to a termination of the relationship with that particular journalist or the entire media industry. She noted that journalists who have experienced such issues with women scientists "start to avoid experts of that gender". The issue of emotions freezes out some of the women who choose to share their expertise with the public.

Existing Opportunities That Raise Women Voices in the Media

Participants identified various initiatives that support women to share their scientific knowledge in the media in Uganda. The initiatives depend on the purpose, location, expertise, and financial ability of a scientist. For example, the Bantu language expert indicated using an FM radio owned by a cultural institution and a WhatsApp group to encourage the use of the endangered languages. The French and Bantu linguists indicated that French speakers have started an online radio, Bonjour, to promote the speaking of French among journalists and women educationists.

Participants indicated that there are various ways the government of Uganda encourages the training and visibility of women scientists. They highlighted the 1.5 extra points given to girls joining public universities in Uganda. The government has also appointed women in positions of leadership in various government agencies, which has given them the necessary prominence to be covered in the media. For instance, the Minister of Science and Technology, the Minister of Health, and the permanent secretary of the same ministry are women. These government officials often appear in the media to speak about science-related issues. Within the university, there is the gender mainstreaming division, which ensures that men and women have equal opportunities in research, innovations, and knowledge transfer. Similarly, the Makerere Research and Innovation Fund ensures a gender balance of PIs when awarding grants to projects.

Participants also highlighted several initiatives by different professional bodies that offer mentorship, training and sometimes funding to women. Some of the organisations identified include the African Women in Agricultural and Research and Development (AWARD), the Association of Uganda Women Doctors, the Forum for African Women Educationists (FAWE), the Association of Women Engineers and Scientists in Uganda, and Uganda Media Women Association.

Increasing Women's Voices in the Media

Participants acknowledged the presence of women's voices in the media. However, they noted that these voices are still few, often peaking during celebration of the International Women's Day. Broadly, participants proposed four mechanisms that can contribute to increasing women's voices in the media. These include support from men, skilling journalists in science reporting, deliberate selection of women scientists as sources of news, and institutional policies that put in place quotas for leadership positions for men and women.

Participants recognised the role men have played in their professional growth. They noted that men have been instrumental in supporting them at various levels including family, at places of work, mentoring them, and including them in research. Men were also credited for appointing women in positions of leadership, which increased their chances of appearing in the media.

> All the time, I have received their [men's] support. My husband supports me through the domestic assistance, by making sure that everything gets settled at home. He as well gives me financial support to go into the field. For example, one time I was in Arua [northwestern Uganda] and we did not have enough money on our RIF [Research and Innovation Fund] project, and he facilitated accommodation for the whole of my team. Besides that, he, on my behalf contacts publishers, and organizing media events for

example, during the launch of a book, and organizing workshops, among others. Scientist B

Some of the participants acknowledged assuming leadership on the recommendation and election by men in associations where women are a minority.

> The support started right when I was still in undergraduate classes through the group work and discussions that were crucial for my performance. I have also been a president of the Uganda Institution of Professional Engineers, so I needed men to win that position because it was not an appointment, but rather an election. Scientist C

Participants suggested that in order to increase women scientists' voices in the media, men should include women in their research teams. They also noted that during times of dissemination, men should cede space for women to speak to the media.

> They should give them [women] platforms and equal voices. For example, if we are working together on a project, when the media come, give me the opportunity to talk about our work, or let us be interviewed together. Scientist D

Participants reported that some of the journalists lack basic knowledge of science, which limits their ability to understand the critical issues and the key actors in the field of science. They proposed that there is a need for skilled journalists in reporting science.

> I noticed that media people do not know much about science. You find when someone does not even know what to ask. They do not dig deep into the real science that you would expect to come out. Scientist J

Participants commended the public broadcaster, Uganda Broadcasting Corporation, for reporting science. However, they noted that private media organisations need to follow the example of the public broadcaster in reporting about science.

Interviewees also observed that the media should be deliberate in selecting women scientists as sources in their stories. Such sourcing may entail choosing a woman whenever such an opportunity presents itself. The female journalists interviewed for this study called for the ongoing empowerment of journalists to ensure that they would be sensitised to seek gender balance when reporting on science issues.

In terms of institutional support, interviewees noted that there is need for policies that support the equal sharing of leadership positions between male and female scientists.

> Let men take deliberate action to give space to women. For instance, at Makerere they should intentionally do a human resource review where they categorically say, 'top management should be occupied by 50% men and 50% women.' In such away, women will come through and eventually their voices will as well be heard in the media. Scientist A

These findings provided a basis for the discussion and recommendation. The recommendations are expected to contribute toward depatriarchalizing the media space for women scientists to fit into the existing situation as emphasised by the appreciation inquiry theory.

Discussion

Women's voices are critical in science and technology and media attempts to deliberately seek them are important in increasing and inspiring other women to participate in the economic growth and development of a country. Studies have already suggested the inclusion of women in the media has a role model effect with a likely impact of increasing the number of women contributing not only to the development of society as experts (García-Holgado et al., 2020). Uganda journalists, therefore, need to deliberately seek the opinions of women scientists whenever they are doing stories in the line of science and technology.

Considering that hegemonic masculinity exists across societies – at international, national, community, religious, family, and other forms – men have a role to play in promoting women and girls in science and technology (Ratele et al., 2019). Men should reflect on masculinities and work toward reforming gender responsibilities with a view to promoting gender justice for women, girls, and boys. As noted in the findings, some men are already supporting women, but the cultural and social barriers are still so strong that men need to work at individual, group, and policy levels to uplift women in science. Men's support for women may require more men's alliances to dedicate efforts to sacrifice their privileges for the sake of promoting women. In that case, women's organisations will need to further engage men and boys about the need to promote women and girls in science for justice and sustainable development in societies. More male involvement in supporting women, especially in doing domestic work, will encourage more women scientists to engage with the media, and more female scientists to participate in writing science stories. As already noted, female journalists are more likely to cover women scientists than male journalists would. Therefore, a conducive environment where men and women can thrive will enable female scientists and female journalists to thrive in sharing science with the public. In addition, keeping a catalogue of women scientists willing to speak to the media would be vital on the part of journalists. Such an effort would be a solution to the outcry by some participants and the ACME (2012) report that indicated that journalists rarely reach out to women experts.

Further, initiatives that bring together women scientists and journalists should be organised by both science institutions and the media to discuss the challenges each party faces in engaging the other. Through these engagements, scientists can learn media literacy and journalists can attain science literacy. ACME (2019) argues that such engagements would increase the trust in each party's ability to contribute toward sharing knowledge with the public. Engagement would reduce the stereotype that women are not authoritative in their fields and that journalists do not understand science and therefore should not be trusted with scientific facts.

To deal with some of the shyness reported among some women, this study suggests that in addition to engagement with journalists, women scientists should constitute themselves into groups of professional support. It has been reported that such peer groups act as sounding boards for raising professional issues (Kreeger et al., 2020). Existing networks such as religious associations, single-parent groups, parents of children with autism, and ethnic associations should be used as building blocks rather than discriminatory groups. Lunchtime meetings, happy hours, WhatsApp groups, virtual meetings, and other initiatives can be incorporated to support women scientists and to share ideas on how to engage the media and participate in other community activities where (media) visibility may arise.

Funding agencies should expand efforts aimed at including women in science. Makerere University has already started increasing women by encouraging them to apply individually and by encouraging men to include women as co-PIs in their RIF projects. Also, the 1.5 points still propel many young women who would never have joined the university to become scientists to get the opportunity to become graduates. However, such efforts are still few in Uganda. Yet, as noted in the findings of this study, women scientists who were PIs on research projects were more likely to be reported about in the media.

Institutions also need to be deliberate about removing barriers to women's promotions, including creating an environment that allows women to balance family and professional careers in science. Such an environment may entail giving women more time in applying for positions and requiring institutions to employ a prescribed quota in top management.

Further, women researchers should be trained in research grant writing so that they can win grants and gain research leadership positions, a prerequisite for higher leadership positions in academia and policy-making agencies at national and international levels. By the principles of prominence emphasised by news media, leading a project and/or a science institution increases the chances of being covered by the media. Such training may be accompanied by mentorship programmes to help girls and women understand their role in technical fields of science. This solution fits well in the appreciative inquiry since instructions such as Makerere are already providing some support and require enhancement.

Furthermore, journals, books, and other publishers can be persuaded to encourage women scientists to engage in media work that will publicise their work. For instance, women scientists can be asked to give a press conference and provide social media handles as a way of giving publicity to their research. Scholars have already noted the importance of reconceptualising science education to include components of science communication for the benefit of society (Lee-Johnson and Henderson, 2019; Phillips et al., 2022; Huber & Baena, 2023). In that sense, women scientists would need to learn the existing communicative patterns of social media such as algorithms of aggregating news, echo chambers, false consensus effects, the spiral of silence, misinformation, and disinformation.

In addition, there can be outreach to further deepen media literacy for women scientists, especially in using social media, to improve visibility and make them visible, as Mathe (2023) and McArthur (2016) propose. Such skills will enable them to tell their stories and interact with influential journalists and media houses. Women's participation will make media spaces more diverse and allow women to participate in using science to develop their communities, nations, and regions.

Lastly, media houses, especially broadcasters, should create time that favours women scientists. While it is difficult to have a programme that fits all women scientists, consulting a range of such experts about the best time they can be available could be a good starting point for including them in the sharing of scientific knowledge. Employing women journalists to interview women scientists can enhance participation. Where women journalists are not available, male journalists who have been trained in gender-sensitive coverage can be employed to engage women scientists in sharing knowledge with the public. Where possible, specific programmes should be designated for women scientists as guests and/or hosts. In addition to women scientists speaking on such programmes, men can also be invited to speak about the success stories of women scientists as a way of appreciating women in practice and encouraging other women to go public in the practice of their scientific professions. In such cases, follow-up mechanisms to keep track of voices should be done for consistent coverage and representation of women in the media.

Conclusion

This study has used the appreciative inquiry theory to highlight the underrepresentation of women in Uganda's media and suggested ways of depatriarchalising the media space in the country. Key to depatriarchalising is the realisation of the dominance of men in society and science in particular, and engaging men to support women in science for justice and sustainable development of Uganda. The chapter recommends science literacy for journalists and media literacy for scientists to reduce the hostility between the two groups with a view of constructing women better in the media. The deliberate choice of women sources for media purposes and institutional support in grant writing, funding, and appointment to top management where they can garner media attention is recommended. Lastly, encouraging publishers and the institutions women scientists work for to support women scientists will go a long way in increasing women's voices in the media as a way of appreciating their role in science. The chapter recommends a broader study involving more research institutions to gain more perspectives about increasing the voices of women in the media in Uganda, the continent, and beyond.

Bibliography

Africa Centre for Media Excellence (2012). *Media organisations must invest in protecting women in journalism.* https://acme-ug.org/tag/women-in-media/ [Accessed 15th November 2024].

African Centre for Media Excellence. (2019). "Barriers to gender equality in the news." Retrieved from https://acme-ug.org/2019/03/07/barriers-to-gender-equality-in-the-news/#:~:text=The%20media%20is%20a%20prism,pay%20gaps%20and%20sexual%20harassment.

Anderson, D. R. (2005). "The importance of mentoring programs to women's career advancement in biotechnology." *Journal of Career Development*, 32(11), 60–73.

Armstrong, A. J., Holmes, C. M., & Henning, D. (2020). "A changing world, again. How Appreciative Inquiry can guide our growth." *Social Sciences & Humanities Open*, 2(1), 1–4.

Azmawati, A. A. (2019). "Mainstreaming gender in media education: Malaysian experience." *Global Media Journal: Indian Edition*, 11(2), 2–16.

Batiibwe, S. M. (2022). "Strategies for retention of women lecturers in mathematical sciences in GovernmentUniversitiesinUganda,"*SN SocialSciences*.https://link.springer.com/article/10.1007/s43545-022-00589-

Bosslet, G. T., Torke, A. M., Hickman, S. E., Terry, C. L., and Helft, P. R. (2011). "The patient-doctor relationship and online social networks: results of a national survey." *Journal of General International Medicine* 26, 1168–1174.

Chesler, C. N. and Chesler, M. (2002). "Gender-informed mentoring strategies for women engineering scholars: On establishing a caring community." *Journal of Engineering Education*, 91(1), 49–55.

Chimba, M., and Kitzinger, J., (2010). "Bimbo or boffin? Women in science: An analysis of media representations and how female scientists negotiate cultural contradictions." *Public Understanding of Science*, 19(5), 609–624.

Cooperrider, D., and Srivastva, S. (1987). "Appreciative Inquiry in Organizational Life." In Cooperrider, D. L., Sorensen, P., Yager, T., & Whitney, D. eds. *Research in Organizational Change and Development* (pp. 81–142). Emerald Publishing Limited.

Crettaz von Roten, F. (2011). "Gender differences in scientists' public outreach and engagement activities." *Scientific Communication*, 33, 52–75.

Dragaš, M. (2012). "Gender relations in daily news chapter headlines: The Representation of gender inequality with respect to the media representation of women (Critical Discourse Analysis)." *Discourse (interdiscursivity)*, 67–78.

Akademie, D. W.. (2023). "Strengthening women's participation and representation in the media: An interview with media scholar Viviane Schönbächler." https://akademie.dw.com/en/strengthening-womens-participation-and-representation-in-the-media/a-65698419

Feeney, M. and Bernal, M. (2010). "Women in STEM networks: who seeks advice and support from women scientists?" *Scientometrics*, 85(3), 767–790.

Fiske, S. T. (2010). Venus and Mars or down to Earth: Stereotypes and realities of gender differences. *Perspectives on Psychological Science*, 5(6), 688–692.

García-Holgado, A., Verduogo-Castro, S., Sáchez-Gómez, and Garciá-Peñalvo, F. (2020). "Facilitating access to the role models of women in STEM: W-STEM Mobile App." In Z. Panayiotis and I. Andri

(Eds.). *Learning and Collaboration Technologies: Designing, Developing and Deploying Learning Experiences*, pp. 466–476. *Journal of Media Literacy Education*, 13(2), 55–70.

Global Media Monitoring Project. (2020). "Toronto: World Association of Christian Communication." https://whomakesthenews.org/wp-content/uploads/2021/08/GMMP-2020.Highlights_FINAL.pdf

Hall, J., and Hammond, S. (1998). "What is appreciative inquiry." *Inner Edge Newsletter*, 1–10.

Hammad, L. (2013). *Building Women's Solidarity to Advance Women's Rights in Bolivia*. A thesis submitted to the University of San Francisco for the award of a Master of Arts in International Studies (MAIS).

Huber, B., and Baena, L. Q. (2023). "Women scientists on TikTok: New opportunities to become visible and challenge gender stereotypes." *Media and Communication*, 11(1), 240–251.

Kreeger, P. K., Brock, A., Gibbs, H. C., Grande-Allen, K. J., Huang, A. H., Masters, K. S., Rangamani, P., Reagan, M. R., and Servoss, S. L. (2020). "Ten simple rules for women principal investigators during a pandemic." *PLoS Computational Biology*, 16(10), 1–9.

Lee-Johnson, J., and Henderson, L. (2019). "Using social media to re(centre) black women's voices in educational research." In R. Winkle-Wagner, J. Lee-Johnson, & A. N. Gasket (Eds.), *Critical theory and qualitative data analysis in education* (pp. 222–235). Routledge. https://doi.org/10.4324/9781315158860-16

Lester, L. (2020). "Media and the environment." In *The Media and Communications in Australia* (pp. 321–326). Routledge.

Long, M., Boiarsky, G., and Thayer, G. (2001). "Gender and racial counter-stereotypes in science education television: A content analysis." *Public Understanding of Science*, 10(3), 255–269.

Lukanda, I. N. (2020). "Cultural values and modern media as drivers of science communication." In T. Gascoigne, B. Schiele, J. Leach, M. Riedlinger, BV Lewenstein, L. Massarani, & P. Broks, *Communicating Science: A Global Perspective*. Canberra: ANU Press, pp. 907–930.

Lukanda, I.N. (2021). "Female voices marginalised in media coverage of science in Uganda, both as authors and sources". *Journal of Science Communication*, 20(2): 1–17.

Lukanda, I. N., Namusoga-Kaale, S., and Claassen, G. (2023). "Media as mediators in a science-based issue: politics, foreign influence and implications on adoption of Genetically Modified Organisms in food production in Uganda." *Journal of Science Communication*, 22(01), 1–22.

Makerere University. (2023). "Gender mainstreaming Directorate." https://gendermainstreaming.mak.ac.ug/ (Accessed December 1, 2023).

Mathe, L. (2023). "Women's political participation in Zimbabwe: Play and content creation on Twitter." *Information, Communication & Society*. 1–16 https://doi.org/10.1080/1369118X.2023.2250442

McArthur, S. (2016). "Black girls and critical media literacy." *English Education*, 48(4), 362–379.

McKinnon, M., and O'Connell, C. (2020). Perceptions of stereotypes applied to women who publicly communicate their STEM work. *Humanities and Social Sciences Communications*, 7(1), 1–8.

Minello, A. (2020). "The pandemic and the female academic," *Nature* https://www.nature.com/articles/d41586-020-01135-9.

Murtiningsih, B. S. E., Advenita, M., & Ikom, S. (2017). "Representation of Patriarchal Culture in New Media: A case study of News and Advertisement on Tribunnews.com." *Mediterranean Journal of Social Sciences*, 8(3): 1–12.

Nakiwala S. A. and Namasinga-Selnes, F. (2020). "Gender in journalism education: addressing shortfalls in male students' enrolment at a media department in Uganda." *Journalism Education*, 9(2), 43–53.

Nasaba, R. M. (2019). Arithmetic of the sound of silence: Adding, subtracting and taking back women's voices in media spaces. *Communicare: Journal for Communication Sciences in Southern Africa*, 38(2), 54–73.

Nassanga, G. L. (2019). "Empowering Rural Farmers to Improve Livelihoods Through Environmental Risk Communication: A Case Study of Uganda." *Agriculture and Ecosystem Resilience in Sub Saharan Africa: Livelihood Pathways Under Changing Climate*, 595–612.

Niemi, M. K., and Pitkänen, V. (2017). "Gendered use of experts in the media: Analysis of the gender gap in Finnish news journalism." *Public Understanding of Science*, 26, 355–368.

North, L. (2016). "Damaging and daunting: Female journalists' experiences of sexual harassment in the newsroom." *Feminist Media Studies*, 16(3), 495–510.

Nyadoi, P., Mbabazi, K. F., Nachuha, S., and Thompson, J. (2023). *Career growth for Uganda's women and girls in sciences: The challenges, opportunities and experiences*. Lewes, DE: AJPO.

Odaga, G. (2020). "Gender in Uganda's tertiary educational distribution." *Social Sciences and Humanities Open*, 2(1), 1-15 https://www.sciencedirect.com/science/article/pii/S2590291120300127

Orgeret, K., Idås, T., and Backholm, K. (2020)." # MeToo, sexual harassment and coping strategies in Norwegian newsrooms." *Media and Communication*, 8(1), 57–67 DOI: 10.17645/mac.v8i1.2529.

Patel, S. S., Hawkins, C. M., Rawson, J. V., and Hoang, J. K. (2017). "Professional social networking in radiology: Who is there and what are they doing?" *Academic Radiology* 24, 574–579.

Phillips, A. A., Walsh, C. R., Grayson, K. A., Penney, C. E., Husain, F., and Women Doing Science Team. (2022). "Diversifying representations of female scientists on social media: A case study from the women doing science Instagram." *Social Media+ Society*, 8(3), 1–17.

Pringle, R. (2020). *Gender at work*. Routledge.

Ratele, K., Verma, R., Cruz, S., and Khan, A. R. (2019). "Engaging men to support women in science, medicine, and global health." *The Lancet*, 393(10171), 609–610.

Rohn, J. (2010). "Women scientists must speak out." *Nature*, 468(733. https://doi.org/10.1038/468733a

Ruder, B., Plaza, D., Warner, R., and Bothwell, M. (2018). "STEM women faculty struggling for recognition and advancement in a 'men's club' culture. Exploring the toxicity of lateral violence and microaggressions: *Poison in the water cooler*, pp. 121–149.

Semujju, B. (2015). "Frontline farmers, backline sources: Women as a tertiary voice in climate change coverage." *Feminist Media Studies*, 15(4), 658–674.

Shah, A., Lopez, I., Surnar, B., Sarkar, S., Duthely, L. M., Pillai, A., Salguero, T. T., and Dhar, S. (2021). "Turning the tide for academic women in STEM: A postpandemic vision for supporting female scientists." *ACS Nano*, 15(12), 18647–18652.

Shillcutt, S. and Silver, K. J. (2018). "Social media and advancement of women physicians." *New England Journal of Medicine*, 378(24), 2342–2345.

Smith, S. L., and Choueiti, M. (2010). *Gender disparity on screen and behind the camera in family films; the executive report*. Geena Davis Institute on gender in media. Los Angeles: University of Southern California Annenberg School for Communication & Journalism.

Stoddard, J., Tunstall, J., Walker, L., & Wight, E. (2021). Teaching beyond verifying sources and "fake news": Critical media education to challenge media injustices. *Journal of Media Literacy Education*, 13(2), 55–70. https://doi.org/10.23860/JMLE-021(13):2-5

Suwana, L. F. (2017). 'Empowering Indonesian women through building digital media literacy.' *The Kasetsart Journal of Social Sciences*. 212–217. DOI: 10.1016/J.KJSS.2016.10.004

The Republic of Uganda. (1995). Constitution. Kampala: Government Republic of Uganda.

The Uganda Gender Policy. (2007). Kampala: Ministry of Gender, *Labour and Social Development*. https://www.rodra.co.za/images/countries/uganda/policy/The%20Uganda%20Gender%20Policy%202007.pdf

Tizikara, C., Nakayiwa-Mayega, F., and Otto, F. (2019). "Investing in women as drivers of growth: A gender-based assessment of the Science, Technology and Innovation ecosystem in Uganda." *African Journal of Rural Development* 4(2), 261–281.

UN Women Europe & Asia. (2020). In Focus: International Day of Women and Girls in Science. https://eca.unwomen.org/en/news/in-focus/international-day-of-women-and-girls-in-science-0

Van Eperen, L., & Marincola, F. M. (2011). How scientists use social media to communicate their research. *Journal of Translational Medicine*, 9, 1–3.

Ward, L. M., and Grower, P. (2020). "Media and the development of gender role stereotypes." *Annual Review of Developmental Psychology*, 2, 177–179.

Williams, C., Kitzinger, J., and Henderson, L. (2003). "Envisaging the embryo in stem cell research: rhetorical strategies and media reporting of the ethical debates." *Sociology of Health and Illness*, 25(7), 793–814.

Women's Leadership Institute Australia (2019). Annual Information Statement (2019). https://www.acnc.gov.au/charity/charities/85010dec-38af-e811-a963-000d3ad24077/documents/98093805-9e1f-ea11-a812-000d3ad1f29c Accessed 15th November 2024.

Wotschack, P. (2019). "Exploring the (missing) gender training gap in Germany: The role of organizations and sectors in continuing training participation." *Social Politics: International Studies in Gender, State & Society*, 26(3), 444–474.

Zink, E. (2016). "Research training, international collaboration, and the agencies of Ugandan scientists in Uganda." In T. Halvorsen and J. Nossum (Eds.). *North–South Knowledge Networks Towards equitable collaboration between academics, donors and universities*. Bergen: African Minds & UIB Global.

17
AFRICAN WOMEN AND LEADERSHIP IN SCIENCE ACADEMIES

Jacqueline Kado

Introduction

Decision-making is at the core of determining the longevity of an individual, institution, community, or nation. Leadership bestows the authority for decision-making on an individual entrusted with safeguarding the longevity of an entity. It is astonishing that, despite the world's gender ratio posited at 101 males for every 100 females, thereby almost a ratio of 1:1 (Ritchie & Roser, 2019), only 33% of the world's researchers are women (UNESCO, 2021). Despite the noteworthy scientific innovations by women globally, their work remains unduly recognized. This is further demonstrated by the fact that only 3% (L'Oreal-UNESCO, 2021) of the Nobel Prizes awarded for science have been given to women.

Research has shown that the life sciences, as a scientific field, has attained gender parity and in some cases even has more women than men in many countries. However, 28% of university graduates are women pursuing engineering courses, compared to 40% who take up computer sciences (Mukhwana et al., 2020). Only 22% of artificial intelligence (AI) professionals are women. The fields of engineering, computer sciences, and artificial intelligence are driving the Fourth Industrial Revolution and are experiencing a skills shortage (L'Oreal-UNESCO, 2021). With such low representation in crucial fields that drive socio-economic development, it is no wonder that very few women take up leadership roles compared to their male counterparts. Their interest notwithstanding, it is also possible that women are not accorded the opportunity to lead in these highly competitive fields. The converse is however true for men, who form the majority of experts in these fields. Men take up leadership roles in significant numbers and have more leadership opportunities at their disposal in the science fields.

This chapter aims to discuss the factors that deter women scientists from vying for leadership positions in science organizations, with a specific focus on the Network of African Science Academies (NASAC). For the status quo to change, the factors that deter the upward mobility of women in the echelons of power in the science field must be addressed. It is only by doing so that SDG5 on *Gender Equality* can be realized in the science sector.

The Network of African Science Academies (NASAC)

NASAC was established on 13 December 2001 in Nairobi, Kenya, and is a consortium of merit-based science academies in Africa (NASAC, 2018). NASAC aspires to make the "*voice of science*" heard by policy and decision-makers within Africa and worldwide (NASAC, 2018). As of November 2023, the membership of NASAC comprised twenty-nine science academies (NASAC, 2023a), including the African Academy of Sciences (AAS) and national academies from Algeria, Benin, Burundi, Cameroon, Congo Brazzaville, the Democratic Republic of Congo, Egypt, Ethiopia, Ghana, Ivory Coast, Kenya, Madagascar, Mauritius, Morocco, Mozambique, Nigeria, Rwanda, Senegal, South Africa, Sudan, Uganda, Tanzania, Togo, Tunisia, Zambia, and Zimbabwe.

Being an Africa-wide organization, NASAC has emphasized attaining gender parity in the short term. Concerted efforts have been made to get more women scientists to take up leadership roles at the academy level with minimal success. At the network level, however, the board has three women members out of six members. This chapter hopes to identify the factors that can help NASAC attain gender parity and become a proponent of attaining SDG5 in the sciences, among the academies, and across Africa. An academy of science is an honorific society, association, or organization (NASAC, 2018) that promotes the use of merit-based science advice to inform developmental policies and propagate scientific values in society and the public in general.

As an honorific society, academies draw their members from the best scientists in the country, irrespective of gender or age, but purely based on scientific merit. Based on the foregoing, it is a cause of concern that only 2 out of 29 NASAC member academies have female scientists as the presidents of these prestigious institutions. This chapter explores possible factors that deter women scientists from vying for leadership positions within the member academies of NASAC.

These factors are worth exploring because they are not only stymieing the work of female scientists in academia but also undermining the UN aspiration in SDG5, which aims to *achieve gender equality and empower all women and girls* (UN Women, 2022). The factors that deter women scientists from vying for leadership positions within the academies have a knock-on effect on the governance of NASAC, which is then deprived of attaining gender parity. The leadership of NASAC depends on the leadership of its member organizations. Six of the presidents of the science academies get elected to serve as members of the NASAC board every three years (NASAC, 2023b).

Underrepresentation in Academic Leadership

The underrepresentation of women in science academy leadership is not unique to Africa, but rather a concern for many scientific institutions around the world. Among the reasons that contribute to this underrepresentation include socio-cultural biases and limited opportunities to support the study and work of women in STEM. According to Education Sub-Saharan Africa (ESSA), women constitute only 2.5% of the vice-chancellors, yet the global average is about 30% (ESSA, 2023). Among the member academies of NASAC, the Academy of Sciences in South Africa took the lead in having the most women among their membership at 24%. The academy in Uganda follows at 13%, and then Cameroonian and Ghanaian academies follow at 11% (Ngila & Boshoff, 2017). The African Academy of Sciences, which is a regional academy drawing its membership from several African countries, has 17% of the fellows as women. The South African academy also has the highest share of women in the academy governance at 31% (Ngila & Boshoff, 2017).

Based on the foregoing statistics, underrepresentation is a real challenge in science academies. A lot still needs to be done to enhance gender equality and diversity in science leadership in Africa. To overcome this challenge, it is prudent that academies embark on implementing policies and practices that nominate, elect, and recognize women scientists first into academy membership. Additionally, there is a need to provide education and training on gender issues and unconscious bias (UNESCO, 2017) to all stakeholders, members, and staff of the academies in the science system. Once women scientists become members, it is critical to embark on initiatives that foster leadership development, mentorship, and networking and enhance visibility for their scientific achievements, within and outside the academies (Klege, 2022). Supporting women's gender roles related to childcare to enable them to achieve work–life balance can also serve to overcome underrepresentation by keeping them in science careers. Academies must also collaborate with other like-minded institutions to champion gender diversity and inclusivity at all levels. The most effective way of doing this is by promoting awareness and advocacy on the benefits of gender equity and equality for the scientific community in particular and society in general (Klege, 2022). This is especially important if gender inclusion is practiced beyond academy membership, but also into academy leadership positions.

Overcoming Obstacles for Gender Parity

Overcoming the barriers that cause gender inequality in academia is not easy but possible to overcome. Identifying the barriers is the first step to overcoming them. Chief among these barriers are the personal biases and stereotypical sentiments harboured by male counterparts towards women in any male-dominated fields like STEM. Another reason is that there are few female role models and mentors who can offer guidance and support for women seeking academic and leadership opportunities in science (Flynn, 2022). Competing professional and personal responsibilities also affects the career progression of many women in science. When faced with this obstacle, most women would sacrifice their careers for family responsibilities if a work-balance alternative is not available. Last but not least, most scientific organizations do not proffer an organizational culture that is conducive to the development of women's leadership skills (Flynn, 2022). In such an environment, it becomes difficult for women to hone leadership skills, and support from peers remains insufficient.

Despite the foregoing, many African women have indeed made significant contributions to the STEM fields. Yet, their election or appointment to positions of leadership within scientific academies has not been commensurate (Diab & Bulani, 2023). Challenges and barriers have remained and there is a need for these to be addressed to promote gender equality and diversity in leadership.

Historically, women have experienced obstacles when seeking employment or applying for leadership positions in STEM professions, more so in Africa. These obstacles may include underrepresentation, lack of inclusivity or diversity, inadequate mentorship, limited recognition through prizes and awards for scientific excellence, and even insufficient but extremely competitive funding options for pursuing studies and research in STEM (Mukhwana et al., 2020). Overcoming these obstacles is a prerequisite for more African women pursuing careers in the STEM fields.

Supportive institutional frameworks together with the enactment of favourable government policies are also essential in the advancement of women in science at the national level. This may include but is not limited to the creation of policies that ensure gender equity and the provision of funding for initiatives that promote diversity and inclusion (Ngila & Boshoff, 2017). Once that is in place, it will be possible for institutions to capacitate STEM education and outreach programmes that target girls and women, which will in turn increase their representation in science academies. These programmes can help nurture and sustain scientific talent among young people (Flynn, 2022). The knock-on effect of this is the enhanced capability of individuals to address and challenge gender stereotypes in STEM fields. In the end, girls and young women are better equipped to pursue STEM careers, thereby increasing the pool of qualified candidates for leadership roles within the science academies.

Acquisition of gender-aggregated data is also important. The data gap can sometimes be the reason why mainstreaming gender in STEM fields is not accomplished (Chigudu, 2019). Research is necessary to collect and analyse data on the representation of African women in science academies. In doing so, areas where progress is being made and where more efforts are needed can then be easily identified and acted upon (Ngila & Boshoff, 2017). The foregoing notwithstanding, it is of significant importance to recognize that the experience of women in STEM is not uniform across sectors, cadres, or even countries in Africa. Other factors such as socioeconomic status, cultural biases, and geographical setting can intersect with gender to create unique barriers to promoting gender equality or equity (Ngila & Boshoff, 2017). These disparities can therefore only be resolved if intersectional approaches are adopted.

In a nutshell, while there has been progress in increasing the representation of African women in leadership roles in science academies, there is still much work to be done to attain gender parity. Efforts to promote gender equality and equity, to provide support and mentorship, and to challenge stereotypes and unconscious biases remain essential in advancing African women in STEM leadership. These initiatives not only benefit individuals but also contribute to the advancement of STEM institutions in Africa and globally.

Response by Science Academies

Science academies must respond differently to achieve gender parity in their leadership. Academies play a pivotal role in the science community and influence spearheading approaches that can mainstream gender in STEM (Diab & Bulani, 2023). Academies set the pace for how institutions address the underrepresentation of women, promote gender equity, and foster diversity in STEM leadership (NASAC, 2017). Specific actions and strategies must, however, be adopted for significant change to be seen towards attaining gender parity. Ten of these actions and strategies, which academies should undertake, are discussed below.

Academies should, among other things:

i   Develop and implement explicit and clear policies backed with a genuine commitment to promote gender diversity and equity within their leadership and membership.
ii Offer training on leadership and support professional development opportunities targeted towards more women scientists from within and outside their membership.
iii Diversify the nomination and voting of members vying for elective positions in academy leadership to include women who qualify by merit not just gender.

iv Publish and track data on the representation of women in the academy and organize leadership accountability for promoting gender equity.
v Support and sponsor mentorship programmes that aim to promote women scientists within the academy to influence academia and STEM institutions.
vi Ensure that the achievements of women scientists are recognized and honoured through scientific awards and prizes while promoting gender diversity in the award committee.
vii Focus on supporting an inclusive work environment that takes account of gender roles like maternity, childcare, and work–life balance for women scientists, especially for those holding leadership positions.
viii Undertake outreach and networking activities that will enhance awareness and participation of relevant actors and agencies in the implementation of gender parity strategies.
ix Organize forums that identify and address unconscious biases and stereotypical views on the capability of women in leadership or any other decision-making role.
x Undertake internal studies or research to collect and collate gender-disaggregated data on all activities to evaluate the progress on attaining gender parity and determine requisite remedial actions.

Science academies in Africa can take the lead in championing diversity and inclusion in STEM. This is possible if emphasis is placed on taking concrete actions that back predetermined strategies for gender mainstreaming systematically (Diab & Bulani, 2023). Better approaches to inclusivity and equitable resource allocation ensure that both men and women have adequate support and opportunities to take up decision-making or leadership roles in the academies.

Changing the Narrative

To break the silence and speak about African women and leadership in science academies requires a paradigm shift. The first step is to speak about the underrepresentation of women in leadership roles in the science academies in particular and in academia in general (Ngila & Boshoff, 2017). The next step is to adopt a multifaceted and collaborative approach that involves various stakeholders such as governments, non-governmental organizations, educational institutions, the public and private sectors, and the scientific community (Mukhwana et al., 2020).

The current narrative is poised to change when science academies commit to:

i Promote inclusivity and diversity by establishing mentorship programmes with role models who inspire girls and young women to pursue careers in STEM.
ii Advocate and lobby governments to implement policies and laws that support gender equity with requisite funding and opportunities in education and employment.
iii Create gender diversity and inclusion committees that set targets and quotas for the representation of women in leadership roles.
iv Undertake research and analyse data on gender trends, disparities, and any other relevant topics that deter inclusivity and diversity in academic promotions or leadership.
v Invest in infrastructure and education resources that support women to pursue science careers or leadership while catering to differentiated gender roles for maternity and childcare.

vi Garner the support of male counterparts to serve as champions for diversity and inclusion and offer their support to gender equity in programmes that nurture leadership skills.
vii Organize events that deliberate on gender equity and diversity issues in academia and science to raise awareness and engage the public.
viii Seek regional and international partnerships that will share information on good practices and lessons learnt in implementing gender inclusion and diversity initiatives in academia.
ix Evaluate progress in improving gender inclusion in academy processes by using standardized metrics for efficient execution of any remedial actions.

Changing the narrative in STEM leadership for women in science academies requires long-term commitment and sustained efforts. African women can lead in science academies if the opportunities are more inclusive and equitable while remaining merit-based.

Conclusion

To promote diversity and inclusion in the science fields and register progress in scientific breakthroughs, the participation of African women in the leadership of science academies is imperative. Even though there are still many obstacles to be resolved, there is also a rising commitment to close the gender gap and elevate African women into leadership positions in STEM. For real change to occur and to create a more conducive and equal environment for African women in science and academia, science academies, governments, and the larger scientific community must work together.

The foregoing notwithstanding, there are still other factors stymieing the work of women scientists in academia, besides the structural and administrative drawbacks. Women scientists have difficulty in obtaining academic grants, scholarships, or fellowships due to having limited proposal writing skills that would progress their careers in science organizations. Gender roles could also be a deterring factor when women take time off from their careers to bear and raise children. This social aspect of gender roles means that career progression is stunted for periods, while that of their male counterparts' progress. Catching up on the lost time taken to provide maternal care to the family is irrecoverable. Careers shift and priorities change, causing a disinterest in taking up any additional roles such as leadership in the academies.

Academies should, therefore, be more proactive and innovative in encouraging qualified women scientists to vie for leadership positions while taking into account their gender roles. To do this, academies will need to mobilize financial resources to support capacity enhancement for women scientists, encourage qualified women scientist to lead academic circles, and better coordinate their efforts on outreach to bring and retain more women pursuing careers in science.

This chapter has highlighted some of the key factors that deter women scientists from vying for leadership positions within the membership of NASAC. Notably, female talents are significantly underutilized, to the detriment of not only the academies but also business enterprises, governments, and the society at large. Maintaining the status quo will not change the statistics unless the ecology that produces them is addressed. Urging individual women scientists to do more will not be sufficient nor will providing leadership training for women scientists alone do the job. A successful strategy must recognize the root causes of the current state, including the relationship between men and women. Both genders must collaborate to change the environment that has so consistently overlooked women's contributions and ascension in leadership roles, up until the presidency. That is the paradigm shift that this chapter hopes to spur among science academies in the membership of NASAC, the meritocracy notwithstanding.

Bibliography

Chigudu, D., 2019. "Strength in Diversity: An Opportunity for Africa's Development." *Congent Social Sciences* 4: 1, https://doi.org/10.1080/23311886.2018.1558715.

Diab, R. & Bulani, M., 2023. *Gender Equality at African Research Universities Alliance (ARUA) Institutions*, Pretoria: Academy of Sciences of South Africa.

ESSA, 2023. *Women Leading*. [Online] Available at: https://essa-africa.org/node/976 [Accessed 30 November 2023].

Flynn, K., 2022. *Academic Leadership by Gender*. [Online] Available at: https://www.investopedia.com/academic-leadership-by-gender-5101144 [Accessed 30 November 2023].

Klege, R. A., 2022. *Strategies for Advancing Women in Academia*. [Online] Available at: https://www.brookings.edu/articles/strategies-for-advancing-african-women-in-academia/ [Accessed 30 November 2023].

L'Oreal-UNESCO, 2021. *For Women in Science*. [Online] Available at: https://www.forwomeninscience.com/

Mukhwana, A. et al., 2020. *Factors that contribute to or inhibit women in science technology engineering and mathematics*, Nairobi: The African Academy of Sciences.

NASAC, 2017. *Women in science: Inspiring stories from Africa*, Nairobi: NASAC.

NASAC, 2018. *NASAC strategic plan 2018–2022*. Nairobi: NASAC.

NASAC, 2023a. *Member Academies*. [Online] Available at: https://nasaconline.org/index.php/2018/11/30/member-academies/ [Accessed 30 November 2023].

NASAC, 2023b. *NASAC Constitution*. [Online] Available at: http://nasaconline.org/wp-content/uploads/2018/02/NASAC-Constitution.pdf

Ngila, D. & Boshoff, N., 2017. *Too Few Women in Science: Why Academies are Part of the Problem*. [Online] Available at: https://theconversation.com/too-few-women-in-science-why-academies-are-part-of-the-problem-84444 [Accessed 30 November 2023].

Ritchie, H. & Roser, M., 2019. *Our World in Data: Gender Ratio*. [Online] Available at: https://ourworldindata.org/gender-ratio [Accessed 30 November 2023].

UN Women, 2022. *SDG5: Gender Equality*. [Online] Available at: https://www.unwomen.org/en/news/in-focus/women-and-the-sdgs/sdg-5-gender-equality [Accessed 26 November 2023].

UNESCO, 2017. *Cracking the code: Girls' and women's education in science, technology, engineering and mathematics (STEM)*, Paris: UNESCO.

UNESCO, 2021. *UNESCO science report: The race against time for smart development*, Paris: UNESCO.

18
EASTERN MARKET WOMEN ACTIVISM IN COLONIAL NIGERIA

A Historical Perspective

Grace Atim

Introduction

Nigerian societies are generally patriarchal in nature, although a few, especially those in Eastern Nigeria, were matrilineal (with tendencies towards matriarchy), and women's views were well respected (Nkiru, 1995). However, in some of the societies that were completely practising patriarchy, women were considered as lower species and were denied a lot of privileges. In such societies, women were considered inferior because of their physical outlook and their role of childbearing and household chores. This was reinforced by customs, traditional practices, beliefs and laws, behind which stood the coercive force of the state. By the time the British colonial authorities held a firm grip on the Nigerian societies, instead of discouraging discrimination against womenfolk, they initiated obnoxious policies that further reinforced patriarchy and also destroyed women's power in Eastern Nigeria. The British colonial authorities came with the Victorian ideal, which relegated women to the background in all spheres of life. In fact, women were required to be inactive in the public sphere and concentrate instead on domestic care work. A practical demonstration of these facts can be gleaned from the manner in which the British colonial authorities treated women in terms of their political appointments. Women were generally not given such an opportunity as a trial to convince them that African women had potential and could do what men were capable of doing and, in certain areas, even better.

To emancipate themselves from oppression and marginalization, women in some cases had to organize themselves to voice out their frustrations and grievances to the colonial authorities, as seen in the popular Aba Women's Riot (Olofu-Adeoye & Atim, 2023). It is against this backdrop that women started protesting for their rights within the period under review. They were protesting against the British obnoxious policies like taxation, as epitomized in the Aba women's riots of 1929. The riot was mobilised by a few women, such as the Oloko Trio; Ikonnia, Mwannedia and Nwugo, the leaders of the protest in Oloko. Ikonnia Nwanyiukwu Enyia, for example, mobilised women from Nchara, Ahaba, Usaka, etc. against the British unfavourable policies. In a nutshell, these women set the pace for feminist movements in colonial Nigeria and beyond, providing the platform for the emergence of feminist activists like Margaret Ekpo (1914–2006), who championed a process of gradual conscientization and enlightened Eastern women politically. It is on the premise of the forgoing background that this chapter analyses Eastern market women's activism in colonial Nigeria, bringing to the fore its relevance to today's gender conversations around women's strategic representation in governance.

Geographical Overview of Eastern Nigeria in the Colonial Period (1900–1960)

The area known as the Eastern Region is strategically located in the south-eastern part of Nigeria with an approximate total land mass of 29,400 square miles (Nwagboso, 2018). It is a region that, in independent Nigeria, comprises the south-south and south-eastern regions in the political dichotomy of the nation. Administratively, the region's initial capital was Calabar. It was later moved to Enugu and finally to Umuahia. The population of this region in 1965 was over 12 million, comprising major and minor ethnicities. Some of the ethnic groups in this region include the Igbo, Ijaw, Ibibio, Efik, Ogoni, Ekio, Urhobo, Itsekiri, Andoni, Ogoni, Abua, Ikwere, Annang, Iyala, Nkum, Nkoro and Ibani.

The region has three types of vegetation. The coastal areas in the south are dominated by mangrove swamps and tidal waterways. Further north of the swamps is the tropical rainforest, however, over a period of time, many of the leafy trees of the forest were cleared for planting palm trees (Information Service, 1956:5). In the northernmost parts of the region is the Guinea Savannah. Major rivers of the region include rivers of the Niger Delta system, such as Qua Iboe, Cross River, Orashi River and Imo River. There is the Obudu Plateau in the north-eastern area, and the Oban and Ikom Hills along the eastern boundary with Cameroon are a few of the highlands in this region (Information Service, 1956:5). Because of the topography of the eastern region, the people are traders, fishermen and farmers and they plant agricultural crops/plants like palm trees, cashew, plantains and pears for subsistence and commercial purposes. The environment of this region also determines the cultural variation of the people. As traditional Africans, the people of this region worship different gods and goddesses in shrines controlled by both men and women. The advent of the British colonial administration in the 19th century truncated most of the cultural and traditional values, as well as the belief system of the peoples of this region, with serious implications for the womenfolk.

The Socio-cultural Background to Eastern Women Activism in Colonial Nigeria

As indicated earlier, most of the societies in pre-colonial Nigeria practised patriarchy, a socio-cultural and political arrangement where women were not considered in the religious, political and economic engineering of their various societies. However, the case of the Igbo society of Eastern Nigeria was quite unique. This is because women had much influence in the religious, political and economic activities of this society. Apart from this fact, the society was matriarchal in the sense that women exercised great power, authority and influence (Samantha, 2013: 14). However, this does not mean male elders were not important; they too had powers and influence in society. In fact, the women – the daughters, wives, mothers and elders – were an essential and important part of everyday life and family. A man could not achieve any standing accomplishment without his wife. However, this was rather a strange system of government to the British colonial authorities by the time they met it in the southern part of the country (Agbasiere, 2000: 48).

Apart from the matrilineal nature of this society, women also had the power to control men through the instrumentality of strikes, boycotts, 'sitting on men' and other strategies. Because of these instruments, women could be assured that their views would be heard and were adequately factored into policy decisions when required (Agbasiere, 2000: 49). In fact, it was a kind of society in which political powers were diffused and shared between women and men. Women were active participants in the village assembly, as well as in community life. At village assemblies, women often spoke on matters of direct concern to them. The socio-political structure of Igbo life required and depended on their active participation. Their views were critical due to the special insight they brought to issues through their spiritual, market and trading duties, as well as their maternal roles (Nkiru, 1995: 447–448).

Women, just like men, achieved status in the society personally, not by their husband's influence. Women were given titles like Omu (queen), *Agba Ekwe*, Umu-Ada (first daughter) and others. The Omu dressed like a male monarch with her insignia of office and had her own palace. She receives homage from both the titled men and women as a female monarch (Nkiru, 1995: 447). There was a Women's Council called the Inyom Nnobi ruled by Agba Ekwe, which titled women and elderly matrons. Men had neither power nor control over this council and it was responsible for the welfare of all women. All decisions taken against women were revoked by this council; it was well coordinated by a network of communication among womenfolk.

In the south-south region, the Ijos had much respect for women, and as such, all their main gods were embodiments of women rather than men. Okaba contends that:

> Temearau is god who lives in the sky; she is a woman because it is woman who bears and produces. Her presence and interest in the world is not as great as that of the spirits. She has no shrine, fetishes or priest. Her assistance in times of great need can be invoked, however by prayer and her protection is procurable if white chalk is rubbed on the head and then blown from the palm of land upwards into the air.
>
> (Okaba 1997:135)

The above quotation portrays the kind of respect Ijos had for their women in the pre-colonial period. Women were well respected to the extent of being equated with God on earth.

Socio-culturally, women's groups among the Ijo preserve a large portion of tradition, culture and history. They were looked upon as the authentic voice of the communal traditions. In basic social functions like marriages and funerals, women dominate the affairs entirely. In some communities among the Ijos, for instance, it is women from the families of the brides and the bridegrooms who initiate and finalize the necessary protocols and in the negotiation process of bride wealth. Furthermore, women were most of the time the custodians of family inventory as they could trace the genealogy of a particular family. As observed by Appah (2003: 67), among the people of Ekpetiama, the first condition for marriage was to investigate the character and status of the mother-in-law's family to establish whether or not they were problematic or not. Other parts of southern Nigeria gave women special attention in the socio-economic, religious and political sectors. This was how women in the southern part of Nigeria were held in high esteem before the British colonial authorities came and destroyed these foundations.

The British Colonial Policies and the Development of Market Women Riots in Eastern Nigeria

The emergence of the British colonial administration destroyed the kinds of respect and prestige women enjoyed in the pre-colonial era. The focus of the British colonial administration was on patriarchy rather than matriarchy and the Victorian Ideal. The British colonial government imposed the system of indirect rule, which was a means of maintaining political authority through the auspices of local, indigenous chiefs. The Native Courts Proclamation No. 9 of 1900 authorized colonial officials to designate 'Native Administrations' within British colonies. However, these were often made without regard to established Nigerian models, models that relied upon both male and female structures of governing authority, as we observed from the foregoing discussion.

By 1914, the colonial administration instituted an indirect rule system in southern Nigeria as well, and Warrant Chiefs were elected. The election of these men excluded womenfolk. Within a few years, the Warrant Chiefs became so exploitative. They seized property, imposed draconian local regulations and began to imprison anyone (women inclusive) who openly challenged their authority. This problem was made more complex when the colonial government announced the implementation of special taxes on the Igbo Market women. These women were responsible for supplying food to the growing urban populations in Calabar, Owerri and other Nigerian cities (Van Allen, 1972). Before the Aba Women riots of 1929, Calabar women protested the market tolls imposed on them in 1924 by mobilizing over 3000 women. In 1925, the Nwaobiala mass protest took place. Already, there was an elaborate network of women marketers which the Igbo, Itsekeri and Ibibio women used to communicate information to organize the women's war. These events culminated in the Aba Women Riots of 1929, which started in Oloko, spreading to other parts of Bendel District, as well as Umuahia and Ugwa. Over 10,000 women took part in these riots, demanding the resignation and trial of Chief Okugo.

The Riot of 1929 set the pace for continuous women's agitations for their political and economic rights in the colonial period and after. It is against this backdrop that in 1938 both women and men organized another mass protest against taxation in Okigwe Division and Owerri Province. The protest was quite violent, leading to the deaths of some women. The protesters attacked and released prisoners, native courts, seized tax tickets, and as well press for inclusion in political appointments. By 1956, women in southern Nigeria organized trade union associations. For example, there was the Aba Women Association, Onitsha Women Association and others. Through these umbrellas, in 1957 a bill was passed in the Eastern House of Assembly amending the financial law. The minimum taxable income for women was raised and children above the age of 16 could be included in tax deductions. These concessions seemed to satisfy the women and their agitations ceased. Other issue which market women protested against included the reduction of garri prices in the markets of Ikot Ekpene during the Second World War (WWII), the imposition of palm kennel extraction and oil mill machines to the detriment of poor and vulnerable women. The fear was that men would use such avenues to deprive women of a source of income. In certain instances, women were protesting not only for their interests but also for the purpose of preserving their land or the community at large.

Exemplary Heroines of the Anti-colonial Struggle in Eastern Nigeria

The revolts in eastern Nigeria were coordinated by powerful women. Among these women was Ikonna Nwanyiukwu Enyia, who was born in 1877 in the family of Mazi Orzi Onyekwu in the Bende Division of today's Abia State. She was one of the pioneers of Aba Women's Riots of 1929, who confronted Chief Okeugo, the Warrant Chief of Oloko, for implementing forced taxes on women (Ehirim, 2009:1). To attack this obnoxious law, Ikonna Nwanyiukwu mobilized women in her neighbouring communities of Umugo, Ahaba, Usaka, Eleogu, Azuiyi, Obeahia, Amizi and Awomuku for a protest march in nudity. Even though she was apprehended, trialled and prosecuted by a commission of inquiry set up by the colonial authority, she was not discouraged from engaging in further protests. Ehirim (2009:1) further contends that 28 years after the Aba Women's riot, 'Ikonna led yet another women protest against the Eastern Nigerian Government of Nnamdi Azikwe. This time it was against the government policy of excessive taxation on men.' Also in 1959, the strong woman mobilized against the government's infectious policy. During this time, it was a protest against the poor quality of food given to innocent school children, and some of them lost their lives. Ikonna Nwanyiukwu was a bold and fearless woman who refused to succumb to the extraneous and fiat powers of the colonial government for the sake of vulnerable women in her community and the Nigerian society at large.

Other women who led the revolts in Oloko were Ikonnia, Mwannedia and Nwugo. They are nicknamed by scholars as the 'Oloko Trio.' These women were known for their abilities and skills. They could instigate the protest and as well tame it once it was getting out of hand; these women were a potent force for the revolts. Nneke Okorie presented herself as another woman's rights activist and social mobilizer. She was a princess and a fearless revolutionary leader of the Akwete kingdom. She was caught and sentenced to two years in Port-Harcourt by the colonial administrator, only to be released by the time the British Administration cancelled women's taxation in southern Nigeria. She later died due to a natural death in 1968 at the age of 102 while the Biafra war was going on.

Another woman of repute who contributed positively during the revolts was Nwanyeruwa. Her major role was to ensure that the protest was peaceful rather than violent. This woman of repute combined her wisdom and age in the protest; under her watch, women protested in song and dance. This strategy was called 'sitting on men' or the Warrant Chiefs until they surrender their insignia of office and resign (Mba, 1982). Nwanyeruwa was an embodiment of inspiration to the womenfolk. She kept emphasizing during the protest that 'women will not pay tax till the world ends (and) Chiefs were not to exist anymore.' Women who confided in her most were said to have kept their monies under her custody so as not to pay taxes. In other words, Nwanyeruwa was serving as a financial institution for these women throughout the period of the riots so that would not avoid payment of taxes by all means. Unfortunately, her peaceful advocacy was rather a colossal failure; hence, the riots turned violent, destroying colonial property and attacking chiefs and their households.

There was also Mary Okezie, one of the earliest elite among the Igbos during the time of the revolt and was a teacher with the Anglican Mission School in Umuocham in Aba. Although she did not take part in the revolt, she sympathized with the women. She was the only woman who submitted a memo of grievance to the Aba Commission of Inquiry in 1930. After the revolt, Okezie emerged as a founder and leader of the Ngwa Women's Association where she worked for the rest of her life to support women's rights.

Margaret Ekpo, born on July 27, 1914, was another exemplary woman leader who united women and promoted female solidarity as a way of fighting for economic rights and expanding women's political rights. She was the brains behind the establishment of the Aba Township Women's Association in 1954. The union motivated women politically and by 1955, women outnumbered men in city voter elections. In 1959, Margaret Ekpo joined Funmilayo Ransome-Kuti in protesting the killing of leaders who opposed colonial practices at an Enugu coal mine, which drew international attention. She was also an active member of the National Council of Nigeria and Cameroon (NCNC), a political party that was at the frontline of African decolonization. Ekpo and Flora Nnamdi Azikiwe were responsible for the formation of NCNC's women's wing. She died on September 21, 2006.

Other women played the role of warriors during these revolts. Among them were Mary of Ogu Ndem and Ihejilemebi. Mary of Ogu Ndem was the overall leader of the women's revolt in Onicha Ezinihitte. According to John Orji (2000:7), she was treated as a very important person (V.I.P.) and caused a tremendous stir of excitement whenever she visited any village. Not only were all the village roads swept and weeded, but valuable sheep and goats would be killed for festive eating. All the women would stand along the road to watch and wait for her. She would come shaded by an umbrella and her deputy leaders would be behind her. She was the great mistress who laid down the rules. Another heroic warrior was Ihejilemebi. She was a woman known for her incredible bravery and strength of character before and during the women's revolt. Before the revolt, she served as the head of women's spy team during local wars and was also a member of the war council (Orji, 2000:8).

It is not surprising that when the women's revolt broke out, she naturally emerged as a warrior who led women to 'sit' on the Warrant Chiefs in various communities, burning the houses of those who refused to resign and collecting their insignia. Throughout eastern Nigeria, women were led by their leaders to condemn obnoxious British policies such as taxation, interfering in market prices and other policies that could sideline women in their businesses. Women adopted different strategies in their protests throughout the colonial and post-colonial periods. This aspect forms the next section of our discussion.

Strategies Adopted by Eastern Market Women Protesters against Colonial Policies

Women adopted both peaceful and violent strategies to project their grievances during the revolts described above. The major tactic in the protest was known as 'sitting on a man.' It was an ancient practice among the Igbo women for shaming a man who was either found maltreating his wife, allowing his cows to eat women's crops, breaking the rules of the market or causing marital disputes generally (Rose, 1999). They adopted this tactic by convening at the targeted man's hut or workplace and dancing, singing songs detailing grievances related to his behaviour, beating on the walls of his home with yam pestles, or, occasionally, tearing the roof from his home, demolishing his hut or plastering it with mud and roughing him up a bit. Women wore ferns on their heads and donned loincloths. They also painted their faces with charcoal and carried sticks wreathed with palm fronds. Therefore, during the riots, women employed these strategies to disgrace their victims.

Women also employed strikes and boycotts as another way of expressing their grievances. In certain instances, they appeared nude, which is believed to have had an ill-omen on those whom their outcry is targeted at. Rose amplifies the implications of women demonstrating in the nude in the following way:

> When bodies hit the streets en masse to oppose the status quo, their power can appear either infinitesimal or so spectacular as to arrest onlookers in their tracks. By suspending audiences between past and future, demonstrating bodies become emblems of what is and what might be: 'laboratories for alternative futures.'
>
> (Rose, 1999:279)

It is an indisputable fact that women's nudity in Africa and perhaps most parts of the world is considered a taboo. In Africa specifically, it is a last resort to expressing dismay over injustices. In the Yoruba culture, deliberate public exposure of the female body is a gesture of extreme gravity and eloquent abomination in the timeless rites of wrongs. Because of this underpinning fact, women in eastern Nigeria used it (nudity) to challenge the imposition of taxation and other obnoxious colonial policies.

Another effective strategy adopted by these women was to discuss their plans secretly and therefore adopt a line of action through an elaborate network of market associations and kinship units. There were numerous such associations in this region. These included the Aba Women Association (AWA), Onitsha Market Women Association, Abak/Midim/Nung Ikot Women's Society and others. They were strategic conduits where numerous women within this region got the necessary information.

Women also adopted violent approaches by attacking European-owned stores and structures housing Barclays Bank. In certain instances, they destroyed prisons and released prisoners, while Native Courts run by colonial officials were not spared. Among the buildings burnt during the 1929 riots were those at Aba, a major administrative centre from which the British name for the rebellion is derived. Other attacks were the European factories at Imo River, Aba, Mbawsi and Amata. Large numbers of police and soldiers and, on one occasion, Boy Scouts were called in to quell the 'disturbances.' On two occasions, clashes between the women and the troops left more than 50 women dead and 50 wounded from gunfire. The lives taken were those of women only; no man, Igbo or British, was even seriously injured. The hefty cost of property damage was paid for by the Igbo women, who were heavily taxed to pay for rebuilding the Native Administration centres (Judith Van Allen, 1972:174). Therefore, the adoption of both peaceful and violent approaches expressed the depth of dissatisfaction which women in eastern Nigeria had with the colonial administration. Their dissatisfaction with the colonial policies led to the establishment of a commission of inquiry, which, in the final analysis, brought reforms to the Native Administration.

Impact of Eastern Women's Protest for Womenfolk in Nigeria

The market women revolt in Eastern Nigeria had impacted greatly the feminist movement in Nigeria generally. Women, for the first time, were able to transform traditional methods for networking and expressing disapproval into powerful mechanisms that successfully challenged and disrupted the colonial administration. The most immediate change that came about was the ceasing of head counting and tax collection. The government did not want further revolts and, in some places, would not see taxes for many years. The colonial administration waited for the provinces to calm down and then gradually introduced the taxes back

(Mallory, 2013:116). But in a way, the riots limited the nature of exploitation the colonial agents set against poor women in Eastern Nigeria.

Another positive impact of market women's revolts in Eastern Nigeria was the restructuring of the Native Administration. The colonial authorities were wary of repeating the same mistake of lumping diverse groups of people together for judicial purposes. To avoid this, the idea of the Native Authority system of indirect rule was implemented with the Native Court Ordinance of 1933 (Allen, 1972: 177). The number of Native Court Areas grew significantly and their boundaries changed as well. Part of the aim of the new structure was to eliminate the corruption that had been inherent in the Warrant Chief System. Though the new system allowed for increased indigenous participation and natives were trained in how to rule themselves, there were a couple of small catches. Beyond women's participation in the Commissions of Inquiry, the women were excluded from the discussion of changes, and many of the reforms implemented had negative consequences for them. The newly reformed Native Administration took over many functions of the village assemblies, seriously affecting women's political participation. No longer did discussions on policy include any adult who could 'speak well.' It was now limited to members of the native courts (Allen, 1972:74). While men who were not members were also excluded from these meetings, their views and interests were well represented. In a nutshell, these reforms instituted following the women's riots took little account of the women's traditional roles. However, the riots brought the reorganization of the administration in south-eastern Nigeria.

The revolts were also instrumental in the emerging gender ideology in Nigeria at large. In other words, the revolts inspired subsequent protests from the 1930s and beyond, especially in Owerri and Calabar Provinces, as epitomized in the Oil mills protest, market control protests, nut cracking machine protest and so forth. On certain occasions, the British Colonial Officers deployed security officers to quell such protests, resulting in the deaths of over 50 women, while more than 50 seriously sustained different degrees of injuries. However, the effects of such protests have given Nigerian women a voice in Nigerian contemporary politics. But this does not imply that women are fully represented in elective and appointive posts today in Nigeria. Their representation is grossly inadequate (Gbamwuan 2015:87) and does not meet the Beijing Declaration for women's participation in politics, as well as the 35% affirmative action plan adopted by the government in the Fourth Republic. Finally, the women's revolts also marked the genesis of the Nigerian road map to political independence that may not have happened if these women had not blazed the trail for nationalism. This gave impetus to others to carry on the struggle, which led to Nigerian nationhood.

Conclusion

This chapter discusses colonial Eastern market women's activism in Nigeria with a special spotlight on the underpinning immediate and remote factors which ignited these riots. The chapter brings to the fore women's stories of bravery, resilience and strength to confront patriarchy. The chapter debates that prior to the British colonial rule, women's rights in this region were held with great respect. Women were incorporated in the socio-economic, political and cultural activities of their various states. However, the British colonial rule saw this as contradictory to their 'Victorian ideal' and not only reversed it indirectly but also imposed obnoxious policies that were at variance with the culture and tradition of the people. The result was immediate revolts by market women who were organized by a few emerging women activists.

As a way of conclusion, the revolts were very fundamental for a good number of reasons. First, it was the first major challenge the British colonial authority had in Nigeria and West Africa at large. This ignited nationalist agitations in Nigeria. Second, the revolts had immediate effects on women in eastern Nigeria, hence the British colonial authority dropped their plan to impose a special tax on the market women. Third, and unknowingly for these women, they were applying the radical feminist approach that calls for a reordering of society in which male supremacy is eliminated in all social and economic contexts. They were also indirectly applying liberal feminist theories whose ultimate goal is to achieve gender equality through political and legal reform within the framework of democracy and informed by a human rights perspective. This has contributed to a heated discourse on gender and social inclusion in contemporary Nigerian politics. Although the market women were not steeped in western education, they set the background for the gender equity question, which advocates for social inclusion in all spheres of development in Nigeria today. Nigerian women today are constantly pressing for their rights in socio-economic, cultural, religious and political spheres of life. Their solidarity struggle has ended up at the level which Deckard (1975) correctly termed 'let us in' to the decision-making process rather than 'set us free.'

Although traditional beliefs and practices confined women in Africa to subordinate positions, eastern Nigerian women were able to make immense and invaluable contributions to societal development politically. They have individually and collectively played dynamic and constructive roles and thus contributed tremendously to societal development (Awe, 1992).

Therefore, in the contemporary period, Nigerian women should intensify advocacy/lobby activities to demand higher percentage of representation in governance, knowing that their foremothers initiated this struggle. This will be strategic in the quest to raise a generation of politically conscious women. They should adopt the 'set us free' clarion call, which would see the emancipation of the womenfolk from the shackles of subjugation, suppression and oppression. This will contribute to liberation from the yoke of poverty, exclusion, discrimination, deprivation, hunger and diseases in the near future.

Bibliography

Agbasiere, T. J. (2000). *Women in Igbo Life and Thought*. London and New York: Routledge.
Appah, S. (2003), 'Women in Ekpetiama'. In Ejituwu, N.C. and Gabriel, A.O.I. (eds), *Women in Nigerian History: The Rivers and Bayelsa State Experience*. Port-Harcourt: Onyoma Research Publications.
Allen, V. J. (1972) *Aba Riots' or 'Women's War'? British Ideology and Eastern Nigerian Women's Political Activitism*. Waltham, MA: African Studies Association.
Awe, B. (eds.). (1992). *Nigeria Women in Historical Perspective*. Ibadan: Sankore/Bookcraft.
Deckard, B. S. (1975). *The Women's Movement: Political, Socioeconomic, and Psychological Issues*. New York: Harper & Row.
Ehirim, C. The Political Editor of *Summit Newspaper*, May, 2009.
Gbamwuan, A. (2015), 'Interrogating the Poor Performance of Women in Nigerian Politics'. In Okpeh, O. and Ikpanor, E. *Themes on Women Studies in Africa: Perspectives from Nigeria*, Vol. 1. Abuja: Donafrique Publishers.
Information Service. (1956). *Eastern Region (Nigeria)*. Enugu: Enugu, Eastern Nigeria Information Service.
Mba, N. E. (1982). *Nigerian Women Mobilized: Women's Political Activity in Southern Nigeria, 1900–1965*. California, Berkeley: Institute of International Studies, University of California.
Mallory, S. K. (2013). *Matriarchy, the colonial situation, and women's war of 1929 in south-eastern Nigeria*. These and Doctoral Dissertation. 537 https://commons.emich.edu/these/537
Nwagboso, C. I. (2018). 'Nigeria and the Challenges of Internal Security in the 21st Century'. *European Journal of Interdisciplinary Studies*, 4(2), 15–33.

Nkiru, Nzegwu (1995), 'Recovering Igbo Traditions: A Case for Indigenous Women's Organizations in Development,' In Martha C. N. and Glover, J. (eds.), *Women, Culture and Development: A Study of Human Capabilities*. Oxford: Clarendon. 447–448

Olofu-Adeoye, A., & Atim, G. (2023). 'A Reflection on the Roles of Nigerian Female Activists in Civil Rights Movements'. *Humanity: Jos Journal of General Studies*. 14, 1, 2–4

Okaba, B. O. (1997), 'Ijo Kinship and Socio-Political Organization'. In Onwuka and Ahiawe (eds.), *Nigerian Heritage*. Owerri: Whyten Publishers.

Orji, J. (2000), '*Igbo Women from 1929–1960*', West African Review, 2(1) 7–9.

Rose, N. (1999), *Powers of Freedom: Reframing Political Thought*. Cambridge: Cambridge University Press.

Samantha, K. (2013), '*Matriarchy, the Colonial Situation, and the Women's of War of 1929 in South-Eastern Nigeria*'. Master's Theses and Doctoral Dissertations.

19
GLOBALIZATION AND AFRICAN WOMEN
Challenges and Opportunities

Josephine Mukabera

Introduction

Background

Processes of globalization have affected economies, societies, and cultures across the globe. Globalization encompasses the dynamic processes of international trade and finance that interconnect and increasingly integrate national economies. These global processes have gained entry into local labor markets, shaping employment structures and relationships, wages and working conditions, opportunities for women and men, and their participation in paid work (Dejardin, 2009). In Africa, processes of globalization resulted in a shift from traditional agrarian economies to increasingly market-oriented systems. As contributors to both the formal and informal economies, African women have found themselves both empowered and marginalized in the wake of globalization.

Women have gained new opportunities for economic engagement through the growth of global markets, yet they still face obstacles in fully integrating into these spaces due to structural inequalities and gender biases. In the realm of education and healthcare, improved access to information and technology has enabled some African women to access educational opportunities and healthcare services that were previously out of reach (United Nations, 2003). Moreover, the global exchange of ideas has also catalyzed discussions around women's rights and gender equality, galvanizing local and international efforts to address pressing issues such as child marriage, female genital mutilation, and gender-based violence (World Vision, 2023). Furthermore, the movement of people across borders, facilitated by globalization, has brought about a diaspora of African women who contribute to the host countries while maintaining strong ties to their countries of origin (Dlamini, 2017; Salau, 2023). Hence, African women living abroad often become agents of change by advocating for their homeland's social and economic development while also embracing and shaping their adopted societies (Kessy and Shayo, 2022).

Recently, researchers have called attention to the importance of intersectionality, considering factors such as class, ethnicity, and rural–urban disparities in examining how globalization affects women differently (Banerjee and Ghosh, 2018). While globalization has opened doors for economic empowerment and increased awareness of women's rights, it has also exposed the fault lines of gender inequalities that persist in various forms (Seguino and Grown, 2006). Challenges such as limited infrastructure, cultural norms, and economic disparities persist, hindering the realization of the globalization benefits for many women (United Nations, 2003). As Africa navigates the currents of globalization, understanding and addressing the diverse experiences of its women will be crucial in constructing a future that embraces both local identities and global interconnections. Based on these ideas, exploring the impact of globalization on African women's experiences enables a more comprehensive understanding of the complex interplay between global forces and local realities, ultimately leading to more informed policies and initiatives that promote gender equality, empower women, and foster inclusive and sustainable development in an increasingly interconnected world. Hence, this review responds to the core question of how globalization has affected the empowerment of women in Africa.

Research Objectives

The purpose of this systematic review is to provide a comprehensive understanding of the relationship between globalization and African women, focusing on the empowerment dimension. The specific objectives related are:

To assess globalization's influence on African women's economic opportunities, including employment, entrepreneurship opportunities, and access to resources.
To identify the cultural changes and challenges faced by African women in the context of globalization, including shifts in norms, values, and identities.
To describe the agency and resilience of African women in shaping gender-equitable responses to the challenges posed by globalization.

Significance of the Study

Gender inequality is a persistent challenge in Africa, and women's empowerment is crucial for achieving sustainable economic growth, social justice, and human rights. As globalization has the potential to exacerbate or alleviate gender inequalities, exploring the topic of globalization and African women is of utmost importance for several key reasons.

As globalization has perpetuated and exacerbated gender inequalities, exploring the topic of globalization and African women allows us to examine how economic policies, labor markets, cultural transformations, and power dynamics intersect to shape women's lives, agency, and access to resources and opportunities. Focusing on women's empowerment, exploring this topic can help assess the extent to which globalization has facilitated or hindered African women's empowerment and how it advocates for policies and practices that prioritize their rights and well-being. In addition, by examining how globalization affects African women's economic, social, and cultural development, we can identify barriers and gaps that can be addressed to ensure more equitable and inclusive development outcomes. This will allow us to advocate for alternative approaches that prioritize social justice and gender equality. Hence, understanding the dynamics between globalization and African women is essential for promoting social justice and sustainable development. As African women's experiences are also influenced by factors such as race, class, ethnicity, and geography, examining globalization through an intersectional lens helps uncover the complex ways in which different identities intersect with global processes.

Finally, by understanding the shared challenges and experiences of African women within the broader context of globalization, it becomes possible to forge transnational networks, exchange knowledge, and collectively advocate for women's rights and gender justice on a global scale. Therefore, exploring the topic of globalization and African women facilitates global solidarity and collaboration among women's movements. This chapter contributes to the existing body of knowledge on the socioeconomic empowerment of African women in the context of globalization.

Examining how global processes affect African women's lives and their socioeconomic empowerment, this chapter builds on globalization theories as it engages with theories related to globalization, such as those discussing economic globalization and cultural globalization and their effects on women. It also contributes to the discussions on women's agency and empowerment theory, examining how African women navigate and respond to the challenges and opportunities presented by globalization.

Key Concepts and the Theoretical Framework

Key Concepts

Globalization

Globalization refers to the deepening of international economic relations, which has accelerated since the 1980s and is associated with greater economic liberalization both internationally and within national economies. It is the increasing interconnectedness, integration, and interdependence of societies, economies, and cultures across the globe. It involves the flow of goods, services, capital, information, ideas, and people across borders, facilitated by advances in technology, communication, and transportation (Jomo, 2003). From a decent work perspective, globalization processes should help reduce, or at least not aggravate, inequalities between men and women. Globalization has profound implications for various aspects of society, including economics, politics, culture, and social relations (Steger, 2017).

From a gender and decent work perspective, the robust demand for temporary migrant care services workers has also opened up new paid jobs for women, which have meant huge financial benefits to their families, communities, and countries. However, the challenge is enhancing the security and quality of employment and reducing gender inequality and the lower segments of global supply chains and enterprises at the edge of production networks where employment is flexible, informal, unprotected, low-paid, and low-skilled.

In the global market for migrant care services workers, domestic workers are less protected and more vulnerable to unfair treatment and exploitative practices than skilled health professionals are. Women are concentrated in the lower segments of global supply chains and enterprises, recasting gender inequalities and women's subordinate labor market position within the global economy. The persistence of gender inequalities in the rest of the economy will continue to shape and limit the choices of women who seek paid employment; it will limit their advantage to fight for better quality jobs and decent work (Dejardin, 2009).

Overall, globalization has expanded economic opportunities, education, and empowerment for women, but it has also brought risks such as labor exploitation, gender-based violence, cultural pressures, and unequal access to resources. This study explores its effects on African women.

African Women

Women and men are often unequally positioned in the economy, perform different socially determined responsibilities, and face different constraints; thus, they are unlikely to respond in the same way to policies and market signals. In developing countries, women workers make up the overwhelming majority of the workforces of labor-intensive export industries and tend to be concentrated in the most vulnerable jobs of global production systems (Dejardin, 2009).

Judith Butler, a prominent gender theorist known for her work in "Gender Trouble" (1990), has been influential in challenging fixed notions of gender and emphasizing its fluid and socially constructed nature. In "Gender Trouble", Butler argues that gender is not an inherent or stable quality but is constructed and performed through repeated actions. According to her, individuals enact and embody gender roles through their behaviors, and these performances contribute to the social construction of gender identities.

Applying Butler's ideas to the question of who an African woman is from diverse African cultures, we can interpret that Butler's framework would view "African woman" not as a fixed or predetermined identity but as a performative construct shaped by cultural norms, societal expectations, and individual expressions. The concept of being an "African woman" would involve the continual performance of gender within the specific cultural, social, and historical contexts of diverse African societies.

Butler's work is more focused on deconstructing fixed categories and challenging the binary nature of gender identity rather than providing specific definitions for identities within particular cultural contexts. Therefore, her approach invites scholars to examine how gender is performed and understood within the dynamic and diverse cultures that make up the African continent.

Women's Empowerment

Women's empowerment came to be articulated in the 1980s and 1990s as a radical approach concerned with transforming power relations in favor of women's rights and greater equality between women and men (Batliwala, 2007).

From the perspective of Kabeer (2005), known for her work on gender and development that emphasizes the importance of agency in the process of empowerment, she defines empowerment as the expansion of people's ability to make strategic life choices in a context where this ability was previously denied to them.

Kabeer identifies three interrelated dimensions of empowerment: (i) *Resources*: Access to and control over resources, including material, human, and social resources, are crucial for empowerment; ii) *Agency*: The ability to make choices and decisions, exercise control over one's life, and act on one's behalf is central to empowerment; (iii) *Achievement*: Empowerment is reflected in the positive outcomes and changes in individuals' lives and in the broader societal structures.

For Cornwall (2007), known for her contributions to feminist research and participatory methodologies, she argues that empowerment is not a linear or universally defined concept; rather, it is shaped by social, cultural, and political contexts. Cornwall's work often highlights the significance of participatory approaches, where individuals actively engage in the process of defining and pursuing their own empowerment. For her, power dynamics, both within communities and at broader societal levels, play a crucial role in shaping the possibilities for empowerment.

To sum up, both Naila Kabeer and Andrea Cornwall highlight the multidimensional nature of empowerment. Kabeer's framework emphasizes the importance of resources, agency, and achievements, while Cornwall emphasizes the contextual and relational aspects of empowerment. Together, their perspectives provide a nuanced understanding of how power, agency, and context intersect in the process of empowerment, particularly in the context of gender and development.

From the above perspectives, women's empowerment refers to the process of equipping women with the necessary tools, resources, knowledge, and agency to actively participate in and shape various aspects of their lives, as well as influence and contribute to societal, economic, political, and cultural changes. Women's empowerment encompasses several dimensions, including economic empowerment (access to employment, entrepreneurship opportunities, and financial resources), social empowerment (equal access to education, healthcare, and participation in public life), and political empowerment (representation and participation in decision-making processes at all levels of governance). It also involves fostering a supportive environment that values and respects women's rights, voices, and contributions while addressing the structural inequalities that limit their potential (United Nations, 2020).

Economic Empowerment

Economic empowerment refers to the ability of individuals, including African women, to have control over economic resources, opportunities, and decision-making processes. It involves improving access to education, employment, entrepreneurship, and financial services to enhance economic independence and well-being (UN Women, 2013). Globalization has transformed economic systems worldwide, including in Africa. It is essential to assess how these changes affect African women's economic participation and livelihoods. Globalization can open up new economic opportunities, such as access to global markets, but it can also lead to economic inequalities and marginalization. Examining the impact of globalization on African women's experiences helps us understand how the dynamics of economic integration affect women's economic empowerment and well-being.

Economic empowerment for women is contingent upon available resources and whether women have the skills to use them, access to economic opportunities, and control over economic benefits that can be used to achieve positive change (Kabeer, 2009). Women can achieve economic empowerment if (1) the resources are available and women have the skills to utilize them; (2) they have access to economic opportunities and control over the economic benefits of those opportunities; and (3) they can use those benefits to make strategic choices leading to positive changes in their lives. Interventions aimed at promoting women's economic empowerment will help in achieving full recognition and realization of women's economic rights, and ultimately sustainable development. Overcoming obstacles faced by women requires society to actively reduce gender discriminatory norms and practices and to ensure that public institutions are accountable for putting gender rights into practice (Kabera, 2009).

This chapter focuses on women because gender equality expected to benefit both men and women leaves more women than men economically insecure, as they are marginalized as economic actors due to structural inequalities. Economic empowerment also contributes to the reduction of gender-based violence, increases women's family-planning possibilities, and slows the spread of HIV.

Finally, investing in the economic empowerment of women and in the promotion of gender equality has broad multiplier effects on human development (SIDA, 2009).

Social Empowerment

Social empowerment refers to the process of enhancing the abilities, rights, and capacities of individuals or communities within the social sphere. It often involves providing individuals or groups with the resources, knowledge, and opportunities needed to participate actively in social, economic, and political aspects of their community or society (Herrmann, 2012). Social empowerment aims to reduce disparities, promote inclusivity, and foster a sense of agency and control over one's social environment. Women's social empowerment refers to the process of enhancing the social status, rights, and opportunities of women in society. It involves addressing and overcoming the various forms of discrimination, bias, and inequality that women may face in different social, economic, and political spheres. Women's social empowerment aims to ensure that women have equal access to resources, education, healthcare, and employment opportunities, allowing them to participate fully and actively in all aspects of society.

Cultural Empowerment

Cultural empowerment refers to the recognition, validation, and promotion of cultural identities, practices, and values, including those of African women. It involves challenging cultural norms and practices that perpetuate gender inequality and ensuring the full participation and agency of African women in shaping and preserving their cultural heritage (Okazawa-Rey & Enns, 2019). Globalization brings cultural exchanges, technological advancements, and changes in social norms and values. These transformations can have both positive and negative consequences for African women. By examining the impact of globalization, we can better understand how it influences women's roles, identities, and cultural practices. This knowledge is crucial for preserving and promoting African women's rights, autonomy, and agency in the face of globalization's cultural dynamics.

Women's Agency and Resilience

Mama (2007) defines the term "agency" as the capacity of individuals or groups to act independently and make choices, while "resilience" signifies the ability to withstand and recover from adverse situations. In development, women's agency refers to their capacity to act independently, make choices, and exert influence over decisions and processes that affect their lives within the context of social, economic, and political development. It involves the ability of women to actively participate in various aspects of development, such as education, employment, healthcare, and community engagement. Recognizing and respecting women's agency is essential for fostering gender equality and ensuring that development efforts are inclusive and empowering (Barrientos, 2006).

Women's resilience refers to their ability to withstand, adapt to, and recover from challenges and adversities in the process of social, economic, and political development. Resilience emphasizes the strength, resourcefulness, and determination of women in the face of obstacles such as poverty, discrimination, and unequal power dynamics (Quisumbing et al., 2018).

This study considered the following elements of women's agency (Barrientos, 2006): *(i) Decision-making power*: Having the ability to participate in decision-making processes at individual, family, community, and societal levels. (ii) *Access to resources*: Access to and control over resources such as land, credit, and technology. Access to these resources empowers women to engage in economic activities, make independent choices, and contribute to their own and their communities' development. (iii) *Education opportunities*: Education equips women with knowledge and skills, enabling them to participate more effectively in various spheres of life and make informed decisions about health and reproductive rights. (iv) *Health and reproductive rights*: Ability to make decisions about their health and reproductive rights, that is, the access to healthcare services, family planning, and the right to make decisions related to their bodies and well-being. The key aspects of women's resilience (Quissumbing et al., 2018) considered are:

(i) *Coping Strategies*: Drawing on social networks, utilizing available resources creatively, and adapting to changing conditions to meet their needs and those of their families. Developing mental and emotional strength to navigate stress and uncertainty. (ii) *Community engagement*: Active participation in *Coping strategies*: Drawing on their social networks, utilizing available resources creatively, and adapting to changing conditions to meet their needs and the needs of their families, community initiatives, and support networks. By coming together, women can share experiences, pool resources, and advocate for changes that enhance their well-being and the overall development of their communities. (iii) *Economic empowerment*: Resilient women often engage in economic activities to secure their livelihoods and contribute to their communities. This may involve entrepreneurship, small-scale farming, or participating in income-generating projects that strengthen both individual and community resilience. (iv) *Advocacy and collective actions*: Challenging discriminatory policies, advocating for legal reforms, or participating in movements that promote gender equality and social justice.

To sum up, women's agency and resilience in development are interconnected concepts that highlight the importance of recognizing and supporting women's ability to act autonomously and adapt to challenges within the broader context of social progress and improvement. Empowering women in these ways contributes to more sustainable and inclusive development outcomes.

Theoretical Framework

This study is guided by a gendered globalization theory as framed by Naila Kabeer, although many other scholars have contributed to the development of that theory. Naila Kabeer, a Bangladeshi-born social economist and professor, has made significant contributions to the understanding of the intersection of gender, development, and globalization. Through extensive research on how globalization impacts women's economic opportunities and social empowerment, Kabeer has highlighted the complex ways in which globalization processes can both empower and marginalize women, depending on various factors such as class, race, and geographical location. One of her well-known works is the book titled *The Power to Choose: Bangladeshi Women and Labor Market Decisions in London and Dhaka* (2000). She has explored the choices and constraints faced by Bangladeshi women in different global contexts. She highlights the way in which changing societal values and norms in Bangladesh widened the labor market options of women in Dhaka as compared with those in London.

It is strategic to link Kabeer's work (2004) on "Gendered Impacts of Globalization: Employment and Social Protection" with the topic of globalization and African women. She highlighted how economic and social changes associated with globalization affect women in various ways:

i   The integration of women into global value chains and the impact of such integration on their working conditions, wages, and overall economic well-being;
ii   The participation of women in the informal economy and how globalization influences the conditions of their work in informal sectors;
iii The gendered aspects of migration, including the experiences of women migrants and the ways in which globalization influences patterns of migration;
iv   How economic changes associated with globalization may enhance or constrain women's agency and decision-making power in various spheres of life;
v   The role of social policies in mitigating or exacerbating the gendered impacts of globalization by supporting or undermining women's well-being in the face of global economic changes.

Focusing on the gendered globalization theory, different scholars and activists in the field of gendered globalization, that is, Connell (2007), Kabeer (2005), Kathy (2008), Moghadam (2005), and Sassen (2001), made significant contributions to the study of gendered globalization, examining its implications on gender equality, women's rights, and the empowerment of marginalized gender groups. Their works provide insights into the challenges and opportunities that globalization presents for gender equity worldwide. This framework examines the ways in which globalization, the process of increased interconnectedness and interdependence among countries and societies, intersects with gender relations. This theory seeks to understand how globalization influences and is influenced by gender dynamics, roles, and inequalities. Gendered globalization theory recognizes that globalization is not a neutral or uniform process. Instead, it affects individuals and communities differently based on their gender identities and roles. The theory highlights that gender shapes and is shaped by various aspects of globalization, including economic, political, social, and cultural dimensions.

The key aspects within the gendered globalization theory connected with our study include the following ideas:

i   Globalization can lead to changes in labor markets and work patterns, affecting men and women differently. Women often face disadvantages in accessing economic opportunities and are often concentrated in low-paid and precarious jobs.
ii   Globalization has facilitated connections between feminist movements across borders, allowing them to collaborate and advocate for gender equality on a global scale.
iii Global trade and investment policies can have differential effects on men and women, and these effects can vary based on factors such as location, class, and ethnicity.
iv   Globalization has led to increased migration flows, and gender plays a significant role in the types of labor migrants engage in. Women are often disproportionately involved in domestic and care work, both within their home countries and as migrants abroad.
v   Globalization can influence cultural norms and values, which, in turn, affect gender roles and expectations in societies.

The gendered globalization theory has prompted policymakers and organizations to address gender-specific issues in the context of global development and international relations. This includes initiatives to promote women's economic empowerment, combat gender-based violence, and enhance women's access to education and healthcare (Grantham et al., 2021).

With a particular lens on African women, historical processes such as colonization, decolonization, and ongoing efforts toward de-westernization have shaped their experiences in global politics. In Africa, colonization left a profound impact on the continent's political and social structures. As African nations gained independence, the process of decolonization aimed to dismantle colonial legacies. However, the struggles faced by African women during this period often remained marginalized. The legacy of colonialism perpetuated gender inequalities, and the postcolonial era witnessed the resilience of African women in challenging these structures (Mbilinyi, 1981; Oyewumi, 1997). Hence, de-westernization in the context of African women's experiences in global politics involves recognizing and valuing indigenous knowledge and diverse feminist discourses that emerge from African contexts. De-westernization empowers African women by acknowledging their agency in shaping political narratives beyond Western paradigms (Narayan, 1997). In that context, postcolonial and decolonial feminisms in Africa provide theoretical frameworks that center the experiences of African women within a global context. These perspectives critique the Eurocentric foundations of mainstream feminism and emphasize the intersections of gender, race, and colonial histories. African women's agency is highlighted as they navigate the complexities of postcolonial societies and challenge oppressive structures (Mohanty, 1988).

Therefore, the impact of gendered globalization on women is not uniform and varies across regions, cultures, and socioeconomic contexts. While some women may benefit from certain aspects of globalization, others may face increased vulnerabilities and inequalities. On the positive side, it has created new opportunities for employment and entrepreneurship, enabling some women to participate in the formal economy. However, globalization has also led to challenges such as increased competition, economic inequalities, and the exploitation of labor, which disproportionately affect women. Additionally, cultural changes and the spread of Western ideals may affect traditional gender roles and contribute to social tensions. While access to education and healthcare may improve for some women in some regions, others may face marginalization and exploitation in the globalized economy. Overall, the impact of globalization on African women is complex, with both opportunities and challenges that vary across regions and socioeconomic contexts. In some cases, globalization has exacerbated violence against women, especially in regions with economic and political instability. Women can be more vulnerable to human trafficking, sexual exploitation, and violence during periods of economic upheaval and displacement. Kabeer (2004) argues that a comprehensive approach is necessary to address the challenges and harness the potential benefits of globalization for women's empowerment and gender equality.

The gendered globalization framework recognizes the gendered dimensions of globalization, including the feminization of labor, gendered patterns of migration, and unequal power relations (Sassen, 2007). Focusing on the effects of globalization on African women, this study clarifies the cultural and economic effects of globalization on African women and describes their determination of women in the face of unequal power dynamics, poverty, and discrimination brought by globalization processes. It, therefore, describes their notable agency and resilience, which have been marked by their active participation in various aspects of development such as politics, economic development, education, healthcare, and community engagement.

Research Methodology

This chapter uses the methodology of systematic review. According to Petticrew and Roberts (2006):

> a systematic review is a research method that involves a structured and comprehensive synthesis of evidence on a particular topic or research question. It aims to minimize bias by systematically identifying, appraising, and summarizing all relevant studies on a specific subject, using explicit methods and predefined criteria.

This systematic review involves identifying, selecting, and synthesizing relevant studies to answer the research question of how globalization has affected the empowerment of African women.

Research design: The study used a systematic review design that involves conducting a comprehensive search of relevant academic journals, books, reports, and gray literature. This systematic search strategy identified thirty-eight studies published between 2000 and 2023 to allow the review to reflect recent developments in the field of gender and development, particularly in the context of globalization.

Search strategy: The study used a systematic search strategy to identify relevant studies published between 2000 and 2023 to ensure that the review includes studies that are methodologically reflective of current research standards. The search terms have included globalization, African women, gender, empowerment, economic, cultural, and social, among others.

Inclusion Criteria

Inclusion criteria in a systematic review define the characteristics that studies must have in order to be considered for inclusion in the review (Higgins and Green, 2011). They help ensure that the selected studies are relevant to the research question and that the review is focused on the specific population, interventions, comparisons, outcomes, and study designs of interest.

Studies published between 2000 and 2023
Studies that focus on African women in the context of globalization
Studies that examine the impact of globalization on economic, social, or political empowerment of African women
Studies that use qualitative, quantitative, or mixed methods
Studies that are published in English
Study selection and data extraction

The identified studies are screened based on predetermined inclusion criteria and the objectives of the study.

The collected information includes the variables assessed related to globalization and African women. These are: (i) the economic globalization's influence on African women: employment, entrepreneurship, and access to resources; (ii) the cultural changes and challenges faced by African women: shifts in norms, values, and identities; (iii) the agency and resilience of African women in shaping gender-equitable responses to the challenges posed by globalization.

(Explored studies are listed at the end of the paper).

Analysis, interpretation, and reporting: The analysis involved identifying common themes and patterns related to the impact of globalization on African women's economic, social, and political empowerment, the strategies they use to resist the dominant narratives of globalization, and the barriers and facilitators of their empowerment. This synthesis involved the qualitative techniques of thematic analysis to synthesize the findings of the selected studies. The study also investigates policy interventions in promoting the empowerment of African women in the context of globalization. The findings are interpreted, and conclusions are drawn based on the synthesized evidence. The findings are presented in a narrative format.

Presentation Results

This part summarizes the key results under the specific themes formulated in line with the study objectives.

The Globalization's Influence on African Women's Economic Opportunities

The assessment of the effects of globalization on African women's economic opportunities will consider the core elements of economic empowerment identified by various scholars. According to Duflo (2012), Kabeer (2005), and Mwaikokesya & Sulle (2020), economic empowerment includes having control over financial resources, earning a sustainable income, and participating in economic activities. Arguably, Kabeer (2005) explains that economic empowerment for women involves not only access to economic resources but also the ability to make strategic life choices, including the power to control resources, access to education and employment, and the ability to participate in decision-making processes within households and communities. In brief, the core elements of economic empowerment are:

i *Financial independence* (having control over financial resources, earning a sustainable income, and participating in economic activities).
ii *Access to resources*: ensuring equal access to and control over resources such as land, credit, and education to engage in economic activities and improve their economic status.
iii *Income generation and employment opportunities*: enhancing opportunities for employment, especially in sectors where women have been traditionally underrepresented.
iv *Entrepreneurship and business ownership*: supporting women in starting and growing their businesses, providing access to markets, and offering training and resources.
v *Skills development*: enhancing women's skills and capabilities through education, vocational training, and other forms of skill development that contribute to increased economic participation.
vi *Social and legal empowerment*: addressing discriminatory laws and social norms that may hinder women's economic progress and ensuring that they have equal rights and opportunities.

With consideration of the papers written by Chachage (2009) and Elson (2000), the economic changes associated with globalization in Africa have had significant impacts on African women's experiences in terms of their access to resources, employment opportunities, and livelihoods. Neoliberal economic policies often resulted in reduced public services and social spending, disproportionately affecting women's access to resources such as healthcare, education, and social protection. The withdrawal of state support for agriculture and the promotion of export-oriented agriculture also undermined women's access to land, credit, and markets, as they were typically engaged in subsistence farming. In Ethiopia, Bekele (2019) states that the growth of multinational corporations (MNCs) created employment opportunities in Africa, particularly in extractive industries and export-oriented manufacturing. However, women employed in these sectors often faced discrimination, wage gaps, and limited access to higher-paying positions and managerial roles (Assie-Lumumba, 2009; Bekele, 2019). Ayenagbo (2022) argues that women remain excluded from the more stable and better-paying jobs in heavy industry because the work requires physical strength.

Additionally, the environmental impacts and land acquisitions associated with extractive industries disrupted local communities in sub-Saharan Africa, affecting women's access to natural resources and traditional livelihoods. Globalization's expansion of international trade, particularly trade liberalization and participation in global value chains (GVCs), presented both opportunities and challenges for African women. While some women entrepreneurs and workers could access new markets and engage in export-oriented sectors, others faced increased competition, job insecurity, and low wages in domestic industries and small-scale enterprises in Tanzania (Mwaikokesya & Sulle, 2020; Udagama, 2012). Trade agreements and intellectual property rights regimes could also hinder women's access to affordable medicines, affecting their healthcare in Tanzania (Udagama, 2012).

Fundamentally, although the industrial development linked with globalization offered women employment opportunities, global economic integration has not always translated into improved economic conditions for African women. It also discriminated against women in access to education, employment opportunities, and entrepreneurial ventures and limited them to access higher-paying positions and managerial roles, which has affected their job security in domestic industries. Moreover, neoliberal economic policies and the lack of government support, which reduced public services and social spending, have affected women's access to resources such as healthcare, education, social protection, land, credit, and markets. Hence, the effects of globalization, marked by increased interconnectedness and integration of economies, have been both opportunities and challenges for women in Africa.

The Cultural Changes Accompanying Globalization on African Women

The assessment of cultural changes accompanying globalization considers how globalization has affected challenging cultural norms and practices that perpetuate gender inequality and the participation of African women in shaping and preserving their cultural heritage. As globalization brings cultural exchanges, those transformations brought both positive and negative consequences for African women in terms of their identities, values, and social norms.

Amoakohene (2007) and Daramola and Anyadike (2017) notice that the spread of Western cultural forms has influenced African women's identities by shaping their self-perceptions and aspirations in Nigeria and Ghana. They argue that the adoption of Western beauty standards and ideals contributed to the marginalization of African women who do not fit these standards, leading to body image issues and self-esteem concerns. This cultural influence also affected women's sense of belonging and cultural pride, as traditional practices and symbols were increasingly overshadowed by Western cultural dominance.

For Oyelaran-Oyeyinka and McCormick (2006), the erosion of traditional cultural practices and the influence of Western values led to shifts in African women's value systems. Traditional values that emphasize communalism, interdependence, and collectivism are challenged by individualistic values associated with globalization, which affect women's sense of identity, their relationships with others, and their understanding of societal roles and responsibilities.

In Zimbabwe, globalization has challenged traditional social norms and gender roles in African societies, affecting women's experiences. As traditional practices erode, women face conflicting expectations between traditional and modern values, leading to role ambiguity and increased pressure to conform to new norms (Kandemiri and Mapira, 2015). The breakdown of extended family systems often accompanied by urbanization and increased individualism impacts women's support networks and social cohesion (Oyelaran-Oyeyinka & McCormick, 2006). Globalization has therefore affected positively and negatively African women in their cultural norms, values, and identities.

Although globalization has brought numerous opportunities and challenges affecting various aspects of societies worldwide, African women, in particular, face distinct cultural challenges and barriers because of globalization. The increased exposure to Western norms and values influencing perceptions of gender roles sometimes clashed with traditional African cultural expectations for women. This pressure to conform to Western standards often conflicts with the deeply rooted values and roles assigned to women in African societies, limiting their ability to embrace new opportunities without facing cultural backlash (Mama, 2006; Nnaemeka, 2013). Additionally, globalization has influenced health policies and access to healthcare in African countries, while we know that cultural norms and practices often intersect with these changes, impacting women's ability to access reproductive healthcare and information. Stigmas surrounding reproductive rights, family planning, and sexual health persist, limiting the empowerment of African women in making informed choices about their bodies and lives (Kabeer, 2005; Mama, 2006).

The Agency and Resilience of African Women in Shaping Gender-Equitable Responses to the Challenges Posed by Globalization

Considering the different articles assessed, the agency and resiliency of African women are undoubtedly remarkable, but they also face several challenges that affect their ability to exercise agency and demonstrate resilience.

African women have demonstrated remarkable agency and resilience in shaping gender-equitable responses to the challenges posed by globalization. Looking at the *economic empowerment and entrepreneurship*, the liberalization of economies has opened up new opportunities, and women have seized these opportunities to establish businesses, engage in trade, and pursue entrepreneurship (Ampofo and Hassim, 2010; Falola & Usman, 2011). African women have engaged in economic empowerment initiatives to challenge economic inequalities and disparities exacerbated by globalization. African women from Rwanda, Tanzania, Uganda, Burundi, etc. have established women's cooperatives, microfinance programs, and entrepreneurship networks to enhance women's economic participation, access to resources, and financial autonomy (Agarwal, 2010). These initiatives empower women economically, enabling them to contribute to their families' well-being and challenging traditional gender roles. Maqutu (2019) explains that African women have been at the forefront of labor rights movements, advocating for fair wages, safe working conditions, and workers' rights. The same author argues that African women have organized unions and fought against exploitative labor practices. Their activism has challenged gender-based discrimination and sought to improve the socioeconomic conditions of workers. Those African women's movements have questioned dominant neoliberal economic policies and advocated for alternative models that prioritize social welfare, economic justice, and redistribution of resources (Chachage, 2017). They have also emphasized the importance of sustainable development that balances social, economic, and environmental concerns and have raised awareness about the adverse impacts of resource extraction, environmental degradation, and climate change on marginalized communities. These movements have advocated for sustainable practices, conservation efforts, and the inclusion of local knowledge and perspectives in environmental decision-making (Kothari and Salleh, 2015). African women have actively participated in movements for environmental justice, especially in contexts where communities are disproportionately affected by ecological degradation, resource extraction, and climate change. They have raised their voices against environmental injustices, advocated for sustainable development, and highlighted the importance of indigenous knowledge and women's perspectives in environmental decision-making (Lahai and Shepler, 2014).

Considering *education and advocacy*, African women, recognizing the importance of education, have advocated for and actively pursued educational opportunities. Education equips them with the knowledge and skills necessary to navigate the changing global landscape (Mama, 2007). Women's advocacy groups have emerged, championing gender equality, women's rights, and social justice. These groups use their agency to influence policy changes, challenge discriminatory practices, and ensure that the benefits of globalization are equitably distributed. They have formed and participated in women's rights movements that advocate for gender equality, challenge discriminatory norms and practices, and strive for women's empowerment. These movements have sought to influence policy agendas, engage in grassroots activism, and raise awareness about the specific challenges faced by women in the context of globalization (Mama, 2000). According to Tripp (2015a), African women have played a transformative role in advocating for labor rights, environmental justice, and women's rights. They have actively sought to increase their participation and representation in decision-making processes at various levels, including politics, governance, and civil society. They have advocated for gender-responsive policies, quotas, and affirmative action to ensure the inclusion of women's perspectives and experiences in shaping agendas and policies. They have mobilized for legal reforms, challenged discriminatory practices, and worked toward empowering women economically, socially, and politically. Smith (2021) underscores that they have formed alliances with global feminist movements, environmental organizations, and social justice groups to amplify their voices, exchange knowledge and strategies, and exert pressure on international institutions and decision-makers.

Finally, Cole and Thomas (2009) argue that African women have engaged in transnational advocacy networks and collaborations to amplify their voices, exchange knowledge, and influence global agendas. They have participated in international conferences, forums, and campaigns to address gender inequalities and promote gender-equitable forms of globalization. Those events provide opportunities for African women to share their experiences, highlight the specific challenges faced by African women, and advocate for inclusive and equitable policies within the global arena (Smith, 2020).

In relation to *health and reproductive rights*, the globalization of health information and initiatives has empowered African women to take control of their health and reproductive rights. Mama (2007) states that women's agencies have played a role in disseminating information about healthcare, family planning, and reproductive rights. Grassroots movements and NGOs led by African women have advocated for improved healthcare infrastructure, access to contraceptives, and the reduction of maternal mortality rates. These efforts contribute to shaping a more gender-equitable healthcare system. In politics, African women have increasingly become involved in politics, at both local and national levels, and globalization has influenced political changes, providing opportunities for women to participate in political processes at all levels (Ampofo and Hassim, 2010). Women's agencies have been critical in pushing for gender-inclusive policies and advocating for women's representation in political leadership. This involvement has helped challenge traditional power structures and foster a more inclusive and equitable political landscape.

In line with *cultural and social transformations*, globalization has brought about cultural exchanges and the dissemination of diverse perspectives. Social movements led by African women have challenged traditional gender roles and norms, advocating for more inclusive and egalitarian societies. They have challenged patriarchal power structures, promoted women's leadership and agency, and sought to transform gender relations within families, communities, and institutions (Ibrahim, 2003). These movements have commented on the exploitative and exclusionary nature of globalization, calling for alternative approaches that prioritize social justice, inclusivity, and environmental sustainability. They have addressed issues such as gender-based violence, access to education, reproductive rights, and political representation (Mama & Zulu, 2007). At the grassroots level, African women have developed innovative approaches, such as community dialogues, women's rights education, and community-led development projects, to foster gender-equitable development and social change (Cornwall & Whitehead, 2007). The cultural production of African women related to art, literature, and media has contributed to reshaping societal norms, challenging gender stereotypes, and fostering a more inclusive and equitable cultural environment (Ampofo & Hassim, 2010).

Particularly, African women's social movements recognize the interconnected nature of gender inequality with other forms of discrimination and marginalization; they address issues of race, class, ethnicity, and sexuality, acknowledging the diverse experiences and identities of African women (Mbilinyi & Dankelman, 2012). These movements have called for inclusive development that recognizes and addresses the needs and priorities of marginalized communities, including women. They have advocated for participatory decision-making processes, community-led development initiatives, and equitable distribution of resources (Omeje, 2014).

To address global gender inequalities, African women's networks have provided platforms for African women to connect with global feminist movements, share experiences, exchange knowledge, learn from global experiences, build solidarity with women from diverse backgrounds, and collectively address the challenges they face. African women have participated in transnational feminist networks that promote collaboration, solidarity, and the sharing of strategies and resources to challenge gender inequalities and advocate for women's rights in the context of globalization (Mohanty et al., 2017). This facilitates the sharing of strategies, lessons learned, and best practices to strengthen women's rights advocacy and challenge dominant models of globalization (Cornwall, & Nyamu-Musembi, 2004).

African women engage in transnational networks to advocate for policy change at both national and global levels. They collaborate with international organizations, civil society groups, and other stakeholders to influence policy frameworks, legislation, and institutional practices to address gender inequalities and promote women's rights (Mama, 2000). African women have joined global advocacy campaigns that focus on diverse issues such as violence against women, reproductive rights, economic justice, and political participation. African women contribute their perspectives, expertise, and experiences to shape the global agenda and advocate for gender-equitable policies (Lwabukuna & Baiocchi, 2016).

Although unlimited achievements reflect evident agency and resilience skills across various sectors, Kabeer (2005) explains that discriminatory practices linked with traditional norms and cultural expectations often limit African women's opportunities for education, employment, and participation in decision-making processes. This hinders the full realization of women's agency as they may face barriers in accessing resources and opportunities. Discrimination is also manifested in cultural practices such as early marriage, female genital mutilation, and unequal inheritance rights, limiting the autonomy and agency of African women. Moreover, African women often face barriers to entrepreneurship, employment, and financial independence (Duflo, 2012). Limited access to credit, land ownership, and markets often constrain their economic agency. Additionally, informal and precarious work conditions prevalent in many African countries disproportionately affect women. Furthermore, African women face significant health disparities, including limited access to healthcare services, maternal mortality, and the burden of infectious diseases such as HIV/AIDS (Sen and Östlin, 2008). These health challenges not only jeopardize their well-being but also affect their ability to exercise agency in various aspects of life, including education, work, and community involvement. Promoting economic empowerment and overcoming health inequities are fundamental to enhancing the resilience and agency of African women.

Through economic empowerment, education, health advocacy, political participation, and cultural transformation, women in Africa actively contribute to shaping a more gender-equitable society amid the complexities of globalization (Mama, 2007).

To conclude, the United Nations (2020) noticed that women's empowerment encompasses several dimensions, including economic empowerment, social empowerment, and political empowerment, as well as a supportive environment that values and respects women's rights, voices, and contributions, and addresses the structural inequalities that limit their potential. In this perspective, the above achievements of African women demonstrate remarkable agency and resilience in shaping gender-equitable responses to the challenges posed by globalization.

Theoretical and Policy Implication

This chapter examines the impact of globalization on African women's experiences with consideration of the intersectionality of their identities, the gendered impacts of economic policies, the influence on power dynamics and cultural transformations, the emergence of transnational networks and movements, and the policy implications for social justice.

In assessing globalization's influence on African women's economic opportunities, the results of the study show that global economic integration has presented both opportunities and challenges for African women. On the one side, the economic changes associated with globalization have had positive impacts on African women's experiences in terms of their access to resources, employment opportunities, and livelihoods (Chachage, 2009; Elson, 2000). For example, in Tanzania, Nigeria, and Ghana, some women entrepreneurs and workers could access new markets and engage in export-oriented sectors. However, other women faced increased competition, job insecurity, low wages, limited access to higher-paying positions and managerial roles, trade agreements, and intellectual property rights regimes, which have affected their access to affordable medicines (Assie-Lumumba, 2009; Ayenagbo, 2022;

Bekele, 2019; Mwaikokesya & Sulle, 2020; Udagama, 2012). This matches the idea of Kabeer (2004), which highlights the complex ways in which globalization processes can both empower and marginalize women, depending on various factors such as class, race, and geographical location. As it was noted that trade liberalization and foreign direct investment have often perpetuated gender inequalities and marginalized women's economic participation in Africa, it is relevant to consider the community's social characteristics and culture while planning and promoting their development. Examining these impacts sheds light on the systemic barriers and challenges African women face in the globalized world. Kinyanjui (2014) argues that planners need to decolonize and de-westernize their planning perspectives so that they can incorporate some of the African forms and norms of livelihood negotiation and specialties.

These results underscore the necessity of considering the gender intersectionality approach in development practices, as it considers the role played by multiple social identities, providing insights into how they shape experiences of discrimination and privilege of social groups in development practice (Crenshaw, 1989). This approach recognizes that people's experiences of privilege and oppression are often influenced by the intersection of various social categories rather than just one. As an example of many African countries, including Rwanda, women from different socioeconomic backgrounds (rural/urban, different ethnic groups, illiterate/literate, etc.) may face distinct challenges and have varying access to resources that may facilitate or limit them to promote entrepreneurship and economic development projects. The culture of different sub-ethnic groups, which limits them to access bank loans or other resources to improve their economic status, is an example. However, policymakers and development practitioners used to ignore that. Therefore, policymakers need to shift toward inclusive and participatory planning that can formulate policies that do not respond to the needs of women in general but rather respond to the particular needs of specific subgroups of women based on their specific experiences.

In line with cultural changes, the results show that globalization has brought cultural exchanges having both positive and negative consequences for African women in terms of their identities, values, and social norms.

In Nigeria and Ghana, the adoption of Western beauty standards and ideals contributed to the marginalization of African women who do not fit these standards, and it has affected women's sense of belonging and cultural pride so that traditional practices and symbols are increasingly overshadowed by Western cultural dominance (Amoakohene, 2007; Daramola and Anyadike, 2017). Further, traditional values that emphasize communalism, interdependence, and collectivism are challenged by individualistic values associated with globalization, which affect women's sense of identity, their relationships with others, and their understanding of societal roles and responsibilities (Oyelaran-Oyeyinka & McCormick, 2006). In Zimbabwe, globalization has challenged traditional social norms and gender roles in African societies, and women face conflicting expectations between traditional and modern values, leading to role ambiguity and increased pressure to conform to new norms (Kandemiri & Mapira, 2015). The pressure to conform to Western standards often conflicts with the deeply rooted values and roles assigned to women in African societies, limiting their ability to embrace new opportunities without facing cultural backlash (Mama, 2006; Nnaemeka, 2013).

Linking these results with the definition of cultural empowerment. Globalization has challenged cultural norms and practices that perpetuate gender inequality and is questioning the participation and agency of African women in shaping and preserving their cultural heritage (Okazawa-Rey & Enns, 2019). African women are tested to show how wise they are in embracing new cultural values brought by globalization processes while protecting their positive cultural ones. Policymakers and development practitioners have to reflect on innovative and creative cultural practices that conciliate both the positive values of globalization and those existing in their countries in favor of women's rights and development. African societies have to review how gender roles are allocated at the family level for more involvement of men if we need to empower women to participate in other community activities and enjoy their right to development.

In the face of globalization challenges of poverty and discrimination, African women developed the skills and power to overcome them. Scholars explained that the liberalization of economies has opened up new opportunities, and women have seized these opportunities to establish businesses, engage in trade, and pursue entrepreneurship (Ampofo & Hassim, 2010; Falola & Usman, 2011). African women's movements have questioned dominant neoliberal economic policies and advocated for alternative models that prioritize social welfare, economic justice, and redistribution of resources (Chachage, 2017). Moreover, African women have formed and participated in women's rights movements that advocate for gender equality, challenge discriminatory norms and practices, and strive for women's empowerment (Mama, 2000). In Rwanda, for example, women's groups participated in reviewing the National Constitution (2003), which now recognizes at least 30% of women in leadership positions and other decision-making bodies. They also contributed to the revision of the law of land ownership and property rights, which now recognizes women. In addition, Maqutu (2019) states that African women have been at the forefront of labor rights movements, advocating for fair wages, safe working conditions, and workers' rights. In politics, they have advocated for gender-responsive policies, quotas, and affirmative action to ensure the inclusion of women's perspectives and experiences in shaping agendas and policies (Tripp, 2015a). In many African countries, like Rwanda, Tanzania, Uganda, Burundi, and others, women have established women's cooperatives, microfinance programs, and entrepreneurship networks to enhance women's economic participation, access to resources, and financial autonomy (Agarwal, 2010).

They have mobilized for legal reforms, challenged discriminatory practices, and worked towards empowering women economically, socially, and politically. Cole and Thomas (2009) argue that African women have engaged in transnational advocacy networks and collaborations to amplify their voices, exchange knowledge, and influence global agendas. Further, the globalization of health information and initiatives has empowered African women to take control of their health and reproductive rights. Social movements led by African women challenged patriarchal power structures, promoted women's leadership and agency, and sought to transform gender relations within families, communities, and institutions (Ibrahim, 2003).

In brief, through economic empowerment, education and health advocacy, political participation, and cultural transformation, women in Africa actively contribute to shaping a more gender-equitable society amid the complexities of globalization. However, this great will that motivates African women to embrace global opportunities is still weakened by local cultural discriminatory practices, a lack of required resources, and health-related barriers. Strengthening networks and supportive partnerships at the global level may reduce those challenges.

By understanding how globalization affects African women, policymakers, activists, and scholars can work toward addressing gender inequalities, promoting women's empowerment, and creating more equitable and sustainable forms of development. By recognizing and addressing these dynamics, we can strive for a more inclusive and equitable globalization that prioritizes the rights and well-being of African women.

Limitations

This Study Encountered Some Limitations

First, some findings from specific studies on globalization and African women are not generalizable to the entire African continent or different cultural, socioeconomic, and geographical contexts within Africa. Second, the diverse sociocultural, economic, and political contexts across African countries add complexity to the study of globalization and African women. Hence, this study did not fully capture the nuanced experiences and dynamics within different African societies, necessitating context-specific analysis. Finally, given the evolving nature of globalization, a comparative analysis over different periods can help address the limitation of not fully capturing the long-term impacts or future trajectories of globalization on African women. Considering these limitations, we adopted a context-specific approach in our study.

Conclusion and Recommendations

The systematic review on globalization and African women provides a comprehensive and up-to-date synthesis of the existing literature on the topic, which could be useful for policymakers, development practitioners, and scholars in the field.

This study made an important contribution to the understanding of the complex relationship between globalization and African women's empowerment. It provides insights into how globalization processes have influenced the economic and cultural empowerment of African women and how African women's agency and resilience facilitated them to overcome the challenges related to globalization. The following objectives guided the study:

To assess the globalization's influence on African women's economic opportunities, including employment, entrepreneurship opportunities, and access to resources.
To identify the cultural changes and challenges faced by African women in the context of globalization, including shifts in norms, values, and identities.
To describe the agency and resilience of African women in shaping gender-equitable responses to the challenges posed by globalization.

From the results, globalization processes have affected African women positively and negatively. Women used the economic and cultural opportunities accompanying globalization to improve their status and their countries. With many achievements described above, African women are active agents, and globalization can offer them new opportunities for challenging existing gender injustices and to express their multiple gender identities. However, some challenges still need to be tackled, for example, the need to find a balance between global and local, that is, to consolidate transnational feminist solidarity without losing sight of local and national women's activism and everyday local resistance and struggles. Although some groups of women are benefiting from the global opportunities, others are not due to their specific localities and identity factors. For example, social groups of women have problems with financial resources or those oppressed by rigid health cultural norms, which affect their economic development. Therefore, the application of the gender intersectionality approach and the formulation of policies that respond to the needs of specific women's groups would benefit more community groups. Based on the above summary, the researcher recommends the following strategies to sustain the agency and resilience of African women in the face of globalization challenges:

Policymakers: To develop and implement gender-responsive policies and frameworks at national and international levels which address the specific challenges faced by African women, promote their rights, and enhance their access to resources, opportunities, and decision-making processes.

Development Practitioners and Local Leaders

To promote inclusive and sustainable economic growth through initiatives that provide access to finance, support women's entrepreneurship, promote gender-equitable employment practices, and address structural barriers to economic participation.

To invest in education and skills development programs: Ensure that education is accessible, inclusive, and of high quality. Promote the acquisition of relevant skills, including digital literacy, to enhance African women's participation in the global economy and decision-making processes.

To support and empower African women's leadership at all levels of society. Increase their representation in decision-making positions, including political, economic, and social spheres. Provide training and mentorship opportunities to enhance their leadership skills and promote their meaningful participation in shaping policies and programs.

To foster partnerships and collaboration with civil society organizations that work toward gender equality and women's rights. Support their advocacy efforts, amplify their voices, and provide resources for their programs and initiatives aimed at advancing the rights and well-being of African women.

To challenge and transform cultural norms and discriminatory practices that perpetuate gender inequality. Promote gender-sensitive approaches to addressing harmful practices such as child marriage, female genital mutilation, and gender-based violence. Engage communities and stakeholders in dialogue and awareness-raising to promote positive social change.

To support transnational collaborations, knowledge exchange, and joint advocacy efforts that amplify the voices of African women, challenge dominant models of globalization, and advocate for more inclusive and equitable forms of development.

To invest in research and data collection that specifically focuses on the experiences, challenges, and aspirations of African women in the context of globalization. This will provide evidence-based insights for policymaking, program design, and advocacy efforts.

Bibliography

Banerjee, S. and Ghosh, N. (2018) Introduction. Debating Intersectionalities: Challenges for a Methodological Framework. *South Asia Multidisciplinary Academic Journal* 19 https://doi.org/10.4000/samaj.4745

Batliwala, S. (2007) Taking the Power out of Empowerment: An Experiential Account. *Development in Practice* 17(4/5):557–565.

Butler, J. (1990) *Gender Trouble: Feminism and the Subversion of Identity*. Routledge.

Connell, R. (2007). *The Southern Theory Global Dynamics of Knowledge in Social Science*. Polity Press.

Dejardin, A.K. (2009) *Gender (In)equality, Globalization and Governance*. International Labor organization. ARTICLE g.pdf

Dlamini, N. (2017). "Becoming him: A Transnational African Diasporic Analysis of Gender Performance in Diaspora." *Gender & Society*, 31(5), 658–681.

Grantham, K. et al. (2021). *Women's Economic Empowerment: Insights from Africa and South Asia*. Routledge

Higgins, J. P., and Green, S. (Eds.). (2011). *Cochrane Handbook for Systematic Reviews of Interventions*. The Cochrane Collaboration. (Available online: https://training.cochrane.org/handbook

Jomo, K.S. 2003. Globalization, Liberalization and Equitable Development: Lessons from East Asia. Programme on Overarching Concerns, ChapterNo. 3. UNRISD, Geneva.

Kabeer, N. (2004) *Gendered Impacts of Globalization: Employment and Social Protection*. United Nations Research Institute for Social Development (UNRISD) https://www.unrisd.org/en

Kabeer, N. (2005). "Gender equality and women's empowerment: A critical analysis of the third Millennium Development Goal 1." *Gender & Development*, 13(1), 13–24.

Kabeer, N. (2009). "Women's economic empowerment: Key issues and policy options", Sida Background Paper, Sussex: Institute of Development Studies

Kathy E. (2008) *Gender and Globalization in Asia and the Pacific: Method, Practice, Theory*. University of Hawaii Press.

Kessy, A T, and Shayo, HE (2022) Tanzania's diaspora engagement: The need for a paradigm shift in diaspora engagement and investment policies, *Research Globalization* 5. https://www.sciencedirect.com/science/article/pii/S2590051X22000168

Mbilinyi, M. (1981). "African Women in Politics: Their Situation and Struggle Within the Political System." In *Women in Africa: Studies in Social and Economic Change*, edited by Nancy J. Hafkin and Edna G. Bay. Stanford University Press

Moghadam, V. M. (2005). *Globalizing Women: Transnational Feminist Networks*. Johns Hopkins University Press

Mohanty, C. T. (1988) "Under Western Eyes: Feminist Scholarship and Colonial Discourses." *Feminist Review*, 30, 61–88.

Narayan, U. (1997). *Dislocating Cultures: Identities, Traditions, and Third World Feminism*. Routledge.

Oyewumi, O. (1997). *The Invention of Women: Making an African Sense of Western Gender Discourses*. University of Minnesota Press.

Petticrew, M., and Roberts, H. (2006). Systematic Reviews in the Social Sciences: A Practical Guide. Blackwell Publishing.

Salau, M.B. (2023) *African Diasporas: History and Historiography*, Oxford University Press.

Sassen, S. (2007). A Sociology of Globalization. W.W. Norton & Company.

Seguino, S. and Grown, C. (2006) *Gender Equity and Elobalization: Macroeconomic Policy for Developing Countries*. Journal of International Development, 18, pp. 1–24.

SIDA (2009) Women's Economic Empowerment: Scope for Sida's Engagement. https://www.enterprise-development.org/wp-content/uploads/SidaEngagement_WomensEconomicEmpowerment.pdf

Steger, M. B. (2017). *Globalization: A Very Short Introduction* (4th ed.). Oxford University Press.

Tripp, A. M. (2015a). *Women and Power in Post-Conflict Africa*. Cambridge University Press.

Sassen, S, (2001). *The Global City*: New York, London, Tokyo. Princeton University Press.

United Nations (2003) Women's Access to Information Technologies Needed to Eradicate Poverty, Create Economically Just, Democratic Societies, Women's Commission Told. https://press.un.org/en/2003/wom1391.doc.htm

UN Women. (2013). Economic Empowerment. https://www.unwomen.org/en/what-we-do/economic-empowerment

World Vision (2023) Empowered Girls Voice their Concerns & Call for Action on Gender Equality, Health, Rights, & Wellbeing at World Vision's Women Deliver Side-event. https://www.wvi.org/newsroom/empowered-girls-voice-their-concerns-call-action-gender-equality-health-rights-wellbeing

Explored Articles

Agarwal, B. (2010). *Gender and Green Governance: The Political Economy of Women's Presence within and Beyond Community Forestry*. Oxford University Press.

Amoakohene, M. I. (2007). "Body Image and Self-esteem among Adolescent Girls in Ghana: Implications for Well-being." *Gender & Development*, 15(3), 395–411.

Ampofo, A.A. and Hassim, S. (Eds.). (2010). *Gender, Politics, and the State in Africa*. Indiana University Press.

Ayenagbo, K. (2022). *Globalization and Women's Employability in Sub-Saharan Africa*. REDFAME.

Assie-Lumumba, N. T. (2009). "Gender, globalization, and African economies: Historical, contemporary, and future perspectives." *Feminist Africa*, 13, 30–51.

Barrientos, S. (2006). "Empowerment and Agency: A Critical Exploration of Agency in Women's lives." *The European Journal of Development Research*, 18(3), 509–528.

Bekele, A. B. (2019). "The Impact of Multinational Corporations on Women Workers in Ethiopia." *Gender Issues*, 36(2), 195–213.

Daramola, O. O., & Anyadike, C. (2017). "Globalization, cultural imperialism and women's body image in Nigeria." In O. O. Daramola & A. A. Oyedele (Eds.), *Gender Issues in Nigeria* (pp. 227–244). Springer.

Duflo, E. (2012). "Women's Empowerment and Economic Development." *Journal of Economic Literature*, 50(4), 1051–1079.

Chachage, C. S. L. (2009). Neoliberalism and Women's Economic Marginalisation in Tanzania." *Nordic Journal of African Studies*, 18(3), 151–169.

Chachage, C. S. (Ed.). (2017). *African Intellectuals and Decolonization*. Springer.

Cole, P., & Thomas, L. (Eds.). (2009). *Gender matters in global politics: A Feminist Introduction to International Relations*. Routledge.

Cornwall, A., Harrison, E., & Whitehead, A. (Eds.). (2007). *Feminisms in Development: Contradictions, Contestations, and Challenges*. Zed Books.

Cornwall, A., & Nyamu-Musembi, C. (2004). "Putting the 'Rights-Based Approach' to Development into Perspective." *Third World Quarterly*, 25(8), 1415–1437.

Elson, D. (2000). "Male Bias in Macroeconomics: The Case of Structural Adjustment." *World Development*, 28(7), 1359–1373.

Falola, T. and Usman, A. (Eds.). (2011). *Women and Globalization in Africa: A Political Economy Approach*. University of Rochester Press.

Ibrahim, A. (Ed.). (2003). *Gender and Citizenship in Africa*. Zed Books.

Kabeer, N. (2005b). "Gender Equality and Women's Empowerment: A Critical Analysis of the Third Millennium Development Goal 1." *Gender & Development*, 13(1), 13–24.

Kandemiri, Y., & Mapira, N. (2015). "Gender Roles and Gender Relations in the Postcolonial Shona society of Zimbabwe." *Gender & Behaviour*, 13(1), 6122–6134.

Kothari, A., & Salleh, A. (Eds.). (2015). *Eco-Sufficiency and Global Justice: Women Write Political Ecology*. Pluto Press.

Lahai, J., & Shepler, S. (Eds.). (2014). *Gendering Global Transformations: Gender, Culture, Race, and Identity*. Routledge.

Lwabukuna, O., & Baiocchi, G. (2016). *African Women at the Helm: Grassroots Leadership for Sustainable Development*. Routledge.

Mama, A. (2000). "Feminism, Gender and the State in an Era of Globalization." *Feminist Review*, 66(1), 17–45.

Mama, A. (2006). "From the Margins to the Centre: Women's Experiences in Contemporary Africa." *Development*, 49(1), 11–18.

Mama, A. (2007). "African Women's Agency in Globalization: Challenges and Opportunities." *Agenda: Empowering Women for Gender Equality*, 21(75),1–7.

Mama, A., & Zulu, S. (Eds.). (2007). *Women in African Parliaments*. Lynne Rienner Publishers.

Maqutu, L. (Ed.). (2019). *Gender and Work in Global Value Chains: Capturing the Gains?* Cambridge University Press.

Mbilinyi, M., & Dankelman, I. (Eds.). (2012). *Gender and Sustainable Development: Case Studies from NCCR North South*. Sage Publications.

Mohanty, C. T., Russo, A., & Torres, L. (Eds.). (2017). *Third World Women and the Politics of Feminism*. Duke University Press.

Mwaikokesya, J. B., & Sulle, E. (2020). "Women Participation in International Trade and Regional Integration Processes in Tanzania." *African Journal of Rural Development*, 5(2), 142–156.

Nnaemeka, O. (Ed.). (2013). *The politics of (m)othering: Women, Identity, and Resistance in Africa*. University of Chicago Press.

Omeje, K. (Ed.). (2014). *Extractive Economies and Conflicts in the Global South: Multi-Regional Perspectives*. Palgrave Macmillan.

Oyelaran-Oyeyinka, B., & McCormick, D. (2006). "Globalization, Structural Change, and Productivity growth." In B. Oyelaran-Oyeyinka & R. L. McCormick (Eds.), *Industrial Development for the 21st Century: Sustainable Development Perspectives* (pp. 1–23). United Nations University Press.

Quisumbing, A. et al. (2018). "Empowerment and Resilience: Insights from South Asia." *Journal of Gender and Development* 26 (2), 199–216.

Sen, G., and Östlin, P. (2008). Unequal, Unfair, Ineffective and Inefficient. Gender Inequity in Health: Why it exists and How we can Change it. Final Report to the WHO Commission on Social Determinants of Health.

Smith, J. (2021). "African Women's Movements: Engaging in Transnational Advocacy Networks and Collaborations". *Journal of Gender Studies*, 35(3), 345–362.

Tripp, A. M. (2015b). *Women and Power in Post-Conflict Africa*. Cambridge University Press.

Udagama, N. (2012). "The Impact of Trade Liberalization on Women's Employment and Wages in Developing Countries." *Gender & Development* 20(1), 57–70.

20
PATHWAYS TO POWER
Religiosity, Economic Opportunities, and IlParakuyo Maasai Women

Lucy W. Massoi and Parit O. Saruni

Introduction

Globally, there is a significant imbalance in gender power dynamics, with men being favoured in terms of authority in decision-making and access to resources (Acosta et al., 2020; Ndlovu and Mjimba, 2021). This inequality is present in several aspects of life, such as education, employment, and economic prospects, and is also evident in religious (Skidmore, 2007) and infrastructural domains. The gender power paradigm highlights the inherent inequality, positioning men in spaces of authority within wider social systems (Pratto and Espinoza, 2001; Pratto et al., 2006). Tackling gender inequality and empowering women is essential, not just for its ingrained significance but also for promoting broader developmental goals, such as economic expansion.

This chapter integrates ideas from qualitative studies on women's empowerment in culturally similar groups, along with the current research. These studies offer a wide-ranging and thorough compilation of the experiences and methods employed by women in many indigenous and pastoralist communities around the world. Research undertaken on the Himba women of Namibia (Inman, 2024) and the Bedouin women of the Middle East (Abu-Rabia-Queder, 2007) provides comparative views. These studies illustrate various diverse aspects of empowerment, showing how social, cultural, economic, and religious factors intertwine to shape women's lives. Moreover, they emphasise the importance of understanding empowerment in different cultural contexts, offering a nuanced perspective that deepens our understanding of the experiences of Ilparakuyo Maasai women in Tanzania.

The Maasai community has a long-standing reputation for its unique socio-economic and political structure, which has firmly established it within a patriarchal system where men hold significant power advantages (Spencer, 1988; Talle, 1998; Hodgson, 2001; Misafi, 2014). The traditional structure has significantly restricted the participation of Maasai women in decision-making processes and their access to resources, resulting in low positions for them. Increasingly, global development efforts intersect with regional cultural and socio-economic norms, resulting in the formation of a separate patriarchal framework (Opoku et al., 2018; Kipngetich et al., 2022).

Even so, the contemporary increase in religiosity and the development of modern development infrastructural systems are reshaping these traditional structures (Baxter, 1994; Massoi, 2015; Kipuri & Ridgewell, 2008; Van Klinken, 2016). The growing prevalence and influence of gender-based movements in Maasai territories are stimulating the emergence of new religious customs and shaping social standards, particularly gender roles (Massoi, 2018). Simultaneously, recent economic developments, such as the construction of the Standard Gauge Railway (SGR) infrastructural projects, are creating new opportunities and prospects for Maasai women. This is disrupting the long-standing traditional patriarchal customs and creating pathways for empowerment.

This chapter explores how developments are giving Maasai women more authority and undermining traditional patriarchal systems, based on prior studies conducted by Massoi in 2015 and 2018. The analysis is based on Naila Kabeer's concept of women's empowerment, which centres on three fundamental aspects: agency, resources, and accomplishments (Kabeer, 1999). Agency refers to the ability of Maasai women to challenge established power structures and cultural norms (Raymond, 2021; Wabende, 2022). Resources are the tools and methods used by these women to exercise their agency (Ankrah, et al., 2020). Achievements are tangible results that indicate changes in self-sufficiency, social status, and societal roles (Chen & Barcus, 2024).

Employing Kabeer's paradigm, we examine the transformations taking place in Maasai territories. We explore how the evolution of religious rituals and economic development is empowering Maasai women to renegotiate and redefine their positions within their group and the wider social context. As an example of these economic developments, we examine the testimony of Neema, a Maasai entrepreneur who has directly seen and experienced these shifts. She says:

> Establishing my own business I felt like sowing a seed in arid terrain. However, thanks to the fresh prospects brought by the standard gauge railway and the backing of my community, it is now thriving. I embody more than simply the identity of a Maasai woman; I am an entrepreneur, a provider, and a powerful representation of transformation.
> *(Interview: Neema, Maasai Businesswoman owner in Parakuyo, Twatwatwa hamlet in Kilosa District)*

This chapter will enrich Neema's story by including case studies, doing comparison assessments with comparable communities, and using infographics such as storytelling. In addition, we will examine probable future trends and obstacles in the empowerment of Maasai women, offering a forward-thinking perspective on this transforming process.

Conceptual Underpinning

Dynamics of Women's Empowerment: A Multidimensional Framework

The notion of women's empowerment, which rose to prominence in the 1980s, is intricate and ever-changing (Misafi, 2014). It involves achieving mastery of one's own life, making choices, and implementing those choices to produce results. The empowerment framework devised by Naila Kabeer enables a thorough understanding of the many and varied facets of women's empowerment.

Women's empowerment, as a theoretical concept, comprises three interrelated dimensions: agency, resources, and achievements (Kabeer, 1999). We analyse the dynamics of female empowerment in Maasai pastoral societies utilising Naila Kabeer's framework for empowerment. This framework allows for the analysis of the cultural background, which is especially important in the Maasai setting due to its distinctive features.

Agency, in the Maasai context, denotes the ability or capability of women to demonstrate autonomy in decision-making and to challenge dominant power structures and cultural norms. Recent studies indicate that the increasing religious devotion, particularly within emerging religious communities, is beginning to alter conventional roles and beliefs, hence empowering Maasai women to voice themselves with greater power (Agadjanian & Yabiku, 2015; Shim, 2021). Resources refer to both concrete and tangible assets that enable women to exercise their autonomy. Maasai women have had more access to resources and expanded economic opportunities because of infrastructure initiatives and other economic advancements (Hallward-Driemeier, 2013; Massoi & Saruni, 2020; Oppong, 2023). Achievements are the concrete or visible results that emerge when an individual takes action and utilises the resources at their disposal. The progress made in empowering women within Maasai villages is visible through noticeable shifts in societal roles, increased participation in decision-making processes, and improved social status within the community (Hodgson, 2001; Temba et al., 2013; Abramovitz, 2018; Rigby, 2022). Researchers employ this approach to examine the impact of shifts in religious and economic opportunities on the conventional patriarchal system in Maasai communities, resulting in the empowerment of women. This study is grounded in current academic research that examines the interplay between religion, economic progress, and gender in pastoral societies (Massoi, 2018; Chambo, 2024).

Women's Empowerment and the Role of Religion

Religion has a complex role in Maasai culture, especially when it comes to the church's impact on women's empowerment. This function has both transformational and restrictive dimensions. Scholastic perspectives acknowledge the church's role as a catalyst for change when it supports gender equality, questions traditions such as polygamy, and confronts injustices faced by women (Riesebrodt & Chong, 1999; Uchem, 2001; Van Klinken, 2016). The transforming nature of religious teachings becomes evident when they condemn actions that contribute to gender inequity, therefore providing women with fresh opportunities for negotiation and empowerment.

On the other hand, an alternative perspective highlights the potentially restrictive aspects of religion, namely when it maintains male authority in issues of spirituality and supports patriarchal systems (Htun & Weldon, 2015). Religion, in some cases, might unintentionally perpetuate pre-existing gender inequalities. The ambivalent impact of religious influence on women's empowerment is shown by neighbourhood religious leaders such as Pastor John Lekanai of the nearby Pentecostal church, who said: "Our community is experiencing a significant shift in attitudes and beliefs". He went on to say: "Our religious beliefs are leading us towards fresh insights, particularly on the role of women. They serve not just as our sisters and moms, but also as leaders and visionaries. The teachings of our church now align with this updated reality" (Lekanai, personal communication). Supporting the former perspective, we argue that, the church may act as a catalyst – transformative mechanism for change in

Maasai culture by offering women greater opportunities for negotiation and empowerment compared to what was previously accessible (Riesebrodt & Chong, 1999; Uchem, 2001; Hodgson, 2011; Van Klinken, 2016). Yet, it also recognises the intricate nature of religious influence, acknowledging that the church may both empower and, in certain circumstances, limit the roles of women in Maasai culture (Spinks, 2003; Htun & Weldon, 2015).

Pastoralism, Religiosity, and Women's Empowerment

The complex interactions between pastoralism, religiosity, and the changing roles of women in Maasai culture are further explored in this part, which builds on the transformational and restricting aspects of religion in women's empowerment within the Maasai community.

The Maasai culture exemplifies a complex relationship between pastoralism, religion, and the empowerment of women. Historical examination reveals that conventional marriage rituals and household arrangements, rooted in pastoral traditions, are currently changing due to religious influence (Scoones, 2021; Scoones & Nori, 2023). The influence of Christian teachings has resulted in a significant cultural shift, which has led to the increased prevalence of monogamy. Furthermore, continuous efforts to diversify the economy are empowering Maasai women to take on fresh roles, effectively reconciling traditional norms with expanding opportunities (Massoi, 2018; Tunyone, 2023). These societal changes have visible and significant impacts on the local society, as emphasised by a respected Maasai elder:

> I have observed substantial alterations in our town, women, once limited to the margins, are progressively establishing themselves as influential individuals in the fields of education and business. The change is not limited to women alone; it encompasses the entire progress of our society.
>
> (*Samuel Ole Mpaayei, a respected Ilparakuyo Maasai elder*)

Based on those observations, our broad framework looks further into the complex systems of Maasai women's empowerment. This analysis examines the evolving roles of religious beliefs and the expanding economic opportunities that are reshaping traditional behaviours within the Maasai community. We aim to get deep insights into the complex process of empowerment in this particular socio-cultural setting by integrating Naila Kabeer's (2005) theory into our analytical framework (see below). This paradigm not only improves understanding of all the elements involved but also functions as a valuable tool for addressing the inherent complexity of empowering Maasai women. Adopting this perspective allows us to have a greater understanding and analyse the significant transformations experienced by women in Maasai society.

Economic Opportunities and Maasai Women's Empowerment

The Maasai community has experienced a significant change in its economic opportunities, primarily attributed to the development of key infrastructure projects such as the SGR (Were et al., 2020). These innovations have not only revolutionised the physical environment, with a particular focus on empowering women (Chambo, 2024; Tunyone, 2023), but have also generated new opportunities for economic participation. The implementation of projects such as the SGR has not only resulted in infrastructure changes but also facilitated the participation of Maasai women in economic activity, hence increasing their access to market opportunities (Brown, 2019). The departure from traditional gender norms has made a significant contribution to the economic empowerment of women in Maasai culture.

Maasai women are increasingly becoming involved in the economy, resulting in changes in their roles and status within their households and in wider society. Wangui (2008) and Dutt et al. (2016) conducted studies on the Maasai culture and found that women, who were traditionally restricted to their homes and subordinate to men in a culture where men dominate, are now becoming more powerful and aggressive in making significant decisions. The change in economic participation represents significant progress in challenging and reshaping traditional gender roles within Maasai culture. The wider implications of these changes extend beyond the Maasai community. The resilience and adaptability of traditional societies are showcased through the empowerment of Maasai women, which is spurred by economic and religious transformations.

The Empirical Site and Methodology

Kilosa District

Kilosa, a district located in the east-central part of Tanzania, approximately 300 kilometres from Dar es Salaam, is currently undergoing a notable transformation characterised by the merging of traditional practices with cutting-edge technology. A significant manifestation of this development is the adoption of the SGR system, which traverses the area, encompassing the Twatwatwa hamlet. The ethnic diversity in Kilosa, particularly the Maasai ethnic group, illustrates the complex interplay between traditional customs and modern influences. The district's heterogeneous ethnic composition, encompassing various ethnic groups alongside the Maasai, strengthens the local religious context. Churches, such as the Catholic, Lutheran, and Calvary Assemblies of God, serve congregations of individuals from diverse backgrounds. According to URT (2013) and Kilosa District Council (KDC) (2016), Kilosa has 438,175 residents, of whom 219,797 are female.

Methodology

This chapter utilises a qualitative research technique, using the concepts of appreciative inquiry (AI), building upon the ethnographically inspired framework established in Massoi's (2018) work. A useful method for studying complicated social phenomena, such as the empowerment of Maasai women, is to focus on finding positive elements and accomplishments (Cooperrider et al., 2008; Bushe, 2012; Venis et al., 2022). The research uses a blend of direct observations, comprehensive interviews, and group discussions. These techniques, based on ethnography, give priority to the viewpoints of participants (Naidoo, 2012) and are specifically designed to align with the AI approach, which focuses on identifying positive aspects and strengths in the experiences of Maasai women, particularly concerning their religious engagement and economic involvement.

We conducted this research from January 2021 to December 2023, with a focus on the Ilparakuyo Maasai community in Tanzania. The participants were intentionally chosen to represent a diverse variety of experiences within the Maasai community. The selection of participants was deliberate to include a wide range of experiences among Maasai women in Kilosa. This ensured variety in terms of age, socio-economic position, and degrees of engagement in church activities and economic enterprises. The objective of this method is to shed light on narratives of achievement and constructive change (Heath & Waymer, 2021). The data were analysed using thematic analysis, specifically focusing on finding themes related to empowerment and positive advancements (Clarke & Braun, 2017). As noted earlier, this study utilises Kabeer's conceptual framework of empowerment (Kabeer, 1999; Mosedale, 2005; Silva, 2022), viewed through the perspective of appreciative inquiry (AI). The study examines how the combination of religion and economic possibilities, namely those provided by the SGR, contribute to the empowerment of Maasai women.

The ethical concerns adhered to the principles outlined by the American Anthropological Association (2012), which included obtaining informed permission, maintaining confidentiality, and demonstrating cultural sensitivity. The research is situated within the framework of Kabeer's empowerment paradigm, supplemented with the concepts of appreciative inquiry. This comprehensive method offers a detailed perspective for analysing the data, specifically emphasising the favourable features of Maasai women's empowerment within the context of religious influence and the changing economic environment (Kabeer, 1999).

Historical Context

This section explores the historical gender relations within the Maasai community. Comprehending historical events is essential for understanding the changing roles of women and cultural norms. This understanding lays the groundwork for analysing how economic opportunity and religiosity may lead to power, emphasising the shift in women's roles in society. The Maasai, renowned for their pastoralist way of life, have historically followed a patriarchal framework in which males have held predominant positions in society, notably in matters of decision-making and resource distribution (Yurco, 2022). Women's roles were mostly focused on household duties and raising children, with restricted prospects for formal education and economic advancement (Kipuri & Ridgewell, 2008; Archambault, 2017; Tian et al., 2021).

Throughout history, Maasai women have played a crucial role in shaping the social and cultural dynamics, even though they have had minimal public power. They have served as caretakers of cultural traditions, such as rituals marking important life transitions, and have played a crucial role in maintaining the family economy via tasks such as creating intricate beading and processing milk (Archambault, 2016). Maasai women have shown remarkable tenacity and adaptation throughout their life stories. Oral histories and traditional songs often emphasise the fortitude and resilience of women amid social obstacles (Wasamba, 2009). The tales, which have been transmitted over generations, provide a substantial qualitative context for understanding the changing position of women in Maasai culture. The Maasai community is experiencing changes in the roles and perspectives of women due to contemporary influences and problems, including climate change and globalisation (de Wit, 2021; Kilonzo, 2022). The historical backdrop provides a foundation for comprehending the present changes in gender dynamics and the empowerment of Maasai women.

Case Studies: Reflecting on Empowerment

We provide three convincing case studies that demonstrate the concrete effects of altering religious beliefs and economic opportunities on individual Maasai women.

Case One: Neema's Path to Entrepreneurship

Neema, who was strongly rooted in traditional roles within the Maasai society, underwent a significant change when she encountered new religious beliefs promoted by local Pentecostal churches, together with the introduction of the SGR, which coincided with her life (Were et al., 2020; Brown, 2019). These influences caused a significant change in her viewpoint, emphasising the possibility of women actively participating in society.

Unfazed by social doubt and the difficult effort of managing her traditional social obligations with her new business endeavour, Neema set off on a path of self-exploration and entrepreneurship. Utilising her adeptness in making traditional Maasai beaded jewellery like earrings, bracelets, anklets, and necklaces, she established a modest business and effectively marketed her items to both tourists and locals in Morogoro. Over time, Neema's business thrived, resulting in a consistent income that surpassed her prior financial contributions to the home. She illustrates: "I recall experiencing a combination of fear and enthusiasm with each creation I crafted. Everything I sold represented more than just a mere transaction; it served as a tangible manifestation of my recently acquired autonomy and resilience". Neema's journey is beyond mere economic autonomy; it has fundamentally reshaped her sense of self and her position within the community. She emerged as a symbol of strength, motivating other women to imagine a life free from the limitations of convention. The narrative effectively illustrates the profound influence of economic possibilities, not only on individual lives but also on the whole social structure of the Maasai society (Lesutis, 2022).

Case Two: Anna's Pioneering Leadership

Anna's involvement with the Maasai community began as an ordinary member of her local Pentecostal church (Meeks, 2020). Nevertheless, as years passed, she became more immersed in religious life, eventually assuming a position of leadership, a job often designated for men. Her path faced several challenges as she experienced opposition from community people who were sceptical about a woman obtaining a major position in the church (Barr, 2021). Anna's fortitude and resolute resolve moved her ahead. She expresses her conviction when she says: "Each stride I made towards leadership was greeted with scepticism, but my unwavering belief and foresight for an improved society for everyone propelled me forward". Anna's ascension to leadership not only brought about a significant change in her position within the society but also acted as a source of inspiration for other Maasai women. Her prominent position within the church afforded her a significant opportunity to champion women's rights and empowerment, leading to a transformation in cultural attitudes and gender roles within the Maasai community (Barr, 2021).

Case Three: Rehema's Educational Goals – A Preview of the Future

Rehema epitomises the up-and-coming cohort of youthful Maasai women, whose aspirations are influenced by changing standards (Barr, 2021). Being a high school student, she personifies the ambitions inspired by seeing the changes of women such as Neema and Anna in her community. Rehema's narrative radiates optimism and aspiration, representing a transformation in the community's mentality towards the significance of women's education (Jamatia, 2023). The phrases she spoke with deep sincerity capture her sentiments: "Witnessing the achievements of women such as Neema and Anna has enlightened me. Education beyond the acquisition of knowledge; is the means to access a realm where I am not limited by traditional practices". Rehema's ambitions highlight the crucial significance of education as a means for ongoing empowerment. The story she told effectively connects to the overarching ideas discussed in this chapter, demonstrating the extensive impact of influential individuals on the younger generation and the crucial function of education in sustaining and enlarging the cycle of empowerment.

Linking Personal Stories to Wider Concepts of Empowerment

Both Neema and Anna exemplify fundamental elements of Kabeer's empowerment paradigm, including agency, resources, and achievements. Their narratives provide tangible illustrations of the overarching theme of empowerment among Maasai women, emphasising the interconnectedness of economic and religious transformations in reshaping their social positions.

Linking Rehema's Aspirations to Wider Concepts of Empowerment

Rehema's educational experience and goals are connected to the overarching ideas of empowerment discussed in this chapter. The narrative exemplifies the cascading impact of empowering women such as Neema and Anna on the subsequent generation, highlighting the pivotal significance of education in perpetuating the cycle of empowerment. Rehema, a high school student, envisions a future where she may surpass the limitations imposed by tradition, aligning with the evolving ambitions of the Maasai youth, including young women. Thus, Rehema can say:

> Education serves as my pathway to success. The sight of women in my town taking charge of enterprises and making influential choices serves as a source of inspiration for me. I have come to see that my aspirations are legitimate and achievable.
> (*Interview: Rehema, Ilparakuyo high school student*)

These case studies provide concrete proof of the significant influence that modifying religious beliefs and economic opportunities have on the lives of Maasai women. Through seeing their own experiences, we get a profound understanding of the formidable influence of empowerment, motivating us to picture a future where opportunities are no longer limited by deeply entrenched patriarchal customs.

Religiosity, Gender Relations, and the Church: Instigators of Transformation

The changing religious structure among Maasai ethnic groups, namely the growing impact of Christianity, has had a profound effect on the dynamics of gender. The shift towards Christian principles of gender equality and monogamy sharply contrasts with the traditional Maasai patriarchal traditions that have supported polygamy and the subordination of women (Hodgson, 2000; Wangui, 2008).Maria, a Maasai woman adds:

> During my upbringing in our culture, the idea of a different lifestyle never entered my imagination. Our customs were firmly established in the practice of polygamy and the subjugation of women. However, the introduction of the church had a transformative impact on our lives. It resembled a beacon of optimism.
>
> *(FGD, Ilparakuyo Maasai woman)*

The alterations in religious devotion have resulted in significant transformations in the customs of marriage and the arrangements of families, giving Maasai women the ability to redefine their positions within society. Christian faith has questioned behaviours like widow inheritance and marital abuse, historically sanctioned under Maasai norms. The church has been a strong proponent of the respect and equitable treatment of women in marriage, resulting in a decrease in polygamy and a rise in monogamous unions, as documented in Kilosa (Massoi, 2015, 2018). This transition has offered women new forums for involvement, challenging deeply established patriarchal norms.

In 2018, Esther, a determined Maasai lady, expressed her viewpoint on the evolving dynamics within her ethnic group. She said that during that time, our duties were limited to conforming to established conventions. We had restricted prospects outside of our residences (Voice of Esther, in 2018). However, the circumstances have evolved. In 2022, Esther's perspective changed as a result of the significant influence of the SGR. In her revised perspective, she articulated that: "The advent of the SGR not only introduced trains but also presented us with unprecedented chances". In addition, she said:

> I have seen women similar to me deviate from traditional roles to engage in business associated with standard gauge railway infrastructure construction. We have assumed the role of contributors within our houses and have taken on the responsibility of making decisions inside our families. The global landscape outside our village has become more accessible, and we are actively embracing and making use of these possibilities.
>
> *(Interview: Esther, 2022, Post-SGR)*

The divergent perspectives from 2018 and 2022 underscore the significant impact of the SGR in transforming the roles and ambitions of Maasai women, demonstrating their tenacity and capacity to adjust in response to change.

Both Neema and Anna embody essential components of Kabeer's empowerment framework (agency, access to resources, and achievements). Their stories provide concrete examples of the dominant topic of empowerment among Maasai women, highlighting how economic and religious changes are intertwined and have influenced their social status. Edward, a Maasai elder said: "It is very impressive to see the Maasai women, such as Neema and Anna, effectively using their power, available resources, and notable accomplishments to actively confront and defy long-established societal expectations".

Indeed, their narratives strongly correspond to the ideas of empowerment that Kabeer has outlined in the framework. The church in Kilosa has significantly contributed to the empowerment of Maasai women by helping them acknowledge their worth and capabilities beyond traditional societal expectations. This empowerment is especially significant for widows, unmarried women, or those who have gone through divorce since they often encounter cultural obstacles. The church's impact is seen as a means of emancipation, offering pastoral Maasai women the assistance and knowledge necessary to navigate difficulties such as climatic fluctuations, land disputes, and extensive land investments. In 2018, Mama Anna Oloishuro, a renowned Maasai leader, contemplated the substantial changes that had already occurred within their society. She recollected as follows:

> I have a vivid memory of a period when women similar to me were seldom given a voice inside our society. However, now, I find myself in a position of high regard and influence within our church and community. The church has equipped us with the means to flourish in an evolving world.
>
> (*Interview: Mama Anna Oloishuro, 2018*)

In 2022, significant advancements occurred with the implementation of the SGR, resulting in further changes to the environment.

Mama Anna Oloishuro said:

> Our community has seen significant changes with the implementation of the Standard Gauge Railway in our area. The construction of the SGR created novel prospects for commerce and interconnection. The combination of this advancement, together with the ongoing endorsement from the church, has bolstered the status of Maasai women even further. We have gained recognition as esteemed leaders in our church and community, and have also engaged actively in area trade and business. The church's teachings on empowerment, together with the economic opportunities offered by the SGR, have enabled us to prosper in this evolving world.

The divergent perspectives by the same person from 2018 and 2022 exemplify the ever-changing nature of empowerment inside the Maasai community and the persistent influence of external forces such as the SGR.

Religion and Gender Dynamics in the Maasai Community: Intricate Interplay of Transformation

The changing religious composition among Maasai ethnicities, namely the growing impact of Christianity, has significantly influenced the dynamics of gender. The shift towards Christian principles of gender equality and monogamy sharply contrasts with the traditional Maasai patriarchal traditions, which have traditionally supported polygamy and the subordination of women (Hodgson, 2000; Wangui, 2008). David, a member of the Maasai community, expressed his thoughts on this transition, saying: "We have seen our traditions being confronted by these novel theological doctrines". While some individuals express concerns about the potential erosion of the Maasai cultural heritage, others see the advantages associated with achieving gender parity. Nevertheless, this transition has encountered obstacles since several members of the community saw the new religious doctrines as a threat to the established Maasai culture. Samuel, a Maasai elder, expressed his apprehensions, stating: "We have preserved our customs for many years, but now they are gradually fading. The church introduces alterations that may not always align with our comfort".

The church has transformed into a venue for advocating women's honour and parity in matrimony, resulting in a decrease in polygamy and a rise in monogamous unions, as documented in Kilosa (Massoi, 2015, 2018). One married Maasai woman, testifies:

> I have seen transformations in our marital unions. The church's teachings and sermons on the importance of respecting women as equals and the encouragement of monogamy have empowered us to have a greater influence inside our families, and polygamy is declining.
>
> *(Interview: Christine, a Maasai woman)*

The intricate interaction between religious and gender dynamics persistently influences the Maasai society, offering both prospects and difficulties as traditions adapt to emerging views. Connecting to Kabeer's framework, it is evident to argue that: "The Maasai community's encounter offers a striking illustration of how alterations in religious convictions may fundamentally transform gender relations" (Edward, a Maasai elder in Ilparakuyo). The phenomenon involves an intricate interaction between the promotion of personal agency and the opposition to external forces, demonstrating the intricate and diverse characteristics of my framework for personal empowerment. The alterations in religion and gender dynamics are interconnected and influenced by the previously described narratives of empowerment.

Applying Naila Kabeer's Framework: Maasai Women's Resource Access

Amidst a deep cultural transition in the Maasai culture, there has been a notable change in women's access to resources, particularly land. The development of religion, namely Pentecostalism, has had a significant impact on this shift by breaking down customary obstacles that previously limited women's access to important resources. The church plays a crucial role in this development, acting as a guiding light for change by actively imparting knowledge to Maasai women about their rights and cultivating an atmosphere of fairness and reverence. The church's teachings transcend the spiritual domain, enabling women to demand their rights and urging males in village committees to acknowledge women as equal citizens with equal and fair access to resources. The shift is palpable, shown in the increasing ability of women to possess property for diverse reasons, such as residential, commercial, and agricultural use. To provide greater clarity on these changes, we refer to the perspectives of the Maasai community: Naima, a Maasai woman, recounts her experience, affirming:

> Previously, the land was exclusively allocated to men—our dads, brothers, and spouses. However, I now see a noticeable alteration. The church has educated us on our rights, and as a result, I now own a little parcel of land where I grow maize and vegetables with great pride. The land represents not just a physical space but also signifies my recently acquired autonomy.
>
> *(Interview: Naima, an Ilparakuyo Maasai woman)*

Similarly, Joseph, an esteemed member of the community, contemplates this profound change, reflecting:

> In our upbringing, we were instilled with the notion that women should not own property. Nevertheless, the teachings of the church have enlightened us to a novel

perspective. I completely endorse my daughter's assertion of her right to our ancestral property. This is a novel trajectory, however, it ultimately leads to a more promising future.

(*FGD: Ilparakuyo Maasai men*)

In the same way, Esther, a young Maasai mother, shares her viewpoint, asserting:

By participating in many workshops, I became aware of the potential for possessing property. It was a previously inconceivable notion. Currently, I am conscientiously putting aside money to acquire a parcel of property. The expedition is arduous, although I have optimism for a more promising future for my offspring.

(*Interview: Esther*)

These voices represent the fundamental nature of the continuous metamorphosis inside the Maasai community. The text emphasises the significant influence of evolving religious convictions and emerging economic prospects on the empowerment of women, especially with their capacity to obtain resources and assert property rights. This transition is consistent with Naila Kabeer's empowerment concept, which highlights the interdependence of resources, agency, and accomplishments in the pursuit of gender equality and economic self-sufficiency within the Maasai society. Nevertheless, despite notable advancements, it is crucial to recognise that obstacles continue to exist, and the achievement of complete empowerment is still an ongoing endeavour.

New Dynamics: Infrastructure Developments and Women Empowerment

The rolling out of the SGR across the Parakuyo grazing fields has brought about a significant change in the traditional pastoral lifestyle of the Maasai population. Commencing in 2018 and approaching finalisation in 2023, this noteworthy endeavour has engaged the participation of both domestic and global corporations. The decision to hire a significant proportion of the local labour has created exceptional chances for the Maasai community, especially the younger generation, who have historically relied on cattle herding for their livelihoods.

Story 1: Transformation of a Maasai Youth

Introducing Julius, a young Maasai individual hailing from the Parakuyo area. Before the implementation of the SGR project, his existence mostly centred on the occupation of tending to and guiding cattle, a customary practice that had been handed down from one generation to the next. Nevertheless, with the establishment of the SGR, he saw a fresh prospect. Julius assumed the position as a security guard in the project, which not only granted him financial autonomy but also acquainted him with a realm outside the savannah. He said:

"I never envisioned myself being in charge of protecting a railway", Julius ponders.

However, this job has had a profound impact on everything. Presently, I can provide financial assistance to my family, and I have begun the process of setting aside funds for my younger sister's schooling. This is a novel direction for me, and I am enthusiastic to discover its destination.

(*Interview: Julius, Ilparakuyo security guard*)

Story 2: The Maasai Women's Collective

Mama Maria, leading a group of Maasai women, decided to capitalise on the economic prospects offered by the SGR. A collective was formed to offer food services to the personnel involved in the project. This effort not only provided these women with financial empowerment but also questioned conventional gender norms within the community. Mama Maria confidently asserts:

> Previously, we were restricted to our residences, but now we operate a thriving enterprise in unison. We have shown our girls that they possess the capability to achieve anything. The transformation of our town is remarkable, and it is very gratifying to be involved in it.
>
> (*FGD, Maasai women*)

Story 3: The Dilemma of Fragmented Grazing Areas

Makena and his family have engaged in the occupation of cattle herding for several generations. Nevertheless, the development of the SGR resulted in the division of their grazing areas. Makena expresses his apprehensions over the future, stating:

> The livelihood of our livestock is contingent upon these territories, which are now divided into two separate halves. Due to circumstances, we have been compelled to adjust and relocate our livestock, which has proven to be a challenging endeavour. We anticipate that the railway will provide sufficient advantages to counterbalance these difficulties.
>
> (*Interview: Makena*)

The implementation of the SGR across the Parakuyo grazing fields is a significant deviation from the Maasai's traditional pastoralist way of life. The building project, overseen by a Turkish company (Yepi-Merkezi), has brought about significant transformations among the surrounding populations. Significantly, it has provided work opportunities to several Maasai persons, including positions such as security guards, machine operators, and chefs. This expansion of income-generating opportunities goes beyond the traditional methods of selling livestock.

Comparative Analysis of Women Empowerment: Maasai and Himba Ethnic Groups

This section examines the processes of empowerment undertaken by the Maasai and Himba ethnic groups, with a specific emphasis on the similarities and differences in their respective paths. Both of these societies, which have traditional male-dominated systems, are presently experiencing significant changes due to a range of external influences. The Maasai community is undergoing religious and infrastructural changes, whereas the Himba ethnic group primarily grapples with changes influenced by the impact of tourism and exposure to globalised media.

Empowerment in the Maasai Societies

Empowerment within the Maasai community is being facilitated by the teachings of Pentecostal churches and the continuing building of the SGR, leading to more opportunities for economic and social engagement among Maasai women (Kipuri & Ridgewell, 2008). These modifications have played a crucial role in questioning established gender norms and enabling Maasai women to express their rights and pursue new means of making a living.

Empowerment in the Himba Societies

The Himba ethnic group's pursuit of empowerment follows a distinct trajectory. The rapid growth of the tourism industry and extensive global media attention are driving the rise in economic independence and changes in traditional gender roles among them. The Himba women have leveraged their abundant cultural history, converting their customary customs into prosperous enterprises that cater to visitors in search of genuine cultural encounters.

Comparative Analysis

To fully comprehend the concept of women's empowerment in various cultural settings, we also examine and compare the experiences of Berber women in Morocco. The Berbers, like the Maasai, had deeply ingrained patriarchal customs. Nevertheless, the main catalyst for their empowerment is their educational progress and active participation in artisanal trades (Kim, 2023). Cooperatives and educational programmes, often driven by NGOs and government efforts, have significantly contributed to the empowerment of Berber women (Laghssais & Comins-Mingol, 2023).

This research highlights the complex and diverse nature of women's empowerment on a global scale, influenced by factors such as religion, economics, and education. The distinctive trajectory of each community exemplifies the tenacity and flexibility of women in response to changing cultural and socio-economic environments.

Future Implications

Looking forward to the next phase of Maasai women's empowerment, it is critical to examine their path under the prism of Naila Kabeer's tripartite paradigm, which includes agency, resources, and achievements.

- **Agency**: With greater involvement in family and communal decision-making processes, we expect Maasai women to further develop their agency in the next years (Woodhouse & McCabe, 2018; Massay, 2020). The increased availability of digital technologies and global communication platforms will give them even more power, allowing them to express their opinions, fight for their rights, and actively engage in social and political discussions.
- **Access to Resources**: The future holds the promise of providing a broader array of resources for Maasai women. In addition to the economic benefits generated by infrastructure projects, there is a high probability that educational resources and technological tools will become more readily available. Enhanced accessibility will empower Maasai women to gain essential skills and knowledge necessary for their economic and personal growth. Policy efforts and changes in education are essential in providing these resources, which are specifically tailored to address the requirements of Maasai women.

Achievements: The concrete results that arise from the Maasai women's exercise of their power and utilisation of available resources can undergo substantial transformation. There is a possibility that we will observe an increase in the presence of women in positions of authority, both within their localities and in broader contexts. Their successes may also manifest as improved financial status, increased educational accomplishments, and greater participation in community development initiatives.

Challenges and opportunities: Nevertheless, there are obstacles to overcome on the journey ahead. It will be crucial to find a middle ground between preserving traditional cultural values and adopting modern societal norms. The community must effectively manage the intricate challenge of safeguarding cultural heritage while simultaneously embracing forward-thinking transformations (Kipuri & Ridgewell, 2008). Furthermore, prioritising the sustainability and inclusivity of economic and social transformations will be of utmost importance.

Conclusion

This chapter examines the current state of transformation of Maasai women and their potential trajectory towards empowerment. Our understanding of this change is improved by including case studies, conducting comparative research, and providing compelling tales. Furthermore, participating in discussions regarding future consequences provides a strategic framework for sustaining these significant changes.

The Maasai civilisation, renowned for its strong patriarchal system and historical practice of polygamy, experienced a remarkable transformation. The existence of local Pentecostal churches, along with major infrastructural programmes, such as the Standard Gauge Railway, has triggered a substantial cultural metamorphosis. This shift in paradigm challenges traditional norms and empowers women to assert their rights and explore innovative ways of making a living.

A significant revelation in this study is the complex interplay between belief systems and the gaining of power. This illustrates the mutually beneficial relationship between religious conversions and infrastructural projects, which simultaneously create new opportunities for Maasai women. This achievement signifies more than a simple change; it reflects a potential framework for empowering women in other marginalised communities. It emphasises the significant influence of religious commitment and infrastructure as catalysts for change.

The trajectory followed by Maasai women demonstrates an outstanding consistency with Naila Kabeer's empowerment framework, which incorporates the elements of agency, resources, and achievements. This builds upon Kabeer's model and provides a concrete example of how religious and economic transformations can empower women to act autonomously for themselves. These modifications yield tangible achievements and have the potential to transform entire communities.

In essence, the task of empowering Maasai women is a dynamic and evolving undertaking that requires continuous support, creative thinking, and participation. Their journey embodies their unwavering resilience and resolve, functioning as a global symbol of gender parity and empowerment. Consistently empowering Maasai women would not only boost the socioeconomic progress of their communities but also yield substantial benefits beyond their immediate environment.

Acknowledgement

This chapter is derived from research presented at the Sixth African Forum of the "African Potentials" project (2016), which was kindly funded by the Japan Society for the Promotion of Science (JSPS) under Grant no. 16H06318. The DFG offered additional research assistance for the collaborative research centre "Future Rural Africa," under "Violent Futures" subproject, thus expanding the study's depth and breadth in 2023. The authors acknowledge the valuable feedback offered by anonymous reviewers.

Bibliography

Abramovitz, R., 2018. *Let It Be Messy: Building Relationships and Exploring Empowerment with Maasai Women in Kenya*. Prescott College.

Abu-Rabia-Queder, S. 2007. "The activism of Bedouin women: Social and political resistance." *HAGAR: Studies in Culture, Polity & Identities*, 7(2).

Acosta, M., van Wessel, M., Van Bommel, S., Ampaire, E.L., Twyman, J., Jassogne, L. and Feindt, P.H., 2020. "What does it mean to make a 'joint' decision? Unpacking intra-household decision making in agriculture: Implications for policy and practice." *The Journal of Development Studies*, 56(6), pp. 1210–1229.

Agadjanian, V. and Yabiku, S.T., 2015. "Religious belonging, religious agency, and women's autonomy in Mozambique." *Journal for the Scientific Study of Religion*, 54(3), pp. 461–476.

Ankrah, D.A., Freeman, C.Y. and Afful, A., 2020. "Gendered access to productive resources–evidence from smallholder farmers in Awutu Senya West District of Ghana." *Scientific African*, 10, p.e00604.

Archambault, C., 2016. "Re-creating the commons and re-configuring Maasai women's roles on the rangelands in the face of fragmentation." *International Journal of the Commons*, 10(2): pp. 728–746.

Archambault, C.S., 2017. "'The pen is the spear of today': (re) producing gender in the Maasai schooling setting." *Gender and Education*, 29(6), pp. 731–747.

Barr, B.A., 2021. *The Making of Biblical Womanhood: How the Subjugation of Women became Gospel Truth*. Baker Books.

Baxter, P. 1994. "Pastoralists are people: Why development for pastoralists, not the development of pastoralism?" *Rural Extension Bulletin*, 4: 3–8.

Brown, D., 2019. Chapter 11: Women's Empowerment and Development in South Sudan Desmond Brown and Robert Dibie. *Women's Empowerment for Sustainability in Africa*

Bushe, G.R., 2012. Appreciative inquiry: Theory and critique. In D. Boje, B. Burnes and J. Hassard, eds., *The Routledge companion to organizational change* (pp. 87–103). London: Routledge.

Chambo, M. 2024. The Effects of Standard Gauge Railway on Land Use and Livelihood Sustainability of the Ilparakuyo Maasai Pastoralists: A Case of Kilosa District, Tanzania. M. A Thesis. Mzumbe University. Forthcoming.

Chen, Z. and Barcus, H.R., 2024. "The rise of home-returning women's entrepreneurship in China's rural development: Producing the enterprising self through empowerment, cooperation, and networking." *Journal of Rural Studies*, 105, p. 103156.

Clarke, V. and Braun, V., 2017. "Thematic analysis." *The Journal of Positive Psychology*, 12(3), pp. 297–298.

Cooperrider, D.L., Stavros, J.M. and Whitney, D., 2008. *The Appreciative Inquiry Handbook: For Leaders of Change*. Berrett-Koehler Publishers.

de Wit, S., 2021. "Gender and climate change as new development tropes of vulnerability for the Global South: essentializing gender discourses in Maasailand, Tanzania." *Tapuya: Latin American Science, Technology and Society*, 4(1), p. 1984638.

Dutt, A., Grabe, S. and Castro, M., 2016. "Exploring links between women's business ownership and empowerment among Maasai women in Tanzania." *Analyses of Social Issues and Public Policy*, 16(1), pp. 363–386.

Hallward-Driemeier, M., 2013. *Enterprising Women: Expanding Economic Opportunities in Africa*. World Bank Publications.

Heath, R. L. and Waymer, D., 2021. University engagement for enlightening CSR: Serving hegemony or seeking constructive change. *Public Relations Review*, 47(1), p. 101958.

Hodgson, D. 2000. *Rethinking Pastoralism in Africa: Gender, Culture and Myth of the Patriarchal Pastoralist.* James Currey.

Hodgson, D. 2001. *Once Intrepid Warriors: Gender, Ethnicity, and the Cultural Politics of Maasai Development.* Indiana University Press.

Hodgson, D.L., 2011. *Being Maasai, Becoming Indigenous: Postcolonial Politics in a Neoliberal World.* Indiana University Press.

Htun, M. and Weldon, S. L., 2015. "Religious power, the state, women's rights, and family law." *Politics & Gender*, 11(3), pp. 451–477.

Inman, Emilia N. 2024 "There Are No True Himbas Anymore: Exploring the Dynamics of the Himba Culture and Land Use in the Face of Change in Kunene Region, Namibia." *Sustainability* 16(4): 1582.

Jamatia, P.L., 2023. "The role of youth in combating social inequality: Empowering the next generation." *International Journal of Social Science, Educational, Economics, Agriculture Research and Technology*, 2(8), pp. 229–238.

Kabeer, N., 1999. Resources, agency, achievements: Reflections on the measurement of women's empowerment. *Development and change*, 30(3), pp. 435–464.

Kilonzo, S.M., 2022. "Women, indigenous knowledge systems, and climate change in Kenya." In E. Chitando et al, eds., *African Perspectives on Religion and Climate Change* (pp. 79–90). Routledge.

Kilosa District Council (KDC) 2016. Kilosa District Socio-Economic Profile. Kilosa District Council

Kim, E., 2023. "Sustainable new product development for ten thousand villages, a fair-trade social enterprise: Empowering women and economic development through problem-based service learning." *Sustainability*, 15(8), p. 6452.

Kipngetich, L. J., Koome, P. M., & Wachira, T. W. 2022. "Effects of socio-cultural factors on the access of women to elective leadership positions in Kenya." *Journal of Policy and Development Studies (JPDS)*, 1(1), 1–10.

Kipuri, N. & A. Ridgewell 2008. A Double Bind: The Exclusion of Pastoralist Women in the East and Horn of Africa: Report. Minority Rights Group International, London.

Laghssais, B. and Comins-Mingol, I., 2023. "Beyond vulnerability and adversities: Amazigh women's agency and empowerment in Morocco." *The Journal of North African Studies*, 28(2), pp. 347–367.

Lesutis, G., 2022. "Infrastructure as techno-politics of differentiation: Socio-political effects of mega-infrastructures in Kenya." *Transactions of the Institute of British Geographers*, 47(2), pp. 302–314.

Massay, G., 2020. "The struggles for land rights by rural women in sub-Saharan Africa: The case of Tanzania." *African Journal of Economic and Management Studies*, 11(2), pp. 271–283.

Massoi, L. W. 2015. "Land conflicts and the livelihood of pastoral Maasai women in Kilosa District of Morogoro, Tanzania." *Afrika Focus*, 28(2): 107–120.

Massoi, L.W. 2018. "Women in Pastoral Societies and the Church in Kilosa, Tanzania." *Journal of African Study Monographs*. Vol. 56 (Supp.), 77–86

Massoi, L. W. & Saruni, P. O., 2020. "Changing Dietary Practices: The New Food Insecurity among The Pastoralists in Mabwegere Village Kilosa District." *Kivukoni Journal*, Vol. 4–7, 120–139.

Meeks, C.A., 2020. Cracking the Stained-glass Ceiling: Leadership Experiences of Black Clergywomen in the Black Church. Doctoral thesis, Northeastern University.

Misafi, H. 2014. "Women's participation in decentralized local governance: The case of pastoral and non-pastoral women in Kondoa local authority, Tanzania." *Afrika Focus*, 27(2): 87–97.

Mosedale, S., 2005. "Assessing women's empowerment: towards a conceptual framework." *Journal of International Development*, 17(2), pp. 243–257.

Naidoo, L., 2012. "Ethnography: An introduction to definition and method. An ethnography of global landscapes and corridors," in L. Naidoo, ed., *An Ethnography of Global Landscapes and Corridors.* IntechOpen.

Ndlovu, T. and Mjimba, V., 2021. "Drought risk-reduction and gender dynamics in communal cattle farming in southern Zimbabwe." *International Journal of Disaster Risk Reduction*, 58, p. 102203.

Opoku, M.P., Anyango, B. and Alupo, B.A., 2018. "Women in politics in Kenya: an analysis of participation and barriers." *Multidisciplinary Journal of Gender Studies*, 7(1), pp. 1506–1530.

Oppong, C. ed., 2023. *Female and Male in West Africa*. Taylor & Francis.

Pratto, F. and Espinoza, P., 2001. "Gender, ethnicity, and power." *Journal of Social Issues*, 57(4), pp. 763–780.

Pratto, F., Sidanius, J. and Levin, S., 2006. "Social dominance theory and the dynamics of intergroup relations: Taking stock and looking forward." *European Review of Social Psychology*, 17(1), pp. 271–320.

Raymond, A., 2021. "Girls' participation in formal education: a case of Maasai pastoralists in Tanzania." *Educational Research for Policy and Practice*, 20, pp. 165–185.

Riesebrodt, M. and Chong, K.H., 1999. "Fundamentalisms and patriarchal gender politics." *Journal of Women's History*, 10(4), pp. 55–77.

Rigby, P., 2022. "Maasai (History, Religious Systems, Rituals)." In *Encyclopedia of African Religions and Philosophy* (pp. 409–412). Springer Netherlands.

Scoones, I., 2021. "Pastoralists and peasants: Perspectives on agrarian change." *The Journal of Peasant Studies*, 48(1), pp. 1–47.

Shim, J.M., 2021. "Religiosity and Individual Agency: Denominational Affiliation, Religious Action, and Sense of Control (SOC) in Life." Religions, 12(2), 117; https://doi.org/10.3390/rel12020117

Silva, H. M. S. V., 2022. "Defining women empowerment: A conceptual study." *International Journal of Multidisciplinary Studies*, 9(2), pp. 105–121.

Skidmore, M. 2007. "Introduction." In M. Skidmore & P. Lawrence, Eds., *Women and the Contested State: Religion, Violence and Agency in South and Southeast Asia*, pp. 1–6. University of Notre Dam Press

Spencer, P. 1988. *The Maasai of Matapato: A Study of Rituals of Rebellion*. Manchester University Press.

Spinks, C. 2003. "Panacea or killer? The impact of Pentecostal Christianity on women in Africa." *The Journal of Women for Women International*, 1(1): 20–25.

Talle, A. 1998. "Male and female in Maasai life: Ageing and fertility." In M.I. Aguilar, Ed., *The Politics of Age and Gerontocracy in Africa: Ethnographies of the Past and Memories of the Present*, pp. 125–149. Africa World Press.

Temba, E.I., Warioba, L. and Msabila, D.T., 2013. Assessing efforts to address cultural constraints to girls' access to education among the Maasai in Tanzania: A case study of Monduli district." *Journal of International Cooperation in Education*, 15(3), pp. 21–37.

Tian, X., Kidokoro, T. and Mwangi, F.M., 2021. "Sociocultural Dimensions of Children's Physical Activity in Contemporary Pastoralist Maasai Society." *International Journal of Environmental Research and Public Health*, 18 (16), 8337.

Tunyone, E. (2023). Large Scale Development Projects and Resource Conflicts Management: Experiences from Kilosa District, Tanzania. Master's Thesis. Mzumbe University.

Uchem, R.N. 2001. *Overcoming Women's Subordination: An Igbo African and Christian Perspective: Envisioning an Inclusive Theology with Reference to Women*. Snaap Press.

United Republic of Tanzania (URT) 2013. Population Distribution by Age and Sex. National Bureau of Statistics, Ministry of Finance, and Office of Chief Government Statistician, President's Office, Finance, Economy and Development Planning, Dar es Salaam and Zanzibar.

Van Klinken, A. 2016. *Transforming Masculinities in African Christianity: Gender Controversies in Times of AIDS*. Routledge.

Venis, R.A., Taylor, V., Sumayani, P., Laizer, M., Anderson, T. and Basu, O.D., 2022. "Towards a participatory framework for improving water & health outcomes: A case study with Maasai women in rural Tanzania." *Social Science & Medicine*, 301, 114966.

Wabende, K., 2022. "Applied Theatre as A Social and Economic agency in Deconstructing Gender Myths." *Pathways to African Feminism and Development, Journal of African Women Studies Centre*, 7(1), pp. 246–262.

Wangui, E.E., 2008. "Development interventions, changing livelihoods, and the making of female Maasai pastoralists." *Agriculture and Human Values*, 25, pp. 365–378.

Wasamba, P., 2009. "The concept of heroism in Samburu Moran ethos." *Journal of African Cultural Studies*, 21(2), pp. 145–158.

Were, J., Chepkwony, G., Oduor, J. and Smith, C., 2020. "Sharing Value-Based Practices of Community Engagement for Geothermal Development: Kenya and New Zealand Partnership." In Proceedings World Geothermal Congress (p. 1).

Woodhouse, E. and McCabe, J.T., 2018. "Well-being and conservation: diversity and change in visions of a good life among the Maasai of northern Tanzania." *Ecology and Society*, 23(1).

Yurco, K., 2022. "Rethinking spaces of gendered livestock ownership: pastoralist women's knowledge, care, and labor. *Social & Cultural Geography*, 25(3), 451–459.

SECTION 5

African Women in Entrepreneurship, Academia and Politics

21
THRIVING IN NEW LANDS
Migrant Women Doing Business in South Africa

Vivian Ojong and John Mhandu

Introduction

Human beings are dynamic and transient by nature. Although migration is portrayed as a crisis, it assists in contributing to the stability of household incomes in fragile economies through remittances and improved food security. It represents an investment in education for the next generation. According to Antonsich, Mavroudi, and Mihelj (2017), migration is viewed as a crisis and social problem for "host" countries. In South Africa, African migrants have faced a plethora of challenges such as xenophobia, harassment, as well as issues related to human rights and integration (Crush, Chikanda and Tawodzera, 2015; Mhandu, 2020; Tevera, 2013). The current study is important because it engages with the discourse of African migration within the South African space with a particular emphasis on highlighting how their experiences reflect forms of bounded solidarity and enforceable trust. According to Flahaux and De Haas (2016), poverty and violent conflict in Africa are seen as the main push factors of mass displacement and migration. This is shown by an increase in the need to improve the lives of African migrants across the continent. The decision to migrate reflects an individual's struggle for survival and presents a consciousness and agency of an individual to migrate. This consciousness is viewed by McAuliffee and Kitimbo (2018), as defined by a social networking capacity, which results in a "mass exodus" of African migrant women into South Africa.

African migration scholarship appears to reduce women's agency and willpower by linking women's migration processes to men's, thereby reducing women's agency. This results in the positionalities of women remaining on the periphery of literature. This chapter examines the ways African migrant women in the informal sector employ their agency to circumvent challenges bedevilling them in the informal economic space. The main argument herein is that African migrant women who are doing business in South Africa employ a plethora of coping and adaptation mechanisms to circumvent the challenges created by acculturation in the host nation-state. As such, coping and adaptation are highly dependent on the migratory status of African migrant women. The majority work in the informal sector due to the inability of the formal economy to absorb the excess labour supply. This chapter adds to the scholarship of African migration and the informal economy with a particular emphasis on how African migrant women in South Africa employ their agency to withstand the challenges they face.

Feminist discourses provide a nuanced and context-specific explanation of how African migrant women thrive in the "New Land". The key tenets of African feminism such as sexuality, oppressive regimes of gender, and patriarchy *inter alia* are used to discuss the experiences of African migrant women in South Africa.

Methodology

Grounded on the interpretivist research paradigm, this qualitative study used 20 in-depth interviews with African migrant women in Durban. Taking a cue from Pervin and Mokhtar (2022), qualitative research was suitable for this study because the main aim was to explain the subjective experiences of the participants that could not be quantified. The adoption of the interpretivist research paradigm is informed by Berryman (2019: 273) who argues that "social construction, language, shared consciousness, and other social interactions" are important in a qualitative study to invent facts. To achieve this goal, in-depth interviews and research questions were structured in a way that best understands "how, when and why". This was related to the philosophical thought of idealism, including social constructivism. All twenty interviews were conducted in a natural setting with no interference. Each interview took approximately one hour. All in-depth interviews were conducted telephonically.

During the fieldwork process, the significance of reflexivity was acknowledged. According to Olmos-Vega, Stalmeijer, Varpio, and Kahlke (2023:242), qualitative researchers should capitalise on reflexivity to "self-consciously critique, appraise, and evaluate how their subjectivity and context influence the research processes". Data saturation was reached on the 18th interview and 2 more interviews were conducted for confirmation purposes. Thematic analysis was used, and data was coded manually. Informed consent forms were read before the interview process and all the participants verbally agreed to participate in the study. The ethical principles of research, namely anonymity, voluntary participation, informed consent, confidentiality, and results communication, were observed throughout the study. To establish trustworthiness, it was ensured that credibility, transferability, dependability, and confirmability remained important in the study. To this effect, member checking was conducted. According to Birt et al. (2016), member checking, also known as respondent validation or participant validation, is very important in qualitative research to validate, verify, or assess the trustworthiness of the results. Data transcripts were presented to participants for validation and feedback. All the participants confirmed that the transcriptions were a true reflection of what they said.

Theoretical Framework

The chapter is informed by Hofstede's (1984) theory of cultural dimensions. According to Hofstede, Hofstede, and Minkov (2010), this dimension explains the extent to which culture embraces the uncertainty of the future. Snitker (2010) adds that Hofstede's theoretical view of uncertainty avoidance explains how members of a society try to cope with anxiety by minimising uncertainty. The main argument of the theory is that uncertainty can create anxiety and members of the society develop coping mechanisms to deal with it. The main argument herein is that cultures with a high level of uncertainty avoidance rely strongly on their set rules and ways of doing things (Hofstede, Hofstede, and Minkov, 2010). On the other hand, the authors maintain that societies with low uncertainty avoidance (a lower level of anxiety) are more relaxed regarding how things are done. This implies that societies, including migrant

Table 21.1 Participants' profile.

Participant	Nationality	Age distribution	Gender	Migration push factors
Participant 1	Zimbabwean	41–45	Male	Economic/War
Participant 2	Congolese	Unknown	Male	War
Participant 3	Congolese	35–40	Male	War
Participant 4	Zimbabwean	46–50	Female	Economic
Participant 5	Cameroonian	35–40	Female	Economic
Participant 6	Zimbabwean	41–45	Female	Economic
Participant 7	Zimbabwean	31–35	Female	Economic
Participant 8	Zimbabwean	30–34	Female	Economic
Participant 9	Zimbabwean	Unknown	Male	Economic
Participant 10	Zambian	31–35	Female	Education
Participant 11	Zimbabwean	Unknown	Female	Economic
Participant 12	Zimbabwean	41–45	Male	Economic
Participant 13	Malawian	Unknown	Male	Economic
Participant 14	Malawian	Unknown	Male	Economic
Participant 15	Mozambican	41–45	Male	Economic/War
Participant 16	Zimbabwean	35–40	Female	Economic
Participant 17	Zambian	46–50	Female	Economic

communities, often attempt to control their uncertainty as much as possible. As an illustration, certain rules and cultural beliefs are not broken to create bounded solidarity and enforceable trust. Against this backdrop, African migrant women's agency within the framework of Hofstede's uncertainty avoidance index and indulgence versus self-restraint were analysed to emphasise how they struggle with two forms of identity, that is, African women and migrant women.

Theoretical insights are also drawn on Portes' and Sensenbrenner's (1993) concept of bounded solidarity and enforceable trust. It is argued that altruistic sources of social capital allow African migrant women to draw resources for survival from others such as family and friends. This is often done out of solidarity with members of the same migrant community according to Portes' (1993) notion of bounded solidarity. Their *modus operandi* is not based on the general values of entrepreneurial spaces but on their loyalties to an African migrant community. Borrowing from Portes and Landolt (2000), it is also argued that their resource transactions are embedded in the opportunity structures. These structures act as guarantors of their survival in the "new lands" and they build enforceable trust through their power. To this effect, it is argued that in the "new lands" African migrant women find themselves, they can utilise the opportunity structures in the South African economy and a cultural disposition for business in their countries of origin to thrive in an environment that is not designed to enable their success. Through the concepts of "bounded solidarity and enforceable trust", they are creating specific niche entrepreneurial spaces that serve as a form of "protected market".

African Immigrant Entrepreneurship

Scholars such as Fatoki and Patswawairi (2012), Fatoki (2014), Ojong and Mhandu (2019), Mlotshwa and Msimango-Galawe (2020), and many others have highlighted the significance of social networks in the business success of immigrant entrepreneurs. According to Fatoki

(2014), social networking is simply social interactions and personal relationships, including the exchange of information and benefits. Social networking is a crucial mechanism that encourages cooperation and the achievement of common goals (Mhandu, 2020; Fubah and Moos, 2022). The authors add that migrants often engage in networking to exchange information on possible resources necessary for business growth. Different types of networks such as social, managerial, business, ethnic, family, and inter-organisational networks and others have been identified in contemporary literature (Fatoki and Oni, 2014; Desta, 2015; Mhandu, 2020). These networks involve relationships with family, friends, family members, and other acquaintances within their migrant community. Studies conducted by Crush, Chikanda, and Tawodzera (2015), as well as Fatoki (2013) have concluded that although networks are important in the success of immigrant entrepreneurship, immigrant entrepreneurs in South Africa encounter barriers such as xenophobia and assimilation, which limits them to co-ethnic networks.

Immigrant entrepreneurs face a plethora of challenges in South Africa. Research conducted by Mhandu (2020) and Crush, Chikanda, and Tawodzera (2015) suggests that African immigrant entrepreneurs face challenges resulting from internal or external factors. In some instances, internal challenges are addressed by the African immigrant entrepreneurs themselves (Panda, 2018). Other external factors such as xenophobia, lack of financial support, lack of access to markets and gender discrimination remain a challenge amongst African migrant women in South Africa. In some instances, entrepreneurship is perceived to be a career for men (Fubah and Moos, 2022). The xenophobic attacks appear to be one of the main challenges affecting African migrant women in the history of South Africa (Ngota, Mang'unyi, and Rajkaran, 2018). Tevera (2013) provides a complementary analysis and argues that xenophobia generates rhetoric that the local citizens use as justification for denying African migrants access to essential services such as public health and education. African immigrants are often referred to by South African citizens as *"makwerekwere"* (Tevera, 2013, Mhandu, 2020; Crush, Chikanda and Tawodzera, 2015). Many African migrants who face xenophobic attacks often feel excluded from mainstream society. Those who are unable to find formal employment or who are not happy with their employment usually venture into entrepreneurship in the host country.

According to Goyayi (2022), African migrants experience deeply entrenched gender inequalities such as sexual and gender-based violence and lack of access to resources and livelihoods. The author maintains that African migrant women have moved to South Africa in search of better services, political stability, and safety. As such, South Africa has witnessed an influx of Sub-Saharan female migrants from 46.4% in 2005 to 47.5% in 2019 (Goyayi, 2022). Against this backdrop, Mafukidze and Mbanda (2008) opine that the feminisation of migration in South Africa is taking place at a time when African migrants face a negative attitude from the host country. Raniga and Fitshane (2022) argue that African female migrants need an essential support system and are characterised by multiple social capital relations that they nurture both in the home country and the host country. Most of these women are undocumented. Irrespective of their legal status, African migrants maintain their social networks as a coping strategy. As argued by Maphosa (2012), their experience of social networks resonates with the idea of social capital, which highlights that migrants help each other by learning about local cultures and resources. Also, African migrants support each other with food security, access to transport, accommodation, and other resources (Hofmann, 2014; Maposa, 2012; Mafukidze and Mbanda, 2008)

Undocumented Migrant Women

The study found that most migrant women doing business in South Africa are undocumented. They face a plethora of challenges because of their legal status. They do not have the right to stay or work in South Africa, which makes them vulnerable to arrest and harassment. Some expressed their fear of being detained and deported if arrested. Commenting on the challenges of migrant women doing business in South Africa, the following participants had this to say:

I came to South Africa in 2011. I have been here for more than 10 years now. The biggest challenge that I can say is related to papers. I am an undocumented migrant and most of the women you see in this saloon do not have papers. We are always on the run especially when home affairs come to raid. We are afraid of being arrested and deported. Now and then the police and the Department of Home Affairs always come to check our documentation. Sometimes it's not only about being arrested. When the police come, sometimes they harass us. They do not give us time to explain. Even the way they grab you into the van is so harsh. There is no time to negotiate. That's how they are, and this is South Africa.

(Participant 6, 2022)

Things were going on well before COVID-19. After the pandemic life changed. Now there are a lot more arrests than before. Every day you hear new operations against foreign nationals. Undocumented migrants like us are always a target. I have family and friends I was working with in my shop, who were arrested last month. As we speak, they are detained in the Lindela Repatriation Centre. We do not know when they will be released or deported. They have been there for more than a month now. The conditions in Lindela are deplorable. Many undocumented migrant women are afraid of being arrested. We have kids to take care of and some of us are unmarried. Imagine what will happen to my kids if I am arrested or detained. We know that we do not have the right to work in South Africa but there is nothing that we can do considering the economic and political problems that we have in our country Zimbabwe.

(Participant 8, 2022)

I am originally from Mozambique, but I grew up in Zimbabwe. My father is from Mozambique and my mother is Zimbabwean. The challenges that we face as women are the same as men. The only difference is that men are hustlers. Surviving in South Africa is very difficult sometimes especially if you do not have proper documentation. I tried to apply for a work permit, but I did not get one. It was rejected twice. As migrants, we need to survive, which is why we are here. I was once arrested just before COVID-19. That was the most difficult time in my life in South Africa. The police approached my shop and arrested me for failing to produce a work permit. Yes, I understand they were doing their job and I cannot blame them. I went to Westville police station and the following day we were taken to Pinetown magistrate court before we were detained in Lindela. I stayed in Lindela for almost a month and was deported to Zimbabwe. That experience I will never forget in my life and it's something that I would not want to experience again. That is my fear. Whenever I work, I am always afraid of being arrested and detained.

(Participant 15, 2022)

The above extract shows different experiences of migrant women doing business in South Africa. The challenges outlined above can be summarised as harassment, long-term detention, loss of customers, deplorable conditions in the repatriation centre, loss of livelihood, and deportation. These challenges are not new in migration scholarship, especially in the context of South Africa. For example, the arrest of undocumented migrants is not a new phenomenon in South Africa. It concurs with several studies done in South Africa. As an illustration, in a study conducted by Human Rights Watch (n.d.), the harassment experiences of Participant 6 confirm these studies. The Human Rights Watch (n.d.) uncovered evidence of physical abuse of undocumented migrants by the South African armed forces. A relative example is that of Benneth Mabaso who informed the Human Rights Watch how he was assaulted by soldiers. According to Human Rights Watch (n.d.), Benneth Mabaso, an undocumented Mozambican migrant, recounts that:

> They stopped the van and took us out to cross-question us. They were wearing camouflage uniforms. We insisted that they had taken our money, and they then beat us badly. When we were on the ground, they jumped on us with their heavy boots. My ribs were very sore. After that, the soldiers took us to the hospital.
> (Benneth Mabaso cited in Human Rights Watch, n.d.)

The case of Benneth Mabaso is consistent with the key finding of this study regarding the harassment of undocumented African migrants doing business in South Africa. More accurately, Participant 9 explains her fear of long-term detention while investigation for her undocumented status is being investigated. She recounts that:

> My biggest fear is to be detained for a long time while the uniformed force is conducting their investigation as to why I am an illegal migrant in South Africa. I have seen this happening to some of my colleagues. By the time they finish their investigation, you will have lost a lot of customers. Customers will never wait for you to be released. Given the chance, I would rather opt for my case to be withdrawn and go home but this option does not exist.
> (Participant 9, 2022)

The above example shows how undocumented African migrant women doing business in South Africa are afraid to remain in detention. However, it is important to note that the experience of harassment discussed above violates the South African Bill of Rights. The South African Immigration Act (Act 13 of 2002) allows the Department of Home Affairs (DHA) to detain undocumented migrants at the Lindela Repatriation Centre for deportation and it does not allow anyone to violate the constitutional rights of detainees. This is strongly supported by the Constitution of the Republic of South Africa 1996 (Act 106 of 1996), which states that:

> Everyone who is detained, including every sentenced prisoner, has the right … to conditions of detention that are consistent with human dignity, including at least exercise and the provision, at state expense, of adequate accommodation, nutrition, reading material and medical treatment.

According to the Constitution of South Africa, since African migrant women experience fear of harassment during arrest, the constitution of South Africa protects their dignity, and no one is allowed to violate their human rights. However, the evidence provided above shows how South African uniformed forces violate the Constitution and harass undocumented migrants during their arrest and in some cases ensure long-term detention, as in the case of Participant 9.

African Migrant Women and the Immigrant Niche

The study found that African migrants in South Africa naturally protect their markets in different ways by concentrating on a specific niche of the labour market. This is a line of work that is represented by an immigrant niche and a sector-specific configuration of social and economic processes. The study found that most work as hairdressers and street vendors and are visible in a narrow band of activities of SMMEs, which are mostly in retail and service rather than in production. They try to protect their niche markets at all costs. The following are extracts that explain how African migrant women protect their markets.

> These days there is too much competition. I am in the garment industry and a fashion designer. I design clothes that compete with international standards. We must protect our markets. As such I sell ethnic clothes that you will never get in South Africa. I have a lot of Nigerian and Cameroonian customers. It is difficult for a person from another country to design the kind of clothes that I make. You must understand the culture first before you start thinking of making Nigerian clothes. I have connections with my colleagues back home. Sometimes they give me material at a cheaper price. We have created a good network.
>
> (Participant 5, 2022)

> Many of us are clustered in the clothing sector. We are involved in making traditional clothes, and African wedding dresses and I carry out general tailoring activities. I have been in this business for more than 15 years. I started it before I came to South Africa. I do not mind about the stiff competition. Our market is well protected. I get material from Zimbabwe and sometimes in Zambia and I transport it to Zambia using truck drivers. They are affordable. I sometimes pay R300 to R500 which is relatively fair. However, if another person is not well connected, they are very expensive, and you won't see the profit. We have our WhatsApp group with other women doing the same business around Durban. Of course, we were significantly affected by COVID-19, and we kept on fighting. The WhatsApp group is used for specific communication, such as challenges and threats to our business, how to make sure that we understand competition and to ensure that we build unity.
>
> (Participant 17, 2022)

> I am a hairdresser. I get my products from Zimbabwe and Zambia. The products from Zimbabwe are tailored for Afro-textured hair using natural ingredients grown and harvested in Zimbabwe. You find that many Zimbabweans, especially those with natural hair, prefer the Zimbabwean-made replenishing conditioner and you cannot find these

products in South Africa. A good example is the products that we get from a shop called 'Manetain Organic' which we get in a retail shop in Chisipite in Harare. They sell more than 150 hair products. Our client in South Africa prefers using these products. Even if we are financially stable, we still need to continue serving the interests of our valuable customers.

(Participant 8, 2022)

A closer analysis of the above extracts shows that African migrant women work hard to remain economically active in niches, irrespective of the challenges they face and even after having reached upward economic self-sufficiency and social mobility. The narratives of Participants 5 and 8 show that African migrant women doing business in South Africa often target their fellow immigrants by providing them with ethnic clothing and hair products that are not found in South Africa. There is a noticeable presence of Nigerians who deal in the clothing sector, and they protect their market by ensuring that the clothing designs compete with international standards and are culturally centred. Against this backdrop, the process of ethnic succession has taken place amongst African migrant women in South Africa. African migrant women doing business in South Africa maintain social ties with members in their home country. They create a network of connections and a mixed embeddedness approach. This approach is concretely related to how they use social networks. An immigrant niche is constructed through family networks. This is well supported by the following extracts.

I would not have made it in my business if it wasn't for my family. They supported me and they continue to support me in my business. They always check on me and, in most cases, they give me maximum support be it socially, emotionally, and financially. Even in terms of labour, my sister is assisting me, and this has grown to be a family business. When I came to South Africa After I finished high school, my family raised capital to assist me in starting my hair salon. This was free of charge, and I never returned the money. So, for me family network is very important.

(Participant 11, 2022)

I can tell you that you will never succeed in business if you are self-centred. I started my salon with the help of my family members. I remember very well that my aunt who is in the United Kingdom played a significant role in my life. The first hair dryer and other types of equipment she gave me for free. Although relatives have mixed motives. Others are happy that you are developing, and others are jealous. In my situation, my relatives and friends back home played a significant role. When I started renting a chair, I did not have enough resources, but my other Zimbabwean colleagues would contribute towards my monthly rentals.

(Participant 1, 2022)

The social networks explained by Participant 11 are often based on solidarity and trust within the family boundaries. This trust is normally generated by kinship and ethnic relationships. These are in unison with a study conducted by Chimucheka, Chinyamurindi, and Dodd (2019). The authors establish that immigrant entrepreneurs who have a low level of experience often rely on social networks. Their business is oriented to networks. As such, African migrant women doing business in South Africa use social networks to build social capital, which in this context refers to resources embedded in the network of relationships of individuals, communities, networks, or societies. Many benefits are derived from networks and are positively associated with innovativeness in business performance. As highlighted by Participant 11, social networks provide access to valuable resources that are available in the opportunity structure. These include cheap labour from family and co-ethnic members and funding. This is a reflection that African migrant women doing business in South Africa have access to valuable transactional networks in their home country. This facilitates the sustenance of their business in the host country. To this effect, it is argued that social networks of African migrant women doing business in South Africa are supported by *"bounded solidarity" and "enforceable trust"*. These immigrants develop a preference for products and goods associated with their natal regions for their symbolic representation. The narrative of Participant 1 shows the role played by social networks in establishing businesses in the host country. This agrees with a study conducted by Mhandu, Ojong, and Muzvidziwa (2018), which concluded that Zimbabwean migrant women hairdressers participating in informal economic activities in Durban utilise multiple avenues such as the use of social networks to sustain their businesses. In doing so, their experiences are both constrained and enabled by the structural forces in which they operate.

Opportunity Structure and Mixed Embeddedness

The opportunity structure and mixed embeddedness are used to explain the rise of African migrant economies in South Africa. The main argument herein is that African migrant women doing business in South Africa assume a common ethno-cultural background and co-ethnic social networks. This is not a new finding in migration scholarship. It confirms the explanation provided by Räuchle and Schmiz (2019), Mhandu (2020), as well as Mhandu, Ojong, and Muzvidziwa (2018). Anecdotal evidence provided in this chapter shows that African migrant women often rely more on resources available in the opportunity structure. Their structural arrangements create opportunities for business growth as they navigate South Africa's formal and informal economic spaces. On the other hand, the mixed embeddedness approach creates opportunities for the interaction necessary for self-employment in terms of migrants' agency. A combination of opportunity structure and mixed embeddedness creates room for survival depending on whether the structural conditions are constraining or enabling. Furthermore, the opportunity structure consists of resources, market conditions, welfare systems, production factors, technological development, and other resources that are necessary for survival in the host nation-state.

African migrant women doing business in South Africa should be contextualised within the mixed embeddedness approach which is a multi-dimensional concept of migrant entrepreneurship. As outlined above, anecdotal evidence of this study reveals that African migrant women doing business in South Africa design clothes that compete with international standards and are exported to other countries. This reflects how African migrant women go beyond serving local markets and operate transnationally. The transnationalism character of migration has also been pointed out by scholars such as Vertovec (2007, 2019) to describe people living in the host country but maintaining ties with their country of origin. This is a key point emphasised by most participants in this study. African migrant women doing business in South Africa are characterised by cross-border networks, which should consist of parties of the overall transnational embeddedness. As such, the mixed-embeddedness approach is key to analysing African migrant women doing business in South Africa. It assists in contextualising the lived experiences of African migrants as a combination of social, economic, and institutional factors central to their economic activities.

Enforceable trust and bounded solidarity are also noticeable amongst African migrants doing business in South Africa and contribute to their ethnic identities. They convert network ties into sources of social capital where they can access and exchange shared resources. To this effect, the concept of bounded solidarity and enforceable trust was used to explain the effects of ethnic networks on the social and economic mobility of African migrant women doing business in South Africa. Evidence of bounded solidarity is drawn from how they get resources from other migrants out of solidarity with members of the same ethnic group. This is based primarily on the loyalties to co-ethnic members. Trust is enshrined in the situations of African migrant women because it is enforceable and is associated with the dynamic structures of social control. Thus, the study establishes that bounded solidarity is central to the lives of African migrant women doing business in South Africa and is the starting point for the cycle of acculturation. It assists in the reaffirmation of their social identity. Enforceable trust is generated by social networks and can sustain collaborative relations.

The returns of bridging and bonding social capital amongst African migrant women thriving in the "new lands" of South Africa are crucial and are closely linked to the outcomes of their economic behaviours. Key findings of this study indicate that structural bridging capital creates inter-ethnic contacts that are associated with the likelihood of business success in the host country. This argument finds complementarity in Kanas et al. (2012) and Patulny (2015) who are of the view that bridging and bonding capital is associated with co-ethnic ties and assists in the mobilisation of resources for business success. As such, evidence from this study shows how African migrant women rely strongly on co-ethnic contacts. They utilise bridging capital to facilitate the exchange of information, social inclusion, and participation in the businesses.

Recommendations

The chapter makes the following recommendations.

1 African migrant women, particularly undocumented, should be incorporated into African entrepreneurship programmes. This is an important initiative which will assist in dismantling the obstacles to business opportunities and economic participation that African migrant women face.
2 Mentorship programmes must be introduced to African migrant women doing business in South Africa. The value of mentors is important, and it should be supported with training, networks, and, if possible, financial support from different stakeholders and the government. Mentorship is important at all stages of business development.
3 The study utilised a non-probability sampling, and the findings cannot be generalised to the entire target population. Therefore, we recommend a quantitative survey to confirm the results' validity and to build a data bank that can be used for further research.
4 The study established that most African migrants doing business in South Africa are undocumented. As such to reduce illegal immigration, in theory, we recommend that the South African Government work together with regional leaders and other governments on reducing "push" factors and securing its land borders.

Conclusion

The chapter describes how African migrants doing business in South Africa thrive and survive in the new lands. They are concentrated in a specific labour market niche. This is a line of work that is represented by an immigrant niche and a sector-specific configuration of social and economic processes. As such, it was established that most African migrant women in South Africa work as hairdressers and street vendors and are visible in a narrow band of activities of SMMEs, mostly in retail and service rather than in production. Most migrant women doing business in South Africa are undocumented and they face a plethora of challenges because of this. Some are discussed in this chapter and include harassment, long-term detention, loss of customers, deplorable conditions in the repatriation centre, loss of livelihood, and deportation. The study establishes that bounded solidarity is central to the lives of African migrant women doing business in South Africa and is the starting point for the cycle of acculturation. It assists in the reaffirmation of their social identity. Enforceable trust is generated by social networks. Theoretical insights are also drawn on Portes and Sensenbrenner's (1993) concept of bounded solidarity and enforceable trust. Altruistic sources of social capital allow African migrant women to draw resources for survival from others such as family and friends. The opportunity structure and mixed embeddedness explain the rise of African migrant economies in South Africa. The main argument herein is that African migrant women doing business in South Africa assume a common ethno-cultural background and co-ethnic social networks.

Bibliography

Antonsich, M., Mavroudi, E. and Mihelj, S. (2017). Building inclusive nations in the age of migration. *Identities*, 24(2), pp. 156–176.

Berryman, D. R. (2019). Ontology, Epistemology, Methodology, and Methods: Information for Librarian Researchers. *Medical Reference Services Quarterly*, (3), pp. 271–279.

Birt, L., Scott, S., Cavers, D., Campbell, C. and Walter, F. (2016). Member checking: a tool to enhance trustworthiness or merely a nod to validation? *Qualitative Health Research*, 26(13), pp. 1802–1811.

Chimucheka, T., Chinyamurindi, W.T. and Dodd, N. (2019). The effect of the use of social networks on the performance of immigrant entrepreneurs operating SMMEs in the Eastern Cape province, South Africa. *Academy of Entrepreneurship Journal*, 25(4), pp. 1–15.

Constitution of the Republic of South Africa 1996 (Act 106 of 1996).

Crush, J., Chikanda, A. and Tawodzera, G. (2015). The third wave: Mixed migration from Zimbabwe to South Africa. *Canadian Journal of African Studies/Revue canadienne des études africaines*, 49(2), pp. 363–382.

Desta, N.T. (2015). *Networking as a growth initiative for small and medium enterprises in South Africa* (Doctoral dissertation, University of the Free State).

Fatoki, O. (2013). The determinants of immigrant entrepreneurs' growth expectations in South Africa. *Journal of Social Sciences*, 37(3), pp. 209–216.

Fatoki, O. (2014). Immigrant entrepreneurship in South Africa: Current literature and research opportunities. *Journal of Social Sciences*, 40(1), pp. 1–7.

Fatoki, O. and Oni, O. (2014). The networking behaviour of immigrant entrepreneurs in South Africa. *Mediterranean Journal of Social Sciences*, 5(20), pp. 284–290.

Fatoki, O. and Patswawairi, T. (2012). The motivations and obstacles to immigrant entrepreneurship in South Africa. *Journal of Social Sciences*, 32(2), pp. 133–142.

Flahaux, M.L. and De Haas, H. (2016). African migration: Trends, patterns, drivers. *Comparative Migration Studies*, 4, pp. 1–25.

Fubah, C.N. and Moos, M.N. (2022). Immigrant entrepreneurship in South Africa: A review and research agenda. *Journal for Transdisciplinary Research in Southern Africa*, 18(1), pp. 1–13.

Goyayi, M. 2022. Protecting the rights of migrant women entrepreneurs in the informal sector. Available at: https://ddp.org.za/blog/2022/04/12/protecting-the-rights-of-migrant-women-entrepreneurs-in-the-informal-sector/

Hofmann, S. G. 2014. Interpersonal emotion regulation model of mood and anxiety disorders. *Cognitive Therapy and Research*, 38(5), pp. 483–492.

Hofstede, G., Hofstede, G. J. and Minkov, M. (2010). *Cultures and Organizations: Software of the Mind.* 3rd Edition. USA: McGraw-Hill.

Human Rights Watch (n.d.). The treatment of undocumented migrants in South Africa, Human Rights Watch. Available at: https://www.hrw.org/legacy/reports98/sareport/Adv3a.htm (Accessed: 28 August 2023).

Kanas, A., Chiswick, B.R., Van Der Lippe, T. and Van Tubergen, F. (2012). Social Contacts and the Economic Performance of Immigrants: A Panel Study of Immigrants in Germany. *International Migration Review*, 46(3), pp. 680–709.

Mafukidze, J. and Mbanda, V. 2008. Low-income African migrant women and social exclusion in South Africa. *Agenda*, 22(78), pp. 172–185.

Maphosa, S. B. 2012. Natural resources and conflict: Unlocking the economic dimension of peacebuilding in Africa. *Africa Institute of South Africa*. Briefing 74, pp. 2–9.

McAuliffee, M. and Kitimbo, A. (2018). *African migration: what the numbers really tell us.* World Economic Forum. Available at: https://www.weforum.org/agenda/2018/06/heres-the-truth-about-african-migration/

Mhandu, J. (2020). Navigating the informal economy: Social networks among undocumented Zimbabwean migrant women hairdressers in Durban, South Africa. *The Mankind Quarterly*, 61(2).

Mhandu, J., Ojong, V.B. and Muzvidziwa, N.V. (2018). Modus operandi and the socio-spatial milieu in which immigrant niche markets vis-a-vis informal economic activities. *Journal of Social Development in Africa*, 33(2), pp. 85–108.

Mlotshwa, S.H. and Msimango-Galawe, J. (2020). The risk of overvaluing networking on small and medium enterprises performance in Gauteng province, South Africa. *The Southern African Journal of Entrepreneurship and Small Business Management*, 12(1):1–13.

Ngota, B.L., Mang'unyi, E.E. and Rajkaran, S. (2018). Factors impeding African immigrant entrepreneurs' progression in selected small and medium enterprises: Evidence from a local municipality in South Africa. *South African Journal of Business Management*, 49(1), pp. 1–9.

Ojong, V.B. and Mhandu, J. (2019). The value of transnational/immigrant entrepreneurship to the development of African countries. *Journal of Social Development in Africa*, 34(1), pp. 141–165.

Olmos-Vega, F.M., Stalmeijer, R.E., Varpio, L. and Kahlke, R. (2023). A practical guide to reflexivity in qualitative research: AMEE Guide No. 149. *Medical Teacher*, 45(3), pp. 241–251.

Panda, S. (2018). Constraints faced by women entrepreneurs in developing countries: Review and ranking. *Gender in Management: An International Journal*, 33(4), pp. 315–331.

Patulny R. (2015). A Spectrum of Integration: Examining Combinations of Bonding and Bridging Social Capital and Network Heterogeneity among Australian Refugee and Skilled Migrants, in Ryan, L., D'Angelo, A., Erel U. (eds) *Migrant Capital. Networks, Identities, and Strategies*, pp. 207–229. Basingstoke: Palgrave Macmillan.

Pervin, N. and Mokhtar, M. (2022). The Interpretivist research paradigm: A subjective notion of a social context. *International Journal of Academic Research in Progressive Education and Development*, 11(2), pp. 419–428.

Portes, A. and Landolt, P. (2000). Social capital: Promise and pitfalls of its role in development. *Journal of Latin American Studies*, 32(2), pp. 529–547.

Portes, A. and Sensenbrenner, J. (1993). Embeddedness and immigration: Notes on the social determinants of economic action. *American Journal of Sociology*, 98(6), pp. 1320–1350.

Raniga, T. and Fitshane, K. 2022. Economic experience of migrant women residing in Gauteng, South Africa: a sustainable livelihood perspective. *Social Work* 58(3), pp. 239–271.

Räuchle, C. and Schmiz, A. (2019). Migrant economies: Opportunity structures and potential in different city types. *Ethnic and Racial Studies*, 42(10), pp. 1766–1787.

Snitker, T.V. (2010). The impact of culture on user research. In *Handbook of global user research* (pp. 257–277). Morgan Kaufmann.

Tevera D. (2013). African migrants, xenophobia, and urban violence in post-apartheid South Africa. *Alternation*, (7), pp. 9–26.

Vertovec, S. (2007). Super-diversity and its implications. *Ethnic and Racial Studies*, *30*(6), pp. 1024–1054.

Vertovec, S. (2019). Talking around super-diversity. *Ethnic and Racial Studies*, *42*(1), pp. 125–139.

22
CHURCH WOMEN AND ENTREPRENEURSHIP
A Case Study of the Evangelical Lutheran Church in Zimbabwe, Western Diocese

Mbongeni Proud Dube

Introduction

Despite socio-cultural barriers that still exist, women have shown remarkable progress and success in entrepreneurship (Mazonde and Carmichael, 2016). Contemporary studies reveal that many women in Africa and beyond continue to defy societal norms and expectations to pursue their dreams. Generally, more women in different parts of the world are becoming entrepreneurs. In greater numbers than ever before, women are stepping away from traditional economic roles and venturing out to start their own businesses (Van Eerdewijk and Mugadza, 2015). In every field imaginable, even the most "masculine," one does not have to look hard to find female entrepreneurs who have overcome seemingly impossible odds to achieve success (Coughlin and Thomas, 2002). This is also true with women in religious spaces; women in the Evangelical Lutheran Church in Zimbabwe (ELCZ), Western Diocese have displayed resilience, determination, and creativity in overcoming the challenges they face as entrepreneurs. Without any doubt, Church women have found innovative ways to navigate these barriers as they create support networks and collaborations with fellow women in business (Mapuranga, 2018). They have proven their abilities, skills, and strength of character by breaking stereotypes and paving the way for future generations of women entrepreneurs. This is evidenced by how they are involved in socio-economic activities that help them support the livelihoods of their families, communities, and the Church. With continued support and empowerment, Church women in the ELCZ, Western Diocese will continue to break barricades and shape the future of business in their communities. Thus, the study seeks to appreciate the achieved and remarkable milestones taken by female entrepreneurs in the ELCZ, Western Diocese.

Background

The Lutheran Church was formed after Martin Luther's teachings were embraced by his followers and spread throughout Germany (*16th century*), and Lutheranism later spread to other countries. According to Söderström et al. (2003:11–14), the ELCZ (*formerly the Evangelical Lutheran Church of Southern Rhodesia*) is an evangelical denomination, founded in 1903 by Swedish and South African missionaries. In the year 2006, the ELCZ passed a new constitution that established Dioceses. Before the birth of Dioceses, the Lutheran Church in Zimbabwe was under one Bishop. Thus, administratively, the Church is divided into three Dioceses (*Western, Eastern, and Central*). The ELCZ Gender Policy (2015:3) highlights that "From 1903, preaching was meant for men only and even pastorate that was trained was male in totality. Women were only assigned to accompany their male counterparts as instruments of praise." This created an atmosphere of having no female voice in line with preaching the Word of God despite the fact that the first preachers were women when they were sent by Jesus to tell the disciples that he was alive (The ELCZ Gender Policy, 2015). In 1987, the ELCZ then enrolled the first female student pastors, which became a breakthrough from male dominance in the Church's pastorate. As the Church continued to reflect its theology, another breakthrough happened in 2015 when the ELCZ became the first Church in Zimbabwe to launch a standalone Gender Policy. The ELCZ Gender Policy was put in place to promote gender justice and equality between genders in the Church and community (The ELCZ Gender Policy, 2015). The ELCZ Gender Policy acknowledges that our traditional set-up is built in a way that promotes gender inequality. There is no doubt that the set-up is male-dominated! The ELCZ, like most religious movements, has inherited from a patriarchal society or transferred the traditional way of dealing with gender matters (The ELCZ Gender Policy, 2015). Although the ELCZ has covered some ground in the area of gender justice, there is still a need for the Church to commit itself more toward achieving gender justice in the Church and Zimbabwe. In the meantime, we applaud the ELCZ for having a Gender Justice Policy, female ordination, female lay leaders and preachers, and for promoting female entrepreneurs in the Church.

Sustainable Livelihood Framework (SLF) and Social Capital Theory

The study will be guided and analyzed through the lens of the Sustainable Livelihood Framework (SLF) and social capital theory. Therefore, the SLF provides a holistic lens to analyze the various dimensions and assets that contribute to sustainable livelihoods. This framework emphasizes the interconnectedness of different components that shape individuals' livelihood strategies (The Department for International Development, 1999). In the context of the ELCZ, Western Diocese, the SLF was resourceful in exploring the factors that enable or hinder Church women entrepreneurs' ability to establish and maintain sustainable businesses. On the other hand, social capital theory focuses on the value of social networks and resources embedded in relationships (Claridge, 2018). Within the setting of the ELCZ, Western Diocese, this theory sheds light on the social connections and resources that Church women entrepreneurs utilize to enhance their entrepreneurial ventures. By employing the SLF and social capital theory as a theoretical framework, this study offers a comprehensive and nuanced understanding of the experiences and challenges faced by Church women entrepreneurs within the ELCZ, Western Diocese. Accordingly, the findings of this study can inform policy interventions and support systems that promote gender-inclusive entrepreneurship within religious communities, ultimately empowering church women to sustain their livelihoods and contribute meaningfully to their communities.

A Review of Entrepreneurship, Gender, and Religion

The intersection of entrepreneurship, gender, and religion is a complex and evolving area of study. While there is a growing body of literature exploring this topic, it remains relatively limited and fragmented. Gielnik (2014) holds that the existing literature provides a rich tapestry of continuities and discontinuities. Existing literature emphasizes the influence of religious beliefs and values on women's motivations for entrepreneurship (Dziva, 2021). Religion can provide a sense of purpose, empowerment, and ethical grounding for their business ventures (Gielnik (2014)). The current study aligns with this theme by examining the role of religious values in shaping women's entrepreneurial endeavors. Hence, this study builds upon the existing literature by focusing on the specific context of the ELCZ, Western Diocese. It aims to deepen our understanding of how religious beliefs and practices in this particular setting influence women's motivations and values in entrepreneurship. Also, the existing literature explores the motivations of women entrepreneurs, especially those in religious spaces (Mapuranga, 2018). There is limited research specifically addressing the interplay between gender, religion, and entrepreneurship within the ELCZ, Western Diocese. More so, studies highlight the socio-cultural factors and barriers that impact women's participation in entrepreneurship within religious contexts (Mazonde and Carmichael, 2016). These factors include traditional gender roles, patriarchal attitudes, and limited access to resources. The existing literature acknowledges the need for better support systems and policies to address these barriers (Gaidzanwa, 2016). The current study aligns with this theme by examining the socio-cultural factors and barriers that church women entrepreneurs in the ELCZ, Western Diocese, face. Thus, the current study aims to fill the gap by providing insights into unique experiences and shedding light on the specific challenges and constraints experienced by women entrepreneurs in the ELCZ, Western Diocese, and offers recommendations for empowering and supporting their entrepreneurial aspirations.

Positionality

I am a young pastor in the ELCZ, who is passionate about women's empowerment and has actively initiated gender empowerment programs within the communities I serve. The insights and perspectives presented in this review are informed by my experiences and commitment to promoting gender equality and supporting women entrepreneurs. In this discussion on entrepreneurship, gender, and religion, I draw upon the gender empowerment initiatives I have undertaken to shed light on the unique challenges and opportunities women face within the ELCZ, Western Diocese. This methodology positionality allowed my study to build and guarantee trust between myself and participants to reach insightful, meaningful, and impactful research that benefits both Church women in the ELCZ and the scholarly board of knowledge.

Methodology

The research made use of the qualitative methodology since it provides a deep and nuanced understanding of complex phenomena (Saunders et al., 2018). While quantitative methods are primarily concerned with numerical data and statistical analysis, qualitative methods focus on exploring subjective experiences, meanings, and social contexts (Corbin and Strauss, 2008). The methodology also allowed the researcher to collect detailed and rich data or firsthand information about the participants' experiences through methods such as interviews, observations, and open-ended survey questions. Bakasa (2016) notes that the qualitative method prioritizes capturing the participants' perspectives and voices, giving them agency in shaping the research process and findings. Saunders et al. (2018) further explain that qualitative methodology emphasizes the importance of understanding the social, cultural, and historical context in which the research is conducted. This enabled the researcher to examine the interplay between various factors and gain insights into how they shape individuals' experiences, behaviors, and perceptions. The study targeted Church women who are involved in entrepreneurship in the ELCZ, Western Diocese. In this research, the writer used non-probability sampling. The chapter also made use of visual images since they significantly increase the work's impact and readability. On data generation, 18 participants *(female Church entrepreneurs)* participated in 2 focus group discussions and 9 in-depth interviews, allowing them to share their entrepreneurship experiences and achievements. Thus, Breen (2007) highlights that focus group discussions are used to explore the group's experiences, generate ideas for a group, and give a deeper understanding of the phenomenon for the purpose of hearing their common experiences, within a social context. Furthermore, Breen (2007) adds that one-on-one interviews ought to probe individual experiences and encourage self-reflection on issues that could be distorted if social pressure were placed on individuals. The sample size for the research constituted 27 participants *(female entrepreneurs in the Western Diocese)*. In each entrepreneurial line, three Church women were chosen.

Defining Entrepreneurship

Entrepreneurship is defined as an activity that involves the discovery, evaluation, and exploitation of opportunities to introduce new goods and services, ways of organizing, markets, processes, and raw materials through organizing efforts that previously had not existed (Shane and Venkataraman, 2000). Hence, entrepreneurs typically possess qualities such as creativity, innovation, risk-taking, and leadership skills. Nieman and Nieuwenhuizen (2003) assert that entrepreneurship plays a crucial role in driving economic growth, creating job opportunities, and promoting innovation in various industries. For Coughlin and Thomas (2002), entrepreneurship is a means of providing economic opportunity for disadvantaged groups, including women, low-wage earners, and minorities. Thus, entrepreneurship is one of the best tactics within the strategic realm empowering women and elevating them to the equal status they are entitled to (Coughlin and Thomas, 2002).

An Overview of the Western Diocese

The ELCZ, Western Diocese, covers Matabeleland South and Matabeleland North, stretching from Beitbridge-Chikwarakwara to Victoria Falls, and the area is hugely characterized by the driest areas in Zimbabwe falling under agro-ecological region five. It consists of 24 parishes and 144 congregations most of them being situated in a rural setup. The Diocese is divided into two deaneries, the Northern and the Southern. This Diocese is also known as the rainbow Diocese since it accommodates different languages *(Sotho, Venda, Ndebele, Shona, and Shangane)*. Despite the presence of the Church in the area, culturally the patriarchal system is dominant and it has led to gender inequalities especially disadvantaging women and girls. Nevertheless, the positive news is that the Diocese has a gender justice department that seeks to promote gender justice through challenging patriarchal structures that push women and girls into peripheries. The impact of the gender justice desk is felt in the Diocese because there has been a rise of women entrepreneurs in the Church. Therefore, it is fair and just to appreciate the achievements of female entrepreneurs in the ELCZ, Western Diocese.

Presentation of Data

Church Women as Business Owners

The biblical Proverbs 31:10-31 model is the encouraging model for women in the Western Diocese who embark on different entrepreneurial projects, searching for change, responding to it, and exploiting it as an opportunity. These religious women identify and pursue value-creation opportunities often in the face of risk and uncertainty (Mapuranga, 2018). Grounded on biblical faith, with God all things are possible, the Lord is my strength, and an encouraging population of the women in the Church work tirelessly to achieve set goals of improving livelihoods and reaching out to the poor in the Church and community. The study shows that based on talents and skills, Church women in the Western Diocese are involved in various entrepreneurship fields. This was reinforced by one participant during a focus group discussion who noted that

> Church women are involved in different businesses based on their passion, talents, resources and locations.
>
> Respondent 5

Tourism

The research also gathered that some women in the Western Diocese are entrepreneurs in the tourism industry. They have lodges to provide top-class accommodation and event management gardens. As entrepreneurial skills are explored, employment creation is achieved, which contributes to the development of well-being in society in general. One Church woman who is in the business of lodges highlighted that

> Investing in properties like lodges has made me a better woman in the Church and community.
>
> Respondent 15

Early Child Development Centers

Value creation opportunities are also pursued through early development. The survey shows that some women in the Western Diocese have managed to secure land and construct early development centers. They spend time and effort, take risks, and earn financial and personal freedom by developing products and services that benefit society. The research shows that most women who run early child development centers are teachers. One of them actually said

> I am doing what I love and I am happy because what I love is giving me money.
>
> Respondent 13

Decoration and Catering

Other Church women earn a living through decoration and catering services. Talent is identified as they work in groups in the Church. This talent is then matched to come up with decoration and catering entrepreneurs. These services are then extended to communities. For instance, Church women doing decoration and catering provide services at weddings, political rallies, and birthday celebrations. This one was confirmed by one respondent who noted that

> Decoration and catering are a good venture because today's world is characterized by various gatherings.
>
> Respondent 6

Chicken Rearing

Farming is broad, and as such, chicken rearing is an entrepreneurial project through which some religious women earn a living. The study acknowledges that some Church women who are involved in chicken rearing produce over 1000 chickens and they have a market ready for them. One Church woman who is involved in chicken rearing shared that

> The chicken project has fast money and if you do chickens in large quantities you will not go wrong.
>
> Respondent 16

Beadworks

Fashion is not static in nature, and as such, continuous innovation is done in designing new handbags, necklaces, bracelets, headgear, and many more bead products. Many women in the Western Diocese are entrepreneurs in beadworks. Trainings are done internally for free since Church women value the sharing of knowledge and skills for the betterment of their livelihoods. It is important to note that the beadwork project has united Church women in different parishes since women who are involved in this project work together. This was supported by one Church woman who stated that

> The beadwork project has empowered us to work together as women of Faith.
>
> Respondent 13

Dress Making, Cutting, and Designing

Fashion, as mentioned earlier, is not static. Some women in the Western Diocese were trained through Church entrepreneurial skills training initiatives and have developed their skills through continuous practice over the years. A number of them are now very good and upmarket designers of women', men', and children's wear. The research also gathered that Diocesan women have their own offices where they sell their clothing products branded with a Church logo as a way of fundraising. Some of the women, who are formally employed in the same industry, make their products after hours based on the Proverbs 31:10-31-woman model. The Church's teachings need to be appreciated because it pushes Church women to use their hands to earn a living. One respondent noted that

> The Lutheran Church's teaching empowers us as women to use our hands and talents.
>
> Respondent 15

The above testimony shows that these religious women do not only spend time praying but also encourage one another to make money. This is the meaning of true Christianity, religion should lead people to abundant life (John 10:10).

Event Centers

Urbanization has led to people realizing the need for fun and gathering, either as friends or families, for parties at whatever level and the importance of gathering outside the usual home. Some women moved with time and managed to secure land for event centers. Some have developed their home stands into event centers. People from different walks of life hire the venues for their gatherings. Entrepreneurs in this project line mainly tape on expertise from those with skills in landscaping and horticulture for proper setup.

Boutiques Businesses

The study also found out that there are Church women who own boutiques. These are small retail businesses that sell fashionable clothing, accessories, or luxury goods. Boutique owners often focus on providing unique and high-quality products, targeting niche markets and a specific customer base.

Retail Shops

Retail shops are physical stores that sell goods and services directly to customers. Some women in the Western Diocese own retail shops and they sell a wide variety of items such as clothing, electronics, home goods, groceries, and more.

Factors Motivating Church Women to Be Entrepreneurs

Findings reveal that women in the Western Diocese join entrepreneurship ventures for various reasons. This is supported by Coughlin and Thomas (2002), who argue that no single factor motivates a woman to build her own company. Her reasons depend upon several personal and external circumstances, both positive and negative. "Recognizing their primary motivations for starting businesses allows us to better understand the global rise of female entrepreneurs and how to better deliver effective programs in support of women-owned businesses" (Coughlin and Thomas 2002:71).

Financial Independence

Among other factors, financial independence was one of the major reasons why Church women ventured into different entrepreneurial lines. Most women highlighted that entrepreneurship offers them the opportunity to earn a living without having to rely on anyone else. This was reinforced by one respondent who noted that

> There is nothing painful and like begging for money from one's husband everytime one needs something.
>
> Respondent 7

The need for financial independence is a reality in the world of women. Women who are not financially independent face many challenges. Kabonga et al. (2021) note that customarily, a woman's role has been that of mother and wife. Thus, Coughlin and Thomas (2002) point out that women who participate in the market economy can increase their status within the household and community. They are also more likely to participate in household decision-making and to demand their legal rights. "Research shows that women's access to and activity within the market economy results in a significant increase in their authority within the household and community" (Coughlin and Thomas 2002:50). Societal norms still discount women as the primary breadwinners in the family. In addition, Bonner et al. (2017) hold that for too long, women's participation in the labor market has been considered secondary to that of men. Thus, women need to run their own businesses so that they can also contribute to the process of economic growth like their counterparts.

Unemployment

The Zimbabwean crisis of high unemployment is also a primary motivating factor for Women in the Diocese to start businesses. This is a response to the situation on the ground. Over 60% of Church women see entrepreneurship as a way of creating employment opportunities for themselves and others. Tom Tom (2017) acknowledges that the unemployment rate in Zimbabwe and the lack of other economic options are the major factors in why women go into business for themselves. During an interview, a Church business woman stated that

> The Zimbabwean situation does not allow one to sit down hence there is a need to run around and make ends meet.
>
> Responded 2

The economic dilemma in the country forces almost everyone to be an entrepreneur, including women in religious spaces. This is evidenced by the number of vendors on the streets.

Flexibility

According to Coughlin and Thomas (2002:12), "The history of women's social role has always been full of constraints, but it could now be translated into opportunities, which is precisely what many women are doing." However, Kabonga et al. (2021) highlight that comparatively, women entrepreneurs' number remains lower compared to male entrepreneurs. During interviews, several Church women shared that they chose to be entrepreneurs because entrepreneurship allows them to work flexible hours that accommodate their family needs. In a focus group discussion, one woman was quoted saying

> Being an entrepreneur has allowed me to be my own boss compared to those who are formally employed but the challenge is that we still have few women participating in entrepreneurship compared to men.
>
> Respondent 9

It has been observed that most women in Zimbabwe and beyond are not able to work for long hours because of family responsibilities yet men can work more hours. Hence, this speaks to existing gender disparities in our communities. Nevertheless, results show that women in the Western Diocese want to break away from the limitations of traditional employment and create businesses that allow them to set their own hours, be their own boss, and determine their own income. Coughlin and Thomas (2002) claim that by starting their own businesses, women are creating an environment where they are in control of where they work, how they work, and when they work.

Passion

Most of the women interviewed in the Western Diocese attested that they started their businesses out of passion. It is clear that this has made them successful because it allows them to do what they love doing. These women have turned their passion into entrepreneurial adventures. This is supported by a Church business woman who noted that

> I love decorating, I can even do it without being paid. I know this is my talent and a gift from God

Starting a business out of passion is key. Without a strong passion for business, it might be impossible for women to flourish in the informal economic sector since they face social and cultural constraints. This is reinforced by Nziku and Struthers (2021) who state that despite the acknowledgment of their economic roles and significance, the contributions of female entrepreneurs to world economics are still understated. Therefore, women in the ELCZ, Western Diocese, seem to be unstoppable because they were motivated by passion to start businesses. These women are fueled by the desire to create something that reflects their values, which allows them to make an impact in their lives and they are driven by a strong desire to make a difference. Looking at the rewards of entrepreneurship, most women business owners seem to agree that the greatest rewards of entrepreneurship come from within (Coughlin and Thomas, 2002).

Financial Empowerment

The ELCZ Gender Justice department always encourages Church women to be financially empowered, because it gives women the power to take control of their lives and make their own decisions. Women usually encounter abuse by their husbands and remain silent since they do not have what is theirs. Hence, this sense of empowerment was attractive to several Church women in the Western Diocese. This is evidenced by one woman who said that

> Being a female entrepreneur is one of the most rewarding roles I have undertaken in life. I am now financially empowered.
>
> Respondent 11

According to Coughlin and Thomas (2002), discrimination and abuse begin at home with the undervaluing of domestic duties, because they do not directly generate income. Therefore, one of the most universal motivations for women starting entrepreneurship in the Western Diocese is the need to be financially empowered.

Personal Motivation

The need for personal fulfillment also emerged as an answer to why women in the Western Diocese venture into entrepreneurship. Findings reveal that most interviewed women share the common motivation of self-fulfillment and the desire for pride or self-esteem. Coughlin and Thomas (2002) maintain that even in the developing world where the primary motivation is economic, the motivation for self-fulfillment is very strong. In addition, Link and Strong (2016) acknowledge that most successful female entrepreneurs are associated with a unique personal motivation. This means that the desire for self-fulfillment is strong in many women. In accordance with the above, one of the respondents stated that

> There is nothing fulfilling like having your own business. It gives you inner peace and prestige as a woman!
>
> Respondent 12

In other words, the above quotation tells us a ruthless story regarding those women who remain constrained by cultural boundaries. This means that we have many women who die silently inwardly and these women will never achieve peace with themselves or that self-fulfillment. There is a need to continue reminding each other that a number of African societies give women little respect for their accomplishments and abilities and therefore crave an opportunity to create their own self-respect. What happens to those women who cannot get that opportunity?

Conquering Encountered Challenges

The chapter acknowledges that women entrepreneurs face more obstacles and challenges due to gender biases, stereotypes, and traditional gender roles. However, the researcher seeks to draw our attention to the resilience and determination displayed by female entrepreneurs in the Western Diocese more than the challenges they face. This study shows how these women worked hard to overcome hurdles set before them. Consequently, the entrepreneurial spirit is commonly about overcoming obstacles.

Gender Roles Women Play at Home

From the inception of their business adventure, most Church women find it difficult to balance family life and business. Family obligations at home hinder women from becoming successful entrepreneurs compared to their male counterparts (Modarresi et al., 2017). Accordingly, there is a need to appreciate businesswomen in the Western Diocese for their tenacity to withstand such challenges. This demonstrates that women are stronger than men and they are not weak vessels. One respondent stated that

> The challenge I continue to face as a female entrepreneur is that I have to focus on my business and family. I have to be a mother, wife and a business woman at the same time.
>
> Respondent 9

These extra societal responsibilities always affect married women in business since they have to balance business and home duties. Fasci and Valdez (1998) also suggest that multiple demands on many women's time reduce the time they can devote to business. On the other hand, this is not so with their counterparts, male entrepreneurs do not have to worry about taking care of children, cooking, and other family duties. Hence, in such an environment, few women are able to survive in business.

Lack of Education and Training

Entrepreneurship training and education are important gears for women business persons to effectively run and operate a business as they keep informed businesspersons on modern and upcoming industry developments (Chinomona and Maziriri, 2015). Lack of education and training emerged as a challenge that Diocesan women faced and are still facing as entrepreneurs. A number of Church women interviewed expressed that it was difficult to start a business without adequate knowledge to run it. In addition, some Church women are running their businesses but lack education and training; hence, this is not giving them the best results. Phillips et al. (2014) uphold that women also tend not to have the relevant education and experience in starting and managing a business, and this, in most cases, leads to less potential for success. Therefore, there is a need for the Church to continue supporting female entrepreneurs through training programs. During a focus group discussion, one Church woman testified that

> Due to lack of knowledge in the business sector, we have made a lot of blunders and this has negatively affected our businesses till today.
>
> Respondent 3

The above statement is a call for help. Most women are willing to acquire more skills in business but a male-dominated society has put up systems and structures that discriminate, frustrate, and hinder women from fulfilling their entrepreneurial dreams. Although entrepreneurship training and education are of greater importance, female entrepreneurs are on the verge of receiving less of these teachings compared to males (Phillips et al. (2014). However, the study continues to view Church women in the Western Diocese as heroes, because they still manage to soldier on with their businesses in an unfair environment. Ibru (2009) argues that many women entrepreneurs lack training and education both in developed and developing countries, and hence the need for training especially in developing economies must be highlighted.

Cultural Constraints

The study reveals that culture has always had traditional expectations for women. As such, this has negatively affected many women who would have wished to venture into business. In many countries, socio-cultural factors do not act in favor of women, where their traditional role is subordination to men, often in patronizing relationships in which the woman's place is in the home rather than the workplace (Hechavarria and Ingram, 2016). The reality is that the African cultural value entails that the man or husband becomes the breadwinner. A woman exhibiting her entrepreneurial prowess is presumed to want to take over the leadership role of a husband. Some Church women in the Diocese shared that due to cultural beliefs in their societies, it was not easy, and is still not easy to be a female entrepreneur. Despite all the cultural constraints, many Church women decided to defile the status quo by starting their own business and they have refused their entrepreneurial dreams to be killed by culture. This was amplified by one respondent who pointed out that

> For a long time, culture has disadvantaged us as women but now it is our time to rise up.
> Respondent 12

In addition, for traditional patriarchal reasons, women are not readily accepted as entrepreneurs running and managing an enterprise (Van Eerdewijk and Mugadza 2015). Thus, it is clear that in various contexts, culture mainly disadvantages women more than men. It is disturbing because women entrepreneurs will definitely face discrimination in male-dominated communities. A study by Barwa (2003) on women entrepreneurs in Vietnam showed that women face additional handicaps due to the prevailing social and cultural gender-based inequalities and biases.

Lack of Capital

The study shows that over 65% of interviewed businesswomen in the Western Diocese acknowledge that lack of capital remains a challenge to women who want to venture into business. A study by Karim (2001) established that financial problems were the most common problems faced by women entrepreneurs and inadequate financing was ranked first. Tur-Porcar et al. (2017) further argue that lack of adequate business capital is an extra outer influence that negatively affects women's private enterprise. However, it is unfortunate because studies reveal that women have less access to capital and networking opportunities than men. Most Church women highlighted that they find it more challenging to secure venture capital and funding than their male counterparts. This is due to various factors like gender biases and discriminatory practices in the venture capital industry. Mandipaka (2014) highlights that male members think it is a big risk to finance the ventures run by women and many financial institutions are skeptical about the entrepreneurial ability of women. Furthermore, a report by the United Nations Industrial Development Organization (UNIDO 2003) suggests that despite the evidence that women's loan repayment rates are higher than men's, women still face more difficulties in obtaining credit often due to discriminatory attitudes of banks and lending groups. The ground is not level between men and women, but women of faith in the Western Diocese remain unshakable. Women entrepreneurs go the extra mile to achieve in business and this must be appreciated and acknowledged. During an interview, one Church woman mentioned that

> It was difficult for me to start a business because no one wanted to lend me money. No one believed that I would own my own boutique.
> Respondent 4

The Impact of Entrepreneurship

Entrepreneurship has a multi-faceted impact on individuals, communities, and the economy. Indeed, the Church women in the Western Diocese have allowed entrepreneurship to transform them, their community, the Church, and the economy of Zimbabwe. This research recognizes the impact of entrepreneurship and the achievements of Church women in business. Tom Tom (2017) advances that "it can be seen that women's entrepreneurship is a growing phenomenon and has had a significant economic impact in the economy of Zimbabwe."

Personal Lives

The research revealed that entrepreneurial projects have positively impacted the lives of women in the Western Diocese. Starting their own business has allowed women to gain financial independence and control over their own finances. Tom Tom (2017) highlights that the engagement of women in the informal economy of Zimbabwe has positive implications for their socio-economic well-being. On the other hand, Coughlin and Thomas (2002) argue that starting and managing a business can boost women's self-confidence and empower them to take charge of their lives. For example, the research established that some of the beadwork products have penetrated the international market. Muzvidziwa (2001) appreciates the effort and sacrifice made by these women, especially their cross-border businesses. Hence, special mention has to be made of the ELCZ's Gender Justice Project, which conducted nationwide training on Beadwork as a form of livelihood development. Such testimonies prove that entrepreneurship can be a powerful tool for women's empowerment. It allows women to break traditional barriers, gain economic independence, and overcome gender inequality. They no longer have to rely on others for financial support. This is supported by a statement from a Church woman who noted that

> Being a business woman has really changed my life, I do not depend on my husband for everything like before. The little I get from my chicken project takes me far.
>
> Respondent 22

It is also central to note that some Church women ventured into businesses in order to assist their husbands since two are better than one. As a result, initiating their own business allows them to take control of their financial situation and help support their husband and family. For instance, there are a number of women who manage to pay school fees for their children and others have built houses because of these projects. The economic situation in Zimbabwe at the moment requires married couples to help each other.

Church

The study also discovered that entrepreneurship has the potential to transform the Church. If the Western Diocese continues to encourage and support female entrepreneurship, it will lead to the economic sustainability of the Church. This is so because findings confirm that women are the backbone of the Church and their support cannot be questionable. Church women seem to be more committed than men. Some Church women in business often generate wealth, which can be channeled into charitable work. Also, most of the Church activities in the Diocese are funded by women who after harvesting from their projects plough back to the work of God. One respondent highlighted that

> I know that my blessings come from God and I have a religious obligation to give back to God my 10%.

This statement was supported by many religious women involved in entrepreneurship in the Diocese. What is interesting about these women is that God seems to have a share in all their resources. Thus, for Muzvidziwa (2020) gender, religious beliefs, and practices shape an individual's engagement in the informal sector.

Economy and Community

The role played by Church women in entrepreneurship must be appreciated because they boost the economy and improve communities in the context of the Zimbabwean economic crisis. Chirisa (2018) recognizes how religious people use religion as a coping mechanism that enhances resilience, enabling individuals to navigate challenging economic conditions and also contributing to economic development. As a result, most women highlighted that they started their business not only for themselves and their families but also for the community. These female entrepreneurs in the Diocese seem to possess a deep understanding of their communities' needs and can use their businesses as a platform to address social issues. They can create products or services that directly benefit their communities, such as providing employment opportunities, supporting local artisans, or addressing specific community challenges. This view aligns well with one Church woman who said the following

> My desire is not to be selfish but I want to plow back to my community.

Without any doubt, female entrepreneurs in religious spaces play a vital role in closing the gender gap in business and strengthening local and global economies. By providing employment opportunities, they empower individuals to support themselves and their families. This reduces the unemployment rate, especially in a country like Zimbabwe, hence improving the quality of life for many.

Role Models and Inspiration

According to the findings, a meaningful number of Church women in the Diocese serve as role models and inspire other women to pursue their entrepreneurial dreams. They demonstrate that it is possible for women to achieve success. Although the patriarchal cultural heritage encountered in certain societies precludes female entrepreneurship, especially in certain developing nations, women owned businesses still flourish at a very high speed (Jonathan and Da Silva, 2007).

The achievement of women has shown a great impact on the lives of many women and girls in the Church and beyond. During a focus group discussion, a woman stated that

> I am happy that I became a good mother and example to my daughter, as we speak my daughter is running her own decorating and catering company.
>
> Respondent 11

Through the determination of these religious women, a lot of women in the Church now see that their dreams and ambitions are achievable and that they too can overcome challenges and obstacles to create successful businesses. In addition, seeing successful women entrepreneurs can also provide them with role models and mentors to learn from and gain guidance and support on their own entrepreneurial journeys. Ultimately, the success of other women entrepreneurs can drive a ripple effect, encouraging and inspiring more women to pursue their own business ventures. This, in turn, helps to break gender stereotypes and promote gender equality.

Conclusion

Church women in the ELCZ, Western Diocese, have made significant achievements in entrepreneurship and their contributions should be recognized and appreciated. Against all odds, these women have demonstrated their capabilities, skills, and determination to succeed. Furthermore, women in the Western Diocese have positively impacted their lives, families, communities, economy, and the Church. Their accomplishments serve as an inspiration and example to aspiring female entrepreneurs in the Diocese and beyond to pursue their dreams and overcome barriers of any kind. However, it is important to acknowledge that there are still gender disparities and challenges that Church women encounter in entrepreneurship. Hence, the Church should continue to support women and encourage more women to pursue entrepreneurial paths.

Bibliography

Bakasa, E. C. 2016, *An exploration of the Livelihood and Coping Strategies of Urban Teachers in Post Economic Crisis Zimbabwe 2009–2015*. University of Pretoria.

Barwa, S.D., 2003, *"Impact of Start your Business (SYB) Training on Women Entrepreneurs" Working Chapter Series No. 1, ILO Office in Vietnam*.

Bonner, K., Hart, M., & Levie, J. 2017, *GEM UK: Wales report 2017: Global Entrepreneurship Research Association*.

Breen, R. L., 2007, A Practical Guide to Focus-Group Research. *Journal of Geography in Higher Education*, 30(3), 463–475.

Chinomona, E., and Maziriri, E. T. 2015, Women in Action: Challenges facing women entrepreneurs in the Gauteng Province of South Africa. *International Business & Economics Research Journal (IBER)*, 14(6), 835–850. doi:10.19030/iber.v14i6.9487

Chirisa, I. 2018, Religiosity and Informal Economic Activities: Enhancing Household Resilience in Zimbabwe. *Journal of Sustainable Development Studies*, 11(2), 12–34.

Claridge, T. 2018, *Introduction to Social Capital Theory*. Social Capital Research.

Corbin C and Strauss A. 2008, *Basics of Qualitative Research: Techniques and Procedures for Developing Grounded Theory*, London, Sage.

Coughlin, J. H., and Thomas, A. R. 2002, *The Rise of Women Entrepreneurs: People, Processes and Global Trends*. Westport, CT: Quorum Books.

Dziva, D. 2021, Women's Economic Empowerment and Religiosity: Exploring the Informal Economy in Zimbabwe. *Journal of African Economies*, 30(4), 567–589.

ELCZ, Gender policy, 2015, *Church and Community Fight Obstacles to Gender Justice, Equality and equity*. 7, Lawley Road, Suburbs, Box 2175, Bulawayo.

Fasci, M.A. and Valdez, J., 1998, A performance contrast of male- and female-owned small accounting practices, *Journal of Small Business Management*, 36(3), 1–7.

Gaidzanwa, R.B., 2016, Women and land in Zimbabwe: State, democracy and gender issues in evolving livelihoods and land regimes', in A. Pallotti and C. Tornimbeni (Eds.), *State, land and democracy in Southern Africa*, pp. 149–166, Routledge, New York.

Gielnik, M. M., Frese, M., Kawuki, A.M., Katono, I.W., Kyejjusa, S., Ntayi, J.M., Orobia, L.R. and Dlugosch, T.J. 2014, Action and Action, Regulation in Entrepreneurship, Evaluating A Sample Business Plan. *Academic of Management Journal*.

Hechavarria, D.M. and Ingram, A.E., 2016, The Entrepreneurial Gender Divide: Hegemonic Masculinity, Emphasized Femininity and Organizational forms, *International Journal of Gender and Entrepreneurship*, 8(3), 242–281. http://dx.doi.org/10.1108/IJGE-09-2014-0029.

Ibru, C., 2009, *Growing microfinance through new technologies*. Federal University of Technology, Akure, Nigeria.

Link, A.N. and Strong, D.R., 2016, Gender and Entrepreneurship: An Annotated References, *Foundations and Trends in Entrepreneurship* 12(4–5), 287–441.

Jonathan E. and Da Silva, T., 2007, Empreendorismo Feminino: Tecendo a Frama De demandas Conflitantes. *Psicologia Sociedade*. 19(1): 77–84.

Karim, N. A., 2001, *Jobs, gender and small enterprises in Bangladesh: Factors affecting women entrepreneurs in small and cottage industries in Bangladesh*, SEED Working ChapterNo. 14, International Labour Office, Geneva.

Kabonga, I., Zvokuomba, K., and Nyagadza, B. 2021, The Challenges Faced by Young Entrepreneurs In Informal Trading in Bindura Zimbabwe. *Journal of Asian and African Studies (JAAS)*, 56(8), 1780–1794. doi:10.1177/0021909621990850.

Mandipaka, F., 2014, *An Investigation of the Challenges Faced by Women Entrepreneurs in Developing countries*: A case of King Williams' Town, South Africa, Free State University.

Mapuranga, T.P. 2018, Ed., *Powered by Faith: Pentecostal Businesswomen in Harare*. Eugene, OR: Wipf and Stock.

Mazonde, N.B. and Carmichael, T., 2016, The Influence of Culture on Female Entrepreneurs in Zimbabwe, *Southern African Journal of Entrepreneurship and Small Business Management* 8(1), a101. http://dx.doi.org/10.4102/sajesbm.v8i1.101.

Modarresi, M., Arasti, Z., Talebi, K., and Farasatkhah, M. 2017, Growth barriers of women-owned home-based businesses in Iran: An exploratory study. *Gender in Management: An International Journal*, 32(4), 244–267. doi:10.1108/GM-03-2016-0069

Muzvidziwa, S. N. 2020, Gender, Religiosity, and the Informal Economy in Zimbabwe: A Critical Analysis. *African Journal of Gender and Religion Studies*, 12(1), 89–107.

Muzvidziwa, V. 2001, Zimbabwe's cross border women traders: Multiple identities and responses to new challenges. *Journal of Contemporary African Studies*, 19(1), 67–80.

Nieman, G.H. & Nieuwenhuizen, C., 2003, *Entrepreneurship. A South African perspective*. 2nd Ed, Pretoria: Van Schaik.

Nziku, D. M., and Struthers, J. J. 2021, *Enterprise and Economic Development in Africa*. Emerald Publishing Limited. https://books.emeraldinsight.com/page/detail/Enterprise-and-Economic-Development-in-Africa/?k1/49781800713239.

Phillips, M., Moos, M., and Nieman, G. 2014, *The Impact of Government Support Initiatives on the Growth of Female Businesses in Tshwane South Africa*.

Saunders, B., Sim, J., Kingstone, T., Baker, S., and Waterfield, J. 2018, Saturation in Qualitative Research and Operations. *Quality and Quantity*. https://doi.org/10.1007/s11135-017-0574-8

Shane, S. and Venkataraman, S. 2000, Entrepreneurship as a Field of Research: The Promise of Entrepreneurship as a Field of Research. *Academy of Management Review*, 26 (1):13–17.

Söderström, H., Bergman, S., and Bergman, T., 2003 *The History of the Evangelical Lutheran Church in Zimbabwe 1903-2003*, Church of Sweden, ISBN 916314073X, ISBN 9789163140730 https://web.archive.org/web/20160304220513/http://www.fjellstedtska.se/ELCZ_100years.pdf.

The United Nations Industrial Development Organization, 2003, *Developing Rural and Women Entrepreneurship*, Vienna.

The Department for International Development 1999, *Sustainable Livelihoods Guidance* Sheets.

Tom Tom, M. 2017, Women in the Informal Economy: A Case Study of Zimbabwe. *Journal of International Women's Studies*, 18(1), 172–185.

Tur-Porcar, A., Mas-Tur, A., and Belso, J. A. 2017), Barriers to women entrepreneurship. Different Methods, Different Results? *Quality and Quantity*, 51(5), 2019–2034. doi:10.1007/s11135-016-0343-0.

Van Eerdewijk, A. and Mugadza, T., 2015, *Resilience in Adversity: The Changing Face of Women's Activism in Zimbabwe 2000–2014, Knowledge Programme Hivos*, The Hague, Netherlands.

23
THE ROLE OF YOUNG WOMEN IN PROMOTING ECONOMIC DEVELOPMENT IN AFRICA

Cherifa Klaa

Introduction

Young women have been contributing for decades to local development processes in many African countries, which have been paying attention to the important role of African women in the different development processes by working to include women as well as promote their roles in those development dynamics. However, it should be kept in mind that the policies that the African countries have embraced to achieve this goal have differed from one country to another due to the social differences between those countries. In some countries, women managed to become active actors involved in small and medium enterprises, which are the main drivers of job creation throughout Africa. In this context, it can be noted that the percentage of African women entrepreneurs who are running start-up companies has reached 24%, which is a high rate compared with other regions of the world.

Although many African governments have large programs to facilitate small and medium enterprises and advanced facilities, they are often characterized by policies that disregard gender equality. As a result, those programs have so far been limited in their impact and scope as they did not prioritize women in planning and leading business and economic programs. A number of African women entrepreneurs have managed to accomplish impressive results in recent years though.

Research Aims

This research aims to assess the role of African women in economic development, with a particular focus on the field of small and medium enterprises. It scrutinizes the real contribution of African women to development and economic life, as well as the size of small and medium enterprises led by women in Africa. And finally, the challenges faced by African women in starting, running, and scaling up businesses are to be depicted.

Research Problem

The role of young African women in the development and economic life in Africa is a question that has arisen in both the academia and political circles across the continent, and this study represents an attempt to answer the following research question: To what extent have women led businesses and commercial and economic programs in Africa?

Methodology

This research chapter relied on the statistical method to display the gap between sexes in Africa in terms of empowerment, women's ownership of land and loans, representative's percentages on boards of directors in African companies, as well as women's contribution to GDP. Besides, the comparative method is also followed in order to compare between African women entrepreneurs with their peers in the world. These two methods complete each other and help to give accurate answers to the research questions.

Literature Review

We have reviewed the literature that focused on the role of young women in the economic development of Africa. And as the studies that shed light on specific African countries have been excluded, the researcher found a relatively small number of studies that tried to scrutinize the subject.

1. Study of Bouée, B.C. (2018)
   This study sought to present a unique contribution to African businesswomen, their incentives, motivations, challenges, and impacts. The author tends to believe that entrepreneurship is the way to promote the status and role of women in Africa.
2. Study of Ayinaddis, S.G. (2023)
   The main purpose of this study was to assess the social and economic factors that affect women's entrepreneurial performance in major small projects in the city of Bahir Dar, Ethiopia. It concluded that the demographic, social, economic, and administrative factors have really influenced women's performance in the field of entrepreneurship, particularly when it comes to small and medium projects and businesses. Therefore, this research recommended improving the economic and social development in order to facilitate the performance of women entrepreneurs in projects in Bahir Dar, Ethiopia.
3. Study of Ojong, N & Simba, A & Dana, L.P (2021)
   This study assesses the state of women's entrepreneurship in Africa and argues that the political, economic, social, and cultural integration of women entrepreneurs, as well as the resources and strategies they use, interact to determine entrepreneurial outcomes.

Research axes: Seeking to address the topic under scrutiny, this chapter is divided into three main axes, which are outlined as follows:

1. The reality of African women's contribution to development and economic life in Africa.
2. The size of small and medium enterprises led by women in Africa.
3. The constraints faced by African women in starting, operating, and expanding businesses.

The Reality of African Women's Contribution to Development and Economic Life in Africa

In an effort to address gender inequality and stimulate inclusive social and economic growth and development, women have been the target of many development initiatives in emerging economies. Many of the economic development initiatives for women revolve around access to financial services and entrepreneurship as avenues for inclusion and empowerment (Nwakanma, 2020: 01). African women are often dubbed "the untapped economic force" that should be an integral part of the programs seeking to address the development challenges facing Africa; a continent where structural and systemic change is a key element to achieving the goal of developing the private sector in a more inclusive manner for both sexes (Reines 2018). It can be noted that to achieve the element of empowerment for women in various sectors, it was necessary to enact laws and policies that achieve this, as national and regional laws and policies by some African countries played a role in determining African women's access to resources and opportunities in paid work, entrepreneurship, and agriculture, which is considered a tool for bringing about social change. In recent years, some West African countries have witnessed progress in gender equality under the law, as in 2010 Senegal adopted a law on gender equality in government, which witnessed a significant increase in the percentage of women in parliament to 43%, and came in second place after Rwanda in Africa in 2020. The Republic of Cape Verde, or as it is called "Cabo Verde", also adopted a law that punishes perpetrators of gender-based violence. However, general regional progress has been fragmented, and no progress has been made. Little focus is placed on expanding women's economic opportunities and their ability to work (Buvinic, O'Donnell, & Shelby, 2020: 08).

Nevertheless, African women still face gender biases in legal frameworks and macroeconomics and have fewer human, social, and financial assets than men. Currently, African women make up the majority of workers in the informal economy, and only a third of women across the continent participate in formal economic activity. Cultural and social norms often do not support their participation. Many ambitious female entrepreneurs lack access to supportive and mentor networks, as well as bargaining power within their households and communities (Reines, 2018). Looking at gender equality in both the workplace and society, we discern four distinct groups of countries that have achieved different degrees of progress according to a report issued by the "McKinsey Global Institute" (Moodley, Kuyoro, Holt, Leke, Krishnan & Akintayo 2019: 06):

1 Leaders (Lesotho, Namibia, Rwanda, South Africa, and Zimbabwe). These countries, mainly in Southern and East Africa, have achieved solid progress toward parity in both work and society with higher GPS on education, more equal participation in professional and technical jobs, and above-average progress toward parity on most societal indicators.
2 Workplace-focused (Botswana, Guinea, Nigeria, Sierra Leone, and Swaziland). These countries have low scores in progress toward gender equality in society but somewhat better scores in progress toward gender equality in the workplace.
3 "Middle of the road" (Angola, Burundi, Cameroon, Democratic Republic of Congo, Ethiopia, Gabon, Ghana, Kenya, Madagascar, Mauritius, Mozambique, Tanzania, Togo, Uganda, and Zambia). These countries have average scores in progress toward parity in work and society relative to other African countries, and all of them have areas of strength. For instance, Ghana has made more progress on higher education and financial inclusion than other countries in the group. Mauritius scores relatively high in access to health and education, while Madagascar has higher-than-average female participation in professional and technical jobs.
4 Room for growth (Algeria, Egypt, Morocco, Tunisia, Benin, Burkina Faso, Chad, Côte d'Ivoire, Liberia, Malawi, Mali, Mauritania, Niger, and Senegal). These countries are still far away from achieving gender equality although differences between North and

sub-Saharan Africa are significant. While North African countries mostly match the global average of gender equality in areas such as women's access to healthcare and have early achieved parity in education, these countries also perform significantly below their peers on work indicators, particularly the labor-force-participation rate.

The greatest development challenge that Africa faces is to create enough, good, equal, and adequate job opportunities to accommodate its growing population, particularly for the youth and women. Although there have been many strategies advocated for harnessing the potential of the demographic power (the fastest growing workforce in the world), to build appropriate infrastructure, support globally competitive and labor-intensive sectors, and train that workforce in various skills, the best way to integrate women was absent from the debates and discussions (Reines, 2018), disregarding the fact that women represent more than half of the African population (nonetheless, they only contributed with 33% of GDP of the continent in 2018). If every country in Africa were working to achieve progress in gender parity and reduce the gap between them, this would lead to an additional $ 316 billion in GDP. This means that increasing the inclusion of women may lead the gross domestic product GDP to increase by 10% by 2025 (Maina & Marks 2020).

According to the sub-Saharan Africa Gender Gap Index, as of 2023, sub-Saharan Africa accounted for 68.2% of the gender gap, meaning that females were, on average, 32% less likely to have the same opportunities as males in the region. Despite the variation in percentages from one country to another, Namibia, South Africa, and Rwanda provided the best results, with a score of 0.8, which showed an average gender gap of about 20%. This achievement placed Namibia among the top nine performers to fill most of the 80% of the total gender gap in the world. Chad, on the other hand, has the lowest performance in sub-Saharan Africa, with a score of 0.57 (Reines, 2018) (Figure 23.1).

It should be noted that African women play an important role in building African societies, as the role of women in Africa differs from one country to another or from one region to another according to the customs, traditions, history, culture, or religion of that country or region (Klaa, 2020: 04). This led to the proclamation of the woman's contract during the period (2010–2020) in Africa in order to advance their developmental role and contribution to economic life (sis.gov.eg, 2018). But there are still difficulties facing the empowerment of women, though they are making a significant contribution to the economy of the continent, as they are more active economically as farmers and entrepreneurs than women in any other region of the world. These women are the ones who grow most of the food in Africa and own a third of all companies operating in it (Empowering African Women: An Agenda for Action, 2015: 5). However, there is a strange paradox at the global level about the relationship between African women and the economy. According to a study conducted by the researcher Dominique Ouattara, women work two-thirds of the working hours and produce more than half of the foodstuffs, but they earn only 10% of the total income, own less than 2% of the land, and receive less than 5% of bank loans (Ouattara, 2018).

Notwithstanding, women in Africa are increasingly represented on the boards of directors of companies, where the percentage of women's representation on boards of directors in sub-Saharan Africa in 2018 reached about 24.3% of the seats on the boards of directors of African companies, and the percentage of women heading boards of directors of African companies is 24.5% compared to 27% worldwide. And despite the move to add more women to corporate boards, women's representation in African companies is still below the global average (Eds. Ekine & Aremu, 2022). Furthermore, African women's participation in industry and service

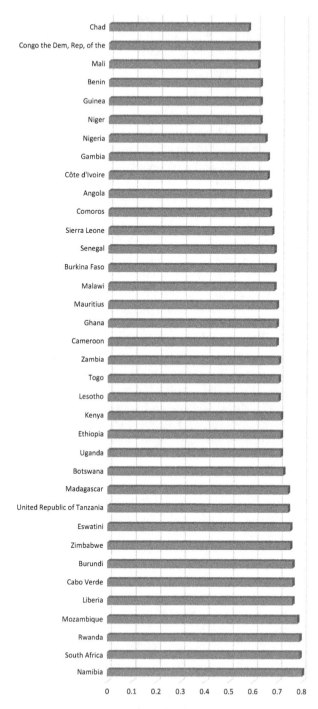

Figure 23.1 Gender gap index in sub-Saharan Africa as of 2023, by country.   Source: Kamer, L, 2023, '*Gender gap index in Sub-Saharan Africa as of 2023, by country*', viewed 21 Aug 2023, from: https://www.statista.com/statistics/1220485/gender-gap-index-in-sub-saharan-africa-by-country/

sector has increased since 2010, yet most female workforce still work most often in agriculture. Sixty percent of women in lower-middle-income countries (excluding women in sub-Saharan Africa) work in agriculture. And in sub-Saharan Africa, the percentage is about 50% of women's workforce, less than 20% in lower-middle-income countries. Overall, women's labor force participation in the agricultural sector has declined from 2000 to 2019 (Djantchiemo & White, 2022), but sub-Saharan Africa still has the highest participation rate in this sector. Regarding entrepreneurship, women entrepreneurs in Africa are considered a force for innovation, creativity, and economic dynamism. Sub-Saharan Africa is the region that has the highest rate of entrepreneurship among women in the world (Maina & Marks, 2020), as the rate of women who run a start-up company has reached 24%. This is what the study (Women in Africa Entrepreneurship: A Path to Women Empowerment?) issued by Roland Berger in 2018 shows. This rate is particularly high compared to other regions, such as Latin America and the Caribbean (17%), North America (17%), the Middle East (9%), Southeast Asia and the Pacific (11%), and Europe/Central Asia (6%) (Bouée, 2018). This fact leads us to ask a question about the volume and scope of small and medium enterprises led by women in Africa.

The Size of Small and Medium Enterprises Led by Women in Africa

Africa has the highest rate of entrepreneurship in the world, and it is the only continent in which women represent the majority of entrepreneurs, according to a World Bank report issued in March 2019 (Ojong et al., 2021:233). According to the Roland Berger Entrepreneurship Study on Women in Africa (2018), female entrepreneurs contributed between $250 billion and $300 billion in African economic growth in 2016, equivalent to about 13% of the continent's GDP, which is the largest emerging market in the world with the potential to add $12 trillion to global GDP by 2025 (Women and the Changing Face of Entrepreneurship in Africa 2020).

Small and medium enterprises are the main drivers of job creation across Africa, accounting for more than 90% of all companies outside the agricultural sector in the region, and the size of formal women ownership of small and medium enterprises currently amounts to about a third of all registered small and medium enterprises in Africa. Women-owned SMEs are likely to have lower annual sales, fewer employees, and smaller volume than those owned by men (Ojong et al., 2021: 233). Government facilitation for women-owned SMEs is particularly important because of the gender gaps that characterize the SME sector and the constraints it faces. The challenges women face in starting, operating, and scaling up enterprises can only be addressed on a large scale through deliberate efforts of government programs and implemented policies, and as in other power relations systems, patriarchal institutions and norms are not reformed without conscious efforts to mainstream gender concerns. Therefore, it means that widespread change in the hierarchy of power can only be achieved through the deliberate actions of state actors to make gender equality a top priority (Reines, 2018).

Many African governments already have large programs to facilitate small and medium enterprises, but they are often characterized by gender-biased policies, in which the status quo is maintained by reinforcing gender inequality. The small and medium enterprises division of the Uganda Investment Authority provides a strong example of the support available. For SMEs, programs offered including entrepreneurship training, business incubation and SME workspaces, mentorship networks, technical skills training to add value, and advocacy on behalf of SMEs, in addition to other programs, have been so far limited in their impact and reach due to their unfair gender nature, given the fact that women are neither mentioned nor given priority in the planning. There are many ways in which this issue can be addressed, from setting targets for women's participation in youth entrepreneurship programs to gathering and integrating sex-disaggregated data from SME databases and working with women's membership organizations, such as the Uganda Women Entrepreneurs Association Limited, in order to improve communication of information about these programs to women across Uganda (Reines, 2018).

In the first decade of the twenty-first century, the African continent witnessed the growth of a new group of businesses that focused on female entrepreneurship and businesses owned or run by women. Doing Business in Africa showed that the three countries with the highest percentage of businesswomen are Ghana (44%), Cape Verde (43%), and Rwanda (41%) (Women and the Changing Face of Entrepreneurship in Africa 2020), with sub-Saharan Africa currently boasting the highest rate in the region. Female entrepreneurship, with one in four women in Africa involved in business, more than double the global average among all businesses in sub-Saharan Africa (including the established ones), nearly one in three owned by women, which is close to the global average of (34%) in sub-Saharan Africa, and it is the only region in which women are more likely than men to work on their own account, and they constitute 58% of the total number. Moreover, about 45% of employers in Africa are women, and it is one of the highest rates in Europe and Central Asia, and the level of total entrepreneurial activity (TEA) for entrepreneurship among women is the highest among those between the ages of 25–34 years and 35–44 years, where women are more involved in entrepreneurial activities than men between the ages of 25 and 34 in sub-Saharan Africa. It is noteworthy that women with higher education are more active (30%) in startup companies compared to men with higher education. Sub-Saharan Africa has the highest rate of female entrepreneurs in the world (27%). The MasterCard Index of Women Entrepreneurs for the year 2017 included two African countries, Uganda (34.8%) and Botswana (34.6%), as the highest percentage of female entrepreneurs in the world (Maina & Marks, 2020).

These patterns are confirmed by a more recent study about developing countries more broadly, according to the MasterCard Women Entrepreneurs Index 2018, which indicated that the countries with the highest number of women entrepreneurs included Ghana, Uganda, and Botswana, with Ghana leading by a score greater than all its peers with the highest percentage of businesswomen (46%); this is attributed to the existence of a long history of female entrepreneurship in Ghana. In fact, sub-Saharan Africa has the highest rate of female entrepreneurs in the world, with about 26% participating adult females in entrepreneurial activity (Women and the Changing Face of Entrepreneurship in Africa 2020), and the Women Entrepreneurs Index in Africa for the year 2021 indicates that Botswana was considered the leading African country in favoring female entrepreneurship, as the country recorded a rate of 56.3, followed by South Africa (54.9) and Ghana (51.1). And according to this index, these countries not only have a high percentage of women-owned companies but also officially support women entrepreneurs (Galal, 2023). In Table 23.1, the location and ranking of the first countries in the Women Entrepreneurs Index for the year 2021 are depicted.

Despite the remarkable progress of many African countries that are witnessing a development in the size of the projects of African women entrepreneurs, most of the companies led by women in many African countries are small companies with few opportunities for growth, and women entrepreneurs are not spread across the continent. For instance, in Botswana, Ghana, Nigeria, Kenya, Uganda, and Zambia, there are disproportionately large numbers of women-led projects (Toesland 2018), as well as twice the proportion of women-led projects in some regions of Africa such as the Sahel region. This fact prompted the African Development

Table 23.1 Leading African countries in the MasterCard Index of Women Entrepreneurs (MIWE) in 2021

Leadind African countries	Bostwana	South Africa	Dhana	Madagascar	Nigeria	Uganda	Ethiopia	Angola	Tunis	Morocco	Algeria	Malawi	Egypt
Mastercard Index of Women Enterpreneurs (MIWE)	56.3	54.9	51.1	44.3	43.8	.43.8	43	42.4	41.7	38.6	38	33.9	32.9

Source: The statistics were taken by the researcher from the following source: Galal, S, 2023, "*Leading African countries in the MasterCard Index of Women Entrepreneurs (MIWE) in 2021*", viewed 16 June 2023, from: https://www.statista.com/statistics/1223158/index-of-women-entrepreneurs-in-african-countries/

Bank's Gender Equality Trust Fund starting in 2023 to provide a grant of $950,000 US; approximately $1 million in gender-based grants to enhance opportunities for women-led businesses in Africa for the Business Links Program for small and medium enterprises in Burkina Faso, Chad, Mali, Mauritania, and Niger. This support grant is expected to supplement a previous grant funding of $3.9 million from the Bank's Transition Support Program that will support nearly 1,400 women-led enterprises that contribute to economic resilience and social cohesion in the region. The Gender Trust Fund will also support the implementation and scale-up of the World Bank's Program of Action for Women in Africa, the Affirmative Finance Action for Women in Africa (AFAWA) that aims to close the $42 billion gender financing gap for women-led African firms by promoting both transferable and non-gender lending. The program will be managed by the G5 Sahel Federation of Chambers of Commerce. In cooperation with financial institutions and intermediaries to support local, small, and medium-sized companies' access to financing directly, it should be noted that the Business Links Program for small and medium enterprises in Africa is in line with the Private Sector Development Strategy (2021–2024) of the African Development Bank, the Gender Equality Strategy (2021–2021), and the strategy (2022–2026) to address fragility and build resilience in Africa. The Board of Executive Directors of the World Bank Group approved the grant on March 23, 2023 (afdb.org, 2023) in order to advance the economic empowerment of African women.

The Constraints Facing African Women in Starting, Operating, and Expanding Projects

Investing in the economic empowerment of young African women and developing their skills is one of the most urgent and effective ways to drive progress on gender equality, poverty eradication, and inclusive economic growth. Despite mounting evidence of the positive outcomes of young women's economic empowerment, young women still suffer from unequal access to education and skills development, and they face barriers to securing decent work and opportunities to thrive as entrepreneurs. Discriminatory laws may restrict young women's access to resources, including land and loans. Young women still bear a disproportionate share of unpaid care work, due to the persistence of traditional roles. For both sexes (unwomen.org, 2023), despite the size of small and medium enterprises led by women in

Africa, there are restrictions they face in starting, operating, and expanding projects, the most important of which can be mentioned as follows.

The Problem of Infrastructure and Lack of Profit

The lack of vital infrastructure limits business growth, and as a result, women entrepreneurs face difficulties in trying to earn a living, as about 39% of the women entrepreneurs who stopped their activity were restricted by the lack of profit, and about 15% of them because of problems in obtaining financing for their projects. In this context, Fatoumata Guirassy, The CEO of Saboutech, a Guinean incubator for small and medium-sized companies and start-ups, explains that women not only lack the means but also do not have the skills required to develop their companies. Hervé Lado mentioned the example of budget management, stressing that female entrepreneurs tend to confuse between company and family budgets and end up using the startup's money to finance unexpected family events. Consequently, business development and expansion quickly reach a threshold and then eventually decline (Bouée, 2018).

The Problem of Financing and Job Creation

With the growth of African economies, they have become more open and dynamic, where women entrepreneurs enter the private sector in greater numbers and assume the mantle of innovation and business leadership that was once dominated by men. There are more businesswomen in Africa than in any other region in the world, where one out of every four women are entrepreneurs, according to Diane Cote, Head of Risk Management at the London Stock Exchange Group. Women entrepreneurs could increase Africa's economic output by $20 trillion by 2050. Contemporary female entrepreneurship is living proof of the potential that can be attained in African economies in the coming decades. However, women entrepreneurs still face various challenges. The African Development Bank estimates that there is a gender financing gap of US$ 42 billion. For women entrepreneurs, it is essential to meet the aspirations of the African Union's Agenda 2063 to advance women in development. Historically, African women have been the cornerstone of their societies due to their dual dedication to providing for their families and growing their businesses. However, these sacrifices can signal a broader societal problem when not coupled with equitable access to markets, job opportunities and employment, and a conductive environment for female entrepreneurship. Job creation has become one of the biggest challenges faced by African companies and governments. With the expected growth of the working-age population on the continent by 40% to one billion people in 2030, there should be a rise of the job creation rate by 12 million jobs annually to keep pace with population growth and prevent the unemployment rate from soaring. This calls for resetting our understanding of the roles of women in African entrepreneurship, reimagining opportunities and models for women's entrepreneurial activity, and also supporting a dynamic economic future for Africa – it is the future driven and supported by female entrepreneurs (Gatiti & Marks, 2020).

Gender Gaps in Business Size and Profitability

Numerous gender inequalities constrain women's ability to promote and expand their businesses, making women-owned businesses less profitable and smaller than men-owned businesses in Africa. Government, the private sector, development actors, and individuals all have a role to play in bridging these gender gaps and creating an enabling environment for the next generation of female entrepreneurs (Maina & Marks, 2020). Despite high levels of entrepreneurship, female entrepreneurs earn a lower income (34%) than men across Africa. In addition, women-owned businesses tend to be smaller. They represent 20% of small companies (less than 10 employees), 10% of companies with between 100 and 500 employees, and only 7% of companies with more than 500 employees, and the difference in size between male- and female-owned companies are partly due to the fact that women have to deal with lower levels of capital investment, in contrast to male-owned companies owning more than six times the value of capital. In this context, it can be noted that in sub-Saharan Africa, there is the highest rate of women who stop working at 10% because of the lack of funding and lack of profitability mentioned as the most important reasons for closure (Maina & Marks, 2020).

The Problem of Financing and Inequality

Inequality in terms of access to funding is another constraint that faces women, as the rate of women's access to finance is significantly lower compared with men. In sub-Saharan Africa, in 2019, the rate of women's access to finance reached only 37% beside 48% for men (Maina & Marks, 2020). This creates additional barriers to accessing banking services, digital finance, loans, or other forms of capital investment. This is exacerbated by the gender gap in access to guarantees as women in Africa own only 38 percent of land alone or collectively. Compared to 58% of men, many women are also at risk of losing land if their husbands die (Maina & Marks, 2020).

Societal-Cultural Dimensions

Women across Africa face a range of barriers to achieve their full potential. From restrictive cultural practices to discriminatory laws and deeply fragmented labor markets. Eliminating gender inequality and empowering women can increase the productive potential of one billion Africans and boost the continent's development process (Empowering African Women: An Agenda for Action, 2015: 5). African women also suffer from the shortage of time as they have to fulfill their household and family tasks that leave them with little time and energy to carry out more productive tasks in the society (Empowering African Women: An Agenda for Action, 2015: 26).

Societies' negative attitude toward women entrepreneurs, cultural influences, and the heavy burden of household responsibilities are considered the main social and cultural problems that affect the start-up and expansion of business of women entrepreneurs (Ayinaddis, 2023: 5) because the supportive environment for women's entrepreneurship requires unified systems with mutual features and a constructive culture in the field of entrepreneurship, including investments, human and financial capital, opportunities for growth, and a mix of innovative and progressive institutional and infrastructure provisions. The gender aspects of policies, laws, and cultural expectations are often opaque and confusing, but they are deeply rooted in norms, practices, and standards, including neutral legal and commercial systems that ensure fair access to the capital. Financial and cultural expectations and practices that support women's businesses foster a productive and supportive entrepreneurial ecosystem for women entrepreneurs (Bullough et al., 2022: 989).

Corruption

For women entrepreneurs operating in Africa, corruption in the home country imposes additional burdens and costs that may hinder not only female entry into entrepreneurship but also the growth of new women-led ventures. Female entrepreneurs are more exposed to corruption, mainly bribery, than their male counterparts due to a lack of financial guarantees, as female entrepreneurs face more difficulties than male entrepreneurs in dealing with corrupt officials because of the lack of strategic capabilities and financial resources. Besides, research indicates that countries with high levels of corruption are more likely to discriminate against females than males and business restrictions related to corruption disproportionately affect female entrepreneurs (Pindado et al., 2023:4).

Land Ownership and Agricultural Problems

The lack of improved technologies to preserve agricultural products is an obstacle for women entrepreneurs working in the agricultural field, as this absence constitutes an obstacle to marketing them, in addition to the lack of storage facilities close to the market, the lack of access to internal markets, and the high prices of imported inputs Such as chemicals, which may impede increase in production capacity (Klaa, 2020: 7).

Moreover, African women have less access to land as their share of land holdings tends to be poorer in terms of equality than that of male farmers, they face discrimination in both formal laws and customary practices as the insecurity of land tenure makes them less likely to invest in their land, and they have limited access to financial services that are necessary for any business expansion as their access to financial services is impeded by legal obstacles, cultural assumptions, and common banking practices (Empowering African Women: An Agenda for Action, 2015:26).

Access to Science, Technology, and Digitization

Startups in Western countries focus more on digital tools and high-tech and advanced technologies; however, African women are showing creativity by creating their own careers and by providing solutions to issues that are not addressed in their environments. As a way forward, the education system in Africa needs to be strengthened. Including basic education and continuing training, young African women must be empowered to choose paths in various fields such as science, technology, and business, expand into the digital sector, and eventually move beyond the domestic sphere (rolandberger.com, 2018). The new information and communication technology constitutes an important challenge facing women, but the most important technical illiteracy is the ineffectiveness of African women in dealing with the elements of power and its determinants in the information space (Klaa, 2020: 6–7).

Conclusion

Young African women play a major role in the development and economic life in Africa through leading small and medium projects, which are considered the best projects to raise the gross domestic product compared to the major projects that women entrepreneurs are unable to do, not even most of the African countries as they have been suffering from violent conflicts that led to chaos and security uncertainty. Despite the great awareness of recent years of the role of women and their economic empowerment in Africa, as well as the various reforms, policies, and measures taken to improve their status, especially in the field of small and medium enterprises. There are still numerous hurdles that they face when trying to begin, operate, and expand their projects, especially the lack of financing opportunities and support provided by governments or financial institutions such as banks that refuse to give loans to young women. Adding to that the dilemma of land ownership really affects their role in the development and economic life in Africa.

Bibliography

afdb.org. 2023. "*Sahel region: African Development Bank to extend nearly $1m in gender-based grants to boost opportunities for women-led businesses*", African Development Bank, viewed 17 Jul 2023, from: https://www.afdb.org/en/news-and-events/press-releases/sahel-region-african-development-bank-extend-nearly-1m-gender-based-grants-boost-opportunities-women-led-businesses-61753

African Development Bank, Empowering African Women: An Agenda for Action, 2015, *Gender Africa Equality Index 2015*, Tunisia.

Ayinaddis, S.G., 2023. "Socio-economic factors affecting women's entrepreneurial performance in MSEs in Bahir Dar City, Ethiopia", *Journal of Innovation and Entrepreneurship*, 23 (12), 05.

Bouée, B.C., 2018. *Women in Africa Entrepreneurship: A path to women empowerment?* Roland Berger, Munich.

Bullough, A., Guelich, U., Manolova, T.S. & Schjoedt, L., 2022. "Women's entrepreneurship and culture: gender role expectations and identities, societal culture, and the entrepreneurial environment", *Small Bus Econ*, Volume 58, 989.

Buvinic, K. & O'Donnell, M. & Shelby, S. 2020. *Women's Economic Empowerment in West Africa: Towards a Practical Research Agenda.* CGD Working Chapter584. Washington, DC: Centre for Global Development.

Djantchiemo, S. & White, T. 2022. "*Figure of the week: Labor trends for women in Africa*", The Brookings Institution, viewed 22 Jul 2023, from: https://www.brookings.edu/articles/figure-of-the-week-labor-trends-for-women-in-africa/

Ekine A. & Aremu, A., 2022. "Making the future of African STEM female", in Ordu, A., & Golubski, C., (Eds), *Foresight Africa: Top Priorities for the Continent in 2022*, DC Brookings Institution, Washington.

Galal, S., 2023. '*Leading African countries in the MasterCard Index of Women Entrepreneurs (MIWE) in 2021*', viewed 16 June 2023, from: https://www.statista.com/statistics/1223158/index-of-women-entrepreneurs-in-african-countries/

Gatiti, Z. & Marks, Z. 2020. "Women and the Changing Face of Entrepreneurship in Africa", chapter presented at *Conference Women and the Changing Face of Entrepreneurship in Africa, Centre for African Studies*, Harvard University, October 1–2.

Kamer, L., 2023. '*Gender gap index in Sub-Saharan Africa as of 2023, by country*', viewed 21 Aug 2023, from: https://www.statista.com/statistics/1220485/gender-gap-index-in-sub-saharan-africa-by-country/

Klaa, C., 2020. "Role of African Women in Development and Economic Life: Reality and Challenges", *International Journal of Inspiration & Resilience Economy*, 4 (1), 4–7.

Maina, I. & Marks, Z. 2020. "Strengthening and Scaling the next Generation of Women Entrepreneurs in Africa", chapterpresented at *Conference Women and the Changing Face of Entrepreneurship in Africa, Centre for African Studies*, Harvard University, October 1–2.

Moodley, L., Kuyoro, M.M., Holt, T., Leke, A., Krishnan, A.M. & Akintayo, F. 2019. *The power of parity: Advancing women's equality in Africa*, Report, McKinsey Global Institute.

Nwakanma, A.P., 2020. "Women, Entrepreneurship, and Economic Development in Africa". In Yacob-Haliso, O., Falola, T. (Eds), *The Palgrave Handbook of African Women's Studies*, Palgrave Macmillan, Cham.

Ojong, N., Simba, A. & Dana, L.P. 2021. Female entrepreneurship in Africa: A review, trends, and future research directions, *Journal of Business Research*, Volume 132, August, 233.

Ouattara, D. 2018. "*La femme va-t-elle enfin trouver sa place dans l'économie africaine?*", viewed 02 Aug 2023, from: https://www.jeuneafrique.com/363165/societe/dominique-ouattara-femme-va-t-enfin-trouver-place-leconomie-africaine/

Pindado, E., Alarcon, S., Sanchez, M., Martínez, M. G. 2023. "International entrepreneurship in Africa: The roles of institutional voids, entrepreneurial networks and gender", *Journal of Business Research*, Volume 166, June, 04.

Reines, R. 2018. *Why women hold the keys to Africa's future*, World Economic Forum, viewed 18 June 2023, from: https://www.weforum.org/agenda/2018/03/why-women-hold-the-keys-to-africas-future/

rolandberger.com. 2018, "*Africa: First female entrepreneurs in the high-tech sector as new role models*", Roland Berger, viewed 19 May 2023, from: https://www.rolandberger.com/en/Insights/Publications/Africa-First-female-entrepreneurs-in-the-high-tech-sector-as-new-role-models.html

sis.gov.eg. 2018. "*Empowering Women in Africa*", viewed 22 June 2023, from: https://www.sis.gov.eg

Toesland, F. 2018. "*Women-led tech startups on the rise in Africa*", United Nations Africa Renewal, viewed 22 Apr 2023, from: https://www.un.org/africarenewal/magazine/august-november-2018/women-led-tech-startups-rise-africa

unwomen.org. 2023. "*Economic empowerment and skills development for young women*", UN Women, viewed 18 June 2023, from: https://www.unwomen.org/en/what-we-do/youth/economic-empowerment-and-skills-development-for-young-women

24
WOMEN IN HIGHER EDUCATION MANAGEMENT IN AFRICA

Trends, Policies, and Practices

Elizabeth A. Owino and Donald Lwala

Background

In recent years, significant strides towards gender equality have been made in various sectors. However, the glass ceiling still persists, particularly in higher education management. Women worldwide, and notably in Africa, continue to face significant underrepresentation in leadership roles within academic institutions. Despite an increasing number of women pursuing higher education and excelling in academic fields, they encounter barriers when ascending to leadership roles. Globally, women outnumber men as tertiary education students (52%) and represented close to 45% of teachers in tertiary education in 2020, as compared to less than 35% in 1990 (Galán-Muros, Bouckaert and Roser, 2023). Internationally, the representation of women tends to eease as academic ranks progress, often resulting in fewer women in senior leadership positions in higher education institutions (HEIs).

Higher Education Management

Higher education management relates to the structures and processes of leadership, governance, and administration in HEIs (Sporn, 2003). As institutions of higher learning, universities are characterized by different roles: teaching, research, and administration, which often require sound and strategic management. With the current competitive higher education environment, institutions must differentiate themselves effectively to meet the market needs. Leadership and management remain the primary success factor in these institutions.

Historical Contexts of Higher Education Management in Africa

Higher education was a colonial reform strategy to develop an educated African elite class capable of serving in the colonial government. Higher education institutions, therefore, became symbols of national pride, self-reliance, and self-respect, and governments were willing to allocate resources and invest in them (Coleman and Court, 1993). Among the earliest HEIs in Africa were Makerere University in Uganda (1922), Egerton University in Kenya (1939), University of Ghana (1948), University of Ibadan in Nigeria (1948), Addis Ababa

University in Ethiopia (1950), and College of Rhodesia and Nyasaland (1952), as observed by Damtew (2003) in (Woldegiorgis and Doevenspeck, 2013). These institutions were mainly concentrated in sub-Saharan Africa. However, after most African countries gained independence, the number of HEIs in the public and private sectors increased enormously. As of 2009, there were over 250 public and 420 private HEIs in Africa (World Bank, 2009). Currently, according to the Statista (2023) database, there are 1,279 officially recognized HEIs in Africa, with Nigeria having the highest number (279), followed by Tunisia (203) and Morocco (148). Like other universities worldwide, African universities' mandate remains threefold: teaching, research, and community service. For these mandates to be achieved, the management of these institutions is key.

The management of HEIs in Africa has followed global trends. Upon independence, most African countries relied on external experts to manage their institutions (Varghese, 2013). However, during and after the national liberation struggles, there were concerted efforts to Africanize the management of all HEIs (Sutton, 1971). Where the independent countries needed high-level professionals to replace the expatriates, competent individuals were identified and sent abroad for training in HE management (Kidd, 1991). Such training focused on management models for HEIs, such as Clark's triangle of 1983.

Clark's triangle is a model that illustrates the governance and management structure of HEIs (Maggio, 2011). The model views HE governance through three lenses: the state, institutional governance, and the market. From the triangle, it is possible to distinguish between a state control model, a Humboldtian model of academic self-rule (where institutions govern themselves and have academic freedom while integrating education and research), and an Anglo-American market-oriented model (which focuses on having HE at the centre of modernization and development) (Dobbins, Knill and Vögtle, 2011).

For the state-control model, the state, through the ministry responsible for HE, oversees the study content, the degree requirements, the examination system, and the appointment and remuneration of academic staff (Dobbins and Leišyte, 2014). On the other hand, the respective HEI is responsible for regulating internal institutional affairs concerning education and research content. This implies that HEIs are not autonomous. Instead, they are rational instruments the state uses for national priorities, although their mandate remains research and education (Dobbins, Knill and Vögtle, 2011).

In many African countries, most HEIs follow the state control model. For example, in South Africa, after the constitution, the primary legislation to which universities are subject is the Higher Education Act (HEA), which "prevails over any other law dealing with higher education" (De La Rey, 2015). One of the objectives of the HEA of 1997 was to establish a single coordinated HE system that promotes cooperative governance and provides for program-based HE to respond better to the country's human resource, economic, and development needs. This was directed at redressing past discrimination, representation, and equity. Additionally, the HEA provides inclusivity and diversity in the council membership at the institutional level concerning race, gender equity policies, and institutional culture. In turn, councils govern, while the vice chancellors (VCs) and executive manage the institutions.

In Kenya, the HEIs have a centralized system of governance where power is concentrated in the hands of the VCs. The presidency makes appointments of the VCs and the principals of constituent colleges. The HEM in Kenya has the power to make decisions about fundamental policies and practices such as mission, enrollment size, the access of students to instructional programs and social community responsibilities, degree requirements, and freedom available to individual faculty members, among other domains (Sifuna, 1998). Three key instruments govern HEI in Kenya: The Universities Act, the University Charter, and the statutes.

The Universities Act of 2012 provides for the development of university education; the establishment, accreditation, and governance of universities; the establishment of the Commission for University Education (CUE), the Universities Funding Board, and the Kenya University and Colleges Central Placement Service (KUCCPS) Board; the repeal of certain laws; and for connected purposes (Kenya, Republic of, Universities Act no. 42 of 2012). The University Charter, on the other hand, defines the university's governance: its objects, statutes, ordinances, regulations, officers, and powers, including those that allow for the award of degrees (www.aston.ac.uk/Fmanagement-structure/statutes-and-ordinances). Section 13 of the Universities Act 2012 provides that a Charter establishes every university in Kenya by the Act of Parliament (Universities Act 2012) and its variations or amendments. Consequently, statutes form the supreme law and ordinances that provide detailed information about the university's running in terms of its governance.

In Uganda, Lwanga et al. (2020) observe that the management of HEIs is based on three factors: market mechanism, institutional mechanism, and organization configuration. HEIs in Uganda comprise universities, business colleges, technical colleges, national teachers' colleges, agricultural colleges, and management institutes, among others. The HEIs operate under the legal and regulatory frameworks provided by the Universities and Other Tertiary Institutions Act (UOTIA, 2001) and other frameworks by the National Council of Higher Education (NCHE), respectively.

The Ugandan HEA provides for the governance structures of HEIs through laws, policies, and rules that act as standard operating procedures. HEIs are directed under the leadership of governing bodies and management who lead these institutions on behalf of the owners or stakeholders. Like in most countries, HEM in Uganda is a function of many elements: The external, economic, technological, social, political, and ethical environment, among other factors (Olum, 2004).

According to UOTIA (2001), the HEM consists of officers like the chancellor, the vice chancellor, the university secretary, the academic registrar, the librarian, the bursar, and the dean of students. Universities have organs of administration that include the university council, the senate, and other academic bodies stipulated as per the law to ensure that a management function is carried out effectively to realize institutional goals.

In the case of Rwanda, the HE system consists of over 29 institutions (17 public and 12 private). Higher Education Council (HEC) is an independent government agency established in 2007 and housed within the Ministry of Education. The HEC is responsible for university admissions policies, the structure of the academic calendar, and student funding programs.

Educational governance in Rwanda is complex, encompassing several actors, including organizational entities from the central government to parents' assemblies via local governmental institutions, faith-based organizations (FBOs), and non-governmental organizations (NGOs). The decentralization process divides the Rwandan administrative structure into two main levels: the central and local government. The organization of the education system follows this differentiation. At the top level, the government is responsible for organizing the educational system through policies and granting accreditations. The local government monitors the functioning of the educational system through specific regulations and resolutions (World Bank, 2011, p. 35). The education system is organized so that a principal heads each college and a dean heads schools, while campus managers or coordinators manage campuses.

The Tanzanian HE sector aims to provide society with advanced knowledge and skills through teaching, research, and consultancy. The HEIs have contributed highly trained personnel to all socio-economic and political sectors (Astin and Astin, 2000). Since independence, the HEM in Tanzania has undergone significant changes. Among the changes have been the establishment of the institution of Science and Technology Policy in 1985 (URT, 1996); the formation of the 1990 Kuhanga Committee; the establishment of the Ministry of Science, Technology and Higher Education in 1990; the inception of the Higher Education Accreditation Council in 1995; and the establishment of the National Council for Technical Education (NACTE) in 1997 (Mollel and Tshabangu, 2014). It is believed that implementing the Education and Training Policy in 1995 brought significant change in HEM.

Through its Education Supplementary Act No. 10 of 1995, the policy opened the door for private-sector participation in education provision (Ishengoma, 2007; Mollel and Tshabangu, 2014). The changes provided some autonomy and opportunity for participation by the respective communities in the management process of their education institutions. The Tanzania Commission for Universities website lists 11 public and 17 private universities, four public and 15 private university colleges, and another 14 centres or institutes it recognizes (Tanzania Commission for Universities, 2013). Public universities are owned and funded by the government. Private universities are privately owned and funded. The balance of tertiary institutions is under their respective ministries and the National Council for Technical Education (NACTE). The National Council for Technical Education governs non-university tertiary institutions that offer technical, semi-professional, and professional courses at certificate, diploma, and degree levels (NACTE, 2006). Institutions under NACTE are categorized into five fields of study: agriculture, natural resources and environment, business and management engineering and other sciences, health, and allied sciences, and planning and welfare.

In 2005, the HE sector proposed the Universities Act, which has provided autonomy to public universities. The Act was presented in the parliament to replace the previous legislation establishing public universities. For instance, the University of Dar es Salam (UDSM) Act No. 12 of 1970 emphasized exaggerated centralization and limited the university's powers to make important internal decisions (Mkude, Cooksey, and Levey, 2003). This was followed by the enactment of Universities Act No. 7 of 2005 in the National Assembly United Republic of Tanzania (URT), 2005.

The Universities Act established the Tanzania Commission for Universities (TCU), referred to as the Universities Act, Part II. TCU is responsible for student admission to universities in Tanzania academic programs and general regulations of the curriculum; the long-term planning, staff development, scholarship, and physical development strategies and programs of universities; recurrent and development budgets for public universities (URT-Universities Act Section 5, 1c).

In essence, TCU ensures university standards regarding curriculum, admissions, staff qualifications, and academic programs. However, their respective councils or governing boards handle the university and university colleges' management and functions (URT-Universities Act, Section 45, 1). The Act has procedures for appointing a university VC. In public universities, the VC is appointed by the chancellor, while in private universities, the VC is appointed by the owner/sponsor. In either of the appointments, the recommendations from the university council are considered (Section 36, 2a, b).

From the above overview, the management structures of HEIs in Africa are more or less similar, with little variation. Most HEIs follow the state model where the governments, through the Acts of Parliament, provide leadership frameworks, including appointing the chief executive officers (CEOs) of these institutions.

Women in Higher Education Management

Although studies on women's leadership show that women are more likely than men to offer transformational leadership which motivates innovation and growth, women are still under-represented in management and leadership roles in HEIs (Cahyati, Hariri and Karwan, 2021; Cheung, 2021). This raises significant concerns about gender parity and inclusion in key establishments, including HEIs, in many countries.

Coupled with this, data on gender is lacking in many parts of the world, making it difficult for stakeholders to appreciate or identify the varied dimensions of the disparities truly. However, it is a fact that the representation of women within the senior leadership of higher education needs to catch up everywhere in the world, with far fewer women than men holding leadership positions (Cheung, 2021).

Progress has, however, been made, so that 39 out of the top 200 HEIs in the world (19.5%) are currently led by women, a slight increase from the 34 universities (17%) led by women in 2019, and much more is still expected (Bothwell, 2020). Bothwell observes that the current statistics for HEI institutions in the top 200 selected individual countries are much more promising (the United States, Sweden, the Netherlands, and the United Kingdom). However, there is a drift when the data is further analyzed. It becomes clearer that women leaders in HEIs are disproportionately more likely to occupy leadership and management positions in smaller colleges or women's universities. This has been particularly observed in South Asian countries, such as India, Pakistan, Bangladesh, and Sri Lanka (Morley and Crossouard, 2015). The same trend is seen in other nations of the world like Japan, South Korea, and Hong Kong, where top national or public universities have not had women in leadership and management positions.

Numerous factors have been cited to impede the representation of women in management roles: Structural, institutional, and individual factors. Structural factors include the recruitment, hiring, and promotion processes that are often informed by images of successful managers in many patriarchal societies. Such successful leaders exhibit images like strength, aggressiveness, and competitiveness. According to the expectation state theory, structural factors refer to several characteristics often associated with men and women, which are taken into account by hiring managers (Berger, Wagner and Webster Jr, 2014). These include competence and authority, which are closely tied to higher status. The cultural and stereotypical beliefs associate these traits with men, resulting in gender imbalance in higher leadership and management positions within organizations.

Socio-cultural factors and gender socialization are also structural factors that have contributed to women's underrepresentation in HEM. Socialization moulds the notion of roles that different genders should take early on in childhood, which evolves with them in adulthood. The phenomenon is explained by Cornell well-known theory of hegemonic masculinity (1987), which postulates that society privileges one version of masculinity above others, guaranteeing men dominant position and subordinate women. Additionally, childbearing and domesticity relegating women to the position of nurturing and rearing children also affect the potential of women, often impeding their opportunity to progress in their careers.

Many institutions have complex organizational structures, processes, and practices about gender issues. The impact of institutional structural factors on the underrepresentation of women in management positions has been well documented. Mwashita, Zungu, and

Abrahams (2020) argue that gendered institutional structures have hampered women's entry into managerial positions. These structures often limit access to networking processes, lack of mentorship, limited training and development opportunities, and job evaluation.

Studies conducted in the African public sector report that women work twice as hard as men to be recognized and promoted to senior management roles (Mott, 2022). In South Africa, Mabokela (2003) observed that women worked harder than men in the institutions, earning them the title "donkeys" of the university. Additionally, because of their cautious nature, women have limited access to social capital and networks compared to men, which can promote their career advancement and leadership roles. Besides, hard work and calculated moves for career advancement are a function of intentional coaching and mentorship. Coaching and mentoring women in HEIs is a strategy for building their capacity while opening new pathways to career progression opportunities. The lack of female mentors and role models is one of the key impediments to women's advancement in HEIs (Doubell and Struwig, 2014).

There is much sacrifice that women must make as they advance leadership and management roles. For example, women who rise to management positions tend to spend a significant amount of time at work, which could have been spent with families (Abate and Woldie, 2022). In support of this view, Dodanwala and Shrestha (2021) indicated that the conflict between work and family remains the most common cause of the glass ceiling for women. Even when women have the skills and opportunities to advance their careers, reconciling the dual realities of career and family together with the traditional gender role remains challenging for women (Dodanwala and Shrestha, 2021). In this light, it can be concluded that academia and family are "greedy institutions" contributing to the plight of women in their career advancement.

Furthermore, women often suffer from the "motherhood penalty," which has been associated with limited opportunities for women to advance in academia and higher education management (Burkinshaw, 2015). The phenomenon of the motherhood penalty is founded on the assumption that women's family commitment can affect their work productivity (Lutter and Schröder, 2020). Motherhood penalty in the organizational context can manifest in many forms, which include discriminatory hiring practices, career inertia, and more stringent performance standards compared to non-mothers and men. In this sense, women have fewer opportunities to grow and excel in their careers.

Like structural and institutional factors, individual factors equally impede women's career advancement in leadership and management roles in HEIs. First and foremost, women have always been described as their own first and worst enemies. Women are obstacles to themselves in the form of internalized oppression, making them fear and not stand up to venture into leadership and management roles. Lack of required self-confidence or self-belief causes one to doubt oneself as well as one's capabilities, causing one to be comfortable with roles that are less challenging or demanding (Perera et al., 2021).

In traditional societies, some women might choose family over careers by opting for shorter work days and taking maternity leaves to care for their children. In a study done in Bhutan, it was found that the government's policy of six months of maternity leave, in a way, is an obstacle for women to ascend to leadership positions in educational institutions. Their opinions were that the Ministry of Education hereafter would not select women leaders through interviews, fearing long maternity leave, which would be deemed to impact their educational institutions (Dawa, 2022).

Gender equality strategies remain elusive regardless of the diversity and inclusion policies adopted in HEIs. There remains a gap between institutional policies that endorse gender equity and actual practices (Aiston and Fo, 2020). Unless HEIs mainstream gender equity in their institutional policies and practices, and without gender equity permeating the institutional cultures across all levels, the policies will remain on paper. Consequently, it may take over half a century before gender parity in HEIs is attained globally as women continue to build up their agency and readiness for leadership in higher education.

Despite the structural, institutional, and personal barriers in HEIs and the wider society, women will continue to seek opportunities for leadership and management. Successful women leaders must find ways to support other women individually through mentorship and leadership development. Therefore, the onus is on universities to be innovative as they mainstream gender in all policies and practices to achieve substantive outcomes in gender parity.

Methodology

For this study, a systematic literature review (SLR) design was used. This is because the SLR method is an explicit and reproducible technique for identifying, evaluating, and synthesizing existing bodies of literature and published work by researchers, practitioners, and scholars (Cahyati, Hariri and Karwan, 2021; Cheung, 2021). According to Okoli, (2015) SLR is appropriate because it is rigorous, systematic, explicit, and reproducible.

In addressing these research questions, the study followed the eight steps of SLR. The first step is identifying the purpose of the SLR. The purpose of this study was to determine the changes experienced in the higher education management landscape in Kenya, Rwanda, South Africa, and Tanzania in the last two decades. The second phase involves the development of a draft protocol outlining the procedures that the methodology should follow to ensure it is rigorous. The third phase involves the determination of the inclusion and exclusion criteria (Table 24.1). The fourth phase includes a literature search, while the fifth stage is data extraction. The sixth stage is a quality appraisal, the seventh is a synthesis of the studies, and the final stage is writing the review.

Table 24.1 Inclusion and exclusion criteria

Criteria	Inclusion	Exclusion	Justification
Criterion 1	All peer-reviewed primary studies	Grey literature, periodicals, news articles	To ensure the validity of findings for generalizability
Criterion 2	All peer-reviewed studies in English	Non-English studies	To English speaking, reviewers can understand the articles
Criterion 3	Studies on HEIs in Kenya, Rwanda, South Africa, and Tanzania	Studies on HEIs outside the geographical location	To ensure that the studies are within the contextual scope
Criterion 4	Studies conducted between 2003 and 2023	Studies earlier than 2003	To ensure that the articles are recent and within the time scope
Criterion 5	Studies on women managers in HEIs	Studies not focusing on women managers in HEIs	To ensure focus
Criterion 6	Empirical studies	Non-empirical studies	To ensure replicability

Source: Authors (2023).

Research Questions

The study had three research questions:

i What are the barriers for women aspiring to leadership roles in selected African countries' higher education institutions?
ii How do national and institutional policies in selected African countries support the inclusion of women in higher education management positions?
iii What are the consequences of the underrepresentation of women in HEM roles in selected African countries?

Literature Search

The researchers sought literature from six electronic databases: EBSCO Host, ERIC, Sage, JSTOR, and Web of Science (WoS). The databases were selected because of their multidisciplinary focus and high impact (Pranckutė, 2021). Some databases required subscriptions; hence, the researchers complemented the search with Google Scholar for broader coverage and open access (Araneda-Guirriman et al., 2023). The search was conducted in October 2023 by combining the following keywords: "underrepresentation," "women in higher education," "women and higher education management," "women in management," and "women in higher education governance."

Extraction and Selection of Data

For the current study (n=100), articles were identified from the six electronic databases. Out of this, (n=25) were removed as they were duplicates, while (n=5) were deleted as they were only abstracts. A total of (n=70) articles were screened, and (n=25) were excluded. Articles sought for retrieval were (n=45), out of which (n=30) could not be retrieved. Articles assessed for eligibility were (n=15), out of which (n=9) were excluded. Therefore, only (n=7) were eligible for review.

Results

Data from this study were subjected to descriptive and thematic content analysis in response to the three research questions. The following section provides the results from the data analysis (n=7) in descriptive and thematic analysis.

> What are the barriers for women aspiring to management roles in higher education institutions from selected African countries?

Several barriers have been found to impede women's ascension to leadership and management roles. In the field of HE, this research question sought to establish these barriers in selected African countries: Kenya, Rwanda, South Africa, Tanzania, and Uganda. In most African countries, the underrepresentation of women in leadership and decision-making roles in HE remains persistent despite efforts by governments and international organizations. Decades of effort through research, training, and networking have yielded little to reduce the numerous systematic barriers to women's leadership in HEIs at socio-cultural, institutional, and individual levels.

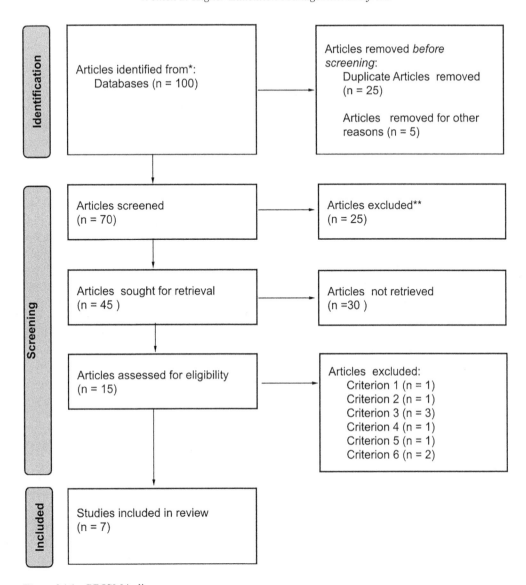

Figure 24.1 PRISMA diagram

Cultures are dynamic, and any group of people operates under common shared values and norms. These shared values and norms give people a sense of belonging and identity. In most African countries, socio-cultural factors and societal values continue to perpetuate oppression against women and discourage women from taking decision-making roles and leadership positions (Abate and Woldie, 2022).

In sub-Saharan Africa, the causes of women's underrepresentation in leadership and decision-making roles are entrenched in the patriarchal culture (Ilesanmi, 2021). The patriarchal system tends to relegate women to subordinate roles, often barring them from ascending to leadership and decision-making roles. The customary law and patriarchal culture often result in the "gendered division of labour," where men are expected to lead and occupy decision-making roles in their homes, community, and national life. In contrast, women are expected to assume subordinate roles (Osituyo, 2018). Studies report that socio-cultural factors significantly limit the number of women actively managing HEIs in Africa (Akala, 2021; Odhiambo, 2011; Onsongo, 2004).

Women are known to be naturally endowed with the ability to multitask. While this is positive, having a work-family imbalance is a factor that impedes the representation of women in the HEM. Studies indicate that women avoid management roles in educational institutions due to their attachment to their families (Chabaya, Rembe, and Wadesango, 2009).

Further, scholars indicate that women who rise to management positions tend to spend a significant amount of time at work, which could have been spent with families (Abate and Woldie, 2022). In support of this view, Dodanwala and Shrestha (2021) indicated that the conflict between work and family remains the most common cause of the glass ceiling for women. Even when women have the skills and opportunities to advance their careers, reconciling the dual realities of career and family together with the traditional gender role remains challenging to them (Dodanwala and Shrestha, 2021). In this light, it can be concluded that academia and family are "greedy institutions" to the plight of women.

Institutional factors equally create barriers to women's entry into management roles in HEI (Mwashita, Zungu, and Abrahams, 2020). These structures often limit access to networking processes, lack mentorship, and have limited training and development opportunities and job evaluation. Moreover, women work twice as hard as men to be recognized and promoted to senior management. This has been observed and confirmed among women in HEIs in South Africa who have been referred to as "donkeys" of the university (Mabokela, 2003). Additionally, because of their cautious nature, women have limited access to social capital and networks compared to men, which can promote their career advancement and leadership roles.

The other issue is limited opportunities for coaching and mentoring. Mwashita et al. (2020) observe that coaching and mentoring aim to develop human capacity, being that in mentorship, a non-judgmental partnership is nurtured based on trust. Therefore, women mentees can experience support and guidance as they grow in their profession. Limited opportunities for these services impede the career advancement of women in HEM.

Human beings have individual and personality differences as a function of their environment and genetic makeup. This can be seen in how women differ in areas such as decision-making, problem-solving, self-efficacy, social awareness, and relationship management, among others. Such individual factors can be causes of the underrepresentation of women in the HEM setting (Mabokela, 2003). Kiaye and Singh (2013) observe that psychological factors such as lack of self-confidence and women's self-limiting behaviour (imposter syndrome) are barriers to women's advancement in HEM. Moreover, studies have also pointed out that women's lack of confidence or self-esteem is a consequence of the imposition of male dominance culture and the socialization belief that male leadership styles are the norm (Mathur-Helm, 2016). The Venn diagram (Figure 24.1) illustrates how social, organizational, and individual factors interact to contribute to the underrepresentation of women in HEM.

How do national and institutional policies in selected African countries support the inclusion of women in higher education management positions?

Figure 24.2 Factors that cause women's under-representation in HEM. Source: Victoria Galán-Muros, Mathias Bouckaert, and Jaime Roser (2023)

Policies are governance tools important in shaping societies as they help regulate people's lives (Otieno-Omutoko and Mwaura, 2014). Countries have several policies that guide service delivery: education, gender, health, employment, marriage, and family relations, among others. Gender policies are statements of institutions on intentions of actions aimed at promoting gender equality by advancing the lives of women, men, boys, and girls in different areas of life, including leadership and education. With effective gender policies, decisions, actions, and projects are designed to influence and determine outcomes. Gender policies must be people-centred and responsive to the target group's needs.

Gender policies in many African countries were not a priority until 2015 when the United Nations (UN) member states adopted the Sustainable Development Goals (SDGs). This marked a notable shift towards prioritizing gender equality, as underscored by the provisions of SDG 5. SDG 5 seeks to empower women and girls by eliminating discrimination against them, such as violence, harmful practices, unrecognized domestic labour, unequal pay, and unequal representation in decision-making and leadership. The provisions of SDG 5 became instrumental in guiding gender policies within the UN member states in Africa. In Kenya, for example, gender equality is enshrined in various national legal and policy documents (Ministry of Education, MO–E, 2007). The 2010 Constitution of Kenya outlaws discrimination based on gender and emphasizes social justice and equal opportunities in education, including gender inclusion and empowerment.

In Rwanda, policy documents show the country's commitment to gender parity. These policy documents include the Girls Education Policy (2008), the National Education Policy (2010), and the University of Rwanda Gender Policy (2016). Besides, the National Gender Policy ensures gender parity as a "mainstream" philosophy in all budgets, policies, and programs. These policies are meant to improve the representation of Rwandese women in HE by mainly focusing on their leadership and management. Similarly, Uganda's National Gender Policy aims to transform Ugandan society into gender-informed citizens (Gender in Education Sector Policy, 2016). Its structure aims to guide all other sectors and levels by conceptualizing gender as important for implementing the country's development programs (Hailu et al., 2023).

Governments and states can influence the representation of women in various leadership positions, especially in higher education management (Abate and Woldie, 2022). Through legislation, governments can guarantee gender equality not only in women's political participation but also in the case of public service organizations. Studies report that the introduction of specific instruments, such as gender quotas in national legislation and constitutions, is imperative in enhancing women's career advancement and promoting their representation of women in top leadership positions (Mwashita, Zungu, and Abrahams, 2020). In Kenya, the commitment to increased gender equality has been enshrined in various legal documents, including the 2010 constitution of Kenya. The government of Kenya established the initial National Policy for Gender and Development in 2000, which included the commitment to building gender-related policies in different sectors. Over the years, the policy has been revised and reviewed with an update of 2019. In 2007, the Ministry of Education, Science, and Technology established the "Gender in Education Policy," which was later revised in 2015. Promoting gender equality has also been enshrined in the National Education Sector Strategic Development Plan for 2018–2022, including sections on enhancing equity and inclusion in higher education. The government has also demanded that all higher learning institutions develop gender equity policies in their employment practices.

Further, the Kenyan government has also rolled out affirmative action policies that encourage the enrolment of women students in HE. Another notable intervention was the establishment of many private universities and women-only institutions, such as Kiriri Women's University of Science and Technology, established in 2003 (Odhiambo, 2011). The university was deemed important in providing much-needed access for women in higher education. Nonetheless, in many African countries, gender policies seem to be ineffective. For instance, Nyoni, He, and Yusuph (2017), when studying the participants in higher education senior leadership in Tanzania, reported that women are still underrepresented, specifically in positions traditionally male. The pattern of male prevalence in senior leadership positions in higher education is visible in countries with diverse policies and legislation for gender equality as far as Tanzania is concerned.

What are the consequences of the underrepresentation of women in HEM roles in selected African countries?

The persistence and pervasiveness of the underrepresentation of women in HEM have significant consequences on the realization of gender equality. These consequences seriously impact individual, societal, institutional, and national efforts aimed at achieving gender equality.

At an individual level, the lack of gender equality impedes access to equal opportunities for women in HEM. Traditional and stereotypical gender roles that perpetuate masculinity and femininity may restrict young people's choices and prospects. Stereotypical classifications of professions and subjects have strong implications for females. They impair learning and prevent females from fulfilling their full potential. Stereotypes lower one's self-assessment and sense of competence, that is, a person's self-concept, and impact career choices (Otieno-Omutoko and Mwaura, 2014).

Additionally, women's underrepresentation results in a waste of valuable human resources. Training women to higher levels where they qualify for leadership roles and failing to utilize them in these positions can have overall negative impacts. The women fail to reach their academic potential, and the nation also loses economic returns on investment. Underrepresentation of women in HEI courses like science, technology, engineering, and mathematics (STEM) can affect the pool of professionals and leaders in those areas in the job market. Consequently, this may maintain, if not worsen, the gender gap.

The underrepresentation of women in HEM perpetuates the gender pay gap, as most women hold middle and lower positions in HEIs. This, in turn, results in lower purchasing power, making women unable to finance their education. Lower levels of education imply low representation of women in the job market. As a result of low levels of education, women are less likely to compete for positions with men and more likely to earn less, hence increasing income inequality. This cycle is, therefore, perpetuated.

Fewer women in HEM may need more role models to encourage them to aspire for leadership positions in HEIs. This is because female role models in patriarchal societies inspire women and challenge gender discrimination in their communities. Women with access to relatable role models are more likely to prosper academically than those without access (Kaziboni and Uys, 2015).

Conclusion

The underrepresentation of women in leadership remains a concern, particularly in realizing sustainable development goals and attaining gender equality. Globally, women are underrepresented in management and leadership roles in virtually all sectors. The existing body of research attributes this trend to numerous structural, institutional, and individual factors that serve as bottlenecks for women's progress and advancement. In Africa, the underrepresentation of women in leadership and management roles remains a hot political and legal issue, with nations such as Kenya and Rwanda coming up with affirmative action policies pushing for the third gender rule in public institutions. The underrepresentation of women in national leadership roles and positions is mirrored in other national institutions, particularly HEIs. This can be attributed to the "glass ceiling" caused by socio-cultural, institutional, and individual barriers. Socio-cultural factors prescribe subordinate roles to women and emphasize their domesticity. Institutional barriers include discriminatory human resource practices that limit women's ascension to leadership roles, lack of mentors, limited social capital, and factors like the "motherhood penalty." From an individual perspective, the underrepresentation of women stems from a lack of self-belief and imposter syndrome that impede women from pursuing their ambitions.

Nonetheless, across the continent, nations have developed different affirmative action policies targeting women and children. In Rwanda, policies such as the Girls Education Policy

(2008) and the University of Rwanda Gender Policy (2016) have been implemented to help improve the enrolment and representation of women in HEM. In Uganda, the government has rolled out the National Gender Policy that targets the representation of women at various levels of society. Within the Kenyan context, gender equality policy is enshrined in various national legal and policy documents, including the Constitution of Kenya 2010. Despite these progressive policies in gender equality, women still remain underrepresented in higher education management positions in these nations, calling for the need for the policies to be reviewed further. Having fewer women in the management and decision-making roles in HEIs has serious consequences, as the views of women might need to be adequately addressed in the boards that make key decisions in these institutions. This can have spillover impacts on the enrolment of women in HE while also perpetuating stereotypes about leadership.

Bibliography

Abate, G.B. and Woldie, A.T. (2022) 'Breaking Barriers to Women's Advancement in the Public Sector in Sub-Saharan Africa'. Available at https://cbie.ca/wp-content/uploads/2022/04/ALT-Research-Report-Begashaw-EN-FINAL.pdf

Aiston, S., & Fo, C. (2020). The silence/ing of academic women. *Gender and Education*, 33, 1–18. https://doi.org/10.1080/09540253.2020.1716955

Akala, B.M. (2021) 'Revisiting education reform in Kenya: A case of Competency Based Curriculum (CBC)', *Social Sciences & Humanities Open*, 3(1), p. 100107.

Araneda-Guirriman, C. et al. (2023) 'Women in academia: an analysis through a scoping review', *Frontiers in Education*, p. 1137866.

Astin, A.W. and Astin, H.S. (2000) 'Leadership reconsidered: Engaging higher education in social change.' *Higher Education* 133.

Berger, J., Wagner, D.G. and Webster Jr, M. (2014) 'Expectation states theory: Growth, opportunities and challenges', *Advances in Group Processes*, 31, pp. 19–55.

Bothwell, Ellie. 2020. Female Leadership in Top Universities Advances for First Time Since 2017. Times Higher Education. https://www.timeshighereducation.com/news/female-leadership-topuniversitiesadvances-first-time-2017

Burkinshaw, P. (2015) *Higher education, leadership and women vice chancellors: fitting in to communities of practice of masculinities*. Springer.

Cahyati, D., Hariri, H. and Karwan, D.H. (2021) 'Women's Leadership in Higher Education: Barriers and Opportunities in Indonesia', *International Journal of Education Policy and Leadership*, 17(9), p. n9.

Chabaya, O., Rembe, S. and Wadesango, N. (2009) 'The persistence of gender inequality in Zimbabwe: factors that impede the advancement of women into leadership positions in primary schools', *South African Journal of Education*, 29(2), pp. 235–251. Available at: https://doi.org/10.10520/EJC32196.

Cheung, F.M. (2021) 'The "state" of women's leadership in higher education', *International Briefs for Higher Education Leaders*, 9, pp. 5–8.

Coleman, J. and Court, D. (1993). *University development in the Third World: The Rockefeller Foundation experience*. Oxford: Pergamon Press.

Dawa, T. (2022). Major Factors Affecting Women's Participation in Educational Leadership: A Case of Bhutan. *Acta Scientific Paediatrics* https://www.academia.edu/92738270/Major_Factors_Affecting_Women_s_Participation_in_Educational_Leadership_A_Case_of_Bhutan

De La Rey, C. (2015) 'Governance and Management in Higher Education', *Higher Education Transformation Summit* [Preprint].

Dobbins, M., Knill, C. and Vögtle, E.M. (2011) 'An analytical framework for the cross-country comparison of higher education governance', *Higher Education*, 62, pp. 665–683.

Dobbins, M. and Leišyte, L. (2014) 'Analysing the transformation of higher education governance in Bulgaria and Lithuania', *Public Management Review*, 16(7), pp. 987–1010.

Dodanwala, T.C. and Shrestha, P. (2021) 'Work–family conflict and job satisfaction among construction professionals: the mediating role of emotional exhaustion', *On the Horizon: The International Journal of Learning Futures*, 29(2), pp. 62–75. Available at: https://doi.org/10.1108/OTH-11-2020-0042.

Doubell, M. and Struwig, M. (2014) 'Perceptions of factors influencing career success of professional and business women in South Africa', *South African Journal of Economic and Management Sciences*, 17(5), pp. 531–543.

Enid Kiaye, R. and Maniraj Singh, A. (2013) 'The glass ceiling: a perspective of women working in Durban', *Gender in Management: An International journal*, 28(1), pp. 28–42.

Galán-Muros, V., Bouckaert, M., and Roser-Chinchilla, J. (2023). The representation of women in academia and higher education management positions: policy brief.

Hailu, M.F. et al. (2023) 'Gender and higher education in African universities: A critical discourse analysis of key policy mandates in Kenya, Rwanda, and Uganda', *Education Policy Analysis Archives*, 31.

Ilesanmi, O.A. (2021) 'Women in/and the Security Sector in Africa', *The Palgrave Handbook of African Women's Studies*, pp. 413–428.

Ishengoma J. M., et al. (2007). *The Debate on Quality and Private Surge: A Status Review of Private Universities and Colleges in Tanzania Boston College & Council for the Development of Social Science Research in Africa* 5, 85–109. https://www.worldbank.org/en/programs/paset/brief/higher-education

Kaziboni, A. and Uys, T. (2015) 'The selection of academic role models by first year University students', *Journal of Sociology and Social Anthropology*, 6(1), pp. 77–86.

Kidd, C.V. (1991) 'University training abroad: Sub-Saharan Africa', *Higher Education Policy*, 4, pp. 41–46.

Lutter, M. and Schröder, M. (2020) 'Is There a Motherhood Penalty in Academia? The Gendered Effect of Children on Academic Publications in German Sociology', *European Sociological Review*, 36(3), pp. 442–459. Available at: https://doi.org/10.1093/esr/jcz063.

Lwanga, D., Mbabazize, M., Katuramu, O., & Barigayomwe, R. (2020). The Management Of Higher Education Institutions In Uganda A Perspective from Thomas Berkeley's Analytical Framework for Management. *International Journal of Scientific and Research Publications*, 10(3), 487–493.

Mabokela, R. (2003) '"Donkeys of the University": Organizational culture and its impact on South African women administrators', *Higher Education*, 46, pp. 129–145. Available at: https://doi.org/10.1023/A:1024754819125.

Maggio, Z. (2011) 'Exploring Burton Clark's triangle of coordination in the context of contemporary relationships between states and higher education systems', *Unpublished manuscript. New York, NY: Department of Administration, Leadership, and Technology, New York University* [Preprint].

Mathur-Helm, B. (2016) 'Women in management in South Africa', in *Women in management worldwide*. Gower, pp. 359–373.

Mkude, D., Cooksey, B., & Levey, L. (2003). *Higher education in Tanzania: A case study*. Cambridge University Press

Mollel, N., & Tshabangu, I. (2014). Women in educational leadership: Conceptualizing gendered perceptions in Tanzanian schools. *Educational Research International*, 3(4), 46–54.

Morley, L. and Crossouard, B. (2015) 'Women in higher education leadership in South Asia: Rejection, refusal, reluctance, revisioning', *British Council report* [Preprint].

Mott, H. (2022) *Gender equality in higher education: Maximising impacts*, British Council: London.

Mwashita, T., Zungu, N. and Abrahams, D. (2020) 'The glass ceiling: Career progression barriers for female employees in the South African hospitality industry', *African Journal of Hospitality, Tourism and Leisure*, 9(5), pp. 1077–1093.

Nyoni, W.P., He, C. and Yusuph, M.L. (2017) 'Sustainable Interventions in Enhancing Gender Parity in Senior Leadership Positions in Higher Education in Tanzania.', *Journal of Education and Practice*, 8(13), pp. 44–54.

Odhiambo, G. (2011) 'Women and higher education leadership in Kenya: A critical analysis', *Journal of Higher Education Policy and Management*, 33(6), pp. 667–678.

Okoli, C. (2015). A guide to conducting a standalone systematic literature review. *Communications of the Association for Information Systems*, 37.

Olum, Y. (2004). Strategic management in institutions of higher learning: The case of Makerere University. *Makerere Journal of Higher Education*, 1, 13–24.

Onsongo, J. (2004) 'Factors affecting women's participation in university management in Kenya'. OSSREA Gender Issues Research Report Series - no. 22. Available at http://ossrea.net/publications/images/stories/ossrea/girr-22.pdf

Osituyo, D. (2018) 'Underrepresentation and career advancement of women in the South African public-sector setting', *International Journal of Women's Studies*, 19(3), pp. 171–186.

Otieno-Omutoko, L. and Mwaura, P. (2014) 'Gender policy as a management strategy in education', in F. M. Nafukho, H. M. A. Muyia and B. Irby, ed., *Governance and Transformations of Universities in Africa: A Global Perspective*, pp. 169–181.

Perera, I. S., Ganeshan, J., & Belitski, M. (2021). *Underrepresentation of women managers in the boardroom: Evidence from the Sri Lankan financial sector*. 12 (2), 23–52. http://doi.org/10.4038/cbj.v12i2.79

Pranckutė, R. (2021) 'Web of Science (WoS) and Scopus: The titans of bibliographic information in today's academic world', *Publications*, 9(1), 12; https://doi.org/10.3390/publications9010012

Sifuna, D.N. (1998) 'The governance of Kenyan public universities', *Research in Post-Compulsory Education*, 3(2), pp. 175–212.

Sporn, B. (2003) 'Management in higher education: Current trends and future perspectives in European colleges and universities', in R. Begg, ed., *The dialogue between higher education research and practice*. Springer, pp. 97–107.

Statita (2023) *Africa: number of universities by country 2021, Statista*. Available at: https://www.statista.com/statistics/1242428/number-of-universities-in-africa/ (Accessed: 31 August 2023).

Sutton, F. (1971). 'African universities and the process of change in Middle Africa', in Kertesz, S. D. ed., *The task of universities in a changing world*, University of Notre Dame Press, pp. 383–404.

Universities and Other Tertiary Institutions Act (UOTIA), 2001

Varghese, N.V. (2013) 'Governance reforms in higher education: A study of selected countries in Africa', in *Policy Forum on governance reforms in higher education in Africa, Nairobi Kenya*. Paris: UNESCO.

Woldegiorgis, E.T. and Doevenspeck, M. (2013) 'The Changing Role of Higher Education in Africa: "A Historical Reflection"', *Higher Education Studies*, 3(6), pp. 35–45.

World Bank (2011). Rwanda education country status report – Toward quality enhancement and achievement of universal nine basic education; AN education system in transition; a nation in transition. Washington D.C.: The International Bank for Reconstruction and Development/The World Bank

Appendix 1

Table 24.2 A list of some female Vice-Chancellors in Africa (past and present)

Sn	Name	Country/Institution	Year of Appointment/ Terms served	Discipline
1	Nana Aba Appiah Amfo	University of Ghana - Ghana	October 2021	Linguistics
2	Prof. Olive Mugenda	Kenyatta University, Kenya	2006-2016	Family studies and Business Administration
3	Prof Joyce Jepkirui Agalo	Machakos University - Kenya	August 2023	Education Communication and Technology
4	Prof. Emily Achieng' Akuno	Jaramogi Oginga University of Science and Technology, (JOOUST) Kenya	August 2023	Music
5	Prof. Teresa Akenga	University of Eldoret, Kenya	June 2013/2 terms	Science (Chemistry and Mathematics)
6	Prof. Theresauo-Akenji Nk	University of Bamenda, Cameroon		Science (Medical Technology; parasitology and Immunology)

(*Continued*)

Table 24.2 (Continued)

Sn	Name	Country/Institution	Year of Appointment/ Terms served	Discipline
7	Prof. Imbuga Mabel	Jomo Kenyatta University, Kenya	August 2008-2018	Biochemistry
8	Prof. Malata Address	Malawi University of Science and Technology	August 2016	Nursing and Midwifery
9	Prof. Ibtisam Eltayeb Eljack Ahamed	Gadarif University of Science and Technology.		Economics and Administrative Science,
10	Prof. Lillian Salami	University of Benin, Nigeria	2019	Human Nutrition
11	Prof Grace Alele-Williams	University of Benin, Nigeria	1985	Mathematics
12	Prof Florence Obi	University of Calabar, Nigeria	2020	Psychology of Education
13	Naana Jane Opuku-Agyemang	University of Cape Coast	2008 -2012	Special Needs Education

Source: Authors (2023)

Appendix 2

Table 24.3 List of the first managers (Vice Chancellors) of HEIs in Africa

Sn	Institution	Name	Gender	Year of Appointment	Discipline
1	Addis Ababa University	Dr Lucien Matte, S.J.	M	1952	Education
2	Egerton University	Prof. Richard S. Musangi	M	1981	Agriculture
3	Makerere University	Frank Kalimuzo	M	1970	Bachelor of Arts
4	University of Nairobi	Josephat Njuguna Karanja	M	1970	History
5	University of Rwanda	James McWha	M	2013	Teaching, research, and educational administration
6	University of Ghana	Dr. Kwame Nkrumah	M	1948	
7	University of Ibadan	Kenneth Dike	M		History
8	University of Zimbabwe	William Rollo	M	1955	African Linguistics

Source: Authors (2023)

25
AN UNBALANCED EQUATION
Exploring Gender Disparity among Academics in Southeast Universities, Nigeria

Abel T. Ugwu and Ngozika Anthonia Obi-Ani

Introduction

Igboland operates within a patriarchal framework, where male preference is emphasized, particularly evident at the micro level within families (Ugwu Comfort, personal communication 2021). Notably, men wield substantial socio-political authority, affording them exceptional and unrestrained privileges rooted in their masculinity. Consequently, they manipulate, reshape, and reinterpret cultural values, often invoking spirits, deities, or ancestral associations to align with their perspectives (Okorie et al 2020). The process of socialization bestows Nigerian men with influence and dominance across all domains, granting them ultimate decision-making power in familial and communal affairs. This autonomy is substantially shaped by the 'culture,' which underscores male supremacy (Okonkwo & Ezumah 2017: 1–2). In Igboland, one's standing is predominantly established by possessions and wealth, frequently passed down through inheritance. As Korieh (2013: 363) points out, 'Igbo inheritance norms predominantly favor males and are translated into cultural norms and meanings.' Consequently, restricted access to productive resources and biased inheritance practices favoring men contribute to women's precarious economic position. Additionally, Olumukoro (2011:1–2) underscores how illiteracy perpetuates the economic and social vulnerability of women. Education, in the form of literacy, stands as a critical determinant of societal advancement. It cultivates in individuals a disposition for continual knowledge acquisition, value integration, and competence. Despite education being a fundamental human entitlement in the nation, women in Igboland have encountered numerous obstacles in accessing equitable education.

However, the turning point for female education in Igboland was intricately tied to the events of the Nigeria-Biafra War from 1967 to 1970, serving as the catalyst for transformative changes in the realm of female education. The colonial era, serving as a structured tool of social marginalization and oppression, led to unequal educational opportunities, favoring men (Uchem 2001:47). This control of education introduced Western gender discrimination, dislodging women from political and socio-economic positions held prior to colonial rule in Igboland. This colonial manipulation persisted post-colonialism. Before the Nigeria-Biafra War (1967–1970), education was predominantly male-oriented (Okoro 2018:65). However, post-war shifts prompted men to shift toward quick-return businesses and skills, altering the educational landscape (Onumonu & Anutanwa 2017:155–159). The aftermath of the war inadvertently granted every child, regardless of gender, a chance at prosperity, dismantling patriarchal norms (Ugwu Celestina, personal communication 2021). Amid these changes, women found increased freedom, challenging traditional educational norms. Nevertheless, despite women's progress in various public domains, they remain underrepresented in academia, with men dominating research and publications. Female academic leaders are scarce, reflecting skewed gender ratios (Ogbogu 2006:1–3). Women hold less than 35 percent of academic posts in Nigerian universities, mainly in lower and mid-tier positions (Ogbogu 2006:3–4). Such gender disparities reveal entrenched institutional biases hindering women's academic advancement (Poole 2005:1–3). While economic challenges discouraged post-war male education, advancements in female education coincided with evolving perceptions of women's roles in Igbo society. However, this transformation hasn't translated into balanced gender relations, especially in academia, where gender bias and skewed research outputs persist. Although scholars have explored factors hindering women's academic productivity, a historical context has been largely overlooked, limiting comprehension of changing female education in Igboland and Nigeria. This study addresses the gap by closely examining gender dynamics in Southeastern Nigerian universities, offering a historical perspective on the issues shaping female academic experiences. The intention is to enrich scholarly understanding of this subject.

This qualitative study, through in-depth interviews, identified 22 key informants made of 5 males and 17 females interviewed between January and July 2021. Focusing on post-civil war educational changes in Igboland, the study uses selected universities—University of Nigeria and Enugu State University Teaching Hospital—as case studies. This study is centered on relative deprivation theory, which explains that a person is likely to feel usually deprived of some desirable thing relative to his/her past, another person or persons, group, ideal, or some other social category (Walker & Pettigrew 1984:302). Thus, the evaluation of social relations and identities by comparison often leads to unfavorable outcomes. Nevertheless, if the evaluation proves to be positive, the individual feels at ease with the realization of self-identity and belonging. However, if the comparative evaluation proves otherwise, the individual experiences relative deprivation. The present gender relation among academics in Southeastern Nigeria universities, when compared, is unequal, with the female academics feeling deprived, most especially when they compare themselves with their male counterparts vis-à-vis research output and general participation in university politics. This pitches them at a crossroad as it creates very challenging situations for their growth in academia and political participation in the university. This has birthed, among female academics, a sense of marginalization and a somewhat new version of 'Igbo feminism,' which they believe will bring them favorably at par or even above their male counterparts in a society that sacrifices the right to equal treatment in the altar of patriarchal tradition.

Literature Review

The study aims to examine gender relations among academics in Southeastern Nigeria universities. To do that, literature studies on patriarchy, religion, education, and gender studies associated with the subject matter are reviewed to fill an important gap in scholarship. Scholars such as Basden (1921), Eze and Okonkwo (2009), Korieh (2013), and Osaji-Nwafili (2021) all agree on the patriarchal nature of Igbo society. Korieh particularly maintains that gender is the basic principle structuring inheritance in Igbo society, with men having ultimate rights (Korieh 2010).

During the first half of the 20th century in Igboland, education was largely the exclusive preserve of the male folks (Okoro 2018). There was a general preference for male children's education over female because parents saw the training of the girl-child as a waste of resources as her fortune lies with her husband's household. Thus, Goodluck (2007) observed that male preference in education tended to result in higher dropout rates for girls either for early marriage or participation in trading or other activities in the informal sector. The coming of the Christian religion did not help matters on the issue of women's subordination, as Uchem argued (2002). For her, the roots of women's subjugation are tied up with human psychology, culture, and religion, buttressed by oppressive uses of the Bible (Uchem 2001). For many centuries, Christians believed that women's assigned secondary status in relation to men was ordained by God and supported by the Bible.

However, the general preference for male children's education was affected by the Nigeria-Biafra War (1967–1970). The war left Igboland desolate, resulting in the need for the men to go into trading businesses that yielded quicker economic returns, thereby giving women the chance to enroll in classes. Since then, enrolment in schools has tilted in favor of the females (Obi-Ani 2017). Paul Obi-Ani (2009) dissected how the war disorganized the educational system in Igboland. Nevertheless, when the war came to a halt in early 1970, Obi-Ani notes that rapid reconstruction measures were put in place with assistance from both local and international goodwill organizations like Rangers Football Club Enugu, UNICEF, and UNESCO, among others. Unfortunately, Obi-Ani's work does not reflect the ensuing notable social changes which included a somewhat rise in female enrolment in education. However, in recent years, there has been a growing awareness of gender equality and equity in the world. (Olufunke 2001). Oke (2001) vividly discusses the exciting trend in the growth of gender awareness and the attention toward gender issues in national and international agenda.

Despite the foregoing, Ogbogu (2011) identifies some of the persisting socio-cultural challenges facing female academic staff of higher institutions in Igboland. Morley (1999) and Ogbogu (2011) argue that female academics carry a dual burden involving academic work and family obligations without help from their male partners. Similarly, Akinjobi (2013) postulates that female academics in Nigeria have a lot of challenges: managing work, love, family, recreation, and so on. This constitutes a lot of stress for them in trying to balance what is traditionally regarded as their gender role and sustaining a career.

For a meaningful progress to be made in the total emancipation of women in academia, there is a need to know how an understanding of gender should shape our approach to the production of knowledge (Dunn 2020). Obonodo (2008) advises that the fact that women occupy a central position in the home and society calls for their full integration into national and international affairs. Similarly, Marika Sherwood (1988) argues that women in politics serve as vehicles for female struggle against their neglect by the men. Similar neglect in the academia prompted M.N. Ezeh and U.U. Okonkwo (2009) to lament how women's scholarship is comparatively underexplored. For Ibrahim and Salihu (2004), viral trainings of women empower them to compete better while adjusting their roles in the society. Similarly, Glover (2021) offers a theoretical understanding of the oppression of women in the society with the dual reading of Marx's gender and class. For the much-desired gender parity in the academia to be attained, there must be an all-round reorientation, including the field of gender studies (McShane 2020).

Methodology, Scope, and Sources of Data Collection

The study adopted mainly the qualitative method of historical research by documenting a descriptive analysis. Both the primary and secondary sources are used for fact-finding and interpretation of results. Through in-depth interviews of 22 persons (male = 5 and female = 17), samples were taken from both female and male academics from the rank of graduate assistant to rofessorial cadre. This gives the research a more balanced and unbiased gender perspective. The scope of the study is restricted to selected universities like the University of Nigeria and Enugu State University of Science and Technology to enable the authors to focus on details of the subject matter. The identities of the study participants have been anonymized.

Overcoming Obstacles: The Journey of Women's Education in Igboland

Colonial schools in Igboland emerged to serve the interests of European missionaries, merchants, and colonizers (Asogwa, personal communication 2021). They taught Christian doctrines, reading, writing, and math, while girls were instructed in domestic skills like sewing, knitting, and embroidery (Gabriel 2000). For instance, the Women's Training Centre in Obowo, established in June 1950, provided daily classes teaching women to create simple embroidered mats, tray cloths, and linen works (Korieh 2010). Corroborating this, Goodluck (2007) noted that male favoritism in education led to higher dropout rates for girls due to early marriage or informal sector involvement. Even if girls pursued education, they often oriented themselves toward domestic-compatible careers guided by parents or relatives (C. Maria, personal communication: 2021). Schools' expansion introduced gender distinctions in Igbo society through salaried employment and leadership access. This gender-based differentiation, stemming from the greater number of educated boys, linked lack of education to diminished prestige (Gabriel: 72). This outlook to some extent characterized post-colonial gender dynamics in Igboland.

The conclusion of the Nigeria–Nigeria War in 1970 marked a turning point in the prioritization and pursuit of Western education in Igboland. Historically, education predominantly favored males during the first half of the 20th century (Okoro 2018:65). This gendered norm shifted post-war, wherein the conflict led to the loss and conscription of Igbo men, leaving women to shoulder the responsibilities as breadwinners, enduring hardships for their families (Obi-Ani 2017:186). The war's aftermath shattered Igboland, compelling many, now-orphaned males, to confront dire economic challenges. Unable to return to school, they turned to business and vocational skills, seeking quick economic relief after the devastating effects of the war (Onumonu & Anutanwa 2017:155–156). This swift transition represented a seismic change, with education's trajectory recalibrating as men shifted from academics to economic pursuits.

Men were not the solitary combatants in the struggle for survival. Post-war, a fresh perception of freedom emerged: the imperative to empower every child, regardless of gender. The war obliterated concentrated investment in male children due to conscription, execution, and wartime biases (Obi-Ani 2017:186). Faced with these harsh realities, women valiantly supported their families, utilizing the post-war landscape (Obi-Ani 2017:186). This shift in gender roles was transformative; women embraced the newfound agency to provide for their families. This empowerment emboldened them to enroll their daughters in school, often without their husbands' consent. Some women even pursued adult education, seeking enlightenment and white-collar opportunities. The expanding freedom among women fostered a marked change in their traditional educational status, resulting in increased female enrollment at all levels of education.

Certainly, the post-civil war economic struggles seemingly favored females, leading to a shift in educational enrollment dynamics that now lean in their favor. Today, maintaining a balance in male–female school enrollment is a challenge for state governments in Igboland (Cress & Hart 2009:475). However, this trend has given rise to a social situation where many women professionals marry men who have attained financial success despite limited education (Obi-Ani 2017). This poses a challenge as it's often men who comprehend the value of research that encourage their wives, particularly those in academia, to pursue their professions. Female academics grapple with myriad challenges. Balancing work, familial obligations, personal life, workplace biases, and societal expectations within a patriarchal structure is intricate. These factors invariably impact their academic responsibilities (Ogbogu 2009:8) and professional advancement. The need to juggle these diverse demands creates a complex backdrop for female academics, influencing their growth and success.

Over time, the Millennium Development Goals (MDGs) placed a spotlight on gender equality by promoting women's education enrollment. Nigeria aligned its policies with the MDGs, particularly the 'education for all' target, recognizing the necessity to bridge educational disparities (Okoroafor & Anuforo 2012:67). Despite the MDGs' contributions and the inadvertent impact of the Nigeria-Biafra war favoring women's education, disparities endure among 21st-century academics in Southeastern Nigerian universities. As the MDGs era concluded in 2015, the global community reached a crossroads. This juncture offered an opportunity to build upon MDGs' successes and momentum, while also embracing fresh ideas for the future. The new agenda prioritized transforming the world to meet human needs while safeguarding gender equality, a core MDG focus. Thus, the post-2015 (Sustainable Development Goals, SDGs) period demands renewed efforts targeting specific child groups, including girls from minority, nomadic, and labor-affected backgrounds, along with those facing gender-based discrimination. Coupled with institutional and cultural practices seen in 21st-century Igboland, these factors have left female academics facing a pivotal moment. This context necessitates an exploration of challenges among female academics in higher education in Southeastern Nigeria, a focal point of this study. Amidst evolving global agendas and local dynamics, addressing gender-based disparities remains paramount.

The educational advancements of women in Igboland, spurred by the Nigeria-Biafra crisis, have yet to manifest as the much-needed gender equality within academic circles. While women now have the freedom to pursue education, their integration into teaching and administrative roles has been marked by complexity (Ogbonnaya, personal communication: 2021). For instance, data from the Academic Planning Unit at the University of Nigeria, Nsukka (2023), reveals a historical disparity. In the 1976/77 academic session, male academics numbered 851, contrasting with 200 female academics. In the 2015/16 academic session, female academics grew to 813, compared to 1,485 males. The pattern remained similar in the 2020/21 session, with 1,827 men and 1,201 women. Ugwu Celestina (personal communication: 2021b) opines that although progress is evident, the number of female academics still lags behind their male counterparts. Literature corroborates that securing and sustaining academic positions in Nigerian universities is demanding for women. Despite portraying themselves as liberal and supportive of social justice, these institutions maintain male-dominated, patriarchal governance structures. Female academics confront daunting hurdles, requiring mental resilience to navigate (Akinsanya 2012).

While some women have achieved noteworthy milestones, they persist as marginalized minorities (Ogbogu 2006). Akinjobi (2013) underscores those female academics in Nigeria grapple with a myriad of challenges encompassing work-life balance, relationships, family, and recreation. These struggles, often linked to gender dynamics, hinder their status and progress.

Inequality in Ivory Towers: Analyzing Challenges of Female Academics in Higher Education

The idea of gender relations in academia seems inevitable because of the perceived inequality between male and female academics. As the universities in Igboland do not operate in isolation, there is a transfer of Igbo cultures into the universities situated in Igboland. Thus, the universities, more often than not, become representations of the society within which they are situated. Therefore, for gender scholars, the essence of the position of women in African culture must be the basis of writing women's history (Okonkwo 2009:1). Lamenting on the issue of negligence of the female scholarship, Okonkwo (2–3) has this to say:

> in the 21st century, it is still appalling to note that scholars focusing on women History seems not to be taken too serious even by colleagues in the academia. The reason for this total neglect remains to the present writer an enigma. As one of the victims of this "ridiculed phobia", I saw the need to study about women history at the university of Lagos, Nigeria at the master's degree level. Such an attempt as a male gender witnessed tremendous criticisms even from leading academics. It is on this notion that I contest that the focus on women history is yet to be understood.

In Okonkwo's opinion, adequate attention is not given to the approach of scholars toward the understanding of women. He further maintained that women mainly carry out studies in African women's history and urged men as well to possess feminine consciousness as the development of keen scholarship is a matter of interest. One informant aptly pointed out that the notion of gender equality in academia is easier spoken of than witnessed. She acknowledged that while some men maintain respectful relationships with their female counterparts, it's disheartening to still encounter male academics in the 21st century who believe women should have a secondary role. These men expect women to carry over their traditional supportive role from the Holy Book into the academic sphere (Agbo U. M., personal communication: 2021b). Uchem (2002) further emphasizes that the subjugation of women finds its origins in human psychology, culture, and religion, often bolstered by selective interpretations of the Bible. This has led to subtle biblical and cultural myths that manipulate women to accept their own oppression and resist liberation (Uchem 2001). Christianity, widely embraced in Igboland, historically reinforced the subordination of women. Such teachings still echo in corporate and academic environments today, where female academics face challenges juggling work and family, encountering obstacles attending conferences due to reasons like husbands' objections, and lacking unbiased mentorship (Ohia & Nzewi 2020). One distinguished professor (Esie Umeano, personal communication: 2021) elaborates that this leads to inappropriate behavior from some male academics and students toward their female counterparts, often causing female academics to be perceived as stern or even labeled as wicked. The informant's advice to married female academics is to carefully manage both domestic responsibilities and academic careers, although this balance isn't as glamorous as it may seem.

Achieving this takes the combined effort of the husband and wife. Speaking from experience, Rammile (2022) opined that it is usually very difficult to maneuver the overlapping challenges associated with her as an academic, a wife, and a church leader in her husband's church. To overcome these hurdles, she needed balance. With proper management of her time, her husband further provided the stand upon which her balance was guaranteed. On the importance of time management as a crucial habit to the success of female academics, another study participant Ezugwu Roseline (personal communication: 2021) agrees with Rammile.

Certainly, the pivotal role of a supportive husband cannot be overstated in this context. It is important to acknowledge that Rammile experienced a similar situation in South Africa, a culture distinct from that of the Igbo. The inherent patriarchy within Igbo society, where husbands are expected to resist such adaptations, exacerbates the challenges for female academics. Walters (2022) concurs with this sentiment, examining the intricacies of conducting doctoral research while caring for her child. She aptly notes that 'finding solitude for writing is hard to obtain with an active toddler at home.' Her observation resonates as academic research necessitates tranquility, mental equilibrium, and undisturbed focus—all elusive with an energetic toddler vying for the mother's time and attention. This is often manifested through frequent and insistent cries. In such circumstances, the pursuit of scholarly endeavors, such as doctoral research, becomes an arduous undertaking.

Uchem (2001:17) highlights how Igbo men embracing a more equitable attitude toward their spouses are ridiculed for not 'controlling their wives.' This reflects a standard where male 'maleness' hinges on women's control. Another study participant, Egodi Uchendu (personal communication: 2021) echoes this, pointing to men's innate desire for control pervading all aspects, even academia. Married male academics often delegate home tasks, enjoying time for academic and leisure pursuits. Female academics lack such luxury, juggling responsibilities. While institutional rules might not overtly hinder female academics, another participant Agbo Christiana (personal communication: 2021) argues that psychological and ingrained biases drive domination and stereotypes. She criticizes the use of psychology, body language, and sensory cues to discriminate against women. Contrarily, Obonga W. O. (personal communication: 2021) stands out, prioritizing collegiality over gender. Raised in a different cultural context, he recognizes the harmful impact of gender biases that seep into academia. He advocates universities as places to counteract such biases, emphasizing enlightenment and equitable treatment. Obonga's view resonates with MC and CNN (personal communications: 2021), applauding his stance on gender relations. As cultural practices at the micro level permeate the macro environment, academic settings mirror these biases. While some cling to outdated traditions, the university is meant to be a hub of enlightenment, fostering parity rather than endorsing inequity. Obonga's perspective resonates, challenging the acceptance of discriminatory norms and advocating for equality's triumph.

However, while maintaining that supporting the female academics who find themselves at crossroads will ensure greater societal transformations, Chigozie (personal communications: 2021), however, seems largely to have a different experience from fellow female academics. According to her, 'my relationship with fellow male academics is not just cordial but mutual. I enjoy much respect from them and this ensures that I don't experience the issues of inequality.' However, when one takes into cognizance the status of Chigozie, the rest of the reason why she enjoys such respect and mutuality with her male counterparts becomes crystal clear. She is an academic doctor in her faculty and also a religious leader. Observably, her academic and religious statuses are the reason she enjoys such respect. Needless to say that her statuses add weight to the measure of respect and recognition from fellow academics, especially the males. This largely suggests that higher status in the academia and in the church serve as the way female academics can gain mutual respect. Anyadike (personal communication: 2021) agrees that, to an extent, status plays a significant role in gender relations in academia. With this benchmark, what should then be the fate of young female academics who have not gained 'higher' status academically and female Muslims, traditionalists, and atheists, among others who are not Christians? Respect and recognition of a human person is like a gift that makes people feel valuable. Irrespective of gender, social, or religious status, everyone deserves respect.

Furthermore, other opinions gathered through oral interviews add a dimension to the understanding of gender relations among academics. For instance, Chidiebere Diyoke (personal communiation:2021) stated that equality in gender among academics can never be achieved if female students keep shying away from 'strenuous' programs in the sciences. He insisted that female students prefer subjects in the arts to such 'strenuous' and often demanding programs in the sciences, particularly engineering, which involves handling of working tools. For him, this accounts for why it is difficult to find female lecturers in the engineering department. From this, it can be deduced that the numerical strength of male academics in the engineering program far outweighs that of the female. This is because of the disinterestedness of the females in choosing to study those areas; a disinterestedness that is informed by the male-induced patriarchal system in Igboland. From childhood, the patriarchal system imbibes in the girl-child the sense that such activities relating to handling tools are meant for boys/men. Young girls are only taught how to manage homes by mainly orientating their childhood experiences with home chores (Agbo, personal communication: 2021a). With this mindset, the girl-child, at a later stage, would not be interested in going on engineering courses. In the same vein, Emenike Mathew (personal communiaction: 2021) agrees with Diyoke while adding that the possibility of gender 'equality as regards the number of academics can never be realized even miraculously'.

Family issues and spousal insecurities persistently hinder female academic achievements. An informant, Nwachukwu (personal communication: 2021), shared a disheartening account where a husband tore his wife's hard-earned certificate, believing her education bred disrespect. Such cases underscore spousal control over women's accomplishments. Married female lecturers also face hindrances—spouses curbing their conference and networking opportunities, eroding academic growth (Aneke, personal communication: 2021). Despite women's academic progress, domestic setbacks, mainly voicelessness in family decisions, impede their choices and careers (Nwankwo, personal communication: 2021). Such challenges disproportionately affect female academics, balancing home and the 'publish or perish' academic mantra. Complexities arise when husbands, traditionalists unversed in dual marital roles, leave domestic duties solely to women. Cooking, cleaning, pregnancy, childbirth, and childcare—largely women's responsibilities—constrain academic pursuits (Agbo, personal communication: 2021). Traditional gender norms foster this divide, as women are encumbered with both domestic and academic obligations. Agbo's experience underscores the impact—her husband's refusal to permit a research interview in Port Harcourt disrupted her PhD studies. Despite making arrangements, yielding to marital expectations undermined her research. This highlights the critical interplay between domestic roles and academic pursuits. Domestic hindrances remain the paramount challenge, revealing the entrenched gender dynamics that impede women's holistic academic development.

Closely related to the above, patriarchy and religion have both posed persistent challenges to female academics in the 21st century. On the part of religion, Uchem (2001:46–47) would note that:

> the missionaries effectively and uncritically implemented the colonial policies, which politically, economically and socially marginalized women. Consequently, women were deposed from their economic, political and social positions, which they had enjoyed in the pre-colonial, pre-Christian and pre-Islamic days. Thus, it is sad to think that religion (Christianity and Islam) have served as the vehicles that transported women's inferiorization and marginalization to Nigeria.

Historically, the patriarchal nature of Igbo society has posed a great challenge to women (Okonkwo 2009:1) just as religion contributed more than an ordinary share to the plight of women in the 21st century (Uchem 2005:11). For many centuries, the Igbo society and the Christian churches believed that women should play a subordinate role to men as this was ordained by God. This has been supported by numerous scriptural passages which are derogatory to the status of women in tune with the times and traditions of their authors and interpreters as well (Uchem 2005: 11). The biblical account of the creation in Genesis Chapter 1 will always stand tall as a reference point for such conscious attitude of assigning secondary and subordinate status to women. The Christian churches have failed to understand that the times, culture, and tradition that prevailed when these scriptural passages were written are different from that of the contemporary Igbo society. Thus, the understanding of the time and culture that prevailed when the Bible was written as distinct from the traditions of the Igbo society will undoubtedly help in the reinterpretation of some of the biblical passages that are anti-women. Commenting on the religious nature of the Igbo, Isichei (1976:24–26) puts it thus, 'the Igbo were nothing if not profoundly religious, and all accounts of their life reflect the fact...religion led the Igbo into some oppression and injustice.' Unfortunately, women are the victims of these religiously and culturally instigated manipulations as both combine to ensure the enduring subordination of women. The pre-colonial Igbo society, though largely patriarchal in nature, had assigned socio-economic cum political roles to women but such roles are subsidiary as the men enjoy the monopoly of power and policy-making from the colonial period to the present (Okoro 2009:28–32). However, the coming of Christianity in Igboland and the interpretation of the Bible from a male-gendered perspective worsened the condition of women as it contributed to ensuring that the secondary status of women to men is upheld. As a result, Uchem (2001: 111) remarked thus:

> it is increasingly clear that what today passes for Igbo culture regarding women is a residue from the interaction of imported Euro-Western concepts of women's inferiority with the original Igbo culture. While Igbo culture has changed considerably following its contact with Western political and religious colonization, the aspects, which culturally subordinate women have remained unchanged. Igbo egalitarianism, which allowed for women's autonomy and inclusion, has been suppressed...contemporary Igbo women's experience reveal that while Igbo men have taken on Western Christian construction of gender, which dis-empowered and inferiorized women, they still hold on to past cultural expectation of women in present changed circumstances. Deprived now of the traditional checks and balances, which formerly curbed male domination, Igbo women now suffer a complicated triple oppression resulting from political colonization,

received Western Christian culture and the unchanged aspects of Igbo culture. Igbo men now dominate and lord it over women by invoking both "our culture" and "our (Church) tradition" … contemporary Igbo Christians have little or no social consciousness of that trend toward gender equality.

Similarly, the Western Christian provision of marriage as written in the Common Law of England ensured that women were subordinated. It should be noted that the pre-colonial Igbo culture recognized a woman's different autonomy even in her traditionally subordinate status. However, Western Christianity came up with the idea of 'the two became one body' as written in Matthew Chapter 19:5, and through such means, the woman's separate identity became socially erased and subsumed under the man (Uchem 2001:116). Yet again, Christianity reinvigorated Igbo women's subordination through the language of the Western Christian marriage ritual and the Pauline code, which ensured that the ritual is worded distinctly to the man and the woman. Through such means, the man is exhorted to 'love' and the woman to 'obey/submit.' This is a double standard for both partners and 'by urging the man to love and the woman to obey, the Christian marriage ritual institutionalizes a man's sense of himself as "head" and "first" and the woman's future life as that of a subordinate, unequal in dignity with the man' (Uchem 2001:117). The fact that this marriage ritual is meant to be 'for better, for worse' punctures any attempt to redefine the marital status and role of women, an indication that the church is not the best place for the redefinition of the secondary status of women. While using herself as an example, Kelechi Omeje (personal communication, 2021) insisted that she had more freedom to pursue her personal goals before marriage. However, ever since she got married, everything has changed, and the most annoying thing is that nothing seems to have changed in her partner's use of time.

The challenging condition of the female academics demands that they fight both the Igbo society that is patriarchal in nature together with the Western Christian religion which manifests itself in dictating double standard marriage system for both male and female, with the former playing a 'head' role, while the later assumes the 'subsidiary/supportive' duty. Another informant (Ekwochi, personal communication: 2021) stated that in her department, when a female academic is of the same cadre as the men, the male academic tends to relate very well but the reverse becomes the case if the male academic is placed higher academically. The same thing applies to the choice of head of department as female academics rarely emerge as heads of department or faculty deans (Fagbemi, personal communication: 2021). The University of Nigeria Nsukka has not had a female vice-chancellor since it was established in 1960. Such could be said of Enugu State University of Science and Technology (The Nation 2023). According to African Check (2019), Prof. Lai Olurode, who specializes in political sociology, development, and gender studies at the University of Lagos, challenges that it is difficult for women to 'rise to positions of authority in the Nigerian university system due to stereotypes and prejudices.' She continued by affirming that 'marriage and motherhood' were usually prioritized for the woman rather than career advancement.

Conclusion

This research focused on Southeastern universities to analyze the status of female academics in post-civil war Nigeria. It attempted to challenge the prevailing patriarchal nature of Igbo society, which undermines the academic productivity of females by attempting the exploration of gender relations among male and female academics. It insisted that male and female academics should be given equal opportunities to pursue their careers irrespective of the orthodox roles assigned by traditional Igbo society. African societies, like Igboland, confronted multifarious obstacles to women's education till the late 20th century. These obstacles have undermined the comparative relevance of female academics in school politics and research. Yet, attitudes and treatment shifted during this era, spurred in part by the unintentional repercussions of the Nigeria–Biafra War (1967–1970). Thorough research and fieldwork revealed that education was male-centric in the early 20th century, preparing men for leadership in families and communities. However, the civil war became a turning point, reshaping Igbo society through its aftermath. The war's devastation and the subsequent reluctance to pursue Western education prompted men to focus on rapid-return businesses and skills, leaving the door open for female education to flourish. This paved the way for some women to join the ranks of university lecturers. Still, their accomplishments face obstacles stemming from domestic and stereotypical challenges, hampering research, political participation and fair treatment. Echoing Dr. Mrs. U. M. Agbo's sentiments, the study suggests that disciplined domestic assistance, support from husbands, and adept time management could empower female academics to excel. This chapter calls for the overcoming of the patriarchal norms, which is essential for the operation of female academics. This approach is also vital for the equitable selection of administrative candidates based on qualifications, not gender. This study underscores the significance of female education's evolution post-war while urging reforms to support women's success in academia.

References

Academic Planning Unit Office Record. (2023), University of Nigeria, Nsukka.
African Check. (2019), "More than 15 Female Vice-Chancellors have led Nigeria Universities but higher education still a man's world", available at https://africacheck.org/fact-checks/reports/more-15-female-vice-chancellors-have-led-nigerian-universities-hi, accessed August 2023.
Agbo, C. C. (2021a), Personal Communication held at Enugu State University of Science and Technology, Enugu.
Agbo, U. M. (2021b), Personal Communication held at University of Nigeria Nsukka.
Akinjobi, A. (2013), "Balancing Acts for African Women Development: Challenges of Women Academics in Africa, the Case of Nigeria", *An International Journal of Language, Literature and Gender Studies*, Vol. 2, No. 6, pp. 20–45.
Akinsanya, O. O. (2012), "The Role of Women in Academics: Issues, Challenges and Perspectives" *JORIND*, Vol. 10, No. 2, ISSN 1596-8308, pp 136–141.
Aneke, N. (2021), Personal Communication held at University of Nigeria, Nsukka.
Anyadike. (2021), Personal Communication held at University of Nigeria, Nsukka.
Anyanwu, C. N. (2021), Personal Communication held at University of Nigeria, Nsukka.
Asogwa, J. (2021), Personal Communication held at Ihakpu-Awka, Nsukka.
Basden, G. T. (1921), *Among the Ibos of Nigeria*, London: Seeley, Service & Co. Limited.
Cress, C. M. and Hart, J. (2009), "Playing Soccer and Football Field: The Persistence of Gender Inequalities for Women Faculty" *Equity and Excellence in Education*, Vol. 42, No. 4, pp. 473–488.
Diyoke, C. (2021), Personal Communication held at Enugu State University of Science and Technology, Enugu.
Dunn, A. R. (2020), "How Should an Understanding of Gender Shape Our Approach to the Production of Knowledge?", *Journal of International Women's Studies*, Vol. 22, No. 2, pp. 1–37.
Ekwochi, E. A. (2021), Personal Communication held at Enugu State University of Science and Technology, Enugu.
Emenike, M. (2021), Personal Communication held at Enugu State University of Science and Technology, Enugu.
Esie, U. (2021), Personal Communication held at University of Nigeria, Nsukka.

Ezeh, M.N. and Okonkwo, U.U. (2009), *Our Women, Our Strength, Issues in African Women History & Gender Studies*, Lagos: Grace Anasiudu Press.

Ezugwu, R. (2021), Personal Communication held at Enugu State University of Science and Technology, Enugu.

Fagbemi, V. Y. (2021), Personal Communication held at University of Nigeria, Nsukka.

Gabriel, A. O. I. (2000), "Women Education in Igboland: A Gender Perspective", *Journal of Gender Studies*, Vol. 1, No. 3, 60–79.

Glover, L. (2021), "Social Reproduction Theory: On Regulating Reproduction, Understanding Oppression and As a Lens On Forced Sterilisation", *Journal of International Women's Studies*, Vol. 22, No. 2, pp. 34–48.

Goodluck, N. (2007), "Male Child Preference and Access to Education: A Study of Aba Urban", B.A. Thesis, University of Nigeria, Nsukka.

Ibrahim, J. and Salihu, A. (2004), *Women, Marginalisation and Politics in Nigeria*, Ilupeju: Global Right Partners for Justice.

Isichei, E. (1976), *A History of the Igbo People*, London: The Macmillan Press Ltd.

Korieh, C. (2010), *The Land Has Changed: History, Society and Gender in Colonial Eastern Nigeria*, Alberta, University of Calgary Press.

Korieh, C. J. (2013), *The Way We Lived: Essays on Nigerian History, Gender and Society*, New Jersey, Goldline & Jecobs Publishing.

Maria, C. (2021), Personal Communication held at Enugu State University of Science and Technology, Enugu.

McShane, J. (2020), "What Does It Mean to 'Decolonise' Gender Studies?: Theorising the Decolonial Capacities of Gender Performativity and De-Colonial Capacities of Gender Performativity and Intersectionality", *Journal of International Women's Studies*, Vol. 22, No. 2, 62–77,

Morley, L. (1999), *Organizing Feminism: The Micro Politics of the Academy*, New York: St. Martins.

Nnadi, E. (2021), Personal Communication held at University of Nigeria, Nsukka.

Nwachukwu, I. (2021), Personal Communication held at University of Nigeria, Nsukka.

Nwankwo, A. (2021), Personal Communication held at University of Nigeria, Nsukka.

Obi-Ani, N. A. (2017), "War and the Occupation of Nsukka and Enugu Areas of Biafra: 1967–1979", Doctoral Dissertation, Nnamdi Azikiwe University.

Obi-Ani, P. (2009), *Post-Civil War Political and Economic Reconstruction of Igboland, 1970–1983*, Nsukka: Great AP Express Publishers Ltd.

Obonga, W. O. (2021), Personal Communication held at University of Nigeria, Nsukka.

Obonodo, E. A. (2008), "Educational Level and Gender: Perception of Women Leadership Role: A Study of Olomoro Community, Isoko South L.G.A Delta State", Unpublished project, Department of Sociology/Anthropology, University of Nigeria.

Ogbogu, C. O. (2006), "An Evaluation of Female Labour Input in the University Educational System in Nigeria", Doctoral Dissertation, Obafemi Awolowo University, Ile-Ife, Nigeria.

Ogbogu, C. O. (2009), "An Analysis of Female Research Productivity in Nigerian Universities", *Journal of Higher Education Policy and Management*, Vol. 31, No 91, 17–22.

Ogbogu, C. O. (2011), "Gender Inequality in Academia: Evidence From Nigeria" *Contemporary Issues in Education Research*, Vol. 4, No. 9, 1–9.

Ogbonnaya, L. (2021), Personal Communication held at University of Nigeria, Nsukka.

Ohia N. C. and Nzewi U. M. (2020), "Socio-Cultural Challenges of Women Development: The Case of Female Academics in Igboland, Nigeria*"*, *Mediterranean Journal of Social Sciences*, Vol. 7, No. 1, pp. 269–278.

Oke, O. A., (2001), *From Conference to Conference: A Bibliography on African Women and Development, 1980-1995*, Ibadan: Rex Charles Publication.

Olufunke, O. A. (2001), *From Conference to Conference: A References on African Women and Development, 1980–1995*, Ibadan: Rex Charles Publication.

Olumukoro, C. A. (2011), "Influence of Literacy Education Programmes on Socio-economic and Psychological Empowerment of Women in Edo and Delta states, Nigeria", Doctoral Thesis, University of Ibadan.

Okonkwo U. U. (2009), "Doctored History: The Challenges of Women History in the 21st Century Africa", in *Our Women, Our Strength, Issues in African Women History & Gender Studies*, ed. Ezeh, M. and Okonkwo, U. U., Lagos: Grace Anasiudu.

Okonkwo, U. T. and Ezumah, N. N., 2017, "Socio-Cultural Factors Affecting the Autonomy of Reproduction Decisions of Married Women in Nsukka L. G. A. of Enugu State, Nigeria", *International Journal of Sociology and Anthropology Research*, Vol. 3, No. 2, pp. 1–12.

Okorie, A., Cristopher C. and Ezugworie C. (2020), "An Assessment of the Traditional Penal Code for Adultery and the Operations of Women's Rights Instruments Among the Igbos, in South-Eastern Nigeria", *International Journal of Political Science (IJPS)*, Vol. 6, No. 4, pp. 33–45. ISSN 2454-9452.

Okoro, S.I. (2018), "The Igbo and educational development in Nigeria, 1846–2015", *International Journal of History and Cultural Studies (IJHCS)*, Vol. 4, No. 1, pp. 65–80.

Okoro, U. (2009), "Perspective on the place of gender in African development", in M. N. E. Ezeh and U. U. Okonkwo (eds.), *Our Women our Strength: Issues in African women History and Gender Studies*, Lagos: Grace Anasidu Press.

Okoroafor, E. and Anuforo E. (2012), "The Millennium Development Goals (MDGs) and the Problem of Policy Implementation in Nigeria", *International Journal of Development and Management Review(INJODEMAR)*, Vol 7, pp. 67–80.

Omeje, K. (2021) Personal Communication held at Enugu State University of Science and Technology, Enugu.

Onumonu, U. and Anutanwa, P. (2017), "Rethinking the Impact of Nigerian Civil War: Commerce in the Post Civil War Nnewi and its Challenges, 1970–2000', *Mgbakoigba Journal of African Studies*, Vol. 6 No. 2, pp. 155–167.

Osaji-Nwafili C. A. (2021), "An Appraisal of Dioke (Adultery) Punishments in Ndokwa Society in the Context of the Entrapment in John 7:53–8:11", *Journal of Research in Humanities and Social Science*, Vol. 9, No. 7, pp. 58–68.

Poole, M. (2005), "Removing the Equality Barriers: Women as Senior Managers and Executives in Universities", Chapter Presented at the *International Association of University Presidents, 2005 XIV Trennial Conference*, Bangkok, Thailand (pp. 1–25).

Rammile, N. (2022), "Balancing Academic Work and Home Life", in *On Becoming a Scholar: What Every New Academic Needs to Know*, ed. Jansen, J., and Visser, D., Cape Town: African Mind.

Sherwood, M. (1988), *Women Under the Sun: African Women in Politics and Production, A References 1983–1985*, London: Institute for African Alternatives.

The Nation Newspaper. (2023), accessed at https://thenationonlineng.net/eight-female-vice-chancellors-in-nigeria

Uchem, R. N. (2001), *Overcoming women's subordination, an Igbo African and Christian perspective: Envisioning an Inclusive Theology with Reference to Women*, Enugu: Snaap Press Ltd.

Uchem, R. N. (2002), *Beyond Veiling: A Response to the Issues in Women's Experiences of Subjugation in African Christian Cultures*, Enugu: Snaap Press Ltd.

Uchem, R., (2005), *Gender equality from a Christian perspective*, Enugu: Snaap Press Ltd.

Uchendu, E. (2021), Personal Communication held at University of Nigeria, Nsukka.

Ugwu, C. (2021a), Personal Communication held at Ihakpu-Awka, Nsukka.

Ugwu, C. C. (2021b), Personal Communication held at Enugu State University of Science and Technology, Enugu.

Walker, I. and Pettigrew, T. (1984), "Relative Deprivation Theory: An Overview and Conceptual Critique", *Article in British Journal of Social Psychology, The British Psychological Society*, Great Britain, Vol. 23, pp. 301–310.

Walters, C. (2022), "The Mom Penalty", in *On Becoming a Scholar: What Every New Academic Needs to Know*, ed. Jansen, J., and Visser, D., Cape Town, African Mind.

26
WOMEN'S POLITICAL PARTICIPATION AND THE PLACE OF PATRIARCHY IN POLITICAL INSTITUTIONS IN OSUN STATE, NIGERIA

Abidemi Abiola Isola

Introduction

The level of women's participation in Nigerian politics since independence has been low compared to their male counterparts and varies from one democratic government to the other. This is not peculiar alone to Nigeria, but it is a general occurrence in Africa. The story of women in the political scene has been that of struggle. Beginning from the colonial era (1900), the discrimination against women has been a recurring struggle in the nation's patriarchal political system. The struggle to correct this anomaly and end the discrimination against women has continued to intensify without desired results. In Africa, the concern for women as a specific group increased with the advent of Western civilisation and formal education as well as globalization. This global emphasis on women's struggle for equality and fairness has created a new awareness among women, particularly in developing countries. In a nutshell, women aimed at creating equal opportunities and responsibilities for increased participation in nation-building Adeleye (2000:3). How can this be accomplished? It is by active participation in political issues, which could also be referred to as political participation. What then is political participation? According to Arowolo and Aluko (2010), political participation is an important act every eligible citizen of a country is expected to be involved in, in order to ensure the development of such a country with no form of gender discrimination (Ajayi, 2007; Enemuo, 2015). One major essence of political participation in any is to seek control, acquisition and dispensation of power in order to organise society, harness and distribute resources and influence individual interests.

Diversity in social, political and cultural situations in each country of the world has led to variations in women's political participation. In spite of this, there is one common feature to women's political experiences across the world, and this is in the aspect of politics, which seems to be reserved for men alone. Consequently, in many parts of the world, especially in developing countries, the level of women's political participation is low when compared to their male counterparts (Adereti, 2003). In Africa, the level of women's political participation cannot be compared with that of men, as the latter seem to have better political opportunities than the former. This is as a result of socio-cultural activities which are discriminatory and economic inequalities, reinforcing women's subordinate place in the society (Adeogun & Isola, 2022). These harmful traditional practices are embedded in a patriarchal culture which stymies women's voices from being heard in the public.

The era of colonialism for Nigerian women was an era of inactivity, especially in politics. This was as a result of colonial administration, which brought with it the assumptions of European patriarchy into Nigerian society, although the Queen of England occupies a pride of place in the political scheme of things in Europe (Omoniyi, 2012). Consequently, Tiger and Fox (1972) sought to bridge the biological and cultural dimensions of humanity, which brought about this assumption on European patriarchy by stating in their book entitled "The Imperial Animal", which postulated that "human social behavior, including colonialism and the oppression of women by men, can be chalked up to the impulse to insure that as many of our genes as possible have a future". It has been argued that a structure of inequality was built during the colonial era in Nigeria. It led to the discrimination against women and promoted male-dominated social systems (Olatunde 2010). Although such structures existed during the pre-colonial era, they were institutionalized as new legal structures under the colonial rule. During this period, women were marginalized in various aspects, economically denied access to loans, and educationally by predetermining their school curricula and ensuring that girls enrolled for domestic science as against other skill-enhancing courses because of the belief that they were expected to be primarily effective mothers and housewives (Olatunde, 2010). "Hence, girls were brought up in the traditional family set up to be passive, obedient, 'ladylike' and always submissive to men. Boys, on the other hand, were encouraged to be aggressive, competitive and independent" (Adereti 2003: 4).

According to Udegbe (1998:20), "societal norms and stereotypes also function as a traditional ideology that relegates women to housewife roles while promoting men as actors, providers and final authority". Similarly, Isiugo-Abanihe (1994) says that "most Nigerian societies are patriarchal and the male or husband is the major decision maker, especially on issues relating to family matter". Sustaining this claim, Olatunde (2010) writes that the division of roles prescribed by most cultures assigns the subordinate position to women. Gender roles are neither natural nor immutable. They are constructed and invented by society. As a result of this traditional norm of boys being more active than girls at the family level, women were behind educationally, economically and socially. This is not to deny the occasional departure from this traditional norm as stated above, as some women rose to the top politically and held leadership positions. Nigeria, for instance, has a very rich history of notable women who also helped their various communities in various ways in the past and are now celebrated as legends (Akinyode-Afolabi & Salami, 2003:9). She further asserted that:

> Oral tradition has it that women played prominent roles in the political history and decision making process of (some) traditional societies. The legendary roles played by princess Inikpi of Igala land and Moremi of Ife as survivors of their societies during warfare, to the extent of sacrificing their lives to ensure victory, were remarkable. Other notable women of valour who helped in directing the course of history of their traditional societies in the precolonial era included Queen Amina of Zaria, Queen Kambasa of Ijaw and Queen Owari of Ilesa.

These women played prominent roles, which have been a source of encouragement for women folk to participate in politics. Today, in the 21st century, women are found virtually in all areas of public life, beginning from the local, state, to the federal level. There are such women like Bosede Osiirewo, Titi Ajanaku, Ebun Oyagbola, Alhaja Sinatu Ojikutu, Sarah Jubril, Kofoworola Bucknor-Akerele, Oluremi Adiukwu Bakare, Biola Babatope, Erelu Olusola Obada, Mrs Janet N. Mokelu, A Young and Late Hajia Gambo Sawaba, Okonjo Iweala, Late Dora Akunyili, Titi Laoye Tomori, to mention only a few, who have been are, at one time or the other, Councillors, Local Government Chairpersons, Senators, Commissioners, Ministers, Special Advisers and Deputy Governors (Adereti, 2003; Chukwuemaka and Eze, 2011; Igbokwe, 2013). These political positions are bestowed on women either through election or appointment, but more importantly, is the awareness of women themselves of their rights.

Nevertheless, the condition of women in Africa in general and in Nigeria's politics compared to that of men, leaves much to be desired due to those factors militating against women that could be either socio-cultural, socio-economical or ideological in nature (Nwankwor & Nkereuwem, 2019). Thus, this chapter tends to expound the historical perspective of patriarchy and women's political participation, globally, nationally and much more among the Yorubas, with a focus on Osun State and how this marginalization can be overcome. In order to highlight the challenges and possibilities associated with women's advancement in Nigeria, the chapter will also outline developments in other African contexts.

The study employed Molyneux's (2002) organizing theory to justify the fact that the presence of gender-biased customary laws and patriarchal cultures in Africa and in particular Osun State can limit the efforts of women's organizations working at the grassroots level towards an increase of representation of women in political participation both in qualitative and quantitative. Molyneux (2002: 183) conceptualized "Bottom up development" as "greater attention to demand from the grassroots, more sensitive policy instruments, and changes in the nature of state-society relations". This implies that women's involvement in the decision-making process using a bottom-up approach should be supported by the government via a sensitive policy instrument which includes every aspect of customary laws that is put in place for the people at the grassroots level, making sure that these laws are not gender biased. Furthermore, it is affirmed by Molyneux's theory that patriarchy is the basis for discrimination against women, and unless the structure is demolished in the society, representation in decision-making process will continue to be poor.

Conceptual Clarification of Patriarchy

The term patriarchy, which is from the Latin word "pater", which means "father", has to do with male hegemony over a group of people or society as a whole, which silences the presence of women in such a group or society, thereby making them redundant. Patriarchy started from the family. It is the main institution where patriarchy originated and spread to every other institution of the society.

This reveals that as a patriarchal unit within a patriarchal whole serving as an agent of the larger society, the family not only encourages its own members to align and conform, but it also acts as a unit in the government of patriarchal state, which rules its own citizens through its family heads (Olutayo, 2001: 100). This unit, in turn, infects the society, whereby men not only see themselves as the head of their own family but heads of their colleagues at their places of work to the extent that they do think that a woman of the same qualification should not earn the same salary as theirs (Adeogun & Isola 2010). This is the reason why the struggle for gender parity must start from the family, believing that once the struggle is won against patriarchal culture, which seems like a "parasite", in the family, then it can be taken care of within the society.

Sultana (2011:1) states that patriarchy is the leading obstacle to women's progress and development. Despite differences in levels of dominion, the same principle remains that men are still in control, although the nature of the control may differ. It is the factor that is responsible for the complete failure of any state to empower women on equal terms with men (Dore & Molyneux, 2002; 224 Rai, 2005; Eisenstein, 2008). The word "patriarchy" in its literal meaning is like the rule of the father or the "patriarch" and originally was used to describe a specific type of male-dominated family, that is, the women, junior men, children, slaves and domestic servants (Sultana, 2011:2).

Bhasin (2006:3) similarly refers to "patriarchy" as male domination. The power relationships by which men dominate women and create a system whereby women are kept subordinate in a number of ways. Such a system makes the voice of women "never" to be heard in the public. Furthermore, Adeogun & Isola (2022) defined patriarchy as the system in which the male head of the household has absolute legal and economic power over his dependent female and male family members. This kind of society is common all over the world, especially on the Africa continent. It is the manifestation and institutionalization of male dominance over women in all sectors of the society (Makama, 2013:117), particularly within the government and the economy, meaning the direct or indirect exclusion of females from these institutions (Adekanye, 2013: 21). This means that men hold power in all the important institutions of the society and that women are deprived of access to such power.

Based on the above definitions, it is not surprising that the concept of patriarchy has become so popular in gender studies, particularly in women's studies. The ideas, principles and values characterizing patriarchy as a system or rule tend to be strengthened by traditional stereotypes and symbolisms, which depict women on the one hand as weak, submissive, temperamental and emotional, and men on the other hand as strong, competitive and rational (Adeogun & Isola, 2010). Justifications for gender roles are based on an implied "sexual division of labour", which sees women, already depicted in this kind of gathered discourse, as either "feminine" or belonging to the so-called weaker sex, consigned to the purely homekeeping functions, including reproduction and child-rearing. The males, because they are regarded as more powerful as regards "body build", are given the so-called bigger tasks, like breadwinners for family sustenance or the laborious responsibilities of running a government, administering the machinery of state power and warmaking (Adekanye, 2013: 21). Patriarchy in essence leads to male dominance in all spheres of the society. Furthermore, women have been raised to believe that they are inherently in need of protection from men. Women who support patriarchy accept their own low standing within it. This belief promotes patriarchy.

Historical Perspective of Women Political Participation and Patriarchy

Since the 4th Beijing World Conference on Women in 1995, the expansion of women's political participation has been a worldwide trend. From the local to global level, women's leadership and political participation are compromised. Women are underrepresented as voters as well as in leading positions, whether in elected offices, civil services, the private sector or academia. This occurs despite their proven abilities as leaders and agents of change and their right to participate equally in democratic governance (Isola, 2014).

Women account for over half the population of most societies and are still underrepresented. Adeogun and Isola (2022:20) posits that "Without the active participation of women and the incorporation of women's perspectives in all levels of decision making, the goals of equality, development and peace cannot be achieved".

According to Akinyode-Afolabi and Salami (2003), in spite of the great desire for women's empowerment in all areas of life, which has been championed by the United Nations and its agencies and many international organisations, the representation of women in government and other public decision-making positions is still very low all over the world. Although it is a different experience in different regions, a situational analysis still points to the fact that there is a huge gender gap between women's and men's representation in political leadership as well as other aspects of public life.

Although the case is different now, with more women coming out of their shells to participate politically, there is still more to be done on the part of women to ensure it increases in number and in quality. Ogunlade (2012) further argued that, despite the enormous achievements of Nigerian women since independence, there are many issues undermining their role and participation in the democratic process in Nigeria. This is not limited to Nigeria or African countries alone; it is a global issue (Fatile, Adepoju, Chineye & Ayeni, 2017, The daily beast, n.d.). Looking at the Inter-Parliamentary Union (IPU) 2022 list of female leaders in the highest position offices in the world who are heads of state/head of government, the total number of female leaders is 30, representing 6.9 per cent of all political leaders in the world. In all, there are 13 women holding the office of Head of State. This represents 8.4 per cent of the total number of Heads of State while 15 women, representing 4.3 per cent are Heads of Government in the world. Women are quite far from 30 per cent said to be the minimum to obtain a balanced gender representation.

Women's participation in politics is important for there to be an improvement in governance in Africa (Ndlovu & Mutale, 2002:72) and globally. There is a need for gender equality in political participation. In several African countries, women hold or have held positions mostly regarded as male conservers. This confirms that women in recent times have played an important role in politics in Africa, and it is an indication that women can still do much more if the parasite called patriarchy can be gotten rid of.

Women's Political Participation and Patriarchy in Some African Countries

Patriarchy, which has been deeply rooted in the culture of most African (and other) countries, cannot be overemphasized in the sense that it is the most entrenched ideology in most African settings. It is an institution that has eaten up the dignity of women and turned the word "Woman" into "Slave" and "Submissiveness" into "Enslavement", thereby highlighting the skewed nature of gender relations. However, there are some countries that have undergone this ridiculous situation and have overcome it to some extent, while others are still struggling to get rid of the "sticky parasite". The following sections highlight developments in other African countries to facilitate ease of understanding the Nigerian context.

South Sudan

South Sudan became the newest country in Africa after decades of war. Women account for over 60 per cent of the population of South Sudan. The decades of war in South Sudan not only deprive women of their independence, but the disturbing and conventional post-war society coupled with discriminatory cultures and abject poverty undermines the promotion of equal rights and the ability for women to actively participate in the development of the newborn nation (Adeogun & Isola, 2010). Women's organizations have fought tirelessly to influence constitution-making in South Sudan. The Transitional Constitution of the Republic of South Sudan, which was endorsed by the president of South Sudan at independence, is a revised version of the 2005 interim constitution; it includes provisions that favour women's participation and gender equality (Ali, 2010: 7). Nonetheless, the interim constitution also recognizes customary law, which supports practice of patriarchy, which majorly facilitates access to property for women and girls through their fathers or husbands. This, in turn, often discriminates against widows and other groups of women. Customs that communities established to maintain widows' access to land, such as wife inheritance by a brother-in-law, often compound this discrimination. According to Aldehaib (2010:7), the common structures of different systems of customary law in South Sudan revolve around family law, which concerns itself with marriage, divorce, custody of children and inheritance. Customary law therefore determines a woman's personal security at home, and in public life as well as her access to resources (Aldehaib, 2010: 7). Mostly, customary law disseminates harmful customs and traditions in the realm of the family, which downgrade women to a minor status. These harmful customs include forced and arranged marriages, forced wife inheritance and bride price (Aldehaib, 2010: 7). All these aid the practice of patriarchy. Customary law perpetuates unjust gender relations that serve the social, psychological and economic interests of men by bringing women into a position of subordination and inequality in the family and the community (Aldehaib, 2010: 7). In 2019, South Sudan ranked 57th position in the world, having 28.5 per cent female representation in the Lower House and 12.0 per cent in the Upper House (IPU, 2019, 2023). This situation has gone a long way to stymie the tireless effort of women's organizations in South Sudan in ensuring that women climb the ladder of decision-making in their country.

Rwanda

It is also important to take a look at Rwanda as a country with challenges but still thrives. Rwanda emerged from one of the most destructive conflicts in modern history with a strong commitment to gender mainstreaming and increasing women's political participation. This would not have been possible without the support and demonstrated political commitment of the government of Rwanda at the higher level of leadership (Brukutwa, 2014; Mutamba, 2005). The Rwandan government turned political commitment into a concrete practical action, which has transformed the level of involvement of women in political participation in that country (Cole, 2011:14).

Rwanda has the highest percentage of women appointed to government in the world. Rwanda ranks first in the world in female representation in parliament with an astounding 56.3 per cent (Inter-Parliamentary Union (IPU) 2016) in the lower house and 34.6 per cent in the upper house. In 2019, Rwanda had 61.3 per cent in the lower house and 38.5 per cent in the upper house. (IPU, 2019). As of October 2023, the percentage of women's representation in Parliament was 61.3 in the lower house and 34.6 in the upper house. This achievement could not have been possible without the support and demonstration of political commitment of the Government of Rwanda at the highest level of leadership (Mutamba, 2005). The Rwanda government, led by the Rwanda Patriotic Front (RPF), prioritized women's representation, adopting a constitution in 2003 requiring women to be granted 30 per cent of posts in all decision-making organs (Gogineni, 2010). This is the same country that over 20 years ago was in the throes of a genocide that consumed its population at a speed unparalleled in modern history. The traditionally patriarchal society thrust its women into the role of rebuilding the country. In essence, the women of Rwanda were proactive in their situation, which paved the way for them to climb up the ladder of authority. Their victory over patriarchy and politics started from the grassroots level. Women formed local councils, headed judicial proceedings, tilled the land and rose through the ranks of government. This was the beginning of peace and reconciliation that whipped the country into the model of development and gender equality (Falola & Jacquemin, 2022).

South Africa

In a conventionally patriarchal society, where the leadership roles in society belong to men and women's primary role is a domestic one, in South Africa, since the end of the apartheid system and the first democratic elections in 1994, women have continued to make gains in politics and governance. In the 1999 elections, South African women earned 30 per cent of representation. Also, in the 2009 elections, women had a very strong showing by winning 178 (44.5 per cent) of the legislative seats in the lower house of parliament and 16 (29.6 per cent) of the 54 seats in the upper house of parliament. This growth has placed South Africa as the fourth-ranked country in the world in women's political participation. In 2019, South Africa ranked the third African country in women's political participation, with 42.7 per cent in the lower house of parliament and 35.2 per cent in the upper house of parliament. It retained third position in 2023 as well, with 45.3 per cent of women in the lower house and 44.4 per cent in the upper house. This outstanding journey began during the struggle for freedom (1956), when many women marched to the union buildings in Pretoria as simulacra to fight for their freedom. It was not a palatable experience, as many of them were arrested and detained. South African women across the racial line have been a source of courage for the entire community. In his statement, Thabo Mbeki, former president, said, "No government in South Africa could ever claim to represent the will of the people if it failed to address the central task of emancipation of women all its element and that include the government we are privilege to lead" (Mbeki in South Africa History online, 2016). This points to the fact that women should be put into consideration when it comes to political matters (Adeogun & Isola, 2022).

Liberia

Liberia, like many democracies, faces the challenge of identifying and implementing strategies in order to ensure equality in the numbers of women and men in national governance and decision-making capacities. Entrenched traditional norms, cultural practices which embrace the practices of patriarchy, limited education of women and institutional frameworks have hindered gender equality in Liberian politics. Every attempt by the global community and local efforts of Liberia did not lead to gender equality in national governance (Sirleaf-Johnson, 2010, Cole, 2011). However, in 2005, the National Election Commission was reconstructed and general elections were conducted. Those elections produced the first ever elected female president of an African country, President Ellen Johnson Sirleaf (Inter-Parliamentary Union, 2010). Liberian election of 2005 voters' registration records show that the number of registrants was split equally between male and female and that voter turnout was higher among women (Cole, 2011). Similarly, the 2011 election voted in again Ellen Johnson Sirleaf for a second term. As an effective female president, she brought about an increase in the number of women in parliament in the country (Isola, 2014). Additionally, African countries such as Senegal, Mozambique, Uganda and Angola have also been highly ranked for their level of women's representation in parliament. Notable improvements have also been celebrated in some Arab countries that have been traditionally associated with low rates of women's participation in politics (Adeoye, 2023).

Having documented the transformation that has been experienced in some African countries, the chapter will now focus on the Yoruba in Nigeria.

Patriarchy among the Yorubas: Osun State in Focus

The Yorubas

Well-documented facts in women and gender studies confirm that women exercised power during the precolonial era in all spheres of life, especially in decision-making. Evidence shows that they wielded political authority and economic influence in the pre-colonial era. This was witnessed by their representation in political institutions and at high levels of government. According to Adefolarin and Ekundayo (2014: n.p.), Yoruba women had occupied public offices at the apex and were involved in formal direct participation in political issues via the institution of Iyalode and the Erelu Ogbon, which are high-ranking female titles accorded with respect in political and social settings. They were also involved in the judicial process and played an exclusive role by controlling their own affairs and that of the community as a whole. Although Yoruba women during this period did not have representation and authority in the Yoruba political system equal to that of their counterparts, there was no sex segregation in politics, and gender was not used as the basis of political role differentiation (Babangida, 1987) (in Adefolarin & Ekundayo, 2014). A very good example of this is that of Prince Moremi, who lived in the second half of the 18th century in Ile Ife, situated now in Osun State. A brave woman who allowed herself to be captured as a result of an invasion during the war in order to learn the fighting tactics of her captors and came back to train her people how to fight a war and who later defeated their enemies. This altruistic nature is worth emulating from Moremi of Ile Ife. (Adefolarin & Ekundayo, 2014). Furthermore, "one can say that women in this era were an integral part of the political setup of their communities, although they assumed responsibilities different from their male counterparts; in most cases these responsibilities were complementing that of men" (Olatunde 2010: Afolabi, 2019). There were extensive provisions for women's involvement in the key leadership position within the Yoruba society (Table 26.1).

According to Noah in 1985 (in Adefolarin & Ekundayo, 2014), the first female Oba, Oba Orumpata, who lived in the 16th century was the only known female Oba in Yoruba land. Before her, Yoruba lands were often attacked by the Nupes, and during the war, many of them were taken captives, but when Oba Orumpato was on the throne, she trained her army in such a way that they were able to attack and conquer Nupe.

The coming of colonialism brought strange educational, religious, economic and political influences and also redefined the role and the place of women. Women were affected by the alienation of land experience. As women lost access to and control of land, they became more economically dependent on men. Consequently, this led to an intensified caution of domestic patriarchy, reinforced by colonial social institutions. This could be referred to as the

Table 26.1 Women Titled Chiefs and Their Complementary Roles in the Precolonial Era in Nigeria

	Name	Town or Village	L.G.A	State	Type Rulership	Date
1	Luwo Gbadiaya	Ife	Ife Central L.G.	Osun	Ooni of Ife	Pre-colonial days
2	Iyayun	Oyo	Oyo L.G.	Oyo	Alaafin	Pre-colonial days
3.	Orompoto	Oyo	Oyo L.G.	Oyo	Alaafin	Pre-colonial days
4	Jomijomi	Oyo	Oyo L.G.	Oyo	Alaafin	Pre-colonial days
5	Jepojepo	Oyo	Oyo L.G.	Oyo	Alaafin	Pre-colonial days
6	Queen Amina	Zazzau	Zazzu	Zaria	Emir	Pre-colonial days
7	Daura	Daura	Daura Emirate	Katsina	Queen	Pre-colonial days
8	Kofono	Daura	Daura Emirate	Katsina	Queen	Pre-colonial days
9	Eye-Moin	Akure	Akure	Ondo	Regent/Monarch	Pre-colonial days (1705–1735 AD)
10	Ayo-Ero	Akure	Akure	Ondo	Regent/Monarch	Pre-colonial days (1850–51 AD)
11	Gulfano	Daura	Daura Emirate	Katsina	Queen	Pre-colonial days
12	Yawano	Daura	Daura Emirate	Katsina	Queen	Pre-colonial days
13	Yakania	Daura	Daura Emirate	Katsina	Queen	Pre-colonial days
14	Walsam	Daura	Daura Emirate	Katsina	Queen	Pre-colonial days
15	Cadar	Daura	Daura Emirate	Katsina	Queen	Pre-colonial days
16	Agagri	Daura	Daura Emirate	Katsina	Queen	Pre-colonial days
17	Queen Kanbasa	Bonny	Bonny L.G.	Rivers	Queen	Pre-colonial days

Source: Olasupo (2006). Renaissance of interest in women Traditional Rulers in Nigeria.

beginning of patriarchy. This was reemphasized by Gusim in 2012 (in Isola, 2014:100), who argued further that the colonial economy was an export-oriented one, which seriously undermined the prestige of the traditional occupations of Nigerian women, while, placing women at a great disadvantage. The women began to "experience oppression in its entire ramification. They were formally marginalised in the scheme of things and they seem to have lost power they possessed during the pre-colonial era" (Abdulreheem, 2007 in Isola, 2014:100).

Osun State

Osun State, which was carved out of the old Oyo State on 27 August 1991. It is in Southwest Nigeria. Osun State covers an area of approximately 14,875 square kilometres, lies between longitude 0400E and 0505″ and latitude 05 558″ and 08 o7″, and is bounded by Ogun, Kwara, Oyo and Ondo States in the South, North, West and East, respectively. The statistics on gender participation by state show that out of 244 contestants in Osun State, women's representation in Osun State since 2007 is 50 (20.5 per cent), while that of men is 194 (79.5 per cent) participating in the political machinery (Oladoye, 2011), which indicates that there is still a wide gap between men and women in the Nigerian public life. Lack of empowerment has implications for women's role in maintaining and influencing national development in Nigeria in general and Osun State in particular. Election results in 1999, 2003, 2007, 2011, 2015 and 2019 (Adeogun & Isola, 2022:93–94) in Nigeria showed a consistent pattern of low representation of women in political participation both at the national, state and local government levels. The exclusion and underrepresentation of women in governance is as a result of many obstacles women face due to social disadvantages and, consequently, interlocking layers of gender inequalities rooted in the power structures at all levels of society (Abokede (2008 in Isola, 2014).

According to Scott (1986) (in Abokede, 2008), institutions are gendered; they pass on to generations of gender ideologies and justify structures of exclusion and injustice. Political parties in Osun State exist within the patriarchal social structure, where men dominate and women are subordinates. Therefore, political parties reflect the dominant practice of society and reproduce gender relations of male domination and female subordination. Abokede (2008: 22) quipped in her documented facts that women are not placed on electoral lists because men do not want them to jeopardize their winning ability. The loyalty of women is not certain. Men believe that by nature women are not secretive, i.e., *obinrin o ni gogongo* (women do not have Adam's Apple). Thus, Derbyshire (n.d.) states that women's voices are not considered as their perspectives are often ignored. The socio-cultural context of Osun State shows that it is a patriarchal society with the prevailing gender power relation where men as the head of the family control everything, including decision-making. Patriarchy is a system of male domination that shapes women's relationships in politics. It is the transformation of male and female into men and women, constructing a hierarchy of gender relations where men are privileged and women are discriminated against. (Eisenstein, 1984 (in Abokede, 2008: 25). The patriarchal culture is leading among the factors militating against women's involvement in political activities in Osun State (Isola, 2014).

Some of the socio-cultural factors that militate against women's progress in political participation are as follows:

1 **Cultural norms and gender role socialization**
   Traditions, customs, sexual stereotyping of social roles and other cultural prejudices practised at home (which is the main institution where patriarchy originated from and spread to other institutions) are among the greatest obstacles to women's attainment of equal rights with men and their full participation in societal activities. Culturally, discriminatory practices against women can be said to have started from the mother's womb. For example, there is this strong traditional belief in Yorubaland that when a pregnant woman experiences brief but painful labour, she is going to deliver a male child because male children take their sword and come out without wasting much time, whereas females delay because they have lots of things to take along (spiritually) when coming to the world, hence the delay (Isola, 2014).

   As children grow, there is the separation of roles, giving the male children recognition of their superiority over their female siblings within the society. The female siblings are taught how to be subject to their male counterparts, how to keep their home in order and not be involved in public issues. Those deep-rooted attitudes and practices form the basis of myriads of problems that contribute to the sustenance of inequality between men and women. Unfortunately, Osun State is still a very traditional society, closely in touch with cultural practices dictated by customary rules and norms (Abokede, 2008; Orisadare, 2019).

2 **Patriarchy and religious institutions**
In religious institutions, patriarchy is also visible, as most rules and regulations tend to discriminate against women. According to Adeogun & Isola (2022), most religious institutions do grant support to male domination by overemphasizing the aspect of women's submission to their husbands, making it sound like slavery. Most religious people handle the issue of submission with too much seriousness than the issue of loving a wife to the point of death as commanded by the same Bible and Al-Quran that talked about both. Overemphasized submission automatically deprives women of their rights. It gives room to subordination, slavery and all forms of violence perpetrated against women (Adeogun & Isola, 2010). As it is known that Osun State is popularly dominated by Christians and Muslims together with a few traditional worshippers, the overemphasized submissive role of women by these religions had helped the spread of patriarchy in Osun State. The Roman Catholic Church played a major role in reinforcing and overemphasizing the subordination of women. The main aspects of Catholicism which affect women include a glorification of motherhood and female suffering, personified in the image of the Virgin Mary, and encouragement to accept one's circumstances on earth in preparation for a better life in heaven. The terrorist attacks against girls and women in some Islamic countries and communities can be traced to this issue of overemphasized submission expected from a girl/woman (Adeoye, 2023).

3 **Political institution and patriarchy**
According to Adekanye (2013: 22), patriarchy can also be seen in the political institution, in the context of men totally dominating a state or country and attempts to persuade such dominance through the grooming of male children into men prepared to take total control of the state power and machinery rule, including the armed forces and security agencies, thereby reducing the status of women in political activities. This implies that since women are most often educated, they have no basis for getting involved in politics. Education serves as an eye-opener for women to be active participants in political concerns. This is most often used against women. A very good case is that of Mrs. Patricia Olubunmi Etteh, former Speaker of the House of Representatives and President of the Women's Caucus of the National Assembly. Mrs. Etteh began her political career as a member of the AD but later switched allegiance to the PDP. She represented the Ayedaade/Isokan/Irewole constituency in Osun State and became the Speaker of the House after the 2007 legislative elections. However, Mrs. Etteh only lasted in the position from 5 June to 30 October 2007. She was soon embroiled in a controversy over the lack of due process and good judgement in the award of contracts worth N628 million to renovate her official residence and that of the deputy speaker, Babangida Nguroje, as well as to purchase a fleet of 12 official vehicles for the House of Assembly (Okome in Isola, 2014).

Mrs. Etteh's problems were soon misinterpreted by the majority of the media as due to her lack of a higher education, and her critics missed no opportunity to remind the nation that she was a hairdresser before becoming a politician and thus lacked the finesse and requisite qualities of the position of Speaker. Some also concluded that Etteh's performance was indicative of women's unsuitability for politics, particularly given the feminist's contention that women have better and stronger moral fibre than men. The National

Assembly underwent a turbulent period of conflicts and contestation between the supporters and opponents of Mrs. Etteh. She was eventually supported by her party, but it was a little too late. After many riotous sessions with open brawls that culminated in the death of an Etteh supporter, Aminu Safana, PDP (Kastina), she finally resigned (Abdulraheem, 2010; Okome in Isola, 2014). In other words, by using the weapon of limited formal education, women are automatically deprived of their political rights to participate in politics, even when they have the skill, but when it is time to cast votes, men make necessary and adequate provisions for the so-called illiterate women to cast their votes to put them in power. The patriarchal culture in Osun State hinders women a lot; husbands don't allow their wives to participate publicly, except a few. So even if there are positions to be filled in governance and husbands do not agree to allow the wives to come forward, they cannot come out on their own (Orisadare, 2019).

There is an urgent need for political actors in Nigeria to draw lessons from the achievements of other African countries. Patriarchy can be overturned when senior male political leaders actively promote women's political participation, as has happened in the African countries presented earlier. Nigeria can draw lessons from other African countries and deepen women's political participation. This will go a long way in overcoming patriarchy and harmful sociocultural norms that deny women their rights.

Way Forward

In order to overcome the many challenges and constraints to women's political participation created by patriarchal structure, the following suggestions are proffered:

1. There is a need for the urgent protection of women from patriarchal subordination. This should start in the family by putting an end to gender role socialization in the sense that males and females should learn to give helping hands to one another when it comes to chore sharing at home or in public places like school, the workplace and religious gatherings, among many other places. This will relieve women of some burden of work. This will enhance women's political participation. Also, women should learn to support one another and give constructive criticism when necessary.
2. There is a need for active introduction of quotas and affirmative action. There are different types of quotas; the best option for Nigerians is the quota, which is officially mandatory because, from the findings, there are patriarchal attitudes in political parties and men seem not ready to share power with women. Rai (in Abokede, 2008:46) argues that despite quotas being important in addressing the exclusion of women from the public political sphere, it is not quota in isolation; they can only form one part of a multi-faceted strategy. Gender quotas should operate within the framework of diversity so as to avoid the domination of women by socially and economically privileged groups in political structures. The constitution should be amended to prohibit laws, cultures or traditions that are against the dignity, welfare or interests of women or which undermine their status.
3. There should be the establishment of a gender ministry with a strong mandate to promote gender parity at the grassroots level with women representatives at the national level as well. This can be achieved by having a women-alone ballot, a gender progressive constitution designed by women leaders in government and civil society, and a 30 per cent quota

of women in national government, which can trigger a transformation in leadership for the voice of women to be heard, putting an end to marginalization.

4 Women leaders should build credibility. This will serve as a source of encouragement to other women, thereby gaining women's confidence in women's leadership when it comes to political matters. Also, the National Orientation Agency of Nigeria should collaborate with the religious leaders and traditional rulers, who are the custodians of culture, through mass campaigns to the general public (Abokede, 2008:42).

Conclusion

This chapter reflected on women's political participation and the place of patriarchy in political institutions globally, nationally and locally among the Yorubas, with a main focus on Osun State in Nigeria. From the above discussion, it is clear that women are victims of subordination as a result of chauvinist culture in Africa in general and Osun State in particular. Some of the factors mentioned in this chapter strongly contributed to the experience of patriarchy in political issues. The central argument of this chapter is that patriarchy is indeed a parasite deeply rooted in families. It works against women's political participation, although it can be overcome, as has been demonstrated in the description of the progress that has been made in some African countries.

References

Abdulraheem, M.M. 2010. Rights of women in the pre-colonial, post-colonial era. Prospect and challenges. In S. Oni and S. Joshua (Ed.) *Gender relations in Nigeria's democratic Governance: Journal of Politicis and Governance*, UPL, 14–24.

Abokede, A.F. 2008. The gender agendas: Bargaining with political parties in Osun State, Nigeria. Ph.D. thesis, Erasmus University.

Adefolarin, A and Ekundayo, D. 2014 *Important report on women and political participation in Nigeria in the fourth republic (1999–2014)*. Social Research and Documentation Group Abuja.

Adekanye, A. 2013. Women in key decision making positions in Nigerian government: Comparative study of federal and selected state governments from the South-West, 1992-2012. BSc. Project, Babcock University.

Adeleye, F. 2000. Creating a new world with new visions: African feminism and trends in the global women's movement. Ph.D. thesis. Obafemi Awolowo University.

Adeogun, T and Isola 2022. A democratic governance and women's political participation in Nigeria. in Oni, E., Fagbadebo, O., Yagboyaju, D. (Eds.), *Democratic practice and governance in Nigeria*, Routledge.

Adeogun, T and Isola, A. 2010. "Patriarchy and customary law as major cogs in the wheel of women's peacebuilding in South Sudan". *Journal of Gender Information and Development Africa*, 5, 53–55.

Adeoye, A (2023). *Contemporary issues on governance, Conflict and Security in Africa*. Palgrave Macmillian.

Adereti, A. F. 2003. 'Comparative analysis of women's political participation in Southwestern Nigeria under three democratic regimes.' Ph.D. thesis, Obafemi Awolowo University.

Afolabi, C. M. 2019. The invisibility of women's organizations in decision making processes in Africa and its implications. https://www.frontiersin.org/research-topics/6474/the-invisibility-of-womens-organizations-in-decision-making-processes-in-africa-and-its-implications---volume-i

Ajayi, K. 2007. Gender self-endangering: The sexist issue in Nigerian politics. *Journal of Social Science*, 14, 137–147

Akinyode-Afolabi, A and Salami, T. 2003. 'Democracy governance in gender audit 2003 election and issues in women's political participation in Nigeria Lagos, Women Advocate Research and Documentation Centre (WARDC).' www.boellnigeria.org/web/112-223.html.28

Aldehaib A (ed) 2010. 'Sudan's comprehensive peace agreement viewed through the eyes of the women of South Sudan.' Fellows programme occasional chapter 3.

Ali, N. 2010, 'Gender and State building in South Sudan.' United States institute of Peace, special Report 298, 2301 constitution Ave. www.usip.org

Arowolo, A. and F. Aluko, 2010. 'Women and political participation in Nigeria.' *European Journal of Social Sciences*, 4, 28–40.

Babangida K. 1987. Opening Address Presented at the Workshop on Better Life for Normal Women Half at Abuja on 14th and 15th September.

Bhasin, K. 2006. *What is Patriarchy?* Women Unlimited: New Delhi.

Brukutwa, G. 2014. Gender equality is not a western notion. https://imaginingequalityglobafunctionforwomen.org/

Chukwuemaka, D. and Eze, S. 2011. Democratization and women's political space in Nigeria: A critical appraisal. *Journal of Public Administration and Governance* 1(1), 13–27.

Cole, S. 2011. *Increasing women's political participation in Liberia: "Challenges and Potential"*. Syracuse University.

Derbyshire, G. n.d. "Gender manual: A practical guide for development policy makers and practitioners': Social development division (DFID) in A. F Abokede, 2008. The gender agendas: Bargaining with political parties in Osun State, Nigeria. Unpublished thesis, Erasmus University, pp. 24–37.

Dore, D. and Molyneux, M. 2002. Histories of gender and the state in Latin America. *Social History*, 27, 45–57.

Eisenstein, G. H. 2008. "Contemporary Feminist Thought" in A. F Abokede, A. F. The gender agendas: Bargaining with political parties in Osun State, Nigeria. Ph.D., thesis, Erasmus University, pp. 20–50.

Enemuo, G. 2015. 'Gender and women empowerment' in R. Anifowoshe and F. Enemuo (Eds.), *Elements of politics*. Lagos: Malt house Press Ltd.

Falola, T and Jacquemin, C (2022). *Identity Transformation and Political in Africa*. Rowman & littlefield.

Fatile, J. O., Adepoju, A., Chineye, E and Ayeni, L. 2017. Women participation in Local governance and Nigeria Democratic System. A study of selected local government in Lagos. (1999-2016). *International Journal of Advanced Studies in Business Strategies and Management*, 5(1). 52–86.

Gogineni, R. 2010. *Rwandan Parliament's Female Majority Focuses on Equality*, www.unwomen.org

Gusim, T. 2012. Empowering women can change everything. www.careforming.org

Igbokwe, I. 2013. Contextualizing gender based violence within patriarchy in Nigeria. www.pambazula.org/gender-minorities/contextualizing-gender-based-violence-within-patriarchy-in-nigeria

IPU 2019. Inter-Parliamentary Union. www.ipu.org/wmn-e/classif.htm

IPU 2023. Inter-Parliamentary Union. www.ipu.org/wmn-e/classif.htm

Isola, A 2014: Women Political participation and Grassroot Democratic Sustainability in Osun State. Unpublished Thesis. Babcock University.

Makama, G.A. 2013. Patriarchy and gender inequality in Nigeria. The way forward. *European Scientific Journal*, 9, 17–23.

Molyneux, M. 2002. Gender and the silences of social capital: Lessons from Latin America. *Development and Change*, 33(2), 167–188.

Mutamba, J. 2005. Case study: Strategies for increasing women's participation in Government. www.un.org/africa/osaa/reports/Democratic%20Governance%20Case%20study%20RWANDA.pdf

Ndlovu, S. and Mutale, S. B. 2002. Emerging trends in Women's participation in politics in Africa. *American International Journal of Contemporary Research*, 3, 11–23.

Nwankwor, C. and Nkereuwem, E. 2019. Nigeria Score card on women participation in Nigeria 2019 election. *Premium Times*. 25 February, 2019.

Ogunlade, A. 2012. Nigerian Women and Democratic Process. *The Nation*. 30 January, 2012, p. 4.

Okome, M.O. 2013. *Women political participation in Nigeria:2007 General elections*. OLUBEN Printers.

Olasupo, S. (2006). Renaissance of interest in women Traditional Rulers in Nigeria. UPL Press

Olatunde, D. 2010. Women's political participation and representation in Nigeria's politics in the last decade. Ph.D. thesis, University of the Witwatersrand.

Olutayo, M. 2001. Gender and Public Office-Holders Perception of Political Recruitment in Oyo State, Nigeria. MSc. dissertation, University of Ibadan.

Omoniyi, M, 2012. Counseling for 21st Century. Political challenges in achieving Nigeria's vision 2020. *European Scientific Journal*, 8(4), 10.

Orisadare, M.A. 2019. An assessment of the role of women group in women political participation and economic development in Nigeria. https://www.frontiersin.org/articles/10.3389/fsoc.2019.00052/full

Rai, M. 2005. *Equal participation of women and men in decision making process with particular emphasis on political participation and leadership*. Addis Ababa.

Scott, J.W. 1986. Gender: A useful category of historical analysis. *American Historical Review*, 91, 1053–1075.

Sirleaf-Johnson, E.J. 2010. African women political participation: Lecture by H. E. Ellen Johnson Sirleaf President of the Republic of Liberia. www.awdf.or

Sultana, A. 2011. Patriarchy and Women's subordination: A theoretical analysis. *Arts Faculty Journal*, 9, 56–74.

Thedailybeast.n.d.www.thedailybeast.com/article/2014/04/02/twodecades/aftergenocide/Rwanda/women-have-made-the-nation-thrieve

Udegbe, A. 1998. *Gender and leadership images and reality*. Vantage Publishers. Parline: the IPU's Open Data Platform

27
YOUNG PROFESSIONAL WOMEN'S PERFORMATIVE AGENCY IN CHALLENGING MEDIA (MIS) REPRESENTATIONS OF WOMEN IN POLITICS

The Case of Zimbabwe

Kuziwakwashe Zigomo

Introduction

Women's under-representation in politics continues to be a challenge, not only in Africa but the world at large. Whilst many scholars engaging with engaging with this phenomenon from different angles, in this chapter I focus on the media's role in the under-representation of women and the opportunities this presents for widening women's political participation and representation, particularly during electoral processes.

Numerous studies have highlighted how unbalanced and biased reporting in the media of women in politics has contributed to their under- (and mis)-representation (Van der Pas & Aaldering 2020, Media Monitoring Project Zimbabwe 2012, Hawkins et al. 2023 and Harmer 2021). This negative reporting has fed into stereotypical representations of women in politics as being 'loose' and immoral, or docile and subservient. The unbalanced reporting on women has also contributed to the limited visibility of women in politics as compared to that of their male counterparts.

Over previous decades, however, social media has increasingly become an interactive political communication tool used by women in politics, mostly young women, to enhance their visibility and interact with their constituents. Yet questions still arise about the effectiveness of social media as a political communication tool and its ability to enhance women's participation and representation in politics. In looking at the case of Zimbabwe, this chapter will show that whilst social media has significantly enhanced women's visibility and participation in politics, its impact on women's representation is less clear.

The chapter argues that whilst social media can work well as a part of a larger and robust campaign strategy for women affiliated with larger political parties, on its own it can be a misleading tool with which to gauge the efficacy of women's campaign strategies and reach particularly, during election periods. Thus, it is a more beneficial campaigning tool for women affiliated with larger political parties than those who are not. Overall, this chapter will show that whilst social media has enhanced women's agency by increasing their visibility and participation in politics, more still needs to be done. Most notably, it has provided women a platform where they can subvert patriarchal discourses to do with conventional gender norms and expectations, which seek to limit their participation by constructing their own representations of themselves which embody both feminine and masculine traits to enhance their participation. However, in as much as social media has provided women with such opportunities, there are also limits to this agency which restrict women's full participation, as demonstrated by cyberbullying and violence against women, as well as the widening gap between those women who have access to digital media platforms and those who do not.

The chapter draws on ethnographic material collected over the 2018 and 2023 elections in Zimbabwe, consisting of a wide range of data collection methods such as participant observation both off and online at political rallies, campaign trails, and political events; elite interviews with women in politics, as well as political analysts and women's civil society organisations (CSOs); and focus groups with the political party supporters and members of the Zimbabwean electorate. The chapter draws on Judith Butler's influential ideas on gender performativity and agency as well as postcolonial feminist theory, mainly Spivak and Mohanty.

Methodology

Theoretical Framework: Butler's Performative Agency & Postcolonial Feminist Critiques

Butler's influential ideas to do with gender performativity and agency have gained much traction in feminist scholarship globally (Akurugu 2021). Butler conceptualises gender 'not as an expression of what one is but as something that one does', which therefore makes it distinct from one's biological sex (Lloyd 1998: 125, Butler 1988, 1999 and 2009). When gender is conceptualised in this way, it is a social construct based on shared meanings and understandings in a given society in relation to what are prescribed as acceptable standards of masculine and feminine traits, attributes, characteristics and behaviours. It is the constitutive acts carried out by members within a given society repeatedly that lend legitimacy to these binary categorisations of what it means to be male and female based on socially acceptable and agreed norms of masculinity and femininity. When one deviates from these norms by 'doing' or 'performing' gender differently outside of these prescribed social norms and expectations, one is sanctioned by their society. Hence, societal gender norms and expectations police the behaviours of the individuals who make up membership in a given society and thus become 'signifiers' or societal markers of what type of behaviour is acceptable and what is not. Failure to comply with traditional or conventional gender expectations and norms (masculine and feminine attributes) in a society results in one being punished or sanctioned (Butler 1988: 522).

Whilst much feminist scholarly focus has been on transgender communities in this regard, here I focus on female subjects, mainly women in politics, who transgress or subvert traditional or conventional, and we may add patriarchal gender norms and expectations in their societies by either challenging them or not conforming to them, i.e., by exhibiting or performing both feminine and masculine traits or attributes. This, for me, is an important area where women exercise their agency, particularly in arenas or spaces which are hostile to them and which seek to exclude them.

It is important to state that although Butler highlights theatrical performances in her approach, here I employ this theory within the domain of politics, which is arguably an interesting site where performances are enacted by those who are vying for positions of power in political office, whether male or female. In this vein, social media has increasingly become a virtual political space where we can observe the performances of women in politics, particularly during campaign periods. We can also observe these performances at campaign rallies and political events, many of which are now broadcasted both offline and online. Political spaces, both offline and online, are also spaces where we can observe discourses to do with expectations of gender norms and expectations as well as how these are sanctioned in a given society by observing how female candidates and politicians interact with their constituents.

Before concluding this section, it is important to consider whether there are any limits to Butler's notion of performative agency, especially when we consider women of colour in the global South. Postcolonial feminist critiques highlight the politics of difference, for instance, in highlighting how women's experiences of oppression in the global South differ from those of their Western counterparts (women in the global North). This has widely been epitomised in the North–South divide and has been referred to as 'double patriarchy' or 'two colonialisms' by postcolonial feminist scholars like Chandra Mohanty, Joyce Chadya, and Elizabeth Schmidt (Mohanty 1984, Chadya 2003 and Schmidt 1994). In considering limits to the agency, in this case, political agency, we are further challenged by other postcolonial feminist scholars like Spivak (1988) to consider how the experiences of more privileged women in the global South not only differ from their Western and European counterparts in the West but also differ from their less privileged counterparts in the global South. This highlights what we have come to know as the rural–urban divide, and it is at this intersectional juncture where we are forced to reckon with the multiple aspects of women's identities in the global South that make their experiences of oppression varied and distinct. These are factors which Western intersectional feminists highlight, such as gender, race and class. Elsewhere, I have argued that other intersectional factors such as age, class, marital status and party identification have proven to be more salient in erecting varied and distinct barriers for women in getting elected in the global South, particularly in postcolonial African states like Zimbabwe. Thus, the wide and growing scholarship on intersectionality, which originated in the global North to highlight the intersectional axes of discrimination for women of colour, needs to go beyond the factors of gender, race and class when considering women of colour in the global South (Zigomo 2022: 527). Overall, when we apply Butler's notion of performative agency to the wide and varied experiences of women of colour in the global South, we may well ask whether there are limits to the agency that is epitomised here. Further questions we might ask here are: agency by whom and for whom? Can women in the global South exercise as much political agency as their female counterparts in the global North? Or can this agency be hampered by global inequalities and racial hierarchies between richer and poorer states? Further to this, can low-profile women in politics exercise the same measure of agency as their high-profile counterparts?

Political spaces, whether offline or online, are platforms where gender performativity takes place, enhancing the participation and visibility of certain women in politics by enabling them to subvert patriarchal discourses which seek to exclude them from the realm of politics, yet these are simultaneously platforms which also exclude other women who either have limited or no access to these platforms. Those who have limited or no access to these platforms have other, more privileged women speak *for* them and purport to understand or represent their needs. Thus, making the realm of politics elite platforms which regulate who can be included and who is not. Consequently, a postcolonial feminist lens brings to light the reality within which agency can be expressed in the realm of politics by highlighting the aspect of global inequalities between the North and the South, as well as wealth disparities within states between the rural and the urban, or the urban rich and the urban poor. However, it is still important to point out that within this prevailing context comprising the plight of women of colour in postcolonial African states, which is characterised by 'two colonialisms' and 'double patriarchy', gendered power relations are continuously shifting, fluid, and dynamic, thus presenting hidden spaces where women are able to express their agency, and these will be highlighted in this chapter.

Data Collection and Methods of Analysis

In considering the gender performativity of young Zimbabwean women in politics, the questions I seek to address are: *How are young professional women in Zimbabwean politics representing themselves on and offline during electoral periods?* And *how do these women in politics both challenge and reinforce gendered stereotypes through their representations of self and their performances of femininity both online and offline?* The data collection for this chapter employed a number of methods. Both online and offline ethnographies of women in politics were conducted. Online via the monitoring of their social media accounts on platforms such as X (formerly Twitter) and Facebook and offline in attendance at campaign rallies, campaign trails, and political events. As this study employs an interpretivist epistemological framework, the worldview of my research participants, who are mainly women in politics (by this I mean women politicians) or are aspiring to be in politics (by this I mean women candidates), was central to my focus. My aim was, therefore, to understand how these women understood themselves and their role in politics. To this end, their performances became paramount to me, including how they referred to themselves, how they presented themselves publicly, their dressing, the words, phrases and metaphors they would use in referring to themselves and what they believed their role in politics was, their entrances into public gatherings and how they positioned themselves in the public eye. Thus, attention was paid to the images they posted (and re-posted) of themselves on their social media accounts, the political messages and public statements they would send to their audiences, and their interactions with their audiences. I further observed them at political events which profiled women candidates both online and offline and paid attention to the coverage they received in the press as well as the language that was used to refer to them. Further to this, I conducted interviews with aspiring women candidates and women politicians, both older and younger, as this allowed me to see the possible variations in their views and experiences. The older age group was within the age bracket of 40 and above, whilst the younger was in the age bracket of 18–39 years. Women across a range of political parties were interviewed; the main groups being the main parties: Zanu PF and the main opposition party, the MDC, now turned CCC, as well as smaller, less established political parties and independents. The women also ranged in terms of their demographics and constituencies in that I made sure to include women of differing marital status: single, divorced and married, as well as women of different professions and who were campaigning in different constituencies mainly in Harare (Harare West, North and East). I further conducted focus groups with some of their supporters of various ages and backgrounds. These data were collected over two election periods in 2018 and 2023. My main method of analysis was an interpretivist discourse analysis, which was conducted on interview and focus group transcripts, news chapter and media coverage, as well as ethnographic field notes.

Setting the Context: Political Discourse on Women in Zimbabwean Politics

Zimbabwe is an interesting case to explore in this chapter because despite it being an authoritarian state, it has boasted of high levels of women's representation in politics, most notably in 2013, when over a third of its Parliament was recorded as being female (UN Women 2013). This made Zimbabwe one of the few African countries in Africa alongside Rwanda, South Africa and Namibia to boast of relatively high levels of women's representation. In that same year, the country also introduced its Proportional Representation (PR) Parliamentary System, which consisted of the provision of an additional 60 seats for women, raising the total number of parliamentary seats from 210 to 270. Women thus occupied 124 out of the 350 parliamentary seats, including 86 in the National Assembly, 60 in the reserved seats, and 26 directly elected in the 210 constituency seats (UN Women 2013). The country has also noted quite generous quota allowances for women in the main political parties, Zanu PF and the Movement for Democratic Change (MDC), now turned Citizens Coalition for Change (CCC).

Yet despite these gains, the dominant political discourse on Zimbabwean women in politics has tended to pit women into two binary categories: being either labelled as 'prostitutes and witches' when they fail to conform to traditional gender norms and expectations or being labelled as 'good wives and mothers' when they do conform to gender expectations. Both categories are limiting for women, as the 'women as prostitutes or witches' frame is a way of sanctioning women who challenge male hegemony or authority and who don't conform to traditional gender roles. One notable example of this is Priscilla Misihairabwi-Mushonga, a self-proclaimed feminist and prominent member of the main opposition, the MDC-T in Zimbabwe, Zimbabwe's ambassador to Sweden at the time of writing (Tshili 2021). Misihairabwi-Mushonga has often challenged gender expectations and norms by encouraging women to compete with men for positions of power and by also encouraging women to protest and support other women in politics, even by unorthodox means through such initiatives like her 'pantyless campaign' (New Zimbabwe 2018). Another example is that of Thokozani Khupe of the main opposition party, who was labelled as a prostitute (colloquially referred to as '*hure*') when she challenged Nelson Chamisa's unconstitutional rise to power in the party after Morgan Tsvangirai's death (AFP 2020). Joice Mujuru was also labelled as 'a loose woman who wears short skirts' and 'a witch' when she challenged Emmerson Mnangagwa's rise to power in the ruling Zanu PF party and became a rival to the former First Lady of Zimbabwe, Grace Mugabe (Thompson 2018 and Mudiwa 2020). Mnangagwa was, at the time, the former Vice President and right-hand man to Robert Mugabe and was installed as Zimbabwe's second president, thus succeeding Mugabe after a military coup which took place in November 2017.

Women who are pitted into the second category of being labelled as 'good wives and mothers' by conforming to gender norms and expectations are hailed for their maternal attributes. This has perhaps been most visible in the prevalent discourse on politicians' wives, mainly the First Ladies, who are often hailed as 'Mothers of the Nation'. Since its independence, Zimbabwe has had three First Ladies – Sally Mugabe, Grace Mugabe and Auxillia Mnangagwa – all of whom were praised for their maternal attributes. All three women exhibited themselves as nurturers and caregivers by establishing their own orphanages. As long as these women play their maternal roles well and do not transgress into the more masculine roles in leadership, they retain some measure of legitimacy; however, should they become overly ambitious in seeking to advance to higher leadership positions, they quickly lose this legitimacy. Ambition is often described as a masculine attribute, and when a woman exhibits this attribute, she is perceived as coming out of her feminine and taking on more masculine attributes, which can be distasteful to the public. Grace Mugabe received much backlash for being ambitious in trying to ascend to the position of Vice President of the ruling party. Her ascension was quickly thwarted when it became evident that moves were being made to make her Zimbabwe's first female president succeeding her husband, resulting in the military coup of November 2017 (Southall 2017: 82). The takeaway here is that when women diligently play their role in being Mothers of the Nation without venturing into the masculine aspects of leadership by seeking to advance themselves to the top levels of leadership reserved for men or by challenging male headship, they are praised for it, yet are never taken seriously in politics. When they do try to ascend, however, or venture into the more masculine roles, they are sanctioned for it by being labelled as deviant, uncontrollable or dangerous women who seek to usurp their husband's authority, much like Grace Mugabe was.

Other women in party structures who conform to gender norms and expectations are often relegated to the women's wings of their party structures, often carrying out administrative tasks and having limited decision-making power or capacity. These women are perceived as being docile and subordinate and are often not taken seriously in politics. Many of the women appointed through the proportional representation system which came into effect in 2013, are appointed by their parties consisting of predominantly male leadership. These women are labelled as '*bakhosi*' (meaning they are ridiculed for having been given their seats 'for free' or out of charity but not on the basis of having earned these on merit). Hence, they are not taken seriously in Parliament as they are not representing any constituencies.[1] This, in turn, creates a type of hierarchy amongst women in Parliament where it is the women who have been voted in by their constituencies who are accorded more respect in Parliament because they are understood to be representing their constituencies, whilst the women who do not have constituencies they represent are not deemed as powerful. These women, who are appointed through the PR system, are also perceived as being pawns in a male agenda and not necessarily representative of advancing the empowerment of other women. Whilst the PR system has been extended for another ten years,[2] it seems to have had adverse effects on increasing women's representation in politics, as many of the women who are appointed via this system have not managed to use it as a springboard to go on and compete for constituencies but have instead remained in those seats, often hindering the advancement of younger women who seek to advance in the party structures.

Against this backdrop, women's limited visibility in politics continues to be a challenge. Men get more media coverage, whilst the limited coverage of women in politics is composed of biased and negative reporting detailing scandals in their personal lives, misogynistic statements about their physical appearance and so on. Offline, other aspects hamper their visibility, particularly when campaigning for elections, in that it is hard for them to campaign because of limited financial resources, hikes in nomination fees and patriarchal norms in their parties where male candidates are often preferred and put forward as candidates over female candidates, particularly in the primaries. In response to these challenges, women are exercising their agency by increasingly turning to social media to enhance their visibility in politics.

Social media is now a powerful political communication tool for women but also a strategic campaigning tool and has been most evident over Zimbabwe's last two elections, to which this chapter now turns its focus.

Analysis and Discussion

A Tale of Two Elections (2018 and 2023)

In this section, I will endeavour to provide an analysis of the campaign strategies female candidates and politicians used in the 2018 and 2023 elections, respectively. As mentioned before, social media is increasingly being used as a strategic campaigning tool for political communication by female candidates, as they use this platform to not only promote themselves, send political messages and interact with their constituents, but it is also a platform from which we can observe their performances of femininity, or masculinity, in the public sphere of politics and read into the inferred meanings of these performances within their given context.

Gender studies scholars have argued that electoral contexts are inherently gendered and that these gendered contexts shape candidates' campaign strategies (Bauer & Santia 2023). Taking Butler's approach, if gender is something which can be performed or 'put on' and not something which is innate or inherent to human nature, then it is natural to assume that political candidates, whether male or female, can 'put on' either masculine or feminine traits or attributes to appeal to their constituents depending on the electoral environment and context. A recent study conducted in the US revealed that in masculine electoral contexts, female candidates adopted more feminine traits or characteristics to appeal to the electorate, whilst in feminine electoral contexts they did not necessarily adopt more feminine traits (Bauer & Santia 2023: 329). However, in Zimbabwe, particularly over the past two previous elections, I find the opposite to be true.

In 2018, the electoral environment proved to be more optimistic for women in that a larger number of female presidential candidates were running for office and even larger numbers at Parliamentary and Local Council levels as compared to 2023[3] (see Table 27.1 and 27.2 below).

Table 27.1 Numbers of Female Political Candidates Who Contested for Local Council by Province (2018 and 2023)

Province	Year (2018)	Year (2023)
Bulawayo	113	62
Harare	143	88
Manicaland	145	96
Mashonaland Central	59	45
Mashonaland East	85	54
Mashonaland West	134	87
Masvingo	85	70
Matebeleland North	125	67
Matebeleland South	100	79
Midlands	154	87
Total:	**1143**	**735**

Adapted from Zimbabwe Electoral Commission(ZEC) verified 2018 and 2023 nomination lists (sources: https://www.zec.org.zw/download/combined-local-authority-results-2018/ and https://www.zec.org.zw/download/nomination-court-results/)

Table 27.2 Numbers of Female Political Candidates Who Contested for National Assembly by Province (2018 and 2023)

Province	Year (2018)	Year (2023)
Bulawayo	38	16
Harare	81	14
Manicaland	22	4
Mashonaland Central	11	1
Mashonaland East	16	6
Mashonaland West	18	8
Masvingo	11	4
Matebeleland North	13	8
Matebeleland South	16	2
Midlands	17	6
Total:	**243**	**69**

Adapted from ZEC verified 2018 and 2023 nomination lists (sources: https://www.zec.org.zw/download/combined-verified-national-assembly-results-2018/ and https://nehandaradio.com/wp-content/uploads/2023/06/Government-Gazette-Extraordinary-Vol.-64-30-06-2023-Electoral-Act-final.pdf)

In the 2018 election, there was also a sizeable number of women running as independents, both at the Parliamentary and Local Council levels, which in itself was unprecedented, as the last female to have contested as an independent in Zimbabwean elections, historically, was Margaret Dongo in the 1990s.

Whilst the numbers of female across the board were notably higher in the 2018 election, they were still significantly lower when compared to their male counterparts (see Figure 27.1. below;[4] Table 27.2. above).

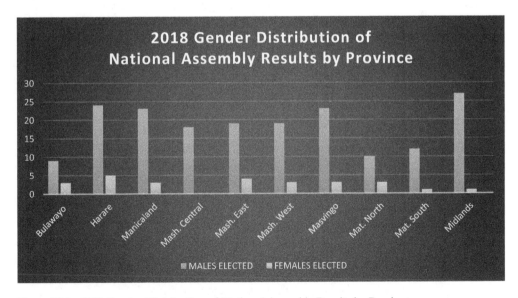

Figure 27.1 2018 Gender Distribution of National Assembly Results by Province

Figure 27.2 2023 Gender Distribution of National Assembly Results by Province

The gender gap became even wider in the 2023 election, with even lower numbers of women contesting for seats (see Figure 27.2[5]). The only exception here is Mashonaland Central, with no females elected in both the 2018 and 2023 elections.

Whilst the 2018 electoral environment was considerably more open and optimistic to the inclusion of women candidates, with more women opting to run, as facilitated by the accessible nomination fees, multiple parties running, a largely female electorate[6] and a new seemingly democratic dispensation in Zimbabwe after the military coup of November 2017, it was still arguably masculine in that women were still significantly under-represented and did considerably worse than their male counterparts across the board. However, when we compare this to the 2023 electoral environment, where significant hikes in nomination fees,[7] limited resources for female candidates to campaign, and even fewer females making it through the primaries in their respective parties, the electoral environment was even more constraining for women and thus arguably even more masculine. This resulted in what we could consider a 'softer' masculine environment, which was more accommodating of women in 2018, as opposed to a 'harder' or 'tougher' masculine environment, which was less accommodating of women in 2023. This was further exemplified by the only female presidential candidate, Elizabeth Valerio, only being permitted to contest after a struggle at the nomination court, proving the environment had become even more hostile to women (The Herald 2023).

The qualitative data presented in this section will show that whilst women adopted more feminine traits and attributes in the 2018 electoral environment, these strategies shifted to more masculine traits and attributes in the 2023 electoral environment, mainly to ensure their survival in an increasingly hostile environment.

Let us begin by looking at the feminine characteristics adopted by female candidates in the 2018 electoral environment. These fit into the 'good wives and mothers' theme, which has been evident in Zimbabwean politics for decades since independence. However, women played this card strategically in their campaigns, as illustrated below.

Maternal 'Motherly' Attributes

These quotes in this section are taken from previous research on female candidates, which is in Zigomo's publication entitled 'Virtue, Motherhood & Femininity: Women's Political Legitimacy in Zimbabwe' (Zigomo 2022: 542 and 543). The first is from a ZESN event for women's presidential candidates in Harare, which took place weeks before the election, on 5 July 2018, where one of the female presidential candidates, Violet Mariyacha, introduced herself in this way;

> Good evening ladies and gentlemen. I'm Violet Mariyacha, *a mother*, politician, human rights activist, businesswoman, songwriter, singer and author. I am running as a presidential candidate for the United Democracy Movement because, *as a mother*, I saw that Zimbabwe needs help like that of *a mother*. The economy [sic] situation as it is, is so bad and Zimbabwe needs healing and *a mum* can do that. Thank you.

The second is Kudzai Mubaiwa, a female political candidate and businesswoman who contested as an independent for the Parliamentary level in Harare Central. Mubaiwa, who is also a mother and wife, stated part of her campaign strategy on her social media Twitter account:

> *I was very deliberate on things like Mothers' Day*. I put in a picture with my little daughter, I've got a little baby, I was carrying her to give a matronly feel and I said 'Happy Mothers' Day to all of the women who have little kids' and what not. And that was one of the posts that was engaged [with] the most on social media and it was by men and women, 'mother we are with you' and what not…I saw some really disastrous candidates, who are male and married, winning in places where some young brilliant single women would have done a fairly better job.

In the first quote, whilst Mariyacha identifies her multiple identities, the most salient one highlighted here is that she is 'a mother' and she hones in on this one characteristic repeatedly to make this stick in the mind of the audience. Whilst this conforms to more conventional gender norms and expectations, this is also strategic, as drawing on the maternal attributes of being a nurturer and caregiver is, in this context, symbolic of the liberation struggle where women carried out the nursing tasks in looking after the wounded soldiers. These more feminine attributes are highlighted to appeal to voters at this event.

Mubaiwa is also intentional and strategic in her deployment of the term 'mother' and in presenting herself as a motherly figure to her audience on her social media account. In doing so, she invokes and appeals to the softer side of the electorate and demonstrates that she has maternal attributes. Again, this fits into very conventional ideas about gender norms and expectations, but it is done strategically so as not to repel the audience but to fit into their stereotype of what a woman should be and ought to be whilst still being capable of running for office. We can see how she later makes the distinction between irresponsible married male candidates who won in some constituencies over highly capable single women, demonstrating that she understands there was an advantage of being married and male in this election over being single and female. Single and divorced women were judged more harshly in this election and deemed incapable of running for office.[8] Thus, being married can be an advantage as it can give one a measure of respectability; however, it still does not denote equality with one's male counterparts, for one can easily be dismissed as a married woman who should be at home looking after her family rather than contesting for political office in the public sphere. So, this becomes a double-edged sword for married female candidates like Mubaiwa.

Wifely or Homely Attributes

In an interview I had with a young single female candidate who contested as an independent in 2018, Linda K Sibanda, she stated:

> I was supposed to run in 2023 and there were certain things that I needed to fix to run in 2023 which was *to get married, have a child*, at least, to boost my profile because most voters don't relate to me. They don't relate to young single educated [women]....It was at the back of my mind, then it became true that 'you are actually not relatable' unless you join a party then you can sneak in like that. But as yourself (here she is referring to herself as a young single and educated woman), no. And there is data to support that young single women...are not the constituents' favourite because as a politician you sometimes have to be picture perfect. So what people don't have or what people aspire to be- show them that...At that time (referring to the time she campaigned in 2017 and 2018) *I was in an intentionally public relationship*, because I couldn't deal with those other aspects. It worked out to my advantage because I didn't get that label (here she is referring to the label of women in politics particularly single women as 'prostitutes' colloquially termed as '*mahure*').
>
> [Linda. K. Sibanda. Independent Candidate. Harare East Constituency. Interview. Harare. July 2023]

Sibanda highlights that part of her campaign strategy was to demonstrate that she was in a serious relationship, which served her well with her younger constituents, but did state later on that not actually being married proved less advantageous for her when relating with her older constituents who felt she would not be able to relate to their concerns as a young single educated woman. This demonstrates that young, single, female candidates like Sibanda are sanctioned by their (mostly older) constituents for not conforming to gender norms and expectations of being a wife and a mother. However, there is an exception to this, which Sibanda highlights in her statement, in that for the constituency to overlook this 'shortfall' (one being female and single), the candidate would need to be contesting within an established political party.

This brings another dimension to this discussion which is important, namely, the credibility that a larger, more established political party gives to women candidates like Sibanda who do not conform to traditional or conventional gender norms and expectations. This was further confirmed in the election results in 2018 where women who were running as independent candidates across the city of Harare, whether married or unmarried, came in third and lost to their counterparts who were running in either of the bigger, more established parties, these being the ruling Zanu PF party and the main opposition party, the MDC, now turned CCC (ZEC 2023). In the next section, we will see that the women who did run in the more established political parties did win, mainly for that reason. And whilst the party ticket proved useful for women in being elected to political office, they did still employ a robust social media strategy, and the notable shift here was one from exhibiting more feminine traits, as we saw in 2018, to exhibiting more masculine traits to adapt to a harsher and tougher electoral environment.

With even fewer women contesting in the 2023 elections than there were in 2018, there was a notable shift to female candidates and politicians exhibiting more masculine attributes and traits in the much more hostile 2023 electoral environment. However, what is worth noting here is that whilst the feminine traits do not completely disappear, we do see masculine attributes becoming more salient or prominent.

'Iron Lady' or 'Strong Woman' Attributes

The first observation to note here is that the fewer ladies who did run in the more established parties, such as the CCC, did make a concerted effort on their social media platforms to refer to themselves as 'strong women' or 'iron ladies'. One notable example of this is the then CCC spokeswoman, Fadzayi Mahere, an advocate by profession and political candidate for Harare Mount Pleasant Constituency. On her Twitter page, where the spokeswoman has a large following of over 600,000 followers, Mahere refers to herself in her profile as 'Zim Iron Lady'. The media subsequently referred to Mahere as the 'Iron Lady' of the main opposition, a term previously attributed to Priscilla Chigumba, the Chairperson of the Zimbabwe Electoral Commission, who was referred to as the 'Iron Lady of Zimbabwean Elections' (Pongo 2023 and Chihota 2018). Another example is a prominent CCC candidate for Sunningdale Constituency, Maureen Kademaunga, who also referred to herself during her campaign as a 'fighter', indicating the masculine attribute of strength in her positioning herself as a 'strong woman'. A pinned post on her Twitter page throughout her campaign with Kademuanga dressed in an elaborate head-wrap and a fur coat has the following caption inscribed:

> I am a girl from a typical working class family, and I represent a tradition that means a lot to me which has always been about *fighting for others*- for oppressed people. It's a tradition I take very seriously. I fight; some days with a fierce fury and some days with a quiet smile.

Whilst these 'strong woman' and 'iron lady' attributes may seem symbolic of Margaret Thatcher at her prime in British politics, they have a deeper resonance in this context when considering Mbuya Nehanda, a prominent historical female figure and freedom fighter who waged the first Chimurenga War against colonial rule in the 1890s to liberate black people from colonial oppression and whose statue was recently erected in Harare's central business district in 2021 (Gershon 2021). According to Zvingowanisei (2023: 72), Nehanda belonged to the Chihera line of traditional Shona cultural ancestry, where women have historically occupied positions of leadership and influence in both the socio-cultural and religio-political spheres of Zimbabwean society. Scholarly works on the radical feminist construct of Chihera by African scholars reveal how Shona women from this ancestral line have historically and continue to traverse, disrupt and subvert patriarchy in Zimbabwean society by exhibiting the attributes of fearlessness, assertiveness, strength and independence (Chitando et al. 2023: 3).

This being said, whilst young female candidates in established parties like Mahere and Kademaunga, who later won the election, did exhibit these masculine traits, other female candidates in less established parties like Elizabeth Valerio, who ran for a presidential seat, still had a maternal motherly figure feel to her ten-day road rally campaign in the lead-up to the election, as her constituents widely referred to her as 'Mother of the Nation'. Valerio, however, lost mainly due to her decision to contest as an independent or under a less-known party.

'Heroic', 'Brave' and 'Courageous' Attributes

Other observable masculine attributes like bravery and courage were also displayed by female candidates running in the established parties as part of their social media campaigns.

One example is Joanna Mamombe, a young female biologist by profession, who ran for a second term for a Parliament seat representing Harare West Constituency. Mamombe was hailed by her followers for her bravery after having previously been abducted by suspected state agents along with her colleagues, Cecillia Chimbiri and Netsai Marova, in May 2020 and surviving this ordeal (Amnesty International 2020). Images and video clips circulated online as to the wounds Joanna and her colleagues incurred, with them lying on hospital beds receiving medical care after escaping their captors. Mamombe was considered brave for not only having survived the ordeal but also for standing up for herself in refusing to go with a state agent into remand whilst still receiving medical care in the hospital.

Fadzayi Mahere also posted a tweet during her campaign on 10 August 2023, of one of her constituents commending her for her bravery. The caption read 'I'm voting for Mahere because we need someone who *fights for our rights*. As an activist and advocate she knows our rights and will stand up for them'. Another constituent posted on the account made the comment, 'I'm supporting Mahere because she has a track record of *bravery* and integrity. She represents the New Zimbabwe we all need'.

The final example of this bravery being exhibited by female politicians is that of Gladys Hlatshwayo, the CCC Secretary for Foreign Affairs, whilst at a press conference, which took place at Sapes Trust just after the elections on 26 August 2023, where the CCC was contesting the election results. Hlatshwayo demonstrated bravery when defending then-CCC spokesman, Promise Mkwananzi, during an alleged state-sponsored attack. As Mkwananzi was reading his speech, a suspected state agent, unidentified, walked up to the podium and manhandled Mkwananzi, taking away his speech (Nehanda Radio 2023). Before the suspected agent could get away, Hlatshwayo, who was sharing the stage with Mkwananzi, quickly intercepted the agent, gripped him firmly and asked him boldly in front of the press, 'who are you'? 'who sent you'? Whilst the agent managed to eventually slip away out of Hlawatswayo's grip, the media press footage of the incident went viral on social media, with Hlatshwayo being labelled as a 'heroine', a 'warrior' and an 'iron lady' by her followers. Hlatshwayo was considered brave and heroic for standing up to a suspected CIO agent and not flinching in the face of intimidation.

Other notable women in Zimbabwean politics who have been hailed for these masculine attributes are Joice Mujuru and Margaret Dongo, both recognised as freedom fighters due to their participation in the liberation struggle. Masculine attributes like strength and bravery are positive attributes and appeal to the electorate not just in Zimbabwe but even in Western countries like the US, as other scholars have noted (Bauer & Santia 2023), so it can be beneficial for female candidates to exhibit these traits when appealing to voters and their audiences. However, this is not necessarily beneficial for women or their empowerment in the long run, as it reinforces the notion that politics is inherently a masculine field. Thus, feminine traits may not appeal as much in such an environment. Consequently, in such hostile environments, women have to tow the line strategically in this regard by exhibiting more masculine or feminine traits depending on the environment. As we have seen, this is a key area where women exercise their political agency, but there are some limitations and challenges to this agency, which I will go on to outline in the final section of this chapter.

It is worth concluding this section by mentioning that there are women historically who have exhibited both feminine and masculine traits in appealing to their constituents. One notable figure in this regard is Joice Mujuru. Mujuru's liberation credentials and motherly feeling became a central aspect of her campaign strategy in 2018 (Zindoga 2016 and Mujuru & Masiyiwa 2018). Thus, whilst it may become strategic for women to display either feminine or masculine characteristics or attributes depending on the electoral environment, in Zimbabwe, influential women like Mujuru have towed the line by exhibiting both masculine and feminine traits. But unfortunately, this has not made them equal to their male counterparts. Neither has it necessarily made them electable. This has been referred to as 'the double bind' women in politics globally often find themselves in, in having to demonstrate both feminine and masculine attributes in politics to be taken seriously whilst still not elevating them to the level of their male counterparts (Mataruse 2022). However, in the global South, particularly postcolonial contexts like Zimbabwe, which are characterised and shaped by militaristic masculinities born out of struggles for independence, this double bind is more so double patriarchy, where women need to show that they are tough enough, like the men, to be capable of running for office but also soft and maternal enough to adhere to patriarchal cultural norms and expectations so they are not sanctioned by their societies. This is reminiscent of the liberation war, where women fought alongside their male counterparts for independence but also had to carry out the more domesticated and administrative tasks in the camps. This is another double-edged sword for women in that, whilst they may be taken more seriously, they are still not seen as equals to their male counterparts.

Challenges and Limitations to Women's Political Agency

Whilst women in politics have used social media as a strategic campaigning and political communication tool through which to exercise significant political agency, there are still some significant limitations and challenges which arise for the full expression of this agency for women, which I will briefly outline in this final section.

The first is cyberbullying and 'slut-shaming' through the dissemination of false information, misinformation and fake news. Whilst social media has been liberating for women, it has also been weaponised against women when rumours circulate about women in politics being in illicit sexual relationships to soil their reputations during electoral periods. This has particularly been the case with younger female candidates like Fadzayi Mahere (CCC) (Open Democracy 2022), Joanna Mamombe (CCC) and Tafadzwa Sihlahla (Zanu PF 2018 candidate) (Zigomo 2022), to name a few. This, however, is not a Zimbabwean problem alone but a more global challenge for women in politics. What is worth noting is that this cyberbullying and slut-shaming of women happens across the political divide and has become a significant decampaigning tool against women candidates during elections. However, even in this regard, women have exercised their agency in standing up for themselves and defending themselves against such discrimination. In 2018, Priscilla Misihairabwi-Mushonga, whilst filing Thokozani Khupe's nomination papers in court, appeared wearing a T-shirt labelled '#metoo #hure' based on an online movement she started (ZWNews 2018). Thus, demonstrating her solidarity with Khupe and all women in politics who have been labelled as prostitutes for challenging male authority. It is also worth noting here that CSOs, particularly women's organisations and the broader women's movement in Zimbabwe, have maintained a somewhat ambivalent stance in assisting women in politics in this regard. Younger female politicians like Mamombe have felt unsupported by the women's movement when facing accusations of illicit affairs with the influential men in their parties, stating that the women's movement tends to be more supportive of older (and subsequently more well-known) female politicians at the expense of younger (less well-known) ones (Zigomo 2022: 536–537). This has not meant that women's organisations have not been supportive of younger women in politics, as organisations such as the Institute for Young Women's Development (IYWD) do considerable work in capacitating younger up-and-coming women in politics, but the work of CSOs in this regard has been significantly hampered by the polarised nature of the political environment in Zimbabwe. The familial ties and matriarchal system of politics where existing networks with older, more established women politicians exist, as well as funding priorities, dictate to a larger extent where resources are deployed.

There has also been virtual 'success-shaming' of women politicians on social media. One example of this is the questioning of one Zanu PF female MP's competency for political office after she was sworn into Parliament in August 2023. The MP in question, Hon. Tatenda Matevera, who was Information, Communication and Technology Minister at the time of writing and whose credentials have been widely questioned on social media along with allegations of her having 'slept her way to the top', demonstrates how women are still victims of online abuse and misogyny (Zim Morning Post 2023).

The digital divide has also widened the gap between the haves and the have-nots, particularly those who have access to social media technologies and those who do not, and thus are often left out of political discourses to do with women in politics. In the weeks leading up to the 2023 elections, the Women Coalition of Zimbabwe (WCOZ), in partnership with the Women in Politics Support Unit (WIPSU) and the Zimbabwe Electoral Support Network (ZESN), hosted a women's candidate debate series platform on Twitter Space. However, network connection issues and inequitable access to data bundles, particularly in peri-urban areas and rural areas, have meant that women without regular and consistent access to social media risk being left out of these important debates and exchanges. Let alone less privileged women who may want to contest but lack sufficient resources to participate in virtual spaces. Tendayi Mpala, an independent candidate who contested in 2018 for Harare West, cited in an interview that one of the lessons she learnt from her campaign was the significant levels of poverty in parts of her urban constituency, which meant that not all of her constituents were able to participate virtually.[9] Thus, the limited reach of social media amongst the urban poor and the rural population is one area which risks robbing less privileged women of their political agency.

Also, young women in politics who are not as high profile can often be more vulnerable to physical violence and abuse by rival party groups, particularly when they are not as well-known on social media or have limited access. Whilst abducted high-profile women like Mamombe were able to tweet and disseminate information about their abduction in a short amount of time before their phones were taken, less privileged women who are low-profile or not as well-known and with limited access to social media technologies may not be as fortunate. One example of this is Moreblessing Ali, a member of the opposition based in Chitungwiza who was not as prominent on social media and who was abducted later in June 2022 but did not survive the ordeal (VOA 2022). This can further impact the ability of women's organisations to more effectively mobilise and crowdfund for less privileged women in both urban and rural areas.[10]

Finally, likes on social media can be deceptive, particularly when they do not necessarily translate into votes – another vital lesson which young female independents learnt in the 2018 election.[11] However, despite these limitations, social media has still proven to be advantageous for women, particularly as part of a larger, more robust campaign strategy. It has particularly proven to be most effective for those women who have employed it as a part of their larger campaign strategy when running for one of the more established political parties.

Conclusion

In conclusion, social media has presented significant opportunities for young women in politics as part of their campaign strategy, particularly for those who have opted to run in the larger, more established parties. It has increased their visibility in politics and boosted their public profiles. Even more importantly, it has been a platform where women have been able to exercise their agency through their performances by displaying either feminine or masculine traits as a strategic campaigning tool in both challenging and reinforcing gendered stereotypes during electoral periods. In this chapter, I have shown how women have shifted in their approach in this regard by looking at qualitative data obtained over two elections in Zimbabwe. The main takeaway here is that women have strategically exhibited gendered traits to either conform to gendered expectations or resist them, and whilst this has shown that women do employ a measure of soft agency in politics in this regard, there are still limits to this agency, which should not be overlooked.

Notes

1. Priscilla Maphosa. Genderlinks Zimbabwe. Interview. Harare. August 2023.
2. As of 2023.
3. Four of the 23 presidential candidates were women. Whilst this is still a low number when compared to their male counterparts, it is still the highest number of females the country has had running at the presidential level in one election. However, in the 2023 elections the number of women further dropped, with only one woman contesting at the Presidential level and barely a total of 70 at the Parliamentary level (ZESN Report 2023 and RAU Gender Audit 2018).
4. Adapted from ZEC's verified National Assembly results 2018 (source: https://www.zec.org.zw/download/combined-verified-national-assembly-results-2018/).
5. Adapted from ZEC's verified National Assembly results 2023 (source: https://www.zec.org.zw/download-category/national_assembly/).
6. According to the Research and Advocacy Unit's gender audit report (2018: 4), female voters registered to vote increased from 52% in 2013 to 54% in 2018. In an Afrobarometer (2017) survey, it was noted that rural women were far more likely to vote than urban women. They were also far more likely to attend a campaign rally (Afrobarometer 2017 survey cited in RAU 2018: 4). As over 60% of Zimbabwean's population is largely rural, this has implications for political participation and voting outcomes on a much larger scale. It is worth further noting that whilst this population group tends to make up the larger composition of political rally attendees and voters, there is no direct correlation between rally attendance and voting behaviour. Finally, due to other factors such as 'Pull-Her-Down' (PHD) syndrome (mainly in the urban towns where women have proven to be less supportive of other women) and assisted voting in rural areas within a highly polarised political environment, the political participation of women in such a context may not translate into a supportive environment for women candidates.
7. Nomination fees saw a steep hike in this election from 1000 USD to 20000 USD at the presidential level and from 50 USD to 1000 USD at the Parliamentary level (AFP 2023).

8 Interviews with single and divorced women corroborated this as documented in Zigomo's article "Women's Political Legitimacy in Zimbabwe" (Zigomo 2022).
9 Tendayi Mpala. Independent Political Candidate (2018). Harare West Constituency. Interview. Harare. July 2023.
10 Kudakwashe Munemo. Knowledge Management Documentation and Advocacy Coordinator. Institute for Young Women's Development (IYWD). Interview. Harare. 11 September 2023.
11 Dudu Nyirongo. Independent Candidate (2018). Harare East Constituency. Interview. Harare. September 2023.

References

AFP-Agence France Presse. 2023. 'Zimbabwe parliament approves steep hike in election fees'. Available at: https://www.barrons.com/news/zimbabwe-parliament-approves-steep-hike-in-election-fees-ca367a09

AFP-Agence France Presse. 2020. 'Zimbabwe's top court says Chamisa not legitimate opposition leader'. *AFP News*. Available at: https://www.barrons.com/news/zimbabwe-s-top-court-says-chamisa-not-legitimate-opposition-leader-01585681804

Akurugu, Constance. 2021. 'Gender performativity in rural northern Ghana: implications for transnational feminist theorising'. *Feminist Theory*, 22(1): 43–62.

Bauer, Nichole and Santia, Martina. 2023. 'Gendered times: How gendered contexts shape campaign messages of female candidates'. *Journal of Communication*, 73: 329–341.

Butler, Judith. 1988. 'Performative acts and gender constitution: An essay in phenemonology and feminist theory'. *Theatre Journal*, 40(4): 519–531.

Butler, Judith. 1999. *Gender Trouble: Feminism and the Subversion of Identity*. New York & London: Routledge.

Butler, Judith. 2009. 'Performativity, Precarity and Sexual Politics'. *Lecture given at Universidad Complutense de Madrid*. June 8, 2009, Madrid, https://aries.aibr.org/storage/antropologia/04v03/criticos/040301b.pdf

Chadya, Joyce. 2003. 'Anticolonial nationalism and the woman question in Africa'. *Journal of Women's History*, 15 (3): 153–157.

Chihota, Elijah. 2018. 'Justice Chigumba the Iron lady of Zimbabwean elections'. *Harare Post*. Available at: https://www.hararepost.co.zw/en/theopinion/662-justice-chigumba-the-iron-lady-of-zimbabwean-elections

Chitando, Ezra, Chirongoma, Sophia and Nyakudya, Munyaradzi. 2023. "Introducing a radical African indigenous feminist principle: Chihera in Zimbabwe". In *Chihera in Zimbabwe: A Radical African Feminist Principle*. Ezra Chitando, Sophia Chirongoma and Munyaradzi Nyakudya (Eds.), pp. 1–31. Cham: Palgrave Macmillan.

Gershon, Livia. 2021. 'Spiritual Medium Mbuya Nehanda defied colonialists in 19th century Zimbabwe'. *Smithsonian Magazine*. Available at: https://www.smithsonianmag.com/smart-news/zimbabwe-unveils-statue-anti-colonial-leader-mbuya-nehanda-180977835/

Harmer, Emily. 2021. *Women, media and elections: Representation and Marginalisation in British Politics*. Bristol: Bristol University Press.

Hawkins, Ian., Roden, Jessica., Attal, Miriam and Aqel, Haleemah. 2023. 'Race and gender intertwined: Why intersecting identities matter for perceptions of incivility and content moderation on social media'. *Journal of Communication*, 73, (6), 539–551.

Lloyd, Moya. 1998. "Sexual politics, performativity, parody". In *Politics of Sexuality*. Terrell Carver & Veronique Mottier (Eds.), London & New York: Routledge: pp. 124–134.

Mataruse, Sisasenkosi. 2022. 'Joice Mujuru and the Zanu PF's women's league 1973–2014: Opportunities and limits of maternal dignity (Musha Mukadzi) and self-preservations'. *Master's Thesis, Rhodes University*.

Media Monitoring Project Zimbabwe (MMPZ). 2012. 'Media representation of women in politics-October 1 to November 30, 2012'. *Report*.

Mohanty, Chandra. 1984. 'Under western eyes: Feminist scholarship and colonial discourses'. *Duke University Press*, 12(3): 333–358.

Mudiwa, Rudo. 2020. 'Prostitutes, wives and political power in Zimbabwe'. In *The Oxford Handbook of Zimbabwean Politics*. Miles Tendi et al (Eds.). Oxford: Oxford University Press.

Mujuru, Linda and Masiyiwa, Gamuchirai. 2018. *Joice Mujuru: The Fighter*. Global Press Journal. Available at: https://globalpressjournal.com/africa/zimbabwe/joice-mujuru-fighter/

Nehanda Radio. 2023. 'Opposition CCC Conference disrupted by over 10 state agents'. Available at: https://nehandaradio.com/2023/08/26/opposition-ccc-press-conference-disrupted-by-over-10-state-agents/

New Zimbabwe. 2018. 'Zim election: Female candidates face scathing abuse'. Available at: https://www.newzimbabwe.com/zim-election-female-candidates-face-scathing-abuse/

Open Democracy. 2022. 'How gendered violence is used to try to silence Zimbabwe's female politicians'. Available at: https://www.opendemocracy.net/en/5050/zimbabwe-politics-sexual-gender-based-violence/

Pongo, Brilliant. 2023. 'What propelled Fadzayi Mahere's political ascent?' *ZimSeen*. Available at: https://zimseen.com/what-propelled-fadzayi-maheres-political-ascent/

Research and Advocacy Unit (RAU). 2018. '2018 Elections: What happened to the Women?' Report. Accessed on 3/12/2023. Available at: https://researchandadvocacyunit.org/publications/elections/elections-in-2018/

Schmidt, Elizabeth. 1994. 'Peasants, traders and wives: Shona women in the history of Zimbabwe, 1870-1939'. *Social History of Africa*. Portsmouth: N.H. Heinnemann.

Southall, Roger. 2017. 'Bob's out, the Croc is in: Continuity or Change in Zimbabwe?' *Africa Spectrum*, 3: 81–94.

Spivak, Gayatri. 1988. "Can the subaltern speak?" In *Marxism and the Interpretation of Culture*. Cary Nelson and Lawrence Grossberg (Eds.). London: Macmillan.

The Herald. 2023. 'UZA leader wins nomination case'. Accessed on: 3/12/2023. Available at: https://www.herald.co.zw/uza-leader-wins-nomination-case-2/

Thompson, James. 2018. 'Analysis: 'Witch', 'Prostitute', women to face sexism in Zimbabwean elections'. *The Zimbabwe Mail*. Available at: https://www.thezimbabwemail.com/opinion/analysis-witch-prostitute-women-to-face-sexism-in-zimbabwe-elections/

Tshili, Nqobile. 2021. 'Misihairabwi appointed ambassador to Sweden'. *The Chronicle*. Available at: https://www.chronicle.co.zw/misihairabwi-appointed-ambassador-to-sweden/

UN Women. 2013. 'Women make up more than one-third of Zimbabwe's new Parliament'. Available at: https://www.unwomen.org/en/news/stories/2013/9/zimbabwe-women-mps-sworn-in

Van der Pas, Daphne and Aaldering, Loes. 2020. 'Gender differences in political media coverage: A meta-analysis'. *Journal of Communication*, 70: 114–143.

VOA. 2022. 'Body of abducted citizens coalition for change activist Moreblessing Ali found dumped in well'. Available at: https://www.voazimbabwe.com/a/6613191.html

Zigomo, Kuziwakwashe. 2022. 'Virtue, motherhood and femininity: Women's political legitimacy in Zimbabwe'. *Journal of Southern African Studies*, 48(3): 527–544.

Zim Morning Post. 2023. 'From soapie star to social media scandal: Former studio 263 actor now ICT minister sparks outrage after shamelessly copying Bill Gates'. Available at: https://zimmorningpost.com/from-soapie-star-to-social-media-scandal-former-studio-263-actor-now-ict-minister-sparks-outrage-after-shamelessly-copying-bill-gates/

Zindoga, Tichaona. 2016. 'Mujuru's fight back- a new dawn for the opposition?' *NewAfrican*. Available at: https://newafricanmagazine.com/11696/

Zvingowanisei, Silindiwe. 2023. "Chihera: Renegotiating the status of women in Shona indigenous culture in Zimbabwe". In *Chihera in Zimbabwe: A Radical African Feminist Principle*. Ezra Chitando, Sophia Chirongoma and Munyaradzi Nyakudya (Eds.), pp. 65–85. Cham: Palgrave Macmillan.

ZWNews. 2018. 'Pictures of Priscilla Misihairabwi-Mushonga wearing HURE jumper. Available at: https://zwnews.com/metoomovement-priscilla-misihairabwi-mushonga-top/

SECTION 6

African Women Thriving and Struggling in Historical Times, Older Age, Diplomacy and Religion

28
EMPOWERING IMAGES OF OLDER WOMEN IN AFRICAN LITERATURE

Pepetual Mforbe Chiangong

Introduction

Societies across the globe ascribe diverse meanings to the aging process. In most communities in Africa, old age is not limited to senescence, that is, "the time-related deterioration of the physiological functions necessary for survival and fertility" (Gilbert 2000) but embodies the continual relevance or "functional determinations" (Silverman 1987, 3; see also Martin 2017) based on sequential age and status. Centred on her keen observation of African and Caribbean migrant communities in the United Kingdom, Linda Bellos sustains a seemly understanding of old age that "[i]t is, of course, not merely a matter of how old people look, it is the continuity and experience that they represent which is significant" (Bellos 2020, 128). In her short story "Age," she therefore glorifies "grey hair." Established on cognitive aptitude, concepts such as fluid intelligence and crystallized ability have been employed to discuss the decline in cognition and "[…] social-cultural influences on general world knowledge" (Bengtson 2005, 12), respectively. These gerontological modes of categorization and engagement with old age have been challenged by some elderly individuals who demonstrate cognitive accuracy through transmission of comprehensive accounts of historical events and wisdoms through orature, serving as central role models to the younger generation (see also Canton 2018). W. Andrew Achenbaum underscores the worth allied with old age in an Asian context by citing an inspiring note from Confucius: "At fifteen, I applied myself to wisdom; at thirty, I grew stronger at it; at forty I no longer had doubts; at sixty there was nothing on earth that could shake me; at seventy I could follow the dictates of my heart without disobeying the moral law" (2005, 21). How Confucius establishes meaning with different age sets is similar to how Amadou Hampaté Bâ discusses old age in a Malian context, with each stage in the life course marked by a rite of passage designed to inculcate relevant knowledge and wisdoms to maturing community members. When asked whether the respect for the elderly is deterrent to progress and development, Hampaté Bâ responded, with storytelling, saying that fostering the teachings of the elderly is progress (Sesana 2005, 5). According to Achenbaum, therefore, "[t] he young have always respected the old's capacity to mentor. They count on the stories that elderly men and women tell to help them to clarify options, and identify pitfalls that lie ahead" (2005: 28).

It is against this backdrop that I embrace the gender lens to consider a selection of creative material from the African continent and its Diaspora, some of which have partly been inspired by important political and historical events outlined below. It is significant to note here that my association with gender in the chapter is centralized on the experiences of women in different cultural contexts that must not necessarily be framed within a specific feminist theory. However, relevant to the study is Jennifer Makumbi's (2020) understanding of *mwenkanonkano*—creating a balance—employed to critique how elderly women overcome differences and negotiate contradictions. Obioma Nnaemeka clearly illustrates the *mwenkanonkano* trope when she remarks that "African women's lives are a balancing act indeed. Fighting on all fronts to contend with external and internal forces, bridge the fissures between public and private, link home and abroad and maintain sanity through it all requires great strength and imagination" (2005, 31). This reflection is embodied in this work as a recognition of the diversity of the continent, challenging simplistic demands that ask "to provide a framework for African feminisms [because]…the majority of African women are not hung on 'articulating their feminism'"; they just do it … it is *what* they do and *how* they do it that provide the "framework" (32, emphasis in the original). While the chapter will examine how elderly women "do" their feminisms in order to create sanity in the society, the major aim is to explore their empowering roles in Africa and African Diaspora communities and further contend, following Carolyn Cooper (1991) that their forms of protest survived the middle passage, acquiring new patterns and strategies inspired by the lived conditions of African slaves on the plantations in the Americas. Cooper explores spirit possession in the Diaspora, centring it at the core of religious practices of people of African descent. She writes that "[a] s metaphor spirit possession doubly signifies both the dislocation and rearticulation of Afrocentric culture in the Americas" (Cooper 1991, 64). Reflecting on Cooper's views and on other genres of orature, I focus this chapter on "And Palm Wine Will Flow," by Bole Butake (Butake 2013a-Cameroon), *The First Woman* by Jennifer Makumbi (Uganda), "The Palm Wine Seller" by Gladys May Casely Hayford (Sierra Leone/Ghana), and "On Aging," and "Our Grandmothers" by Maya Angelou (USA), to centre the different gender perspectives from which elderly African and black women stand as emboldening tropes in their societies. The chapter is not concerned for the time being with the experiences of ageism (see Chiangong 2021), sexism, racism, (dis)ability, and classism experienced by women, especially at a later age. It focuses, instead, on how elderly women navigate some of these intersecting categories of discrimination to challenge marginalization and, in doing so, assert themselves as women in all imaginable ways.

Historical Reality and Political Agency

In spite of the immeasurable value embodied in old age, I concur with Achenbaum above that old age is a social and cultural construct. These paradigms for Michael Mangan involve diverse generations laying

> their own 'spin' on its construction (Mangan 2013, 238) and furthering this view, old age is gendered, sustaining how elderly women are distinguished from men. Aligned with the latter supposition, Sothembiso Nyone, quoted in Nagueyalti Warren, states that "(Women's) faces are maps of the hardships they have gone through. The older women get, the prouder they should be
>
> (Warren 2008, 357)

Warren uses Nyone's words to introduce the section on "Ageing" in *Temba Tupu! (Walking Naked): Africana Women's Poetic Self-Portrait*, a collection of poetry from female writers of African descent. Nyone's aphorism is instructive, as it demands a critique on African and black women's old age from an empowering perspective, yet upholds that the gender *wahala* is far from over.

African literatures, for the most part, introduce us to elderly female characters who in critical conditions demonstrate assertiveness, resilience, and defiance towards specific power structures. The agency embodied in their identity, largely unappreciated, has been an integral part of African communities. Abena Busia clarifies this tendency of overlooking women's political power and overall contribution to society as "having no *official* voice of *recognized* history" (1991, 88). Known in history to embody ancestral knowledge as they collaborate with other women to challenge and unsettle irrelevant control of their livelihoods, Nalova Lyonga, and Roselyn Jua refer lyrically to them as "natural democrats" (1993, 175) and "movers and shakers behind every "true" or great revolution" (1993, 180), respectively. These empowering images of elderly African womanhood, mostly at the grassroots, have no doubt existed for centuries and still salient in African and African Diaspora spaces where democratic principles and freedom are curtailed. When elderly women mobilize for a protest, they transcend often restricting heteronormative gender barriers and taboos by wearing men's clothing, exposing their naked bodies, adopting intractably defiant attitudes, and interrogating patriarchal order. This form of protest, which Naminata Diabate calls "naked agency and insurgent nakedness" (2020, 22) "[...] are most highly context-driven mode of dissent, insurgent nakedness is not just one thing with multiple interpretations. It is many things. It is a different code to decipher deeper cultural and societal accounts each time it is used, not only in its interpretation but also in its constitution" (2 & 3). Gender performativity in this context, therefore, allows elderly women the desire to impose their identities, demanding a broader recognition and appreciation, instead of essentialization of the force personified in them.

Based on forms of protests established by their ancestors, Roselyn Jua and Nalova Lyonga explore the contribution to the cultural and political order of the Anlu of Komland and the Takumbeng women all of the North West Region of Cameroon, which have served as background to creative literature. Both groups came to prominence on the political landscape in 1958 and 1990, respectively, to protest for peace and justice in their communities in the face of colonial control and pre-independent/postcolonial multi-party political rows. The Anlu women, as Jua recalls, were instrumental in changing the course of history in Komland as their rebellion was not only anticolonial but contributed to the establishment of a desired post-independent political leadership in the then British Southern Cameroons; which they deemed had the interest of grassroots communities at heart. Jua recounts in "Women in the Democratic Change in Cameroon" that the political determination and will of the Anlu in 1958 "influenced the outcome of the 1959 elections in [...] favour of the Kamerun National Democratic Party (KNDP) and also changed the whole course of history as far as Southern Cameroons was concerned" (1993, 181). What is remarkable about the rebellion of the Kom women was the non-negotiable and collaborative stance that they embraced to disrepute the Kamerun National Congress (KNC) whose leader was rumoured to sell their land to the Igbos of Nigeria, coupled with the fact that the native authority had imposed contour farming on them, an agricultural mode they said was never practised by their ancestors; so they revolted against this regulation and in doing so supported the KNDP's bid to Premiership. In the wake of their mobilization and protests, Eugenia Shanklin writes that in the course of its three-year "reign of terror," *anlu* demanded the shutting down of markets and schools, defied both traditional and colonial authorities, and set husbands against wives, church member against church member, brother against brother. School attendance fell by as much as 50–70 percent. *Anlu*, also interfered with the all-important death ritual, as well as with the traditional all-male governing organizations—*mukum* and *kwigoyn*—and the women taunted the Fon, the semi-divine ruler [...] calling him by name and ignoring his commands. When the palace of Laikom burned, *anlu* forbade people to go and rebuild it.

(Shanklin 1990, 159)

Shanklin further specifies that during their protests

[...] the women were draped in rags and leaves, others in men's torn trousers and old dirty caps. All were singing and chanting, shouting obscenities (159). In similar circumstances, the Takumbeng women, predominantly postmenopausal, as Fonchingong et al chronicle were from "Bamenda metropolitan areas [who] came into limelight in the context of Cameroons democratic transition [...]. By virtue of their numerical strength and collective mobilization for a common cause, the women were able to overcome many impediments (2009: 126; see also Chiangong, 2011; Kah, 2011) in the early 1990s.

P. T. Tanga further notes that the Takumbeng women participated in "political agitations [...] reinforced and encouraged by the women's secret society, the Takumbeng. The group became transformed against the backdrop of these popular agitations and disgruntleness and as a result impacted on the national contemporary politics" (2006, 1). Ritual performance was an important component of the elderly women's rebellion.

Elderly Women, Words, and Ritual

In Butake's (2013a) play, "And Palm Wine Flow," we encounter elderly women who, as discussed above, take the precursors of political violence to task, toppling a dictatorial institution in the process. Kwengong is introduced to us as the first wife of Shey Ngong, the Chief Priest of the land of Ewawa. After rituals of invocation have been performed at the sacred grove by the Chief Priest and at the twin-streams, by the women's cult, led by its elderly members, Kwengong is possessed by the spirit of Earth-goddess and commissioned to seek justice for the people of Ewawa. She relates to her husband the events at the twin-streams that lead up to the death of Fon (King) Chila Kintasi:

When I got to the twin-streams, there was a large gathering of women, mostly the elderly ones. They were all naked, stark naked. It seemed that they had been performing some rites. Upon my arrival they raised a great shout and one of them placed a pot of some portion on my head. Go to the Fon! Go to the palace! They shouted. And make him drink! Then I knew what I was carrying.

(276; see also Chiangong 2011)

It is worth mentioning that elderly female characters in the play orchestrate the women's rebellion against the rule of Chila Kintasi and significantly supervise the actions of

Earth-goddess. Through the performance of the said rituals, Kwengong as Earth-goddess is embodied by a spiritual potency capable of dismantling the autocratic leadership of the Fon.

I engage Kwesi Yankah's concept of surrogate performance and spoken word to explore the intervention of Earth-goddess and the elderly women through their use of utterances and their bodies. According to Yankah, surrogation and the spoken word in Akan oratory embody the akeayme who are "social mediators of speech, or rather speech specialists in the artistic reporting [...]" (1995, 8). The speech specialist whom Yankah studies for the most part speaks on behalf of the king through his role as a diplomat and an orator. An understanding of his concept of surrogate performance supports the cultural and political context that inspires the utterances that Earth-goddess delivers at that critical moment of encounter with Chila Kintasi. Surrogation entails "[speaking] on another's behalf [...]." Yankah notes that "[w]ithout their (akeayme) voice, a royal communicative act is incomplete [...] [It is] the exercise of performance through an agent, instrument or intermediary" (8). Given that surrogation has been employed in different contexts of communication, including modern politics, Earth-goddess acts as a surrogate to the Chief Priest and the elderly women, also authorities of the land, rather than that of Chila Kintasi. The utterances that she delivers are spiritually profound and do no resonate with ordinary speech but reflect that which is empowered by wisdoms emanating from the ancestors and from the elders. Therefore the content of the words that Earth-goddess delivers at the palace is constructed with "acoustic energy [...]" (Yankah, 10), which when performed overthrow Chila Kintasi's despotic rule. To Yankah,

> the spoken word [has] an immediate impact: a capacity to make or break, a potential of instantly enhancing the sociopolitical status of its practitioner as well [...]. In certain societies, the spoken word in [...] religious contexts as divination may have a performative or magical potency—the power to alter reality [...] [marked by] the use of right formulas (10).

Therefore, after leaving the twin-streams, Earth-goddess heads towards the palace of Chila Kintasi. She recounts the outcome of her spiritual-bound journey to her husband telling him that "[...] I walked straight into the inner court. Of course, the whole place was deserted. Not a single body around. When I opened my mouth to speak, I could not recognise my own voice;"

> Chila Kintasi! Chila Kintasi!
> Come out and receive the wares
> The women over whom you wield
> Great power have sent you!
> Come out, I say, and receive the goods
> Sent by those you dishonour so! [...]
> *(... spotlight shows Fon completely dazed)*
> Here are the wares the women commanded deliverance to their Fon!
> Here are the fruits they urged me to feed the crocodile that swallows its own eggs.
> Receive them, oh Fon, and rejoice!
> And may they make your belly swell with fat!
> May they make you call another feast before the sun goes to sleep!
> (277)

The notion of surrogation and spoken word as demonstrated in the rendition of Earth-goddess illustrates her total control of the situation. Acting as a surrogate to the Chief Priest and the elderly women's cult members, the person to whom her oratorical skills are addressed is helpless. Earth-goddess' choice of words, profoundly metaphorical, is embedded in inherited wisdom, accompanied by an eloquence that completely unsettles Chila Kintashi who would rather die than consume the "savoury juice from the vaginas [...]" of the women "whom You [Chila Kintasi] wield power [...] Drink the liquor [...] and feel the power of power" (277 & 278). That he would die than ingest the "liquor," indeed, actualizes his death, which happens after Earth-goddess performs the above words. Language employed in a gender-sensitive context is to Susheila Nasta "[...] both source and womb of creativity, a means of giving birth to new stories, new myths, of telling the stories of women that have previously been silenced. It can also become 'a major site of contest, a revolutionary struggle'" (1991, xii). In the words that Earth-goddess speaks, therefore, one captures her resolve, wit, and performance, which Yankah specifies are traits that are, generally, embedded in elderly women's oratory skills. Butake (2013b) further accentuates the importance of the elderly women in changing the political statusquo when in "Shoes and Four men in Arms," which Kehbuma Langmia is also preoccupied with in *Titabet and the Takumbeng* (2004), they confront police brutality in the awake of protest marches over the cost of living happening in an unnamed place. The rape of women is employed by the military to instil fear and terror in the population. To weaken and unarm the military sent out by the political order to contain the marches, the elderly women's cult, Kil'u, intervenes. While the military celebrates rape as an enjoyable pass-time, the women equally use the tragedy associated with rape as a counter-discourse. Amidst eerie and sarcastic laughs, the elderly women, whose voices are heard from backstage, invite the military to rape them. Recognizing the elderly women's voice and discerning the power embodied in their acts of rebellion, the soldiers are troubled by the invitation and flee the scene as they describe the women as "Very old and very dangerous women" (2013b, 371; see also Chiangong 2011, 2014).

Gender Discourse and Generational Bond

Similar to Bole Butake, Jennifer Makumbi equally takes up the gender question from an empowering perspective in her critically acclaimed novel, *The First Woman*. The life of Nsuuta, an elderly visually impaired Buganda woman, is focalized through Kirabo, the pre-teenage female protagonist who has inherited skills of storytelling from her great grandmother. Kirabo views Nsuuta as "too tall and erect for an old woman and too dignified for a witch [...]" (20). In a further account, she admits that "[s]he had no idea old people could be so beautiful" (20). Nsuuta, Kirabo further details "was practically blind, [though] behind her blindness she could see" (13). Nsuuta is an outgoing and daring character demonstrated in how she relates with Kirabo and other characters in the novel. Nsuuta, who the society considers a witch, is visually impaired and lives by herself except when she receives visits from Kirabo. The latter's visitations enable her to put to use her value as an elderly woman when she communicates ancient notions of Buganda feminisms, history of her community, and other relevant wisdoms, some of which are rooted in legends and myths, to Kirabo. She expatiates on broader Ugandan feminisms through the concepts *kweluma* and *mwenkanonkano*, both embodying diverse meanings in Buganda culture, to enable Kirabo to understand her body and locate her agency in a culture that is strictly patriarchal. The body is central to both concepts and crucial to already existing debates on African feminisms, yet the Baganda flavour in the novel is focused on sexuality, marriage, self-assertion, growth, beauty, education, and religion. While *kweluma* on the one hand emerges from the impediment of gender relations rooted in Uganda's ancestral past, it underscores the failure of some women's support of each other due to their incapability to inhibit patriarchal energy; *mwenkanonkano* on the other hand seeks gender equity and equality, but importantly accentuates mutable Ugandan feminisms that emerge from specific experiences of women aligned with age, sexuality, ethnicity, attractiveness, class, skin tone, religion and with the spaces that they embody. Nsuuta, therefore, accentuates in the text that different political, social, and cultural realities determine the feminisms that emerge in the Buganda community. Therefore, when it comes to exercising her feminist identity and asserting herself as a woman, she advises Kirabo to remember that [...] we are our circumstances. And until we have experienced all the circumstances the world can throw to us, seen all the versions we can be, we cannot claim to know ourselves. (31)[...] Even though we are all women, we stand in different positions and see things differently (70). Similar to the activities of the women's cult in Butake's play, Nsuuta underscores the need for mobilization and communal action, which she is convinced will mend what she describes as the "roof leaks" (70) of *kweluma* that develops when patriarchy flourishes.

Kirabo tells us that she is possessed by a second self, with one of them described as "the evil self, the one who quickened her breath and brought vengeful thoughts" (13) driving her to fly to specific spaces, including swinging on the church steeple. The energy that Kirabo builds up when she is faced with gender bias drives her to this extreme situation. As readers, we, probably, are aware that Kirabo has a significant drive to not conform to heteronormativity, but being a child, she is convinced that such a rebellious spirit is rooted in witchery. Generally, this evil part of her body emerges when she is faced with demands of patriarchy that ask her to not climb the jackfruit tree and to

> sit properly! [...]You cannot sit like men. Always kneel [...] you will not offend anyone that way [...] When you sit on a chair, cross your legs at the ankles to—(13). Although she always does the contrary, her body, nevertheless, always reacts in a specific way when such demands are made. For instance, she "[...] blinked once and next her evil self was out of her body and into the room. She flitted from wall to wall, like a newborn ghost lost. She flew with eyes closed because the emotion was too intense. For a long time, she swooped and darted, her mind raging over this foul body that made people spit, she swooped and darted, swooped and darted, a bat spooked in daytime (13).

She decides to find a cure of her "evil self" by consulting the elderly Nsuuta, who seemingly embodies Kirabo's characteristics and actually finds the witch-identity imposed on her, a compliment.

Kirabo's encounter with Nsuuta is informative as the reader is notified that the latter also possesses a second self, which as Kirabo tells us, employs it to put men at her service. It is known in literature that women who openly challenge heteronormativity are often perceived either as mentally unstable, as Lucia in Tsitsi Dangarembga's *Nervous Conditions* or as witches. After several visits to Nsuuta's homestead, to rid herself of her evil other, Nsuuta informs her that her desire is rooted in a crisis and develops each time she attempts to suppress a rebellious tendency whenever the urge emerges. Nsuuta concludes that with her second "evil" self, Kirabo is actually a special girl. Outlining the necessity for her to claim her "evil" self, Nsuuta tells Kirabo that every woman, including Kirabo's grandmother Alikisa, possesses a second "evil" self, especially when they feel squeezed (23). She reveals to Kirabo that Alikisa

> occasionally [...] hates being a woman. Did you know she loved to run naked in the rain when we were young? (23). Through Nsuuta, Kirabo learns the wisdom of the Muganda woman's role in her community. She also learns from her that her original self, whom male ancestors had destroyed in their women, was till embodied. Based on a myth, Nsuuta recounts that in the ancient times, the men had taken control of women's power and access to land sending them off to the sea that contains water considered to possess "no shape, it can be this, it can be that [...] inconsistent [...] untamed (55) and unpredictable.

Being forced to relocate to the sea, women have since then been associated with the attributes of water. Nsuuta further reveals that the ancients "had such irrational fear of the nature of women that they should try anything to keep them under control", (55). It is through irrational fear of women that it becomes crucial to inform the younger generation, particularly through orature, about the authority of their ancestors. This need is equally articulated in Sindiwe Magona's novel, *To My Children's Children* (1990), in which the protagonist writes a letter that archives her life as an aspiring young woman, particularly in Apartheid South Africa to her great-grandchildren. The epistolary frame that Magona's narrative takes serves the purpose of storytelling, a genre she embraces to archive relevant knowledge for her great-grandchildren. This knowledge about transmission helps to locate orature as a crucial tool for conveying the past to the younger generation, an approach which preoccupies Nsuuta in *The First Woman*.

However, what is important about Makumbi's gender agenda is how Nsuuta takes over the narrative of the woman's body in *The First Woman* to accentuate that the original and powerful status of Baganda women constructed the political and social systems until it was unsettled by Western notions of modernity, dominated by capitalism and the fight over the acquisition of land, over which the men claimed victory. In spite of this patriarchal presence, some of the girl children like Kirabo are still born with the qualities of the first women. The women's body, especially the genital, is considered in the novel by male characters as foul, which deserved to be covered, driving Kirabo's grandmother and other women into perceiving it as "ruins" and " the burden" (65). Yet, as seen in "And Palm Wine Will Flow," other female characters in the novel perceive their intimate parts as a site of rebellion, where the overall strength of the woman is located; "[...] what little power women have is found there" (Makumbi 66). The elderly woman's naked body not only threatens masculinity but also challenges patriarchal, sexist, and ageist gazes with the goal of troubling hierarchies between people and testing restrictive gender and age boundaries. This concern is equally expressed in Nagueyalti Warren's poem, "When I Am old" in which she repeatedly stresses how she will position her body at old age;

> When I am old I will walk naked in the rain, eat chocolate for breakfast... When I am old I will walk naked in the rain, celebrate my flab with ice cream—[...] When I am old I'll walk naked in the rain, my sag giggling and maybe give a toothless smile to all surprised eyes.

(2008, 387)

Imagining the thought-flow and actions of the speaker in Warren's poem, the naked body of elderly women is symbol of celebrating life, but importantly a site to stage their presence unabashed at crucial moments similar to the one described in Butake's play. Based on this feminine expression of the body, the goal of Nsuuta is, therefore, to convince Kirabo not to destroy and eventually bury her so-called evil self, because that is exactly where her agency is entrenched. Her agency enables her to flout patriarchal rules and do just the opposite of what that order expects of her. Nsuuta encourages Kirabo to challenge gender barriers that make them "shrink" and inter their female presence and bravery (67) just as we will see, below, in a poem by Gladys May Casely Hayford.

Challenging the Male Gaze

The lives of elderly women, particularly when they are marginalized, serve as a source of wisdom, providing precepts of existence to younger women as seen so far in "And Palm Wine Will Flow" and *The First Woman*. Lucile Clifton affirms in her poem, "miss rosie," that indeed elderly women have suffered oppression "wrapped up like garbage [...] wet brown bag of a woman [...]" (2008, 371). That notwithstanding, younger women have undeniably drawn inspiration from observing how elderly womanhood has survived being reduced to waste. As observed in "And Palm Wine Will Flow," in "miss rosie" but also in *The First Woman*, younger female characters eschew marginalization lived by their ancestors as they reject the circumstances under which their elderly role models have been subjected to; often left in poverty rooted in all kinds of *–isms*. We find a similar trope of resilience in "The Palm Wine Seller," by Gladys May Casely Hayford who presents an elderly female subject, Akosua, hawking palm wine down the streets to "illusioned boatmen" (2008, 360) in blistering sun. Apparently, the poet persona, an anonymous character, observes the happenings around Akosua as the latter goes about her business. The unspecified character reports on the attitude of the boatmen who overlook her "fallen bosom," her "Knotted thin black arms" and dwell on her fair body, "jet-black hair [...] [and on] lips that form a cupid's bow whereon love's dew lies" (360). These, seemingly, menacing gazes from the boatmen further focus on "the roundness of her bosom, Brilliance of her eyes [...] Velvet gleam of shoulder, [...] Soft caressing hands" (360). The initial impression that the reader gets is that Akosua trades in demanding conditions, yet her demeanour stresses her corporate forthrightness and energy. In spite of her age demonstrated through metaphors of "lips creased in by wrinkles, Eyes dimmed with the years, Feet whose arch was altered [...] selling palm wine In the broiling heat [...] filled unto the brim" (360), Hayford positions her on the streets as a heroine of her gender, of her age and of the space which she currently personifies.

The empowering stance of Akosua as she performs her trade is demonstrated in the repetition of "Akosua selling Palm Wine," which appears in all of the nine stanzas of the poem, sometimes twice in each stanza, informing on her persistence and defiant attitude presented in a deriding sexist and capitalist space. What Hayford seeks to underscore in the poem is the subject's determination to survive, which equally serves as an inspiration to the poet persona who, evidently on more than one occasion, spots Akosua go up and down "our" street selling palm wine. Moreover her keen observation of the behaviour of the disillusioned boatmen provides a sheet of protection over Akosua who is determined, under precarity to provide for the child strapped to her back. The poet, equally demonstrated in our early discussion of other works, seeks to challenge essentialist notions often associated with African womanhood by creating an omniscient perspective that observes Akosua and reports on her activities to the reader. Moreover, the said speaker in the poem also communicates to readers how Akosua's determination is embedded in the charm that radiates through her fair body and jet-black hair, luring the boatmen's gazes towards her. What is thought-provoking about the poem is that Hayford does not communicate the ulterior motive of the boatmen. The speaker, equally, does not expatiate further on this subject, offering Akosua goddess-like qualities, which she employs to dominate, often threatening sites, like the streets. I imagine that Akosua is aware of these gazes, but the power that her silence conveys carries with it an interventionist trope that serves as an ethical motif to the boatmen and a gender incentive to her keen observer whom I imagine is a young girl. Akosua's attitude towards the boatmen and the people around her, in my view, unconsciously sets empowering standards for anyone should they find themselves operating in such and even more dangerous circumstances.

Anchoring the Diaspora

Maya Angelou (2008a, 370) seems to respond to the conditions presented by Hayford in "The Palm Wine Seller," through her poem "On Aging." The speaker in the poem places the limelight on a still energy-driven aging body, drawing the curtain on views that project female old age as that which is "sitting quietly, Like a sack left on the shelf [...], with stiff and aching bones which cannot climb the stairs" (370). The subject therefore issues out firm instructions to her entourage asking them not to offer any sympathy and demands emphatically that they "Hold! Stop! Don't pity me! Hold! Stop your sympathy!" The elderly poet persona eschews a rocking chair in spite of hurting bones. Aiming to invert her community's gaze from often stereotypical renditions about old age, the elderly poet persona celebrates old age as breath, "Cause tired don't mean lazy And every good bye ain't gone [...] [for] I'm the same person I was back then [...]" (370).

While the poet persona in Angelou's poem reprimands pitiful gazes directed at elderly female bodies, she is actually demanding that an ageing female body should not be understood in the context of strength, but more in the framework of tenacity, agency, resilience, and determination. One may imagine that Angelou connects the thematic concern in "On Ageing" with events in "Our Grandmothers" (2008b, 262), another of her poem explaining why old age should rather be celebrated and not shunned or pitied. In "Our Grandmothers," Angelo pays tributes to a number of female ancestors, particularly those of African descent, whose presence altered the trajectory of history for disadvantaged people in their societies. The grandmothers she lists in her poem are "Sheba and Sojourner, Harriet and Zora, Mary Bethune and Angela, Annie to Zenobia" (265) some of whom laid the foundation for the emancipation of people of African descent from enslavement to the civil rights movements in the United States through their leadership, activism, philanthropy, education, and scholarship. She venerates the spirits of these ancestors, particularly with the goal to chronicle the lived reality of black mothers during slavery. The attempts of black grandmothers to seek freedom for their children and prevent them from being (re)sold to slave owners are constantly threatened by "loud longing of hounds and the ransack of hunters crackling the near branches" (2008a, 262).

Hidden in the cane bushes, the mother's determination in "Our Grandmother" is constantly echoed in the following lyrical rendition; "I shall not, I shall not be moved" when she "gathers her babies, their tears slick as oil on black faces, their young eyes canvassing mornings of madness." In this traumatic uncertainty, the children ask; "Momma, is Master going to sell you from us tomorrow" (262). The horrors of enslavement, coupled with racial indignities, remind us of why the speaker in Angelou's "On Ageing" has slowed down and spends time just listening to her body. The body she listens to embodies archival material marked with ancestral rhythms of history, of fights, of spirituality, of rebellion, and of hope that is passed on from the continent of Africa and from one generation to another. The elderly female body as documentation also resonates with what happened in the North West Region of Cameroon way before the 1950s, which Butake and Langmia embed in their theatre. Therefore, listening to her body, the speaker in "On Aging" personifies silence and reflection on the consequences of being uprooted from the African continent, surviving the middle passage and plantation labour and the quest for freedom; but it is also about intently listening to how society perceives old age as debilitating and as it associates that only with the vagaries of the ageing process.

Enslaved people embodied African religious practices, such as the one explored in "And Palm Wine Will Flow," together with Christianity, which served as a source of communal strength, survival, preservation of their dignity, identity and importantly inspired patterns of revolt. The poet persona in "Our Grandmothers" is deeply religious. She embodies the "Holy Spirit," in spite of rejection by white churches. She, however, finds determination in a spiritual world that enables her to seek "the tents of the free" (264). The African grandmother's repetition of "I shall not, I shall not be moved" captured in almost all the stanzas of the poem conveys her will, in spite of the risk involved, to escape enslavement with her children. Her search for freedom is not marked by self-pity but a "cry [...] in a new voice" (263). The quality of her cry unburies her agency which "[...] cannot fit your tongue, for I have a certain way of being in this world, and I shall not, I shall not be moved" (263). Angelou concludes the poem by accentuating the determination of her ancestors who sang their way to self-dignity, veracity, and emancipation.

One of the grandmothers, Mary McLeod Bethune, who Maya Angelou cites in her poem, wrote in her will in 1955 that

"I leave you hope. The Negro's growth will be great in the years to come. Yesterday our ancestors endured the degradation of slavery, yet they retained their dignity. Today, we direct our strength toward winning a more abundant and secure life. Tomorrow, a new Negro, unhindered by race taboos and shackles, will benefit from more than 330 years of ceaseless struggle. Theirs will be a better world. This I believe with all my heart".
(The National WWII Museum, 2020)

The degradation of enslavement that Mary McLeod Bethune speaks about is convoluted with gender, patriarchy, class, age, and (dis)ability. These and more categories are encountered by elderly women of African descent, but which they have contested in different but significant ways.

Conclusion

The texts explored in this chapter are situated in diverse cultural contexts in which elderly women of African descent have expressed momentous ways, feminisms if you like, of responding to ubiquitous forms of political control and gender-related suppressions. Not only the forms of protest but also the self-determination strategies embodied by the elderly female characters have challenged narrations of subservience and decline of the female body in order to espouse tropes of (re)appropriation of cultural values and centralization of lost historical identities through ritual, folklore, agency, and resistance. In the process, the elderly women recuperate gender and cultural identity, which serve as emancipatory pathways to societal concerns. To underscore the emancipatory worth that accompanies the presence of elderly people in any space, I revert to Linda Bellos who in her process of venerating old age perceives the end of life for the elderly as ritual and celebration. She notes that

> [t]here is, to my mind, something rather good about attending the funerals of old people who lived long, fruitful and varied lives. It offers an opportunity not only to celebrate that life but also gain a tangible essence of our having a history. Grey hair in some ways represents the notion of history as well as age and experience.
>
> (2020, 127)

Therefore, the different elderly women discussed in the chapter have offered us enriching contexts in which they operate, using their bodies as tropes of freedom. Their embodied strategies attain the objectives of determination, irrespective of where they are located. Their shared ancestry serves as a communal language that has informed the reader of the complex historical trajectory of the African continent that is rooted to a considerable extent in political violence, male dominance, slavery, and institutionalized racism. The hope is that this study contributes to existing African and African Diaspora conversations on gender relations in a bid to seek, establish, and affirm the connections and continuities of these historically endowed identities.

References

Achenbaum. A.W., 2005, 'Ageing and changing: International historical perspectives of ageing,' in Malcolm L. J., et al. (eds.), *The Cambridge Handbook of Age and Ageing*, pp. 21–29, New York, Cambridge University Press.

Angelou, M., 2008a, 'Our grandmothers,' in Nagueyalti W. (ed.), *Temba Tupu (Walking Naked): Africana Women's Poetic Self-Portrait*, pp. 262–265, Trenton, Africa World Press, Inc,

Angelou, M., 2008b, 'On ageing,' in Nagueyalti W. (ed.), *Temba Tupu (Walking Naked): Africana Women's Poetic Self-Portrait*, p. 370, Trenton, Africa World Press, Inc.

Bellos, L., 2020, 'Age,' in Margaret Busby (ed.), *New Daughters of Africa*, pp. 127–132, Oxford, Myriad Editions.

Bengtson, L. V., 2005, 'The problem of theory in gerontology today,' in Malcolm L. J. et al. (eds.), *The Cambridge Handbook of Age and Ageing*, pp. 3–20, New York, Cambridge University Press.

Busia, A., 1991, 'Rebellious women: Fictional biographies – Nawal el Sa'adawi's *Women at point zero* and Mariama Bâ's *So long a letter*,' in Susheila N. (ed.), *Motherlands: Black Women's Writing from Africa, the Caribbean and South Asia*, pp. 88–98, London, The Women's Press, Ltd.

Butake, B., 2013a, 'And palm-wine will flow,' in *Dance of the Vampires and Six Other Plays*, pp. 243–284, Bamenda, Langaa RPCIG Publishers.

Butake, B., 2013b, 'Shoes and four men in arms,' in *Dance of the Vampires and Six Other Plays*, pp. 331–378, Bamenda, Langaa RPCIG Publishers.

Canton, L., 2018, 'Ageing in a faraway land,' in Carmen C. (ed.), *Imagining Ageing: Representations of Age and Ageing in Anglophone Literatures*, pp. 13–17, Bielefeld, Transcript.

Chiangong, P. M., 2011, *Semiological interpretation of the plays of Gilbert Doho, Bole Butake and Hansel Ndumbe Eyoh*, Bayreuth, Bayreuth African Studies.

Chiangong, P. M., 2014, 'A critique of morality: An existential reading of elderly characters in two of Bole Butake's plays,' in John N. N., *Perspectives on Cameroon Art, Archaeology and Culture: Papers in Honour of Professor Bole Butake*, pp. 181–198, Yaounde, Editions CLE.

Chiangong, P.M., 2021, *Old age in African literary and cultural contexts*, Newcastle upon Tyne, Cambridge Scholars Publishing.

Clifton, L., 2008, 'Miss rosie,' in Nagueyalti W. (ed.), *Temba Tupu (Walking Naked): Africana Women's Poetic Self-Portrait*, Trenton, Africa World Press, Inc.

Cooper, C., 1991, "Something ancestral recaptured': Spirit possession as trope in selected feminist fictions of the African diaspora,' In Susheila N. (ed.), *Motherlands: Black Women's Writing from Africa, the Caribbean and South Asia*, pp. 64–87,London, The Women's Press, Ltd.

Diabate, Naminata, 2020, *naked agency: Genital cursing and biopolitics in Africa*. Durban, Duke Press.

Fonchingong, C. C. et al, 2009, 'Traditions of women's social protest movements and collective mobilisation: Lessons from Aghem and Kedjom women,' in Emmanuel Y. V., *Civil Society and the Search for Development Alternatives in Cameroon*, pp. 125–141, Dakar, African Books Collective.

Gilbert, F. S.t, 2000, 'Aging: The biology of senescence,' In *Developmental Biology*. Sunderland, Sinauer Associates Inc. https://www.ncbi.nlm.nih.gov/books/NBK10041/, accessed 04.10.2023.

Hayford, M.C.G., 2008, 'The Palm Wine Seller,' in Nagueyalti W. (ed.), *Temba Tupu (Walking Naked): Africana Women's Poetic Self-Portrait*, pp. 360–361.Trenton, Africa World Press, Inc.

Jua, R., 1993, 'Women's role in democratic change in Cameroon,' in Nalova L., et al. (eds.). *Anglophone Cameroon Writing*, pp. 180–183, Bayreuth, Bayreuth African Studies.

Kah, H. K., 2011, 'Women's resistance in Cameroon's western grassfields: The power of symbols, organization, and leadership, 1957–1961,' *African Studies Quarterly* 12 (3), 67–91

Langmia, K., 2004, *Titabet and the Takumbeng*. Bamenda: Langaa Research and Publishing.

Lyonga, N., 1993, 'Natural democrats: Women and the leadership crisis in Cameroon literature,' in Nalova L., et al. (eds.), *Anglophone Cameroon Writing*, pp. 175–179, Bayreuth, Bayreuth African Studies.

Magona, S., 1990, *To My Children's Children*. Claremont, David Philip Publishers Ltd.

Makumbi, J., 2020, *The First Woman*. London, Oneworld Publications.

Mangan, M., 2013, *Staging Ageing: Theatre, Performance and the Narrative of Decline*, Bristol, Intellect.

Martin, S., 2017, *Dancing Age(ing): Rethinking Age(ing) in and Through Improvisation Practice and Performance*, Bielefeld, Transcript.

Nasta, S., 1991, 'Introduction,' in Susheila Nasta (ed.), *Motherlands: Black Women's Writing from Africa, the Caribbean and South Asia*, pp. xiii–xxx, London, The Women's Press Ltd.

Nnaemeka, O., 2005, "Mapping African feminisms," in Andrea Cornwall (ed.), *Readings in Gender in Africa*, pp. 31–41, London, International African Institute.

Sesana, K. R., 2005, 'Amadou Hampate Bâ and Tierno Bokar,' *Wajibu* 20(3), 4–6.

Shanklin, E., 1990, 'Anlu remembered: The Kom women's rebellion of 1958–61,' *Dialectical Anthropology* 15(2/3), 159–181.

Silverman, P., 1987, 'Introduction: Life course perspectives,' In Philip S. (ed.), The *Elderly as Modern Pioneers*, pp. 1–16, Bloomington, Indiana University Press.

Tanga, P.T., 2006, 'The role of women's secret societies in Cameroon's contemporary politics: The case of Takumbeng,' *African Journal of Cross-Cultural Psychology and Sport Facilitation (AJCPSF)*, 8, 1–17.

The National World War II Museum, New Orleans, 2020, 'The extraordinary life of Mary McLeod Bethune,'https://www.nationalww2museum.org/war/articles/mary-mcleod-bethune. Accessed 09.10.2023

Warren, N., 2008, 'When I am old,' in Nagueyalti W. (ed.), *Temba Tupu (Walking Naked): Africana Women's Poetic Self-Portrait*, p. 387.Trenton, Africa World Press, Inc.

Yanka, K., 1995, *Speaking for the Chief: ökyeame and the Politics of Akan Royal Oratory*. Bloomington, Indiana University Press.

29
WOMEN'S EXPERIENCES OF GROWING OLDER IN A RURAL ECONOMY IN GHANA

Abdul-Aziz Seidu, Joshua Okyere and Bright Opoku Ahinkorah

Introduction

The demographics of the world are changing rapidly. With improvements in medicine and advancement in science and technology, the human population is now living longer than before. This improvement in life expectancy and longevity also means that the ageing population is likely to rise in the foreseeable future. Particularly, older people residing in rural areas are likely to face harsh consequences of ageing in Ghana. This chapter elucidates women's experiences of growing old in rural economies in Ghana.

The chapter begins by discussing the concept of ageing and the global, regional, and national statistics on ageing. It then delves into national policies on ageing in Ghana. The chapter further examines the lived experiences of older women in rural areas, focusing on their social experiences, economic experiences, and health challenges. Additionally, this chapter illuminates the positive, agentic roles of older women in rural Ghanaian society. The intersectionality of gender and rurality in Ghanaian women's experiences with ageing is also explored. The chapter concludes by discussing existing opportunities to improve the quality of life of women as they navigate through their later years.

Concept of Ageing

Ageing is a complex and multifaceted concept. Hence, different conceptualization of ageing has been proposed based on the dimension from which proponents view it. While some view ageing from a chronological standpoint, there are other scholars who view it from a biological position (Maltoni et al. 2022: 101300; Räsänen 2023: 1–3). From a chronological standpoint, ageing describes the passage of time from an individual's birth to the present date (Lachman et al. 2015: 20–31). In other words, it reflects an individual's age in terms of years, months, and days that have elapsed since their birth. Usually, chronological ageing is adopted as a prima facie approach to define how old a person is and categorize them based on their time of existence. It is on the premise of chronological ageing that we have categories such as adolescents (10–19 years), young people (15–24 years), and older people (60 years and above). However, chronological ageing provides a myopic perspective to the experiences of growing old. This limitation gave birth to the concept of biological ageing.

Biological ageing, also known as functional ageing, transcends the argument of time that would have elapsed since birth to address "different biological and physiological developmental factors such as genetics, lifestyle, nutrition, and comorbidities" (Maltoni et al. 2022: 101300). This perspective suggests that ageing arises because of gradual cellular damage, which predisposes the individual to declined cognitive and physical capacity to function, and ultimately death (Sattaur et al., 2020; WHO, 2015). For instance, the functional ageing perspective would be concerned about the extent to which a chronologically older person is able to perform daily tasks such as eating, walking, sleeping, communicating, and participating in social activities.

There is also yet another perspective to the concept of ageing: the social conceptualization of ageing. Across many countries and different cultures, ageing is socially constructed as a transition through certain life events. While menstruation marks a transition to womanhood, retirement is considered a marker of old age (WHO, 2015). As such, society ascribes certain norms and expectations to persons who are considered to be aged.

In Ghana, like in many sub-Saharan African countries, the cultural context plays a key role in shaping the behaviour, actions, responsibilities, and limitations of older people (Essuman & Mate-Kole 2021: 1–11). Traditionally, it is believed that older people (i.e., 60 years and older) should retire from active work and rely on their children to support them with the necessary economic, emotional, and health needs. This is reflected in the Akan adage that says, "When your parents take care of you for your teeth to erupt, you in turn take care of them until their teeth come off" (Essuman & Mate-Kole 2021: 5). Consequently, it is common to see many older people in Ghana returning to their rural communities where they originally resided to retire and be with the extended family. This provides an opportunity for the older person to enjoy the companionship of an extended family system and be confident of constant support in any means possible. Hence, it is uncommon to see older people's or long-term care homes in Ghana.

Having explored the concept of ageing and old age in Ghana, it is imperative to understand the demographics of this population. As such, the next section of this chapter discusses the global, regional and national statistics on ageing. Exploring these statistics is crucial for contextualising the Ghanaian experience within the broader framework of global ageing trends. Analyzing statistics on ageing at different levels allows us to identify patterns, variations, and potential influencing factors that contribute to a more nuanced understanding of the ageing phenomenon.

Global, Regional, and National Statistics on Ageing

The demography of the world is quickly changing. According to the World Health Organization (WHO) as of 2020, there were approximately 1 billion people aged 60 years or older. This figure is projected to further increase to nearly 1.4 billion by 2030. This means that by 2030, 1 out of every 6 human beings would be aged 60 years or older (WHO 2022a). The WHO further reports that in 2020, the number of persons at age 60 or older outnumbered the total global population of children under five (WHO 2022a). This has significant ramifications for the world's demography in the next three decades. In terms of gender differences, the United Nations Department of Economic and Social Affairs [UNDESA] (2019) indicates that women constitute 58% of the population aged 65+ years. It is expected that by 2030 and 2050, women will continue to dominate the proportion of older people in the world, 57% and 56%, respectively (UNDESA 2019).

In sub-Saharan Africa, it is projected that the population of persons aged 60 years or older would reach 67 million by 2025, and 163 million by the year 2050 (WHO African Region 2022). While the recurring pattern shows an upward trend in the population of older persons, there are some variations regarding the magnitude of increase across the individual sub-Saharan African countries. For a country like Nigeria, it is projected that the population of older people would triple by 2050 (Mbam et al. 2022; 1243–1250). In Ethiopia, there is an estimated 6.1 million older people, constituting 5.3% of the country's total population (UNFPA ESARO 2022).

The situation in Ghana is similar to what has been observed across other African countries. Evidence from the 2021 Ghana Population and Housing Census revealed that the population of older people has increased from 213,477 in 1960 to 1.9 million in 2021 (Ghana Statistical Service 2022). Of the 1.9 million older people in Ghana, 56.7% were females. Moreover, the Census report indicates that a quarter of all older persons in Ghana are multidimensionally poor, with the most profound poverty being reported in the Savannah region (Koduah et al. 2015: 1–20). Given that the Savannah region is predominantly rural, the statistics provide a basis to prioritize the older women's experiences of growing old.

The next section digests Ghana's national policies on ageing to map out their contribution to the livelihoods of older women in rural communities of Ghana.

National Policies on Ageing in Ghana

Historically, social protection policies for the older people trace their origins to 1965 with the enactment of the Social Security Act (Alidu et al. 2016: 154–172). This legislation led to the extraction of lump-sum amounts from an established Provident Fund, which was subsequently allocated to provide benefits for invalidity and survivors among older people (these terms are in the original legislation). Subsequently, multiple policies have been implemented. Among the existing policies is the national health insurance exemption for older people, livelihood empowerment against poverty (LEAP) and the National Ageing Policy (Essuman & Mate-Kole 2021: 1–11). In 2004, the Kufuor government introduced the National Health Insurance Scheme (NHIS) with the aim of reducing out-of-pocket-payment for healthcare services (Ghana Statistical Service 2022). Under this scheme, individuals were required to register at the National Health Insurance Authority (NHIA) and pay a premium to grant them an active status that would enable them to seek healthcare for free. However, considering the economic constraints that often characterize some key populations, the health insurance exempted older people from paying a premium (Essuman & Mate-Kole 2021: 1–11), thus, bringing about some level of economic relief while increasing their accessibility to healthcare coverage. However, this exemption is only applicable if the individual is 70 years or above. The implication is that "younger-old" persons (i.e., 60–69 years) do not benefit from this policy, therefore, they pay the premium on their national health insurance. Another limitation of the NHIS is that it fails to cover all health needs of older people. For instance, Okyere and Kissah-Korsah (2023: 5) argue that the NHIS makes no provision for older people who would require palliative care.

In 2008, the government of Ghana initiated the LEAP Programme as a component of its national social protection (Fuseini et al. 2019: 760–773). The primary goal of the LEAP Programme is poverty reduction, achieved by elevating and stabilizing consumption patterns, while also fostering accessibility to essential services and opportunities for those in extreme poverty and vulnerability (Ministry of Gender, Children and Social Protection 2023). At the beginning, the LEAP Programme was rolled out in the Wa West and Wa East districts in the Upper West region of Ghana. After its success in the two districts, the programme was scaled up to other districts within the region and subsequently rolled out in other regions in Ghana (Fuseini et al. 2019: 760–773). While the LEAP Programme places emphasis on persons living with disabilities, orphaned, and vulnerable children, it also includes persons aged 65 years and older as key beneficiaries. Fuseini et al. (2019: 765) assert that beneficiaries of the LEAP Programme received stipends and in-kind transfers such as benefiting from free registration and renewal of their national health insurance premiums. However, the current scope of the LEAP programme is restricted, since it primarily encompasses a small subset of older people who fulfil the role of caregivers for orphaned and vulnerable youngsters (Government of Ghana 2010; Kpessa-Whyte 2018: 403–408). Consequently, a significant proportion of older people who are economically disadvantaged and do not have caregiving responsibilities are marginalized and left out.

The year 2010 marked an important trajectory in Ghana's history of advancing the wellbeing and welfare of older people. The National Ageing Policy was formulated in 2010 to serve as a guide on the key areas of focus in ageing or aged programmes and interventions. This policy was titled, "National Ageing Policy: Ageing with Security and Dignity" (Essuman & Mate-Kole 2021: 8). Thus, highlighting the importance of social welfare and dignified living for older people in Ghana.

Primarily, the national aging policy aimed at ensuring the comprehensive integration of older individuals into mainstream society, encompassing social, economic, and cultural aspects (Government of Ghana 2010). This goal sought to enable older people's meaningful participation in the national development process to the greatest extent possible. Specifically, the policy focused on nine thematic areas: defending the rights of older people, facilitating older people's involvement in social development, poverty alleviation, enhancing the health and wellbeing of older people, housing and living arrangements, galvanizing family, community support, facilitating financial security, and prioritizing the gender differences in ageing (Government of Ghana 2010). The policy recognizes the rights of older people to uphold their personal independence, with a specific emphasis on accessing basic necessities such as nourishment, clean water, housing, apparel, medical care, education, skill development, employment, and other income-generating pursuits. Furthermore, the National Ageing Policy recognizes that older people often face the challenge of ageism and accusation of witchcraft which leads to victimization and abuse (Government of Ghana 2010; Kpessa-Whyte 2018: 403–408). To improve the living conditions and financial security of older people in rural areas, the National Ageing Policy proposes to make micro-credit readily available to them (Government of Ghana 2010).

Lived Experiences of Older Women in Rural Areas

Having placed the concept of ageing in perspective and explored the policy nuances of growing old in Ghana, this section sheds light on the lived experiences of older women in rural areas. The social, health, and economic lived experiences are also illuminated.

Social Experiences

Older women in rural communities in Ghana often suffer a double burden of social ascription. Double burden of social ascription in this context means that older women are cherished by the society and are at the same time abused and chastised. This is what Van der Geest (2002) refers to as the ambivalence towards older people: respect for them on the one hand and resentment towards them on the other hand.

On the one hand, older women in Ghana's rural areas are perceived as repository of knowledge regarding traditions, norms, and belief systems. As such, they are often consulted on major social practices. For instance, older women are consulted during adolescent rites of passage such as the Akans' "Bragro" and the Krobo's "Dipo" rites to advise the adolescent girls about menstruation, menstrual hygiene, marriage, and pregnancy-related issues (Kutufam 2021: 116–136). Also, older women play an active role in advising younger women in the community and in their respective households about issues related to pregnancy, keeping a traditional home, and child nurturing and feeding practices. This is reflected in the Akan saying that, "*Yɛkɔ Abrewa Tia hɔ Bayi Bɔne*". It loosely translates as going to the old woman for advice. Thus, highlighting the significance of older women to the social structure of the Ghanaian rural setting.

On the other hand, there is a preponderance of literature that suggests that some older women in rural areas face elder abuse (Crampton 2013; Danyoh et al. 2018: 4; Malmedal & Anyan 2020: 299–313; Sossou & Yogtiba 2015: 422–427). According to the WHO (2018), elder abuse refers to:

> [...] a single or repeated act, or lack of appropriate action, occurring within any relationship where there is an expectation of trust, which causes harm or distress to an older person. This type of violence constitutes a violation of human rights and includes physical, sexual, psychological, and emotional abuse; financial and material abuse; abandonment; neglect; and serious loss of dignity and respect.

As noted earlier, in Ghana, many elder women, particularly those residing in rural areas, are labelled as witches (Crampton 2013; Danyoh et al. 2018: 4; Malmedal & Anyan 2020: 299–313; Sossou & Yogtiba 2015: 422–427). This accusation of witchcraft tends to emanate from situations where in a given household or family, the younger generation face many challenges, including the inability to find employment, the inability to conceive and bear a child, or the experience of ill health of the younger generation in the household (Crampton 2013). In such scenarios, older women are blamed for the difficulties being experienced in the family. This may be due to the traditional belief that recognizes the existence and power of witchcraft in the traditional Ghanaian system. The belief is that there are good witches, "*Bayi pa*" and bad witches, "*Bayi bone*" as expressed in Twi (Crampton 2013). It is believed that an older woman would use her witch powers to ensure the success of the younger members of the family. Therefore, if the welfare and wellbeing of the younger members of the family retards, then the older woman in the house is sometimes accused of being the cause of every misfortune.

The situation is further worsened by some religious bodies who tend to be the lead accusers of older women as the architects of the misfortunes of the younger generation in a given household (Essuman & Mate-Kole 2021: 1–11). From the perspective of some of these neo-prophetic religious bodies, older women are possessed by evil spirits that control and direct them to cause mayhem in their respective families (Ayete-Nyampong 2014; Baffoe & Dako-Gyeke 2013: 347–363). Given that most Ghanaians are religious; they tend to easily believe this viewpoint that older women in rural areas are witches. Hence, they maltreat older women in their households, subjecting them to undignified life.

The proliferation of maltreatment and accusation of older women as witches is evident in the existence of witch camps, especially in rural areas in Northern Ghana (Mabefam 2023: 1–18). To escape persecution and potential harm, those accused of witchcraft sometimes find refuge in these witch camps. The camps provide a form of sanctuary, offering protection from the threats they face in their home villages. However, life in these camps is often challenging, as the individuals are separated from their families and communities, and they may experience stigmatization even within the camp setting. Social maltreatment of older women in rural Ghana has the potential to lead to significant physical injuries and adverse psychological impacts. In some situations, witchcraft accusations against older women have led to what Adinkrah (2020: 275–294) describes as "grannicide" – that is, the intentional killing of older women by their grandchildren.

Health-Related Experiences

Aside from the numerous infectious and parasitic diseases that older women are predisposed to (example: malaria), they face a higher burden of non-communicable, chronic, and degenerative diseases. A report from the WHO African Region shows that 43% of all causes of death in Ghana are due to non-communicable diseases with the most prevalent diseases being cardiovascular diseases, stroke, diabetes, cancers, and respiratory diseases (WHO 2022b). Yet, the health infrastructure and capacity to handle the health needs of older women remain underdeveloped. These diseases experienced by older women in the rural areas significantly affect their quality of life and therefore require palliation. However, there is a scarcity of affordable palliative care services to alleviate the physical and psycho-emotional distress faced by older women grappling with life-limiting conditions (Okyere & Kissah-Korsah 2023: 1–11).

The existing preconditions in Ghana's rural communities further exacerbate the ill health experience of older women. Notably, most rural communities in Ghana still rely substantially on unclean sources of cooking fuel such as charcoal, firewood, and kerosene (Tabiri et al. 2022: 480–489). Such sources of cooking fuel have been found to significantly increase the risk of hypertension, especially among older persons (Ayebeng et al. 2023: 1–9). Given that women are culturally ascribed to the gender role of cooking, older women's continual use of unclean cooking fuel would result in higher prevalence of hypertension and respiratory conditions among this cohort. This is likely to worsen their health expenditure. To mitigate these health risks, transitioning to cleaner cooking technologies, such as improved cook stoves or alternative energy sources like liquefied petroleum gas (LPG) and solar cookers, could offer a viable solution. Implementing such alternatives could not only reduce health risks but also alleviate the economic burden associated with healthcare expenditures for older women in these communities. It is imperative to promote and facilitate the adoption of cleaner cooking practices to enhance the overall wellbeing of older individuals in rural Ghana.

Transportation and distance are major barriers that impede the healthcare utilization behaviour of older women in rural areas. In many instances, healthcare centres are situated far from the homes of these women. This assertion is corroborated by Agyemang-Duah et al.'s (2019: 1–12) study that revealed that despite the availability of the LEAP Programme and cash transfer, older women in rural communities were still unable to access healthcare due to issues related to far distance to the nearest healthcare facility and inability to find a reliable source of transportation. Hence, older women often rely on family members or community members for transportation, which might not always be readily available. This tends to result in delayed or forgone medical care, which can have serious ramifications for the health and wellbeing of elder women in rural settings in Ghana.

Despite the availability of the LEAP Programme and the NHIS (see above), older women residing in Ghana's rural communities encounter significant financial barriers in their decision to seek formal healthcare. One study that aligns with this assertion is that of Appiah et al. (2020: 1–15) which suggests that older women are 1.2 times more likely to experience financial barriers in accessing formal healthcare than older men. The financial barriers faced by older women compared to their male counterparts could be due to the years of wage differentials that tend to be in favour of men. Particularly, this challenge of not being able to meet the financial requirements of seeking formal healthcare is profound among older women who did not receive any support from their family and the oldest old women (i.e., 85 years and above) (Oduro Appiah et al. 2022).

Unfortunately, the current set-up of the NHIS fails to sufficiently cater to the healthcare requirements of older people due to several factors (Kpessa-Whyte 2018: 403–408). Initially, the eligibility criteria for receiving free healthcare benefits from the programme resulted in a segment of older people below the age of 70 being excluded from coverage. Furthermore, the procedural inefficiencies inherent in the administration of retirement income benefits for pensioners, coupled with the limited coverage of the retirement income security system among older people, pose significant challenges for individuals aged 60–69 in their efforts to enrol in the NHIS (Kpessa-Whyte 2018: 403–408). Furthermore, the current exemption policy of the NHIS, which only applies to individuals aged 70 and above, is insufficient. This is particularly problematic considering that prevalent health conditions among this age group, such as arthritis, stroke, hypertension, heart diseases, and diabetes, are not included in the NHIS-approved list of services that are funded by the Scheme (Kpessa-Whyte 2018: 403–408; Okyere & Kissah-Korsah 2023: 1–11). The current coverage offered by the NHIS for older people does not adequately address the health issues associated with aging, leaving this population particularly susceptible to both man-made and natural degenerative diseases related to ageing.

To compound issues, there is evidence suggesting that most older people lack access to adequate health information (Hilson 2016: 547–563). Consequently, older women lack understanding of what they can do to manage morbidities associated with old age. It is possible that the inadequate health information received by older women may be due to a matter of supply. Healthcare providers may be lacking knowledge and expertise regarding geriatric care (Hilson 2016: 547–563). Hence, their inability to divulge comprehensive information to elder women.

All these health-related challenges underscore the failure of ageing policies like the LEAP and NHIS to properly target the group of older people who require much health support. It seems the extant policies and initiatives tend to treat the aged as a homogenous group, disregarding the vast heterogeneity that exists in this group. Therefore, any intervention, policy, or initiative aimed at eliminating the health and financial challenges faced by older women in rural Ghana must appreciate and account for the heterogenic characteristics of this vulnerable population.

Economic Experiences

A comprehension of the economic experiences of older women in rural areas of Ghana demands an appreciation of the socio-cultural context. This is because older women's economic experiences are influenced by a nuanced interaction between traditional livelihood activities, physical constraints related to ageing, and the intricate dynamics of resource and market access. Although women frequently make substantial contributions to their households and communities through activities such as subsistence farming, their economic autonomy can be impeded by a range of obstacles.

Subsistence farming constitutes the backbone of economic engagement in rural areas (Demedeme & Opoku 2022: 13–23). As such, older women in rural residences in Ghana tend to be more engaged in such economic activities. To support the older women's engagement in farming as a source of livelihood, the government of Ghana through the Business Advisory Centre and Rural Enterprise Programme provides the necessary grant money to ensure that they become self-reliant (Demedeme & Opoku 2022: 13–23). This provision ensures that rural-dwelling older women have a source of livelihood to fend for themselves.

Coping with Challenges

As noted above, older women often face many challenges, including verbal abuse, neglect, and disrespect (Lamptey et al. 2018: 199–208). In response to these challenges, older women in rural settings adopt varied coping mechanisms. A common strategy is turning to divine intervention. As indicated earlier, Ghana is a highly religious country. Irrespective of the type of religion, older women hold the belief in a supreme being who has control over whether or not a phenomenon occurs. Hence, in instances where an older person is faced with abuse, disrespect and neglect, they turn their eyes to whatever spirits they believe in for solace and renewed hope that things will get better someday (Lamptey et al. 2018: 199–208; Danyoh et al. 2018: 4).

Avoidance and keeping to one's self is another common mechanism adopted by older persons to cope with the abuse, disrespect, and neglect that they encounter. This coping strategy has been reported in a qualitative study by Lamptey et al. (2018: 199–208). Similarly, Danyoh et al. (2018: 4) also report in their study that about 34.8% of older people adopted the strategy of avoidance. Perhaps, the preference for this coping strategy may be due to the point it limits the tendency for escalation. However, such coping strategies can be maladaptive as they would in the long run result in loneliness and heightened sense of anxiety.

Intersectionality of Gender and Rurality of Ghanaian Women's Experiences with Ageing

The term "intersectionality," coined by Crenshaw (2013: 23–51), originally referred to the compounding effects of inequalities within individuals. Initially, it explored the convergence of race, class, and gender inequalities (Carastathis 2016; Carbado et al. 2013: 303–312). Choo and Ferree (2010: 129–149) later examined it as a process amplifying oppression. Intersectionality empowers the study of those in multiple marginalized groups. It broadened to encompass various demographics, power dynamics, and societal systems (Carbado et al. 2013: 303–312). Recently, intersectionality has delved into socio-economic status and geography (Roy et al. 2020: 1188–1197). Calasanti and Giles (2018: 70) introduced a life course perspective, addressing how older adults face late life with intertwined categorical memberships subject to inequalities. They highlighted that ageing itself can be a disadvantaged status, despite previous privilege.

Growing older in rural areas is especially challenging due to limited access to the support of both formal service and informal support from family members. Alongside tending to grandchildren, meals, household chores, and community involvement, older women actively participate in various agricultural tasks encompassing planting, weeding, watering, harvesting, processing, and food storage. Remarkably, the roles of older wives in rural areas closely resemble those of their younger counterparts (Warner & Balcombe 1996). Older female farmers undertake demanding journeys to markets, often accompanied by grandchildren, carrying substantial loads of farm produce for sale.

Furthermore, in numerous rural areas, aged women head households primarily due to spousal loss. Despite their substantial agricultural contributions, rural-dwelling older women lack access to agricultural support initiatives such as extensions and credit. Hindered by factors like insufficient awareness among decision-makers stemming from inadequate research dissemination highlighting domestic responsibilities, societal status, incorrect assumptions, and illiteracy, men continue to dominate loans and land control. Paradoxically, Ghana's primary farmers are women, constituting 47 percent of the agricultural labour force and contributing up to 70 percent of total food production (World Bank Group 2018). Hence, essential research into women farmers' roles, significance, and constraints is pivotal for crafting policies aimed at enhancing productivity and fostering socio-economic development.

The Agency of the Older Women in the Social, Economic, Political, and Religious Spheres

So far, the discussions elucidate the challenges that older women face in their socio-economic, political, and religious spheres. Nonetheless, older women have demonstrated a strong agency in these spheres. As posited by social gerontologist, Nana Araba Apt (McGadney-Douglass, Douglass, Apt & Antwi, 2005), older women in Ghana are perceived by the society as repositories of knowledge on all social and health issues. As such, they tend to assume the role of advisers in the household, encouraging their daughters to seek healthcare for their grandchildren. Furthermore, older women in Ghana are known to take up caregiving for their spouses, children, and other relatives – a task that requires a lot of commitment, sacrifice, and grit to successfully execute. Thus, underscoring the remarkable strength and resilience of older women in Ghana.

The role of older women in politics and governance has also been documented in previous studies (Owusu-Mensah, Asante & Osew, 2015; Sood, 2021). Particularly, within the Akan community, the succession and inheritance system bestows upon the Queen Mother the exclusive and prerogative right to nominate the potential chief (Owusu-Mensah, Asante & Osew, 2015: 1–16). As a result, any eligible candidate aspiring to become a chief must first receive endorsement from the Queen Mother. She selects the deserving, untarnished royal heir known for their strong moral character within the community and the broader society (Owusu-Mensah, Asante & Osew, 2015: 1–16). This demonstrates how the discerning judgement, moral aptitude, and commitment of queen mothers (usually older women) to preserving cultural values contribute significantly to the seamless continuation of traditional governance structures, fostering a sense of continuity and stability within the community. It is not surprising that Sood (2021) refers to queen mothers as the maternal activists of the 21st century.

Navigating through Later Years: Opportunities for Quality of Life

Amidst the gloom of growing old in rural Ghana, there are still some opportunities that can be leveraged to help older women navigate through their ageing process. Primarily, the existence of the NHIS is one of the key opportunities. Indeed, the current nature of the NHIS has several limitations. Going forward, it is imperative for the NHIS to expand the bracket of fee exemption to all older people by moving the threshold of 70 years and older to 60 years and older. This will ensure that women aged 60–70 years who lack financial and social support from their immediate family would have a national social welfare policy to rely on. The resultant effect could be an improvement in healthcare utilization among older women in rural Ghana and improvement in their general quality of life.

The time is right for the NHIS to consider expanding the benefits package available to older people in Ghana. This expansion must reflect the changing health needs of this vulnerable population. Hence, treatment and medications for hypertension, diabetes, chronic respiratory conditions, and cancer must be fully absorbed by the NHIS. Moreover, this expansion must include the integration of palliative care services and rehabilitation services to older people. Implementing these changes in the health insurance regime in Ghana would ensure that there is synergy between policy and the needs of older women in Ghana.

As has been highlighted above, one major limitation of the LEAP Programme has been its target of older people who fulfil the role of caregivers for orphaned and vulnerable youngsters (Government of Ghana 2010; Kpessa-Whyte 2018: 403–408). This implementation strategy needs to be reviewed and amended to ensure that all rural dwelling older women receive cash transfer irrespective of whether or not they perform caregiving roles to orphaned and vulnerable children. By implementing this action in the LEAP Programme, the dignity and welfare of older women would be guaranteed. Also, initiatives such as the Rural Enterprise Programme must be scaled up to all rural communities in Ghana to help better the economic life of older women through the receipt of grant money for agribusiness and other small enterprises.

The current National Ageing Policy lacks comprehensiveness. It does not provide strong, actionable plan that must be implemented to address the new health threats that confront older people, particularly women in rural areas in Ghana. Therefore, it is imperative for the 2010 National Ageing Policy to be reviewed. Any revision to the policy must necessarily provide clear strategies, targets, and activities to address the health, socio-economic, and psychological wellbeing of older women. On the socio-economic front, a revised National Ageing Policy must provide strategies that can be implemented to ensure that older women who work in the informal sector are captured by the Social Security and National Insurance Trust. This is critical as it will help the government accumulate capital sufficient to cater for the economic needs of the older when they retire from active economic work.

Some years ago, the Community-Based Health Planning and Services (CHPS) was introduced as an initiative to improve primary health care and facilitate universal health coverage by reducing distance-related barriers to healthcare accessibility. This initiative can be leveraged in response to the older women's challenge of delayed healthcare due to transportation and distance difficulties. The government of Ghana through the Ministry of Health and the Ghana Health Service must post specialist geriatric healthcare providers as part of the cadre of healthcare providers available in these CHPS facilities. In doing so, healthcare will be more accessible to older people. Hence, we will be contributing to the effective management of the adverse health outcomes experienced by older women in rural areas as diseases such as hypertension, cancer, diabetes, and chronic respiratory diseases would be comprehensively managed in facilities closer to the end user. This could promote adherence to medications and treatment and improve the quality of life of the older people.

Conclusion

It is evident that ageing as a woman in rural settings of Ghana is not linear but rather nuanced with complexities. This chapter projects older women in rural areas as key stakeholders and actors in social construction and socialization of the younger generation. Nevertheless, they often experience maltreatment, abuse, name calling, and accusations of witchcraft. Moreover, while there are bits and pieces of policies that have implications on the older population in Ghana, these policies have been limited in scope and comprehensiveness. We conclude that ensuring an enabling environment for quality ageing in rural areas, there must be a conscious effort to break off the cultural and religious beliefs that propagate ageism. The younger generation must be reoriented to understand that ageing is part our lives as humans and that this process can be demanding and complex. Therefore, exercising patience and tolerance when dealing with older people would facilitate the promotion of dignified and respectful ageing. Our contention is that enhancing rural transportation services and creating user-friendly healthcare facilities tailored to the needs of older individuals would constitute effective steps in reducing physical accessibility obstacles to the utilization of formal healthcare services. Also, expanding the health insurance coverage scope and benefits package coupled with an upward adjustment of the LEAP Programme cash transfer would help alleviate poverty among older women in rural Ghana. The country must increase the supply of healthcare providers skilled in geriatrics to match up the increasing demand for such services. We acknowledge that getting a pool of specialized healthcare providers in geriatrics might take time. Therefore, we propose that geriatric care be actively included in the preservice training of all health and allied healthcare providers. This will help create a large pool of general practitioners who can provide adequate geriatric information and services.

References

Adinkrah, M., 2020. "Grannicides in Ghana: A study of lethal violence by grandchildren against grandmothers." *Journal of Elder Abuse & Neglect, 32*(3), pp. 275–294.

Agyemang-Duah, W., Peprah, C. and Peprah, P., 2019. "Barriers to formal healthcare utilisation among poor older people under the livelihood empowerment against poverty programme in the Atwima Nwabiagya District of Ghana." *BMC Public Health, 19*(1), pp. 1–12.

Alidu, S., Dankyi, E. and Tsiboe-Darko, A., 2016. "Aging policies in Ghana: A review of the livelihood empowerment against poverty and the National Health Insurance Scheme." *Ghana Studies, 19*(1), pp. 154–172.

Appiah, J. O., Agyemang-Duah, W., Peprah, C., Adei, D., Peprah, P., and Fordjour, A. A. 2020. Transportation barriers to formal healthcare utilisation and associated factors among poor older people under a social protection programme in Ghana. *Journal of Transport & Health, 19*, 100965. doi: 10.1016/j.jth.2020.100965

Ayebeng, C., Okyere, J. and Dickson, K.S., 2023. "Influence of type of cooking fuel on risk of hypertension among reproductive-age women in sub-Saharan Africa: insights from nationally representative cross-sectional surveys." *International Health, 16*(3), 325–333

Ayete-Nyampong, S., 2014. *A study of pastoral care of the elderly in Africa: An interdisciplinary approach with focus on Ghana.* AuthorHouse.

Baffoe, M. and Dako-Gyeke, M., 2013. "Social problems and social work in Ghana: Implications for sustainable development." *International Journal of Development and Sustainability, 2*(1), pp. 347–363.

Calasanti, T. and Giles, S., 2018. "The challenge of intersectionality." *Generations, 41*(4), pp. 69–74.

Carastathis, A., 2016. *Intersectionality: Origins, contestations, horizons.* University of Nebraska Press.

Carbado, D.W., Crenshaw, K.W., Mays, V.M. and Tomlinson, B., 2013. INTERSECTIONALITY: Mapping the Movements of a Theory1. *Du Bois Review: Social Science Research on Race*, *10*(2), pp. 303–312.

Choo, H.Y. and Ferree, M.M., 2010. "Practicing intersectionality in sociological research: A critical analysis of inclusions, interactions, and institutions in the study of inequalities." *Sociological Theory*, *28*(2), pp. 129–149.

Crampton, A., 2013. "No peace in the house: witchcraft accusations as an 'old woman's problem' in Ghana." *Anthropology & Aging Quarterly*, 34(2): 199.

Crenshaw, K., 2013. "Demarginalizing the intersection of race and sex: A black feminist critique of antidiscrimination doctrine, feminist theory and antiracist politics." In *Feminist legal theories* (pp. 23–51). Routledge.

Danyoh, J.D., Dampson, D.G. and Dzakadzie, Y., 2018. "Abuse or disabuse: Coping with elderly abuse in the Asaiman Municipality, Ghana." *European Journal of Research and Reflection in Educational Sciences*, *6*(4), pp. 1–12.

Demedeme, G. and Opoku, C.B., 2022. "Economic empowerment of rural women: Assessing the effectiveness of the rural enterprise program (REP) in Ghana, West Africa." *Journal of Agricultural Extension and Rural Development*, *14*(1), pp. 13–23.

Essuman, A. and Mate-Kole, C.C., 2021. Ageing in Ghana. *Aging Across Cultures: Growing Old in the Non-Western World*, Springer Nature, pp. 1–11.

Fuseini, M.N., Enu-Kwesi, F. and Sulemana, M., 2019. "Poverty reduction in Upper West Region, Ghana: role of the livelihood empowerment against poverty programme." *Development in Practice*, *29*(6), pp. 760–773.

Ghana Statistical Service (GSS), 2022. One-quarter of the elderly in Ghana are multidimensionally poor. https://census2021.statsghana.gov.gh/presspage.php?readmorenews= MTc2ODIyNTE2NS4yMjU1&One-quarter-of-the-elderly-in-Ghana-are-multidimensionally-poor#:~:text=The%20Ghana%20Statistical%20Service%20(GSS,and%201%2C129%2C906%20(56.7%25)%20females

Government of Ghana, 2010. National ageing policy: Ageing with security and dignity. https://www.mogcsp.gov.gh/mdocs-posts/national-ageing-policy-ageing-with-security-and-dignity/

Hilson, G., 2016. "Farming, small-scale mining and rural livelihoods in Sub-Saharan Africa: A critical overview." *The Extractive Industries and Society*, *3*(2), pp. 547–563.

Koduah, A., Van Dijk, H. and Agyepong, I.A., 2015. "The role of policy actors and contextual factors in policy agenda setting and formulation: maternal fee exemption policies in Ghana over four and a half decades." *Health Research Policy and Systems*, *13*(1), pp. 1–20.

Kpessa-Whyte, M., 2018. "Aging and demographic transition in Ghana: State of the elderly and emerging issues." *The Gerontologist*, *58*(3), pp. 403–408.

Kutufam, D.V., 2021." Dipo and the Adolescent Krobo Girl: Redemption of a Contested Puberty Rite for Contemporary Sexual Health Education." In *Dialectical Perspectives on Media, Health, and Culture in Modern Africa* (pp. 116–136). IGI Global.

Lachman, M.E., Teshale, S. and Agrigoroaei, S., 2015. "Midlife as a pivotal period in the life course: Balancing growth and decline at the crossroads of youth and old age." *International Journal of Behavioral Development*, *39*(1), pp. 20–31.

Lamptey, I., Boateng, A., Hamenoo, E. and Agyemang, F.A., 2018. "Exploring the experiences of elderly persons cared for by family caregivers in Ghana." *Int j innov res adv stud*, *5*, pp. 199–208.

Mabefam, M.G., 2023. "Journeying into the experiences of persons accused of witchcraft: Rethinking development theory and practice," *Critical African Studies* 15(3), 356–373.

Malmedal, W. and Anyan, C., 2020. "Elder abuse in Ghana–A qualitative exploratory study." *The Journal of Adult Protection*, *22*(5), pp. 299–313.

Maltoni, R., Ravaioli, S., Bronte, G., Mazza, M., Cerchione, C., Massa, I., Balzi, W., Cortesi, M., Zanoni, M. and Bravaccini, S., 2022. "Chronological age or biological age: What drives the choice of adjuvant treatment in elderly breast cancer patients?" *Translational Oncology*, *15*(1), p. 101300.

Mbam, K.C., Halvorsen, C.J. and Okoye, U.O., 2022. "Aging in Nigeria: a growing population of older adults requires the implementation of national aging policies." *The Gerontologist*, *62*(9), pp. 1243–1250.

Ministry of Gender, Children and Social Protection, 2023. Livelihood Empowerment Against Poverty (Leap). Republic of Ghana. https://www.mogcsp.gov.gh/projects/livelyhood-empowerment-against-poverty-leap/

McGadney-Douglass, B. F., Douglass, R. L., Apt, N. A., and Antwi, P. 2005. "Ghanaian mothers helping adult daughters: the survival of malnourished grandchildren." *Journal of the Motherhood Initiative for Research and Community Involvement* 7(2), pp. 112–124.

Oduro Appiah, J., Agyemang-Duah, W., Fordjour, A.A. and Adei, D., 2022. "Predicting financial barriers to formal healthcare utilisation among poor older people under the livelihood empowerment against poverty programme in Ghana." *GeoJournal*, 87, pp. 333–347.

Okyere, J. and Kissah-Korsah, K., 2023. "Barriers to the integration of palliative care in Ghana: evidence from a tertiary health facility." *Palliative Care and Social Practice*, 17. doi: 10.1177/26323524231179980

Owusu-Mensah, I., Asante, W., and Osew, W. K. 2015. "Queen mothers: the unseen hands in chieftaincy conflicts among the Akan in Ghana: Myth or reality." *The Journal of Pan African Studies*, 8(6), 1–16.

Räsänen, J., 2023. "When biological ageing is desirable? A reply to García-Barranquero et al." *Journal of Medical Ethics*. doi: 10.1136/jme-2023-109329

Roy, M., Bhatta, T. and Burnette, J.D., 2020. "Intersectional effects of gender, education, and geographic region on functional health disparities among older adults in India." *Journal of Aging and Health*, 32(9), pp. 1188–1197.

Sattaur, Z., Lashley, L.K. and Golden, C.J., 2020. "Wear and tear theory of aging." *Essays in Developmental Psychology*. https://nsuworks.nova.edu/cps_facbooks/732

Sood, A. 2021. "The queen mothers of Ghana: Maternal activists of the twenty-first century." *Journal of the Motherhood Initiative for Research and Community Involvement*, 12(2). https://jarm.journals.yorku.ca/index.php/jarm/article/view/40632

Sossou, M.A. and Yogtiba, J.A., 2015. "Abuse, neglect, and violence against elderly women in Ghana: Implications for social justice and human rights." *Journal of Elder Abuse & Neglect*, 27 (4–5), pp. 422–427.

Tabiri, K.G., Adusah-Poku, F. and Novignon, J., 2022. "Economic inequalities and rural-urban disparities in clean cooking fuel use in Ghana." *Energy for Sustainable Development*, 68, pp. 480–489.

UNFPA ESARO, 2022. Rapid review of healthy ageing and long-term care systems in East and Southern Africa. https://esaro.unfpa.org/en/publications/rapid-review-healthy-ageing-and-long-term-care-systems-east-and-southern-africa

United Nations, Department of Economic and Social Affairs, Population Division, 2019. World Prospects 2019, custom data acquired via website. https://www.un.org/development/desa/pd/news/world-population-prospects-2019-0

Van der Geest, S. 2002. "From wisdom to witchcraft: Ambivalence towards old age in rural Ghana." *Africa*, 72(3), 437–463.

Warner, M.W. and Balcombe, K., 1996. *How Useful is Gender in Explaining the Economic Roles of Africa's Rural Peoples? An Application of Logistic Regression Analysis*. University of London, Wye College, Department of Agricultural Economics.

World Bank Group, 2018. *Democratic Republic of Congo Systematic Country Diagnostic: Policy Priorities for Poverty Reduction and Shared Prosperity in a Post-Conflict Country and Fragile State*. World Bank.

World Health Organization (WHO), 2018. "Elder abuse". www.who.int/news-room/factsheets/detail/elder-abuse

World Health Organization (WHO), 2022a. *Ageing and health*. https://www.who.int/news-room/fact-sheets/detail/ageing-and-health#:~:text=Every%20country%20in%20the%20world,in%202020%20to%201.4%20billion

World Health Organization (WHO), 2022b. *Beating noncommunicable diseases through primary healthcare*. https://www.afro.who.int/countries/ghana/news/beating-noncommunicable-diseases-through-primary-healthcare#:~:text=In%20Ghana%2C%20NCDs%20account%20for,becoming%20common%20in%20health%20facilities

World Health Organization, 2015. *World report on ageing and health*. World Health Organization.

World Health Organization, African Region, 2022. *Ageing*. World Health Organization. https://www.afro.who.int/health-topics/ageing

30
THE ROLE OF ELDERLY WOMEN IN BOTSWANA

A Perspective from African Theological Feminist Gerontology

Tshenolo Jennifer Madigele

Introduction

This chapter seeks to examine the multifaceted roles played by elderly women in Botswana and analyse the ways in which African Theological Feminism can provide a comprehensive understanding of their experiences. It highlights the cultural, social, and spiritual dimensions that shape the lives of elderly women, emphasizing the need for a nuanced theological perspective that recognizes and celebrates their contributions. For the purposes of this chapter, the term "elderly person" refers to individuals aged 65 years and above, acknowledging that some sources may use 60 years as a standard measure for categorizing elderly individuals. This chapter uses the term "elderly person" instead of "older person" to be clear and respectful. "Elderly" suggests wisdom and shows someone is a senior figure in the community, which can be seen as more polite in some situations (Taylor, 2011). This change in words aims to refer to people in this age group in a positive and respectful way, highlighting their experience and important role in the community. The pivotal question is: "What is the role of elderly women in Botswana?"

Ageing is a multifaceted process that extends beyond mere chronological advancement, encompassing economic, social, and physical dimensions. Traditionally, societal perspectives have often depicted ageing as a phase marked by decline, emphasizing vulnerabilities in older individuals. Social welfare policies, such as pensions and care homes, have reinforced a perception of dependency and stigmatization of the elderly, highlighting the risks associated with the ageing process (Biggs and Powell, 2001; Twigg and Martin, 2014). It is from this background that criticisms have surfaced, pointing to the inadequacy of this discourse in addressing the structural inequalities faced by older individuals, especially those from diverse social backgrounds (Rotarou and Sakellariou, 2019).

The population of elderly individuals was around 43 million in 2010. Forecasts from the World Health Organization (WHO) anticipate a substantial increase to 67 million by 2025 and a staggering 163 million by 2050. Similarly, in Botswana, the ageing population has witnessed growth, constituting 6% of the total population in 2011, up from 5% in 2001, with projections indicating a rise to over 8.5% in 2021 and an anticipated 20% by 2050 (WHO, 2022).

A rapid situational analysis in 2019, supported by the World Health Organization (WHO) and conducted by the Ministry of Health, identified significant gaps in the care of older individuals. These gaps include the absence of specific policies and laws addressing their needs and rights, a misalignment of the healthcare system with the requirements of older adults, insufficient data on their health status, and a notable prevalence of non-communicable diseases. Additional challenges encompass high poverty levels, accusations of witchcraft, unhealthy eating habits, and substantial tobacco and alcohol consumption rates.

In response to the identified gaps in elderly care in Botswana, the Ministry of Health, in collaboration with the World Health Organization (WHO), has taken proactive steps to address the challenges of an ageing population. One significant initiative is the development of the Healthy and Active Ageing Strategy for the period 2021–2026. Additionally, the Ministry of Health has embraced the WHO Integrated Care for Older People (ICOPE) assessment and monitoring card, piloted in October 2022. Aligned with WHO's global guidelines on Integrated Care for Older People, Botswana has adapted these guidelines to suit its health facilities. To operationalize the ICOPE guidelines, the Ministry of Health has introduced a health monitoring tool in the form of an assessment card (WHO, 2022).

It has become evident that the ageing process is intricately shaped by a convergence of variables, including age, gender, ethnicity, socio-economic status, historical events, and the social location of individuals. In light of this complex interplay, the spotlight must be directed towards evaluating the effectiveness of policies in addressing the welfare of the elderly. This scrutiny is particularly crucial as the elderly, especially women, are susceptible to experiences of marginalization and poverty. The initiatives undertaken by Botswana's Ministry of Health, in collaboration with the World Health Organization, to develop strategies like the Healthy and Active Ageing Strategy and the adoption of the WHO Integrated Care for Older People (ICOPE) assessment and monitoring card, highlight the importance of proactive measures in mitigating the health challenges associated with an ageing population.

This chapter embarks on a thorough exploration of the diverse roles and challenges associated with elderly women in Botswana, placing a crucial spotlight on the imperative necessity for African Theological Feminist Gerontology. The unfolding discussion follows a structured approach, delving into the historical and cultural context, examining the invaluable contributions of elderly women, and meticulously addressing the challenges they encounter. These challenges, encompassing economic hardships, health issues, social stigmatization, and unhealthy habits, are highlighted for their potential to curtail the agency and strategic contributions of elderly women within the spheres of family, community, and nation. In acknowledging the paramount importance of reclaiming and amplifying the agency of elderly women, we introduce African Theological Feminist Gerontology as a pivotal framework. Grounded in the intersections of theology and feminism, this framework aims not only to bolster the current contributions of elderly women but also to proactively shape a future where barriers are dismantled, ensuring they are recognized as valuable community members rather than mere recipients of aid.

Historical and Cultural Context

To understand the role of elderly women in Botswana, it is essential to consider the historical and cultural context. Traditional Batswana society has long recognized the importance of elderly women as custodians of culture, knowledge, and wisdom. However, with the advent of modernization and changing gender dynamics, their roles have undergone significant transformations (Ingstad, et al., 1992). In Botswana, people understand ageing, known as "*botsofe*," by comparing it to an idealized past. This term includes physical changes, spiritual influence, and accumulated knowledge that happen as someone gets older. Common signs, like wrinkled skin and using canes, indicate the onset of *botsofe*, much like in the past. Ageing is not just about physical changes; it also represents cultural authority, spiritual connection, wisdom, and political influence. The process of ageing is a gradual negotiation within families, communities, and broader social contexts. Tswana people distinguish between social elderhood (*bogolo*) and senescence (*tsofetse*), considering them as different but related aspects of *botsofe*. While elderhood traditionally came before senescence, nowadays, factors like chronic illnesses can make people show signs of ageing at a younger age. This shift not only affects how old someone is considered but also changes the social importance of being an elder (Tlou and Campbell, 1984; Burke, 2000). Thus, ageing was aligned with social significance.

The concept of ageing or *botsofe*, therefore, was traditionally associated with longevity and experience. Nowadays, the experience of old age is intertwined with dealing with multiple health issues, reflecting a shift from the earlier perception of ageing (Livingston, 2003).

The difference between frailty associated with old age and illness is significant. In the past, the physical signs of ageing, like bent posture or slowed gait, developed gradually over many years but did not necessarily prevent the elderly from being active and working. However, illness could lead to a sudden withdrawal from productive activities. The extreme frailty observed in very old individuals was seen as a transition towards spiritual potency, resembling the becoming of an ancestor. This perspective highlighted the cyclical nature of life. The frailty of the very old, with slow movements and speech, often led to them being affectionately referred to as "children," emphasizing the care and love they received. This contrasted with illness, which in recent times has increasingly characterized old age as a period marked by pain, social disruption, disordered ageing, and a decline in personal strength (Burke, 2000).

In the past, when elderly women got older, they were respected, and people thought their declining health indicated spiritual strength. People even brought them small gifts for blessings. Nowadays, elderly women often face chronic illnesses like cancer and diabetes. Unlike before, many people do not attribute these illnesses to spiritual causes. Instead, elderly women seek medical care at clinics. Limited resources sometimes make it hard for them to access traditional healthcare. The goal of treatment is often to ease symptoms rather than cure. Additionally, there is a broader health crisis, including the impact of HIV and AIDS, leading to more illness and disability, especially among children. Urban areas lack the support needed, so sick or disabled individuals often return to the homes of elderly women in rural villages. This changing health situation is seen as a result of lifestyle changes and modernization, impacting how elderly women experience ageing and health in Botswana (Livinston, 2003). Therefore, the traditional view of ageing as a period of spiritual strength and gradual physical changes has shifted. Elderly women now often contend with chronic diseases, and the interpretation of their health has moved away from spiritual explanations to a more medicalized understanding.

In essence, the understanding of ageing in Botswana has evolved from a focus on physical changes and cultural significance to a more complex scenario involving health challenges and economic shifts. In the past, elderly women were traditionally seen as productive and respected members of society. They held roles of authority and knowledge and were actively involved in productive activities, contributing to the community's well-being. However, there has been a shift, and elderly women now encounter new challenges. These challenges are related to changes in the economy, which have altered the traditional roles and significance of elderly women. Money has become crucial for care, and the old age pension programme, starting at 65, has redefined the concept of being old. The pension programme, by setting 65 as the age of eligibility, contributes to redefining what it means to be old in Botswana. This chronological marker becomes a tangible measure for determining who is considered elderly and eligible for state support (Livingston, 2003).

Many older women in Botswana face tough challenges, especially because there are more elderly women than men. Unlike elderly men, who often have respect and power through possessions such as cattle and important roles in family and community matters, elderly women have less economic power. They still play vital roles in cultural practices like arranging marriages, but they rely more on money sent by family members in cities. This makes them financially dependent. So, while they are important for cultural traditions, their financial situation is often difficult, and it is important to understand and address their specific challenges (Ingstad, 1994).

Contributions of Elderly Women

Amidst the challenges faced by elderly women in Botswana, it is crucial to recognize and celebrate their invaluable contributions to family, community, and the nation. African Theological Feminist Gerontology emerges as a transformative framework that not only acknowledges these contributions but actively seeks to recover, amplify, and enhance them in the face of evolving societal dynamics.

Elderly women in Botswana play a pivotal role within the family structure, often assuming caregiving responsibilities for grandchildren and extended family members. Their wisdom, nurturance, and experience become crucial in providing emotional support and stability, especially in cases where parents have migrated to urban areas. Despite health challenges, these women remain resilient pillars, ensuring the well-being and cohesion of their families. African Theological Feminist Gerontology recognizes and uplifts the importance of these caregiving roles, framing them within a spiritual and cultural context that empowers elderly women to navigate and thrive despite the challenges.

Elderly women in Botswana play a significant role in the social, economic, and cultural fabric of their communities. Traditionally, elderly women are highly respected and revered for their wisdom, experience, and guidance (Ingstad, et al., 1992). They often serve as matriarchs within their families and communities, providing nurturing care and passing down cultural traditions and values to younger generations. In many rural areas of Botswana, elderly women are the primary caregivers for their grandchildren and other family members, especially in cases where parents have migrated to urban areas in search of employment opportunities (Lindsey et al., 2003; Onen et al., 2019; Mhaka-Mutepfa and Wright, 2022).

Elderly women often serve as the backbone of family units. With extended families being a common structure in Botswana, as indicated, these women frequently take on caregiving roles, not only for their grandchildren, but also for other relatives. This responsibility can be particularly pronounced in the context of the HIV and AIDS epidemic that has significantly impacted Botswana, leading to an increase in grandparent-headed households. Elderly women thus provide emotional support and stability, helping to maintain family cohesion during challenging times (Tlou & Campbell, 1984; Madigele & Tshelametse, 2023a). These gendered role expectations, cultural stereotypes, and family responsibilities are perceived as roadblocks for women in leadership (Shaibu, 2013).

However, elderly women are actively advocating for changes in societal attitudes. They are using their influence to challenge stereotypes and promote gender equality in leadership roles. Having experienced various challenges and barriers in their own journeys, they are playing a crucial role in mentoring and guiding younger women aspiring to leadership positions. Their insights into overcoming societal and cultural obstacles are invaluable (Madigele and Tshelametse, 2023b).

Additionally, elderly women often hold important positions within local community structures, where they contribute to decision-making processes and provide support and advice to community members. This phenomenon is rooted in the traditional roles and responsibilities that elderly women have played in many societies throughout history (Livingston, 2003).

Traditionally, elderly women in Botswana are revered as custodians of the cultural heritage. They are responsible for passing down traditions, stories, and cultural practices to younger generations. This role is crucial in preserving the identity and continuity of Botswana's diverse ethnic groups. Elderly women often lead ceremonies and rituals, imparting wisdom and guiding the moral compass of their communities (Bagwasi and Sunderland, 2013). As leaders of most families, elderly women are the major stakeholders in nations' social responsibility programmes, and the success of these programmes is questionable without their input (Raditloaneng, 2012). Hence, elderly women's inadequate representation in political and corporate decision-making can prove to be costly to public and private sectors since organizations' decisions on social responsibility programmes may be affected.

Economically, elderly women contribute through both formal and informal sectors. While participation in the formal workforce might be limited due to age or health factors, many engage in informal activities such as agriculture, craft making, and small-scale trading. These endeavours not only provide a source of income but also contribute to the local economy and community well-being. Additionally, through managing household resources and making financial decisions, they play a critical role in sustaining their families' livelihoods (Shaibu, 2013; Madigele and Tshelametse, 2023a). As grandmothers and heads of households, they nurture children, help with education, and provide personal and career guidance, making sure that grandchildren grow into responsible citizens. However, such wisdom may be hindered by constraints of inadequate representation in positions of power and national decision-making (Kang'ethe, 2013).

Despite their progressive contributions, elderly women in Botswana may face several barriers that deter their participation in political leadership roles. Sociocultural norms, deeply rooted in patriarchal traditions, often perpetuate traditional gender roles and may limit the acceptance of elderly women in positions of political authority. Additionally, a lack of support structures and resources, in terms of both education and campaign resources, could present challenges for elderly women who aspire to engage in political leadership. Furthermore, elderly women, influenced by these sociocultural norms and potential resource constraints, do not find the necessary encouragement or avenues for training and networking that could enhance their political participation. As a result, despite being significant consumers of local policies, elderly women might be less inclined to actively participate in political leadership roles in Botswana (Mandiyanike, 2023).

Elderly women in Botswana face several challenges (see below). These include health issues, limited access to healthcare services, economic vulnerability, and sometimes social isolation. The government and various non-governmental organizations (NGOs) have been working towards addressing these challenges through policies aimed at improving healthcare access, providing social support programmes, and promoting economic empowerment initiatives targeted at the elderly. Elderly women in Botswana continue to be resilient pillars of strength within their families and communities despite the challenges they face (Ingstad, et al., 1992; Madigele, 2021).

Challenges Faced by Elderly Women

The invaluable contributions of elderly women in Botswana are undeniable, as they play pivotal roles within families, communities, and the nation. However, it is crucial to acknowledge that despite their significant contributions, these resilient women face numerous barriers that as Minimise to their capacity to provide and make maximum contributions. Amidst their crucial caregiving responsibilities for grandchildren and extended family members, elderly women encounter challenges stemming from the forces of modernization, urbanization, and evolving family dynamics. The changing attitudes of the younger generation towards caregiving, coupled with the erosion of traditional support networks, contribute to potential isolation and feelings of uncertainty and loneliness among elderly women.

The impact of modernization on the social structures of communities and families in Botswana has been profound, leading to significant changes in the socio-economic landscape. The migration of adolescents and working-age groups to urban centres, coupled with the effects of HIV and AIDS, has transformed rural populations, creating imbalances in family systems (Clausen, 2000). The elderly, predominantly women, and children now dominate rural households, leading to an overrepresentation of dependent members, including the elderly, children, and the disabled (Clausen, 2000). The impact of modernization on family dynamics has resulted in a heightened sense of dependency among elderly women, particularly on their children (Ingstad et al., 1992). The changing attitudes of the younger generation towards caregiving have led to potential isolation and the erosion of traditional support networks. Elderly women find themselves grappling with uncertainty about their future, experiencing feelings of isolation and loneliness (Ingstad et al., 1992).

The evolving role of elderly women is closely tied to the changing attitudes of the younger generation towards caregiving. The burden of caring for grandchildren, combined with challenges in resource management, raises concerns about future care and support for the elderly (Ingstad et al., 1992). The younger generation's shift towards individual economic pursuits and changing family structures contributes to the challenges faced by elderly women in maintaining household viability.

Modernization also brought the shift from subsistence to cash economic structures which altered the socio-economic activities of rural communities in Botswana. Traditional support systems that once relied on basic agriculture have given way to a heavy reliance on the market for the production of goods and services (Kollapan, 2009). This transition has had far-reaching consequences for the elderly population in terms of economic security, access to resources, and the traditional family support system.

One of the major challenges faced by elderly women in Botswana is the changing family dynamics and societal structures resulting from migration and urbanization. The departure of young, able-bodied individuals in search of opportunities has created a void in rural areas, leaving the elderly to manage households and juggle basic agriculture to support their children who have migrated to urban areas (Kollapan, 2009). The increasing trend of migration has contributed to the neglect of elderly family members, as fewer individuals are available to care for the frail elderly at home (Specht and Graig, 1987). Historically, the traditional extended family system served as a robust support structure for elderly women in Botswana. However, with the influence of modernization and shifting family dynamics, this support system has weakened over time (Ingstad et al., 1992). The decline of the extended family has contributed to economic insecurity and a loss of control over essential resources, including livestock and land, creating a vulnerable situation for elderly women.

The impact of modernization on the socio-economic status of the elderly in Botswana is evident in the challenges they face. Modernization has led to the marginalization of the subsistence agricultural sector, resulting in poverty among the elderly (CSO, 2001). Loss of social and economic support from economically active family members, combined with negligence by children and the community, further exacerbates the challenges faced by elderly women (CSO, 2001). The weakening of institutions that traditionally functioned as sources of social and economic support has contributed to their vulnerability.

The changing economic landscape, coupled with a loss of control over vital resources, presents economic challenges for elderly women in Botswana (Ingstad et al., 1992). The impact of modernization on traditional family structures and values contributes to economic insecurity, affecting the livelihoods of elderly women. Limited access to resources such as livestock compounds the economic challenges faced by this demographic.

Poverty among the elderly, particularly older women, is a pressing concern in Botswana. The shift from subsistence agriculture to unproductive agricultural activities generates unsustainable income, leading to situations of chronic poverty (Nyanguru, 2007). The World Bank indicates that the poverty gap ratio for households with elderly members is higher than the national average in several African countries, including Botswana (Nyanguru, 2007).

As noted earlier, in Botswana, the retirement age for government and other sectors is fixed at 65 years, irrespective of the individual's capability to continue serving productively. This policy may contribute to the economic challenges faced by the elderly, as many are forced into retirement regardless of their capacity to contribute meaningfully to the workforce (Sucre, 2002).

Despite being primary caregivers, elderly women in Botswana often struggle to secure adequate healthcare for themselves. Access to modern healthcare facilities becomes a significant challenge, posing a threat to the overall well-being of elderly women (Ingstad et al., 1992). This creates a situation where those who provide essential care to their families face obstacles in obtaining necessary care for their own health needs.

Identified Gaps in the Roles and Challenges of Elderly Women in Botswana

As this chapter has highlighted above, elderly women in Botswana confront many challenges rooted in societal shifts, economic transitions, and obstacles to healthcare accessibility. A critical gap in this context is the absence of tailored social policies to meet the unique needs of elderly women in Botswana (Clausen, 2000). This deficiency in targeted policies poses a risk of exacerbating existing challenges, particularly in accessing healthcare services and ensuring economic security. Without robust policy frameworks, elderly women may continue to encounter barriers hindering their access to essential services and support systems. This prevents elderly women from fulfilling their strategic roles in families, communities, and the nation.

Botswana has witnessed significant transformations due to modernization and urbanization, contributing to the erosion of the traditional extended family system (Kollapan, 2009). Historically, this extended family structure served as a crucial support system for elderly women. The diminishing role of this extended family dynamic amplifies economic challenges and social isolation among elderly women, underscoring a noticeable gap in familial and community support systems.

Despite being primary caregivers, elderly women in Botswana face obstacles in accessing modern healthcare facilities for their own health needs (Sucre, 2002). This healthcare accessibility gap emphasizes the necessity for targeted interventions to address the specific health concerns of elderly women and ensure equitable access to healthcare services.

The changing economic landscape, influenced by modernization, has resulted in economic insecurity among elderly women in Botswana (CSO, 2001). The loss of control over essential resources, such as land and livestock, intensifies their vulnerability, emphasizing the urgency of interventions addressing resource management and economic empowerment.

Shifts in societal values and priorities have led to changing attitudes towards caregiving, raising concerns about the future care and support for elderly women in Botswana (Nyanguru, 2007). This intergenerational gap in understanding and support underscores the importance of promoting respect for the contributions of elderly women and fostering inclusive caregiving practices.

Furthermore, the HIV and AIDS epidemic compounds the challenges faced by elderly women in Botswana, increasing their vulnerability and burden of care (Kollapan, 2009). Addressing the specific needs of older women in HIV and AIDS prevention and treatment programmes is essential to mitigate the impact of the epidemic on this demographic.

As highlighted above, a significant gap in terms of gender equality is the underrepresentation of women in leadership positions across various sectors, including politics, business, and academia. Despite progress in recent years, women continue to be disproportionately underrepresented in top decision-making roles. This gender gap in leadership not only hinders the full utilization of diverse perspectives and talents but also perpetuates stereotypes and inequalities. Closing this gap requires comprehensive efforts to address systemic barriers, unconscious biases, and discriminatory practices that limit women's access to leadership opportunities.

Traditional cultural norms often confine women to specific roles, limiting their opportunities for career growth and financial independence (Clausen, 2000). The perpetuation of these gendered expectations reinforces stereotypes, hindering women from pursuing diverse career paths and contributing to an imbalanced division of labour within society.

Moreover, the mismatch between a retirement age of 65 and delayed entry into stable employment due to high unemployment rates creates a significant gap (Sucre, 2002). Women find themselves with limited time to establish financial security, save for retirement, or ascend to leadership positions within organizations before reaching the retirement age. Additionally, high unemployment rates contribute to the delayed and unstable employment experienced by women, affecting their ability to secure long-term financial stability (Kollapan, 2009). The unpredictable nature of employment opportunities poses challenges for women in planning for retirement and accumulating savings.

The absence of robust social security systems exacerbates the challenges faced by women during unemployment or retirement (CSO, 2001). This lack of support leaves women vulnerable to financial hardships, making it challenging to maintain their quality of life after retirement or during periods of unemployment.

Addressing the identified gaps requires a multifaceted approach encompassing cultural reform, a reconsideration of retirement age policies, gender-inclusive employment practices, and the establishment of robust social safety nets (Clausen, 2000). By challenging traditional norms, reassessing retirement policies, and implementing inclusive measures, societies can strive towards gender equity, fostering an environment where women can navigate their careers and retirement with dignity and financial security.

African Theological Feminist Gerontology

In light of the preceding discussions on the crucial contributions of elderly women in Botswana and the formidable challenges that threaten to constrain their roles, this exploration of African Theological Feminist Gerontology serves as a pivotal link in understanding how religion, specifically in the context of African theological feminism and feminist gerontology, can offer liberative pathways for the elderly women. The role of religion is deeply embedded in the lives of elderly women in Botswana, and acknowledging its liberative potential is key to securing their ongoing contributions.

Religion often acts as a central force in the lives of elderly women, influencing their beliefs, values, and daily practices. Recognizing this, the following sections will delve into African theological feminism and feminist gerontology separately, providing concise summaries of each. The aim is to establish a foundation for the subsequent synthesis of these frameworks into African Theological Feminist Gerontology. This synthesized framework will provide a holistic approach to empower elderly women in Botswana, ensuring the continuity of their agency and productivity within families, communities, and the nation.

African theological feminism, as a conceptual framework, addresses the intersectionality of gender, culture, and spirituality. It emphasizes the importance of integrating feminist perspectives within African religious and cultural contexts, challenging patriarchal structures that may hinder women's agency. By incorporating this framework, we aim to explore how it can contribute to the liberative potential of religion in the lives of elderly women, fostering an environment where their contributions are valued and enhanced.

Feminist Gerontology, on the other hand, focuses on the ageing experiences of women, considering the unique challenges and strengths they bring to the ageing process. It recognizes the diverse ways in which women age and advocates for policies and practices that address their specific needs (Oduyoye, 2001). As we discuss Feminist Gerontology, we will highlight its relevance to the challenges faced by elderly women in Botswana, providing insights into how it can inform strategies to overcome barriers and promote their continued agency.

The subsequent synthesis of African theological feminism and Feminist Gerontology into African Theological Feminist Gerontology aims to create a comprehensive framework. This framework will not only acknowledge the spiritual and cultural dimensions of elderly women's lives but also address the multifaceted challenges they encounter. By intertwining these perspectives, we seek a formula that ensures the liberation of elderly women, allowing them to exercise agency and maintain their roles as productive and valued members of their families, communities, and the nation.

African theological feminism

African theological feminism is a multifaceted framework that integrates theological perspectives with feminist insights within the African context. This concept emerges as a response to patriarchal interpretations of theology, seeking to deconstruct oppressive structures and amplify the voices of women in theological discourse (Oduyoye, 1995). This framework traces its roots to the intersection of traditional African spirituality and Christian theology. Mercy Oduyoye emphasizes the need to re-evaluate theological narratives through the lens of gender equality (Oduyoye, 1986). This framework challenges patriarchal interpretations embedded in religious doctrines.

African theological feminism recognizes the intersectionality of gender with other social categories such as race, class, and ethnicity. This perspective acknowledges the unique challenges faced by African women, considering the historical, cultural, and economic contexts that shape their experiences (Oduyoye, 1995). At its core, African theological feminism seeks to empower women and promote their liberation within theological spaces. It advocates for the recognition of women's agency and contributions, challenging traditional notions that have often marginalized women in religious narratives (Oduyoye, 2001).

A central tenet of African theological feminism involves a critical examination of patriarchal theology prevalent in many African religious traditions. Oduyoye argues that patriarchal interpretations of religious texts have contributed to the subordination of women and a feminist theological lens is necessary for a more equitable understanding (Oduyoye, 1995). African theological feminism engages in the reinterpretation of sacred texts to unveil hidden narratives of women's agency and significance. By deconstructing androcentric readings, this framework aims to restore a balanced perspective that acknowledges the spiritual equality of men and women (Oduyoye, 1986).

The impact of African theological feminism extends beyond theological discourse into societal structures. By challenging patriarchal norms within religious frameworks, this concept contributes to broader conversations about gender equality, women's rights, and social justice in African communities (Oduyoye, 1995). In the case of elderly women in Botswana, African theological feminism becomes a catalyst for social change, advocating for the recognition of their contributions, dismantling stereotypes, and promoting their continued agency within the changing dynamics of the nation. While African theological feminism has made significant strides, it faces challenges and criticisms, including resistance from conservative theological circles and the need for broader societal acceptance. Negotiating the complexities of cultural traditions and theological reinterpretation poses ongoing challenges (Dube, 2001).

The narrative of African theological feminism, rooted in the intersection of traditional African spirituality and Christian theology, calls for the re-evaluation of theological narratives through the lens of gender equality (Oduyoye, 1986). As this framework challenges patriarchal interpretations embedded in religious doctrines, it simultaneously opens a gateway to explore how these principles can be applied to the distinct context of elderly women in Botswana. The need for a more nuanced understanding of the experiences of older women becomes apparent, leading to the incorporation of Feminist Gerontology to complement the broader goals of African theological feminism.

The forthcoming section will delve into Feminist Gerontology, summarizing its core tenets and principles. By understanding the intersections of gender and ageing, we can bridge the gap between acknowledging the transformative potential of African theological feminism and addressing the specific needs and contributions of elderly women. This integration aims to provide a comprehensive approach that enables elderly women in Botswana to exercise their agency and continue being productive members of their families, communities, and the nation.

Feminist Gerontology

Feminist gerontology, a multidisciplinary field critically examining the intersection of ageing, gender, and social structures, has emerged to address the unique experiences and challenges faced by older women. In the context of our discussion on elderly women in Botswana, feminist gerontology proves essential as it challenges androcentric perspectives within gerontology, recognizing that ageing experiences are shaped by gender and intersecting identities (Calasanti & King, 2005). This framework emphasizes the importance of incorporating feminist theories to understand the complexities of ageing, longevity, and the well-being of older women. Central to feminist gerontology is the recognition of intersectionality, considering how various social categories such as gender, race, class, and sexuality intersect to influence the ageing experience (Calasanti, 2004). This aligns with the diverse experiences of older women from different backgrounds, providing a crucial lens for analysing the challenges and contributions of elderly women in Botswana.

Feminist gerontology critically examines power relations inherent in the ageing process, challenging ageism and gender-based discrimination. It sheds light on how societal expectations and stereotypes contribute to the marginalization of older women (Bytheway, 2005). In the context of Botswana, where elderly women face challenges in caregiving responsibilities, feminist gerontology prompts a re-evaluation of societal attitudes towards care, addressing the specific needs and experiences of ageing women in this cultural context.

The focus on the body in feminist gerontology is also relevant to our discussion, emphasizing the embodied experiences of ageing women. This perspective challenges beauty standards, explores the impact of age on body image, and critiques the medicalization of women's bodies in the ageing process (Gilleard & Higgs, 2011). Understanding these aspects is crucial for comprehending the challenges faced by elderly women in Botswana and how societal norms and expectations impact their well-being.

Furthermore, feminist gerontology extends beyond academia to influence policy and advocates for the rights of older women. It calls for policies that address economic disparities, healthcare access, and social support systems, recognizing the diverse needs of ageing women (Estes & Associates, 2012). This aligns with the broader discussion on the challenges faced by elderly women in Botswana, where policy considerations are crucial for improving their well-being and societal recognition.

While feminist gerontology has significantly contributed to the understanding of ageing, it faces challenges, including resistance from traditional gerontological perspectives and the need for more inclusive research methodologies. Some critics argue that the field may not fully capture the experiences of women from marginalized groups (Bryson, 2007). As we transition to the next section on African theological feminist gerontology, the integration of feminist gerontology with the previously discussed African theological feminism will provide a comprehensive approach to address the specific needs and contributions of elderly women in Botswana. This will enable them to exercise agency and continue being productive members of their families, communities, and the nation.

African Theological Feminist Gerontology

The formulation of African Theological Feminist Gerontology as an interdisciplinary approach that combines theology, feminism, and gerontology to address the challenges faced by elderly women in Botswana is an original contribution. This formulation arises from a deep awareness of the significant contributions made by elderly women in Botswana and a recognition of the necessity to sustain and empower them. African Theological Feminist Gerontology represents a unique lens through which to understand and address the multifaceted issues affecting elderly women, offering holistic solutions firmly grounded in cultural understanding and gender-sensitive perspectives.

The concept of African theological feminist gerontology recognizes that elderly women in Africa face a unique intersection of challenges related to gender, theology, and ageing. This intersectionality highlights the need for an inclusive approach that considers the spiritual dimensions of ageing within specific cultural and religious frameworks.

As has been highlighted above, elderly women in Africa often play crucial roles as caregivers, transmitting cultural values and wisdom to younger generations (Clausen, 2000). However, the impact of modernization, economic shifts, and changing family dynamics presents challenges, including economic insecurity and social isolation (Kollapan, 2009). African theological feminist gerontology seeks to frame narratives of empowerment and resilience for elderly women. By integrating theological perspectives that emphasize the dignity and worth of every individual (Oduyoye, 2001), this concept challenges ageist stereotypes and advocates for the recognition of the agency and contributions of elderly women.

The centrality of spirituality in African theological feminist gerontology aligns seamlessly with the positive contributions of elderly women in Botswana that have been previously outlined. This concept acknowledges the profound spiritual dimensions of ageing, recognizing that faith and cultural beliefs play pivotal roles in shaping the coping mechanisms and overall well-being of elderly women (Chepngeno-Langat et al., 2012).

In the context of Botswana, where elderly women serve as custodians of cultural heritage, spiritual and cultural dimensions are integral to their identity and contributions. The framework of African theological feminist gerontology, by emphasizing a holistic approach to gerontological studies, encourages a deeper exploration of these dimensions. This approach transcends the conventional focus solely on physical and economic aspects of ageing. Instead, it delves into the spiritual and cultural aspects, providing a more comprehensive understanding of the experiences of elderly women in Botswana.

The acknowledgement and appreciation of the spiritual and cultural dimensions within the gerontological discourse, facilitated by African theological feminist gerontology, serve as a powerful link to the positive contributions of elderly women in Botswana. This framework not only enriches academic perspectives but, crucially, amplifies the voices of elderly women, ensuring that their cultural roles are preserved and appreciated.

In the context of Botswana, where elderly women are revered as custodians of cultural heritage, the emphasis on spiritual and cultural dimensions aligns seamlessly with their enduring contributions. By recognizing these dimensions, African theological feminist gerontology becomes a catalyst for sustaining the enduring value and agency of elderly women. It reinforces the positive trajectory highlighted earlier, ensuring that the cultural leadership roles, caregiving responsibilities, and economic contributions of elderly women continue to be valued and celebrated within the broader societal context of Botswana.

In essence, this framework provides a meaningful bridge between theoretical understanding and practical application, contributing to the preservation and appreciation of the multifaceted roles played by elderly women. By doing so, African theological feminist gerontology actively contributes to the ongoing positive impact of elderly women in Botswana, ensuring that their agency and contributions remain integral to the cultural fabric of the nation.

African Theological Feminist Gerontology: Sustaining the Gains in Botswana

In the dynamic landscape of Botswana's evolving social structures, African Theological Feminist Gerontology stands as a beacon, recognizing the profound impact of modernization and urbanization on the traditional extended family system (Kollapan, 2009). This framework emphasizes the importance of cultural preservation amid societal transformations. Despite the erosion of the traditional family structure, elderly women in Botswana continue to be cultural custodians, passing down invaluable wisdom to younger generations. Their role as cultural torchbearers is pivotal, ensuring the preservation of Botswana's rich heritage and traditions. By intertwining feminist perspectives and theological insights, this approach fosters a deeper understanding and respect for the contributions of elderly women in caregiving roles.

Moreover, the framework becomes a bridge across the intergenerational gap in caregiving attitudes. Elderly women, as primary caregivers, offer not only practical support but also impart cultural values. African Theological Feminist Gerontology fosters inclusive and culturally sensitive caregiving practices, recognizing the significance of their contributions. Through this approach, the intergenerational exchange of wisdom and care becomes a cornerstone in maintaining family cohesion and cultural continuity.

In acknowledging the existing gap in healthcare accessibility (Sucre, 2002), the framework does not merely identify challenges but actively advocates for positive change. Integrating theological and feminist perspectives calls for healthcare systems that recognize the spiritual and gender-specific dimensions of ageing. Elderly women's well-being is not just a medical concern but an essential aspect of their holistic existence, deserving culturally competent and empowering interventions.

In the economic landscape, the vulnerability of elderly women is recognized, but African Theological Feminist Gerontology focuses on empowering interventions. The framework calls for community-centric approaches, valuing indigenous knowledge and cultural perspectives. By restoring control over essential resources like land and livestock, elderly women become active contributors to the economic fabric of Botswana, ensuring sustainability.

Addressing shifting societal values and caregiving attitudes, the framework advocates for fostering respect for the contributions of elderly women. It envisions a society where their capabilities, experiences, and wisdom are valued, challenging stereotypes and promoting inclusivity in caregiving dynamics. In this way, the interconnectedness of spirituality, feminism, and caregiving becomes a source of strength.

In the face of challenges compounded by the HIV and AIDS epidemic, African Theological Feminist Gerontology proposes a holistic approach to prevention and treatment programmes (Kollapan, 2009). It emphasizes compassion, understanding, and community support, ensuring interventions are not only medical but also culturally competent and empowering. Through this, elderly women become resilient agents of change, contributing to the community's well-being.

The framework challenges traditional gender norms, offering theological insights that support gender equality. It advocates for the representation of women in leadership positions, asserting the capabilities of elderly women in decision-making and political realms. By challenging restrictive roles and promoting inclusivity, African Theological Feminist Gerontology uplifts the status of elderly women in Botswana, recognizing them as valuable contributors to societal flourishing.

In discussions around retirement age policies, the framework considers the unique challenges faced by elderly women due to delayed and unstable employment. It supports inclusive policies that acknowledge the diverse experiences of women in the workforce. Through community-supported initiatives and robust social security systems, African Theological Feminist Gerontology ensures the dignity and well-being of elderly women during periods of unemployment or retirement.

In essence, African Theological Feminist Gerontology does not merely illuminate challenges; it accentuates the profound and positive contributions of elderly women in Botswana. By intertwining theological and feminist dimensions, the framework advocates for cultural reforms that recognize and amplify the strengths of elderly women, ensuring their continued impact on the cultural, social, and economic fabric of Botswana.

Conclusion

This chapter delves into the multifaceted experiences of elderly women in Botswana, addressing their roles and challenges and identified gaps across societal, economic, and healthcare dimensions. The discernible absence of tailored social policies creates barriers, while shifts in traditional family structures contribute to economic vulnerability and social isolation. The compounding factors of HIV and AIDS intensify the challenges faced by elderly women. Introducing the concept of African Theological Gerontology, which intertwines theology, feminism, and gerontology, offers a holistic perspective. Recommendations advocate for culturally sensitive reforms, a reconsideration of retirement age policies, gender-inclusive employment practices, and the establishment of robust social safety nets to bolster support for elderly women in Botswana.

References

Bagwasi, M. M., & Sunderland, J. (2013). Language, gender, and age(ism) in Setswana. In L. L. Atanga, S. E. Ellece, L. Litosseliti, & J. Sunderland (Eds.), *Gender and language in Sub-Saharan Africa: Tradition, struggle and change* (pp. 53–78). John Benjamins Publishing Company.

Biggs, S., & Powell, J. L. (2001). "A Foucauldian Analysis of Old Age and the Power of Social Welfare." *Journal of Aging & Social Policy*, 12, 93–112.

Burke, C. (2000). Life at the Margins in Botswana: From Sitting in Class to Sitting and Doing Nothing. Chapter presented at the workshop entitled *"Recovering the Legacy of Schapera,"* University of Botswana, Gaborone, May 25–26.

Bryson, L. (2007). Review The Futures of Old Age: John A. Vincent, Chris R. Phillipson and Murna Downs (eds) SAGE, London, 2006, 255pp, ISBN-10: 1412901081, ISBN-13: 978—1412901086, £19.99 (pbk). *Critical Social Policy*, 27(4), 574–576. https://doi.org/10.1177/02610183070070040905

Bytheway, B. (2005). "Ageism and Age Categorization." *Journal of Social Issues*, 61(2), 361–374.

Calasanti, T. (2004). "New Directions in Feminist Gerontology: An Introduction." *Journal of Aging Studies*, 18(1), 1–8.

Calasanti, T., and King, N. (2005) 'Firming the Floppy Penis: Age, Class, and Gender Relations in the Lives of Old Men', *Men and Masculinities*, 8(1), 3–23.

Central Statistics Office. (2001). *Population and Housing Census*. Gaborone: The Government Printer.

Chepngeno-Langat, G., Falkingham, J. C., Madise, N. J., & Evandrou, M. (2012). Concern about HIV and AIDS among older people in the slums of Nairobi, Kenya. *Risk analysis: an official publication of the Society for Risk Analysis*, 32(9), 1512–1523. https://doi.org/10.1111/j.1539-6924.2011.01765.x

Clausen, F. (2000). "Morbidity and Health Care Utilization Among Elderly People in Mmankgodi Village, Botswana." *Epidemiol Community Health*, 54, 58–63.

Dube, M. W. (2001). *Other Ways of Reading: African Women and the Bible*. Atlanta, GA: Society of Biblical Literature.

Estes, C. L. (2012). *Social Policy and Aging: A Critical Perspective*. Thousand Oaks, CA: Sage. https://doi.org/10.4135/9781452232676

Gilleard, C., & Higgs, P. (2011). "Aging Abjection and Embodiment in the Fourth Age." *Journal of Aging Studies*, 27(2), 121–132.

Ingstad, B. (1994). Elderly People at the Village Level. In *The Situation of the Elderly in Botswana: Proceedings from an International Workshop*, (pp. 29–41). Gaborone: National Institute of Research.

Ingstad, B., Bruun, F., Sandberg, E., et al. (1992). "Care for the Elderly, Care by the Elderly: The Role of Elderly Women in a Changing Tswana Society." *Journal of Cross-Cultural Gerontology*, 7, 379–398. https://doi.org/10.1007/BF01848700

Kang'ethe, S. M. (2013). "Feminization of Poverty in Palliative Care Giving of People Living With HIV and AIDS and Other Debilitating Diseases in Botswana. A Literature Review." *Journal of Virology & Microbiology*, 17. http://www.ibimapublishing.com/articles/JVM/2013/772210/772210.pdf

Kollapan, J. (2009). The Rights of Older People-African Perspective. In *International Symposium on the Rights of Older People, Age Concern England in collaboration with Help Age International and International Federation on Ageing*. November, Ethiopia.

Lindsey, E., Hirschfeld, M., & Tlou, S. (2003). "Home-Based Care in Botswana: Experiences of Older Women and Young Girls." *Health Care for Women International*, 24(6), 486–501. https://doi.org/10.1080/07399330390199384

Livingston, J. (2003). "Reconfiguring Old Age: Elderly Women and Concerns Over Care in Southeastern Botswana." *Medical Anthropology*, 22(3), 205–231. https://doi.org/10.1080/01459740306771

Madigele, T. J. (2021) 'Who cares for them? Analysing Provision of Care and Assistance among the elderly people in Botswana: Communal Contextual Pastoral Theology'. *African Theological Journal for Church and Society* 2(1): 57–77.

Madigele, T. J., & Tshelametse, R. (2023a). "Religion and Income Inequality among Retirees in Botswana: A Communal Contextual Theological Approach." In E. Chitando et al., eds., *Religion and Inequality in Africa*. London: Bloomsbury.

Madigele, T. J., & Tshelametse, R. (2023b). "Surviving Multiple Pandemics. Socio-Economic Impact of COVID-19 among the Elderly in Botswana: A Call for a Holistic Pastoral Approach." *Scriptura*, 122(1), 1–12.

Mandiyanike, D. (2023). The marginalised majority: The case of Botswana women in local government (1999–2019). In T. Chari & P. Dzimiri (Eds.), *Military, politics and democratization in Southern Africa* (pp. 233–251). Springer.

Mhaka-Mutepfa, M., & Wright, T. C. (2022). "Quality of Life of Older People in Botswana." *The International Journal of Community and Social Development*, 4(1), 104–126. https://doi.org/10.1177/25166026211064693

Nyanguru, A. C. (2007). The Economic and Social Impacts of the Old Age Pension on the Protection of the Basotho Elderly and their Households. Chapter presented at the *Charlotte Maxexe Conference*, Pilanesburg, South Africa, 12–15 June 2007.

Oduyoye, M., 1986, *Hearing and knowing: Theological reflections on Christianity in Africa*, Orbis Books.

Oduyoye, M. 1995. "Christianity and African Culture," *International Review of Mission*, 84, 77–90.

Oduyoye, M. A. (2001). *Introducing African Women's Theology*. Sheffield Academic Press.

Onen, B. L., Harris, C., Ignatowicz, A., Davies, J., Drouvelis, M., Howes, A., Nkomazana, O., Onen, C. L., Sapey, E., Tsima, B., & Lasserson, D. (2019). "Ageing, Frailty and Resilience in Botswana: Rapid Ageing, Rapid Change. Findings From a National Working Group Meeting and Literature Review." *BMC Proceedings*, 13(Suppl 10), 8. https://doi.org/10.1186/s12919-019-0171-z

Raditloaneng, W. N. (2012). Socio-Economic Factors in Rural Water Scarcity: A Case Study of Molepolole Village in Botswana. *American Journal of Human Ecology*, 1(3), 95–101. https://doi.org/10.11634/216796221504193

Rotarou, E. S., & Sakellariou, D. (2019). "Structural Disadvantage and (Un)Successful Ageing: Gender Differences in Activities of Daily Living for Older People in Chile." *Critical Public Health*, 29, 534–546.

Shaibu, S. (2013). "Experiences of Grandmothers Caring for Orphan Grandchildren in Botswana." *Journal of Nursing Scholarship*, 45(4), 363–370.

Specht, R., & Graig, G. J. (1987). *Human Development: A Social Work Perspective* (2nd Ed). Prentice Hall.

Sucre, Z. (2002). Botswana Statement at the Second World Assembly on Ageing Madrid, Spain. www.globalaging.org/health/world/2009/botswana.htm (accessed 3/2/2010).

Taylor, A. (2011) Older Adult, Older Person, Senior, Elderly or Elder: A Few Thoughts on the Language we use to Reference Aging. British Columbia Law Institute. Blog. https://www.bcli.org/older-adult-older-per

Tlou, T., & Campbell, A. (1984). *History of Botswana* (pp. 20–70). Macmillan Botswana.

Twigg, J., & Martin, W. (2014). "The Challenge of Cultural Gerontology." *The Gerontologist*, 55, 353–359.

WHO. (2022). "Botswana to Be a Better Place to Grow Old." https://www.afro.who.int/countries/botswana/news/botswana-be-better-place-grow-old

31
YOUNG AFRICAN WOMEN'S LEADERSHIP IN RELIGIOUS STUDIES AND THEOLOGY

A Review with Special Reference to the School of Religion, Philosophy, and Classics, University of KwaZulu-Natal, South Africa

Lindiwe Princess Maseko

Introduction

The history of women's participation in leadership within African academic and religious contexts is a narrative of perseverance and struggle, as this has been known to be a male-dominated arena. For a very long time, women have been excluded from positions of leadership as their contributions have been undervalued. Until the birth of the Circle of Concerned African Women Theologians in 1989, which became a beacon of hope, leadership roles for women within academic institutions were a far-fetched dream because of societal norms, patriarchal religious, and cultural traditions. These left women at the periphery of academic religious decision-making processes. As a discipline, Religious Studies in Africa was shaped by male scholarship since the 1960s (Chitando 2016). Phiri concedes that scholarship in religious studies and theology in Africa has tended to be dominated by men, with women facing numerous obstacles (Phiri 2009). At first, the pioneering scholars in the study of religion were Europeans and later African males took over from the Europeans as they left the continent. In taking over, male theologians overlooked to account for gender dynamics in the study of religion. The patriarchal system, which favoured male interests, resulted in the exclusion of women from religious studies (Chitando 2016).

In this chapter, I argue that accessing theology and religious studies by young/emerging African women (such as myself) and others is opening up leadership possibilities for African women. Through researching key issues that affect the lives of African women within faith communities, young/emerging African women are challenging patriarchal norms. I utilise personal reflections as one who is travelling the journey, as well as reviewing research by young/emerging Africans who have graduated from a public university in South Africa. Their courage and creativity confirm their leadership in the field, preparing them as the vanguard in women's liberation within faith communities in Africa.

Overcoming Exclusion: African Women in Theology and Religious Studies

In one of their chapter contributions, Phiri and Chitando (2023) highlight the prevalence of male leaders in Africa due to the patriarchal ideology which restricts leadership to men, assuming women are perpetual followers. Writing on "Major Challenge for African Women Theologians in Theological Education from 1989 to 2008," Phiri (2009) accounts for the challenges that women faced. First, she includes the challenge of enrolment which was connected to the systemic factors. In her account, studying theology was connected to ordained ministry by the first missionaries in Africa (Phiri 2009:111). Second, a number of women who wanted to study theology through state universities failed to satisfy the expected qualification since they did not receive a full school education (Phiri 2009:111–112). This was due to the cultural view that in the event that funds were scarce to educate children, priority was given to the boy child. This is because families have tended to look up to the boy child as a provider as compared to the girl, who is expected to be married. Tamale and Oloka-Onyango (1997:3–4) cited by Chitando share that "women in Africa were a rare commodity in the annals of academia and were Africa's true 'drawers of water and hewers of wood" (2016:134).

Writing from an Evangelical Lutheran Church in South African context, Chisale (2020:1) shares that women dominate numerically in church, however, the top leadership positions are still held by men. According to her, "Those who dominate church leadership and management positions in the church are men" (Chisale 2020: 2). Women seem to be supportive of their fellow female leaders' inclusion theoretically, however, in practice, they cannot always guarantee that support. Pui-Lan (2000) also argues that though women constitute the majority in churches, they are marginalised in the power structure of the church and the life of the congregation. This is due to the fact that gender ideology has "socialized women to internalize the notion that men are born leaders and women are designed to be followers and servants of men" (Chisale 2020). Oduyoye (2001:10) avers that "when examining the role of women in religion in Africa, whether Islamic faith, or African Traditional Religion either Christianity, two questions must be interrogated: first, "what responsibilities do women in structures of religion? How does religion serve or obstruct women's development?"

Further, it is very important to identify how religion promotes or hinders women's leadership in the faith communities and beyond and also to mobilise male scholars and activists to partner with women to advance women's leadership (Manyonganise, Chitando and Chirongoma 2023a).

In the context of Zimbabwe, Chirongoma and Moyo (2023) have argued that the exclusion of women, particularly young women, from key leadership and decision-making forums in almost every structure of society remains an elusive topic in academic discourses. Nevertheless, one way of looking into the leadership of young women within the faith communities is also to acknowledge Indigenous Knowledge Systems, particularly proverbs, to open space for women's leadership (Manyonganise, Chitando, and Chirongoma 2023a). Writing from a Nigerian context (Nwachuku 1992:65) submits that in religious spaces, where women are observers rather than active participants, female voicelessness continues to encourage the perpetuation of rites and rituals that foster female oppression. Due to this reality, it should be noted that women in leadership positions represent the voice of the masses in the church who happen to be women as they appreciate the lived experiences of women on the periphery (Chisale 2020:4). Barring young Christian women from leadership and decision-making positions is not favourable to the development of faith communities, as well as academic, political, and economic sectors (Chirongoma and Moyo, 2023).

Given its significance, the Circle of Concerned African Women Theologians (the Circle) must be acknowledged in the history of the struggle for women's leadership in religion and theology. However, prior to that it is important to note that Mercy Amba Oduyoye was the only woman from Africa who had theological publications. She was the lone theological voice of African women, as Kanyoro (2006: 20), shares. In the same struggle for visibility in leadership, Kanyoro and Oduyoye in their early writing posit that "…as long as men…remain the authorities on culture,-rituals, religion, African women will continue to be spoken of as if they were dead" (Oduyoye and Kanyoro 1992:1). The Circle played a key role ensuring that women's issues were not taken for granted (Chitando 2016). Ayanga (2016) submits that the Circle sought to guide and contextualise the desire of women to be the voice of the voiceless. One of the objectives included research, writing, and publication on significant issues that affected African women in religion and culture (Ayanga 2016, Nadar and Phiri 2013). Another objective was, "coming together at national, regional and Pan-African conferences and workshops to share their research findings and to hear each other's stories" (Ayanga 2016: 1). The other objective was mentorship. Through this mentorship, young and emerging women in religion, academics, and culture are assisted to realise the value of their own experiences, as well as their fellow women (Ayanga 2016). African women scholars who are both activists in theology and those involved in religious studies, challenged prevalent approaches to the discipline of religion (Chitando 2016:135). Historically, male theologians have tended to describe religions in general terms; however, female scholars have been more interested in re-claiming women's voices, from a diverse of contexts and religions in Africa (Chitando 2016:136). For example, through the Circle, more emphasis was on HIV and its impact on women and girls in Africa (Chitando 2016). Despite all these challenges, the Circle has proved its commitment to empowering women in Africa to be in leadership roles in religion and society. It has proved this through its critical perspectives on patriarchal notions of leadership (Phiri and Chitando 2023).

The struggle by women to access space in African theology and religious studies has, in turn, contributed to the shortage of women leaders in religion and society. However, as this chapter illustrates, the participation of young women in African theology and religious studies at one academic institution is making a significant contribution to the discipline and to the increase in the number of women leaders in religion and society. In order to ensure that women contribute effectively to leadership in religious contexts, promoting women's access to studying religion and theology has been key. This chapter reviews how young women in a specific public institution are emerging as strategic actors in African religious studies and theology. Hence, the objective of this chapter is to review how the young women studying Gender and Religion contribute to, first, African religious studies and theology, and, second, to women's leadership in religion and society. This chapter, therefore, is both a celebration and critical review of the contribution of young women in the Department of Gender and Religion, School of Religion and Theology at the University of KwaZulu-Natal, South Africa, to both African religious studies and theology and women's leadership in religion in Africa.

Research Methodology

The research method that this chapter engages is qualitative research. The qualitative research method enables the researcher to select and collect data, interpret it through systematic literature review from secondary documentation, and further apply thematic analysis of the content. Creswell (2013:4) and Creswell (2014:32) outline that the qualitative method is an assumed worldview, or a possible theoretical lens, and study of research problems inquiring into the meaning individuals ascribe to a social-human problem. Qualitative research locates the observer in the world and examines the lives of people under their condition (Yin 2015:7–9; Denzin and Lincoln 2011:3). For this chapter, I collected data through the Document Analysis method and partly informal interviews. According to Bowen (2009:27), "document analysis is a systematic procedure for reviewing or evaluating documents both printed and electronic (computer-based and Internet-transmitted) material." Document analysis needs one to examine and interpret data to stimulate meaning, grasp, and develop empirical knowledge (Corbin & Strauss, 2008; Rapley, Rapley, 2007a, b). As instruments for data collection, I have used 10 academic documents known as "theses or dissertations" that have been produced at the particular institution. Apart from secondary sources, I have also used informal interviews to compile the history of Gender and Religion at the institution under study. To select my data instruments, I used a non-probability purposive sampling method.[1] I selected my research instruments based on the following criteria: first, I focused on dissertations produced by "female" (recognising gender diversity) students in Gender and Religion Department in the School of Religion, Philosophy and Classics at the University of KwaZulu Natal. Second, my attention was solely on nine Master's and one doctoral dissertation. The information in the nine Master's theses and one doctoral dissertation had the themes I needed to reflect on. These themes included; "Religion, Women and Gender-Based Violence," and "Religion, Women and Sexual Reproductive Health and Rights (SRHR)," "Religion, Culture, Women," and "SRHR, Religion, Women and Sexuality." Third, I looked at the nine Master's and one doctoral dissertations that date back from 2013, which is 10 years from the time of writing. The purpose for focusing on a 10-year period as to review on the most recent scholarship from young/emerging women African women in Gender and Religion. Fourth, I was focusing on dissertations written on regional context. That is, dissertation written by young female students from and within Southern Africa, including Zimbabwe, Zambia, and South Africa. Fifth, I focused on a diversity of religious affiliations which included Christianity, African Traditional Religion, and Islam.

By using these criteria, this chapter evaluates what the young/emerging African women researchers have contributed to African theology and religious studies, as well as how this academic exposure has impacted the young women's leadership in their faith communities. These theses are posted on research sites like Google Scholar and the University of KwaZulu Natal, College of Humanities Research Space,[2] where I accessed them. I focused partly on the summaries and main arguments of these young/emerging African women scholars.

The Gender and Religion Department

The Gender and Religion Department is under the School of Religion, Philosophy and Classics at the University of KwaZulu Natal in South Africa. Through the leadership of Professor Isabel Apawo Phiri,[3] the Gender and Religion Department was birthed between 2003 and 2004.[4] As a programme which stems from the Circle, the idea was to increase the number of African women who received theological training. There was a need to develop a course specifically for women and core themes were prioritised. One of the core themes was HIV and AIDS because women of the Circle were leading in HIV conversations and research in Africa.[5] Second, because women in the Circle realised that African women as a group were disproportionately affected by the virus and therefore had to contribute to the knowledge production in this area (Nadar and Phiri 2013: 632) in order to promote effective responses to the pandemic. Hence, in 2002 at the Circle's third Pan-African Conference in Addis Ababa, Ethiopia, the issue of HIV and AIDS was discussed. This commitment to engage in research on HIV and AIDS was expressed, including ensuring that oppressive patriarchal ideologies that promoted women's vulnerabilities were challenged (Nadar and Phiri 2013). The conversation on HIV and AIDS was born under the theme: "Sex, Stigma, and HIV and AIDS: African Women Challenging Religion, Culture and Social Practices" (Nadar and Phiri 2013). In support of this, the Ecumenical HIV and AIDS Initiative in Africa (EHAIA),[6] a programme within the World Council of Churches (WCC), shaped a robust partnership with the Circle in the fight against HIV and AIDS. As a result, HIV and AIDS became part of the curriculum in Gender and Religion by that time. Nadar and Phiri (2013) add that the University of Oslo and the University of KwaZulu-Natal had a collaboration of a three-year joint research project called *Broken women healing traditions*, as an Indigenous resource for gender critique and social transformation in the context of HIV and AIDS.

The second central focus was on gender. Phiri notes that the Circle promoted the teaching of gender issues in the theological curriculum by making gender a concept in theological analysis. A gendered approach to theology refers to exposing the injustices that exist in the church, culture, and the Bible in the relationship between men and women (Phiri 2009:112). In her path to becoming a professor in the fields of gender and religion, Sarojini Nadar[7] explains that her journey was "carved through deep personal reflections on how the futures of women and young girls are determined and shaped by religious and cultural norms, which dictate what, how and when she can make choices about herself."[8] Hence, the Gender and Religion programme aimed to promote the recognition on how religious and cultural norms have affected the choices to young girls and women. When one thinks of these two combined themes (HIV/AIDS and Gender), surely the programme developed a life-changing curriculum. In their words, Nadar and Phiri (2013:632) acknowledge that, "the epistemological frameworks that gender and religion studies generate has caused significant paradigm shifts within HIV knowledge production both on the popular and academic level." The Gender and Religion programme aimed to draw students from across the world. The students were enrolled from different religions including Christianity, African Traditional Religion, and Islam.[9] From the beginning of the programme, more women than men have been enrolled in the programme. I am convinced that the Religion and Gender programme at the University of KwaZulu-Natal has gone a long way in equipping young and emerging women scholars with leadership knowledge and skills within African religious studies and theology, on the one hand, and within the faith community, on the other hand.

Defining Leadership

Defining leadership is complex. For the purpose of this chapter, I will use some of the definitions from the relevant scholarship within the discourse of women, religion, and leadership by Manyonganise, Chitando, and Chirongoma as the guiding scholars. As cited by Chitando (2023:27), Winston and Patterson (2006:7) define a leader as

> one or more people who selects, equips, trains, and influences one or more follower (s) who have diverse gifts, abilities, and skills and focuses the follower (s) to the organization's mission and objectives causing the follower(s) to willingly and enthusiastically expend spiritual, emotional, and physical energy in a concerted coordinated effort to achieve the organizational mission and objectives.

Some of the features of this leadership include humility, critical thinking, active listening, positivity, and so forth (Winston and Patterson 2006: 7). In addition, Akpa et al. (2021) aver that leadership can be viewed as a process that involves influence, that is seen as occurring within a group, and leadership as involving a common goal (2021: 274). Chitando (2023:28) also defines effective leadership as one that "requires that leaders be open to and tolerant of minorities."

Although we have seen how interesting leadership can be, women's religious leadership is a contested matter within the global religious arena (Manyonganise, Chitando and Chirongoma 2023a). In fact, there are many factors that hinder African women's leadership. Ngunjiri and Christo-Baker (2012) argue that these obstacles that exist for African women to become leaders are a reality regardless of where they live or come from. They range from economic, social, cultural, and spiritual violence (Chitando 2023). Since then, we have these as a challenge, scholars like Lari et al. 2022 who have argued that patriarchy concentrates on men's interests before women, which needs a call to challenge gender norms related to leadership. Leadership is mostly associated with men (Chitando 2023: 29). This results in viewing women as less fit or acceptable for leadership positions and women's leadership as rated as less effective by peers, subordinates, and top management compared to their male counterparts (Fazal et al., 2020: 3). Religion itself is another barrier to African women's leadership (Chitando 2023). Religion both upholds and impedes women's leadership abilities and ambitions (Manyonganise et al. 2023a, b and c). I want to agree with Chitando, who argues that "no serious scholar of leadership can afford to ignore the significance of women's leadership" (2023:28). Hence, the need to celebrate what the Gender and Religion young women are contributing in the field of religion and theology. In addition, it is important to reflect on how they influence women's leadership in religion and society. In the following section, I provide a summary of how I have been empowered in my journey as a young and emerging African woman scholar in religion and theology.

Positionality: From the Periphery to Active Engagement

I write this chapter as a fortunate young, black, African, woman from Southern Africa, Zimbabwe, Mnene Mission in Mberengwa District. I am a beneficiary of studying Religion and Theology (academically and professionally) in Africa and beyond. At the age of 19, I had an opportunity to enroll for my academic studies, doing a Bachelor of Arts Theology (B.Th.) and Religious Studies Honours Degree from 2014 to 2017) at Midlands State University in Zimbabwe. For me to study religion and theology at this time, I received financial support from the Good Shepherd Lutheran.[10] *In 2019, through the College of Humanities relief fund bursary, I had another opportunity to study for a Bachelor of Theology Honours degree in Gender and Religion, at the University of KwaZulu Natal, in the School of Religion, Philosophy and Classics. Through a Gender, Religion and Health Programme Scholarship, I had another opportunity to pursue a Master's degree (In Gender and Religion at the University of KwaZulu Natal in 2022). Currently, I am doing my doctoral studies in Gender and Religion at the University of KwaZulu Natal (UKZN).*

Besides academics, I am a beneficiary of other theological- and ecumenical-related platforms. For example, I joined the Ecumenical Church Leaders Forum in Zimbabwe[11] *as a junior peace facilitator in the programme called Conflict, Prevention, Management, Resolution and Transformation (2016 and 2018). Through supportive theological mentors, I have benefited from the Ecumenical HIV and AIDS Initiatives and Advocacy (EHAIA) as a youth representative for the Church of Sweden's Regional Partner Consultation meeting which was held in Naivasha, Kenya, in 2016. I have participated in the Global Ecumenical Theological Institute-GETI "Translating the Word, Transforming the World," organised by the WCC at Tumaini University in 2018. Outside Africa, I have benefited from the Bridging Gaps programme of intensive study in contextual theology in the Faculty of Religion and Theology of VU University and Protestant Theological University, Amsterdam in 2021. I have benefitted from Helene Ralivao Fund offered by the Lutheran World Federation as one of the pioneer students in Africa to be part of the Training and Research Programme on Theology, Gender Justice and Leadership at Tumaini University Makumira, Tanzania, in 2022. I have had an opportunity to be a keynote Speaker at the African Theology Students' Research Conference on Gender and Pandemics in Nairobi, Kenya, under the mentorship of dedicated African men and women. In addition, I participated in the All-Africa Conference of Churches (AACC) 9th Ecumenical Theological Institute, in Abuja, Nigeria, in 2023.*

My academic journey in the Department of Gender and Religion at UKZN has provided me with a deep understanding of the intersectionality between gender, culture, and religion. It has allowed me to explore the experiences and challenges faced by women in academia and their contexts. My voice has been enhanced to speak on African women's experiences within their cultural and religious contexts, in particular my own context. I have become part of a community of young African women who are leaders in their own right. As a result, I am honoured and respected in my community, and I am seen as an inspiration to many young girls and women back in Zimbabwe, particularly in Mnene, my home area in Mberengwa. Whilst I appreciate the definitions of leadership in my previous section, for this chapter, I want to view leadership from grassroot terms. There are many different ways of being a leader, yet some qualities are simple and are from humble beginnings. By this, I mean that one can have the opportunity to represent, advocate and inspire a small community. Hence, being able to speak before my colleagues in class is an act of leadership. It requires confidence, communication skills, and the ability to articulate my thoughts effectively. Voicing my opinions and advocating for the issues that affect women at both the academic and communal levels is also a form of leadership. It is about raising awareness, initiating conversations, and creating positive change. Furthermore, being able to offer advice and engage in meaningful conversations on these matters demonstrates leadership qualities. Being proactive in addressing women's concerns and seeking solutions, I believe it is a form of leadership. This is supported by Manyonganise, Chitando and Chirongoma (2023a:9) who maintain that "religious leaders (women and men and) with theological education that emphasizes gender justice are more likely to respond to women's leadership than those without such education."

I have also come to realise that leadership involves perseverance and determination in the face of cultural barriers and societal expectations placed on girls and young women. By pushing beyond some barriers from my village and staying committed to my studies, I have exhibited leadership qualities. Leadership is about having the strength to endure and the determination to succeed despite the challenges that you meet along the way. The ability to continue or begin again from where you left of. Leadership means standing up and speaking out about topics that are often considered strange. Leadership, to me, is about pursuing justice, truth, and serving all members of society. In her contribution titled "The Missing Voice: African women doing theology," Nyambura Njoroge inspires me when she urges "us" women to wake up, and rise up again from our sleep and offer our gifts to knowledge. She urges as follows: "we need to say our bit and to take our rightful place in the church and society so that we do not impoverish our continent and our world by our absence and lack of participation" (Njoroge 1997:78).

I want to acknowledge Manyonganise, Chitando and Chirongoma (2023a) who agree that most of the women leaders at higher levels in society have been inspired and mentored for leadership in faith communities. Indeed, in my journey from the marginalised to the centre, I had the privilege of learning from my African women mentors, as well as some progressive male theologians who support young women's participation in religious studies and theology, as well as leadership in religion. Their guidance, wisdom, and experiences have greatly contributed to my growth. Being open to learning from others and embracing different perspectives is an essential aspect of leadership. It has taught me that leadership is not limited to formal positions of authority, but rather, it is a mindset and a set of skills that implies determination, mentorship, discipline, and a willingness to learn from others. According to Nyambura Njoroge "...reaching out, recruiting, mentoring, and opening doors for others are the hallmarks of collaborative model of facilitating empowering, effective, and responsible leadership" (Njoroge 2005:34).

Despite the challenges of navigating patriarchal figures within the religious space, I have learned that sometimes writing from personal experience is more powerful than simply speaking. Through Gender and Religion studies, I have not only found my voice but also reclaimed my place as a recognised young woman in my context. I am truly grateful for the academic journey and the support that the Gender and Religion Department at UKZN has provided. Being a black, African woman, is one factor that indeed highlights the lack of understanding of equal gifts in theological leadership abilities, as Njoroge (2005) notes. Yes, it is not easy to speak in a male-dominated arena, but I can assure you this: when a girl speaks, when a young, black, African woman speaks, she speaks from her experience, and the narratives positively change! In the following section, I review the contributions of my predecessors in the field of Gender and Religion at UKZN. This is in the context of the central thesis of this chapter, namely, that young women who access theological education are prepared for leadership in academia and in faith communities.

The Contribution of Young Women in Gender and Religion at the University of KwaZulu Natal

In this section, I will focus on the contribution to leadership in religious studies, theology, and religion made by UKZN Gender and Religion young/emerging African women scholars.

I will focus only on 10 women who have navigated this subject by writing on the lived experiences of women within their religio-cultural contexts. I have specifically selected them as they are emerging in the field of gender and religion. In addition, because they are contemporary writers contributing from their traditional religio-cultural contexts. I will specifically summarise their narratives according to the specific given themes in my introduction, what they aimed to achieve through research and writing during their course of either Masters or Doctoral studies in Gender and Religion. The themes for the dissertation review include "Religion, Women and Gender-Based Violence," "Religion, Women and Sexual Reproductive Health and Rights (SRHR), "Religion, Culture, Women," and "SRHR, Religion, Women and Sexuality."

Religion, Women, and Gender-Based Violence

In the context of religion and gender and sexual violence against women, Mayam Bodhanya researched her Master's dissertation on "Women's Health Seeking Behaviour in the Context of Sexual Violence, Sexual Health Rights, and the Muslim Community: A Case study of Hope Careline Counselling" (Bodhanya 2016). Through a qualitative empirical approach and thematic work analysis, her thesis focuses on the health-seeking behaviour of Muslim women who experienced gender-based sexual violence (GBSV) and who accessed counselling careline within KwaZulu Natal Province in South Africa. Her main aim is to trace the extent to which the religious beliefs of the women influenced their health-seeking behaviour of accessing a counselling careline in the context of sexual health rights within the Muslim community.

In her contribution, Bodhanya (2016) employs critical feminist theory by engaging with other theorists who have done some work in Islam and feminism. Bodhanya (2016) highlights that religion influences the health-seeking behaviour of women in various ways as follows. First, in the sense that in the study she carried, the change of religion is a major contributor that denies women's health-seeking behaviour in this context. In her research, it emerged that after changing religion from Islam to Hinduism, some women could not seek help from Muslims again as they felt guilty as they were judged for changing the religion in the first place. Hence, a woman in this case finds it difficult to go back to the Muslim religious leaders for counselling (Bodhanya 2016:22). In this case, Bodhanya argues that religion may be advantageous by barring women from returning to ask for support. This is because it will create an opportunity for women to get in touch with the careline, which offers counselling services that are ethically compliant with certain of their values (such as allowing women to wear scarves during session). However, negatively, religion in this context is portrayed as promoting silence and fear to speak to the Muslim religious leaders just because of the change of religion.

Second, in her research, religion is seen as influential and a discouraging factor for some women who grew up in a Muslim society and therefore are unable to speak up about the sexual violence they experience in marital relationships. Bodhanya (2016) argues that the inability to talk about sexual matters portrays a direct influence of religion that hinders the health-seeking process in the context of GBSV. She argues that this is because in the Islamic faith, some women do not have a say, since a wife has to "do what her husband wants her to do" (Interview in Bodhanya 2016:72).

Third, Bodhanya (2016) alludes that religion is positively influential to women's health-seeking behaviour. As they draw from their perception of their connection to God and find their strength in God. Apart from the fact that religion can contribute both positively and negatively, Bodhanya (2016) suggests that there is a need for new ways of viewing health-seeking behaviour in the Muslim community in the face of the taboo factor around sex and the silence around GSBV. This includes intersectional knowledge production in the field of Gender, Religion, and Health, which adds a voice to the field since sexual health has mostly been considered in fields such as medicine, psychology, and sociology. Through her research, Bodhanya (2016) has contributed new knowledge to the multilayered understanding of GBSV in the Muslim community, which is a stepping stone in women leading within patriarchally dominated spaces and contexts. Bodhanya's academic research is a voice of advocacy on un-silencing the silenced women who experience the realities of sexual and gender-based violence but who are unable to share these experiences due to religious beliefs and norms.

Retaining focus on religion and GBSV, Nokulunga Zamantshali Portia Dlamini adds her voice through her doctoral thesis entitled, "Unmasking Christian women survivor voices against gender-based violence – A pursuit for a feminist liberative pastoral care praxis for married women in the Anglican Church of Southern Africa" (Dlamini 2022). Dlamini (2022) focuses on Christian women survivor voices in the Anglican Church. Using a feminist liberative pastoral care approach, Dlamini's (2022) research aims to understand Christian married women's knowledge and perceptions of gender-based violence. It also seeks to explore how the Anglican Church of Southern Africa (ACSA) in the Diocese of Natal handles GBV as a pastoral challenge. The thesis seeks to critique the theological practices and pastoral care interventions which the ACSA uses for the advocacy and healing of its women members. Further, the study endeavours to establish how the denomination engages the afflicted and the wounded. It also proposes pastoral care guidelines, drawing insights from African women's theology and the praxis of narrative theology that could assist Christian married women in the context of pervasive GBV (Dlamini 2022:19).

Dlamini (2022) uses qualitative narratives of some women survivors in her study and employs the frame of African women's theology. In doing this, her aim is to highlight GBV as a reality that is caused by a "constellation" of ideas. These include physical, economic, patriarchy, toxic theologies, and others. These factors leave some of the women in the Anglican Church vulnerable to GBV. Traditional culture and practices, as well as religion, are key agents to GBV. In her research, she probes how and why Anglican Christian women suffer from pathologies of culture and religion within marriage and how this situation has a negative impact on women's personhood and identities. Dlamini (2022) highlights narratives of pain where GBV is continuous in the church due to silence, which is a norm in the church. Consequently, it causes mental health illnesses such as stress, anxiety, and depression. From this analysis, Dlamini (2022) highlights marriage as a site of oppression for some women.

Second, in her analysis, Dlamini (2022) talks about exposure to GBV, where some women endure suffering and often are left in submission and victimisation. She cites that "women feel trapped in marriages where they have no power or voice and no resources to make their lives manageable" (Dlamini 2022:176). This type of dependency allows space for abuse because the wife will be subjected to abuse as she is a receiver in this marriage all the time, Dlamini argues. Dlamini further maintains that the act of control and accepting control are products of socialisation which are connected to the traditional ideology of femininity and masculinity that has become a norm in a quite number of African contexts. Thus, she calls this, "hinderance and determining factor of worthiness" (Dlamini 2022:176).

The third aspect in her analysis I relate to is how culture and religion are conspirators of Domestic and Gender-Based Violence (DGBV). Although marriage is a designated holy sacrament, a gift from God, to some extent, religion and culture are misinterpreted to promote abuse. From her research, Dlamini found out that it is not surprising that some women in the Anglican Church still believe they have to stick to their marriages until death separates them from their spouses, and "culturally victory in marriage is evident when women resist" (Dlamini 2022:178).

Fourth, Dlamini (2022) looks at how the ACSA handles DGBV. She found out that Church ideas, traditions, and terminology are still used in conservative ways. In addition, Dlamini (2022) probes how faith communities can support women in abusive marriages besides the prayer mechanism. Through her study, some narratives have established safe spaces for vulnerability, recognition, and healing. This has allowed women to flourish through emancipation and restorative justice. Dlamini (2022) suggests that women survivor voices in the church can be privileged through empowerment and advocacy programmes in the church and the incorporation of professional specialist services so as to build networks between social workers, psychologists, counsellors, the law enforcement, and the church. Dlamini's research provides valuable insights into the strategies that should be used within the church to holistically approach DGBV.

Religion, Women, and Sexual and Reproductive Health and Rights

Writing from an Islamic point of view, Farhana Ismail submitted her Master's on women's sexual agency. Her thesis has the title "An analysis of the discursive representations of women's sexual Agency in online Fatwas[12]: A case study of askimam.org" (Ismail 2015). Ismail uses a feminist post-structural methodology with a legal interpretive framework located in classical texts to analyse the *fatwas*. In her study, she explores the discourse surrounding women's sexual agency through a case study of fatwas on Deoband[13] *Mufti* Ebrahim Desai's[14] *fatwa* forum, askimam.org. In her research, she identifies Desai's *fatwas* on askimam.org as a discursive construction of sexual agency. Following that, she assesses the degree to which these *fatwas* facilitate women in negotiating their choices regarding their sexual and reproductive health. Ultimately, she examines the degree to which the Qur'an and hadith[15] foundational sources are incorporated into the discursive depictions of women's sexual agency. According to Ismail (2015), an analysis of the *fatwas* reveals competing and complementing discourses on women's sexual agency. One of the analyses revealed that the petitioners struggle with the contradiction between their unrealistic expectations of reciprocity within contemporary marriage and their pietistic devotion to the legal history of marriage. They support women's choices in the sexual sphere by citing many aspects of health. Some *muftis* respond by utilising an ethical framework to accommodate women's sexual needs and refusals, and by advocating for mutuality through benevolent masculinity. Physical health issues associated with sexual orientation are within a scientific ethical framework, which links sexual rights to physical health, in contrast to other aspects of health that are handled in the legal context as spiritual issues. However, her study demonstrates how *muftis* have the ability to connect sexual rights to psychological and emotional aspects of health. It also demonstrates the ability to embrace an ethical framework that incorporates various forms of medicine and complementary therapies (Ismail 2015). Ismail discusses the *fatwas* created by Desai and his pupils (including his own *fatwa*), which emphasise mutuality, health, and well-being. These online *fatwas* provide insight into Deoband *muftis'* conception of marriage, preserving marriage stability while adhering to legal logic. She also explores the use of the Qur'an and hadith in this context and the Internet's role in reshaping conventional ideas and conventions, potentially redefining gender interactions. Ismail's research contributes to promoting the significance of understanding women's sexual reproductive rights. Also, it promotes women's empowerment within the Islamic frameworks.

Another academic contribution is from Mariam Bibi Khan in her thesis, "Negotiating between health based contraceptive concerns and piety: The experiences of Muslim wives in the greater Durban area" (Khan 2016). Khan (2016) pursues her qualitative empirical study through the feminist paradigm, employing phenomenological research design. She seeks to comprehend the lived experiences of South African Muslim women in the Greater Durban area, negotiating (within the gendered space of marriage) between their health based contraceptive concerns and their pietistic concerns to observe God's will through the course of being "good wives." Findings in her study indicate that the interviewed women from Greater Durban do not perceive themselves to be negotiating between health-based contraceptive concerns and piety. Contraception is understood in terms of their pietistic desire to follow

God's will and is tied to practical health issues. The South African Muslims in Khan's study "face moral conflicts by prioritising domestic responsibility and sexual availability to their spouse irrespective of personal desire" (Khan 2016: vi). According to her,

> [T]through their desire and motivation to please God, women find themselves negotiating and renegotiating their living conditions as a claim of their agentic positions in the process of pietistic self-making (Ismail 2015). This continuous process is fuelled by their ultimate desire for peace in their homes, the overall objective of marriage, and their pietistic aspirations of acquiring Heaven.
>
> (Khan 2016)

Expressing the same interest in women's sexual and reproductive health rights (SRHR), Martha Mapasure (2016) submitted her Master's dissertation on "The Roman Catholic Church and Contraception." Through a qualitative approach of guided reflection questions and face-to-face interviews in Pietermaritzburg, South Africa, Mapasure focuses on African married Catholic women's engagement with Catholic teachings on contraception presented in *Humanae Vitae*.[16] By applying African sexual ethics theories, her aim in this study is to learn these women's understanding of Catholic teaching on contraceptives. She also seeks to find out from their understanding whether Catholic teachings on contraception pay attention to women's sexual and reproductive health rights. Further, she sought to establish the married African Catholic women's opinion on gender orientation in the Catholic Church and how that affects women's health.

Her study indicates that Catholic teachings on contraception in *Humanae Vitae* do not sufficiently address women's sexual and reproductive health rights. Hence, from her findings, these Catholic married women are yet to be given full recognition to participate in church decision-making on teachings such as *Human Vitae* that affect women's health.

Religion, Culture, Women, and Sexual and Reproductive Health and Rights

Mutale Mulenga Kaunda contributes to the discourse on culture, women's sexual agency and femininity through her Masters's thesis titled, "A search for life-giving marriage: The Imbusa initiation rite as a space for constructing wellbeing among married Bemba women of Zambia" (Kaunda 2013). In her empirical study, Kaunda analyses whether and how *Imbusa*[17] initiation rite is used to construct "subordinate femininities" among married Bemba women of Zambia. The Bemba Zambian female identities are constructed during the process of *Imbusa* initiation. Bemba women are urged to maintain a low profile, be non-aggressive, be sex objects, and also "soft self." All this is oriented through *"banacimbusa"* (also known as "classified bedroom stories"), where *Imbusa* women are instructed to talk softly to their husbands.

Kaunda (2013: 46) proposes a life-giving marriage which for her is *Imbusa* that promotes gender justice. For her, this means that *banacimbusa* need to undergo a process of transformation, consciousness-raising, and internalisation of theories from African feminist scholars. Further, she argues for a feminist *banacimbusa* as one which is decisively and consciously works to dismantle patriarchy and hierarchy structures in marriage and society. In her argument, a feminist *banacimbusa* will foster gender equality and awaken women from oppression to social imbalance. Moreso, in this scenario, a feminist *banacimbusa* will enable women to advocate for their rights by disclosing the resources required to think about marital equality. In essence, Kaunda (2013) advocates for these concepts: a progressive *banacimbusa*,

banacimbusa to be schooled in issues that are a current discussion among Africa women and male theologians such as gender justice (Kaunda 2013:48). Also, she pursues the need for a booklet containing common content of *Imbusa* teachings for coherence. She also notes the need for an African feminist *Imbusa* pedagogy and a holistic approach to sexuality.

Pursuing the same theme of culture, femininity, and reproductive health rights, Lindiwe Princess Maseko writes on "A feminist critique of the Karanga people of Zimbabwe's understanding of infertility as a woman's reproductive health right," in her Master's thesis. Maseko (2021) writes from an African feminist view and appraises the Karanga people of Zimbabwe's understanding of infertility. Her study uses a non-empirical qualitative method and theoretically, she adopts an African women's narrative theology and reproductive justice framework to understand the lived reality of women within the Karanga heteropatriarchal context. In her study, she acknowledges fertility as a traditional, cultural, and religious key concept that is valued among the Karanga. However, she notes that the concept of fertility among the Karanga influences their understanding of infertility and portrays it as problematic. Infertility is a religio-cultural construct embedded within a patriarchal systemic of Karanga that leaves some Karanga women in a state of vulnerability as fertility defines femininity (Maseko 2021). In her research, she reveals that the Karanga understanding of infertility lacks a "just" theological discourse that goes beyond Karanga women's biological progeny in responding to infertility. She suggests and recommends Karanga understanding of infertility should be transformed and recognise infertility in a way that affirms the reproductive health and rights of a Karanga woman in contemporary Zimbabwe (Maseko 2021).

In promoting women's reproductive rights within religion and culture, Tania Missa Owino (2016) writes her Master of Theology dissertation titled: "Mediating Human Rights and Religio-Cultural beliefs: An African Feminist Examination of Conceptualisations of Female Genital Cutting (FGC) in the United Nations Children Fund (UNICEF) Documents." In her study, which uses a reproductive rights framework within a feminist discourse analysis, Owino explores how UNICEF frames, conceptualises, and addresses and has responded to the practice of Female Genital Mutilation in Africa. She illustrates how the discourse on human rights and religio-cultural beliefs is mediated and represented in the UNICEF documents.

The survey reveals significant changes in the past years, including the renaming of female genital mutilation (FGC) as "female genital mutilation/cutting" by UNICEF. This has been a shift from focusing on health repercussions to recognising cultural values and a shift from a human rights perspective to a collective approach. The study suggests that tackling FGC from a human rights standpoint is insufficient. Her research calls for collective action within local communities. There is a need of changing mindsets and attitudes about FGC. There is a need to investigate alternate rites of passage through which local communities could continue to reap the advantages of transferring traditional teachings from childhood to maturity (Owino 2016).

Religion, Women, and Sexual Diversity in Christian Churches

Writing about Queer theology on Sexuality, Siphelele Sabathile Mazibuko (2021) adds her voice to the discourse on gender and religion in Africa. In her Masters' thesis titled "Isitabane of faith: An Auto-ethnographic Exploration of Isitabane lived reality in the Shembe Faith Tradition, using the queer theory and phenomenology approach," Mazibuko (2021) examines the lived reality of *isitabane*[18] (queer) within the independent Shembe faith tradition, KwaZulu-Natal, South Africa. She focuses on the embodied experience of queer persons within the African Independent Church (the Nazareth Baptist Church) through narrative. She explores the experience of participants who witnessed her navigating her journey as a queer individual in the hetero-patriarchal church. According to her research and experience, there is discrimination, isolation, exclusion, and homophobic attacks due to individuals different sexual orientations. This is due to gender identity, invisibility, and silenced individuals through biblical scriptures, culture, and tradition embedded in patriarchal systems. Mazibuko (2021) shares her experience as a queer young woman within this church, and how faith people responded to this identity in South Africa. In her study, she focuses on snapshot themes and extracts the dominant following themes: understanding lesbian sexuality as rejection of men rather than women's attraction, a connection between male violence and lesbian sexuality, a link between faith heterosexuality and reproduction, and others. Mazibuko (2021) points out the challenges of the essentialist perspective of ideological notions of gender and sexuality in association with the sex assigned at birth. She writes that the Shembe faith tradition and other African Independent Churches ought to be engaged in a Contextual Bible Study, which may assist the church in reformulating its vocabulary, policies, and related theories, in order to enable it to collectively engage and negotiate gender and sexual identities, as well as issues relating to gender and sexuality in a life-affirming way (Mazibuko 2021). From her study, there is hope that many silenced queer voices will be heard.

In the same discourse, Tracey Sibisi (2021) produced a Master's thesis on "Queering the queer: engaging black queer Christian bodies in African faith spaces." Through a qualitative research and phenomenological approach, Sibisi (2021) examines how the Christian church responds to queer bodies within spaces of faith. She focuses on understanding the systemic realities engaging the experiences of black queer Christian individuals as the starting point of theological reflection. Her focus also extends to the systemic realities that inform the experiences of queer bodies within the Christian church. She argues that "dominant constructions of gender"[19] as a challenge to queer individuals in Christin church in South Africa are informed by heteronormativity and patriarchal systems (Sibisi 2021:9). These constructions of gender continuously infiltrate the lives of many queer individuals as they try to find a sense of belonging in these Christian faith spaces (Sibisi 2021).

From conducting this research, Sibisi (2021) shares that Christian churches that identify as queer are still following conservative norms and ideas that oppress LGBTIQ people. For example, there are still identify individuals who identify as men or women or as boys and girls. However, they do not acknowledge non-binary individuals and bi-sexual individuals (Sibisi 2021). Thus, influencing queer bodies to only exist within the binaries informed by the systemic realities that favour the dominant bodies (Sibisi 2021).

Through her study, Sibisi (2021) contributes to literature within the field of gender and religion, engaging the lived experiences of nine queer bodies within the South African queer faith landscape. In her research, Sibisi calls for inclusive spaces of worship for all individuals regardless of their sexual orientation. To bridge the social gap that exists between the process of socially moving from heteropatriarchal religious spaces into queer places of worship, Sibisi (2021) suggests a need for research that engages possible interventions. By doing this, she envisions that such a study may uncover ways to free queer bodies from heteropatriarchal worship spaces. This way, they can manage to create their own places of faith.

In her academic contribution, she also mentions the necessity of establishing potential interventions through individuals who may begin to queer queered religious spaces in order to fully embrace all bodies within the church. This can be achieved with the help of *izitabane*[19] within the church. She outlines aspects within the queered image of God and the church that individuals might use to develop processes that incorporate all bodies as the body of Christ. The primary objective is to come up with transformational interventions that will move diverse church members towards challenging disruptive and exclusive beliefs that negatively affect LGBITQ individuals (Sibisi 2021).

Ultimately, the examination of the Gender and Religion Master's and doctoral dissertations above has highlighted some important themes. Four themes have been highlighted. These are "Religion, Women and Gender Based Violence," "Religion, Women and SRHR," "Religion, Culture, Women and SRHR," as well as "Religion, Women and Sexual Diversity in Christian Churches." These themes have highlighted the lived realities of women in religion, culture, and society in general. In this next section, I seek to interpret the significance of these contributions to young women's participation and contribution to leadership in African theology and religious studies and leadership in religion and society.

A Significant Contribution to Theology and Religious Studies in Africa and African Women's Leadership

In this section, I will discuss how the young/emerging women in Gender and Religion in Africa have contributed to the broader knowledge of theology and religion. I will answer two critical questions which read: "How are young/emerging African women scholars in Gender and Religion at UKZN contributing to the African religious studies and theology academia?" Second, "How are they adding to African women's leadership within religion and society?" In this section, I aim to show the significance of involving women in the discourse on religion and theology.

Bringing to the Fore the Lived Experiences of Women in Religion

Young women in Gender and Religion are part of the ongoing initiative of women who are brave enough to write about themselves and their fellow women in their own religio-cultural contexts. This is a source of theology. To support this, Oduyoye has argued that "theology is an expression of faith in response to experience" (Oduyoye 2001:22). The topics they have reflected on come from their religio-cultural experiences. It is significant to realise that the Gender and Religion emerging scholars have contributed to not only "experience of women" but also diverse experiences of women in Southern Africa. These young/emerging African women scholars are contributing within different geographical contexts like Zimbabwe, Zambia, and South Africa. They are not only bringing lived realities of women from one African culture or one religion per se. Some of them are writing from within the Islamic faith and others from diverse strands of Christianity. In doing so, they are also bringing on board the Bemba, Zulu, and Karanga cultures. Others bring challenging religious and cultural norms on women's sexuality, sexual and reproductive health, and sexual and reproductive rights. The nature of this kind of a contribution is knowledge production. Knowledge is not produced in a vacuum. Knowledge is produced from context to context, by learning what other individuals are going through. The dissertations and theses by the young/emerging African women scholars confirm the leadership and ability of African women to research into and reflect on their own lived experiences. They are not waiting for researchers from other parts of the world to lead the research.

Reflecting on "Taboo" Topics

Connecting from writing on women's contextual experiences, the Gender and Religion young emerging scholars are not afraid to research into and reflect on taboo topics. Due to the social upbringing and some African cultural nuances, many women find it difficult to talk about some topics, even though they affect them. These are usually called *taboos* or matters that cannot be spoken about in public. For instance, where I come from, the Karanga people from Zimbabwe believe that "sexual language is a taboo" (Shoko 2007:23). Usually elders refer to sexual terminology as *zvinyadzi* or embarrassing. Nevertheless, looking at the reviewed work above, the Gender and Religion women students have deconstructed that norm. This is not because some of us are disrespectful of our cultural norms. However, it is because of the urgency of handling such matters in an academic setting, for example, in the classroom. For us, these so-called taboo topics are not embarrassing. They present an opportunity for us to begin unveiling what is behind them. We ask ourselves: "Are they life giving or life denying, particularly for women and girls?" We talk and write about them as a way of advocacy to deconstruct life-denying norms that are hidden in the name of being taboo subjects. As we have seen, issues of women's sexual abuse and sexual violation in church(s) are enveloped in prayer. They mature until they claim the lives of women. Women's abuse in their own homes is called "bedroom stories" which are not likely to be discussed in public. Diverse sexuality is another silent matter that has been unfolded. Hence, the contributors have shown how some individuals struggle for spaces of faith just because of different sexual orientation. In support of young women's work such as this, Oduyoye (2001:13) advocates for "parameters that identify cultural elements that are life affirming for women in Africa…in search of women's full humanity and participation in religion and society." It is through this academic space that young women are given an opportunity to freely and bravely speak about what they encounter in their respective societies. Without this academic privilege of writing, as women we would not have the ability to express such deep theological reflection on contextual realities seen in these dissertations. For us, this represents academic and activist leadership in religion and theology, as well as advocacy in faith spaces in Africa.

Fresh Perspectives to Religion and Gender Literature in Africa

Through their dissertations, the Gender and Religion young/emerging scholars are producing new perspectives on religion and gender in Africa. As mentioned earlier, the reviewed contributions date 10 years back from 2013 to 2022. While I acknowledge the literature or material that existed before these 10 dissertations, I interpret their dissertations as "fresh" because they are emerging and they have written on influential topics in this field. More critically, the dissertations are "women" oriented. This is a creation of women's emancipation in religious spaces, where theology is read and drawn from a woman's perspective. Manyonganise, Chitando and Chirongoma (2023a:9) argue that empowerment gives voice to women. It begins when women's experiences are written and presented by women. Hence the importance of doing research from the experiences of young African women. Writing from a Venda perspective (Mudimeli 2011) has argued for studies that take into account:

> …African women who are still marginalized within the church parameters, to empower them to stand up and be counted in the leadership structures of their churches. Women should be able to assert themselves and offer resistance regarding negative cultural and

religious constraints that affect them. An empowerment perspective or approach will help women to challenge the religious and cultural discourses that impact on their lives negatively and deny them access roles as leaders in the church.

(Mudimeli 2011:7–8)

In support of women's perspective in religion and theology, Oduyoye comments on the urgency of liberation. She submits that involving women in theology and religion is a paradigm shift that prioritises African women's own understanding in research (Oduyoye 2001). It is important to include young women in research because it matters when they conduct it instead of men, who are the dominating gender discourses in Africa. I will discuss this in more depth in the subsection that follows.

Enhancing Young African Women's Voice in Academic Spaces and Society

The concept of perspective discussed above also gives women an opportunity to use their voice. The concept of women's voice portrays both academic contribution and African women's leadership in society. Academically, the contribution of young/emerging African women ensures that we have both established African women academics and up-and-coming scholars whose work is valued as sound and informative. Using the Circle mantra "publish or perish," Ayanga (2016:4) alludes that research writing and publishing enables African women's voices to be heard. It also allows their reflections to be recognised as valid (Ayanga 2016). This fulfills the words of Phiri and Nadar (2006) who talk about the need of women's voices to be heard in the academy as a way of developing bold and innovative theoretical spaces. For young African women within the institutions, slowly but surely, contributing academically is a stepping stone to ensuring that women's voices are heard and that women are encouraged to take up leadership in society. This also enables them to be in solidarity with other women who are struggling for full liberation (Lorde 1984; Ayanga 2016).

Conclusion

Young/emerging women students in Gender and Religion at UKZN are making a significant contribution to the study of religion and gender. They are transgressing space that has been dominated by men. They are demonstrating leadership and courage and providing leadership in scholarship. However, since the themes that they address are existential and practical, they are also opening spaces for women's leadership in religion and society. Some theological institutions and university departments of religious studies or theology are not themselves immune to sexism, patriarchy, and corruption (Ayondukun, 2021). However, they can be incubators of revolutionary actions that promote women's leadership (Manyonganise et al., 2023:9). Although in many African (and other) societies, acknowledging a woman's wisdom is difficult, the contributions by the young/emerging women scholars summarised above remains valuable. I appreciate the reflections on the Gender and Religion young/emerging African women students' work as a legacy itself in academics and in society. I celebrate the Gender and Religion Department at UKZN as a liberative space for women in religion and leadership. Broadly, I commend the Gender and Religion young/emerging African women's dissertations for providing other students with these life-affirming and inspiring learning resources. Their contributions can be used by other institutions in Africa and beyond as motivation for encouraging more women interested in religion and theology. Through our research and writing, we aspire to serve as mentors for other young women. From the output of the young/emerging African women scholars whose work I have reviewed, it is clear that women's leadership in African theology and religious studies, as well as religion in society, will be assured for now and in the foreseeable future.

Notes

1 Definition developed from the review of the following: Elfil and Negida (2017), Shorten and Moorley (2014), Tyrer and Heyman (2016), van Hoeven et al. (2015), and (Berndt 2020).
2 https://researchspace.ukzn.ac.za/items/118c644e-26e1-47dd-b439-e58da68522bd (Accessed 24 January 2024).
3 Professor Isabel Apawo Phiri served as the Continental Coordinator of the Pan African Circle of Concerned African Women Theologians from 2002 to 2007 (Phiri 2009:106).
4 Interview held with one of the core pioneers on 18 January 2024.
5 Interview 18 January 2024.
6 Initially, Musa W. Dube, then later, Ezra Chitando and Nyambura Njoroge were some of the leading scholars, researchers, and activists in EHAIA.
7 At the time of writing, Professor Sarojini Nadar is a director of the Desmond Tutu SARCHL Research Chair in Religion and Social Justice. In 2008, she served as the Director of Gender and Religion program, where she was also a co-founder (https://desmondtutucentre-rsj.uwc.ac.za/prof-sarojini-nadar/). Accessed 24 January 2024.
8 https://live.fundza.mobi/home/library/non-fiction-books/because-science-is-fun/sarojini-nadar-professor-of-the-f-words-faith-and-feminism/. Accessed 24 January 2024.
9 Interview held 18 January 2024.
10 The Good Shepherd is a Christ-centred community Lutheran Church project with the mission to support orphans at Mnene Parish, Zimbabwe. This initiative was born in 2000. "In 2002, Bishop Dr. Ambrose Moyo from Zimbabwe personally asked Good Shepherd Lutheran Church in Raleigh, North Carolina to help the Mnene Parish and Good Shepherd." The Good Shepherd Lutheran Church directly sponsored orphans in need of education, food, supplies, and prayers. Since its inception, it has supported orphans until they are able to sustain themselves following post-secondary education. https://gslchurch.org/serve/the-world. Accessed 25 January 2024.
11 The Ecumenical Church Leaders Forum is a Faith Based Institution focused on Peace Building in Zimbabwe founded in 2008 and registered as a trust in August 2010 (Maseko 2021:341).
12 A *Fatwa* means a verdict or judicial pronouncement given by a religious legal scholar (*mufiti*) in response to a question posed by a petitioner (*mustafti*). The fatwa-issuing mufti is pious and possesses superior religious knowledge so that his advice will be aligned with God's judgment. Ismail (2015:10).
13 A legal school thought from India (Ismail 2015).
14 Desai is identified as the author and acknowledged religious authority figure of askimam.org, where every fatwa on the site is approved and sanctioned by him (About Us, askimam.org, [Online] Available at: http://askimam.org/about). Accessed 23 November 2015 in Ismail (2015:13).
   Desai is based at Darul Iftaa Mahmudiyyah in Sherwood, Durban, a training institute for muftis. Askimam.org 2011, About Us. Available from: http://askimam.org/about. Accessed 15 October 2015 in Ismail (2015:14).
15 Traditions, sayings, and deeds narrated from the Prophet Muhammad (Kodir 2007: 202) in Ismail (2015:2).
16 *Humane Vitae* refers to one of the Catholic Church's encyclicals (Mapasure (2016).
17 Imbusa initiation is a transition ritual which is preserved as a means to cross boundaries, changes in times, and social status (Rasing 1995:34). It is usually pressured that the bride is a virgin before she is married. It is a significant rite for women who are about to enter marriage (Kaunda 2013).
18 *Isitabane* is a derogatory isiZulu term, used to refer to gay men (Moletsane, Mitchel and Smith, 2012: 255). However, as for most derogatory terms, the term "isitabane" does not consist of a direct meaning but is related to disgust and hatred for queer people. This word is also used for lesbian, bisexual, trans people, and intersex individuals (Mazibuko 2021:14).
19 "Izitabane" used to discriminate and insult the queer community (Sibisi 2021:25).

References

Primary Sources

Masters and Doctoral Dissertations of the Contributors

Bodhanya, M. 2016. Women's health-seeking behaviour in the context of sexual violence, sexual health rights, and the Muslim community. A case study of Hope Careline Counselling (Master's dissertation. University of KwaZulu Natal: Pietermaritzburg, South Africa).

Dlamini, N. Z. P. 2022. Unmasking Christian women survivor voices against gender-based violence: A pursuit for a feminist liberative pastoral care praxis for married women in the Anglican Church of Southern Africa (Doctoral dissertation. University of KwaZulu Natal, Pietermaritzburg: South Africa).

Ismail, F. 2015. An analysis of the discursive representations of women's sexual agency in online fatwas: a case study of askimam. Org (Master's Dissertation: University of KwaZulu Natal: Pietermaritzburg: South Africa).

Kaunda, M. M. 2013. A search for life-giving marriage: the Imbusa initiation rite as a space for constructing wellbeing among married Bemba women of Zambia (Master's dissertation. University of KwaZulu Natal, Pietermaritzburg: South Africa).

Khan, M. B. 2016. Negotiating between health-based contraceptive concerns and piety: the experiences of Muslim wives in the greater Durban area (Master's dissertation. University of KwaZulu Natal, Pietermaritzburg: South Africa).

Mapasure, M. 2016. The Roman Catholic Church and contraception: Exploring married African Catholic women's engagement with Humanae Vitae (Masters dissertation. University of KwaZulu Natal, Pietermaritzburg: South Africa).

Maseko, L. P. 2021. Feminist critique of the Karanga people of Zimbabwe's understanding of infertility as a woman's reproductive health right (Master's dissertation. University of KwaZulu Natal, Pietermaritzburg: South Africa).

Mazibuko, S. S. 2021. Isitabane of faith: an auto-ethnographic exploration of Isitabane lived reality in the Shembe faith tradition (Masters' dissertation. University of KwaZulu Natal, Pietermaritzburg: South Africa).

Owino, T. M. 2016. Mediating human rights and religio-cultural beliefs: an African feminist examination of conceptualisations of Female Genital Cutting (FGC) in the United Nations Children Fund (UNICEF) documents (Masters dissertation, University of KwaZulu Natal: Pietermaritzburg: South Africa).

Sibisi, T. M. 2021. Queering the queer: engaging black queer Christian bodies in African faith spaces (Masters Dissertation. University of KwaZulu Natal, Pietermaritzburg: South Africa).

Secondary Sources

Akpa, V. Askhia, O. & Adeleke, A. A. 2021. "Leadership: A Review of Definitions and Theories." *International Journal of Advances in Engineering and Management*, 3(1), 273–291.

Ayanga, H. O. 2016. "Voice of the voiceless: The legacy of the Circle of Concerned African Women Theologians." *Verbum et Ecclesia*, 37(2), 1–6.

Ayondukun, E. O. (2021). Theological Education and Leadership: A Response to Leadership Challenges in Africa. *Insights Journal*, 6(2), 60–71.

Berndt, A. E. 2020. "Sampling methods." *Journal of Human Lactation*, 36(2), pp. 224–226.

Bowen, G. A. 2009. "Document analysis as a qualitative research method." *Qualitative research journal* 9(2), pp. 27–40.

Chirongoma, S. and Moyo, M. 2023. "Gender discrepancies in Zimbabwean religio-cultural and political leadership: A case study of young Christian women in the Midlands province." In Manyonganise, M., Chitando, E. and Chirongoma, S., eds., *Women, Religion and Leadership in Zimbabwe, Volume 1: An Ecofeminist Perspective* (pp. 123–146). Cham: Springer Nature Switzerland.

Chisale, S. S. 2020. "'Deliver us from patriarchy': A gendered perspective of the Evangelical Lutheran Church in Southern Africa and implications for pastoral care." *Verbum et Ecclesia*, 41(1), pp. 1–8.

Chitando, E. 2016. "Religion and Masculinities in Africa: An Opportunity for Africanization." in A. Adogame et al., eds., *African Traditions in the study of religion, diaspora and gendered societies.* (pp. 133–146). Farnham: Ashgate.

Chitando, E. 2023. "Theorising African Women's Leadership: An Overview." In (Manyongansie, M., Chitando, E. and Chirongoma, S. 2023) *Women, Religion and Leadership in Zimbabwe, Volume 1: An Ecofeminist Perspective,* (pp. 25–43). Cham: Springer Nature Switzerland.

Corbin, J. & Strauss, A. 2008. *Basics of qualitative research: Techniques and procedures for developing grounded theory* (3rd ed.). Thousand Oaks, CA: Sage.

Creswell, J. W. 2013. *Qualitative Inquiry & Research Design: Choosing among Five Approaches.* Los Angeles, CA: Sage

Creswell, J. W. 2014. *Research design: qualitative, quantitative, and mixed methods approaches.* Thousand Oaks, CA: Sage.

Denzin, N. K. and Lincoln, Y. S. eds. 2011. *The Sage handbook of qualitative research.* Sage.

Elfil, M. & Negida, A. 2017. Sampling methods in clinical research: An educational review. *Emergency* 5 (1), Article e52, 1–3.

Fazal, F. et al. 2020. "Women Leadership and Organizational Barriers: A Socio Economic and Ethical Point of View." *Journal of Legal, Ethical and Regulatory Issues,* 23(5), 1–10.

Kanyoro, R.A. 2006. Beads and strands: threading more beads in the story of the circle. *African women, religion, and health,* pp. 19–42.

Kodir, F. A. 2007. *Hadith and Gender Justice: Understanding the Prophetic Traditions.* Cirebon: Fahmina Institute.

Lari, N. Al-Ansari, M. & El-Maghraby, E. 2022. "Challenging Gender Norms: Women's Leadership, Political Authority and Autonomy." *Gender in Management,* 37 (4), 476–493.

Lorde, A. 1984. *Sister outsider: Essays and speeches,* Crossing Press, Berkeley, CA.

Manyonganise, M., Chitando, E. and Chirongoma, S. eds., 2023a. *Women, Religion and Leadership in Zimbabwe,* Volume 1: An Ecofeminist Perspective. Springer Nature.

Manyonganise, M. Chitando, E. and Chirongoma, S. eds., 2023b. *Women, Religion and Leadership in Zimbabwe,* Volume 2: Engagement and Activism in Religious Institutions. Springer Nature.

Manyonganise, M. Chitando, E. and Chirongoma, S. 2023c. "Introduction: Women, Religion and Leadership in Zimbabwe." In Manyonganise, Chitando and Chirongoma, eds., *Women, Religion and Leadership in Zimbabwe, Volume 1: An Ecofeminist Perspective* (pp. 1–21). Cham: Springer Nature Switzerland.

Moletsane, R. Mitchell, C. & Smith, A. (2012) How to do research: a practical guide to designing and managing research projects. Facet Publishing.

Mudimeli, L. M. 2011. 'The impact of religious and cultural discourses on the leadership development of women in the ministry: A vhusadzi (womanhood) perspective' (Doctoral dissertation, University of South Africa)

Nadar, S. and Phiri, I. A. 2013. "Gender and HIV and AIDS. In I. Phiri and D. Werner, eds., *Handbook of Theological Education in Africa.* Oxford: Regnum Books International

Ngunjiri, F. W., & Christo-Baker, E. A. (2012). Breaking the Stained Glass Ceiling: African Women's Leadership in Religious Organizations. *Journal of Pan African Studies,* 5(2), 1–4

Njoroge, N. J. 1997. "The missing voice: African women doing theology." *Journal of theology for Southern Africa* 88: 77–93.

Njoroge, N. J. 2005. "A new way of facilitating leadership: Lessons from African women theologians." *Missiology* 33(1), 29–46.

Nwachuku, D.N. 1992. The Christian widow in African culture. *The will to arise: Women, tradition, and the church in Africa,* pp. 54–73.

Oduyoye, M. 2001. *Introducing African women's theology* (Vol. 6). A&C Black.

Oduyoye, M.A. and Kanyoro, R.A. 1992. The will to arise: women, tradition and the church in Africa.

Phiri, I. A. 2009. "Major Challenges for African Women Theologians in Theological Education (1989-2008)." *International Review of Mission* 98(1), 105–119.

Phiri, I. A. and Chitando, E. 2023. "Women's Transformative Leadership and Africa's Holistic Development: The Role of the Churches." In Manyonganise, M. Chitando, E. and Chirongoma, S., eds., *Women, Religion and Leadership in Zimbabwe,* Volume 2: *Engagement and Activism in Religious Institutions* (pp. 19–34). Cham: Springer Nature Switzerland.

Phiri, I. A. and Nadar, S. 2006. "Treading softly but firmly": African women, religion, and health. In I. A. Phiri and S. Nadar, eds., *African women, religion, and health*, pp. 1–16. Maryknoll, NY: Orbis Books.

Pui-Lan, K. 2000. *Introducing Asian Feminist Theology*. Sheffield Academic Press.

Rapley, T. 2007a. Doing Conversation, Discourse and Document Analysis. *Qualitative Research Kit*.

Rapley, T. (2007b) Doing Conversation, Discourse and Document Analysis. London: Sage.

Rasing, Thera. 1995. *Passing on the rites of passage: Girls initiation rites in the context of an urban Roman Catholic Community*. London: African Studies

Shoko, T. 2007. *Karanga Indigenous Religion in Zimbabwe: Health and Well-being*. Ashgate Publishing, Ltd.

Shorten, A. & Moorley, C. 2014. "Selecting the sample." *Evidence Based Nursing*, 17(2), 32–33.

Tamale, S. and Oloka-Onyango, J. 1997. "Bitches at the academy: Gender and academic freedom at the African university." *Africa Development/Afrique et Développement*, 22(1), pp. 13–37.

Tyrer, S. & Heyman, B. 2016. "Sampling in epidemiological research: Issues, hazards and pitfalls." *British Journal of Psychiatry Bulletin*, 40, 57–60. doi:10.1192/pb.bp.114.050203

van Hoeven, L. R., Janssen, M. P., Roes, K. C. B. & Koffijberg, H. 2015. "Aiming for a representative sample: Simulating random versus purposive strategies for hospital selection." *BMC Medical Research Methodology*, 15 (90). https://doi.org/10.1186/s12874-015-0089-8

Winston, B. E. & Patterson, K. 2006. "An Integrative Definition of Leadership." *International Journal of Leadership Studies*, 1(2), 6–66.

Yin, R. K. 2015. *Qualitative research from start to finish*. Guilford publications.

Informal Interviews

18 January 2024- informal Interview with the Gender and Religion senior beneficiary
24 January 2024 -informal Interview with the Gender and Religion senior beneficiary

Internet Sources

https://berkleycentre.georgetown.edu/people/esther-mombo
https://berkleycentre.georgetown.edu/people/ezra-chitando
https://desmondtutucentre-rsj.uwc.ac.za/prof-sarojini-nadar/
https://gslchurch.org/serve/the-world
https://live.fundza.mobi/home/library/non-fiction-books/because-science-is-fun/sarojini-nadar-professor-of-the-f-words-faith-and-feminism/
https://researchspace.ukzn.ac.za/items/118c644e-26e1-47dd-b439-e58da68522bd

32
ALUTA CONTINUA! AFRICAN WOMEN THEOLOGIANS' CONTRIBUTIONS TO INCLUSIVE THEOLOGICAL EDUCATION

Towards the African Union's Agenda 2063

Moses Iliya Ogidis

Introduction

The coming of missionaries to the continent of Africa brought with it many benefits such as education, specifically theological education for training people for ministry and teaching. This chapter focuses on theological education which is the foundation of education within the African continent. The Bible is greatly upheld as the final authority by Christians and it plays an important role in theological education in Africa. Scholars such as Makhulu (1990), Wahl (2013), and Mashabela (2017) have unearthed the importance of theological education in Africa. This chapter acknowledges their roles and contributions to the field of theology and the importance of theological education. Wahl (2013: 1–2) affirms that many scholars have made valuable contributions on theological education from various points of view. There exist many models when it comes to theological education within the continent of Africa.

Amanze (2008: 3) rightly notes the growth of theological colleges, Bible schools, Christian universities, and institutions of theological education by extension across the continent. These institutions are owned by various denominations in Africa and beyond. For instance, Wood (2023) asserted in 2018 in Rwanda the government passed a law requiring local churches to meet in a "legal" building and have a "legal" pastor. A legal pastor was required to have an associate degree in Bible or theology by later that year. This shows the value of theological education in the continent generally because many pastors or teachers are not theologically trained, but are often trained in other fields. Theological education provides a sound platform for the development of the Africa we want, as articulated by the African Union in its blueprint, "Agenda 2063."

However, most of the notable scholars or giants in African theological education are men due to gender social construction and cultural norms that exclude women from the onset to study theology in various countries of Africa (Phiri 2009). This chapter discusses this gender aspect by focusing on the roles and contributions of some notable African women theologians of the 21st century. It also reflects on how they were able to change the narrative regarding African women's access to theological education. It recognizes how their struggle for gender inclusiveness in theological education can be sustained in the spirit expressed by the Evangelical Church Winning All (ECWA) anthem which says: "The vision of our founders shall not die in our own hands" (ECWA program 2022). This means that the baton needs to be passed on from one generation to the up-coming African women and men (as allies) to keep the fire of scholarship burning for generations to come. In a way, having balanced theological education from both men's and women's perspectives is like a bird using two wings to fly; however, when it is dominated by one gender it is like a bird with one wing. It cannot fly.

Aluta continua, which is a Portuguese saying meaning "the struggle continues" and, in this context, it is in reference to theological education to be inclusive especially in writing balanced theology and from the realities of both men and women (A Dictionary of African Politics, 2019). *Aluta continua* is a slogan that expresses the struggle by African women to be included in African theological education. This chapter discusses the contributions of two African women theologians to women's theological education in Africa.

Methodology

This chapter employs the descriptive method in analysing data. This method contributes by describing how two great African women theologians have changed the theological education in the 21st century in Africa and beyond. While the quantitative method concentrates on numbers and percentages, the qualitative method focuses on the why, along with the what and the how many (Vyhmeister 2001: 126). Descriptive research provides data about the subject of the study, describing the "who, what, when, where and how" of a situation. It provides a systematic description on the roles and contributions of the selected women to the paradigm shift of theological education in Africa and beyond that is as accurate and factual as possible.

Theological Education in Africa

The idea of Christianization of the continent came with a lot of baggage, such as theological education, health, religion, and contentious notions of civilization. The Church in Africa has a rich history of theological education from the Northern part of the continent since the first century A.D. Even in the New Testament, there are references to Africans such as Simon of Cyrene in Matthew 27:32, Mark 15:21, and Luke 23:26. There is also Apollos in Acts 18:24 who came from Alexandria in Egypt and the Ethiopian Eunuch in Acts 8. This shows how connected Africans were with the gospel and the knowledge they received and how it was passed down informally or formally from one generation to another. That is why the history of theological education in Africa will not be complete without mentioning the Northern part of the continent and also the early Church Fathers who were mostly Africans. Even though this work will not deal with these Church Fathers in detail, it is important to refer to them as this helps to show how they also helped in shaping the theological education on the continent. Tertullian who was from Tunisia wrote extensively on theological issues. Athanasius of Alexandria developed early church Trinitarian theology. Augustine of Hippo, Aurelius of Carthage (modern-day Tunisia), Clement of Alexandria, Cyprian of Carthage, and Origen of

Alexandria all contributed to the growth and development of theological education, both in Africa and the entire world (Hinson, 2021). Despite their great contributions to the study of theology, some of them had wrong ideas about women, including having problematic biblical interpretations. Such ideas include women being the misbegotten males, the weaker sex, and inferior among many others. Consequently, details of their ideas about women are not the aim of this chapter but to trace how theological education can be traced back to them.

Nevertheless, the influence of the Church Fathers towards theological education in Africa cannot be underestimated, particularly in light of the fact that they influenced the coming of missionaries and colonizers to the continent. On the other hand, nothing seems to be documented about church mothers or the roles of women during the period of the early African church fathers (Mombo and Joziasse 2011). Laura Swan (2001: 32–70) in her book, *The Forgotten Desert Mothers: Saying, Lives, and Stories of Early Christian Women*, notes the sayings of some early women such as Amma (meaning mother) Matrona, Amma Sarah, and Amma Syncletica. In her work, Laura shows how they also contributed to the growth of the church but since they were not able to write for themselves, little was known about them and their contributions. Neither are they being studied in our universities, theological institutions, and Bible colleges. This can be due to a lack of written documents about them and their theology. One cannot deny the dominance of males in the history of the church and theological education on the continent since the first century AD. Their theology is well appreciated but nothing was said about women. This is due to the fact that for a long time, women did not have access to writing, thereby preventing them from having their works studied in theological institutions.

Furthermore, Pauw (1980: 264–265) observed that with the advent of Christian missions or the coming of missionaries during the latter half of the previous centuries (18th and 19th), both Catholic and Protestant missions trained indigenous people, specifically men, from an early stage to serve as teachers, catechists, or evangelists and were later ordained as ministers in their respective denominations. Theological education on the continent began as a means of training men specifically for evangelism to their fellow indigenous people. Makhulu (1990), Amanze (2008: 3) and Walls (2013: 8) affirm that the aim of theological education in Africa was its emphasis on training church ministers who could preach and evangelize the local people in their various communities. This confirms that the reason for initiating theological education in Africa by the missionaries was to be able to train locals to reach their members of society. However, women were excluded from participating in theological education during this early period.

Amanze (2008) states that theological education is necessary because is open and accessible to equip all believers to establish the Kingdom of God in this world. In summary, evangelism is the central point for theological education that was started in Africa with the coming of the missionaries. However, it is important to note the dominance of men who are seen as the custodians of theological education. Thus, it is unlikely for one to attend most of the universities, seminaries, and Bible colleges without learning about African Church Fathers. However, not much is said about the roles of the women (the Church Mothers) during their time. This generated some questions in the mind of the researcher:

> Does this mean women were not active in theological conversations during this early period? Were there no women who contributed to the people's understanding of God (theology)? Why are most of the theological institutions not teaching about the roles and contributions of these women?

Mwaniki (2021: 1) notes that theology has been defined by men and in terms of God's relationship with the male gender. This gender disparity is partly because of selective reading of the Bible to deny women ordination to the priesthood and senior positions of leadership in the church. This was further captured by Wood (2001), and Onyango (2003: 77–78) who indicated that the women were trained to go and teach the subjects in their villages, and how to help their husbands in the church. Most of the women were trained in different capacities of the church excluding ordination which was believed to be for men and leadership. Therefore, training women for ministerial leadership and ordination was not a welcome idea during the early time of theological education in Africa. In the following section, the chapter will review the contributions of two leading African women theologians to the opening of theological education in Africa to women.

The Background of Mercy A. Oduyoye and Esther Mombo as Theological Educators

This chapter provides a brief background to two leading African women theologians; who they are, and their journey to theological education. These two have been selected due to their distinguished status in the field. This chapter acknowledges that there are other African women theologians who have contributed to theological education in the continent. However, it has settled on these two due to their outstanding leadership and long service. They have successfully challenged male dominance in African theological education. In describing their journeys, the essay shall use their first names initially. However, when referring to their scholarly contributions, the chapter shall resort to the names they have used in their publications.

Mercy Amba Oduyoye, who is considered as the mother of the Circle of Concerned African Women Theologians (the Circle), is a pioneer in championing women's access to theological education in Africa. Pui-Lan (2004) and Fiedler (2017: 11) indicate that Mercy Amba was born on 21 October 1934, to Reverend Charles Kwaw Yamoah and Mercy Yaa Dakwaa Yamoah. The firstborn of nine children, she was named "Amba," which means a girl born on Saturday and "Ewudziwa" after her grandfather, Kodwo Ewudzi Yamoah, on the eighth day after her birth.

Mercy studied in Asamankese during her first three years of primary school and continued in a small Asante village called Akyinakrom where her father began his first ministerial appointment. She also went to a Methodist boarding school for girls. She went on to attend a government-supported co-ed school in Accra, known as Achimot for her secondary education and completed her certificate there in 1952 (Oduyoye 2004: xii; Fiedler 2017: 11). From 1953 to 1954, Mercy attended the Teacher's Training College at Kumasi College of Technology (presently the Kwame Nkrumah University of Science and Technology). After completing her Post-Secondary Certificate of Education (Teachers Certificate A, Ministry of Education Ghana), she taught at Asawase Methodist Girls' Middle School from 1954 to 1959, near Kumasi. She went to the University College of Ghana, Legon in 1959, and in 1961; she received the Intermediate Bachelor of Divinity from the Theology Department of the University of London. She continued for another two years to obtain an honours degree in the Study of Religion (Oduyoye 2004: xii). Even though it was not her idea to study theology but was encouraged by Noel King, a professor of history at the University of Ghana, this marks her journey into the field of theology from 1959 to 1963. In 1964, Mercy graduated from the University of Cambridge, UK, with a Bachelor of Arts (Honours) degree in theology focusing on Tripos Part III, Dogmatics (1963–1965). She went on to receive a Master of Arts

(Honours) degree in theology from the same university in 1969 (Oduyoye 2007 interview with Smith).

The second woman whose contribution this chapter will discuss is Esther Moraa Mombo. She was born in Kisii in Kenya and brought up by her maternal grandmother. Esther was born in 1957 in the village of Birongo, located in Kisii County; she is the eldest of eight children and was born into a Quaker family. Esther attended her primary and secondary education in Kisii before she moved to Nairobi to attend high school, and after high school, she moved in with a relative who promised to send her to college, which never happened (Ngunjiri 2010: 106). Right from childhood Esther's quest for knowledge was evident and this knowledge is focused on theology that was influenced by her grandmother. The passion continued till she fulfilled her dreams and aspirations. Her desire from childhood is not without challenges which are stated below in the words of Esther Mombo as captured by Ngunjiri (2010: 106–107):

> An uncle of mine said to my grandmother and my mother that he would take me and would help me to continue with school. But I ended up in his house working as the house girl. I was a relative, yet they turned me into their house girl! I helped to bring up two children. I woke up at 5 (am) to go get milk, then get back and prepare breakfast. The house was not hers, she shared it with another family. I could not sleep in the sitting room, since that was not theirs. I and another girl from the other family slept in the kitchen. I slept next to the fridge for a year… I took care of the children as though they are mine, and other women make comments like how come you have a good house girl. I did that because they were my uncle's children even if I was being paid, they were still his children. After a year I left for my parent's place not my grandmother' place… I remember when I left that home, I told my aunt that I have taken care of my children while you did your degree, but I will get more degrees than you. I came from a very poor home where we have a house for our parents, and the other house that has chickens, calves, and goats is where we children slept… I kept telling my mother one day I will drive to my aunt's house. I told her I was not just meant to be a house girl. At the time you could get a job as an untrained teacher. My father did not want me to go back to school because now he wanted me to contribute economically to our family's upkeep.

Reading the experiences that Esther went through in her early stages, one would expect that they would have been enough to frustrate her in relation to her furthering her education. However, she never gave up on her dreams. She demonstrates the fact that challenges are bound to be experienced in life. When this happens, giving up is not the solution. Instead, one must press on with passion and sustain the desire to impact the next generation for good. In her case, this was with regards to ensuring women's access to theological education in Africa and beyond. Esther was motivated and encouraged by her grandmother to become a woman preacher; this shows her grandmother's influence on her life. She later received her bachelor's degree in divinity from St. Paul's United Theological College (presently known as St. Paul's University) before pursuing her Master's degree in Philosophy in Ecumenism at the University of Dublin, Trinity College in 1986. After completing her master's degree, she went back to Kenya and began teaching in an Anglican Bible College. It was in the process of teaching in the Anglican institution that she became a member of the Anglican Church. Later, she went back to the United Kingdom to commence her doctorate in church history at the University of Edinburgh. She finished her study in 1998 and then she went back to Kenya where she took a teaching job with St. Paul's United Theological College, now known as St. Paul's University, Limuru, Kenya (Corey 2021: 218).

Mombo's quest to access theological education for herself and other women in Africa has been a struggle with a satisfying ending. For her, it ranges from her gender, age, and even marital status where several men think she is out there aiming at breaking marriages. Mombo experienced marginalization from childhood, because she went against the norm by getting extensive education and resisting early marriage. This continued as her first theological teaching position at a theological school in Eldoret where she was treated with suspicion because she was a woman and single (Kwaka-Sumba & Roux 2017: 138). Mombo has dedicated her professional life to challenging the exclusion of women, gender-based violence, and discrimination against women in churches, as well as challenging patriarchy and power dynamics within the leadership of the church in Africa (Ngunjiri 2010: 110).

The two African women theologians this chapter focused on faced several challenges in their quest to make theological education inclusive. In the following section, the chapter shall provide an overview of the contributions by Oduyoye and Mombo to women's struggle for theological education in Africa.

The Contributions of Oduyoye and Mombo to Women in African Theological Education

Oduyoye often proclaims that "a one-winged bird cannot fly." She has consistently maintained that a one-sided theology cannot be balanced and life-affirming when it does not bring out the voices of women and their contributions to theological education. The birth of the Circle of Concerned African Women Theologians is one of the greatest contributions that Mercy Amba Oduyoye has bequeathed to theological education in the continent. The Circle was born out of her desire to bring the voices of women in doing theology within the continent of Africa. Kanyoro (2006: 3) cites Oduyoye (1997: 1–2) how "the Circle is unique in being the initiative and vision of one woman, which gained enthusiastic welcome, and support of EATWOT (Ecumenical Association of Third World Theologians) women in Africa and subsequently that of many more."

The ecumenical space in which Oduyoye worked provided the incubatory space for the Circle of Concerned African Women Theologians. It was gathered that for a long time, she was the only African woman writing theology and getting her work published. This opened the door for her in the ecumenical space. According to Kanyoro, when she met Mercy in 1988, she had files, lists, and letters from many African Women. All they needed do was to "sort, thread and make them into nice strands" for them to become the Circle of Concerned African Women Theologians (Kanyoro, 2006: 20–21). The Circle of Concerned African Women Theologians was officially inaugurated in 1989 at Trinity College, Legon, Ghana. The committee that was set up was made up of women from Africa who were members of EATWOT (Kanyoro, 2006: 21). Furthermore, Fiedler (2017: 43) observed that

> The humble beginnings of the Circle that culminated in the 1989 convocation have led to an impressive movement in Africa. The Circle has attained growth in geographical coverage, leadership as well as administrative development. After the first convocation in 1989, Circle women from Africa and beyond gathered at the second convocation in 1996. This second was followed by a third convocation in 2002. The fourth convocation was held in 2007.

The impact and growth of the Circle, which was born out of Oduyoye's (1996) vision, has given prominence to women's theological education, both in Africa and beyond. Their theology is more practical and engaged than remote and abstract. They do theology from the experiences of women, including in their interpretation of the Bible. For example, Musa Dube has approached the biblical text from her African experiences to deconstruct oppressive patriarchy ideology on women and children. Fiedler (2017: 26) went further to affirm that "theological institutions have remained vital to the development of the Circle. Theological institutions that offer training to women which are same as that offered to men are crucial in this development." There are now several universities, and theological institutions in Southern, West, East, and also North Africa teaching African Women's Theologies. Even though, not all of the universities and theological education accept such in their curriculum. Even gender studies probably due to patriarchal and cultural norms found within such countries in Africa. To this effect, Kanyoro (2006: 27) made the following observation: "The institutions of theology such as seminaries and universities would be used to create network circles to encourage women to learn from one another about writing for publication."

One of the major contributions of the Circle to theological education in Africa and beyond is through the production of relevant and informative theological literature. African women theologians such as Oduyoye, Mombo, Musimbi Kanyoro, Musa Dube, Nyambura Njoroge, Fulata Moyo, Sophia Chirongoma, and others have provided valuable reflections on African women's experiences within the religious sector. For instance, there is literature on African Biblical and cultural hermeneutics, African women in Religion and culture, among several other publications, and their usage in various theological institutions in Africa and beyond (Fiedler 2017: 144–61). Such contributions of the Circle theology and its inclusion to theological education are also part of the influence on Esther and her contributions to theological education starting from St. Paul's University Limuru Kenya where she is currently teaching and as the leader of the Circle Eastern Africa chapter.

Mombo's contributions to women's theological education in Kenya and beyond are significant. As this chapter has already highlighted, the missionaries mostly invested in men as the ones who would carry the message of the Good News in Africa. This approach shut out several women, not only because of gender but also due to the selection process of who is qualified. As a result, certain categories of women have not been considered eligible (Mwaniki, 2019: 495). This was evidenced in the history of St. Paul's Theological College from its inception, where women only came with their husbands and were taught the basic elementary things such as sowing, knitting, how to be hospitable, and helping the husband in the ministry. This was one of the challenges that Mombo challenged during the time she began working with the college, before it became a university.

Mombo contributed significantly to the idea of engendering theological education, especially at St Paul's, given that from its inception theology had been strictly for the ordination of men and preparing them for ministry. Mombo and Heleen Joziasse (2011: 3) noted that "the college was not prepared for women students both in its physical and social space let alone theological space. The women had to create their own space in a male-dominated institution which was theological education was linked with ordination." Therefore, challenging gender-based theology is one of the major issues that Mombo has had to confront. Mombo and Joziasse (2011: 3–4) affirm the movements that brought about engendering theological education in Africa and brought out the plight of women to the light, namely, the "Ecumenical Decade of Churches in Solidarity with Women (1988–1998). The second is the Circle of Concerned African Women Theologians."

Many women benefited from Mombo's struggles for an inclusive theological education at St. Paul's University Limuru Kenya because of her roles in the university. Corey (2021: 219) observed that "Mombo is committed to students who have historically been disenfranchised from theological education. Drawing them in, she works to create a space for them. At St. Paul's, these students are predominantly women." While this is an accurate observation, it is important to acknowledge that Mombo has also supported men from disadvantaged backgrounds in their quest for theological education. For Mombo (Corey, 2021: 219), theological education needs to be stripped of clericalism and it needs to be gender sensitive in its curriculum. Mombo's quest at St. Paul's University Kenya has led to many women being ordained in the Anglican Church of Kenya and the Reformed Church of East Africa, among many other denominations. Mombo's contribution to theological education in the Anglican Church made her to be well-known within the church in Kenya, as well as across the general Anglican Communion where she is invited to contribute to one cause or the other. This was well captured by Mombo and Joziasse (2011: 113)

> The reason I felt it was important to give theology to the people of God, is because I no longer consider the ordained ministry as the pre-requisite to theological education. To me, ordination is just one of the ministries. If a woman is called to serve God whether she works with children, teaches at a Bible college, or she is working with the youth, anything that a woman does to serve God, is for me an important ministry in the church. I feel that there is a need to critique and rethink the traditional hierarchical perception of Christian ministry where non-ordained forms of ministries are regarded as insignificant, and hence given to women.

Mombo's radical approach to theology is much needed in most of our theological education institutions in Africa where theology is meant for men. There are instances where there are women learning theology but they are not ordained upon graduation due to the traditional theology of excluding women from the ministries of word and sacrament by such denominations. Mombo's quest for the inclusion of women in ordination is a selfless fight since she is still a lay person who has fought for the inclusion of women in the church but she is not ordained. Her desire is for the inclusion of women in theological education and engendering ordination that appears then to be for men and women excluded. As noted by Corey (2021: 220–224), some of Mombo's other contributions include her roles in the Circle of Concerned African Women Theologians, at the international, regional, and national levels. Mombo's communal concerns expand beyond her local community through her participation in the Anglican Communion and as a contributor to most of the debates within the Anglican Communion at the international level (Corey 2021: 223). Mombo's desire is for a holistic theological education and she has sought to seize on every opportunity she has to journey with those that are marginalized in society, especially women but also men. She has been able to secure PhD scholarship for some of her male students to further their studies. The aim is to reconstruct and deconstruct the oppressive and marginalized status of women and men when it comes to theological education.

Another key contribution by Oduyoye and Mombo to theological education in Africa as well as by other African women theologians that have advanced in their theological education is mentoring the young and upcoming theologians. For example, Oduyoye's idea of forming the Circle emerged out of her commitment towards mentoring more African women theologians. Similarly, Mombo has consistently stated that mentoring is an important strategy in terms of transferring learning and life experiences. She argues that although mentoring takes many forms, it is important in facilitating the leadership development of the younger generation. This is very evident in the life of the African women theologians. Their act of mentorship cuts across gender, status, age, nationalities, etc. Their focus is that theology should be life-affirming to all people irrespective of age, status, race, and nationality, among others. Their mentoring is holistic, dealing with individual life, studies, social, moral, mental, and even spiritual dimensions, creating a sense of community and unity in doing theology. Their contributions are vital towards achieving Agenda 2063 of the African Union, with special reference to promoting holistic development of the continent.

Lessons for Up-Coming African Scholars

The lessons drawn in this chapter are specifically for up-coming theologians to strengthen and fortify the study of theology, especially within Africa. This is to appreciate the rich diversities and uniqueness of what God has blessed the continent and uses them in our understanding and struggle to make a change in our communities and churches. One of the lessons is by *improving the status of the Circle*. The Circle, right from its inception, has contributed greatly to the theological education and engendering theology. Previously theological education in Africa appeared to be for only men, but the Circle has been creating room for women to study theology and to be trained on gender, African women theologies, and related themes in most of the universities and theological seminaries. This can be channeled towards the achievement of the African Union's Agenda 2063. The up-coming African theologians need to learn from the footsteps of the older generation so that the momentum is maintained as the continent seeks to achieve gender justice. Just as Mombo (2019: 459) affirms, the power of the theological educators and preachers is very important and this rests on the shoulders of up-coming African women and men. There is a need for them to join hands for a balanced theological education where both women and men have the space to contribute. Furthermore, Kanyoro (2006: 160) notes that

> When trained women theologians begin to make connections between what happens at home and in church with the view to suggesting a change in the name of justice, they have to be cautious about disturbing the set order… But for us in Africa, it does not matter how much we write about our theology in books, the big test before us is whether we can bring change into our societies.

The African men and women who would have been empowered with quality theological education are to go back to the societies and be at the forefront of the struggle for peace, justice and development. In particular, African women's writings should strive to bring change and transformation in the church and society (Mombo, 2013: 858–860; 2019). This is a legacy the upcoming theologians need to emulate and maintain in order to ensure that religion becomes a positive social force in the quest for a more advanced continent. Men who seek to promote gender justice and development will be serving as allies in the Circle's quest to overcome patriarchy. The role of men and boys in partnering with the Circle is meant to avoid marginalizing them in the struggle. This can also create imbalances in society when it is all about the girl child as we are seeing in most countries in Africa and less on the boy child, forgetting that both live in the same communities (Phiri 2009: 5; Mombo 2013: 860).

There is a need for up-coming young African women theologians to address current realities and also develop a curriculum that addresses real-life issues that people are going through in society (Mombo 2019: 459). This will sustain the Circle's activism in challenging oppressive cultures and promoting life giving interpretations of the Bible. Their writings and publications are bringing out the uniqueness of the African realities, especially the experiences of women and how they engaged in doing their theology that is more "functional than ontological." Mashabela (2017: 3) affirms that Africans need an education that engages their context and realities. This challenges Eurocentric theology to allow Africans to lead and shape their African theological education. African theological education can bring the value of the theological curriculum when approached both from the traditional and African women lenses to prepare theological students (men and women) to engage in suitable economic development and liberation that is centred on the African needs and realities. This decolonizes theological education in Africa and empowers the faith community to be effective agents in development.

The story of revolutionary icons such as Oduyoye and Mombo needs to continue to be told. African women theologians are at the forefront of transformative theological education. Going forward, young African women theologians should be empowered by the insights of leading African women theologians such as Isabel Phiri, Musa W. Dube, Musimbi Kanyoro, Teresa Okure, Nyambura Njoroge, and others. They are pioneers in the quest to have a theological education curriculum that is gender sensitive. This was well captured by Mwaniki (2019: 494) when saying that "the Circle has been instrumental in developing and promoting African women's hermeneutics of African women's ways of reading the Bible."

Oduyoye, Mombo, and the Circle faced and are still facing challenges such as discrimination, stigmatization, being named as feminists or "those that want to break marriages with wrong theology." Phiri (2009: 5) notes some challenges faced by women theologians in Africa relate to the primary issue of identity. She writes that "the real struggle that the Lusophone Circle has epitomised for the Circle is about identity of the African women theologians against the desire to be inclusive in our definition of who is an African woman theologian." Other challenges include resistance from family members who have ideas based on gender social construction of women becoming subjected to the leadership of men. This idea has been carried over into theological education. Other challenges faced by Oduyoye, Mombo, and the Circle include some male (and female) colleagues who are not cooperative in their various work places, as well as organizational structures that exclude women from leadership.

The generation of these two great African women theologians has led the way in empowering women in the church and society. Kanyoro (2006: 160) affirms the need for activists who are comfortable with challenging the text of the Bible through critical analysis and hermeneutics in other to bring out the life-affirming aspect of the texts. Therefore, the prophetic task, as Kanyoro (2006: 176) avers, is that of addressing issues that diminish life. African women engaged in theology, are participating in a prophetic mission. As up-coming theologians, there is a need to take this prophetic task seriously by speaking to the real issues of life that the church is facing and also critically analysing cultural norms that are oppressive to humanity. Kanyoro (2006: 177) also notes that "we must listen to each other. To seek justice is to break the boundaries of injustice" and such injustice includes the misrepresentation of women by men and misinterpretation of the Bible. This entails listening to both genders and the communities we come from and breaking those boundaries that create a rift between our theology and the realities that people go through. The mothers of African women theologians have laid a very solid and concrete foundation that the up-coming African theologians, both men and women, need to build upon.

This chapter also notes the challenges that upcoming theologians may face in their area of engagement. Mombo and Joziasse (2011: 96) argue that studying theology, particularly for women, means appropriating power (especially religious power), which traditionally has been a preserve of men. Therefore, the women themselves need to rethink and struggle between feeling called to ministry and the pressure and suspicion that as a woman one simply cannot be called. Church regulations also constitute an obstacle for women. There are church regulations on who should be taught theology, where people should learn theology, and how they should do theology. The church serves as custodian of church traditions that exclude women from access to theological education, including ordination. Breaking such traditions by women is never easy, but Oduyoye and Mombo and other women theologians have set the pace for the upcoming theologians to maintain and, where possible, even exceed. There are other challenges which include: the economy regarding payment of fees and the low number of female students going for theological education since it is still linked with ordination in most African countries. Similarly, the challenges of being single, single mothers, being seen as the weaker sex, widowhood, gender, and sexual-based violence, pandemics, disabilities, etc. play a role in preventing African women from pursuing theological education.

Conclusion

In conclusion, the future of theological education that is gender sensitive is very possible. In turn, this will make a significant contribution towards the success of the Africa Union's Agenda 2063, which envisages a peaceful, integrated, and prosperous Africa. Having a gender-balanced theological curriculum will go a long way in contributing towards this vision. This chapter discussed the roles and contributions of Oduyoye and Mombo in promoting inclusive theological education in Africa. It has highlighted the challenges they have faced and their resilience in seeking to ensure that as many African women as possible have access to theological education. The chapter challenges young African theologians (both male and female) to draw lessons from the sacrifices and insights of Oduyoye, Mombo, and the Circle. Only when women and men can partner in church and society can ambitious development blueprints such as Agenda 2063 succeed. Thus, the slogan should persist: *Aluta continua!*

References

A Dictionary of African Politics. 2019. Oxford: Oxford University Press. Online www.oxfordreference.com/display/10.1093/acref/9780191828836.001/acref-9780191828836-e-23

Amanze, J. N. 2008. "Paradigm Shift in Theological Education in Southern and Central Africa and Its Relevance to Ministerial Formation." Chapter that was to be presented at the *IV Congress of the World Conference of Associations of Theological Institutions on 5th June 2008*.

Corey, E. 2021. "Esther Mombo (1957-)," in *Twentieth Century Anglican Theologians: From Evelyn Underhill to Esther Mombo*. Edited by Stephen Burns, Bryan Cones, and James Tengatenga. West Sussex, UK: John Wiley & Sons Ltd.

ECWA. 2022. Women Fellowship Lafia District Church Council Sing Songs Service Program.

Fiedler, R. N. 2017. *A History of the Circle of Concerned African Women Theologians (1989–2007)*. Mzuni Press.

Hinson, T. 2021. "Fathers of the Reformation: Africans in the Early Church," April 21, 2021. https://africa.thegospelcoalition.org/article/fathers-of-the-reformation-africans-in-the-early-church/ (31/03/2023)

Kanyoro, M. R.A.. 2006. "Beads and Strands: Threading more Beads in the Story of the Circle," in *African Women, Religion, and Health: Essays in Honor of Mercy Amba Ewudziwa Oduyoye*. Edited by Isabel Apawo Phiri and Sarojini Nadar. Cluster Publications.

Kwaka-Sumba, T. and E. le Roux. 2017. "African Women's Leadership – Realities and Opportunities," in *African Christian Leadership: Realities, Opportunities, and Impact*. Edited by R. J. Priest and K. Barine. Maryknoll, NY: Orbis Books.

Makhulu, W. K. 1990. "Theological Education in Africa: Quo Vadimus," In *Theological Education in Africa: Quo Vadimus?* Edited by J. S. Pobee and J. N. Kudadjie. Asempa Publishers.

Mashabela, J.K., 2017. "Africanisation as an agent of Theological Education in Africa," *HTS Teologiese Studies/Theological Studies* 73(3), a4581. https://doi.org/10.4102/hts.v73i3.4581

Mombo, E. 2013. "Mentoring Younger scholars in Theological Education," In *Handbook of Theological Education in Africa*. Edited by I. A. Phiri and D. Werner. Regnum Books International.

Mombo, E. 2019. "Considerations for an Inclusive Global Theological Education: Old Issues, New Questions," *The Ecumenical Review* 71(4), 449–460.

Mombo, E. and H. Joziasse. 2011. *If You Have No Voice, Just Sing! Narratives of Women's Lives and Theological Education at St. Paul's University*. Zapf Chancery for CIRCLE St. Paul's Chapter.

Mwaniki, L. 2019. "Enhancing Theological Education for Women in Africa: The Role of African Women Theologians and the All Africa Conference of Churches," in *Pan-African Women of Faith and A Vision of Inclusive Global Theological Education*. The Ecumenical Review. World Council of Churches, John Wiley & Sons Ltd.

Mwaniki, L. 2021. Third Teac International Webinar-25th May, 2021. Women in Leadership in Theological Education – Challenges and Opportunities. https://www.anglicancommunion.org/media/456832/TEAC_Webinar_Women-in-theological-education-challenges-and-opportunities_Lydia-Mwaniki_2105-en.pdf (Accessed on 27/03/2023)

Ngunjiri, F. W. 2010. *Women's Spiritual Leadership in Africa: Tempered Radicals and Critical Servants Leaders*. State University of New York Press.

Oduyoye, M. A. 1996. "The Impact of Women's Theology on the Development of Dialogue in EATWOT," *Bangalore Ecumenical Association of Third Word Theologians (EATWOT)*, 19(1), 11–33.

Oduyoye, M. A. 1997. *Transforming Power: Women in the Household of God. Proceedings of the Pan-African Conference of the Circle of Concerned African Women Theologians*. Sam-Woode Ltd.

Oduyoye, M. A. 2004. *Beads and strands: Reflections of an African woman on Christianity in Africa*. Orbis Books.

Oduyoye, M. A. 2007, October 22. Interview with Yolanda Y. Smith.

Onyango, E. (Ed.). 2003. *For God and Humanity: 100 Years of St. Paul's United Theological College*. Zapf Chancery.

Pauw, C. M. 1980. *Mission and Church in Malawi. The history of the Nkhoma Synod of the Church of Central Africa, Presbyterian, 1889–1962*. BMP.

Phiri, I. A. 2009. "Major Challenges for African Women Theologians in Theological Education (1989–2008)," *International Review of Mission*, 98(1), 105–119. https://doi.org/10.1111/j.1758-6631.2009.00009.x

Pui-Lan, K. 2004. "Mercy Amba Oduyoye, and African Women's Theology," *Journal of Feminist Studies in Religion*, 20(1), 7–22.

Swan, L. 2001. *The Forgotten Desert Mothers: Sayings, Lives, and Stories of Early Christian Women*. Paulist Press.

Vyhmeister, N. J. 2001. *Quality Research Papers: For Students of Religion and Theology*. Zondervan.

Wahl, Willem Petrus. 2013. "Towards Relevant Theological Education in Africa: Comparing the International Discourse With Contextual Challenges." *Acta Theologica*, 33(1), 266–293. http://doi.org/10.4314/actat.v33i1.14 ISSN 1015-8758 © UV/UFS http://www.ufs.ac.za/ActaTheologica

Walls, Andrew. 2013. "Theological Education From its Earliest Jewish and African Christian Beginnings – Some Currents in the Wider History of Christianity," in *Handbook of Theological Education in Africa*. Edited by I. A. Phiri and D. Werner. Oxford, UK: Regnum Books International.

Wood, L. M. 2001. "Engendered Communal Theology: African Women's Contribution to Theology in the Twenty First Century." *Feminist Theology*, 9(27), 36–56 https://doi.org/10.1177/096673500100002704

Wood, L. M. 2023. "MACU and Rwanda Challenge Partner to Educate Pastors," 7 February 2023 https://christianstandard.com/2023/02/macu-and-rwanda-challenge-partner-to-educate-pastors/ (accessed on 02/04/2023)

33
CALLING THE CHURCH TO ACCOUNT
A Theological Response to the Silent Pandemic of Sexual and Gender-Based Violence against Women in Nigeria's Mainline Evangelical Churches

Henry Marcus Garba and Moses Iliya Ogidis

Introduction

In the era of the early Church Fathers, there was the conviction that the church is truly the pillar and foundation of truth and was embraced as the path to salvation by the fathers of the Second Ecumenical Council in 381 AD (Afonsky, 2001, p. 89). Even in modern times, the church is believed to be the custodian of truth in all aspects. There is a call to stand by it and proclaim it to people in order to set them free from all kinds of oppression. Meanwhile, there is the conviction that the Bible is the word of truth and when rightly interpreted, aims at transforming people's lives and educating them on how to grow in their relationship with God, as well as to get guidance on how God intends people to live with each other. However, in contemporary society, women and girls, under the watch of the church, are unprotected from violence, which Dieudonne rightly captured the explanation thus, "violence has taken various names and faces in our midst: political, military, social, economic, sexual, gender-based and racial. It can be loud or quiet and brutal or silent" (Tshiakany, 2007, p. 54). Unfortunately, when violence is being carried out within the biblical narratives, in most cases, it is not named as sexual and gender-based violence (SGBV), nor is it referred to as rape, especially within the marriage settings that this chapter discusses. SGBV is viewed in this chapter as a game of power (who wills the power and over whom: the predator and the prey).

The Nigerian society is affected by various forms of violence, both reported and unreported. Nigeria is a country in Africa with the largest population of over 200 million people (Olarewaju, 2021, p. 1), with three major languages (Hausa, Yoruba, and Igbo) and numerous others. The country is also a religious nation with three major religions (Christianity, Islam, and Traditional Religion), which sometimes determine the social and political existence of the Nigerian people. Indeed, in Nigeria, Christianity in its denominational diversity plays a leading role in shaping and enforcing ethical norms and consent practices. Christian institutions are helping address the diverse social and ethical needs that affect society. For instance, it is historically observed that Christianity represents a powerful potential resource to address social issues like trafficking, slavery, etc. Throughout history, Christian faith-based organizations and congregations have continued to mobilize significant resources for social intervention (Knight, Casassa, and Kagotho, 2022, p. 194). However, given the broad character of this engagement, this study focuses on how mainline evangelical churches within Nigeria deal with the silent pandemic of SGBV that perhaps has become like cancer-eating the fabric of the church. This prompted some questions that guide the research: "How are the mainline evangelical churches in Nigeria handling sexual and gender-based violence? Why has the World Health Organization (WHO) not declared sexual and gender-based violence as a pandemic? How is sexual and gender-based violence affecting the mental, social, and spiritual lives of the survivors within the church? And how is the church dealing with the silent pandemic eating the fabric of the church?"

This study employed narratives and storytelling within the framework of African Women's Theology as a methodology for data analysis in order to bring out the reality of what women are going through in society and reflect on the ways religion contributes to women's challenges. The narratives and storytelling aim at deconstructing the oppressive cultures, and interpretation of the Bible that reinforce the subordination of women. It also aims at reconstructing new ways of relationships that are not oppressive but life-affirming, giving a better environment for women to live. African women's theology is a contextual liberation theology that recognizes the full humanness and equality of women and men made in the image and likeness of God. It seeks an understanding of God that is not bound by the limitations of the patriarchal system (Oduyoye, 1995). It takes women's experiences as its starting point, focusing on the oppressive areas of life caused by injustices such as patriarchy, colonialism, neo-colonialism, racism, capitalism, globalization, and sexism. It sees a need to include the voices of all women, not just theologians because it acknowledges that most African women are engaging in oral theology. African women's theology must be bilingual, which is "speaking the language of the academy and that of their communities not just linguistically, but culturally and socially" (Phiri and Nadar, 2006, p. 6).

Sexual and Gender-Based Violence: A Pandemic or a Priority

SGBV is any form of sexual activity that occurs to women and girls without their consent. Such sexual activities include unwanted touching of body parts, sexual assault or battery, rape, sodomy, coerced nudity, incest, and sexual harassment. The perpetrators can be family members, friends, husbands, colleagues at the workplace, or neighbors where threats are made to the victims to instill fear in them not to speak out. SGBV occurs frequently worldwide, which leaves no country or community untouched. Additionally, it is believed that gender stereotypes, social norms, cultural standards, and gender discrimination all play a significant role in the perpetuation of violence against women and girls. However, the WHO has not declared sexual violence against women and girls a pandemic but considers it a health priority; hence, the approach of the WHO is to raise awareness and demand action to end violence against women (Adams and Fortune, 1995, p. vii).

Meanwhile, violence is in diverse forms, ranging from domestic abuse and sexual assault to sexual (online) harassment, humiliation of women and girls, divisiveness, racism, suppression, sexism, inequality, etc. Such heinous practices are silently affecting the church and society, which also threatens the integrity of contemporary Christianity. Foremost, Some of the shades of sexual violence include coercion, child and forced marriages or female genital mutilation, sex trafficking, forced prostitution, and exploitation which can be described as a form of modern-day slavery, rape, and sexual torture, which are routinely used as tactics of warfare (Riecher-Rössler and García-Moreno, 2013, p. viii). At the center of these negative realities happening within societies are women and girls who have always been victims of femicide, which leaves them with psychological, emotional, and mental scars, but with few social, cultural, or religious options.

Moreover, violence against women is not a minor issue, but it is usually reported as a short news item or "in other news" (Anne-Marie, 2019, p. 8). This suggests, particularly, that SGBV has not caught the attention of relevant authorities (especially the mainline churches under consideration) to consider it a pandemic nor is it a very serious societal problem that requires urgent consideration. However, a report suggests that a significant number of women have experienced physical or sexual violence at some point in their lives (Anne-Marie, 2019, p. 8). Further, SGBV suggests a manifestation of inequality, domination, and discrimination. It stems from social norms and expectations that reinforce inequality and place women's and girls' choices outside of the realm of their control. Even though both genders can experience violence, SGBV against women and girls is higher and on the increase (Klugman et al., 2014, p. 62). Geraldine Terry in her introductory note on *Gender-based Violence* opines that violence occurs in all cultures and both male and female, however, it is more common in some societies than in others, more against women than men, and is also differentiated by the extent to which societies punish or condone them (Terry and Hoare, 2007, p. xv).

Though SGBV has not been declared a pandemic, the Declaration on the Elimination of Violence against Women in 1993, which is a sub-category of gender-based violence, makes it an issue of concern that needs the response of not only government and non-governmental institutions but also religious and cultural groups (Terry and Hoare, 2007, p. xiv). Besides, the widespread prevalence culture of SGBV that supports the evil against women in countries like Nigeria, South Africa, Cameroon, Kenya, Rwanda, Zimbabwe, and Uganda to mention a few, makes it important for the church and Bible scholars to oppose and disrupt the underlying violence. This is why this chapter examines the theological response of the mainline evangelical church in Nigeria on the silent pandemic of SGBV against women and girls. An example of some mainline evangelical churches that this chapter refers to are the conservative denominations such as the Evangelical Church Winning All (ECWA), Church of Christ in Nations (COCIN), and Evangelical Reformed Church of Christ (ERCC). These evangelical denominations uphold the patriarchal and literal (face value) interpretation of the Bible in not addressing the pandemic of SGBV in their churches. This chapter, however, calls for a re-examination of the public theology of these mainline evangelical churches in Nigeria, which in turn occasioned a theological response.

Sexual and Gender-Based Violence in the Bible

Given the central role played by the Bible among mainline evangelical churches in Nigeria, it is strategic to provide an overview of how SGBV features in the Bible. The Bible is the collection of stories of people who lived in ancient times and is documented for the generations to come to be able to learn from them and correct what needs to be reassessed for a better society. It is described as a "violent book" inscribed with abundant traditions that bear witness to the pervasiveness of gendered aggression and abuse that range from strange rape to acquaintance rape, and gang rape (Blyth, Colgan, and Edwards, 2018, p. 1). There are several examples of SGBV throughout the Bible. Even though biblical authors may not refer to these examples as SGBV nor relegate these biblical rape texts to discussions yet, considering the characteristics of what SGBV means, they are also classified within the category in this work (Scholz, 2010, p. n.p.). This section only discusses a few of them, both from the Old and New Testaments. This section analyses the texts from a gender perspective, examining how men and women are sexually abused and how gender-based violence existed before the present time in the 21st century. This chapter did not exegete the passages under consideration but deployed gender analyses only.

Affirmatively, SGBV against women and girls is possibly, a calculated plan by male predators that are mostly close to the survivors who now become the prey. For instance, 2 Samuel 13:1–22 is the story of Tamar, the daughter of King David who was raped by her half-brother Amnon. For this chapter, this was a calculated and planned rape and incest that Amnon committed. Reading 2 Samuel 13:1, Tamar was described as beautiful, meaning, she was one of a kind among the women of that time. The conspiracy began in verse 2 of the same chapter (13) when Amnon became obsessed with the beauty of his sister until he was fundamentally disturbed because of that. Amnon sought the advice of his close friend, Jonadab, who coached him on how to get his sister, Tamar; some bad advice that led to SGBV against Tamar by Amnon. Thus, the conspiracy for the SGBV on Tamar was championed by Jonadab, Amnon's adviser, who in verse 5 states, "Go to bed and pretend to be ill." Hence, Cooper-White avers that "There is a conspiracy of men aiding and abetting the perpetrator of the crime and a male conspiracy of silence after the act"(Cooper-White, 2007, p. 26).

Consequently, the story of Tamar's rape or incest is further described by Cooper-White as

> a tale of the exercise of power and domination. From the narrator's point of view, this is a 'true crime' story, but the crime is portrayed in the context of the book of Samuel, not as a crime against a person, but rather as a property crime.
> (Cooper-White, 2007, p. 28)

Foremost, the exposure to male sexual assault of women and girls resonates with the prevalent practice of sexual dominance as the very foundation of gendered authority (Sheller, 2018, p. 50). Also, reading the story of Tamar was all about who wills power and over whom: the predator and the prey. That was why immediately Amnon raped Tamar, the next thing was hatred that he developed against her in verse 15 of 2 Samuel 13 where it reads, "then Amnon hated her with intense hatred. In fact, he hated her more than he loved her" (NIV). The narrator in this context focused more on the idea of power than what happened to Tamar later, but he recorded how Amnon was killed.

Societies are defined by how they treat their most vulnerable; Tamar's scenario and the tone of some other biblical narratives suggest the reality of sexual violence against women and men in the biblical world. Many of our existing societies can be categorized as a systemic "rape culture." For example, based on the social construction in Nigeria, some married women do not believe there is rape in marriage. It is frequently described as an unquestioning belief that men are naturally sexually aggressive and dominant and that women are the natural targets of that sexual aggression and must resist unwanted overtures. This suggests that women should try to avoid rape because rape happens, and sexual assaults are accepted as inescapable eventualities (Goodwin, 2020, p. 202). Indeed, SGBV raises social concerns that impede humans from flourishing. There are other examples of rape cases in the Bible, including the story of Dinah, Lot's daughters, and Bathsheba. These examples help shape the minds of contemporary Christians about understanding and dealing with the evil of sexual violence (Moniz, 2019). This is demonstrated in the story of Tamar and the aftermath of Amnon's evil act. Similarly, Cooper-White postulates,

> Whether the act is rape, sexual harassment, battery, or the sexual abuse of a child all our approaches toward prevention as well as intervention and healing will fail until we recognize these not as acts of passion, lust, or temper but as acts of power and aggression often using or targeting sexual body parts or sexist language – simply because this is the area of greatest vulnerability and greatest violation.
>
> (Cooper-White, 2007, p. 26)

Furthermore, a careful examination of some passages in Psalms, 22:14-15, 6:6, 42:3, 56:2, 57:4; and 117:13, suggests the lamentations and petitions uttered by victims of radical evil, pain, and violence (McClure and Ramsay, 1998, p. 1). These lamentations and petitions are not limited to a particular time or space, nor do they reflect the whispers and cries of designated pain and violence. Instead, they reflect the cultural settings of Bible times. For example, the text of Ezekiel 16:36–37 denotes God's punishment upon Israel, the unfaithful wife, which Amy Kalmanofsky describes as one of the most violent sexual texts because of how violence is condoned (ed. Kalmanofsky, 2020, p. 9). God's brutal punishment by exposing Israel's nakedness indicates rape, as stated by Mary Shields (2001, p. 136). Nevertheless, the Old Testament in Deuteronomy 22:23–25 describes rape as "evil" and prescribes a death sentence for such behavior by the perpetrator. The New Testament is not specific about rape but warns strongly against sexual immorality (activities), not only in the physical act but including thoughts (Matthew 5:28; Mark 7:20-23; 1 Corinthians 5:11; 6:15-16; 7:1-2).

Apart from the texts mentioned above, there are more instances of female sexual assault in the Bible, such as Genesis 34 and Judges 19 which offer two explicit rape stories found in the Bible. The books of Genesis 12 and 20 also contain implied episodes in which Abraham proposes Sarah's marriage to foreign rulers. Therefore, Harold Washington proposes that it is imperative to note that an examination of biblical rape narratives suggests that ancient Israel practice a "rape culture" with patriarchal ideology whereby sexual assault is viewed as a manly act and women are regarded as intrinsically rapable (Washington, 1997, p. 352).

Sexual and Gender-Based Violence: A Silent Pandemic in Nigerian

Having provided an overview of SGBV in the Bible, this section turns to an analysis of the issue in the context of Nigeria. The status of women in Nigeria has a way of placing them in an oppressive situation where they face violence daily. Womanhood is determined by patriarchy (Barr, 2021, n.p.), which is a system that reposes power among male members of society, and it is evident in their language use that is oppressive to women specifically (Emeka-Nwobia & Umezurike 2019, p. 43). In Nigeria, social and cultural norms contribute to the creation of hierarchies which result in the thriving of patriarchal norms. Mercy Oduyoye notes how culture structures the subordinate place of women to be completely dependent on men for their viability in the community. Hence, women are usually construed as objects of pleasure to be bought, owned, and discarded at will by men, both in marriage and outside marriage

(Oduyoye, 1995, p. 13). The marginalization and abuse of women within Nigeria tend to be supported by traditional customs within the country where the culture of silence appears to be the central theme as is discussed below. This is the main reason why SGBV has become a silent pandemic and how women are fighting such menaces even in the church.

As noted earlier, Nigeria is the largest country in Africa when it comes to population. It is also highly religious. However, the reality of SGBV that is eating the fabric of the country includes the church. This includes the mainline evangelicals, the focus of this chapter. Notably, "The Nigerian society is plagued by cases of sexual abuse in all sectors, from educational, political, economic and to socio-cultural vis-a-vis religious sectors. Furthermore, its effects have been unevenly felt by all and sundry" (Ituma, Uroko, and Eskay, 2013, p. 499). SGBV is a reality in Nigeria and the churches, with many cases going unreported due to some reasons characterized by fear, stigmatization, preaching, and teaching on perseverance that is one-sided. An example is the death of Osinachi Nwachukwu, a gospel singer whose death is allegedly connected to her husband through domestic violence. Her death opened up a can of wombs about SGBV against women (Ugwu and Atima, 2022). Therefore, one cannot deny the existence and effects of SGBV on the victims especially women and children either Christian, Muslim, or traditional religion. From the WHO's report, Margaret-Mary Mezie-Okoye and Folusho Alamina submit that although SGBV has been observed as one of the fastest-growing crimes all over the world, its actual prevalence is usually unknown because of gross underreporting to the appropriate authorities (Mezie-Okoye and Alamina, 2015, p. 79). However, studies have shown that one in four women may have experienced beaten, coerced into sex, or abused in one way or another (which this work refers to as sexual and gender-based violence, SGBV) by an intimate partner and up to a third of adolescent girls report their experience as being forced (Effa et al. 2009; Emeka-Nwobia and Umezurike, 2019, p. 40). Ipole notes:

> Some wives are suffering and dying silently at the hands of their husbands. I may not be far from the truth if I say that it appears these days, that marriage is topping the list of silent killer diseases. Many precious lives have been sent to their early grave by their husbands. Many more women are walking corpses.
>
> (Ipole, 2018, p. xxxii)

Alas, the woman has been misunderstood, mistreated, misinterpreted, and manipulated for many centuries; hence, she suffers abuse in most societies around the world. All these are because her roles and functions are not understood by the man. Women are just like men's property being treated as slaves like what the husband bought with money (Ipole, 2018, p. 4). As mentioned earlier, the majority of cases of SGBV in Nigeria go unreported because of the fear of being socially stigmatized or blamed for the incident (Emeka, Odika, and Igboanugo, 2022, p. 78). Hence, it is observed that about two million Nigerian girls experience sexual abuse annually and that only 28 percent of rape cases are reported, with only 12 percent resulting in convictions (Akimbobola, 2012).

The Approach of Evangelical Churches to Sexual and Gender-Based Violence

The Evangelicals are the denominations that uphold the sacredness of the Bible. They uphold literal (face value) interpretations and appear to be influenced by culture and patriarchy to cement the oppressive sexual abuse women and girls are going through without allowing justice to prevail on the perpetrators. Common trends in locating Evangelicals are summed by Timothy Larsen thus,

> Orthodox protestants adhere to the global Christian network that developed from the revival movement of the eighteenth century. Evangelicals hold to the Bible as divinely inspired and the final authority in matters of faith and practice; they emphasize God's atoning work through the death and resurrection of Christ; the role of the Holy Spirit in a person's life to bring about conversion and the ongoing life of fellowship and service to God and others, including the task of proclaiming the gospel to all people, and they emphasize the atoning work of Christ on the cross.
>
> (Larsen, 2007, p. 1)

The use of "Evangelicals" in this chapter is within the context of Nigeria whereby some conservative churches hold onto traditions and culture. Consequently, the Bible is interpreted not to challenge SGBV, especially the perpetrators (men) as it is discussed in this chapter. The Evangelicals tend not to consider passages like Deuteronomy 22:25-27 when approaching, especially within the context of marriage. Observably, "The very nature of evangelical faith should naturally lead us to confront the truth about domestic violence. However, what is straightforward in theory is often messy and vexing in practice" (Nason-Clark, Kroeger and Fisher-Townsend, 2011, p. 29). This is commonly seen in the way most evangelical churches (ECWA, COCIN, and ERCC) approach SGBV from the biblical perspective and contextualize it in their teachings, Bible studies, sermons, and even conferences. For instance, the women in one of the bible studies on rape believe that there is no rape in marriage because the man has the right to the woman's body, whether she likes it or not.[1] This is because many of the evangelicals in Nigeria are conservatives who uphold more of the spiritual and patriarchal interpretation of the Bible. Any other interpretation that challenges such views is perhaps considered heretic and barbaric (Ogidis, 2021).

Due to the high level of religiosity in the country (Nigeria), men utilize the privileges as instruments to oppress, subordinate, and abuse women in the name of marriage and what the religious books are saying (Emeka-Nwobia and Umezurike, 2019, p. 42). SGBV is a well-known problem among Christians (churchgoers included) and Muslims in Nigeria, but the evangelical churches appear not to give it the attention it requires to prevent the perpetration of abuse among couples. Pastors and church leaders in Nigeria are in a dilemma in addressing the issue of SGBV among their congregations, which is further complicated by the misapplication of biblical texts. This was evidenced when some students at one of the evangelical seminaries in Nigeria were asked about the role of the church in addressing SGBV. They responded that the women need to persevere in their marriages and continue to pray that God will change them.[2] Though we are sometimes committed to spreading the good news of justice and peace as Christians, at times speaking up against SGBV seems like an incredibly difficult and even impossible undertaking.

On the other hand, religious communities that are supposed to be havens for survivors or victims of SGBV are often not safe places. The clergy who are supposed to advocate for justice and peace for SGBV survivors have become lascivious and caught up in the sexually violent practices against women and girls. Regrettably, church denominations have not been able to lead in advocacy against the sexual abuse of women and girls nor sufficiently condemn the horrific behavior because the perpetrators have sometimes been church leaders and ordained ministers (Stirling et al., 2004, p. 7). Meanwhile, it is observed that the abuse of power by religious leaders has a hoary existence with different narratives painted throughout Christian history, hence, the horrific sexual violence of clergy (Catholic) against the laity was so rampant in medieval Christendom, as observed by Anson Shupe (Shupe, 2010, p. xi). Recently, the issue of the Catholic clergy's involvement in exploitative sexuality has overwhelmed the media; hence, reigniting events of the historical past (Best and Jenkins, 2017, p. 111). The heinous situation in Catholic history is no different in modern times as evident among the ECWA, ERCC, and COCIN. Sadly, many evangelical (ECWA, ERCC, and COCIN) clergy have sexualized their ministries, with unfavorable reports spreading about them taking advantage of women and girls who come to them in trust for help or counseling. Consequently, evangelical Christians are hesitant to speak out against sexual abuse in society or to even acknowledge it (Fortune and Poling, 2008, p. 39; Cooper-White, 2012, p. viii). Meanwhile, Ipole wrote about some of the narratives of women experiencing SGBV:

A woman who has been married for close to twenty years is living in hell in her matrimonial home. Her husband takes undue advantage of the fact that the Bible says women are weaker vessels, therefore, he can bully, beat, kick, batter her, brutalize, and dehumanize her. The worst part of it is that the husband does all these things to his wife not minding who is present and in whichever place.

(Ipole, 2018, pp. 1–2)

These are the realities that many women and children go through at the hands of their husbands, fathers, and uncles. Unfortunately, most members of the clergy are not trained (theologically from the seminaries) on how to address the situation of SGBV and resolve to pray and counsel with the survivors or victims.[3] The awareness against SGBV in many Christian communities and churches is very dim. In a similar vein, Adams and Fortune assert that ministers with no training are not confident to confront abuse cases but would rather default to counseling survivors, especially women, to stay with their partners and work out their communication differences, and it appears similar things are taught in the seminaries within Nigeria (Adams and Fortune, 1995). This is not to look down on the counseling of the survivors/victims, but not being equipped to confront the perpetrators leaves the victims vulnerable to possible violence in the future. Church leaders in ERCC, COCIN, and ECWA settings are very much aware of the existence of SGBV among their members because every week, members call the pastor for help and spiritual guidance. However, the sermons condemning SGBV seem to be inadequate to deter perpetrators from carrying out the abuse, especially against women and children.

Cultures of violence lead to negating the rights of women and [girls] (Bataringaya et al., 2021, p. 4). Therefore, SGBV is a violation of basic human rights with short-term consequences such as fear, anxiety, and low self-esteem. Apart from being an important public health issue, it has spiritual consequences that require the urgent attention of the church. However, one of the ways that SGBV is supported is because people uncritically follow religious leaders and shy away from critiquing them since they are considered representatives of God on earth. Also, it is unfortunate that the churches (ECWA, COCIN, and ERCC) that are supposed to prevent SGBV against women and girls and promote and protect victims by providing security and fighting against SGBV are sometimes found in the mess by shielding the perpetrators of such vile practices.

In different contexts, there is sometimes a perceived tolerance for sexual harassment in both church and society due to the religious and communal nature of the African culture;

hence, the culture of silence and avoidance of shame has contributed to the escalation of sexual violence, especially against women and girls. SGBV is not often reported by the victims, but it is occasionally condoned for fear and shame, especially from the side of the victim. For instance, the case of Osinachi's death on the 8th of April 2022 after an alleged prolonged assault by her spouse (Ikechukwu, 2022) is proof that victims of domestic violence including SGBV do not report the assault. In many instances, churches and Christian victims are concerned about how exposing perpetrators of sexual violence will tarnish the family, the church, or the denominational reputation. However, the church sometimes insists only on praying for a change of heart on the part of the perpetrators, and justice for victims of SGBV is not upheld. Therefore, it is difficult to comprehend complicity when sexual violence against women and girls is disregarded, downplayed, or even covered by pertinent authorities within the evangelicals under the name of perseverance in marriage. Regrettably, the abuse has been criminalized in a way that ignores the core of battering because existing systems have failed to address persistent, predictable, and nonphysical expressions of the abuser's attempt to dominate SGBV survivors (Stark and Buzawa, 2009, p. 18).

Another way in which SGBV is being condoned within the evangelical settings is the "theology of perseverance." The theology of perseverance according to Ogidis, affirms that marriage is for endurance, whereby emphasis is placed on the woman to persevere no matter the circumstance she faces in the marriage while less emphasis is placed on the man to persevere in marriage (Ogidis, 2022, pp. 46–64). That is why the theology of perseverance within some ECWA, ERCC, and COCIN churches is not well balanced since both couples are not addressed equally on the same. Furthermore, the women who happen to be the victims of the theology of perseverance in most cases end up being silent in accepting their fate since all that they are reminded of is what Ephesians 5:22 says, that wives are to submit to their husbands. Foremost, many of these married women persevere physical assault, which paradoxically asserts that the woman's body is insignificant. Hence, women have been targets of disrespect, abuse, prejudice, and oppression because of the idea of perseverance.

Another reason is over-spiritualizing SGBV where the perpetrators are not challenged to stop the evil acts in most cases, but the survivors are mostly told to pray and fast. For instance, Tracy notes how one abused woman shares her experience when she went to the church seeking help about SGBV, they did not prioritize her physical and emotional well-being but offered spiritual platitudes: "Pray, pray more. God can change anyone. God can change him… you just pray more, and God can work this out for you" (Tracy, 2011, p. 31). Spiritualization of SGBV goes in line with the theology of perseverance where several women within the evangelical churches (ECWA, ERCC, and COCIN) in Nigeria are told to pray and less emphasis is placed on the perpetrator of the violence. It is in this context that one finds that marriage appears to be more honorable than human life itself. That is why many women within these churches in Nigeria are dying in silence since all they are told when they report such a situation is to seek God's face through fervent prayer, while the church appears to be silent on the perpetrators of the violence. The silence of women in this context also contributes to the continuation of the violence while the family and church keep quiet. However, could it be that most leaders are silent because they lack what to do. Tracy noted that as evangelical leaders who believe in the veracity and power of God's Word, this is a particularly vexing dilemma, tempting leaders to overlook abuse in their families. It is hard to face a problem when one feels one lacks the knowledge and power to deal with it (Tracy, 2011, p. 33).

Moreover, the perpetrators of SGBV mostly prevent the victims from seeking help; they regulate their interaction with people who will be of help, punish them when they know they are seeking help, or cause them to lie that they are doing well and are happy in an abusive marriage (Stirling et al., 2004, p. 240). Also, in a way some of the women believe that whatever they are going through is part of the marriage with the idea of "for better or worse" and "till death do us part" as part of the vow they took during the wedding. Baffour Takyi, & Jesse Mann observed that,

> If the numerous stories and statistics presented of women who are killed by their spouses, battered, raped, and violated in many other ways around the world do not prick the conscience of the church, then one must conclude that we are faced with a deeply ethical and moral crisis. That the churches should be selective in their understanding of violence, their mission for social justice and their witness to the marginalized is a serious indictment of their credibility.
>
> (Takyi and Mann, 2006, pp. 61–78)

The evangelical church cannot continue to pretend as if SGBV is not happening within the confines of the church where members are perpetrators, victims, and survivors. SGBV is a challenge for the church and puts the responsibility of intervening on the clergy, social workers, certified Christian educators, and professional Christian counselors within the evangelical churches to account for how they have been handling the issues. Similarly, how can the leadership of the church respond theologically to this silent pandemic eating the fabric of the church? There is a need to call the evangelical churches within Nigeria to account for the kind of theology they are teaching, and preaching when it comes to SGBV. Tracy also notes that "given the clear biblical teaching on the prevalence of physical abuse among believers as well as unbelievers it is surprising that evangelicals so frequently assume that family violence rarely if ever happens in their congregations" (Tracy, 2011, p. 37).

Calling the Church to Account: A Theological Response

Just as sexual violence is prevalent in ancient sacred texts, it is also prevalent in contemporary society (Kalmanofsky, 2020, p. 3). SGBV is both a social and spiritual issue, which, therefore, needs a spiritual and theological response. The evangelical churches (ECWA, COCIN, and ERCC) within Nigeria need to wake up to the reality by confronting the church when it comes to SGBV and the theological response they need to teach, preach, and study. A realistic and effective way of addressing the problem of SGBV is to see it clearly in its more subtle and disguised forms. Going through the passages of the Bible, an individual will realize the reality of SGBV right from the Old Testament down to the New Testament. This can be confirmed by what Tracy wrote, "Believers are certainly not exempted from committing SGBV. There are numerous examples from the Bible such as Tamar, David, etc." (Tracy, 2011, p. 35). The evangelical churches in Nigeria need to take the bull by the horns since their members are not exempted from SGBV. Calling the church to account means responding to this question: "How is the church interpreting the Bible in other to address SGBV?"

Using African women's theology in addressing SGBV begins from the experiences of women in the Bible and how it has been interpreted through the ages to silence SGBV and its reality, especially in the lives of Nigerian evangelicals. African women theologian's hermeneutics of life is their central focus which Jesus' model appears to be the key to addressing the silent pandemic of SGBV. Biblical teaching on SGBV, as well as the realities that women experience requires a different approach by pastors. There is a need for church leaders and pastors to teach against SGBV. Pastors within the evangelical churches need to be trained or empowered on how to use gender lens in analyzing and interpreting the Bible especially those that contain SGBV and ways of addressing their situation (Tracy, 2011, p. 37). Furthermore, Tracy notes that,

> Historically, evangelicals have been slow to address sexual and gender-based violence. Evangelical pastors rarely preach on abuses. Few evangelical seminaries offer courses on abuse in general or sexual and gender-based violence. Evangelical churches rarely have specific protocols or resources for ministry to violent families. When churches do respond to sexual and gender-based violence, they often do so in unsound and harmful ways.
>
> (Tracy, 2011, p. 40)

For evangelicals within Nigeria to respond to SGBV theologically, there is a need to consider what some African women theologians are proposing in their theological discourse as a way of interpreting Biblical text. Mercy Oduyoye, the mother of African women's theology argues that, given African women's experiences of suffering through SGBV and other ways, Jesus cannot be interpreted using Western patriarchal dogmas (Oduyoye, 2006, p. 32). For Oduyoye, Jesus possesses mother-like qualities; Jesus suffers with the poor and is oppressed by SGBV. Jesus, like a mother, empathizes by incarnating into the experiences of those who suffer to change their predicament through caring, loving, and offering hope (Oduyoye, 2006, pp. 35–46).

The evangelicals in Nigeria are not immune from SGBV issues because it is composed of male and female believers. Hence, it is bound to be confronted with the challenges of gender dominance like any other human institution. The difference, however, could come from the fact that the church is regarded as a divine institution and is seen as the mother of all God's people, who loves them equally and unconditionally, without siding against one over the other, as seen in Deuteronomy 22:25-27 (Okoli and Okwuosa, 2020, p. 4). Okure affirms that the interpretation of the Bible is a process of seeking to better the living conditions of people irrespective of gender, race, social status, etc. (Okure, 2000, p. 194). Thus, reading the Bible is to search for its liberation strands to life. Okure starts with the experiences of the people, arguing that, in the beginning, it was life with God, and later came the Bible (Okure, 2000, p. 194). This is not to denigrate the Bible but rather to take a hermeneutical lens of life to read across the Bible as one interprets passages that deal with SGBV.

Conclusion

The evangelical church has been at the forefront in promoting justice; however, mainline evangelical churches such as ECWA, COCIN, and ERCC in Nigeria have not contributed significantly to the response to SGBV against women and girls both in academia and in public theology. The reason for this passive response perhaps is because of their stereotypical gender roles that chastise women and girls to control them, the lack of adequate training of clergy on SGBV, and the religio-cultural setting of the evangelical church and the Nigerian society. Meanwhile, the biblical accounts of sexual violence focus on condemning the actions and highlighting their consequences rather than condoning or glorifying them. The lack of taking appropriate measures against SGBV has destructive effects on individuals and communities. Within the context of declining social capital, the importance of finding some religious-social support for women and girls remains absolute (Mercer, 2005, p. 145). Accordingly, women and girls form a significant number of mainline evangelical churches, and the religiosity of Nigerian society puts the church at the forefront in mediating social capital for both families and an agent of societal transformation. Therefore, Nigeria's evangelical churches have the responsibility of providing appropriate and effective SGBV as well as breaking barriers that limit the full potential of women and girls through teaching, promoting the value of human life, and providing justice for victims of SGBV.

Notes

1 ECWA Women Fellowship District Church Council Lafia, Nasarawa State Nigeria. 11/09/2023 at Lafia headquarters.
2 Class discussion on biblical interpretation on addressing challenges in marriage at ECWA Theological Seminary Karu Nigeria Abuja on 12/09/2023.
3 Class discussion on biblical interpretation on addressing challenges in marriage at ECWA Theological Seminary Karu Nigeria Abuja on 12/09/2023.

References

Adams, C.J., Fortune, M. (Eds.), 1995. *Violence Against Women and Children: A Christian Theological Sourcebook*. New York, NY: A&C Black.

Afonsky, G., 2001. Christ and the Church. In *Orthodox Teaching and Tradition*. St Vladimir's Seminary Press. New York, NY: Crestwood.

Akimbobola, Y., 2012. Social media stimulates Nigerian debate on sexual violence [WWW Document]. Afr. Renew. URL https://www.un.org/africarenewal/web-features/social-media-stimulates-nigerian-debate-sexual-violence (accessed 6.11.23).

Anne-Marie, I., 2019. *Reporting on Violence Against Women and Girls: A Handbook for Journalists*. de Fontenoy, France: UNESCO Publishing.

Barr, B.A., 2021. *The Making of Biblical Womanhood: How the Subjugation of Women Became Gospel Truth*. Grand Rapid, MI: Baker Books.

Bataringaya, P., Jahnel, C., Jähnichen, T., Uwimbabazi, P. (Eds.), 2021. *Overcoming Violence: Challenges and Theological Responses in the Context of Central Africa and Europe*. Zürich: LIT Verlag Münster.

Best, J., Jenkins, P. (Eds.), 2017. "Clergies Sexual Abuse: The Symbolic Politics of a Social Problem." In *Images of Issues: Typifying Contemporary Social Problems*. New Brunswick, NJ: Transaction Publishers, pp. 105–130.

Blyth, C., Colgan, E., Edwards, K.B. (Eds.), 2018. *Rape Culture, Gender Violence, and Religion: Biblical Perspectives*. Cham, Switzerland: Springer.

Cooper-White, P., 2007. "The Rape of Tamar, the Crime of Amnon." In Nyabera, F., Montgomery, T. (Eds.), *Contextual Bible Study Manual on Gender-Based Violence: Tamar Campaign*. Springfield, VA: Tucker Multimedia, LLC.

Cooper-White, P., 2012. *The Cry of Tamar: Violence Against Women and the Church's Response*, Second Edition. ed. Minneapolis: Fortress Press.

Effa, E.F., Okokon, E.O., Nwagbara, A.B., Bello, S., 2009. "Pattern, De-terminants and Mental Consequences of Sexual Violence Among Female Undergraduate Students in Calabar Southern, Nigeria." Available at https://www.svri.org/forums/forum2009/presentations/Nwagbara.pdf

Emeka, I.D., Odika, B.T., Igboanugo, N.G., 2022. "Sexual Violence in Nigeria: A Challenge to Sustainable National Security and Development." *JUPEB Journal of Development and Educational Studies (JJDES)* 1(1), 76–88.

Emeka-Nwobia, N.U., Umezurike, G., 2019. "Discourse of Silence! Exploring Gender-Based Violence at Home and Religious Settings in Southeastern Nigeria." *IDOSR-Journal of Arts and Management (IDOSR-JAM)* 4(1), 40–49.

Fortune, M.M., Poling, J.N., 2008. *Sexual Abuse by Clergy: A Crisis for the Church*. Eugene, Oregon: Wipf and Stock Publishers.

Goodwin, M., 2020. *Abusing Religion: Literary Persecution, Sex Scandals, and American Minority Religions*. New Brunswick: Rutgers University Press.

Ikechukwu Nnochiri, 2022 "Osinachi's Death: FG Files 23-count charge against husband, Nwachukwu." www.vanguardngr.com/2022/05/osinachi-death-fg-files-23-count-charge-against-husband-nwachukwu/ (accessed 06.11.23)

Ipole, E., 2018. *Submit to Your Husband in Everything*. Jos: Andex.

Ituma, E.A., Uroko, F.C., Eskay, M., 2013. "The Problem of Sexual Abuse in Nigerian Socio-Religious Society." *International Journal of Research in Social Sciences* 5, 498–512.

Kalmanofsky, A. (Ed.), 2020. *Sexual Violence and Sacred Texts*. Eugene, Oregon: Wipf and Stock Publishers.

Klugman, J., Hanmer, L., Twigg, S., Hasan, T., McCleary-Sills, J., Santamaria, J. 2014. *Voice and Agency: Empowering Women and Girls for Shared Prosperity*. World Bank Publications, Washington DC.

Knight, L., Casassa, K., Kagotho, N., 2022. "Dignity and Worth For All: Identifying Shared Values Between Social Work and Christian Faith-Based Groups' Anti-sex Trafficking Discourse." *Journal of Religion & Spirituality in Social Work: Social Thought* 41, 193–212.

Larsen, T., 2007. "Defining and Locating Evangelicalism." *Cambridge Companion to Evangelical Theology* 1–14.

McClure, J.S., Ramsay, N.J. (Eds.), 1998. *Telling the Truth: Preaching About Sexual and Domestic Violence*. Cleveland, OH: John McClure.

Mercer, J.A. 2005. *Welcoming Children: A Practical Theology of Childhood*. Danvers, MA: Chalice Press,.

Mezie-Okoye, M.-M.M., Alamina, F.F. 2015. "Sexual Violence among Female Undergraduates in Tertiary Institution in Port Harcourt: Prevalence, Pattern, Determinants and Health Consequences." *African Journal of Reproductive Health* 18(4), 79–85.

Moniz, Erin. 2019. "A Tale of Two Rapes: What Tamar and Bathsheba Teach Us About Power, Consent, and Sexual Violence." *CBE International Blog/Magazine*, June 5, 2019. Available at https://www.cbeinternational.org/resource/tale-two-rapes-what-tamar-and-bathsheba-teach-us-about-power-consent-and/. Retrieved on July 21, 2023

Nason-Clark, N., Kroeger, C.C., Fisher-Townsend, B. (Eds.), 2011. *Responding to Abuse in Christian Homes: A Challenge to Churches and their Leaders*. Eugene, Oregon: Wipf and Stock Publishers.

Oduyoye, M.A., 1995. *Daughters of Anowa: African Women and Patriarchy*. Maryknoll: New York Orbis Books.

Oduyoye, Mercy Amba, 2006. "The Christ for African women." In V. Fabella, Mercy A. Oduyoye (Eds.), *With Passion and Compassion: Third World Women Doing Theology: Reflections from the Women's Commission of the Ecumenical Association of Third World Theologians*. Maryknoll, NY: Orbis Books, pp. 35–46.

Ogidis, M.I., 2021. "A Rereading of 1 Timothy 2:12 for Gender Justice in the Evangelical Church Winning All." In I.A. Phiri, C. Shava (Eds.), *The Africa We Pray For: On a Pilgrimage of Justice and Peace*. Geneva: WCC Publication & Globethics.net.

Ogidis, M.I., 2022. "'Till Death Do Us Part': Addressing the Theology of Perseverance within Nigerian Christian Marriage by Re-Interpreting Pauline's Concept of Marriage." *African Multidisciplinary Journal of Research* 7, 46–64.

Okoli, A. B., Okwuosa, L. 2020. "The Role of Christianity in Gender Issues and Development in Nigeria," *HTS Teologiese Studies/Theological Studies* 76, no. 4, pp. 1–8.

Okure, T. 2000. "First was Life not the Book." In Okure, T. (Ed.), *To Cast Fire Upon the Earth: Bible and Mission Collaborating in Today's Multicultural Global Context*. Natal: Cluster Publications, pp. 194–214.

Olarewaju, O.A., 2021. Insecurity in Northern Nigeria: Implications for maternal and child health. Clinical Epidemiology Global Health vol. 12, pp. 1–3.

Phiri, I.A., Nadar, S. (Eds.), 2006. *African Women, Religion, and Health. Essays in Honour of Mercy Amba Ewudziwa Oduyoye*. Pietermaritzburg: Cluster Publications.

Riecher-Rössler, A., García-Moreno, C. (Eds.). 2013. *Violence Against Women and Mental Health*. Basel: Karger Medical and Scientific Publishers.

Scholz, Susanne. 2010. *Sacred Witness: Rape in the Hebrew Bible*. Minneapolis: Fortress.

Sheller, M. 2018. *Mobility Justice: The Politics of Movement in an Age of Extremes*. Brooklyn, NY.: Verso Books.

Shields, E.M.. 2001. "An Abusive God? Identity and Power/Gender and Violence in Ezekiel 23." In A. K. M. Adama (Ed.), *Postmodern Interpretation of the Bible: A Reader*. St Louis: Chalice Press.

Shupe, A. 2010. *Spoils of the Kingdom: Clergy Misconduct and Religious Community*. Urbana and Chicago: University of Illinois Press.

Stark, E., Buzawa, E.S. (Eds.), 2009. *Violence Against Women in Families and Relationships*. Santa Barbara, CA: ABC-CLIO.

Stirling, M.L., Cameron, C.A., Nason-Clark, N., Miedema, B. (Eds.), 2004. *Understanding Abuse: Partnering for Change*. Ontario, Canada: University of Toronto Press,

Takyi, B.K., Mann, J., 2006. "Intimate Partner Violence in Ghana, Africa: The Perspectives of Men Regarding Wife Beating." *International Journal of Sociology of the Family* 32, 61–78.

Terry, G., Hoare, J. (Eds.), 2007. *Gender-based Violence* Oxfam, GB: Oxford.

Tracy, S.R., 2011. "Abuse and the Gospel: Calling the Evangelical Church to Truth." In Catherine Clark-Kroeger, Nancy Nason-Clark, and Barbara Fisher-Townsend (Eds.), *Responding to Abuse in Christian Homes: A Challenge to Churches and Their Leaders*. Eugene, OR: Wipf & Stock, pp. 28–46.

Tshiakany, M.D. 2007. "The Story of the Good Samaritan." In F. Nyabera, T. Montgomery (Eds.), *Contextual Bible Study Manual on Gender-Based Violence*. Nairobi: The Fellowship of Christian Councils and Churches in the Great Lakes and the Horn of Africa.

Ugwu, A., Atima, M., 2022. *Breaking the Silence on Domestic Violence in Nigeria: We Must All Be Advocates*. Niger: Health Watch. https://articles.nigeriahealthwatch.com/breaking-the-silence-on-domestic-violence-in-nigeria-we-must-all-be-advocates/

Washington, H.C., 1997. Violence and the Construction of Gender in the Hebrew Bible: A New Historicist Approach. *Biblical interpretation* 5, 324–363.

34
AFRICAN WOMEN IN DIPLOMACY AND THE QUEST FOR GENDER JUSTICE

Primrose Z.J. Bimha

Introduction

Traditionally, diplomacy was defined as a medium for the conduct of international relations, with diplomats serving as instruments of foreign policy (Sharp 2009: 55). Diplomacy's key functions include the promotion and protection of national interests through relations with other states, bilaterally or multilaterally. Diplomats are individuals trained and appointed by a government to represent their state's interests. They perform a wide range of duties, including, but not limited to, negotiating agreements with other states or international organisations, advocating positions on a wide range of human security issues, responding to conflicts, and providing consular services to citizens at home and abroad.

According to realist traditions, diplomats are classified as reflections of their sovereigns who act by the logic inherent in the anarchical system of power distributed between self-interested and self-helping state actors (Sharp 2009: 54). A major determinant of a state's power and influence in the global political economy is the effectiveness of their diplomacy and diplomats (Sharp 2009: 54). Countries that enjoy a strong reputation in diplomacy often demonstrate excellence in four elements of power, namely, diplomacy, defence, finance, and trade (Sharp 2009: 56). Since men hold the majority of leadership roles in ministries of foreign affairs, defence, finance, and trade, they are more likely than women to be tasked with representing their states' political and economic interests. It is also important to note that women are underrepresented in top positions and overrepresented in administrative support roles (Karin Aggestam & Ann Towns 2019).

Male dominance in politics and diplomacy is evidenced by the following statistical references. Women remain underrepresented in diplomacy, as they make up 20.5% of ambassadors and permanent representatives, globally (United Nations Development Programme [UNDP] 2023). Between 1992 and 2019, women represented a paltry 13% of negotiators, 6% of mediators, and 6% of signatories in peace processes worldwide (United Nations [UN] Women 2022b). Out of 193 UN member states, only 34 women serve as elected Heads of State and Government (UNDP 2023). The global proportion of women at different levels of government worldwide is far from parity levels: 34% of local government seats, 26% of parliamentarians, and 21% of cabinet ministers (UNDP 2023).

For centuries, women have been excluded from decision-making processes which affect them politically, socially, and economically (Awino 2018). It used to be that the closest women could influence foreign policy was if they were either related to or married to diplomats or foreign service officers (Minarova-Banjac 2018). "Until the mid-twentieth century, the most extensive contribution made by women to diplomacy was as the wives of diplomatic and consular officers" (Fritsche & Hall 2002: 1). Their contributions were usually limited to supporting their husbands through domestic duties such as the upkeep of diplomatic offices and households, as well as presiding as hostesses in the facilitation of meetings, or providing voluntary community services (Fritsche & Hall 2002). Lenine and Sanca (2022) also noted that the wives of diplomats and ambassadors acted as informal spies even though they were primarily viewed as diplomats' companions.

Diplomats are typically appointed by the Heads of State and Government in their countries. There are two types of appointment: political diplomats and career diplomats. In reality however, it may be difficult to separate the two. For example, all the participants interviewed for this study noted that ambassadorial appointments were mostly informed by camaraderie ties between political leaders (president and ministers), or forming relationships with key personnel, such as directors and deputy directors, who have links to the presidency or cabinet. Since politics is a male-centric domain, such networks are more likely to work in favour of men.

Many gender advocates emphasise that the representation and participation of women in decision-making is important because they constitute half of the world's population and potential (UNDP 2023). Furthermore, incorporating a wide range of experts, leadership styles, and multiple perspectives is seen to be a means to ensure better quality outcomes when it comes to setting, implementing, and evaluating development-oriented projects. Ultimately, equal participation in decision-making enables a more accurate reflection of the composition of society thereby enhancing the legitimacy and relevance of decisions made in politics and diplomacy (Bimha 2021). Since diplomacy involves the expression and protection of states' economic and political interests more women need to be involved in decision-making in this sector. Therefore, in addition to ensuring parity in terms of cabinet and parliamentary seats, parity in terms of diplomatic appointments is essential.

It is important to conduct studies on the inclusion of women in diplomacy as a means to celebrate their contributions and document their experiences. By so doing, we can gain insights into, and reflect on progress made, or lack thereof. Identifying challenges and opportunities faced by women in the sector could also contribute towards restructuring diplomacy's heavily patriarchal structures and masculinist codes of conduct. As noted by Onditi (2019: 377), the adoption of gender equality as a norm in international relations could be a game changer in shaping foreign policy and diplomatic engagements.

Commitment to Ensuring Women's Empowerment and Gender Equality

Intergovernmental organisations such as the UN and the African Union (AU) have been at the helm of spearheading and reiterating the importance of gender equality as a norm. During the 2023 International Day of Women in Diplomacy, marked on 24 June, the UN reiterated the importance of ensuring the inclusion and survival of women in diplomacy. Strategies aimed at ensuring women's participation on equal terms with men at all levels of decision-making relating to the achievement of sustainable development and human security are vital (UNDP 2023). Thus, the AU's Strategy for Gender Equality and Women's

Empowerment 2018–2028 was developed in support of Sustainable Development Goal (SDG) 5: To "achieve gender equality and empower all women and girls" (AU 2019: 6). It is, therefore, clear that institutions that are pertinent to Africa's participation in global governance have expressed commitment towards adopting gender equality as a norm.

The increased participation of women in diplomacy is an essential approach towards achieving gender parity and shifting towards more gender-diverse foreign policymaking institutions and strategies. Many gender advocates contend that the legal recognition of women's equal status is a necessary first step. According to Buchholz (2023), there are only "14 countries which offer full legal protections to women", and none of them is situated in Africa. These include Belgium, Canada, Denmark, France, Germany, Greece, Iceland, Ireland, Latvia, Luxembourg, Netherlands, Portugal, Spain and Sweden (Buchholz 2023).

At least 44 out of 55 AU member states have ratified the Protocol to the African Charter on Human and Peoples' Rights on the Rights of Women in Africa (AU 2023). The AU continues to emphasise that women's empowerment and gender equality (WEGE) strategies should include a commitment to Agenda 2063's aim to ensure "the attainment of full gender parity with women occupying 50% of elected offices at state, regional and local bodies, and 50% of managerial positions in government and the private sector" (AU 2023). Women in diplomacy are accounted for in this aspiration due to the emphasis on parity in representation in regional and local bodies or managerial positions in government. Since the status of women in diplomacy is underresearched, there is a dearth of information on the distribution of African women in diplomacy at various levels. It is hoped that governments will commit to collating data on this as a means of determining how far they are from ensuring gender justice.

The foregoing section highlighted the worrying dynamics in terms of women's participation in decision-making roles that are linked to governance and diplomacy. This has been attributed to centuries of patriarchy, gender-based discrimination, and harmful stereotypes which led to and perpetuate a lack of transformation. Disappointingly, it has been predicted that gender equality may only be realised in 300 years (UN Women 2022a). The next section will discuss the purpose of the study and the research process. This will be followed by reflections on insights from interviews and literature, in relation to gender-biased appointments, heteropatriarchal norms in the division of labour, and gender-based violence. The chapter concludes by offering some recommendations on how noted challenges can be mitigated.

Methodology

The discussion in this chapter is based on a collation of findings relating to the question: *How do African women in diplomacy navigate masculinised norms and gendered division of labour?* The question was informed by two main objectives. First, the researcher sought to investigate the impact of masculinised norms on participants' workplace experiences. Second, the study sought to identify strategies adopted by women in diplomacy to navigate challenges by these norms.

Initially, the researcher sent email invitations to diplomatic missions of African states based in the Republic of South Africa, where she resides. This form of purposive stakeholder sampling was adopted to ensure the researcher's capacity to facilitate in-person interviews. While the researcher sought to interview at least 20 participants, some potential respondents either ignored or rejected the invitation. Since the initial response-rate was low, the researcher relied on four respondents who volunteered to participate, to reach out to persons they thought would be interested in the study. Therefore, a snowball sampling technique was adopted to access more participants. Snowball sampling is characterised by accessing more participants through referrals from willing participants (Atkinson & Flint 2004). Eventually, the sample included 10 African women (2 ambassadors, 2 personal assistants to ambassadors, 3 foreign service officers, and 3 political desk officers currently serving in their home countries). Their contributions were labelled according to pseudonym identifiers: A1 and A2 (ambassadors); PA1 and PA2 (personal assistants to ambassadors); FSO 1, FSO 2, and FSO 3 (foreign service officers); and PDO 1, PDO 2, and PDO 3 (political desk officers). The PDO interviews were conducted via Zoom video calls, and the rest were conducted in-person.

Each participant was briefed on the purpose of the study in writing. Consent forms were emailed to the participants prior to the interviews. Once the forms were signed and returned, interviews were scheduled and conducted according to participants' availability and preferred meeting space. Participants were informed of their right to withdraw at any stage of the research process. They were also informed that they could choose not to respond to questions they were not comfortable with answering. The names of embassies, ministries, or governments represented by the participants were withheld for ethical reasons, to ensure confidentiality. Participants' identities were concealed using pseudonyms in the reporting of findings.

Interviewing is an effective way to gain insights into people's perspectives through their own narratives, explanations, and examples (Willner 2011). This qualitative approach gives the researcher the opportunity to collect rich and detailed information about how participants understand and explain their experiences (Yin 2008). The interviews lasted between thirty minutes and an hour each. They were based on a schedule of semi-structured questions relating to gendered dynamics in the diplomacy sector. All interviews were recorded using a digital voice recorder. The audio files were stored in a password-secured OneDrive, only accessible to the researcher. They were transcribed verbatim by the researcher, and typed transcripts were analysed to establish relevant themes and quotes. Thematic analysis is a suitable method for "identifying, analysing and reporting patterns (themes) within data" (Braun and Clark, 2006: 79). The researcher adopted this flexible approach by familiarising with the data through reading of transcripts, generating codes, and identifying themes relevant to the research question and objectives. Relevant quotes were identified to support the reporting of findings for this chapter.

It is important to note that focusing on women in diplomacy through the lens of representation at the senior level (e.g., heads of mission) provides a limited understanding of the impact of gender dynamics on women's inclusion and survival within the heavily patriarchal realm of diplomacy. By incorporating the experiences of junior-level officers we gain further insight. It should be noted that approaching women in diplomacy for interviews is difficult owing to the safeguarded and heavily securitised nature of their work. Therefore, women in diplomacy tend to be unapproachable for discussions on their vocational experiences. As *PDO 1* noted, "when you are working in Foreign Affairs, you don't just talk to anyone. What happens at work stays at work". While it is understandable that working in diplomacy requires adherence to secrecy protocols, gendered experiences that remain unshared or unquestioned will lead to the perpetual undermining of women's rights. Women in diplomacy can contribute towards the identification of challenges and sharing of perspectives regarding the status of women in diplomacy without divulging any classified institutional information. It is worth noting that the works of Awino (2018), Onditi (2019), as well as Chideya, Dlamini-Mnthambo, Kerubo and Umutoni (2021) which are cited in this study, were based on insights shared by African women in diplomacy – at various levels, from clerical roles to ambassadors.

African Feminist Perspectives

Patriarchy is a social system which ensures that men hold the greatest power, leadership roles, privileged access to economic opportunities and resources, as well as religious and cultural authority (United Nations International Children's Emergency Fund [UNICEF] 2017: 7). Heteropatriarchy is a social and political system that affirms the notion that men and boys hold authority over girls and women (Arvin, Tuck, and Morrill, 2013: 13). Furthermore, heteropatriarchy endorses compulsory heterosexuality, and upholds patriarchy as natural and normal (Ngidi 2022: 41). Therefore, in addition to emphasising male dominance, institutions that promote heteropatriarchy inculcate queerphobia.

This study contributes to a growing body of literature on the experiences of African women in diplomacy by investigating how they navigate gendered power dynamics through an African feminist lens. Overall, feminist scholars investigate the detrimental effects of patriarchal oppression (Nkealah 2006; Nzomo 2015). They do so by adopting a range of analytical and activist techniques. An African feminist approach is relevant because it is dangerous to generalise gendered experiences simply because the patriarchal subjection of women transcends borders. Western liberal feminists tend to be perceived as anti-men, anti-religion, and anti-culture, whereas African feminists tend to emphasise that they do not seek to denigrate men, religion, or culture (Nkealah 2006:134). Furthermore, they adopt a range of analytical and activist techniques by exploring context-specific challenges. For example, recognising that Black African women continue to be marginalised because their contributions are subjected to the pervasive masculinist and militant nature of postcolonial regimes (Gqola 2001; Magadla 2013). This perspective enables us to examine the allocation of decision-making roles by state leaders based on political networks and camaraderie relations, for example.

An African feminist standpoint should be centred on promoting inclusive gender-responsive governance that is representative of the diversity of interests of the governed (Nzomo 2015: 28). While the AU does not purport to be an African feminist institution, its commitment to gender quality through the framework of "a Theory of Change" centred on promoting women's leadership, voice, and visibility (AU 2019: 10) responds to African realities. The strategy entails, (1) policy and institutional reforms, (2) strengthening a continuous flow of information about gender justice through various media channels, and (3) mobilising cultural practitioners to develop and implement policies that promote women's equal and fair representation (AU 2019:10).

In addition to African feminists' perspectives, the researcher also drew on insights from Lenine and Sanca (2022) who recommended the analysis of gender dynamics through the lens of Feminist International Relations. Similar to existing literature, this study found that diplomatic institutions reproduce gender hierarchies in ways that negatively impact the career trajectories of female diplomats (Lenine & Sanca 2022: 103). If their professional conduct is deemed too soft or feminine for senior diplomatic roles, they do not reach top posts, and some of them even abandon the profession to protect cultural interests such as duties associated with wifehood or motherhood.

Since heteropatriarchy values male dominance and heterosexuality, institutions such as diplomacy inculcate queerphobia. Although queerphobia was not mentioned in any of the interview transcripts and literature compiled for this study, it is important to note that gender justice struggles are diverse. While some researchers have undertaken studies on the marginalisation of queer persons in education and work environments, the researcher could not locate studies specific to African diplomats. African women are not only heterosexual, and gender-based violence is not only about violence against women and girls. Therefore, future studies on transformative inclusion should expand beyond the dominant heterosexist focus. An intersectional approach that takes into account race, sexuality, and class is important for studies of oppression within institutions (Lenine & Sanca 2022: 112).

Gender Bias in Appointments

One of the main reasons why there are so few women ambassadors is because such positions have mainly been occupied by men who are presumed to have innate diplomatic traits such as assertiveness and tactfulness. Heads of state and government, and ministers responsible for foreign affairs and international cooperation, often make decisions regarding postings to foreign missions. They are more likely to appoint men, either based on innate patriarchal assumptions or political networks. A respondent in a study on Canada-based African women in diplomacy noted that, for a woman to become an ambassador, she "has to convince not only the Minister and the President but also the members of the Parliamentary Committee on Foreign Affairs, that she is competent" (Chideya et al. 2021: 35). *A1* noted that the majority of those who have to be convinced sometimes express concerns regarding gender and age, yet this seldom happens when men are shortlisted for such positions. Despite the increased participation of women in diplomacy, they are generally posted to less significant posts. *A2* noted that she and other female colleagues had been posted to economically insignificant duty stations in southeast Asia and parts of Africa, whilst deployments to key capitals such as Beijing, New York, Geneva, London, and Addis Ababa, just to name a few, were reserved for male diplomats.

Black African women continue to be marginalised because their contributions are subjected to the pervasive masculinist nature of political regimes (Magadla 2013). This assertion can be linked to examples of gendered challenges experienced by women in diplomacy. For instance, some female ambassadors have noted that "their male counterparts from other parts of the world do not afford them the same respect they show other male colleagues and do not take them seriously" (Chideya et al. 2021: 35). Minarova-Banjac (2018: 33) referred to the fact that some women adopt masculine norms and practices to succeed in their diplomatic careers. Such women are usually described as "iron ladies or men in skirts", differentiating them from typical feminine identity markers (Minarova-Banjac 2018: 33). For example, *A1* noted that despite being a human rights advocate at heart, she focused on promoting military interventions instead of mediation, in response to crises in neighbouring states because such a posture could guarantee her appointment to special envoys responding to peace and security challenges on the continent. *A2* noted that she thrives by tapping into her feminine energy by exhibiting her maternal instincts as a mother figure within her political party and society. She believed that this strategy earned her recognition and deployment to foreign missions where there is a heavy emphasis on humanitarianism. The foregoing examples correspond with Minarova-Banjac's (2018: 33) supposition that sometimes female diplomats try to be like men so that they can be taken seriously, or they will focus on negotiating soft issues and obtaining legitimacy from adopting a maternal posture.

FSO 3 noted that representatives at foreign missions are expected to act in line with their state leaders' foreign policy interests. Therefore, such appointments are often sensitive and reserved for close mates or allies. This usually applies in cases of tokenism. Aggestam and True (2020) noted that women who are appointed on a token basis usually play along masculine norms and scripts, and they are co-opted due to the unlikelihood that they will contest or disrupt the masculinist nature of politics and diplomacy. *FSO 3* indicated that her dream to one day become an ambassador could be actualised if she pursued one or two of the following strategies: by being affiliated with senior political figures within the ruling party, or developing close relationships with senior colleagues who are close to the president. It is, therefore, evident that some work needs to be done regarding the culture of favouritism. *FSO 3* also noted that when it came to deployments to foreign missions, male staff also had to gain favour with those in power or with influential politicians and senior bureaucrats. While it can be argued that favouritism also affects men in diplomacy, that should not be grounds to condone this style of recruitment.

The Impact of Heteropatriarchal Norms and Division of Labour

According to Minarova-Banjac (2018: 23), as women began to enter into male-dominated professions and workspaces, they had to adopt male-defined feminine identities; expressing submission through obedience to evade being labelled as problematic. The PAs, FSOs, and PDOs noted that presenting hyperfeminine traits helped them to gain favours at work. When it comes to being selected to attend high-level meetings as note-takers or protocol staff, senior officials and diplomats prefer to move around with subservient officers. While they understand the importance of demonstrating interest and commitment to foreign policy objectives by speaking to senior officials about challenges and possible solutions, they often choose not to verbalise their thoughts and ideas for fear of being categorised as wayward. The author, who is a former political desk officer, felt infantilised by senior male diplomats who treated her like an unruly child by questioning who she thought she was when she challenged their perspectives during departmental meetings. She took the opportunity to call out these demeaning tendencies during a staff training session, leading to some men admitting to subconsciously viewing her as a young girl who was in the space to quietly learn from the elders. Based on the foregoing examples, it is evident that intergenerational dynamics also affect women's potential to participate equally in diplomatic settings.

To get ahead, in terms of promotion to director roles or heads of mission, one ought to play along with the rules of the game. Foremost by simply observing how and why others (mostly men) made it to the top, and second, by adopting work strategies that appeal to those who are responsible for promotions and determining ambassadorial appointments. While hard work pays off, the dominance of heteropatriarchal norms undermines prospects for women's equal participation. For example, women's contributions to peacemaking and peacebuilding remain limited. *A1* emphasised that when it comes to actions such as mediation, member states have to choose mediators and envoys composed of skilled negotiators, military personnel, and political elites who are likely to be well-received and engaged with, on an equal footing, by parties to the conflict. Therefore, when it comes to military or security strategies, the dominance of masculinist codes undermines women's inclusion and equal participation.

Heteropatriarchy is strongly rooted in sociocultural relations. Before the 1970s, women in diplomacy were subjected to a marriage ban. The ban required them to leave their diplomatic careers if they got married (Minarova-Banjac 2018: 26). Unsurprisingly, men were not held to the same standard because for them, getting married or becoming a father did not lead to significant challenges in executing their diplomatic duties. Although the marriage ban no longer exists, little to nothing has been done to cater for the combination of challenges associated with being married or having children whilst pursuing a career in diplomacy. The demands of diplomacy, which include travelling outside one's country and not having a say in postings, pose a major challenge for many women. Due to the social expectation for women to be mothers or spouses first, foreign service jobs do not accommodate the demands posed by domestic roles and responsibilities.

Dominant African cultural and religious patriarchal values require women to play a key role in cleaning, cooking, and performing care duties to ensure the well-being of children, husbands, the elderly, and sometimes sick family members. Thus, some women have had to make tough decisions between being praised for their presence and diligence in executing domestic duties or working hard to demonstrate their professional efficiency by dedicating most of their time to state duties. Heteropatriarchal expectations can deter women from taking up roles in diplomacy due to the incompatible demands of their work and gender identity (Bimha 2021). *FSO 2* noted that she often faced the challenge of being labelled as an unserious mother by her in-laws because she travelled so often to the extent that her children spent more time with the domestic helper, who was not their mother. She also referred to instances whereby some people noted with great concern that she was not fulfilling her conjugal obligations because she had to leave her husband "so often". By contrast, men are often hailed for being ambitious breadwinners if they travel abroad for work, without being questioned about abandoning their marital or family duties.

In a 2021 interview, Dr Ngozi Okonjo-Iweala, the first woman, as well as the first African to be elected to the position of World Trade Organisation (WTO) Director-General, emphasised that men ought to "more equitably share domestic and caring work… pointing out sexism when they see it…[and] make space for women, and mentor and sponsor them" (TED 2021). Her contributions as former Minister of Finance, as well as Former Minister of Foreign Affairs, attest to her familiarity with the gendered challenges associated with working in diplomacy. All the interview participants also noted the importance of support, and the need for cases of sexism to be dealt with in a manner that promotes gender justice. They also emphasised the importance of mentorship and sponsorship by both, men and women, who have made it to the highest levels in diplomacy. Sometimes diplomats do not provide mentorship to their female officers, either due to lack of interest in the officers' career development or owing to ingrained gender stereotypical views. *FSO 1* noted that some senior diplomats felt threatened by talented juniors, so they tend not to be interested in sharing information or sponsoring the promotion of such officers. Therefore, attitudinal barriers are a major cause for concern.

FSO 2 sadly noted that she experienced a lot of stress when she was selected to represent her country on a Europe-based mission (country details withheld for ethical reasons) because her husband could not join her as an accompanying spouse. The husband (head of the family) was not willing to go because there were no prospects for him to pursue a formal career as an expert in his field while living abroad. Women often accompany male spouses even if doing so is detrimental to their career goals. Some accompany their husbands as housewives while others are willing to work in different sectors, often in lowly paid positions or care-based roles. Several participants noted that they preferred to be posted within their regional economic community (REC) blocs for proximity to their spouses if their husbands could not accompany them. They also noted that most husbands preferred it when their wives were deployed to duty stations within the same regional bloc. In terms of women being deployed abroad, the ideal destinations for male spouses, due to job prospects, included Canada, the United States of America (USA), and the United Kingdom (UK). The cultural and religious emphasis on men being the heads of households means that decision-making rules are often skewed in favour of men. So, if a woman is married to a husband who does not favour her career progression in diplomacy, she may end up quitting or staying on condition that she would have to forgo opportunities that undermine her family's interests.

According to Chideya et al. (2021: 19), women in political leadership roles are more likely than men to be divorced, widowed, or separated. Women in such positions are also more likely than men, to be single and childfree, suggesting that such careers tend to hold greater appeal for women who do not have cultural responsibilities that may undermine their career prospects. The *PAs* and *PDOs* agreed that being single often guaranteed women access to postings in busy and economically vibrant destinations in the USA or Europe. However, single mothers tend to face additional challenges due to the single-income status of their households and the demands of single parenting. Chideya et al. (2021: 35) noted that "the issue of multitasking becomes a reality for most female diplomats who have to combine the role of motherhood with the responsibilities of their office". They have to protect the interests of their countries as well as build networks through events such as cocktail functions, dinner parties, and weekend activities like golf – all that may clash with domestic duties. While some flexibility may be exercised in terms of opting for daytime events like lunches, they do not always have the power to decide. The dominant written and unwritten rules of engaging in the male-dominated sphere undermine flexibility. It is hoped that in future, men will contribute more to household duties, and when they take up lead roles in diplomacy they should be conscious of the gender dynamics which may affect their views on when, where, and how to conduct meetings to accommodate gender diversity. Given that diplomats demonstrate the will to learn and adapt to different cultures, it should not be difficult for them to do the same when it comes to gender dynamics.

A major challenge which undermines gender sensitivity relates to the dominance of patriarchy's unquestioned endorsement of male privileges. *A2* noted with great concern that in some instances, ambassador designates' credentials were declined owing to would-be receiving states' preference to work with a male representative. Therefore, the promotion of transformative inclusion should continue to be championed within states, as well as at the AU and UN levels. Citing examples of best cases and calling out cases of unfairness is important. Considering the highly secretive nature of diplomacy, this may not happen in the foreseeable future, but it is not entirely impossible.

Gender-Based Violence (GBV)

An often-cited statistic is that one in three women globally have experienced physical and/or sexual violence in their lifetime, mostly at the hands of an intimate partner (World Health Organisation [WHO] 2021). This is a stark reminder that women from different walks of life are at risk of, or have already experienced, gender-based violence. Shockingly, some researchers have reported that more than 50% of women they interviewed in African contexts, agreed that domestic violence is justified on cultural grounds associated with the social power and household headship roles assigned to men (AU 2019: 37). It does not help that heteropatriarchal values enshrined in different cultures and religions tend to condone violence against women. Gendered dynamics are regulated by endorsing the dominance of fathers or male partners, thus emphasising the importance of women's submission to men, including in abusive situations.

Gender-based violence in the workplace was noted as a major cause of workplace insecurity. *PA1* noted that some women were coerced into engaging in sexual relations with senior male staff to ensure appointments to diplomatic stations of their choice. She indicated that some women experienced harassment in the form of groping, inappropriate comments regarding their dress or appearance, and in some cases, stalking. While some diplomatic institutions have reporting mechanisms in place, workplace harassment, assault, and rape are generally underreported. Some of the reasons cited for this include self-preservation, to evade the burden imposed by reporting and undergoing grievance processes. Other reasons cited included fear of not being believed, fear of being shamed, and fear of being excluded from promotion or senior appointment processes that are often presided over by men. All the participants echoed Minarova-Banjac's (2018: 28) claim that complaints relating to violence and harassment against women are often not taken seriously. They noted that in some cases of harassment, remedies included: issuing verbal and written warnings, change of departments, or redeployment to different duty stations. This often applies to cases of GBV perpetrated by staff below the consul and ambassador levels. Most cases relating to violation by senior diplomats go unchecked or lead to the transfer of the survivor.

Despite the increase in awareness campaigns, GBV is very difficult to talk about and it remains underreported in workspaces and society at large (Labour Research Service [LRS] 2021). This corresponds with *PDO1*'s supposition that few women report experiences of workplace harassment or sexual violence. Reasons for this range from the work-related interests noted above, to fear of disclosing such matters to partners or family members. The anticipated burden of undergoing formal hearings or mediation sittings was also cited as a deterrent. In a thesis on gender equality in Kenya's diplomatic service, Awino (2018) noted that most participants identified sexual harassment as a factor contributing to gender inequality in the diplomatic service. While gender conscientisation workshops have been held to ensure staff training, GBV persists. The same applies to society at large. Despite an increase in GBV awareness efforts, women continue to experience various forms of GBV at alarmingly high levels, mostly at the hands of men they know (at home, work, school, or in their communities). This means that women in diplomacy or any other work sector are at risk of experiencing GBV in multiple spaces, and at any stage in their lifetime. According to UN Women (2019), patriarchal sociocultural values are a major barrier to ending GBV because violence against women is considered to be "a private matter that should be dealt with privately". Additionally, women fear reporting violence since they might be told that they have encouraged such acts because of their dressing style, appearance, attitude, behaviour, or situation (location) at the time of harassment or violation, among other factors.

It is concerning that despite the high prevalence of GBV, there is no available data on violence against women in diplomacy. Due to the secrecy emphasised by diplomatic institutions, it is also rare to come across media reports relating to GBV in such institutions. In addition, institutions such as the AU and UN should also be scrutinised for the part they play in underreporting and not paying much-needed attention to GBV within their structures, as well as in the conduct of their work (e.g., peacekeeping). Reports of male officials demanding sex from female job candidates to guarantee appointments at the AU level have surfaced in recent years. An African Union Commission (AUC) "investigation of allegations of harassment against women and other institutional malpractices" revealed that among other challenges, harassment (including sexual harassment), bullying, intimidation, and impunity undermined the rights and safety of personnel (AU 2018). The report noted that staff who reported experiences of harassment indicated that such violence was usually perpetrated by male supervisors "over female employees in their charge, especially, but not exclusively, during official missions outside the work station" (AU 2018). It was further noted that the categories of staff most vulnerable and exposed to such violence included: "short-term staff, youth volunteers and interns" who are more likely to be exploited on account of the insecurity of tenure (AU 2018). Interviewees claimed that such cases were not reported "as this would be counterproductive to the victims" (AU 2018). Furthermore, the absence of a dedicated sexual harassment policy in the AUC worsened the effects of such experiences.

According to Khumalo, Msimang, and Bollbach (2017: 10), "women suffering from domestic violence have significantly lower propensities to turn up for work on time, to work productively while at work and to stay on the job". Gender-based violence survivors are also likely to miss work due to injuries, legal proceedings, and post-traumatic stress. Therefore, workplace programmes aimed at creating safe spaces and providing relevant assistance are important. Due to the complex and sensitive nature of GBV cases, it was not ethically fathomable to explicitly seek information from research participants regarding their personal experiences of GBV without the guarantee of post-interview psychosocial, medical, legal, or other forms of relevant support. Since most participants' interview revelations and key findings from the literature noted the worrying trends of underreporting and lack of institutional support, the theme of GBV within the context of the study reaffirmed the contention that the inclusion of women in diplomacy has not gone far enough to challenge the dominance of heteropatriarchy. This limits women's ability to function as diplomats in their own right, free from harassment or violation. While the researcher could not establish whether all AU members have sexual harassment policies to govern the conduct of staff in foreign affairs and at diplomatic missions, it would not be surprising to find that many of them do not. Reports regarding the unsafe nature of diplomatic spaces undermine prospects for women to aspire to enter or stay in such workspaces. The threat of sexual exploitation or harassment further undermines equal access to opportunities and freedom from fear or violence.

Conclusion

This chapter sought to establish how African women in diplomacy navigate masculinised norms and gendered division of labour. It noted that challenges faced by African women in diplomacy can be categorised into three main themes, namely, gender-biased appointments, heteropatriarchal norms in the division of labour, and gender-based violence. To a large extent, ascending to senior roles requires one to adopt strategies which have traditionally worked for men to attain the same roles, even if it means committing less to one's feminine identity and cultural gender roles. In institutions where allegiance to male political figures and their interests guarantees career success, women often find it difficult to advance calls for gender justice (Nzomo 2015). Therefore, although hard work may pay off, political networks often influence ambassadorial appointments. As a result, women remain overrepresented in junior administrative roles and underrepresented in senior decision-making roles (Aggestam & Ann Towns 2019). In addition to gender-bias in appointments and allocation of roles, violence against women threatens women's professional prospects at all levels, and navigating such challenges may require one to step out of the system completely.

Recommendations

Further research needs to be conducted to create a database of African women in diplomacy and collate information regarding their workplace experiences. A range of methods should be adopted, including surveys, in-depth interviews, focus group discussions, and workshops. Such research should be conducted by feminist researchers, in collaboration with governments and organisations such as the AU and UN. Multistakeholder research should also be followed by the implementation of relevant gender justice frameworks.

To address gender-biased appointments, it is important to ensure equal access to education and opportunities, as well as gender parity at all levels. The AU has already set up relevant frameworks and guidelines, and member states have the liberty to work towards ensuring gender equality policies and practices through their state apparatus and multistakeholder projects. Insights can also be drawn from the 1979 Convention on the Elimination of All Forms of Discrimination against Women (CEDAW) – which continues to serve as the international bill of rights for women. The legal protection of women should include the right to equality in marriage. While this is far from achievable due to established heteropatriarchal norms, it would be a step in the right direction. Culture is never static. Therefore, provisions for equality within marriage are practicable (Bimha 2023). Political leaders, feminist groups, as well as religious and cultural leaders should engage in sustained efforts to ensure the legal and social recognition of such values. Family laws should ensure women's right to work in professions of their choice and promote collaborative decision-making about career decisions, domicile of choice, and sharing of household and childcare responsibilities. In addition to legal protections and campaigns aimed at promoting new ways of living that cater for gender justice, it is also important to shed light on exemplary cases to inspire members of society. For example, interviews, documentaries, or written testimonies by women situated at various levels of leadership in diplomacy and other sectors.

Annual gender spotlighting reports from different sectors, government ministries, and diplomatic missions are necessary instruments, not only for data collection but also for setting and implementing gender justice goals regularly. Norm entrepreneurship is required to ensure the popularity and familiarisation with principles such as gender equality. Therefore, framing women's economic empowerment as a significant contributor to socioeconomic well-being and political success is necessary (Onditi 2019: 382). Gender education from early childhood to tertiary levels should be compulsory to tackle all forms of gender-based discrimination and violence. Public education through community meetings, religious and cultural leaders, mass media, and social media platforms will also go a long way in informing people from different walks of life about the importance of gender justice.

Unfortunately, due to low levels of enrolment and retention in education, women make up 60% of illiterate adults in Africa (AU 2019: 26). Hence, the assertion that women are usually unqualified in terms of education or specialisation. For women to participate fully in politics and international relations, they need to be equally educated and have full grasp of relevant issues, concepts, and tools required to address key challenges, for example, the Sustainable Development Goals (SDGs), Agenda 2063, the African Continental Free Trade Area (AfCFTA), the Protocol to the African Charter on Human and Peoples' Rights on the Rights of Women in Africa (Maputo Protocol), and CEDAW, among others.

Since education and employment opportunities do not provide a full solution to noted challenges, it is important to develop strategies to eliminate widespread heteropatriarchal norms and division of labour. The AU (2019: 27) suggested that gaps in participation and performance of girls and boys in most African countries could be attributed to the dual roles often played by girls, as learners and caregivers. Dual burdens persist for women when they leave school and enter the world of work. Another challenge which was identified by participants is access to childcare support facilities to reduce the impact of work and domestic role demands. As earlier noted, women struggle with balancing work and domestic demands, and they often do not receive adequate support to reduce this double burden. When they do, such support is often provided by unpaid or underpaid women and girls. African women diplomats stationed in countries with high-income levels face the additional challenge of available, yet expensive childcare services, which are usually only available during the day (Chideya et al. 2021: 37).

Women should be granted access to opportunities at all levels, without fear of being intimidated, harassed, or violated. The findings noted in this chapter revealed that the inclusion of women in diplomacy has not gone far enough to eradicate violence against women. Most institutions do not have relevant support systems or disciplinary measures. Therefore, women bear the burden of working in fear or forging ahead professionally, even when traumatised. Furthermore, gender justice initiatives remain exclusionary owing to the queerphobic posture maintained by most African states. As a result, there is a dearth of research on issues such as homophobia and transphobia in diplomatic institutions.

References

African Union (AU). 2018. 'Outcome of the Investigation of allegations of harassment against women and other institutional malpractices in the African Union Commission.' viewed September 2023, from https://au.int/en/pressreleases/20181122/outcome-investigation-allegations-harassment-against-women-and-other

African Union (AU). 2019. 'AU strategy for gender equality & women's empowerment 2018–2028.' viewed 20 September 2023, from https://au.int/sites/default/files/documents/36195-doc-52569_au_strategy_eng_high.pdf

African Union (AU). 2023. 'Maputo protocol on the rights of women in Africa: Commemorating 20 years.' viewed 12 September 2023, from https://au.int/en/newsevents/20230705/maputo-protocol-20-years#:~:text=As%20at%20June%202023%2C%2044,the%207th%20of%20June%202023

Aggestam, K., & Towns, A., 2019. 'The gender turn in diplomacy: A new research agenda.' *International Feminist Journal of Politics*, 21(1), 9–28.

Aggestam, K., & True, J., 2020. 'Gendering foreign policy: A comparative framework for analysis.' *Foreign Policy Analysis*, 16(2), 143–162.

Arvin, M., Tuck, E., & Morrill, A., 2013. 'Decolonizing feminism: Challenging connections between settler colonialism and heteropatriarchy.' *Feminist Formations*, 25(1), 8–34.

Atkinson, R. and Flint, J. (2004). Snowball sampling. In: Lewis-Beck, M.S., Bryman, A. and Liao, T.F. (eds.) The SAGE Encyclopaedia of Social Science Research Methods. Thousand Oaks: California, 1, 1043–1044.

Awino, O.N., 2018. 'Gender inequality in the conduct of international relations in Africa: A case study of diplomatic service in Kenya.' Doctoral dissertation, University of Nairobi.

Bimha, P.Z.J., 2021. 'The status of African women in foreign policy.' *E-International relations*. viewed 12 September 2023, from https://www.e-ir.info/2021/05/06/the-status-of-african-women-in-foreign-policy/

Bimha, P.Z.J., 2023. 'The politics of gender reform in West Africa: Family, religion, and the state by Ludovic Lado.' *African Journal of Gender and Religion*, 29(1), 148–159.

Buchholz, K., 2023. 'Only 14 countries have full equal rights for women.' *World Economic Forum*. viewed 2 September 2023, from https://www.weforum.org/agenda/2023/03/only-14-countries-have-full-equal-rights-for-women/

Chideya, F.Z., Dlamini-Mnthambo, S., Kerubo, J., & Umutoni, S.K., 2021. 'African women in diplomacy: The rising role: Kenya, Rwanda, South Africa and Zimbabwe'. viewed 2 September 2023, from http://www.southafrica-canada.ca/wp-content/uploads/2020/05/Women-in-Diplomacy-in-Africa-website.pdf

Fritsche, C., & Hall, R., 2002. 'Opportunities and challenges for women in diplomacy.' Robertson Hall, Princeton University, on 3 April 2002. viewed 20 August 2023, from https://lisd.princeton.edu/sites/g/files/toruqf506/files/Fritsche_Lecture.pdf

Gqola, P.D., 2001. 'Contradictory locations: Black women and the discourse of the Black Consciousness Movement (BCM) in South Africa.' *Meridians: Feminism, Race, Transnationalism* 2(1), 130–152.

Khumalo, B., Msimang, S., & Bollbach, K., 2017. 'Too costly to ignore – The economic impact of gender-based violence in South Africa.' *KMPG Human and Social Services.* viewed 2 August 2023, https://assets.kpmg.com/content/dam/kpmg/za/pdf/2017/01/za-Too-costly-to-ignore.pdf

Labour Research Service [LRS]. 2021. 'Addressing gender-based violence in the workplace'. viewed 2 August 2023, from https://www.lrs.org.za/2021/11/23/addressing-gender-based-violence-in-the-workplace/

Lenine, E., & Sanca, N., 2022. 'Gender, feminism and diplomacy: Analysing the institution through the lenses of feminist international relations.' *Organizações & Sociedade*, 29, 98–122.

Magadla, S., 2013. 'The personal is the international: For Black girls who've considered politics when being strong isn't enough.' *Politikon*, 40(3), 585–596.

Minarova-Banjac, C., 2018. 'Gender culture in diplomacy: A feminist perspective.' *Culture Mandala*, 13(1), 20–44.

Ngidi, N.D., 2022. '"I feel scared of being a girl": Adolescent girls' conversations about heteropatriarchal sexual violence in South African townships.' *Geoforum*, 134, 40–47.

Nkealah, N.N., 2006. 'Conceptualizing feminism (s) in Africa: The challenges facing African women writers and critics.' *The English Academy Review*, 23(1), 133–141.

Nzomo, M., 2015. 'Women and political governance in Africa: A feminist perspective: Pathways to African feminism and development.' *Journal of African Women's Studies Centre*, 1(1), 26–47.

Onditi, F., 2019. 'The making of "gender diplomacy" as a foreign policy pillar in Kenya and Namibia, in Onditi, F., Ben-Nun, G., D'Alessandro, C. & Levey Z. (eds.), *Contemporary Africa and the foreseeable world order*, pp. 377–397. Pretoria: Human Sciences Research Council.

Sharp, P., 2009. *Diplomatic theory of international relations*. New York: Cambridge University Press.

Tastad, C., & Bass, D., 2020. The route to true gender equality? Fix the system, not the women, *World Economic Forum.* viewed 2 August 2023, from https://www.weforum.org/agenda/2020/01/gender-gap-equality-income-wages-solution

TED. 2021. *6 essential lessons for women leaders | Julia Gillard and Ngozi Okonjo-Iweala.* viewed 2 August 2023, from https://www.youtube.com/watch?v=xg5uD-D1QvY&t=409s

United Nations International Children's Emergency Fund (UNICEF). 2017. *Glossary of Terms and Concepts UNICEF Regional Office for South Asia.* viewed 2 July 2023, from https://www.unicef.org/rosa/media/1761/file/Genderglossarytermsandconcepts.pdf

United Nations Development Programme (UNDP). 2023. *Breaking Barriers: Empowering Women in Diplomacy for a More Inclusive Future.* viewed 20 September 2023, from https://www.undp.org/bosnia-herzegovina/blog/breaking-barriers-empowering-women-diplomacy-more-inclusive-future

United Nations Entity for Gender Equality and the Empowerment of Women (UN Women). 2019. *Take Five: "Patriarchal culture is one of the biggest barriers in ending violence against women".* viewed 2 August 2023, from https://eca.unwomen.org/en/news/stories/2019/02/take-five-patriarchal-culture-is-one-of-the-biggest-barriers-in-ending-violence-against-women

United Nations Entity for Gender Equality and the Empowerment of Women (UN Women). 2022a. *Achieving full gender equality is still centuries away, warns the United Nations in a new report*, media release, 7 Sept 2022. viewed 20 September 2023, from https://www.unwomen.org/en/news-stories/press-release/2022/09/press-release-achieving-full-gender-equality-is-still-centuries-away-warns-the-united-nations-in-a-new-report

United Nations Entity for Gender Equality and the Empowerment of Women (UN Women). 2022b. *Facts and figures: Women, peace, and security.* viewed 20 August 2023, from https://www.unwomen.org/en/what-we-do/peace-and-security/facts-and-figures

Willner, R., 2011. 'Micro-politics: An underestimated field of qualitative research in political science.' *German Policy Studies*, 7(3), 155–185.

World Health Organisation (WHO). 2021. *Devastatingly pervasive: 1 in 3 women globally experience violence.* viewed 2 August 2023, from https://www.who.int/news/item/09-03-2021-devastatingly-pervasive-1-in-3-women-globally-experience-violence

Yin, R.K., 2008. *Case study research: Design and methods.* California: Sage Publications.

INDEX

Abak/Midim/Nung Ikot Women's Society 256
Aba Township Women's Association 255
Aba Women Association (AWA) 253, 256
Aba Women's Riot 250, 253
Abbot, Pamela 221
Abrahams, D. 348–349
academics, in Southeast Universities, Nigeria 362–372; challenges of 367–371; data collection 365; economic challenges 363; Igbo society 365–367; literature review 363–364; social relations and identities 363
access to resources 296
Achebe, Chinua 72, 74
Achebe, Nwando 74
Achenbaum, W. Andrew 411
achievements 297
Adadevoh, Ameyo Stella 112
Adefolarin, A. 382
Adeleye, F. 375
Adeogun, T. 378–379
Adepoju, A. A. 176
Adichie, Chimamanda Ngozi 15, 71, 73
advocacy and collective action 266
Affirmative Finance Action for Women in Africa (AFAWA) 339
African Agricultural Technology Foundation (AATF) 205
African Centre for Media Excellence (ACME) 238
African Continental Free Trade Area (AfCFTA) 111, 511
African Development Bank 339
African drama, women in 5, 70–83; constructive representation of 73–77; deconstructive representation of 71–73; in *Ebibi* and *Ajari* analysis *see* Ebibi and Ajari

African Union Commission (AUC) 509
African women 3–8, 15–17, 29–30, 32, 39, 46, 48, 50, 111, 114, 116–119, 122, 147–148, 151–152, 169–179, 184–186, 219, 236, 243–249, 263, 268–279, 332–335, 338–342, 367, 381, 412, 446, 454–455, 467, 469, 474–484; in artistic works and media 22; autonomy *see* autonomy; economic development *see* economic development, in Africa; in entrepreneurship 3; in entrepreneurship, academia, and politics 9–11; in entrepreneurship and management 20–21; and globalization *see* globalization; in historical times, older age, diplomacy, and religion 21–22; in leadership *see* leadership; in literary works 4–5; in older age, diplomacy, and religion 11–14; older women *see* older women, in Africa; pandemics and climate change 3, 6–7, 18–20; playwright's representation of 5; science, technology, engineering, and mathematics 7–9, 20
African Women in Agricultural and Research and Development (AWARD) 236
Afrobarometer (2017) survey 405
Afuh, Margaret 31, 34, 42
agency, women 296, 303; historical reality and political agency 412–414; and resilience 265–266; resiliency of 272–275
Agenda 2063 511
Aggestam, K. 505
agricultural production 169–170, 172–173; and food insecurity 174; and food security 176; and health, impact of 170
Agu, Dilichukwu 74
Agyemang-Duah, W. 429
Aidoo, A. A. 58, 73

Index

Ajanaku, Titi 377
Ajari 5
Akamanzi, Clare 148
Akinjobi, A. 364, 367
Akinyode-Afolabi, A. 379
Aki-Sawyerr, Yvonne 148
Akpa, V. 457
Akunyili, Dora 377
Alberts, Bruce 203
Aldehaib, A. 380
Al Dowaha 5, 46, 52
Alliance for Science 206
Aluko, F. 375
Amaefula, Rowland C. 75
Amanze, J. N. 476
Amari, Raja 5, 46–47
American Anthropological Association 288
Amina, B. J. Z. 21
Amoakohene, M. I. 271
And They Didn't Die 59
Angelou, Maya 420
Anglican Church of Southern Africa (ACSA) 462
Anglophone-ameroon literature: An introduction (2015) 31
Anglophone Cameroonian women writers *see* contemporary Anglophone Cameroonian women writers
Annan, Kofi 204
Anyadike, C. 271
Appiah, J. O. 430
appreciative inquiry (AI) 3, 287–288
Aquinas, Thomas 117
Arab-Muslim societies 5, 47–48, 51
Arowolo, A. 375
artificial intelligence (AI) 226, 243
Ash, Joyce 29, 31
Asheri, Jedida 33, 39
Ashuntantang, J. 32, 42
Association of Uganda Women Doctors 236
Atanga, L. 42
Atim, Grace 8
Autonomy 12, 39, 49, 54–55, 265, 272, 275, 277, 285, 289, 293–296, 348, 362, 370–371; context of patriarchy 59–61; educational autonomy 65–68; reproductive autonomy 61–65
Auxiliary Sisters 213
Awino, O.N. 509
Ayanga, H.O. 455, 469
Ayinaddis, S.G. 333
Ayozie, Favour 5

Babatope, Biola 377
Baderoon, G. 29
Bakare, Oluremi Adiukwu 377
Bakasa, E. C. 318
Banda, Astridah 122–131

Barwa, S.D. 327
Basden, G. T. 363
Bedwin Hacker 46–47, 55–56
Behold the dreamers 41
Bekele, A. B. 271
Bemba Zambian female identities 464
Bennett, Judith 53–54
Berryman, D. R. 304
Best friends (2009) 37
Bethune, Mary McLeod 421
Betika, D.P. 42
Bhasin, K. 378
Bime, B.F. 42
Bimha, Primrose Z. J. 13
Birchall, Jenny 52
Birt, L. 304
Bodhanya, M. 461
Boko Haram 136
Bold Hearts 140
Bollbach, K. 510
Borokinni, J. 176
Boswell, B. 29
bottom-up approach 377
Bouée, B.C. 333
Bouraoui, Nina 5, 46–47, 51–52
Bowen, G. A. 456
Boyce Thompson Institute for Plant Research 206
Breen, Jennifer 71
The Bride Price 66
Brundtland, Gro Harlem 165
Buchholz, K. 502
Bucknor-Akerele, Kofoworola 377
Buganda community 417
Buganda culture 416
Bunce, M. 184
Burkina Faso 229
Burnley, Gwendoline 40
Busia, Abena 413
Butake, Bole 32, 414, 416
Butler, Judith 263, 391
Byanyima, Winnie 16

Calasanti, T. 431
Campaign for Female Education (CAMFED) 177
campaign trails 391
Campbell, K. K. 156
Canadian International Development Research Centre 207
Canadian International Food Security Research Fund (CIFSRF) 207
capitalism 4, 487
Carr, E. S. 155
Catholic women 7; *see also* church women, in ELCZ

Index

CGIAR (Consortium of International Agricultural Research Centres) 206
Chachage, C. S. L. 184, 270
Charles, Nnolim 72
Chazovachii, B. 184
Chideya, F.Z. 503, 508
Chikanda, A. 306
Chiluba, B. C. 124
Chiname T. B. 187
Chirisa, I. 329
Chirongoma, S. 454
Chisale, S. S. 454
Chita, J. 123
Chitando, A. 15, 22
Chitando, E. 454
Chitando, Mutsawashe 6, 457
Choo, H.Y. 431
Chris, O. C. 76
Christian women and COVID-19 pandemic 101, 486–487; Democratic Republic of Congo 136–137; health and conflict 135–136; Nigeria 137–141
Christmas Carols in June (2019b) 31
Chuku, Gloria 75
Church of Christ in Nations (COCIN) 488
church women, in ELCZ 9–10; background 316–317; beadwork project 321; boutiques businesses 322; business owners 320; in chicken rearing 321; Church and support 328–329; cultural constraints 326–327; decoration and catering 320–321; dress making, cutting, and designing 321–322; early child development centers 320–321; economy and community 329; encountered challenges 325; entrepreneurship 317–319, 327–328; event centers 322; financial empowerment 324; financial independence 322–323; flexibility 323–324; gender roles, at home 325–326; lack of capital 327; lack of education and training 326; overview, of Western Diocese 319; passion 324; personal lives 328; personal motivation 325; positionality 318; programs, to support own business 322; qualitative methodology 318–319; retail shops 322; role models and inspiration 329–330; Social Capital Theory 317; Sustainable Livelihood Framework (SLF) 317; tourism 320; unemployment 323
Circle of Concerned African Women Theologians 455
Citizens Coalition for Change (CCC) 394
civil society organisations (CSOs) 391
Clark, Helen 165
Clark, John Pepper 75
climate change 172; and gender in Africa 189; painful realities of 189–190; St Therese Mission Catholic Women 187; United Nations 2030 Sustainable Development Goals 186
Climate Change Act 178
climate change crisis 184, 190–191, 194; appreciative inquiry 188; natural resources in 185
climate change impacts (CCI) 7; in Africa 189; agricultural production *see* agricultural production; Democratic Republic of Congo 171; environmental and ecosystem degradation 169; Ethiopia 172–173; human health 174–177; Madagascar 173; Nigeria 175; ocean and Savannah ecosystems 170; vector-borne diseases 170; in Zimbabwe 189–190
climate change resilience 7, 184–186, 189; march of women 194–195; single women and 190–191; tobacco farming 192–194
Cole, P. 273, 277
colonialism 4, 487
colonialization 75
colonisation 45
Commission for University Education (CUE) 347
Community-Based Health Planning and Services (CHPS) 433
community engagement 266
Connell, R. 267
Constitution of Kenya 2010 355, 358
contemporary Anglophone Cameroonian women writers 4, 29–43; empowering stories 30; historical context of 30–33; imperfect perfections 36–38; in/of *Icy Foreign Lands*, stories of woman 41; literary historiographies 29; literary productions 29; and male-authored literature 33; patriarchal oppression 33; prospects for 41; under punitive socio-economic conditions 34–36; reflections and recreations of women's fortitude 38–40
contraception 463
1979 Convention on the Elimination of All Forms of Discrimination against Women (CEDAW) 511
Conway, Gordon 203
Cooper, Carolyn 412
Cooperrider, David 232
Corey, E. 481
Cornet, Anne 212
Cornwall, Andrea 263–264
corruption 342
Coughlin, J. H. 319, 322–325, 328
Council for Scientific and Industrial Research (CSIR) 201–202
Council of Churches in Zambia (CCZ) 123
COVID-19 pandemic 6–7, 16, 226; Agnes Mahomva's Leadership in 148–151; Christianity, health, and conflict in Congo

and Nigeria 135–136; clinical cases 87–100; conveying messages on radio 127–128; female filmmakers on 113–114; human communication and interaction 125; networking 126–127; nuns, work of 129; pastoral care 128–129; preventive equipment 129; social distancing 139; women's leadership *see* women's leadership, during pandemic; women with disabilities, in Church 139–140
Crenshaw, K. 431
Crush, J. 306
cultural and social transformations 274
cultural disposition 9
cultural empowerment 265, 276
cultural norms 384–385
cultural practices 49
cultural productions 5
cultures of violence 493
customary law 380

Damascene, Jean 72
Dana, L.P. 333
Dangarembga, Tsitsi 59, 62, 417
Dankelman, I. 187
Daramola, O. O. 271
Darkwah, A. K. 111
data gap 246
The deadly honey 38
Deckard, B. S. 258
Declaration on the Elimination of Violence against Women 488
Democratic Republic of Congo 6, 161, 170–171, 244, 334; Christianity, health, and conflict in 135–136; pandemic background 136–137; women in church 137–138
Department of Microbiology at UCT 202
Diabate, Naminata 413
Dialmy, Abdessamad 54
diplomacy 11–14, 21–22, 500; African Feminist Perspectives 504–505; career diplomats 501; foreign policy 501; gender-based violence (GBV) 508–510; gender bias in appointments 505–506; global political economy 500; heteropatriarchal norms and division of labour 506–508; male dominance in 500; methodology 502–503; political diplomats 501; recommendations 510–512; women's empowerment and gender equality 501–502
discrimination against women 376
discriminatory laws 339
Djebar, Assia 46
Dlamini, N. Z. P. 462
Dlamini-Mnthambo, S. 503
Dlamini-Zuma, Nkosazana 16
Dodanwala, T.C. 349, 354
Doe, Samuel 157

Doh, Emmanuel Fru 31
Domestic and Gender-Based Violence (DGBV) 462
The Dominican Missionary Sisters of the Sacred Heart of Jesus 125–126
The Dragon's Funeral 75
Dróżdż, D. 192
Dube, Mbongeni Proud 9
Dube, Musa 480, 483
Duflo, E. 270
Duhan, R. 60
Dutt, A. 287
Dziva, D. 129

Eastern market women 8
Eastern women activism, in Colonial Nigeria 8; anti-colonial struggle 254–255; British Colonial Policies 253; geographical overview of 251; market women's revolts in 256–257; socio-cultural background 251–252; strategies 255–256
Ebibi and *Ajari* 5; analysis of women in 77–81; characterization of women characters in 76–77; contradictory representations of women 81–82
Ebila, Florence 70, 78
Ebola epidemic 6, 156
ecological degradation 185
Economic Community of West African States (ECOWAS) 118
economic development, in Africa 10, 34, 432, 483; corruption 342; development and economic life 333–337; financing and inequality 341; financing and job creation 340; gender gaps in business size and profitability 340–341; infrastructure and lack of profit 340; land ownership and agricultural problems 342; literature review 333; methodology 333; research aims 332; research problem 332–333; science, technology, and digitization 342; small and medium enterprises 337–339; societal-cultural dimensions 341
Economic Development and Poverty Reduction Strategies 217
economic empowerment 264–266, 272
Ecumenical HIV and AIDS Initiative in Africa (EHAIA) 456
education and advocacy 273
Education Sub-Saharan Africa (ESSA) 244
Education Supplementary Act No. 10, 348
Ehirim, C. 254
Ekpo, Margaret 251, 255
Ekundayo, D. 382
elderly women, in Botswana 12, 437–450; African theological feminism 445–446; African Theological Feminist Gerontology 445,

447–450; challenges 442–443; contributions of 440–442; feminist gerontology 447; historical and cultural context 438–440; identified gaps in the roles and challenges of 443–445
The Elders 134, 141
11 September 2011 terrorist attacks 48
El Fani, N. dir. 46–47, 54
Ellen Johnson Sirleaf Foundation 161
Elson, D. 270
EMBO, in Basel 201
Emecheta, Buchi 66, 73
empathy 116–117
empowerment 155; in cultural contexts 283
Eneta vs Elimo (2007) 37
Enid Kiaye, R. 354
entrepreneurship: and business ownership 270; church women, impact of 327–328; defined 319; gender, and religion 317–318
environmental justice, in broiler farming 191–192
EPRS 192
Ethiopia 177
Evangelical Church Winning All (ECWA) 475, 488
Evangelical Fellowship of Zambia (EFZ) 123
Evangelical Lutheran Church in Zimbabwe (ELCZ) *see* church women, in ELCZ
Evangelical Reformed Church of Christ (ERCC) 488
Ewa and other plays (2000) 37
Ewusi, J. 31, 42
Eze, Godstime 5, 74
Ezeh, M.N. 363–364
Ezike, Enugu 74

Facebook 234
Faculty of Agronomy 214
Fasci, M.A. 326
Fatoki, O. 305–306
Fawole, O. I. 118
Federal Government 139
feminine traits 391
feminine wisdom 111; empathy 116–117; intuition 117–118; nurturing 118; resilience 119
Ferree, M.M. 431
Fiedler, R. N. 479
financial independence 270
Fitshane, Z. 306
Flowers in the desert (2009) 34
focus groups 142
Foncha, Anna 40
Footprints of Destiny (1985) 40
Ford, J. D. 123
Forum for African Women Educationists (FAWE) 219, 236
Fourth Industrial Revolution 243

Francophone Cameroon 31, 36
Fricker, Miranda 117
Fritch, J. 156
Fubara-Manuel, Jessie 6
Furman, Nelly 71
Fwangyil, Gloria Ada 70

Garba, Henry Marcus 12
Gates, Bill 129, 131
Gauthier, Xaviere 74
Geena Davies Institute on Gender in Media 226
gender-aggregated data 246
gender-based sexual violence (GBSV) 461
gender-based violence (GBV) 160, 508–510
gender bias 226, 334, 363; in appointments 505–506
gender differences 427
gender disparity 9, 110, 225, 477; academics *see* academics, in Southeast Universities, Nigeria
gender equality 159, 244, 246, 501
gender gaps 20, 151, 210, 225, 248, 329, 335–337, 340–341, 357, 379, 398; in 2023 election 398; in business size and profitability 340–341; in STEM 20
gender inequality 186, 283
gender parity 246
gender role socialization 384–385
gender stereotypes 116
Genetically Modified Organisms (GMOs) 200–201
Gielnik, M. M. 318
Giles, S. 431
Girls Education Policy (2008) 356
Girls in ICT mentorship programme 220
Global Climate Change Adaptation Index (GAIN) 172
globalization 8, 487; African women's economic opportunities 270–271; agency and resiliency of 272–275; cultural changes 271–272; cultural empowerment 265; cultural pressures 263; development practitioners and local leaders 279; economic empowerment 264–265; economic liberalization 262; gender-based violence 263; gender identities 263; global supply chains and enterprises 262; informed policies and initiatives 261; labor exploitation 262; limitations 278; recommendations 278–279; research methodology 269–270; research objectives 261; significance of study 261–262; social empowerment 265; structural inequalities and gender biases 260; theoretical and policy implication 275–278; theoretical framework 266–268; women's agency and resilience 265–266; women's empowerment 263–264
global media 4

Global North 4, 23
Global South 19
Global Terrorism Index 135
global value chains (GVCs) 271
Glover, L. 364
Going Home 31
Goodluck, N. 364
Goyayi, M. 306
Gqola, P.D. 29
Graburn, Nelson 73, 77
Greitemeyer, T. 117
Greitens, Eric 119
Guirassy, Fatoumata 339
Gukurume, S. 184

Haram, Boko 118
Hashim, Iman 48–49
Hassan, Samia Suluhu 16
He, C. 356
Healing Stings 31
Hertfelt, Marcel 210
heteropatriarchy 506–507
Higher Education Act (HEA) 346
higher education management (HEM) 10, 361; background 345; extraction and selection of data 351; gender equality strategies 350–351; gender parity and inclusion 349; gender socialization 349; historical contexts of 345–349; leadership and management roles 350; literature search 351; market needs 345; methodology 351; motherhood penalty 350; research questions 351; results 351–357; socio-cultural factors 349; structural factors 349
HIV/AIDS 19
Hlatshwayo, Gladys 402
Hofstede, G. J. 304
Hooks, Bell 68
human health 174–177
humanitarian organisations 137–138, 141
Huxman, S. S. 156

Ibrahim, J. 364
Ibrahim, S. G. 21
Ibru, C. 326
Ice, R. 156
Illuminating Hidden Harvests (IHH) Initiative 174
Ilparakuyo Maasai women, in Tanzania: comparative analysis 296; future implications 296–297; gender-based movements 284
information and communication technology (ICT) 8, 226
Inklings from My Ink (2018) 31
Instagram 230
institutional biases 363

Integrated Care for Older People 438
International Centre for Research on Women 170
International Consortium of Applied Economic Research (ICABR) 205–206
International Food Security Research Fund 207
international organizations 163
Inter-Parliamentary Union (IPU) 2022 379
intra-household analysis 123
intuition 117–118
Irobi, Esiaba 72
Isiko, A. P. 130–131
Islamic State in West Africa Province (ISWAP) 136
Ismail, F. 463
Isola, A. 378–379
Isola, Abidemi Abiola 10
Iweala, Okonjo 377

Jelloun, Tahar Ben 4–5, 46, 50
Joziasse, H. 484
Joziasse, Heleen 480
Jua, Roselyn 413
Jubril, Sarah 377
Justice Coalition for Religious (JCOR) 127

Kabeer, N. 263–264, 266–268, 270, 275–276, 284, 286
Kabonga, I. 323
Kado, Jacqueline 8
Kahlke, R. 304
Kamaara, Eunice 6
Kanas, A. 312
Kanyoro, Musimbi 483
Kanyoro, R.A. 480, 482–483
Karim, N. A. 326
Kathy, E. 267
Kaunda, M. M. 464
Kayem, Maidem 39
Kenya 346
Kenya University and Colleges Central Placement Service (KUCCPS) Board 347
Kerubo, J. 503
Khan, M. B. 463
Khumalo, B. 510
Kikwete, Jakaya 165
Killian, Caitlin 49
Kimmel, M.S. 68
Ki-Moon, Ban 165
Kithuka, E. 124
Kitimbo, A. 303
Klaa, Cherifa 10
Kleinman, A. 106
Kongnyuy, Eugene 38
Korieh, C. 362–363
Kruah-Togba, Cornelia 148
Kuhn, Thomas 117
Kyoto Protocol 171, 179

Index

Lado, Hervé 339
Landolt, P. 305
land ownership and agricultural problems 342
leadership 334; academic spaces and society 469; African Women in Theology and Religious Studies 454–455; defining 457–458; gender and religion department 456–457; positionality 458–460; religion and gender literature *see* religion and gender literature; research methodology 455–456; "taboo" topics 468; women's leadership *see* women's leadership, during pandemic, women scientists, for leadership positions
Le Garçon Manqué 5, 46
L'Enfant de Sable 4, 46
Lenine, E. 501, 504
Lerner, Gerda 73, 81
lesbian sexuality 466
Lewis, D. 29
LinkedIn 234
liquefied petroleum gas (LPG) 429
literary productions, of Anglophone Cameroonian women 29–30
literary representation 64
live-lihood empowerment against poverty (LEAP) 426
The lock on my lips 31, 36
Löffler, C. S. 117
Lola, Nkamanyang 42
L'Oreal/UNESCO Prize 207
Lukanda, Ivan Nathanael 8
Lwala, Donald 10
Lwanga, D. 347
Lyonga, Nalova 413

Maasai community 283
Maasai women empowerment, in Tanzania 9; case studies 289–290; economic and social engagement 296; economic opportunities 286–287; empirical site and methodology 287–288; grazing areas 295; and Himba Ethnic Groups 296; in Himba Societies 296; historical context 288; infrastructure developments 294; and infrastructure developments 294; multidimensional framework 284–285; Naila Kabeer's concept of 284; pastoralism and religiosity 286; religion and gender dynamics 292–293; religiosity, gender relations, and church 290–292; religious rituals and economic development 284; resource access 293–294; and role of religion 285–286; socio-economic and political structure 284; transformation of Maasai Youth 294
Maathai, Wangari 70
Madagascar 173, 177

Madigele, Tshenolo Jennifer 12
Mafukidze, J. 306
Magona, Sindiwe 418
Mahere, Fadzayi 401–402
Mahomva, Agnes 7, 148–151
Majid, Anouar 48
Makerere University 225
Makhulu, W. K. 474, 476
Makuchi 42
Makumbi, Jennifer 11, 412, 416
Mama, A. 66, 265, 273
Mamombe, Joanna 402
Manda, S. 123
Mandipaka, F. 327
Mangan, Michael 412
Maniraj Singh, A. 354
Mann, J. 495
Manyonganise, M. 124
Mapasure, Martha 464
Maphosa, V. 187
Maputo Protocol 511
marginalisation 45
Marshall, K. 131
masculine attributes 402
masculine traits 391
Maseno, Loreen 102
Mashabela, J.K. 474
Masika, R. 186–187
Massoi, Lucy W. 9
MasterCard Index of Women Entrepreneurs (MIWE) 338–339
Mathe, L. 239
Mazibuko, S. S. 466
Mbanda, V. 306
Mbantenkhu, M.F. 42
Mbeki, Thabo 381
Mboumien, S. 42
Mbue, Imbolo 41
McArthur, S. 239
McAuliffee, M. 303
McCormick, D. 272
media coverage of science, in Uganda 225; achievements and challenges 228–229; discriminates against women and portrays 226; discussion 238–239; efforts to amplify women voices 230–232; findings 233; gender bias and underrepresentation in 227–228; gender biases 226; gender disparity 225; gender representation 228; intervening factors 229–230; media construction and representation 234–235; opportunities 236; scientists and research 233–234; theory and methodology 232; women's voices in media 236–237
mediatisation 125
Meinke, Holger 206

Mes Mauvaises Pensées 5, 46
Metu, Somtochukwu 5
Mhandu, J. 9, 305–306, 311
migrant women, in South Africa 267; bounded solidarity and enforceable trust 305; coping and adaptation mechanisms 303; cultural dimensions 304; data saturation 304; immigrant entrepreneurs 305–306; and immigrant niche 309–311; opportunity structure and mixed embeddedness 311–312; qualitative study 304; significance of reflexivity 304; social constructivism 304; trustworthiness 304; undocumented migrant women 307–309; women's agency 303
Millennium Development Goals (MDGs) 64, 366
Minarova-Banjac, C. 505–506, 509
Minkov, M. 304
Misihairabwi-Mushona, Priscilla 394
Mlambo-Ngucka, Phumzile 16
Mlotshwa, S.H. 305
Mnangagwa, Emmerson 151
modernization 442–444
Moghadam, V. M. 267
Mokelu, Janet N. 377
Mokhtar, M. 304
Molyneux, M. 377
Mombo, Esther Moraa 13, 477–480, 482, 484
MONESCO 137
Morley, L. 364
Mortimer, Mildred 45
Movement for Democratic Change (MDC) 394
Moyo, M. 454
Msimang, S. 510
Msimango-Galawe, J. 305
Mua, Josepha 40
Mubaiwa, Kudzai 399
Mubvurungwa communal area 185–186; gendered climate change crisis in 189
Mubvurungwa women 195
Mucheke River 185, 190–191
Mucheke River Garden project 194
Muchemwa, Kizito 68
Mugabe, Grace 394
Mujuru, Joice 403
Mukabera, Josephine 8
Mukuka, N. N. M. 124
Mumtaz, Z. 59
Munyao, M. 124
Murray, S.A. 40
Muslim women 48
Mustapha, M. L. A. 177
Muzvidziwa, N.V. 311
Muzvidziwa, S. N. 329
Muzvidziwa, V. 328
Mwaikokesya, J. B. 270
Mwale, N. 122–123

Mwaniki, L. 477
Mwashita, T. 348–349, 354
Mwiine, Amon Ashaba 8

Nadar, S. 456, 469
Narismulu, P. 61
narratives, in public communication 156
National Ageing Policy 427
National Council for Science and Technology (NCST) 218
National Council for Technical Education (NACTE) 348
National Council of Nigeria and Cameroon (NCNC) 255
National Education Policy 356
National Election Commission 381
National Gender Policy 356
National Health Insurance Authority (NHIA) 426
Nationally Determined Contribution (NDC) 171
National Strategy for Transformation 2017–2024 (NST1) 215
Nchami, Azanwi 40
Ncube, Gibson 4, 48
Ndiyah, Florence 34, 42
Ndlove, S. 187
neocolonialism 487
Nervous Conditions 59, 62, 65–66
Network of African Science Academies (NASAC) 243–244
Nfah-Abbenyi, J.M. 32
Ngcobo, Lauretta 59
Ngocobo, S. 110
Ngong, Grace Fien 37
Ngongkum, Eunice 31, 35
NGO Support Group 139
Ngozi, Elizabeth Oluwafunmiso 7
Ngu, M.N. 42
Ngunjiri, F. W. 478
Ngwa Women's Association 254
Nieman, G.H. 319
Nieuwenhuizen, C. 319
Nigeria 177–178; background 138–139; Christianity, health, and conflict in 135–136; Christian women and humanitarian organisations 140–141; climate change impacts (CCI) 175; Nigerian society 486
Nigeria-Biafra War 10, 362, 364, 372
Njoroge, Nyambura 483
Nkamanyang Lola, P.K. 31, 36
Nkealah, Naomi 4, 29, 46
Nnaemeka, O. 29, 40, 412
Nomadic Voices of Exile: Feminine Identity in Francophone Literature of the Maghreb (1999) 46
non-governmental organisations (NGOs) 20, 142, 442

Nostalgia 37
Nsah, K.T. 31
Ntube, N. 42
nurturing 118
Nwabueze, Emeka 72, 75
Nwanya, Agatha Njideka 76
Nwaozuzu, Uche 5, 78, 81–82
Nwapa, Flora 73–74
Nwogwugwu, Ngozi 7
Nwoke, B. E. B. 177
Nyoni, W.P. 356
Nziku, D. M. 324
Nzuh, N.A. 31, 42

Obada, Erelu Olusola 377
Obi-Ani, Ngozika Anthonia 10
Obi-Ani, P. 364
Obonodo, E. A. 364
Oduyoye, M. A. 13, 446, 454, 477–479, 490
Ogbogu, C. O. 364
Ogidis, Moses Iliya 12
Ogunlade, A. 379
Ohaeto, Ezenwa 74
Ojikutu, Alhaja Sinatu 377
Ojong, N. 333
Ojong, V.B. 305, 311
Ojong, Vivian 9
Okoh, Julie 73
Okonjo-Iweala, Ngozi 16
Okonkwo, U.U. 363–364
Okure, Teresa 483
Okyere, Joshua 12
older women, in Africa 11–12, 21, 411–422; challenges 419–420; diaspora 420–421; elderly women, words, and ritual 414–416; gender discourse and generational bond 416–419; historical reality and political agency 412–414
older women, in rural areas 428–434, 440; concept of ageing 424–425; coping with challenges 431; economic experiences 430–431; global, regional, and national statistics 425–426; health-related experiences 429–430; intersectionality 431–432; national policies on ageing, in Ghana 426–427; quality of life 432–433; social experiences 427–429
Olmos-Vega, F.M. 304
Oloka-Onyango, J. 454
Onditi, F. 501
Onitsha Market Women Association 256
Onitsha Women Association 253
Onwueme, Tess 73
Opoku, Bright 12
Organisation for Women in Science (OWSD) 207–208
Organisation for Women in Science for the Developing World (OWSD) 207–208

Orji, J. 255
Orlando, Valérie 46
Osaji-Nwafili C. A. 363
Osiirewo, Bosede 377
Owino, Elizabeth A. 10
Owino, T. M. 465
Oyagbola, Ebun 377
Oyedepo, Stella 74
Oyelaran-Oyeyinka, B. 272

Palczewski, C. H. 156
pandemics and climate change 3, 6–7, 18–20, 23; COVID-19 pandemic clinical cases 87–100; female agency 111–114; and feminine wisdom 111, 114–119; focus group discussions 100–103; results and discussions 103; spirituality 104–106
Pandor, Naledi 22
Paris Agreement 171, 179
participant observation 142
Partnership for Evidence-Based COVID-19 Response (PERC) 148
patriarchal culture 236
patriarchal discourses 11
patriarchal stereotyping 73
patriarchy 4, 59–60, 226, 487; political institution and 385–386; and religious institutions 385
Patswawairi, T. 305
Patterson, J. J. 186
Patterson, K. 456
Patulny, R. 312
Pauw, C. M. 476
Pavari, N. 128
Pearce, A. 123
Penitent Sisters 213
pension programme 440
Pepper, Michael 204
Perkins, S. 156
Pervin, N. 304
Phillips, M. 326
Phiri, I. A. 454, 456, 469, 483
Phiri, K. 186–187
policy decisions 252
policymakers 151, 279
political ethos 158
political events 391
political participation, of women 10; conceptual clarification of patriarchy 377–378; historical perspective of 378–379; in Liberia 381–382; Osun State 383–386; in Rwanda 380–381; in South Africa 381; in South Sudan 379–380; Yorubas 382–383
political rallies 391
political representation of women 9–11, 34–35, 159, 165, 179, 193, 215, 227, 246, 251–252, 255, 257–258, 263, 274, 277; Butler's

performative agency and postcolonial feminist critiques 391–393; campaign strategies 390; challenges and limitations 403–405; cyberbullying and violence against women 391; data collection and method analysis 393–394; political discourse 394–396; women's agency 391
Portes, A. 304–305
PRISMA diagram 353
Promise (1969) 33, 39
prostitution 136
public universities 348
Pucherová, D. 39

qualitative data 398
qualitative interviews 142
quality of decisions 58
quality of life 444
queer young women, in North Africa 45–56; gender identities 51; liminal identity 51–52; refusal and challenges 52–53; singleness and heteropatriarchy 53–55; understanding, impact of Muslim 48–50

racism 487
Rammile, N. 368
Raniga, T. 306
rationality 60
Räuchle, C. 311
The Rebellion of the Bumpy-Chested 74
regional economic community (REC) 507
religion and gender literature 22; gender-based violence 460–463; sexual and reproductive health and rights 463–464; sexual diversity in Christian churches 464–467
religious authorities 131
religious communities 492
religious institutions 385
reproductive autonomy 61–65
research design 269
resilience 119
"Resonate initiative" 220
rhetorical leadership 7; collective goals 156; Ebola 161–165; empowerment 155; global pandemics 165–166; Liberia, political turmoil of 157–158; narratives, in public communication 156; political agency 155; political communication style 155; women's empowerment 156; women's rights 158–161
Rifaat, Alifa 46
Roberts L, I. 104
Rocogoza, Marklin 221
Rohn, J. 229
Rotimi, Ola 72
Rubaya, Clemence 5
rural economies 123

Rural Enterprise Programme 433
Rustles on Naked Trees (2015) 31
Rwanda 277, 356; educational governance in 347
Rwandan Association for Women in Science and Engineering (RAWISE) 220
Rwandan women, in science, innovation, and technology (SIT) 8, 10, 276–277, 334–335, 338, 347, 352, 356–357, 380–381, 394, 474, 488; academic authorities 221; colonization and 1994 genocide against Tutsi 213–214; Gacaca law development and implementation 209; gender equality promotion 209; gender gap 209; historical background of 211; historical context of formal education 212–213; household management programme 209; participation and leadership 221; political participation 209; post-genocide era 214–217; scholarship opportunities 221; women's agency 219–221; women's capacities 217–219

Sadiqi, Fatima 45
Saharso, Sawitri 49
Salami, Irene 73–74
Salami, T. 379
Salihu, A. 364
Salway, S. 59
sampling procedures and data collection 188–189
Sanca, N. 501
Saruni, Parit 9, 287
Sassen, S. 267
Saunders, B. 318
Savannah ecosystems 170
Schmiz, A. 311
Schönbächler, Viviane 229
Science, Innovation, and Technology (SIT) 8
science, technology, engineering, and mathematics (STEM) 7, 17, 357
Science Academies 246–247
Scott, J.W. 384
search strategy 269
secondary education 213–215
The secret lives of Baba Segi's wives (2010) 39
Seidu, Abdul-Aziz 12
self-actualisation 54
Sembatya, Nakiwala Aisha 8
Sensenbrenner, J. 304
sexism 487
sexual and gender-based violence: approach of Evangelical Churches to 491–495; in Bible 488–490; biblical teaching on 495–496; in Nigerian 490–491
sexual and gender-based violence (SGBV) 12, 486
sexual and reproductive health rights (SRHR) 464
sexual autonomy 39

sexual dominance 489
sexual harassment 493
sexualities 56
sexual orientation 468
sexual violence 490, 494
Shanklin, Eugenia 413
"She Can Code" initiative 220
Shelby, Mike 203
Sherwood, M. 364
Shillcutt, S. 230
Shrestha, P. 349
Shula, H. 124
Shupe, Anson 493
Sibanda, Linda K 400
Sibisi, T. M. 466
Silver, K. J. 230
Simba, A. 333
Simba, H. 110
Sirleaf, Ellen Johnson 7, 148, 155–166, 381–382; *see also* rhetorical leadership
skills development 270
Smith, A. 273
Snitker, T.V. 304
social and legal empowerment 270
social conceptualization 425
social empowerment 265
social expectations 47
social experiences 427–429
socialisation 45
social networking 306
social norms 391
Social Security Act 426
social service systems 134
social values and norms 226
societies, defined 489
sociocultural norms 441
Sofola, Zulu 73
Solberg, Rolf 74
South African Bill of Rights 307
South African Department of Science and Technology 204–205
South African Immigration Act 307
South African Women in Science and Engineering (SAWISE) 207
Southeastern Nigeria 10
Soyinka, Wole 72, 74
Spiker, Julia A. 7
spirituality: prayer 104–106; self-talk 104–105; spiritual care-sharing knowledge and resources 105–106
Spivak, Gayatri 392
Srivastva, Suresh 231
Stalmeijer, R.E. 304
Standard Gauge Railway (SGR) 284
Stoddard, J. 231
Stoner, M. 156
Stratton, Florence 75

Strengthening Capacity of Religious Women in Early Childhood Development (SCORE ECD) Project 126
Struthers, J. J. 324
Sub-Saharan Africa (SSA) 169, 426
sub-Saharan Africa Gender Gap Index 335
Sulle, E. 270
Sultana, A. 378
supportive institutional frameworks 246
Sustainable Development Goal (SDG) 6, 8, 355, 502, 511
Switzerland 228
systematic literature review (SLR) design 351

Taku, O.K. 42
Takyi, B.K. 495
Tamale, S. 454
Tamba, Pochi 37
Tande, D. 42
Tanga, P. T. 414
Tanyi-Tang, A. 31, 37
Tanzania 348
Tawodzera, G. 306
tertiary education 214–217
theological education: missionaries and colonizers 476; Mombo, Esther 477–479; Oduyoye, Mercy Amba 477–479; Oduyoye and Mombo, contributions of 479–482; problematic biblical interpretations 476; up-coming theologians 482–484
Things Fall Apart 72
Thomas, A. R. 319, 323
Thomas, L. 273
Thomson, J. 7
TikTok 230
Titabet and the Takumbeng (2004) 416
Tolbert, William 157
Tomori, Titi Laoye 377
Tom Tom, M. 323, 328
To My Children's Children (1990) 418
total entrepreneurial activity (TEA) 338
Tripp, A. M. 273
Trout, L. J. 106
True, J. 505
Tsaaior, J.T. 61
Tur-Porcar, A. 327
Twitter 230
Two Plays: Visiting America and Marienuelle (2006) 37

Uchem, R. N. 367–368, 370
Udegbe, A. 376
Uganda 178, 230, 347
Uganda Investment Authority 337
Uganda Women Entrepreneurs Association Limited 338
Ugbabe, Ahebi 74

Index

Ugwu, Abel T. 10
Ukala, Sam 72
Umuokoro, Matthew 76
Umutoni, S.K. 503
UNESCO Convention against Discrimination in Education 217
United Kingdom 228
United Nations (UN) 202–203, 275, 355
United Nations Department of Economic and Social Affairs (UNDESA) 425
United Nations Framework Convention on Climate Change (UNFCCC) 171, 179
United Nations Millennium Development Goals (MDGs) 161
Universities Act 347–348
Universities Funding Board 347
University of Rwanda (UR) 216–217
University of Rwanda Gender Policy 356, 358
UN Women (2019) 509

Vaarst, M. 192
Valdez, J. 326
Valerio, Elizabeth 398
Varpio, L. 304
vector-borne diseases 170
Vera, Yvonne 68
Vertovec, S. 311

Wahl, Willem Petrus 474
Walker, Alice 76
Walls, Andrew 476
Walters, C. 368
Walulya, Gerald 8
Wangui, E.E. 287
Washington, Harold 490
Way, Yossa 6
The "WeCode" 220
WhatsApp 234–235
White Sisters 213
WHO Integrated Care for Older People (ICOPE) 438
Wild-Wood, Emma 6
Winston, B. E. 456
Wittenberg-Cox, Avivah 117
Wittstock, Clinton 205
The Wives Revolt. The Dragon's Funeral 75
women: in church groups 134; in diplomacy *see* diplomacy; education 56; higher education management *see* higher education management, in Africa; political participation *see* political participation, of women; political representation of *see* political representation of women; sexual and GBV against women 12; sexuality 55; theological education, in Africa *see* theological education; Women Coalition of Zimbabwe (WCOZ) 404
Women Entrepreneurs Index 338

Women in Politics Support Unit (WIPSU) 404
women scientist, for leadership positions: narrative 247–248; Network of African Science Academies (NASAC) 244; overcoming obstacles, for gender parity 245–246; Science Academies 246–247; underrepresentation in academic leadership 244–245
women scientists, in Africa: Canadian International Development Research Centre 207; CGIAR (Consortium of International Agricultural Research Centres) 206; Genetically Modified Organisms (GMOs) 200–201; International Food Security Research Fund 207; L'Oreal/UNESCO Prize 207; OWSD 207–208
women's empowerment and gender quality (WEGE) strategies 502
women's leadership, during pandemic 6–7, 13, 18–19, 87–107, 122–131, 134–142, 145–152; COVID-19 147–148; Ebola Virus outbreak 147; gender inequality 145; HIV/AIDS 147; limitations and future directions 152; public health 151; sexual and gender-based violence 145
Woods, David 199
World Bank 134, 337, 443
World Bank by Trading Economic 173
World Council of Churches (WCC) 140
World Declaration on Education for All 218
World Economic Forum (WEF) 202–203
World Health Organization (WHO) 425, 437–438, 487
writing books 203–204
Wuyts, C. 215

X (formerly Twitter) 230, 234

Yankah, Kwesi 415
Yerima, Ahmed 72
YouTube 230
Yusuph, M.L. 356

Zambia Association of Sisterhoods (ZAS) 130
Zambia Conference of Catholic Bishops (ZCCB) 123
Zanu PF party 394, 400
Zigomo, Kuziwakwashe 11
Zimbabwe 7, 178, 456; climate change in 185, 189–190; environmental crisis 186; globalization 276; political discourse on women in 394–396
Zimbabwe Electoral Support Network (ZESN) 404
Zine, Jasmin 48
Zungu, N. 348–349
Zvingowanisei, Silindiwe 401

www.ingramcontent.com/pod-product-compliance
Lightning Source LLC
LaVergne TN
LVHW081710070225

803225LV00005B/445